Computer-Aided Design and Manufacturing

Computer-Aided Design and Manufacturing

Farid M. L. Amirouche
University of Illinois at Chicago

PRENTICE HALL, Englewood Cliffs, New Jersey 07632

Library of Congress Cataloging-in-Publication Data

AMIROUCHE, FARID M.L.
  Computer-aided design and manufacturing / Farid M. L. Amirouche.
    p. cm.
  Includes bibliographical references and index.
  ISBN 0–13–472341–4
  1. Computer-aided design.   2. CAD/CAM systems.   I. Title.
TA174.A48 1993
670′.285—dc20   92–27575
                                                       CIP

Acquisitions editor: Doug Humphrey
Production editor: Merrill Peterson
Supervisory editor and interior design: Joan Stone
Copy editor: Peter Zurita
Cover designer: Ben Santora
Prepress buyer: Linda Behrens
Manufacturing buyer: Dave Dickey
Editorial assistant: Jaime Zampino

©1993 by Prentice-Hall, Inc.
A Simon & Schuster Company
Englewood Cliffs, New Jersey 07632

Printed in the United States of America

10 9 8 7 6 5 4 3 2 1

ISBN 0-13-472341-4

Prentice-Hall International (UK) Limited, *London*
Prentice-Hall of Australia Pty. Limited, *Sydney*
Prentice-Hall Canada Inc., *Toronto*
Prentice-Hall Hispanoamericana, S.A., *Mexico*
Prentice-Hall of India Private Limited, *New Delhi*
Prentice-Hall of Japan, Inc., *Tokyo*
Simon & Schuster Asia Pte. Ltd., *Singapore*
Editora Prentice-Hall do Brasil, Ltda., *Rio de Janeiro*

*To my son Larby and
my daughter Anissa*

Contents

2   INTRODUCTION TO COMPUTER-AIDED DESIGN   22

3   METHODOLOGY IN DESIGN AND CAD/CAM   45

Preface

With the advent of today's computer technology, we are experiencing a new twist in the way we teach our courses and especially in the manner we educate students on the topic of design. Today, our engineering graduates find themselves facing greater responsibility and challenges in making decisions on companies' product design and manufacturing. Students in most cases need to have the ability to interact with the so-called CAD/CAM systems and understand the basics of the process of design and manufacturing in order to communicate better and be more productive.

The intent of this book is to bring together in one volume the most important areas of design, analysis, and manufacturing in which computers and computer graphics have had a great impact in the past decade and will continue to do so in years to come. The book content is tailored for advanced juniors and seniors and first-year master's degree students. The book should appeal to a large body of engineering fields, especially mechanical engineering. The emphasis in the entire book is on the integration of three disciplines: CAD, CAE, and CAM. Our future engineering students will find themselves more active in all stages of design. This will be possible only with the integration of those disciplines and the blending of man and machine to meet tomorrow's challenges and highly competitive markets. In this book, both design, including analysis, and manufacturing are given equal coverage. Instructors will decide which chapters to use according to their school curriculum. Using the book out of sequence will in no way affect the continuity of the material presented. As a matter of fact, some chapters, such as Chapters 1 and 2, could be assigned as outside reading. Chapter 3 explains the basic concepts of design and shows the effectiveness of computers and computer graphics in today's design process. Illustrative examples are given to stimulate the interest of students in the assigned projects. Chapter 4 is unique; in a sense, it serves as the basis to computer graphics. The derivation of transformation matrices and description of curves encountered in engineering are illustrated through numerous examples.Chapter 5 provides a basic understanding of solid modeling and its integration in today's design and manufacturing. In Chapter 6, the finite-element method is introduced, emphasizing the simplest concepts of mechanics that students learn at the sophomore and junior levels. Applications of CAD/CAM technology are provided in Chapter 7. The manufacturing part of the book is covered in Chapters 8 through 14.

Chapter 8 gives a general introduction to manufacturing. The evolution of manufacturing processes from manual to CNC and DNC machines are fully explained. The programming aspects of CNC machines through APT are presented into two chapters, namely 9 and 10. A complete description of APT geometry and motion statements are described making use of simple yet practical examples. Robotics Technology is introduced in Chapter 11 and 12. These two chapters provide the most comprehensive description of robotics today and their industrial applications. The economics of robots and their purchase justification as well as payback returns are presented for the first time through meaningful exercises. To extend further our understanding of Computer-Aided Manufacturing, selected topics on Group Technology, work cells, and process planning are covered in Chapter 13.

New concepts of Computer-Integrated Manufacturing (CIM) are presented in Chapter 14. This includes a state of the art architecture of CIM and its implementation. The book's last chapter (15) presents some views as to what factors should be considered when purchasing a CAD/CAM system in order to remain competitive.

It is important to note that a full coverage of matrices is presented in appendix A. Many of us teaching a course in CAD/CAM might need a week or two to review matrices. This appendix is very helpful to students. Appendix B gives a listing of a 2D finite element truss developed based on concepts presented in Chapter 6. The intent of this appendix is to give students a platform where they can modify the program input/output to better interact with CAD in general.

A Glossary of CAD/CAM terminology is provided at the end of the book.

The presentation in this book takes a problem-solving approach to the topics, guiding the students through a series of worked-out problems. The book is an outgrowth of years of teaching and research in CAD/CAE/CAM at the University of Illinois at Chicago and the University of Cincinnati. This includes videotaping the course called Introduction to CAD/CAM offered to off-campus engineering students in the Chicago area.

Depending on the students' background and the teaching philosophy, a laboratory class could be introduced to complement the course. The author advises that students be introduced to a CAD graphics package to learn the parallels between theory and practice.

Each chapter of the book ends with a set of problems and assignments written to guide the student through the course. In Chapters 4, 5, 6, 9, 10, and 13 the homework problems could be done in a CAD laboratory where students will get some practice using CAD/CAM workstations or simply PCs equipped with the appropriate software.

This book is written on the assumption that students have had no prior exposure to CAD/CAM; hence the terminology is kept simple and stimulating. Clearly, in a subject as broad as CAD/CAM, not all the subjects can be included. But I believe that if the students are engaged on a number of the projects outlined in this book, they will absorb the materials better.

The author expresses his appreciation for the valuable input from the University of Illinois at Chicago students who took his course Introduction to Computer-Aided Design and Manufacturing (ME 347). I am indebted to the reviewers for their useful suggestions and comments which have undoubtedly enhanced the quality of this book: especially Dr. Ronald L. Huston, my all time friend and colleague, University of Cincinnati; Dr. Tienko Ting, University of Bridgeport; Dr. Dave Janak, University of Cincinnati; and Dr. Musa Jouaneh, University of Rhode Island. I am equally grateful to my students Mr. Steve Tai and Mr. Tarun Arora for their dedication in preparation of parts of the manuscript and illustrations. Without their help this book wouldn't have been possible. I would like to also thank Mr. Nandan Mehta for his efforts. For those who helped contribute to this book by providing me with pictures of their company products, many thanks—especially Ms. Julie Carroll and Ms. Kristine Von Elm from the Center of Engineering Design, University of Utah; Ms. Ann Smith from the ABB Robotics; my friend Mr. Mark Lawry from SDRC; Mr. Vipul Kinariwala from EMRC; Mr. Tom Cole, Public Relations from Boeing Corporation; Mr. Peter May, Algor Inc.; Professor Bob Mabrey of Tennessee Technical University; and Mr. Doug B. Carter, Cincinnati Milacron. I would also like to extend my appreciation to Mr. Peter Zurita for doing an excellent job in editing the book and my friend Mr. Doug Humphrey for his continuous efforts in bringing this book to production.

Finally, I would like to thank my wife Ginger for her patience, support and understanding. She provided me a great deal of motivation to complete this book.

Sometimes we forget the most important people in our lives, those that are responsible for us being here today. For that I would like to thank my father Med Larbi and my mother Yakout for the love they gave me and the appreciation they taught me about education. For my kids, Larby and Anissa, I love you very much.

Farid M.L. Amirouche
Chicago, IL

ABOUT THE AUTHOR

Farid M.L. Amirouche earned a bachelor in engineering science, a Masters in Applied Mechanics and Aerospace, and a Ph.D. in Mechanical Engineering from the University of Cincinnati. He is currently an associate professor in mechanical engineering at the University of Illinois at Chicago. He is the author of over one hundred publications of professional journals and proceedings. For the past five years, he has been conducting research in the area of Computer-Aided Design and Manufacturing (CAD/CAM), multi-body dynamics, rotorcraft systems, vibration and control of flexible constrained mechanical systems and biomechanics. His work has been supported by government agencies such as U.S. Airforce Office of Scientific Research (AFOSR), National Science Foundation (N.S.F.), National Aeronautics and Space Agency (NASA), Veteran Hospital and a number of private industries. He has also served as a DOE fellow where he worked at Argonne National Laboratory on the implementation of robotics in the IFR fuel cycle. His professional activities include N.S.F. panelist, chairman/co-chairman at ASME or ASEE conferences. Dr. Amirouche is a member of ASME, ASEE, AIAA and SAE.

Computer-Aided Design and Manufacturing

chapter 1

Historical Perspective on Digital Computers

1.1 INTRODUCTION

In this era of high technology and computer sophistication, it is inconceivable to talk about computer-aided design and computer-aided manufacturing without first looking back to see where it all began. The essence of computing began in the early 1940s. Though the issue of who first invented the "stored-program computer" is controversial, its history can be traced back to ENIAC (Electronic Numerical Integrator and Computer).

1.2 HISTORY OF THE COMPUTER

Throughout history, humans have always attempted to design and invent mechanisms that would ease the burden of their labors. Until the nineteenth century, these mechanisms could help only with physical work. Not until late in that century were mechanisms designed to assist with mathematical work: computers developed to perform addition and multiplication. These adding machines (also known as third-generation computers) were built from gears, springs, and other mechanical parts. They were limited in functions but did not make mistakes in operations and were faster than calculations done by hand. Complex electromechanical computers were later developed to perform advanced calculations. They used a binary (base-2) logic architecture to symbolize entities and functions. For logic operations, 1 represented a value and 0 represented no value. In a binary representation, addition, subtraction, multiplication, and division were easily performed. For example, to calculate the values 10 and 2 using the four math operators (addition, subtraction, multiplication, and division), we must convert the values to binary numbers (see Appendix 1-1 for further details):

$$(10)_{10} = (01010)_2$$

$$(2)_{10} = (00010)_2$$

To perform addition:

$$\begin{array}{r} 01010 \\ + \ 00010 \\ \hline 01100 \end{array} \qquad (01100)_2 = (12)_{10}$$

To perform subtraction:

$$\begin{array}{r} 01010 \\ - \ 00010 \\ \hline 01000 \end{array} \qquad (01000)_2 = (8)_{10}$$

Mastery of the binary system made the modern computer possible.

Figure 1.1 General view of 'ENIAC', the 1st general purpose Electronic Calculator (Courtesy of UPI/Bettmann newsphotos).

The electromechnical computer was large, cumbersome, and costly to build and maintain. Developments in electricity and electrical circuits made it possible to build an electronic computer using the same binary logic architecture. The cost, speed, and space advantages of this electronic computer were a great improvement over its predecessor. Refinements and advances were made in computer hardware and logic circuits. The creation of an electronic digital computer with memory storage, such as ENIAC (Figures 1.1 and 1.2) paved the way to today's fourth-generation computers.

The story of ENIAC began in the spring of 1941. In a proposal to the U.S. Army, the Moore School offered a machine that could compute ballistic trajectories at least 10 times faster than the differential analyzer the Army possessed. Its modification later became the Electronic Numerical Integrator and Computer, or ENIAC for short.

ENIAC operated at 100,000 pulses per second and thus became the first computer to exploit fully the vacuum-tube technology of the time. The processing speed of ENIAC was very slow by the standards of today's supercomputers, which operate at 100 megapulses per second (CRAY I) to 400 megapulses per second (CRAY XMP, Cyber 205). The machine's organization was dominated by input and output hardware.

Located at the University of Pennsylvania, ENIAC was about a block long and weighed almost 3 tons! When it was turned on, all the lights in Philadelphia dimmed. An operator was at the machine around the clock to change burnt-out light bulbs. Its computation speed was greater than existing electromechanical machines, and it solved problems that were beyond the reach of man at that time. ENIAC's cost was estimated as high as $3.5 million. Today, a microprocessor, or chip, with the same computational efficiency costs $14 or less.

Figure 1.2   ENIAC at the Moore School, 1946 (Courtesy of UPI/Bettmann).

ENIAC caused a hardware revolution in computing. The 18,000-vacuum-tube ENIAC proved that electronic technology could be used to make fast, powerful, reliable general-purpose computers. It began the modern age of electronic computers.

The fourth generation of computers began shortly after the creation of ENIAC, between 1946 and 1952. The computers that were introduced were all based on ENIAC technology and architecture. Today's fourth-generation computers, including the CRAY II and III, are far more advanced, with computing capabilities that seemed impossible in the 1950s.

1.3 DISADVANTAGES OF THE EARLY MACHINES

There were three major problem areas related to the design of the early machines: (1) Communication between man and machine was difficult, (2) maintenance was high and reliability was low, and (3) the computers generated tremendous heat.

Programming the early computers required a great deal of skill and knowledge of each machine's language code because no standard programming language yet existed. All programming had to be written directly in machine languages. There were no predefined functions such as math symbols to indicate mathematical operations. Programming lacked all the timesaving advantages of symbolic representation used today.

In the 1950s, some improvements were made in programming, but the cost of owning a computer was still so high that ownership remained limited to large corporations in the aerospace and aircraft industries. This trend continued into the 1960s, when the prices of computers ranged from $100,000 to tens of million of dollars. It was not until the 1970s, with the advent of hardware and software and the introduction of the microprocessor, or chip, that computer prices began to decline. This is when many smaller industries and businesses were able to invest in computer technology. Today, the chip stores more information, performs calculations 20 times faster, and is several hundred thousand dollars cheaper to manufacture than the block-long ENIAC. The microprocessor has revolutionized the computer world and has made computers affordable to almost everyone.

1.4 COMPUTER HARDWARE

All the physical machinery that makes up a computer is known as hardware. Computer hardware can be divided into four main categories: (1) input devices, (2) output devices, (3) a central processing unit, and (4) memory. Figure 1.3 illustrates the relationship of these categories.

1.4.1 Input Devices

An input device (also known as a reader) is any device that allows the user to communicate with the computer. Communication is usually through an established set of

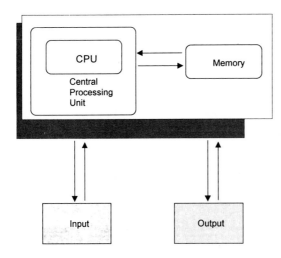

Figure 1.3 Computer configuration.

codes that interprets the input information requested. Some examples of input devices are card readers, paper tape readers, scanners, keyboards, mice, and joysticks.

1.4.2 Output Devices

Output devices are also employed by the computer to communicate with the user. Output devices provide output in two forms: soft copy and hard copy.

The most popular output device provides soft copy, computer output in a nontangible form. The video display unit (VDU) offers the most efficient form of output. The earliest version of the VDU was constructed of a cathode-ray tube (CRT). It used electron beams projected onto a phosphor-coated screen that emitted light when struck by the electron beams. A different form of VDU produces a three-dimensional display that incorporates diffracted laser beams to portray an object in three-dimensional space. This device is still under development.

The second type of output device delivers information in the form of hard copy, such as a printout on paper. It requires more time to print information on paper than to display it on a screen. The most popular hard-copy output device is the printer. There are several types of printers, including line printers, dot-matrix and thermal printers, and laser printers.

1.4.3 Central Processing Unit

The central processing unit (CPU) is the heart of the computer. It is responsible for three functions: (1) manipulating data from memory locations, (2) monitoring and controlling information flow from input and output (I/O) devices and within itself, and (3) carrying out instructions stored in memory. The CPU is constructed of two parts: the controller and the arithmetic-logic unit (ALU). The CPU interacts with memory to receive and store data or information.

The controller receives and interprets instructions from either an outside source (such as a disk drive) or built-in hardware (such as a chip). From these instructions, the controller (1) retrieves the main memory addresses where data is stored, (2) transfers data to the ALU along with instructions to act on it in some way, and (3) moves the results back to the main memory. The controller is always receiving information on what to do next and acts accordingly by its own instruction rules.

The ALU is a complex logic circuit designed to carry out arithmetic operation. These operations are usually addition and subtraction. However, there are ALUs available to handle multiplication, division, and more complex mathematical functions.

A variety of CPUs are available today. They vary in speed, memory management capabilities, and unit of information (word) that is transferred between memory and CPU. A word is made up of a finite number of bits, or binary digits. Table 1.1 shows CPU parameters.

The clock speed defines the number of cycles a chip performs in 1 second. The higher the number of cycles a CPU can run, the faster it can process the data. All processors must rely on a binary code for operation.

1.4.4 Memory

The memory of the computer is composed of basic cell units called binary digits, or bits. Eight consecutive bits are grouped, forming one byte. Bytes are then arranged into words. A word's length depends on the computer design. A word usually occupies one memory location. The main memory stores information including program instructions to be carried out by the controller and also data to be processed by the ALU. The main memory can also store intermediate results while the ALU executes a different portion of the program.

Two types of memory are available: writable memory and read-only memory. Writable memory, also called random-access memory (RAM), is designed to allow information in memory to be changed. The CPU uses RAM to receive the input data. Read-only memory (ROM) cannot be altered. Some typical uses of ROM are

TABLE 1.1   CPU CONFIGURATIONS CURRENTLY AVAILABLE

CPU	Word length	RAM	Clock speed
Personal computers: microcomputers (4–16 bits per word)			
INTEL 8086	8 bits	640 KB	4–6 MHz
8088	8 bits	1 MB	4–6 MHz
80286	16 bits	16 MB	6–20 MHz
Personal computers: minicomputers (16–32 bits per word)			
INTEL 80386SX	32 bits	4 GB	16–33 MHz
80386	32 bits	4 GB	16–33 MHz
80486	32–64 bits	—	—
Large computers (32–64 bits or more per word)			

self-testing a computer, engaging during startup, and information bus architecture control.

Regardless of how large the main memory of a given CPU is, it is still finite and small compared to the magnitude of data the CPU must process. The function of the main memory is to contain instructions and data of the program currently being executed. The relationship of CPU, ALU, and the main memory is given in Figure 1.4. The transfer of information takes place through the information bus. Because computers must be able to access an enormous amount of data, far in excess of the main memory, other devices are necessary to store the excess data permanently. These are known as secondary memory.

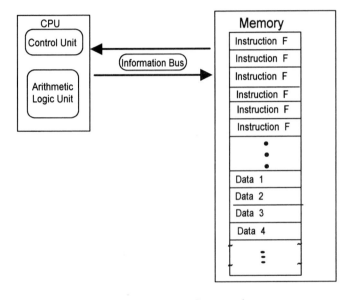

Figure 1.4   Relationship of CPU and memory.

Various types of secondary memory are available. Let us look at some examples.

Compact Disk Read-Only Memory (CD-ROM).   CD-ROM is considered a breakthrough in external storage media. CD-ROM uses the technology of the music industry. A 5-inch CD can contain the information of up to 1200 regular floppy disks.

As a read-only memory device, CD-ROM is ideal for inexperienced users who might erase valuable software. CD-ROM allows the disk to be written only once. It is less sensitive to problems that might damage information on floppy disks and requires less space. CD-ROM systems are currently very expensive, ranging in price from $500 to thousands of dollars. But as improvements and refinements are made, the cost will drop.

Magnetic Disk.   One of the most commonly used storage devices is the magnetic disk. Typically, a magnetic disk consists of six or more metallic platters with concentric tracks. Data are stored on these tracks as either a series of magnetized and nonmagnetized spots on a standard-sized platter 14 inches in diameter. There may be up to 256 tracks, each capable of storing from 3500 to 15,000 characters. The disk is capable of storing 20 to 1000 megabytes (1 megabyte equals 1 million bytes). Data can be transferred from a magnetic disk at a rate ranging from 300,000 to 1.5 million bytes per second. A magnetic disk is not only used as a storage medium but also as an input/output device. Information on a disk can be read repeatedly, and new data can be stored on it simply by writing over the old information.

Magnetic Tape.   Magnetic tape is similar to the tape used on a tape recorder, except it possesses superior quality and durability. Data are stored as a series of magnetized and nonmagnetized spots recorded on a continuous strip of magnetic oxide-coated plastic material. Information can be stored on magnetic tape in various densities ranging from 200 to 6250 bytes per inch (bpi). Tape speed ranges from 37.5 to 200 inches per second, resulting in transfer rates of 7500 to 1,250,000 bpi. Magnetic tape, similar to the other devices, can be used as an input/output medium and can be reused by overwriting. Magnetic tape is widely used for transferring information between computer installations that are not linked together.

Floppy Disk.   The floppy disk operates on the same principle as the conventional magnetic disk, except the platter is made of flexible plastic, hence the name *floppy disk*. Floppy disks are compact media for information storage. They can also be used for input and output operation. They are stored in a plastic or cardboard sleeve for protection. Floppy disks come in three standard sizes: the 8-inch floppy has a memory capacity of 250 kilobytes (1 kilobyte equals 1000 bytes) to 1.5 MB, the $5\frac{1}{4}$-inch floppy has a memory capacity of 125 KB to 1.5 MB, and the $3\frac{1}{2}$-inch floppy has a memory capacity of 360 KB to 2 MB. Memory storage capacity is dependent on the density of the magnetic disk and whether both sides can be used.

Usually, the floppy cannot hold as much data as a conventional disk and its data transfer is not as rapid. However, because the floppy is inexpensive compared to its storage capacity and access speed, it is especially suitable for small and low-cost microcomputers. Various peripherals connected to the computer are displayed in Figure 1.5.

1.5 PROGRAMMING LANGUAGES

Computer programming instructs a (digital) computer what to do and when to do it. A computer language is the means whereby the computer communicates with humans, and vice versa, via input/output devices. Computers do not inherently possess cognitive thought. Programs provide instructions on how to act and react to a limited situation. They do possess a library of binary codes and corresponding values, characters, memory locations, graphics, and other functions built into the computer's hardware. There are currently three levels of computer languages: machine language, assembly language, and high-level languages.

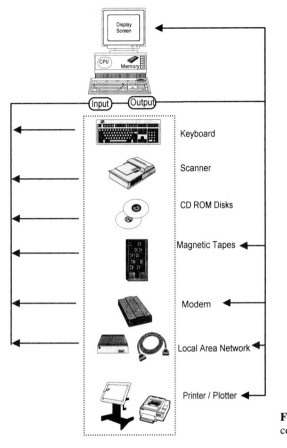

Keyboard

Scanner

CD ROM Disks

Magnetic Tapes

Modem

Local Area Network

Printer / Plotter

Figure 1.5 Peripherals connected to a computer.

1.5.1 Machine Language

Machine language (ML) is the object code the computer understands. ML is composed of an operation code and an operand. Operation code is a binary command or function code that tells the computer what to do. The operand is the binary code that is to be manipulated. For example, a computer hardware engineer designs a computer to recognize the first six bits as an operation code and the following eight bits as the operand. This system recognizes 001111 as a subtraction function in operation code. Suppose we were to write a program line to perform $19 - 8$. The numeric values must first be converted to a binary equivalent (a symbolic table is used when converting characters). The program line should read

$$001111 0001001 100001000$$

where 001111 is subtraction
       00010011 is the operand 19
       00001000 is the operand 8

The nature of ML makes programming tedious and difficult. The makeup of 0's and 1's in a binary code causes optical confusion when reading (discerning each bit length and what it represents) and debugging the program.

1.5.2 Assembly Language

Assembly language was designed to replace ML with an easier-to-discern English-like mnemonic code. A program written in assembly can be translated to ML by an assembler. For each ML statement, there is an equivalent assembly statement.

Machine language and assembly are considered low-level languages due to their complexities. Programming in either requires extensive memorization of all codes by the programmer and comprehensive programs to instruct the computer in every aspect of operation. ML and assembly are "customized" for each computer design. An ML program written for computer A may not work on computer B due to a different configuration in logic design. ML and assembly are machine-oriented.

1.5.3 High-Level Languages

High-level languages (HLLs) were developed to provide users with easier programming. HLLs combine several ML statements into one statement or symbol. The computer comprehends HLLs through a compiler. A compiler is a low-level language that checks for errors in programs written in HLL (source code) and translates them into equivalent low-level language (object code) programs. The disadvantage of HLLs is the time lost in compiling. HLLs are popular due to their ease of programming. Users find HLLs easier to master than their counterparts because of HLLs' Englishlike algorithms. HLL programs can be operated on different systems with few or no changes in the program.

There are different versions of HLLs because each HLL is written for a specific area of application. Let us look at some widely used HLLs.

COBOL.   COBOL (*Common Business-Oriented Language*) was developed in 1959 for business applications in the area of file processing and is designed in a format that simulates composition writing. This language is best adapted to less skilled computer operators. Because COBOL is relatively easy to read and understand, it is most adaptable to operators with no previous computer training. It is used for numeric and alphabetic data processing and file management.

FORTRAN.   The FORTRAN (*For*mula *Tran*slation) language was developed at IBM between 1954 and 1957 for the scientific and technical field to compute complex mathematical problems. The same mathematical hierarchy of operation rules used by mathematicians is incorporated into FORTRAN's math solver. Solving complex (and tedious) math formulas using FORTRAN is easy because programmers write in an identical sequential order the same math operations they would use to find an answer. FORTRAN can handle the simplest math operation to the most complex operations (such as using arrays by writing programming lines that are similar to conventional math formulas).

However, there are several drawbacks to FORTRAN: (1) it has an inadequate ability to read, write, and manipulate text; (2) its program flow control commands are difficult; and (3) subroutines cannot call themselves to repeat the same subroutine function. A FORTRAN programming field has a body of 80 columns. Columns 1–5 are for the statement number. If an instruction (within the field for a FORTRAN statement) calls for that particular statement number, the corresponding FORTRAN line will be executed. Column 6 is a continuation field. If a FORTRAN statement line is too long to fit on the line space provided, the symbol + or $ is entered in the sixth column of the next line to continue. A single FORTRAN statement can have a maximum of 20 lines. Column 7–72 holds the FORTRAN statements that make up the program. Columns 73–81 make up the identification field. Any information entered in this field is ignored by the compiler. A C entered in column 1 of a statement line will cause the whole line to be ignored by the compiler. The main characteristics that make FORTRAN a very popular language today are its loops, conditionals, formatted I/O, and functions and subroutines.

Pascal.   Named for Blaise Pascal, a French mathematician, Pascal is a general-purpose programming language. It was developed by Niklaus Wirth at the Eidgenössische Technische Hochschule in Zurich, Switzerland, during the early 1970s. Pascal can be applied in areas of intensive mathematical solution, business data/file processing, and system programming. Pascal is somewhat lacking in controlled structured flow (e.g., statement line numbers) but is strong in data structure (file) manipulation.

Pascal's programming structure is as follows:

1. Program name
2. Declared variables used by the program and variable type specification (character, real number, integer, etc.)
3. Subroutine program (procedure)
4. Main body of program
5. End statement (to terminate processing)

Pascal uses English-derived statements to instruct the computer. The statements used by Pascal resemble simple sentences in English. For example, suppose you want the computer to print the word *hello*. To accomplish this task using Pascal, you enter "write in ('hello')". Grammarlike symbols are used to instruct the computer to interpret the statements of the program. Such symbols include the semicolon (;), used to indicate the end of a statement, and the period (.), used to indicate the end of the program.

The mathematical capabilities of Pascal rival those of FORTRAN. Pascal has the unique function of determining the remainder of a division problem only. The operator is 'mod' (from *modulo*) and can be created by a "write-in" statement.

Pascal has a very easy formatting route that uses an eight-character line that can be divided into six equal segments (columns). Complex formatting can be done by declaring spaces for output of data. "M:N" would be placed next to the value or variable to be printed. M is the total space allotted for output of characters, and N is taken from M for decimal numbers. This simplified format makes data, file, and text manipulation much easier.

Repeated use of an equation or a set of equations can be placed in a function and a procedure, respectively, to save space in memory. A function within the main program is referred to as a global variable. A function within a procedure is referred to as a local variable. A procedure is similar to a subroutine in FORTRAN, except a procedure must be placed before the main body of the program.

The Pascal structure requires a "begin" statement to declare statements to be executed. Other statements, such as VAR (variable) and CONST (constant), define variables to be used in the program.

Conditionals used by Pascal are similar to those used by FORTRAN but simpler. All logical operators are in symbol form, as shown in Table 1.2.

Compound conditionals use the same conjunctions as FORTRAN. The "if-then" statements used in Pascal are almost identical to the FORTRAN versions, except Pascal cannot call statement line numbers.

BASIC.   BASIC (*B*eginner's *A*ll-*P*urpose *S*ymbolic *I*nteractive *C*ode) was developed in the mid-1960s by John Kemeny and Thomas Kurtz at Dartmouth College. BASIC was designed to be an all-purpose programming language for beginners. BASIC programming resembles the strong mathematical support of FORTRAN and the data and file manipulations of Pascal. BASIC has statement line numbers so that structured flow can be controlled. BASIC is unique because of its modified compiler. After each statement line is entered, the compiler automatically checks for errors in statement use.

BASIC is used widely in personal computers. Several versions of BASIC are available. Some versions are able to do much more than others. The language is still

TABLE 1.2 LOGICAL OPERATIONS IN FORTRAN AND PASCAL

Definition	FORTRAN	Pascal
Greater than	.GT.	>
Less than	.LT.	<
Equal to	.EQ.	=
Greater than or equal to	.GE.	>=
Less than or equal to	.LE.	<=
Not equal to	.NE.	<>

used to teach computer programming to elementary and high school students. (Many computer games that were popular during the late 1970s were written in BASIC.)

Direct mode uses a limited range of BASIC statements. In direct mode, one can operate all mathematical operations and simple print statements, change default values, and operate some I/O capabilities. Direct mode was intended to give a quick demonstration of various programming features and I/O abilities.

Programming mode requires a structured program format. Unlike Pascal and FORTRAN, a program name is not required to begin a program. Each statement requires a line statement number. A comparison between direct mode and programming mode is given in Table 1.3.

BASIC can use all the programming techniques of FORTRAN. BASIC has similar conditional structures and the simple formatting style of Pascal. The line statement number structure, loop procedure, function and subroutine method, and overall appearance of BASIC are similar to those of FORTRAN.

C.   C is a programming language developed in 1972 by Dennis Ritchie at AT&T Bell Laboratories. C was originally developed to run with the UNIX operating system, but the popularity of C made it available on non-UNIX systems. It also followed in the path of BASIC and Pascal of being easy to use. C's strongest ability lies in the area of system software.

The technique of running a C program is relatively easy:

- To call a program file, enter **$CAT filename**
- To compile a program file, enter **$CC filename**
- To execute a program file, enter **$A.OUT**

To run a program, the compile and execute commands must be entered. To enter a comment (that the compiler will ignore), "/* " starts the comment space and "*/ " ends it. Because the name of the program does not appear, comments are in-

TABLE 1.3 COMPARISON OF DIRECT MODE
AND PROGRAMMING MODE IN BASIC

Purpose	Direct mode	Programming mode
Tell the computer to print "hello"	Print 'hello'	10 print 'hello' 20 END RUN
Add 3 and 5 and display answer	Print 3 + 5	10 print 3 + 5
Add 7 and 9 and display answer	Print 7 + 9	20 print 7 + 9
Add 2 and 3 and display answer	Print 2 + 3	30 print 2 + 3 40 END RUN

serted to describe what the program is used for. A semicolon (;) is placed at the end of statements, as in Pascal, to mark the end of a programming line. Brackets are used to surround a block of statements to indicate that it should be treated as a single routine.

C possesses the same mathematical capabilities as FORTRAN and the simplicity of Pascal. The same techniques applied to the other languages can also be operated by C. C does require some practice, but if one is well versed in C, one can apply it to very powerful applications.

The programming language and format of C is much simpler than FORTRAN and BASIC, requiring a less rigid format and much simpler and abbreviated commands.

Ada/Ed.   Ada/Ed was developed by the U.S. Department of Defense around 1975 for controlling and consolidating various computer parts and systems that essentially contain their own computer language. It was named after Augusta Eda, who was supposedly the first "computer" programmer (1842). The power of Ada/Ed lies in its ability to perform several operations on several computers at the same time. Ada/Ed can use the full capability of multitasking (parallel processing) computer architecture available as a programming language. Unlike other current high-level programming languages, which perform tasks in a sequential order as dictated by the programming language, Ada/Ed allows several operations to run concurrently, thus saving computational time as well as money.

Ada/Ed is a prototype HLL compiler that verifies a set of data, passed from one part of the computer to another. If the program contains errors (in data calculation or manipulation), the Ada/Ed compiler will notify the user. New York University's computer science group has a version of the Ada/Ed language, known as SETL (Set Language). The language terms (statements) are based on set theory. Just as HLLs allow a statement to encase several low-level statements for convenience of programming, SETL allows several conventional high-level statements to equal one SETL statement. For example, a 30,000-line SETL program can equal up to half a million lines in a conventional high-level language. Two other high-level programming languages for parallel processors are STRAND (Argonne Laboratories) and KL1.

The benefits of Ada/Ed are ease in programming and shorter computational time. An Ada/Ed-type high-level language is currently under development and refinement. The syntax used by Ada/Ed must be developed to the point where it can be as easily understood as FORTRAN and Pascal are today.

1.6 COMPUTER CATEGORIES

Although the internal components of different types of digital computers are basically alike, computers can be grouped into the following categories:

Supercomputer

Mainframe computer

Minicomputer/workstation

Microcomputer/workstation

Stand-alone personal computer

Computers can be categorized according to word length, which represents the width of the internal data transfer paths of the compiler.

The supercomputer can be defined as the computer that is currently the world's fastest and most powerful. Today's supercomputer is capable of operating at speeds of 20 million operations per second.

The mainframe is also a very powerful computer that generally has a word length of 32 bits or more. It has a large main memory and is capable of fast processing. The mainframe is often used to solve complex engineering and scientific problems such as interactive calculations in fluid dynamics analysis, heat transfer analysis, and stress analysis. Mainframes are also used in large-scale data processing operations such as payroll, corporate accounting, production scheduling, and maintenance of large databases.

The minicomputer is less powerful than a mainframe and usually has a word length of 16 bits. Because the minicomputer is not very expensive, it is cost-efficient in commercial and industrial applications. The minicomputer is relatively small; therefore, it is often used as part of large testing equipment.

The microcomputer has a word length of 8 bits. The applications of a microcomputer are numerous, however; they usually perform a small specific task within a large system.

The stand-alone computer performs processing within its own environment. It is slower than the other classes of computers, and its abilities are more limited. Advances in computer technology are slowly merging the mini, macro, and stand-alone categories into one. Some stand-alone computers now possess 32-bit processors and an expansive active memory that rivals the abilities of mainframe computers of the early 1980s.

In today's market, it has become more difficult to classify computers by word length. A 32-bit minicomputer called a supermini has been developed, along with 16-bit and 32-bit microcomputers called the supermicro and megamicro, respectively. A large minicomputer is capable of the functions of a mainframe, and a large microcomputer is capable of the functions of a minicomputer. The size and complexity of any computer system depend on the functions required of the computer.

1.7 GRAPHICS USING THE LINE PRINTER

Computer line printers are used for printing the desired input/output listings (such as files and program output) in special formats. Considerable progress has been made in generating graphics. Through character manipulation, programs were written to display graphs, waves, and figures by simply using the character symbols available in the corresponding programming languages. Some computer languages have greater capabilities than others in handling characters and are easier to program.

1.8 THE FUTURE ROLE OF COMPUTERS

The world of computers is going through a dynamic transition due to the low cost of manufacturing and high demand. Faster systems are being built to meet the needs of computing in production. An odd situation has occurred due to the development of faster computers: operating system software improvements are beginning to lag behind hardware improvements. Operating system software is designed to manage computer hardware system operations and allows compatible software to interact and operate within the computer. Debates over standardization of an operating system have divided the computer industry and threaten to hinder the progress of computer technology. UNIX has been accepted as the standard operating system for multitasking. Many computer manufacturers have built their system to run UNIX because of its flexibility and power. Recently, AT&T joined Sun Microsystems to update UNIX. Many other computer companies objected to this partnership because AT&T and Sun will have advance information on the new UNIX. With this information, AT&T and Sun will have an unfair advantage in developing hardware compatible with the new UNIX operating system. Other companies have united to create their own new UNIX version. Known as the Open Software Foundation, Hewlett-Packard, DEC, and others will compete with AT&T/Sun in influencing the new computer market. UNIX, DOS, and other current operating systems will be obsolete with the introduction of the next generation of computers.

As computers evolve from their present state, they will be able to assume more difficult tasks—tasks that require actual thought. These fifth-generation computers will contain artificial intelligence. Artificial intelligence is the capability of the computer to perform deductive and inductive thinking. From information it collects, the computer will make a "guess" using inductive logic when a solution is not available.

Hardware for the fifth-generation computers is presently being built. Examples of such computers include the psi II and the multi-psi workstation, which contains a 16-bit parallel processor and incorporates a high-level parallel processing language called KL1 (similar to Ada/Ed). This new generation of computers will have parallel processing as an architectural base to carry out several operations concurrently. The term *fifth-generation* is currently used to refer to computers with parallel processors. But some experts maintain that these same computers will have artificial intelligence built into their operating systems. The design for the artificial intelligence programs is still at the research level.

PROLOG (*Pro*gramming *Log*ic) is intended to be the language for the fifth-generation computers. PROLOG uses symbolic logic along with certain rules to make decisions and reach conclusions. Its mathematical operators and rule of mathematical hierarchy are similar to those of FORTRAN. Among the symbolic logic rules that PROLOG uses are rules of inference (e.g., *modus tollens,* dilemma, hypothetical syllogism), replacement rules (e.g., De Morgan's, exportation, contraposition), rules of conditional proofs, and rules of indirect proofs.

PROBLEMS

1.1 Compare the computing (processing) speeds of today's (8088 low-end) PC/AT with the ENIAC machine.

1.2 (a) List the characteristics of the computer's available memory. (b) How are the peripheral tapes and disks used for additional memory storage?

1.3 (a) Briefly list the advantages of high-level languages. (b) Compare the advantages of Ada/Ed-type language with FORTRAN.

1.4 How does the computer process data as compared to the normal human thinking process?

1.5 Briefly compare and contrast the advantages and disadvantages of using computers.

1.6 Convert $(15.3)_{10}$ and $(103)_{10}$ to binary numbers, and $(72.68)_{10}$ to base 6.

1.7 How do current fourth-generation computers differ from third-generation computers?

1.8 What were the disadvantages of using the early third-generation computers?

1.9 Briefly describe output devices and input devices.

1.10 What are the benefits of using a VDU as opposed to a printer?

1.11 What are the functions of a CPU?

1.12 What is a word? What is a bit?

1.13 Describe the types of programming languages available.

1.14 What is the function of a compiler?

1.15 Of the high-level languages discussed in this chapter, which would you prefer and why? (Would you like even better a language from your previous experience?) How would your preferred language help you in the field of mechanical engineering?

REFERENCES

1.1 Bensant, C. B., and Lui, C. W. K., *Computer-Aided Design and Manufacture,* 3d ed., Halstead Press, New York, 1986.

1.2 Coddington, L., *Quick Cobol,* 2d ed., Elsevier North-Holland, New York, 1978.

1.3 Etter, D. M., *Structured Fortran 77 for Engineers and Scientists,* 2d ed., The Benjamin/ Cummings Publishing Co., Menlo Park, CA, 1987.

1.4 Hancock, L., and Krieger, M., *The C Primer,* 2d ed., McGraw-Hill, New York, 1986.

1.5 Metropolis, N., Howlett, J., and Rota, G., *A History of Computing in the Twentieth Century,* Academic Press, Orlando, Fla., 1980.

APPENDIX 1-1:
MACHINE REPRESENTATION OF DATA
ON DIFFERENT *BASES*

The most frequently used number systems are: binary, octal, decimal, and hexadecimal. The binary number system uses the numbers {0,1}, the octal number system {0–7}, the decimal number system {0–9}, and the hexadecimal (HEX) number system {0–9, A,B,C,D,E,F}. Those number systems are said to be the *base* of the numbers. Table A.1 denotes such a representation. What follows are conversion procedures to represent numbers in different *bases*:

A.1 TABLE OF NUMBERS

Decimal	Octal	Hexadecimal	Binary
0	0	0	0000
1	1	1	0001
2	2	2	0010
3	3	3	0011
4	4	4	0100
5	5	5	0101
6	6	6	0110
7	7	7	0111
8	10	8	1000
9	11	9	1001
10	12	A	1010
11	13	B	1011
12	14	C	1100
13	15	D	1101
14	16	E	1110
15	17	F	1111

A.2 REPRESENTATION OF NUMBERS FROM *BASE 10*
TO ANOTHER *BASE*

The technique to convert an integer number from *base 10* to another *base* is:

1. Divide the *base 10* number by the new base number, i.e., divide by 2 when converting to *base 2,* divide by 8 when converting to *base 8,* etc.
2. The remainder of the division in step 1 is a digit of the number in the new *base.* This digit is located at the left of the decimal point in the number of the new *base.*
3. If the result of the division is bigger or equal than the new *base* number, repeat

step 1. Else, the resultant number is located to the left of the previous digit, i.e., as the most significant digit.

Example

a) Convert the number 105 from *base 10* to its correspondent number in *base 8*.

$$105_{(10)} \text{ to } \underline{?}_{(8)}$$

		remainder
8	105	1
8	13	5
	1	1

$105 \div 8 : \text{result} = 13, \text{remainder} = 1$

$13 \div 8 : \text{result} = 1, \text{remainder} = 5$

$\text{result} \leq 8, \text{stop}.$

Answer: $105_{(10)} = 151_{(8)}$

b) Convert the same number from *base 10* to *base 2*.

$$105_{(10)} \text{ to } \underline{?}_{(2)}$$

		remainder
2	105	1
2	52	0
2	26	0
2	13	1
2	6	0
2	3	1
	1	1

Answer: $105_{(10)} = 1101001_{(2)}$

c) Similarly, the conversion to *base 16* could be done as:

$$105_{(10)} \text{ to } \underline{?}_{(16)}$$

		remainder
16	105	9
	6	6

Answer: $105_{(10)} = 69_{(16)}$ ∎

To represent a real number given in *base 10* to another *base,* the previous procedure for the integer part shall apply to the number to the left-hand side of the decimal point. The following procedure is followed for the fractional part.

1. Obtain the fractional part and multiply it by the new *base* number.
2. The integer part of the resultant product in step 1 is the digit of the fractional part of the number in the new *base*. It is located to the right side of the decimal point and of the previous digits if any.
3. If the fractional part of the product in step 1 is equal to zero, stop. Else, the fractional part of the multiplication is used to repeat step 1 until the desired precision is reached.

Example

a) Convert $.15_{(10)}$ to *base 16*.

$$.15_{(10)} = \underline{?}_{(16)}$$

integer

	.15
	× 16
2	.40
	× 16
6	.40
	× 16
6	.40
	× 16
6	.40

Answer: $.15_{(10)} = .266_{(16)}$

b) Convert $.120_{(10)}$ to *base 8*.

$$.120_{(10)} = \underline{?}_{(8)}$$

integer

	.120	
	× 8	$\longrightarrow$ $(.120)(8) = .960$
0	.960	
	× 8	$\longrightarrow$ $(.960)(8) = 7.680$
7	.680	
	× 8	$\longrightarrow$ $(.680)(8) = 5.440$

integer

5	.440
	× 8	$\longrightarrow$ (.440)(8) = 3.520
3	.520
	× 8	$\longrightarrow$ (.520)(8) = 4.160
4	.160
	× 8	$\longrightarrow$ (.160)(8) = 1.280
1	.280
	× 8	$\longrightarrow$ (.280)(8) = 2.240
2	.240

Answer: $.120_{(10)} = .0753412_{(8)}$ ∎

A.3 A GENERAL REPRESENTATION OF NUMBERS IN DIFFERENT *BASES*

The procedure to obtain the decimal representation of any number in another *base* obeys the following expression:

$$\text{Decimal value} = \sum_i b^i \cdot d_i$$

where b is the *base* number, b^i is the positional weight, and d_i is the positional value. The left digit next to the decimal point has the position $i = 0$, the value of i increases to the left digits, and decreases to the right digits.

Example

$$1101101_{(2)} = 2^6 \cdot 1 + 2^5 \cdot 1 + 2^4 \cdot 0 + 2^3 \cdot 1 + 2^2 \cdot 1 + 2^1 \cdot 0 + 2^0 \cdot 1$$

$$= 64 + 32 + 8 + 4 + 1 = 109_{(10)}$$

$$110.11_{(2)} = 2^2 \cdot 1 + 2^1 \cdot 1 + 2^{-1} \cdot 1 + 2^{-2} \cdot 1$$

$$= 4 + 2 + .5 + .25 = 6.75_{10}$$

$$151_{(8)} = 8^2 \cdot 1 + 8^1 \cdot 5 + 8^0 \cdot 1 = 64 + 40 + 1 = 105_{(10)}$$ ∎

chapter 2

Introduction
to Computer-Aided Design

2.1 INTRODUCTION

Computer-aided design (CAD) is the creation and manipulation of pictures (design prototypes) on a computer to assist the engineer in the design process. CAD has developed over the past quarter century into an indispensable tool for the technology, design, and manufacturing industries. CAD revolves around the integration of the best characteristics of three major elements: CAD hardware, software, and user.

The blending of computers and the human ability to make decisions provides the optimum CAD system. Its primary functions are in designing, analyzing, and manufacturing. Although most novices think of CAD as an electronic drafting board, its functions stretch beyond drawing pictures. An analysis of the object drawn with CAD can be made interactively on the screen, where physical information can be extracted. In engineering, finite-element analysis, heat transfer analysis, stress analysis, dynamic simulation of mechanisms, and fluid dynamic analysis are common operations performed with CAD.

2.2 HISTORY OF CAD

In a sense, CAD represents the evolution of computer graphical representation of information. It was created by the aerospace and automotive industries as a method of increasing the rate of technological development and reducing many tedious tasks of the designer. Patrick Hanratty began early research in the development of computer-aided design while working for General Motors Research Laboratory in the early 1960s.

Graphical representation in computers can be traced back to the beginning of digital computers. In the mid-1950s the SAGE (Semi-Automatic Ground Environment) Air Defense Command and Control System used computer graphics (Figure 2.1). SAGE changed radar information into computer-generated pictures. It also made use of the light pen, which allowed the user to choose information by pointing at the appropriate area displayed on the CRT.

A milestone in the development of computer graphics was the pioneering work of Ivan Sutherland. In 1963, Sutherland's doctoral thesis, describing the sketch pad, began laying the theoretical basis for computer graphics software. The sketch pad consists of a cathode-ray oscilloscope driven by a Lincoln TX-2 computer. Pictures could be displayed on the screen and manipulated by the user with a light pen. The use of systems based on the sketch pad has become known as interactive graphics. The sketch pad clearly showed the potential for a CRT as a designer's electronic drawing board with graphic operations, including scaling, translation, rotation, animation, and simulation. However, in the early 1960s, these systems were very expensive. The only users were large industries that could justify their high cost.

In the late 1970s and the 1980s, hardware with faster processing speeds, larger memory, and smaller size became widely available and affordable to various smaller industries.

Figure 2.1   The SAGE digital computer was used by the U.S. Air Force to track and identify aircraft flying through U.S. air space. (Courtesy of UPI/Bettmann.)

2.3 CAD GRAPHICS GENERATOR

The lack of early computer graphics made the interpretation of computer output strenuous on the designer because it appeared in a numeric format. What was needed was a means whereby the designer could communicate with the results of the computer. This was made possible by the development of the graphic generator, which forms the basis of CAD today. A graphical program is much better at describing a design to the average user. The adage "A picture is worth a thousand words" is still true.

General-purpose CAD graphic programs use the Cartesian coordinates to organize the data for display and visualization. The x, y, and z axes describe the position and space that entities occupy. By manipulating the values of the arrays, which contain all points that the object occupies, one can scale (magnify or reduce) the object, rotate the object about any axis, and translate (move) the object to another location in the same reference axis.

2.3.1 Scaling

To scale a drawing, the magnification factor must be supplied by the designer. Once the computer receives the scaling size, the so-called configuration matrix is multiplied by the appropriate transformation matrix to yield the desired scaled geometry. This will be discussed in detail in Chapter 4. It is worth mentioning that some CAD systems have a ZOOM/PAN key that allows the user automatically to magnify the geometry to either two or four times its size. The original drawing could be reproduced by a simple regenerate command.

2.3.2 Rotation

Rotating an object involves a procedure similar to that used in scaling. The rotation is usually defined with respect to a point or an arbitrary line. In CAD, the user is asked to select the points or axes of rotation in addition to the angle of rotation (clockwise or counterclockwise). The CAD workstation, through its software, will then automatically display the rotated object. Though this operation seems simple, the mathematics involves multiplication of matrices defining the geometry and the rotation. In Chapter 4, all the rotations will be discussed for two- and three-dimensional space.

2.3.3 Translation

Translation is moving the object from one destination to another. The amount of movement on each axis is usually defined by the user. The program will then define the move conditions for the object and display it accordingly. Different CAD systems provide the user with several options for translation in which the new destination could be given through the absolute coordinates by providing the corresponding changes in the *x*, *y*, and *z* coordinates. Another option is specifying a particular point position using the cursor or entering the incremental positioning of the location of the new position. It is important to note that the translation is done with respect to a reference point, assumed to be zero if not supplied. This option allows the user to take advantage of several reference frames to translate the object on the screen.

2.3.4 Geometry Representation

Early graphics programs modeled entities by wireframe drawings. Wireframe drawings are made up of lines, points, and curves representing the outline of the object (Figure 2.2). It requires some imagination for the viewer to envision the appearance of the object. There is a hatch function (as in AutoCAD and others) that hides the lines that should not appear on a particular view to improve the visualization of the drawing. Hidden line removal is an important feature in displaying graphics in dif-

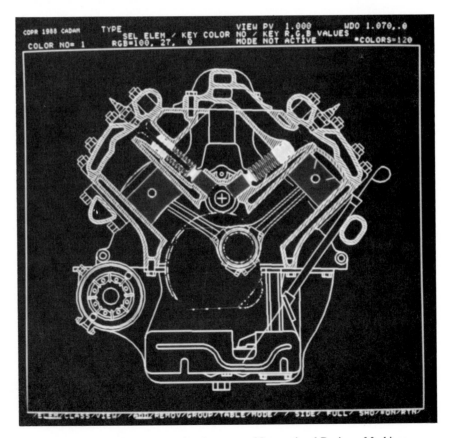

Figure 2.2   Wireframe drawing (courtesy of International Business Machines Corporation).

ferent views. Although the computer may understand the volume inside the wireframe it occupies, the viewer may not. The introduction of solid modeling (Figure 2.3) resulted in a significant improvement in design interpretation. This enhancement is vital to the design and yields a conceptualized picture of how the object would look in the real world. Current CAD programs can reproduce the actual picture of the object being designed. A recent development in computer representation of graphics is stereolithography (by 3D systems). It uses a computer-guided laser to develop three-dimensional prototype parts using photosensitive liquid plastic (Figure 2.4). The technique is based on using the same data that produced CAD drawings, and the machine turns out plastic prototypes. The parts are made by mathematically slicing CAD designs into thin cross sections. An ultraviolet beam traces each layer in a vat of photosensitive chemicals that solidify as they are irradiated. The stereolithography apparatus (SLA) machines produce parts at a rate of one vertical every 2 hours.

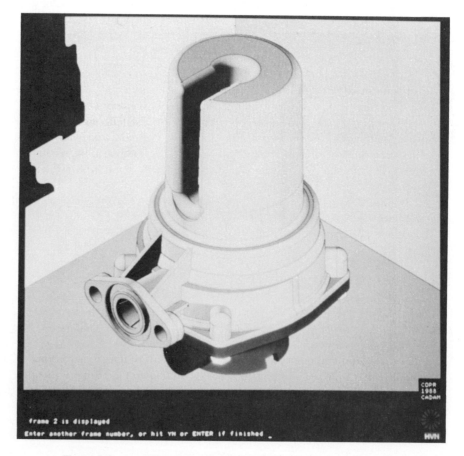

Figure 2.3 A solid modeling drawing (courtesy of International Business Machines Corporation).

Figure 2.4 A CAD system that uses stereolithography (courtesy of 3D systems, Inc.).

As computer capabilities improved, programmers discovered that these graphics programs can do more than just draw objects. They are used in conjunction with analysis and manufacturing programs to create an environment in which products can be made to the highest quality standards. This adds a new dimension to productivity and customer satisfaction.

2.4 OBJECTIVE OF A CAD PROGRAM

The computer's memory capacity and processor speed are the two top considerations when selecting a CAD software package. For example, a moderately complex detail drawing generally consists of approximately 2000 CAD entities. A good CAD package in a production environment should be able to redraw at a rate of 2000 entities per second at a screen resolution of 1024 × 768 pixels. Observations of the speed can be made by zooming, panning, or redrawing (regenerating) a large drawing of approximately 10,000 entities. Some software includes both redraw and regenerate commands. The regenerate function updates everything on disk, whereas redraw updates only a local integer base that controls the current screen image.

The features previously described are used in almost all CAD systems that are mainframe- or minicomputer-based. Other features included in the software are the ability to perform simple calculations such as areas, volumes, centroids, moments of inertia, and centers of mass (Figure 2.5).

Desirable features of CAD software packages are "user-friendly" communication, geometry creation (2D and 3D), dimensioning and labeling, and editing ability.

CAD must be developed to be user-friendly. There are criteria for such a system:

1. The program must be designed so that the user spends more time on the design than on commands.
2. The number of steps necessary to activate any command must be minimized.
3. Any command that affects the database should have protection against accidental deletion or reorganization.
4. The menu should be arranged for easy interaction with the user.

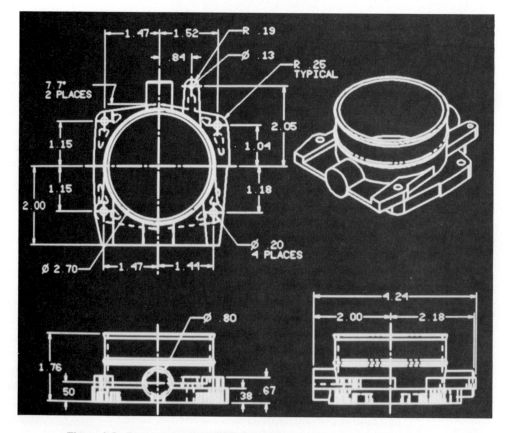

Figure 2.5 Drawings made by PC-based CAD software (courtesy of International Business Machines Corporation).

5. A set of nested commands should be accessible in the midst of drawing, editing, or dimensioning without affecting the progression of the current command. That is, the user can view options during the current command.

6. The overall appearance of CAD should be a neat layout format, as simple as possible.

2.5 DRAWING FEATURES IN CAD SOFTWARE

Geometry creation is the construction of shapes through the manipulation of lines, arcs, surfaces, and curves. Virtually all CAD software is capable of drawing lines, circles, arcs, rectangles, polygons, points, splines, closed curves, and double lines. Entities such as polygons and curves are usually stored as mathematical equations under a file or function name. Variables used in these equations are either adjusted by the user or by the program itself to fit each particular need. Superior CAD programs offer various tools to assist designers in accomplishing their task. These tools include on-screen feedback of absolute, relative, or polar coordinates; rubber band lines; grid and object snaps; and parallels, perpendiculars, and tangents to existing entities. A complete set of object snaps is important to speed the creation of the geometry.

For mechanical design, other features must be included, among them automatic fillets and chamfers, automated crosshatching, the ability to construct circular or rectangular arrays of selected objects, and automatic calculation of areas and section properties.

Every designer relies on a trial-and-error approach that requires the ability to edit a drawing repeatedly. Editing includes deleting, inserting, scaling, rotating, zooming, and even crosshatching.

2.5.1 Editing

All CAD programs have editing features that range from confusing to simplistic. The editing command usually includes functions such as erase, trim, extend, scale, rotate, stretch, undo, move, copy break, mirror, mirror copy, group, ungroup, and change entity characteristics.

Additional features, such as zoom/window, are used to magnify specific areas for more accurate editing.

2.5.2 Dimensioning and Labeling

The first important characteristic of dimensioning relies on its associative function. This means when an object is stretched, scaled, moved, or rotated, the arrows and leaders change to reflect the new geometry.

The second consideration lies in the format of its labels, which include ordinate, baseline, and chained dimensions; control of text size and location; decimal precision; choice of arrowhead style; and dual unit dimensions and tolerances.

It is beneficial for the user to have a set of editing commands that allows quick switching between formats.

2.6 TYPICAL CAD COMMAND STRUCTURE

Most CAD programs have a common structure displayed in menu form that allows the user to select the appropriate option in designing, plotting, filing, and other operations. The commands are grouped to form a command branch as described here.

2.6.1 Command Branch

The command branch outlines the following options:

- PLOT (to access print capabilities)
- DRAW (to access drawing)
- UTILITIES (to access, check, or alter defined parameters such as printer drive file or tolerances)
- FILE (to create or manipulate files)
- VIEW (to access the command to display drawings from various vantage points)

Each option has its own menu from which the appropriate functions to generate the desired drawing are selected. For example, on the draw function menu we will find a series of sublistings, such as LINE, POINT, ARC, and CIRCLE, and each sublisting can be made up of a variety of helpful commands, for example:

```
- DRAW
  LINE
  *DRAWN FROM:
        - POINT TO POINT
        - VERTICAL
        - HORIZONTAL
        - FROM A POINT AND TANGENT TO
        - PARALLEL AT A DISTANCE
        - TANGENT TO TWO CURVES
        - INTERSECTION OF TWO PLANES
        - FROM A POINT AT AN ANGLE
```

For drafting purposes, the line can appear as DASHED, SOLID, or other. Those options can be selected from a menu as follows:

```
*LINETYPE
      - DASHED
      - CENTER
      - SOLID
      - HIDDEN
```

In addition, we can select the color for the line (entity) as follows:

```
                    *LINE COLOR
                      - RED
                      - GREEN
                      - BLUE
                      - YELLOW
                      - CYAN
                      - WHITE
                      - VIOLET
```

For instance, if you need to draw a circle, the following selections can be made:

```
        CIRCLE
        *DRAWN FROM:
             - A CENTER AND RADIUS
             - A CENTER AND TANGENT TO A LINE
             - A CENTER AND TANGENT TO AN ARC
             - A CENTER AND A POINT ON THE CIRCUMFERENCE
             - TANGENT TO TWO LINES
             - TANGENT TO TWO CURVES
             - TANGENT TO THREE CIRCLES
             - THROUGH THREE POINTS
```

Most of the entities that form the object to be drawn are selected from menus like these.

2.6.2 MACRO

CAD software packages are equipped with a powerful function called MACRO. This option allows the user to assemble a set of commands to be executed under one name, which is referred to under the MACRO subroutine. The most commonly repeated series of commands can be stored under MACROs to save time in CAD drawing. For example, a MACRO dimensioning command will combine the following statements under one MACRO name:

- Locate the position of the selected entity
- Measure the entity using predefined units and tolerances
- Format dimensioning labels using predetermined layout such as fonts
- Locate text arrows

2.7 COMPUTER HARDWARE

The CAD software package is designed to run under three types of computer systems: mainframe, personal computer, and workstation.

2.7.1 Mainframe

To be able to use the CAD software on a mainframe, a special workstation is needed. This workstation is designed to handle data exchange at a rate of 1200 to 9600 baud. All CAD processing is performed in the mainframe; the workstation is used only to display graphics. In most cases, the CAD workstation does not perform any calculations. There are a few machines that possess some local processing capabilities such as dynamic rotation, translation, and limited animation display. The advantages of a mainframe in conjunction with the CAD workstation are expanded memory and processing speed. However, the drawbacks are cost and maintenance of a mainframe (Figure 2.6).

2.7.2 Personal Computer (PC)

Today's personal computers are becoming more powerful and represent a real challenge to mainframe computers. A personal computer is a stand-alone machine with its own processor, operating system, memory, and graphics capabilities. A typical PC selected for CAD operation would have a 16-bit processor (Intel 80286 mi-

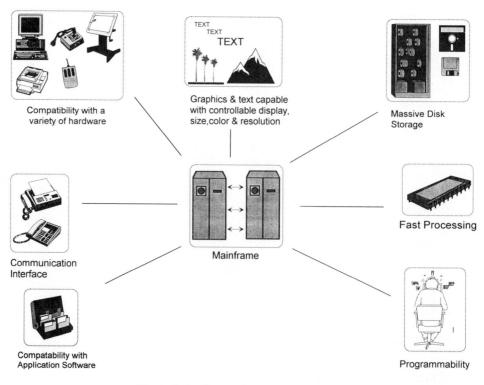

Compatibility with a
variety of hardware

Graphics & text capable
with controllable display,
size, color & resolution

Massive Disk
Storage

Communication
Interface

Fast Processing

Mainframe

Compatability with
Application Software

Programmability

Figure 2.6 Characteristics of a Mainframe.

croprocessor) or a 32-bit processor (Intel 80386 or 80486 microprocessor), parallel processing architecture, 16 megabytes (or more) of RAM, and the UNIX, DOS, or OS/2 operating system for multitasking.

Currently, there are many CAD software packages that can run on a PC, among them AutoCAD, VersaCAD, and CADKEY. The price ranges from $500 to several thousand dollars. Most CAD programs use the same I/O devices as for general computer use. Much CAD hardware is available.

2.7.3 Workstation

A CAD workstation consists of three components: the host computer, input devices, and output devices. Figure 2.7 shows a typical CAD workstation. The host computer is where all the software is located and where all processing takes place. In the stand-alone type of CAD workstation, the host computer (CPU) is integrated in the machine. The others have the mainframe as a separate unit.

A workstation is superior to a PC because it is designed to communicate with a larger array of computers and mainframes. The standards for PCs have risen significantly over the past few years to match the capabilities of a workstation.

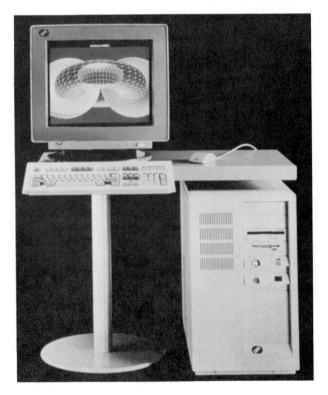

Figure 2.7 A typical CAD workstation (courtesy of International Business Machines Corporation).

2.8 CAD HARDWARE (ACCESSORIES)

Because of today's increasing demand for more power and higher speed, hardware is constantly being improved and redesigned.

The accessories and peripherals to a CAD system are divided between the input and output. However, some hardware devices can be categorized as both input and output.

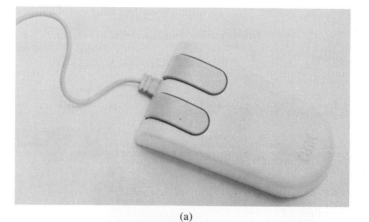

(a)

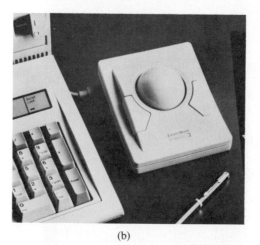

(b)

Figure 2.8 (a) A mouse (courtesy of International Business Machines Corporation) (b) A trackball (expert mouse, expert mouse is a trademark and Kensington is a registered trademark of Kensington Microwave Limited).

2.8.1 Input Devices

In CAD applications, these devices make it possible for a user to communicate with a database to modify existing drawings or create new drawings. A variety of input equipment for CAD packages is available. The most common devices used for design are potentiometer devices (mouse, trackball, joystick), light pens, digitizers, and keyboards. All control the cursor in simple executions.

   Potentiometer Devices.   There are two types of potentiometers: the rotary potentiometer, which controls object rotation. and the slide potentiometer, which controls linear movement. Analog motion applied to controls of the potentiometers is converted to (binary) digital values to be read by the computer.

   The mouse and the trackball are potentiometers (Figure 2.8). In both, a plastic ball is used to track the desired motion of the cursor. The plastic ball turns internal potentiometers, which convert analog motion to digital data. The trackball has the plastic ball face up, where the hand controls the trackball positioning. The mouse is an upside-down version of a trackball. The motion of the mouse on a flat surface causes the ball to turn the internal potentiometers.

   The joystick (Figure 2.9) is another potentiometer device. The joystick moves the cursor in the desired direction. Internal potentiometers sense the joystick motion and act accordingly. The joystick can be moved right, left, forward, and backward. Two types of joystick are available: absolute and rate. The absolute joystick moves the cursor in the direction of the joystick with a finite distance proportional to the values measured by the movement of the joystick. The rate joystick moves the cursor at a speed defined by the position of the joystick. Some rate joysticks have an acceleration rate defined by the amount of displacement of the joystick from its neutral position. A hybrid joystick has been designed with the characteristics of both types.

Figure 2.9 A joystick.

Light Pen.   A light pen (Figure 2.10) is a light-sensitive scanner that identifies a position on the screen display. Although there are a variety of light pen designs, the basic concept is defined as follows: A photocell at the tip of the pen senses light from the screen display. The device then measures the corresponding sweep made by the screen display electron beam from the moment the light is sensed. In addition, an adapter or translator built into the light pen activates the sensing device.

Figure 2.10   A light pen (courtesy of International Business Machines Corporation).

Digitizers.   A touch digitizer (Figure 2.11) has a sensor overlay on the display screen. It senses location upon physical contact on the screen and indicates its corresponding location and/or command to the computer. Although the touch digitizer has a resolution up to 0.01 inch, users find it difficult to manipulate. A digitizer board is a more user-friendly device and is suited for drawings that require some accuracy.

A digitizing unit consists of a tablet and a pencillike stylus (Figure 2.11b). The tablet is an electronic device that consists of a rectangular grid of embedded wires operated by electrical impulses. A stylus is usually moved over the tablet, and its position with respect to the tablet is determined by decoding the stylus signal.

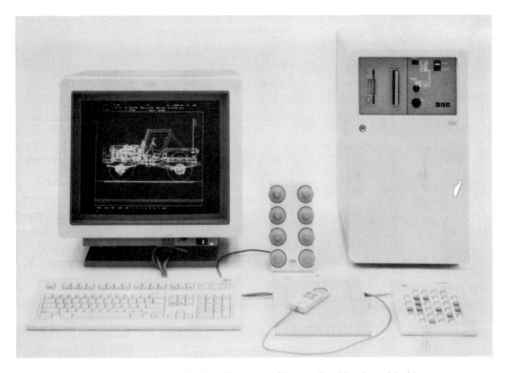

Figure 2.11   A tablet digitizer (courtesy of International Business Machines Corporation).

The digitizer is better than the joystick because it measures the absolute position of a point, whereas the joystick measures only changes between points.

Keyboards.   A keyboard (Figure 2.12) is a versatile input device used for activation of functions (such as special function keys or special key assignment), data or information input, and cursor manipulation. A variety of keyboards for CAD systems are available. They are alphanumeric, numeric, or function keyboards.

The alphanumeric keyboard resembles a standard typewriter keyboard. The numeric keyboard is similar to the number keypad of a simple calculator. The function keyboard has a set of unspecified keys that can be assigned special functions. For most CAD systems, labeled function keyboards are designed to run CAD commands and be able to display valid function keys (function keys that can be activated concurrently.)

The standard keyboard for most CAD systems and computers has a combination of all three types. The alphanumeric keyboard contains approximately 75 keys. Currently, the enhanced keyboard is the standard; it has 101 keys, including 12 function keys and 3 lighted mode indicators.

Figure 2.12   A keyboard (courtesy of International Business Machines Corporation).

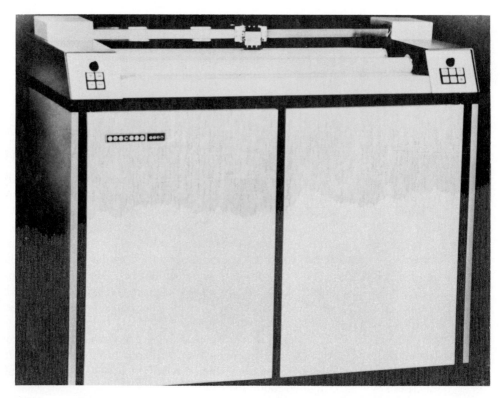

Figure 2.13   An electronmechnical pen plotter (courtesy of CalComp Inc.).

2.8.2 Output Devices

The output of a CAD system can be either temporary or permanent (hard copy). Temporary output can be displayed on the CRT. If hard copy is desired, a peripheral device is needed. This device, called a plotter, can be of two types: electromechanical or electrostatic.

Electromechanical Pen Plotter.   Currently, three types of pen plotters are being used: the drum, the flatbed, and the belt bed (Figure 2.13). In each device, the plotting tool moves across the plotting surface in small increments of approximately 0.001 to 0.01 inch.

The paper of a drum plotter is wrapped around a drum, which rotates by a digital stepping motor. Transverse motion is obtained by the plotting tool moving back and forth across the paper, and longitudinal motion is achieved by rolling the paper back and forth.

The paper of a flatbed plotter is placed on a flat surface and the marking tool moves on it. The belt bed plotter is a combination of drum and flatbed plotters.

The advantage of a pen plotter is that its multiple pen heads can produce various line widths and different colors. Unfortunately, pen plotters are slow.

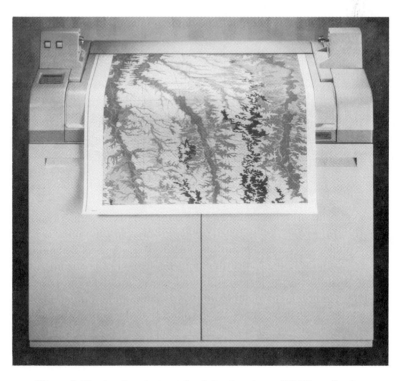

Figure 2.14   A color electrostatic plotter (courtesy of CalComp Inc.).

Electrostatic Plotter.   The electrostatic plotter (Figure 2.14) is a faster alternative for producing hard copies. The plotter consists of wire nibs with a density of up to 200 nibs per inch. Special paper, which accepts electrostatic charges from the nibs, is passed over dark liquid toner particles. These particles are attracted to the charged area and produce markings.

The electrostatic plotter operates faster than a pen plotter. Hard copies have low resolution and accuracy. Copies are produced in one color only.

2.9 VIDEO DISPLAY UNIT (VDU)

The video display unit (VDU) is one of the fastest computer output devices available. It provides temporary storage output and can quickly be revised for further updates by the computer. This temporary storage is referred to as soft copy because the output does not come in a tangible form.

The original CRT design has now reached the level of a high-resolution display capable of reproducing 35-mm-picture-quality display.

Despite these innovations in video technology, the designs still resemble the original CRT. The basic construction of a VDU consists of (1) an electron gun, (2) a focusing system, (3) a directional system, and (4) a phosphor-based coated screen (Figure 2.15).

The electron gun generates the source of electrons, which are concentrated into a beam by a focusing system and positioned onto the screen by the directional system. Upon being struck by electrons, the phosphor-based coat emits light, which is displayed by the screen.

Electron Gun.   The electron gun generates electrons by thermionic emission. A high voltage is applied to a metal source in the electron gun to generate electrons. A vacuum tube, coated with metal, is charged by high voltage to accelerate the electrons in the direction of the screen.

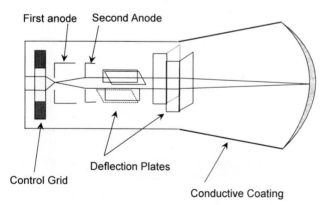

First anode   Second Anode

Control Grid

Deflection Plates

Conductive Coating

Figure 2.15   Schematic of a video display unit.

Focusing System.   The focusing device uses an electronic or magnetic field to concentrate the electrons into a narrow beam. If the beam is relatively wide, the screen would produce a picture similar to an unfocused camera picture.

Directional System.   The electron beam is positioned on the screen by the directional system. Directional devices, plates charged with either the electrostatic or electromagnetic field, bend the electron beam in the desired direction by varying the intensity of the field. Directional systems usually consist of a horizontal and a vertical control directional device. For graphic applications, the electromagnetic field is preferred because of its better positioning accuracy.

Phosphor-Based Coated Screen.   The composition of phosphor determines the color, luminosity, and clarity characteristics of the VDU screen. One sees the radiated phosphor pattern, not the electron beam, when the VDU is in use. Phosphor is composed of a variety of alkali metal tungstate salts with specific impurities added to affect color, luminosity, and refresh time. The refresh time is the time necessary for the phosphor to return to its unexcited state after being struck (excited) by electrons. Refresh time is an important consideration in the design of the VDU. The electron beam must sweep the screen to maintain a display (by exciting the phosphor). The time interval between electron sweeps is determined by the refresh time. If the refresh time is long, an annoying flickering effect will occur, due to the rapid change in light intensities. The refresh time should be short (about 1/40 second for a flicker-free display) so that the frequency of sweep should not be noticeable to the viewer. This will result in a constant picture display intensity.

Although the foregoing may imply that the refresh time should always be short, there are instances when a longer time is necessary, as with the direct-view storage tube (DVST). The image written by the electron beam is maintained by the phosphor storage surface. The DVST system writes the image once, and a flood of beams maintains the image on the screen. If the image has to be edited, the entire picture is erased before the new one is redrawn.

The number of displays with a short refresh time outrank the number of DVST-type displays in production. A variety of these displays are available. The two main types are raster scan and vector scan.

Raster Scan Display.   Raster scan display (RSD) sweeps the screen from the top left corner in a series of left-to-right passes while declining in incremental steps with the electron beam (Figure 2.16). The intensity of the electron beam varies to create shadings and colors. The left-to-right passes represent a line of resolution. The points that make up the line are called pixels. A pixel is the smallest entity that can be displayed by the VDU. In essence, the smaller the pixel size, the better the quality of resolution. The number of pixels is constant for each line, which make the thickness of the line constant. A typical RSD (e.g., for a personal computer) can range from 256 (low-resolution) to 512 (medium-resolution) to 1024 (high-resolution) lines. Each pixel is stored in a specific memory location for graphics.

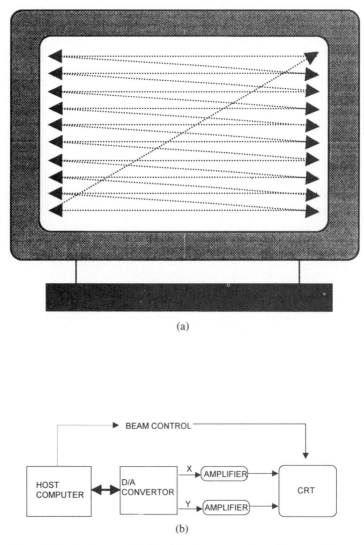

Figure 2.16   Raster scan display: (a) raster scan pattern, (b) system layout.

Resolution is a function of the memory available in the computer. For instance, a 512 × 512 pixel resolution requires about 256 KB of memory (for an 8-bit microprocessor), whereas a 32,000 × 32,000 pixel resolution requires memory measured in gigabytes (using a 32-bit or higher microprocessor). The type of graphics capabilities desired must be matched to the right type of hardware. It would be wasteful to run a 32,000 × 32,000 pixel resolution using a computer equipped with an 8-bit processor (a time-consuming operation) or a 256 × 256 pixel resolution on a 32-bit processor computer (a high-cost operation). In the area of CAD application, it would be prudent to invest in the 32-bit or higher computer because of the important need for graphics quality. The construction of a color display on an RSD is similar to that of a CRT. Instead of one electron gun, the color display for an RSD has three. They are arranged in a triangular formation with each gun controlling a primary color (red, green, or blue). A similar triad configuration of different phosphor dots matches the color of each electron gun to produce the specific color. A shadow mask is placed between the electron gun and the screen to filter out any unmatched color beams for each specific phosphor dot. By varying the intensity of each electron beam, many shades can be produced. The combination of phosphor dots can produce a variety of colors, limited by the design of the display and computer.

Vector Scan Display (VSD).   VSD differs from RSD in the pattern of electron beam sweep. Instead of following a fixed pattern, the beam draws the image. The directional devices are actively controlled by the graphics generator to draw the image. The computer devotes memory (in the same way as RSD does) in setting up an array map of the screen. An equation specified or generated by the graphics package of an application program controls the direction and intensity of the electron beam. From a specified point, the equation or vector generator would define points on which the beam must travel. VSD is considered to produce better graphics than RSD, but the number of entities that can be drawn is limited. Colors can be produced on a VSD using layers of phosphor coats that emit a specific color for each excitation energy intensity. The colors available for a VSD are limited by the phosphor that can be added to the screen.

VSD is plagued by technology limitations. The refresh sweep for a complex drawing may cause the display to flicker due to the increased time necessary to draw the entire image. The colors are limited due to the inadequate arrangement of phosphors on the screen and the time necessary to accelerate or decelerate the electron gun to provide the necessary intensity to cause emission of that particular color of light. Innovations in video displays are coming at a fast pace and might make the VSD a viable choice in the near future.

PROBLEMS

2.1 Describe briefly a raster scan display and a vector scan display.

2.2 Why can't a vector scan display produce as many colors as a raster scan display?

2.3 Briefly identify and describe the various potentiometric devices. What are the benefits of using these devices?

2.4 Give the components of a CAD workstation and briefly explain their relationship.

2.5 Describe the various plotters available. Which plotter provides the best-quality drawings? Which plotter provides the fastest copy of drawings?

REFERENCES

2.1 Appletone, E. L., Image Processing and Visualization, *DEC Professional,* July 1989, p. 38.

2.2 Berkeley, P., *Computer Operations Training: A Strategy for Change,* Van Nostrand Reinhold, New York, 1984.

2.3 Chang, D., PCs Offer More Options for Less Money, *Mech. Eng.,* May 1989, p. 68.

2.4 Hordeski, M. F., *CAD/CAM Techniques,* Reston, Reston, Va., 1986.

2.5 Medland, A. J., and Burnett, P., *CAD/CAM in Practice: A Manager's Guide to Understanding and Using CAD/CAM,* Halstead Press, New York, 1986.

2.6 Naecker, P. A., Workstations and Graphics Terminals: Room for Both, *DEC Professional,* July 1989, p. 48.

2.7 Nilssen, A., Workstations Still Hold the Edge, *Mech. Eng.,* May 1989, p. 68.

2.8 Poor, A., 16-Bit VGA Cards Stretch the Standard, *PC,* July 1989, p. 145.

2.9 Teicholz, E., *CAD/CAM Handbook,* McGraw-Hill, New York, 1985.

chapter 3

Methodology in Design and CAD/CAM

3.1 INTRODUCTION

The design process has changed tremendously in the past decade. The new technology of computer-aided design and computer-aided manufacturing has revolutionized the procedures used in conceptualizing and designing mechanical parts, electrical networks, and architectural designs, among others. To understand the advantages CAD/CAM has brought to this field, we now review the process of the classical approach in design and study how it is done in the context of the computer-assisted approach. Therefore, in this chapter we present the classical methodology of design, as well as the computer-assisted method, and draw some conclusions on how best to use the concept of CAD/CAM to design efficiently.

3.2 CONVENTIONAL APPROACH TO DESIGN

To engineers, design means creating something new by enhancing existing designs or by altering existing ones to perform new functions. Design is not restricted to engineers but is practiced by a large body of professionals including artists, sculptors, and composers.

A design is usually produced to satisfy the need of a particular person, group, or community. Therefore, to design a product, one needs to know the problem constraints and then propose a solution that will operate within those constraints. Constraints are algebraic equations that are functions of the design parameters. They are usually in the form of equality and inequality conditions that must be met by the objective function. In the process of designing something, it will become apparent in most cases that more than one solution exists or perhaps none does. Hence a question one would ask would be, "What is the best or optimum design solution?" To answer this question, the engineer might need further information in terms of social and economic variables pertaining to the use of the product being designed. We often face decisions on factors involved in the design when specifics are not known. This ordinarily requires experience and professional judgment.

Traditionally, the design process involves draftspersons and design engineers, who, once they have completed their jobs, usually present the blueprints (layouts) of the product to the manufacturing or production division. The latter employs machinists, welders, and manufacturing engineers who will try to produce or make the product according to the specifications given by the design people. Minor modifications in terms of dimension precision are not referred to the design engineer, and the product is usually tested under the newly modified constraints by the manufacturing engineer. In many cases, analysis is limited to some basic require-

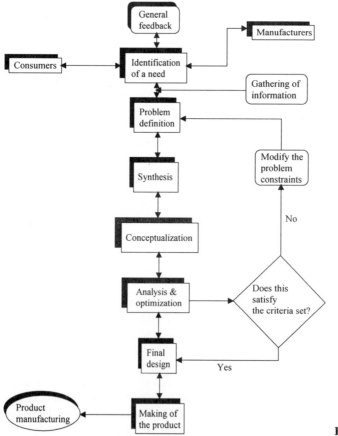

Figure 3.1 The steps in design.

ments—minimum and maximum loads or ranges for certain loads, for example. Product performance failure is usually due to a lack of analysis. Professional judgment played a major role in the early days as a substitute for such analysis. It was not until malfunctions and failures had started to cause the industry to pay enormous sums of money to the victims, when insurance and liability costs were increasing at a rapid rate, that it became essential that more analysis and testing be done before the final approval of any design. This is especially true for the automobile and commercial aircraft industries. A design module that illustrates the steps in design is shown in Figure 3.1.

3.3 DESCRIPTION OF THE DESIGN PROCESS

The steps in design are defined here as described by G. Ditier in *Engineering Design*.

1. Problem definition
2. Conceptualization
3. Synthesis
4. Analysis
5. Manufacturing

They constitute a short summary and should serve as a guide to any project.

3.3.1 Problem Definition

A well-defined problem is the key to a successful design solution. The design process involves many stages that require careful thinking; the problem definition helps everyone focus on the objectives of the problem and the things that must be accomplished. Engineers should not overlook the importance of this crucial first step in design, nor should they act hastily in stating the problem. The problem definition must be broadened in a reasonable fashion to make sure that the ultimate solution is the desired one.

The problem definition should include the following:

1. A statement of objectives and goals to be achieved
2. A definition of constraints imposed on the design
3. Criteria for evaluating the design

Engineers will seek an optimum solution to the design problem in keeping with these requirements. It is essential that the problem definition be used as a guideline to keep the focus on what has to be done to avoid unnecessary design requirements.

3.3.2 Conceptualization

This second step in design usually requires that the engineers use ingenuity, experience, and knowledge to work out a preliminary concept of what the design should look like. Conceptualization is the process whereby a design satisfying the problem definition is formulated. This might involve the creation of a model that is ultimately tested for problem definition verification. This phase can be either very exciting or very frustrating. The latter experience could be the result of a poor problem definition. In the conceptualization process, it is often desirable to look at some existing designs to see if they can be adapted to meet the proposed problem definition. Complex problems must be broken into smaller problems; only then can the overall design solution be identified. In any case, conceptualization consists of generating a model in the mind and translating it back into forms and shapes to conform to a realistic model.

3.3.3 Synthesis

According to Ditier, synthesis is defined as "the process of taking elements of the concept and arranging them in the proper order, sized and dimensioned in the proper way" (p. 35). This is one of the most challenging tasks an engineer faces. A successful and effective design relies a great deal on the synthesis aspect of the problem. At this stage, the information required for the proposed conceptualization is organized and a plan is devised for achieving that particular design. The synthesis aspects of a problem could be handled by a group of engineers. To achieve a profitable synthesis decision, all the elements affecting the design, including product design, cost, and labor, must be considered.

3.3.4 Analysis

Analysis is concerned with the mathematical or experimental testing of the design to make sure it meets the criteria set forth in the problem definition. The engineer must test all possible factors important to the design. For instance, the engineer breaks the design problem into categories, such as stress analysis, vibration, thermodynamics, heat transfer, and fluid mechanics. In each category, the design as a whole or parts of the design are tested for the ability to serve their particular function. A safety factor is usually added to make sure the design works within certain safety limits.

A complex design, as for an automobile, is divided into parts. For instance, if we are concerned with the car suspension, we usually represent the body of the car by a mass, M, and the suspension by simple springs and dampers (linear or nonlinear). A vibration analysis is then conducted for extraction of the spring and damper parameters that yield the most comfortable ride. See Figures 3.2 and 3.3 for possible models used to simulate the vibration response of a car subjected to different road conditions.

Developing models (such as lumped models) requires ingenuity and experi-

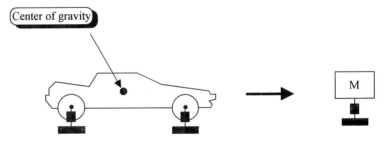

Figure 3.2   Vibration analysis of a car.

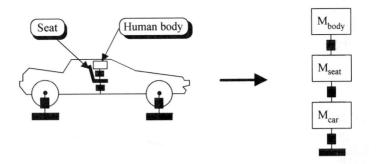

Figure 3.3   Vibration analysis of a car carrying a human body.

ence. It is important that the models developed be realistic, simple, and mathematically testable. If a model is too complex, it will most likely take longer to analyze and hence will cost more. But if the model is too simple, it might be unrealistic; that is, predictions from its analysis might not be typical of the proposed design. It is important to try to keep the model simple, but it must exhibit behavior that is close to that of the actual design, based on good engineering judgment. Ultimately, for all analyses, of heat transfer, fluid, or stress, we must be sure that the models we develop are adequate and exhibit the characteristics of the mechanical design part or product.

Experimentation in analysis is another critical step in design. For instance, one might be apt to use a lumped mass model representing a car and analyze its behavior with different vibration stimulus or conduct a modal analysis experiment in which a real automobile is tested in the laboratory making use of shakers, transducers, and Fourier analysis. The experiment usually represents a more realistic model and gives a better feel for how a particular design is going to perform under the normal conditions (see Figure 3.4).

In addition to mathematical and experimental verification in analysis, we have the so-called engineering science of checking by making use of the feel of a product. It is customary to touch products and parts for comfort, cushion, rigidity, and so on. Engineers can make use of their experience to judge whether the product meets the customer's requirements.

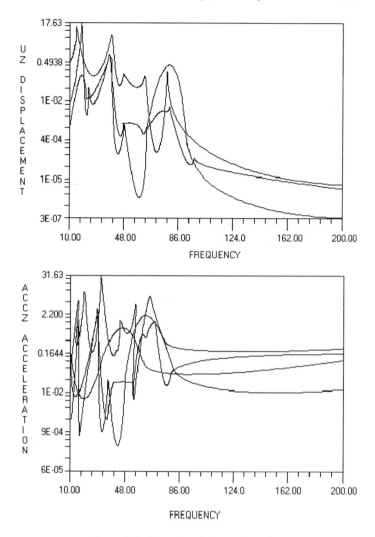

Figure 3.4 Example of structural testing.

In what follows is an example that demonstrates how a proposed idea is developed through the basic set of principles given for design. Because there is no unique answer for these types of design problems, they are mainly used to guide students through the thinking process involved in defining a concise problem statement and proposing an initial adapted solution.

Example 3.1   Handicapped Car Seat Design Project

Product Being Considered

A system is to be designed that will enable a handicapped person to enter, drive, and exit an automobile while remaining in a wheelchair. A commonplace wheelchair is assumed in the design.

Recognition of a Need for the Product

Automobile access is difficult for a person confined to a wheelchair. The product being proposed here would be of great benefit in reducing the burdensome nature of this activity for the handicapped.

Definition of the Problem

Options that make driving an automobile more convenient for a person in a wheelchair are continually being overlooked. A design that would allow a person in a wheelchair to gain access to a car while remaining in the chair would answer this need. It is desirable that the scheme permit easy conversion to seating for a driver who is not handicapped to allow other persons (loved ones, auto mechanics, etc.) to operate the car when necessary.

Solution

Gathering Information

To begin to solve this problem, various sources of information should be considered, including these:

1. Dimensions of wheelchairs in common use
2. Threshold height of various car interiors to serve as a guideline in designing the lift mechanism
3. Ergonomics—the spacing inside the car cabins being considered for this design application
4. Conflict considerations—room available in car bodies for housing the mechanism this feature would require
5. Market demand—is there a demand for this product, and should a survey be conducted to determine the extent of this demand?
6. Financing
7. Engineering and economic considerations
8. Interviews with handicapped people
9. Safety regulations
10. Brainstorming

Conceptualization and Evaluation

With the foregoing discussion in mind, we have considered a transport mechanism that would operate in a manner similar to a loading ramp on a semitrailer, with certain modifications, of course (see Figure 3.5).

The mechanism would feature a transport table or platform that would be located inside the vehicle during normal operation. Instead of providing height and angle (rotation) adjustment as the truck ramp does, it would have to function with a lateral movement to take the platform outside the car and then an actual vertical (translation) capability to lower it to the ground. This could be accomplished by a driver motor located under the front passenger seat that would provide the lateral

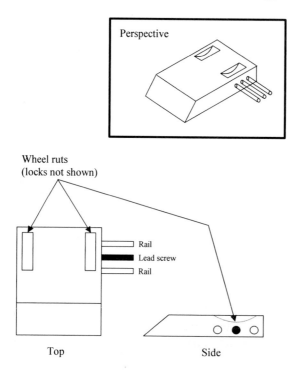

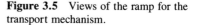

Figure 3.5 Views of the ramp for the transport mechanism.

movement by transmitting its power through a lead screw to the platform. Another drive motor located under the ramp itself could control a scissor-jack type of mechanism that would accomplish the task of lowering the platform to the ground.

Two wide and shallow ruts spaced for the chair's wheels in the surface of the platform to help settle the chair would be advisable in the interest of safety. A width of 3 to 4 inches for the ruts would allow for variations in wheelchair design and make it easy for the user to land in these ruts. Once in the ruts, the user could reach down and flip a wheel lock, which would fix the chair to the platform. The user would then activate the into-car transport mechanism by pushing a switch conveniently located on the platform.

The interchangeable normal driver seat should be designed such that it can be perched on the same platform that the wheelchair will rest on, and it should be able to snap into the same rut-lock system.

Once in the car, the driver, whether in a wheelchair or the interchangeable normal driver's seat, should be able to use seat belts conveniently. It would be advantageous if an adjustable headrest to prevent whiplash could be mounted from the ceiling of the vehicle to provide this important measure of safety. (Wheelchairs are not equipped with such protective devices.)

If subjected to a thorough design sequence, this proposal, like any design proposal, would undoubtedly undergo some evolution, and its stronger and weaker points would be revealed—the weaker ones, it is hoped, being supplanted by better ideas. If this design can be implemented in such a way as to meet the functional constraints of the design and can be produced economically, it would be a welcome innovation for the handicapped. Many people who could otherwise drive were it not that vehicle entry and exit prevents them from doing so would benefit from this wheelchair lift mechanism.   ∎

3.4 COMPUTER-AIDED DESIGN (CAD)

CAD/CAM has gained tremendous popularity in the past decade, and it is becoming an absolute tool for any engineering task. Its application is broadening, and its success is due mostly to the mass production of powerful microprocessors and their low cost.

Computer-aided design is the blending of human and machine, working together to achieve the optimum design and manufacture of a product (see Figure 3.6). The computers' graphics capability and computing power allow the designers to fashion and test their ideas interactively in real time without having to create real prototypes as in conventional approaches to design.

A typical CAD/CAM system involves both design and manufacturing operations. Complex products are designed and analyzed, and their manufacturing plans are produced. The products are given the form they will have in the final stage.

How design steps are enhanced by making use of the CAD/CAM system can be demonstrated by analyzing each design step. For instance, the designer or engineer formulates the problem statement by interacting with various sources of information, as shown in Figure 3.7. From a CAD/CAM workstation, the designer can access a large body of selected information pertaining to the particular design problem at hand.

Because most companies are product-oriented and specialize in the manufacturing of certain products, it is in their best interest to build a technical library in which specific data are stored.

Complex geometries are handled with ease on a CAD/CAM workstation, allowing the user to spend more time on the design aspect of the problem.

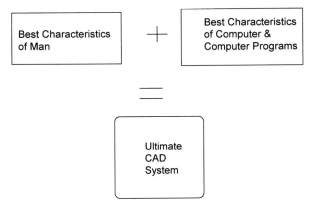

Figure 3.6   Characteristics of CAD.

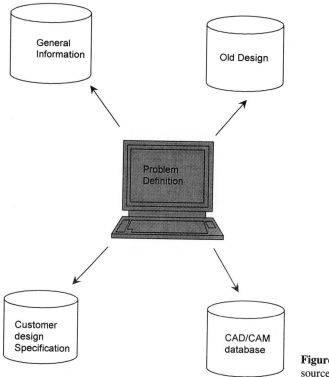

Figure 3.7 Interaction with various sources of information.

The various design advantages CAD offers could be grouped in three areas: drafting and design, wireframe modeling, and geometric modeling.

3.4.1 Drafting and Design

Today, basic drafting and design work are done by engineers on personal computers and workstations. All drafting software operates in the same way. Points and lines that comprise a drawing are entered into the drafting system through any of the input devices available. Generally, a set of cross hairs is used to indicate the starting points of drawings. The drawing process is also aided by pull-down function menus putting the system into different modes to construct basic elements with minimal user input. Most of the drawing packages provide a number of ways to change the drawing once it is entered into the computer. A line editor deletes lines or shows line lengths and angles. Undo commands permit the last element or specific objects to be deleted.

Most of the functions provided by drafting software are intended to increase ease of use. For example, a specific area can be "zoomed in on" to reveal greater detail, and a drawing can be moved horizontally or vertically using the "pan" function. A grid, or series of equally spaced points, can be displayed on the screen to aid in the drawing process. The grid can help in the drawing of straight lines and give the operator a feeling of scale. Another function, called "snap," causes entered lines to "snap" to the nearest grid point. A copy function permits an object to be copied anywhere else in the drawing. Another resource in computer-aided drafting is symbol libraries, which can be purchased or developed for specific applications such as piping. A symbol library contains hundreds of predefined objects that can be called up and placed in a drawing. Other aids are automatic dimensioning, hidden line removal, and the facility of test inclusion anywhere on the drawing using the keyboard. Layering is an important function whereby the drawing is split into distinct overlays. This function helps simplify the creation of drawings and makes plotting easier because the various separate layers can be plotted in different colors. Most of all, the design layouts or blueprints are stored in the computer and can be transmitted directly to the manufacturing division without paperwork.

3.4.2 Wireframe Modeling

Most of the drafting packages on the market allow the user to develop wireframe models, which represent 3D part shapes with interconnected line elements giving the simplest geometric representations of objects. Wireframe models require less computer time and memory space and provide little information about surface discontinuities on the part. They are created by specifying points and lines in space. The interactive terminal screen is usually divided into sections showing various views of the model. The CAD system constructs lines based on user-specified points and commands chosen from an instruction menu. The generalized representation of the creation of a wireframe model created on the display terminal is shown in Figure 3.8.

The designer can temporarily erase selected lines from the screen without deleting them from the model to obtain a clearer view of the area under construction. After completing the model, the user can blank out hidden lines to give the model a solid appearance.

3.4.3 Geometric Modeling

Geometric modeling is associated with surface and solid modeling. Wireframes contain no information about the surfaces themselves, nor do they differentiate between the inside and the outside of objects. Many ambiguities of wireframe models are overcome by surface models, which define part geometries precisely and help produce NC (Numerical Control) machining instructions where definition of structural boundaries is difficult. Surface models are created by connecting various types of surface elements to user-specified lines.

Solid modeling is used to define geometry and volume unambiguously; it provides the ultimate way to describe mechanical parts in the computer. Unlike wireframe and surface modeling, solid modeling provides the accuracy needed for precise

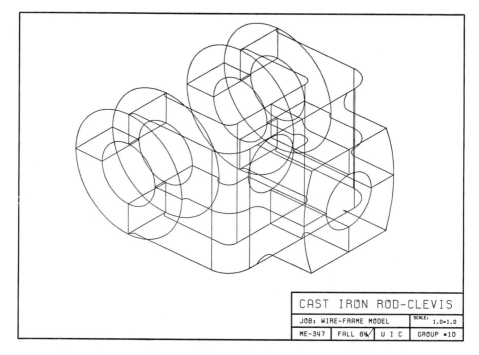

CAST IRON ROD-CLEVIS

JOB: WIRE-FRAME MODEL			SCALE: 1.0-1.0
ME-347	FALL 84	U I C	GROUP #10

Figure 3.8 Example of a wireframe model.

mechanical design. It has the potential to create a database that provides a complete description of the part to downstream applications.

Solid models are constructed in two ways: with primitives or with boundary definition. Both of these methods develop complex geometries from successive combinations of simple geometric operations. The primitive approach allows elementary shapes such as blocks and cylinders to be combined in building-block fashion. The user positions these primitives as required and then creates a new shape with the proper Boolean logic command. In the boundary definition approach, two-dimensional surfaces are swept through space to trace out volumes. A linear sweep translates the surface in a straight line to produce an extruded volume, a rotational sweep produces a part with axial symmetry, and a compound sweep moves a surface through a specified curve to generate a more complex solid. Each of these construction methods is best suited to a particular class of shapes. Most industrial parts with planar, cylindrical, and other simple shapes can be modeled with primitives, but complex contoured components such as automobile exhaust manifolds and turbine blades are easier to model using the boundary definition method. An example of a solid model made using SDRC's IDEAS software is shown in Figure 3.9.

The solid modeling representation of objects is discussed in greater detail, with full illustrations and examples, in Chapter 5.

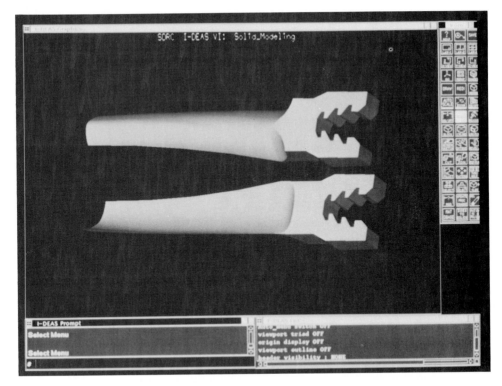

Figure 3.9   An example of solid modelling (courtesy of SDRC, Milford, Ohio).

3.5 PARAMETRIC AND VARIATIONAL DESIGN

Designing and drafting are the preliminary steps carried out in the manufacture of a component. Traditional mechanical CAD/CAM systems are effective tools in improving the efficiency of the drafting process, but they cannot handle the task of design and drafting at the same time. This forces the engineer to think simultaneously about all the design requirements and engineering relationships for each design approach.

Several new CAD/CAM systems claim to meet the needs of engineers engaged in the preliminary design of mechanical products. These systems should enhance the level of productivity of the engineers when creating or modifying designs. Two approaches that are gaining popularity for providing flexibility in the design process are parametric design and variational design.

3.5.1 Parametric Design Systems

In a parametric design, the engineer selects a set of geometric constraints that can be applied for creating the geometry of the component. The geometric elements include lines, arcs, circles, and splines. A set of engineering equations can also be used to define the dimensions of the component. This simple concept of a parametric system can be explained using the following two illustrations.

First consider Figure 3.10, which represents a block with a portion removed from its side. The figure can be drawn by defining the geometries that make up the block as follows:

1. Solve P_1 (origin)
2. Solve L_1 (horizontal line from origin)
3. Solve P_2 (known distance on line from P_1)
4. Solve L_2 (vertical line at 90° from P_2)
5. Solve P_2 (known distance on line)
6. Solve L_3 (horizontal line at −90° from P_3)
7. Solve P_4 (known distance on line from P_3)
8. Solve L_4 (vertical line from P_4 at −90°)
9. Solve P_5 (point at distance from P_1 at 45°)
10. Solve arc (known radius, start, and endpoint)

Thus on the basis of a given set of geometric constraints, the basic dimensions of the component can be defined. The set of geometric constraints would be regarded as a set of instructions that when executed will create the geometry desired. Hence any change to the known entities will yield a different picture altogether. So the objective is to create a geometric relationship between entities to minimize time and effort spent on design.

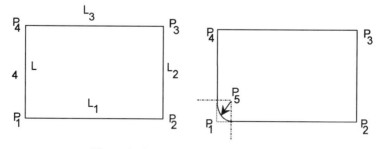

Figure 3.10 Parametric design of a block.

Another approach to this incorporates engineering equations. This can be illustrated using Figure 3.11, wherein M_t is the driving motor and D_1 the diameter of the drive shaft. M and D correspond to the mass and density of the belt, respectively, L_1 to the length. By solving the set of engineering equations as described by Figure 3.11, the geometry of the drive shaft can be defined.

Parametric design systems help users in manipulating the length, angle, and pitch of a particular component. These systems also have the ability to record engineering relationships within a design; they enable users to pinpoint the complex rela-

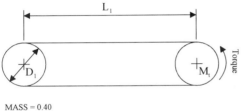

MASS = 0.40
DENSITY = 1.78
WEIGHT = MASS * DENSITY
C1 = 0.05 * FORCE
D = 2 * C1

Figure 3.11 Parametric design of a drive shaft.

tionships that exist among parts of an assembly. A simple example would be the meshing between two gears. Thus the use of parametric design clarifies users' understanding of the engineering aspects of a component. Moreover, the parametric system can produce designs that are more meaningful than those generated by traditional CAD/CAM systems. Designers, analysts, and production engineers can work with the same solid model, extracting and adding information according to need.

The drawback of this system is that it is constrained to the set of geometric or engineering relationships provided by the engineer for creating the design of a component. The limited set of geometric constraints can make it difficult to change a parametric design model once the initial conditions have been set. These systems are best suited for design tasks that do not involve many variations in the design approach. Note that software like IDEAS from SDRC is equipped with such an option in design and is therefore an excellent tool for design. Such software gives the designer flexibility to avoid redrawing objects and minimizes the time involved in arriving at a final product design.

3.5.2 Variational Design Systems

This technique can simultaneously solve a set of geometric constraints and engineering equations with important relationships within and among the elements of design. Essentially, the design is governed by a set of engineering equations relating its geometry and functions.

Unlike the parametric approach, a variational system is able to determine the positions of geometric elements and of any set of geometric constraints; in addition, it is structured to handle the coupling between parameters in the geometric constraints and the engineering equations. The variational design concept helps the engineer to evaluate the design of a component in depth instead of considering only the geometric aspects to satisfy the design relationships. This can be illustrated by the following example.

Figure 3.12 shows a planar two-link manipulator. L_1 and L_2 are the respective lengths of arms 1 and 2. These arms are connected by revolute joints and have one degree of freedom: rotation about the z axis. The global coordinate system is given by X_1 and X_2. The local coordinate systems of the arms are shown in the figure, where Θ_1 and Θ_2 represent the angles between the arms.

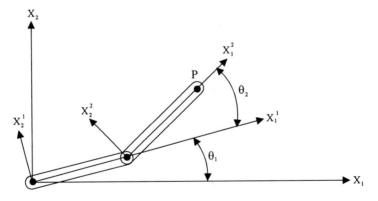

Figure 3.12 Robotic Manipulator.

The position of point P_1 can be given using the following two constraint equations

$$P_x = L_1 \cos \Theta_1 + L_2 \cos (\Theta_1 + \Theta_2) \tag{3.1}$$

$$P_y = L_1 \sin \Theta_1 + L_2 \sin (\Theta_1 + \Theta_2) \tag{3.2}$$

where P_x and P_y represent the components along the x_1 axis and the y_1 axis, respectively.

Differentiating the position vector with respect to time, we get velocity components of point P_1.

$$
\begin{aligned}
V_x &= -L_1 \sin \Theta_1 \cdot \dot{\Theta}_1 - L_2 \sin (\Theta_1 + \Theta_2) \cdot (\dot{\Theta}_1 + \dot{\Theta}_2) \\
&= \dot{\Theta}_1[-L_1 \sin \Theta_1 - L_2 \sin (\Theta_1 + \Theta_2)] - L_2 \sin (\Theta_1 + \Theta_2) \cdot \dot{\Theta}_2
\end{aligned} \tag{3.3}
$$

$$
\begin{aligned}
V_y &= L_1 \cos \Theta_1 \cdot \dot{\Theta}_1 + L_2 \cos (\Theta_1 + \Theta_2) \cdot (\dot{\Theta}_1 + \dot{\Theta}_2) \\
&= \dot{\Theta}_1[L_1 \cos \Theta_1 + L_2 \cos (\Theta_1 + \Theta_2)] + L_2 \cos (\Theta_1 + \Theta_2) \cdot \dot{\Theta}_2
\end{aligned} \tag{3.4}
$$

V_x and V_y represent the velocity components of point P_1, and their selection will determine the angular displacements and how that point is going to move.

To calculate the values of the angles, we need to solve for the combined set of equations resulting from the constraint functions and the equations of motion, which could be expressed as

$$[M]\{\ddot{\Theta}\} + [C(\Theta, \dot{\Theta}] = \{F\} \tag{3.5}$$

where

$$\{\Theta\} = \{\Theta_1, \Theta_2\}$$

The constraint equations at the velocity level can be written as

$$[J][\dot{\Theta}] = [g(t)] \tag{3.6}$$

where $[J]$ is the Jacobian constraint matrix resulting from combining Equations (3.3) and (3.4) and $[g(t)]$ is the velocity profile of the prescribed point, which should be known where $[M]_{ij}$ denotes the generalized mass matrix and $[C]$ the matrix combining all the nonlinear terms in $\dot{\Theta}$ such as coriolis forces, quadratic velocity, etc. and F represents the external forces such as gravity. Amirouche in "Computational Methods in Multi-Body Dynamics" gives a complete derivation of these equations. This example shows how in variational design, parameters such as the mass of the links, lengths, joint torques, and $\Theta_i (i = 1, 2)$ (needed for creating the geometry of the links and the configuration of the planar robot) are found through a set of engineering equations that must be integrated with respect to time to yield the desired motion. Once that is known, a set of instructions, as in the parametric design, must be used to display the position of the links. In effect, this example shows how engineering equations could be combined with geometric constraint conditions to form the design equations.

Variational design has the ability to incorporate optimization into the design environment. The engineer can specify both equality and inequality design constraints. The objective function is a set of both dependent and independent variables that are optimized (minimized or maximized) relative to one or more independent variables. Figure 3.13 shows a nonoptimized design, wherein the sides of the rectangle are not in contact with the boundary of the circle. The objective is to minimize the area bounded by the rectangle at a constant value. The optimized result is as shown in Figure 3.14.

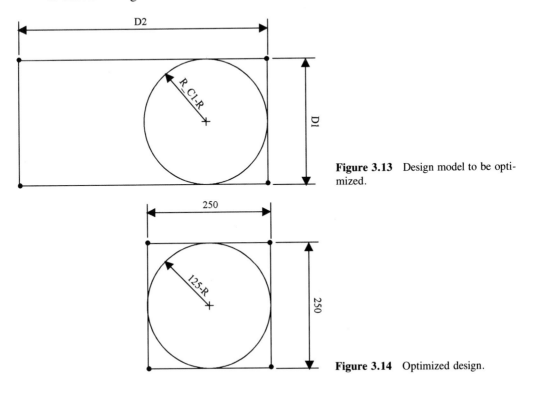

Figure 3.13   Design model to be optimized.

Figure 3.14   Optimized design.

3.6 ENGINEERING ANALYSIS AND CAD

Analysis is of two types: analytical and experimental. Both are generally performed at several stages of design to analyze product criteria and performance (see Figure 3.15).

3.6.1 Analytical Methods

In the analytical approach, different types of analysis can be carried out using various software available for computer-aided design (Figure 3.16). These include finite-element analysis, kinematic analysis and synthesis, and static and dynamic analysis.

Finite-Element Analysis. Finite-element analysis (FEA) is a computer-assisted technique for determining stresses and deflections in a structure. The method divides a structure into small elements with known shapes for which a math-

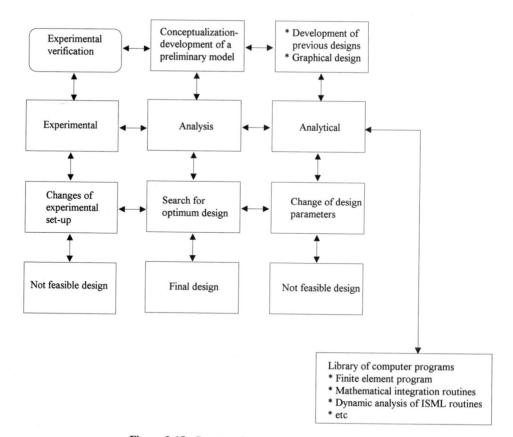

Figure 3.15 Process of engineering analysis in design.

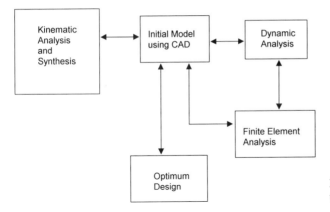

Figure 3.16 Interfacing analysis functions with CAD.

ematical solution can be found; then the global problem is solved using an assembly procedure. Interactive FEA software developed to date requires that the user know how to prepare the program inputs. The program then formulates and solves the problem and provides the necessary output.

The first step in FEA is the creation of a model that breaks the structure into simple standardized shapes and plots it on a common coordinate grid system. The coordinate points are called nodes and serve as the locations in the model where output data is provided. Nodal stiffness properties are then calculated by the finite-element program for each element and arranged into matrices within the computer. These parameters are then processed with applied loads and boundary conditions or calculations of displacements, natural frequencies, strains, and so on.

In most cases, finite-element models are developed for prototype designs for which experimental data exists so that FEA results can be cross-checked and design modifications can be made. Modifications are also tested for actual prototypes. This concept of the finite-element method is presented in Chapter 6, which provides some good examples of its implementation.

Kinematics and Synthesis.   Mechanisms are devices used to transfer motion and/or force from a given source to an output device. The efficiency with which this transfer is accomplished relies on the mechanism design. General-purpose programs like Lincages, IMP, KADAM2, Unigraphics, and MCADA are available today to assist engineers in the kinematic analysis and synthesis of those systems. Kinematics starts with the mechanism design. It calculates large displacements, velocities, and accelerations of mechanisms without regard to the forces acting on them. The mechanism assumes zero degrees of freedom, which means that each degree of freedom (coordinate) is constrained to a particular type of motion. The advantages of combining the software packages on the study of mechanisms with CAD enable the design to optimize the output and eliminate interferences between links.

Synthesis analysis is concerned with coming up with the best characteristics of a mechanism through a set of computer iterations. The designer provides the parameters of the mechanism, and the program develops the alternatives.

   The first step before doing a synthesis analysis is deciding various parameters of the mechanism, such as number of links, joints, joint types, and connectivity of links by specifying which links are fixed. The basic linkage types are defined as kinematic chains within the program. The synthesis analysis is then carried out, and the mechanism structures satisfying the design objectives are determined. These programs are generally used to design four-bar linkages, although they can be used to design six-bar linkages. Some kinematic synthesis programs use graphics to make the software user-friendly. The user specifies points and motion vectors via interactive graphics that can be easily moved about the screen. After a number of points have been specified, the program displays all possible locations of additional points to complete the mechanism. Some software also allows the user to animate the mechanism on the screen to check for criteria such as clearances of moving links (see Figure 3.17).

   Static Analysis and Dynamic Analysis.   Static analysis combines motion analysis with mass properties and force input data to determine positions and joint

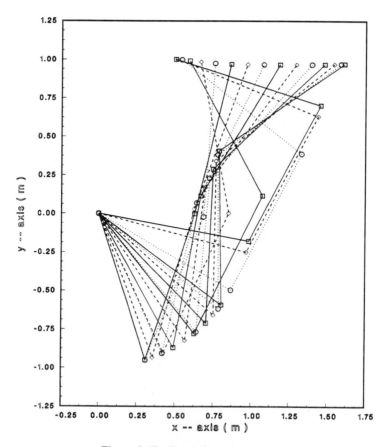

Figure 3.17   Simulation of mechanisms.

reaction forces of mechanisms at rest. Static analysis can also be done on mechanisms at various points in their range of movement if zero velocity is assumed. Static models can have multiple degrees of freedom. Motion and force are uncoupled in this type of analysis. In static analysis, we are mostly concerned with the reaction forces on the mechanical systems and their joints' interconnection forces. Knowing these latter forces is useful in stress analysis to determine engineering criteria such as performance, reliability, and fatigue.

Dynamic analysis uses mass properties and forces to calculate positions, velocities, accelerations, and joint and constraint reaction forces of all model parts when motion is coupled to forces in the system. Analysis is done in discrete steps within a specified time interval. Each degree of freedom in a dynamic model is associated with an independent coordinate for which the analyst has to specify both the initial position and velocity. The computer models for dynamic analysis include geometric data and mass properties of the structure as well as applied forces. The model is generally created through part, joint, marker, force, and generator statements that are typed by the user.

Part statements define the geometry, mass, and moment of inertia of each rigid part of the structure. Joint statements describe contacts between moving parts that hold the assembly together. Joints can be specified as providing translational and rotational movement, including that of revolute, screw, spherical, universal, cylindrical, and translational joints. Marker statements provide a point or coordinate system fixed on each part orienting it to other parts and together defining the overall configuration of the system. Internal reaction forces are selected from a library of standard force elements such as dampers and linear springs. User-written routines can also be used to define additional parameters. Basic geometric data from CAD programs can be sent through direct interfaces. Because complete geometric description is not required, mechanical analysis can be used early in the design cycle, before the final configuration is known. Engineers can design the system knowing only mass and inertia characteristics.

The dynamic analysis output is typically available in tabular form. Graphics can be produced showing output such as force versus time or force versus displacement characteristics. In some cases, animation is reproduced from the combination of output data from the dynamic analysis and geometry representation of the object. Software capable of performing such a task includes ADAMS, DADS, DISCOS, DYAMUS, DARS, and DYNACOMBS.

3.6.2 Experimental Testing

The second aspect of analysis deals with experimental methods in which testing is conducted on prototypes and models either to extract material properties or to validate performance characteristics of a particular design.

Testing in the conventional design process is done to qualify the design after manufacturing. The goal in computer-aided design is to use testing throughout the development cycle and to make better use of the test data through more advanced analysis techniques and to integrate these with other disciplines involved in design.

Initial testing can be done on a prototype or on different components to understand model response to certain loading conditions. Experimental data is extremely useful to the analysis for models where analytical solution is not reliable. It can also be used to refine computer finite element models for large scale analysis. The integration of experimental testing with analytical analysis results in a more effective tool in engineering analysis. Computer-aided design provides the ultimate tool for combining such methods with the graphics capabilities to allow the designer to arrive at more realistic and more effective designs in a minimum span of time.

Additional experimental analyses include fatigue testing to estimate part life from strain gauge measurements, modal testing to extract natural frequency and mode shapes, response functions, and a number of engineering functions in heat transfer, fluid dynamics, and thermodynamics.

Example 3.2   Analysis of a Strap and Solder Joint

A design analysis of the strap and solder joint to determine the failure mechanism of the joint is illustrated using both the conventional design analysis and the computer-aided design analysis.

The interconnect straps, as shown in Figure 3.18, are used to connect the power module and the splitter combiner board.

Solution   An analysis of the strap and solder joint was carried out to determine the failure mechanism. Two possible reasons led to the analysis:

1. Because of the different materials (with varying coefficients of thermal expansion) to which the interconnect straps connect, the failure is expected to be fatigue of the solder joint due to thermal cycling.
2. Power amplifiers are assembled in fixtures, which in turn include alignment pins. These alignment pins did not line up with the solder pads on the module, causing the straps to be bent backward. This bending of the straps to mate with the second solder pad creates an entirely different loading state than simply jumping from one pad to another along the same line.

Therefore, two finite element models would have to be created.

Analysis 1.   Model the strap such that the solder pads are in line, allowing the strap to be aligned "straight." The loading is based on deflections due to thermal expansion only. Goal: Determine strap stresses and loads transferred to the solder joint.

Analysis 2.   Model the strap with rotations that would simulate the bending of the strap. The loading would include bending and thermal expansion considerations. Goal: Determine strap stresses and loads transferred to the solder joint.

It is obvious from the design of the strap that it was intended to absorb deflections along the axis of the part. Once soldered, the strap is very stiff when deflected in a sort of shearing or bending direction. The forces that are being transferred from the interconnect strap to the solder joint can be determined from these

INTERCONNECT STRAP CONNECTION

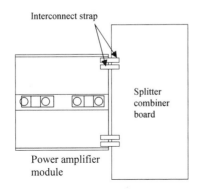

Figure 3.18   Interconnect strap solder joint.

two analyses. At this point, a new model simulating the solder pad–strap interface will have to be analyzed.

Conventional Design Analysis

Material properties (per Netallon, Inc., supplier and tests conducted on the material):

Copper alloy 102, half hard
Tensile strength: 40.5–41.5 Ksi
Yield strength: 2–7 Ksi < tensile strength
Modulus of Elasticity (E): 17×10^6 psi
Thermal expansion: 9.8×10^{-6} in./°F

Applying Castigliano's Theorem: Curved Beams. The deflections of curved beams can be handled very effectively using Castigliano's Theorem if the radius of curvature is much larger than the radius of gyration. The ratio for this analysis is 20 : 1. This approximation was made to determine an initial force value to use as the load for the eventual finite-element analysis.

$$\text{Deflection} = \frac{\pi}{2} \times \frac{FR^3}{EI} \tag{3.7}$$

$$0.002 \text{ in.} = \frac{\pi}{2} \times \frac{F(0.0225)^3}{2(17 \times 10^6)(9.688 \times 10^{-10})}$$

The force for a 0.002-in. deflection is 1.8 lbsf.

Tangential Stress: Curved Beams.

$$\text{Stress} = \frac{-M(r_n - r)}{Ar(r_c - r_n)} \tag{3.8}$$

where A = area of strap
    r_n = neutral axis
    r_c = centroidal axis
    $r_n < r_c$ for curved beams

Thus,

$$r = \frac{A}{\int \frac{dA}{r}} \qquad (3.9)$$

Thus, considering the x-section of the Interconnect strap shown in Figure 3.19,

$$A = (0.093)(0.005) = 0.00465 \qquad (3.10)$$

$$I = \frac{(0.093)(0.005)^3}{12} \qquad (3.11)$$

$$r_n = \frac{0.000465}{0.093 \times \int \frac{dr}{r}} \qquad (3.12)$$

$$\text{Stress} = \frac{-M(0.022 - 0.025)}{(0.00465)(0.0225 - 0.022)(0.025)}$$

$$= M(5.172 \times 10^5) \qquad (3.13)$$

$$M = F \times d$$

$$\text{Stress} = F(d)(5.172 \times 10^5) \qquad (3.14)$$

where d is the height of the strap (Figure 3.19) and F is the force acting on the strap. Therefore,

$$\text{Stress} = F(0.030 \text{ in.})(5.172 \times 10^5) \qquad (\text{where } F = 1.8 \text{ lb})$$

$$= (1.8)(0.030)(5.172 \times 10^5) \text{ psi}$$

$$(\text{Stress})_{\text{Calc}} = 28,000 \text{ Psi}$$

$$(\text{Stress})_{\text{Yield}} = 33,500 \text{ Psi}$$

Computer-Aided Design Analysis

A finite-element Model is built and analyzed using ANSYS. The flat sections of the

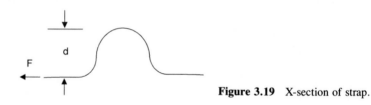

Figure 3.19   X-section of strap.

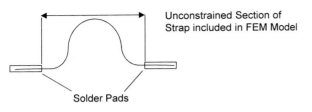

Unconstrained Section of
Strap included in FEM Model

Solder Pads

Figure 3.20   Unconstrained section of strap.

strap are soldered to pads on adjacent modules, and the unconstrained portion of the strap that must absorb the deflections of the modules due to thermal expansion is shown in Figure 3.20.

   Model Development.   Quadrilateral shell elements are used to define the structure. The elements have six degrees of freedom per node available. This is an important feature that allows the analysis of two operating conditions with one model:

1. Strap absorbing deflections in the *x* and *z* directions due to thermal expansion alone.
2. Strap being bent to account for the misalignment of the adjoining solder pads.

   A total of 175 nodes are defined and these are used to generate a mesh of 24 by 6 nodes. A curved surface can be approximated fairly well by keeping the angle over which the element covers at or below 15 degrees. This is the determining factor for deciding the number of nodes and elements required. Thus 144 total elements are used for the analysis. The constraints and loads are then added to the model (Figure 3.21).

   Constraints.   To simulate the movement of the strap due to thermal expansion, one end (right side) of the model is totally constrained against all deflections and rotations. Because the strap is soldered on both ends, it cannot move in the *y* direction and thus is also constrained on the left side in the *y* direction. This portion of the model is identical to both the first and second analyses. However, for the first analysis, rotations about the *y* axis are constrained, which keeps the applied loads in the *z* direction from rotating the model about this axis. For the second analysis, in which a rotated model is required to simulate the bending of the strap, *y*-axis rotations are included.

   Loading.   The predicted load of approximately 1.8 lb in the *x* direction is distributed evenly along the left side elements. Because loads are applied at the nodes, the corner nodes receive 1/12 of the total load and the other end nodes receive 1/6 of the total load. A load of 1.5 lb is distributed in the same manner along the left side in the positive *z* direction.

   FEA Results

Three models are built for each analysis case. Separate models are built to verify the *x* and *z* loads first by comparing the resulting deflections. The model with the 1.8 lbf

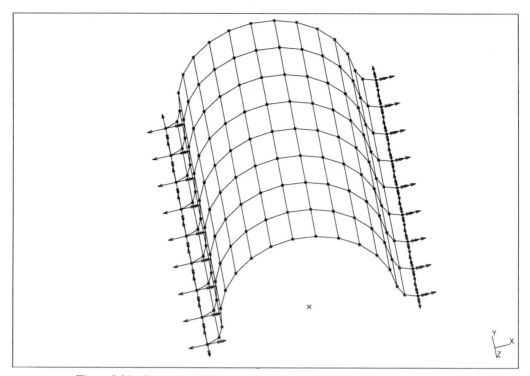

Figure 3.21 Constraints: RHside-ALL, LHside-Y Disp., Load Configuration: X-Dir. - 1 lbf, Y-Dir. - 1.5 lbf.

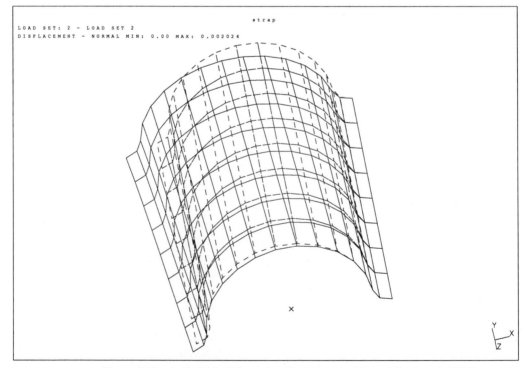

Figure 3.22 Analysis 1: Deformation file, Top view, Max. deflection - 0.0035″.

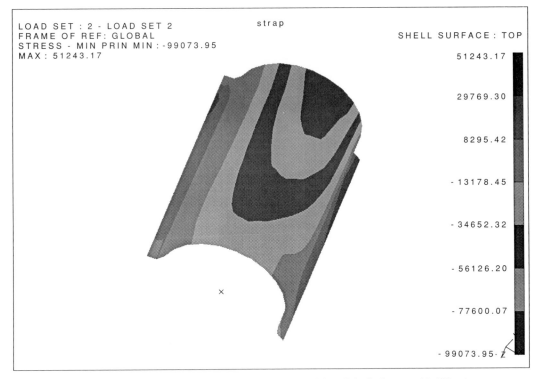

LOAD SET : 2 - LOAD SET 2   strap
FRAME OF REF: GLOBAL   SHELL SURFACE : TOP
STRESS - MIN PRIN MIN : -99073.95
MAX : 51243.17   51243.17

                                                                   29769.30

                                                                    8295.42

                                                                  - 13178.45

                                                                  - 34652.32

                                                                  - 56126.20

                                                                  - 77600.07

                                                                  - 99073.95 · z

Figure 3.23 Analysis 1: Stress contours, Max. Principal stress: 11,400 psi.

axial (x direction) load produces deflections of 0.0037 in. Thus, the load is too large. By reducing the load gradually, eventually a load of 1.0 lbf produces the required 0.002-in. deflections required. Similarly, the 1.5 lbf load along the z direction produces the 0.0005-in. deflection required. Once the independent loads are determined, they are superimposed onto one model to determine the final stresses and deflections.

Analysis 1.   The deflections obtained from the 1.0 (x-direction) load and the 1.5 (z direction) load are plotted (Figure 3.22). Slight rotations are still obtained although the y-axis rotations are constrained. Much larger deflections are seen in the x direction, although a larger force was applied in the z direction. Thus, this verifies that the strap is much "stiffer" to loads applied in the z-direction.

The stress contour obtained (maximum principal stresses) for this loading case are also plotted (Figure 3.23). The maximum stress observed is 11,400 psi. This is much lower than the approximated value of 23,000 psi. Thus, under this loading, the strap has a factor of safety of approximately 3, which is acceptable.

Analysis 2.   The deflections obtained for the identical loading as in Analysis 1, but with the y-axis rotations allowed are now studied (Figure 3.24). Maximum deflections are twice those seen in Analysis 1. Thus, the strap is actually being bent or rotated as a result of the z-direction loads by resulting in a moment.

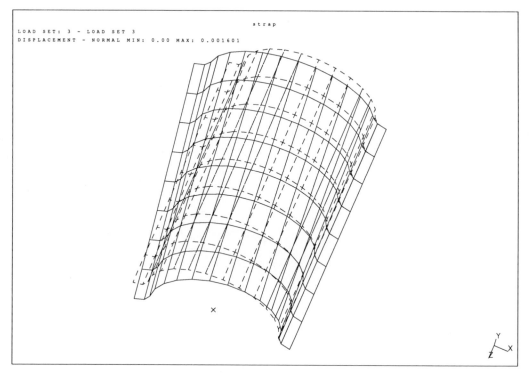

strap

LOAD SET: 3 - LOAD SET 3
DISPLACEMENT - NORMAL MIN: 0.00 MAX: 0.001601

Figure 3.24 Analysis 2: Deformation file, Top view, Max. deflection - 0.007″.

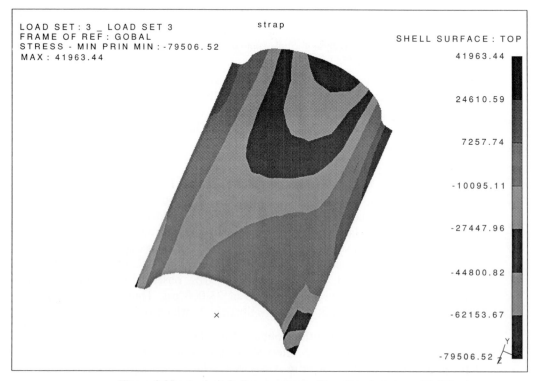

LOAD SET: 3 _ LOAD SET 3   strap
FRAME OF REF: GOBAL   SHELL SURFACE: TOP
STRESS - MIN PRIN MIN: -79506.52
MAX: 41963.44   41963.44

                                                      24610.59

                                                       7257.74

                                                     -10095.11

                                                     -27447.96

                                                     -44800.82

                                                     -62153.67

                                                     -79506.52

Figure 3.25 Analysis 2: Stress contours, Max. Principal stress: 23,400 psi.

The stress contours (maximum principal stress) obtained from the given loading are illustrated in Figure 3.25. As can be seen, the stresses produced from the bending action effectively double the stresses. The maximum stress was 23,400 psi. Thus, for very small deflections, which in turn bend the strap, very high stress values are produced.

Conclusion   The results obtained from the analysis agreed fairly well with those obtained from the classical analysis. It is obvious that corrections must be made to the fixtures to allow the straps to be aligned properly to avoid high-stress bending situations. A further redesign of the strap itself to allow it to absorb deflections in more than one direction would further increase its factor of safety. ■

Example 3.3   Using CAD in Steel Frame Design

This example shows how CAD is used in the analysis and design of a tower crane. The analysis is carried out on a simplified version of the tower crane. The designer uses the computer for defining and redefining the structural attributes to control and perform the analysis and design. The software used for carrying out the analysis was from IDEAS [38] by SDRC.

The classification of the Computer-Aided Design process is shown in Figure 3.26. In the problem definition section, the engineer defines the layout of the structured model—how the structure is supported, the initial properties of the structural members, and the applied loads. The steps followed during the design are illustrated in Figure 3.27.

Since the software has interactive computer graphics, the engineer gets a con-

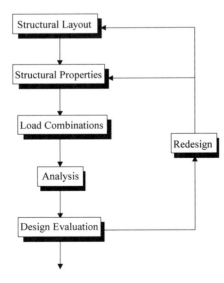

Figure 3.26 A classification of the computer-aided design process.

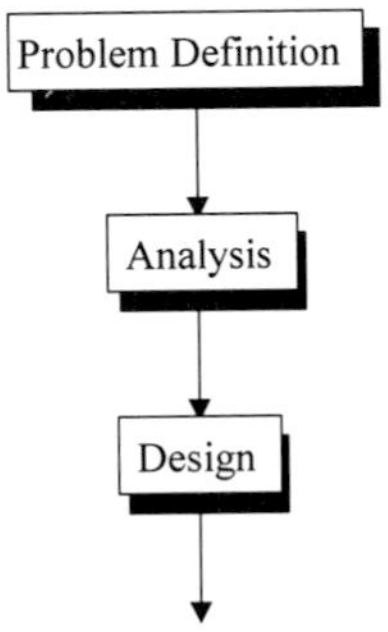

Figure 3.27 Steps followed in the design process.

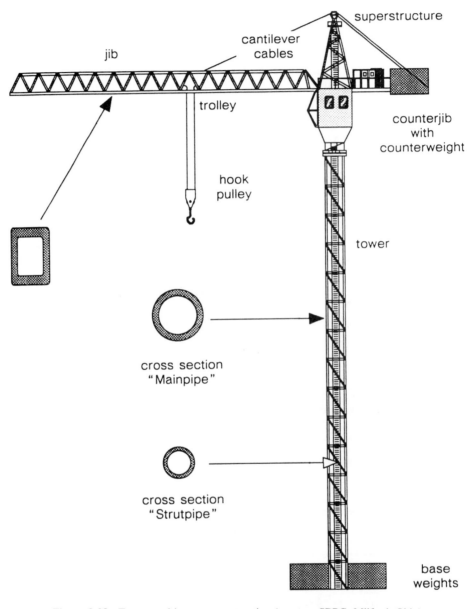

Figure 3.28 Terms used in crane construction (courtesy SDRC, Milford, Ohio).

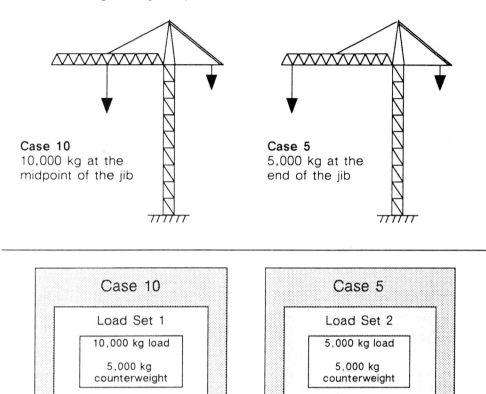

Figure 3.29 Boundary conditions for the tower crane model (courtesy of SDRC, Milford, Ohio).

tinual graphical feedback. Another advantage of using CAD is the ability to change the type of unit measurement at any phase in the design. The terms used in the design and analysis of a crane are listed in Figure 3.28, which also shows the cross sections used in the construction.

The support conditions are represented clearly in the problem definition stage. So any type of support conditions, including spring and skew supports, can be assigned to any node of the structure. The finite element model of the crane is created by defining the nodes and creating beam elements. The boundary conditions are then defined in terms of restraints and loads on the tower crane as shown in Figure 3.29.

The next phase is using the software to solve the problem. This is the process of determination of forces at each finite element in the model. In the post-processing

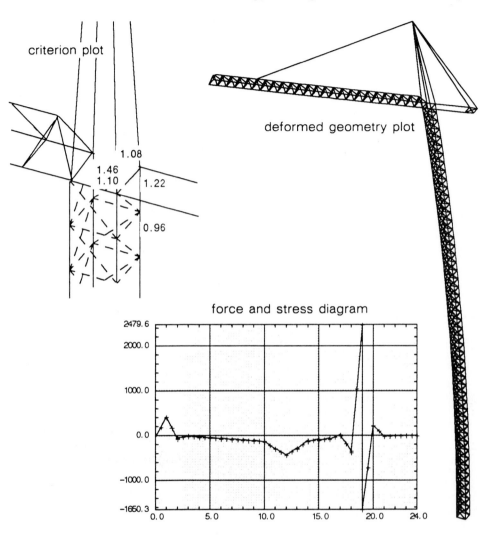

Figure 3.30 Force and stress diagrams, deformation plot (courtesy of SDRC, Milford, Ohio).

phase an analysis data set is selected for processing. The deformed geometry plot is displayed. It is possible to modify and redisplay the deformed geometry. The force and stress diagram can be plotted on the screen. The deformed geometry plot and force and stress diagrams are shown in Figure 3.30. The designer can also study the displacements of the structure on application of different loading conditions. This is illustrated in Figure 3.31.

LOADCASE : 1
DISPLACEMENT – MAG MIN: 0.00E+00 MAX: 1.96E–01

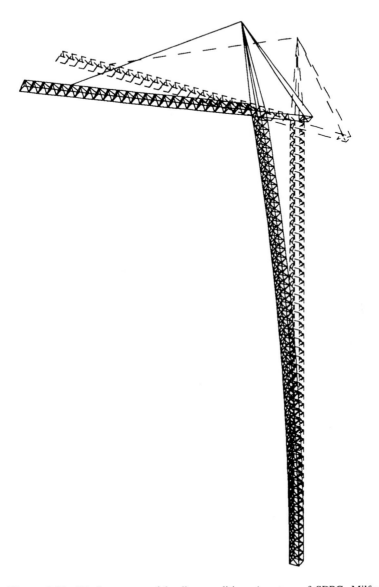

Figure 3.31 Displacement and loading conditions (courtesy of SDRC, Milford, Ohio).

Moreover, the engineer can interact with the structure at this design stage and use the alternative paths to the solution of the problem, as the following facilities are available:

1. Modular generation
2. Frame combination
3. Selective addition and deletion of members
4. Distortion of dimensions
5. Separate analysis or design for any substructure by separating it

Once the final design is achieved, the engineer can utilize the facility in CAD to select which drawings are to be made and to specify the bare particulars.   ∎

3.7 COMPUTER-AIDED ENGINEERING (CAE)

What is computer-aided engineering? According to J. R. Lemon, CAE is defined as a product design and development philosophy that brings together three key engineering elements in an integrated environment for all engineering functions within each stage of the product development cycle. These three elements are applications (performance, structural integrity, reliability, costs, etc.); facilities (hardware/software); and technology, data, and information management. Thus, the CAE approach results in the restructuring and streamlining of the entire engineering process itself instead of the automation of specific steps in the current process such as has been the case in computer-aided design (CAD) and computer-aided manufacturing (CAM) activities.

The main focus of the CAE approach is to place emphasis in terms of time and money in the initial conceptual design phases. This revised allocation of resources results in extensive analysis and testing to guide product design iterations in the computer as opposed to making physical prototypes. This is a major departure from current methods in most mechanical industries, where prototype manufacture and tests are the fundamental means to evaluate product performance and quality. However, the need for prototypes is not eliminated, but the reduction in the number of prototypes needed before full production can go ahead results in time and cost savings.

The CAE approach to mechanical product development emphasizes system analytical modeling and analysis techniques at the earliest phase of design, that is, conceptual design. The process starts with an integrated set of total system simulations of the entire product. Each alternative product concept is mathematically modeled as

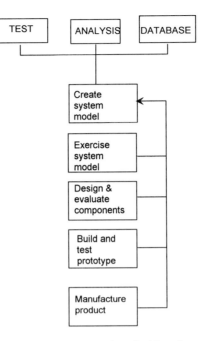

Figure 3.32   CAE structure as described in reference [30].

an entire system. At this point, overall product designers have the flexibility of defining significantly varying or revolutionary concepts in order to minimize weight, reduce energy consumption, and maximize performance for acceptable product concepts.

Detailed component and subassembly design specifications are derived from system models by exercising computer simulations under severe environmental conditions and external product loadings. In addition, internal loads, duty cycles, and constraints acting on components and subassemblies at interfaces and connection points are derived from system models. System modeling and early development of product alternatives within the computer are essential differences compared with today's developments that rely on physical prototypes and build-and-test methods. The CAE approach to manufacturing new products is shown in Figure 3.32.

An isolated approach to automation using CAD/CAM technology does not provide sufficient engineering effectiveness to meet most current manufacturing needs. The new CAE approach attempts to integrate and automate various engineering functions in the entire product development process:

1. Design
2. Analysis
3. Testing
4. Drafting
5. Documentation
6. Project management
7. Data management
8. Process planning
9. Tool design
10. Numerical control
11. Quality assurance

Improved product quality, increased market share, and improved profitability depend upon efficient and effective CAE integration and implementation. This is why CAE implementation has become a strategic issue within most companies in worldwide mechanical-related industries.

3.8 INTEGRATED DATABASE MANAGEMENT SYSTEMS IN CAE

Various supporting data systems of other applications are interfaced with the central product data management system via translators. This communication capability forms the basis of effective integration of tests, analysis, design drafting, and documentation and manufacturing functions.

The application database management systems (Figure 3.33) associated with each particular application workstation handle active data required and/or developed by the application itself. When a particular application task is completed, appropri-

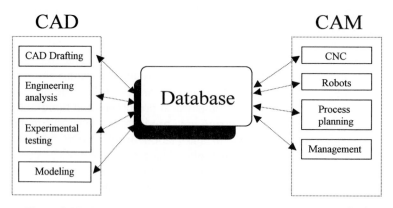

Figure 3.33   Database management system as described in reference [30].

ate data are transferred to the product computer and are used at the product level in conjunction with data and information developed by other applications. When the data are transferred from an active application status, they are processed and checked through an intermediate set of procedures and techniques to assure that they conform to requirements, desired formats, and completeness on the product computer. Similarly, when a product development project is completed and moves into production, product data are transferred from the product computer to the corporate data management system on a mainframe. Corporate data, of course, must be secure and protected for very long periods of time, especially in industries in which liability requirements are important.

3.9 CAE PRODUCT DEVELOPMENT

As in conventional design, CAD/CAM processes rely heavily on testing prototypes. CAE, which is considered an advancement beyond CAD/CAM, involves computer simulation of an entire system or product. Though CAD/CAM addresses only the physical description of the product, the CAE process goes on to analyze functional characteristics such as vibration, noise, and service life. Computer simulation is used to determine precise loads early so that components can be designed based on that criterion. This practice is in contrast to the traditional build-and-test approach in which component design testing relies greatly on computer simulation.

Computer simulation reduces the time and cost associated with product development. More importantly, CAE designs are optimized due in part to the engineering effort oriented toward the evaluation of alternative designs.

The heart of the CAE development process is the symbolic system model of the mathematical representation of the entire structure in the computer. The model is created by combining data on individual components and subassemblies. These data can come either from finite-element analysis, modal testing, or data banks, depending upon which types of data are more readily available. The system model is tested and refined in an iterative process until a detailed optimum configuration is created. The first simulation is generally coarse and not necessarily intended to yield precise results. However, successive simulations suggest changes that produce an increasingly refined model. The next step is to apply loads determined from coarse modeling to model individual components. Because component designs can alter the overall performance of the system, the refined component models are inserted back into the system model, which is tested once again. These designer iterations gradually transform coarse component descriptions into increasingly optimal finite-element models. A prototype is then built and tested with modal analysis and stress testing techniques. The results of these tests can indicate whether further changes to the system model are necessary. Prototype testing thus provides data for refinement of the system model, while the model guides the designer in understanding prototype behavior. After the prototype is redefined, the final configuration is released to manufacturing.

3.10 CAE IMPLEMENTATION

Implementation of an overall CAE system and its associated technologies must be planned carefully. Implementation should proceed step by step because it is not possible to switch off today's design, development, and manufacturing processes and switch on the CAE approach at the same time.

As a first step toward CAE implementation, existing problems should be solved to gain knowledge in the new capabilities and behavior within the computer. A design audit is not simply a learning exercise, but it is an important step to extend a basic product to a family of new products or to fix problems that may have developed.

The next phase involves new product design and development. The CAE tools should be applied to a new and unique product design for which new concepts have the potential of providing strategic product quality and market share advantages. An optimum hardware system along with a similar integrated and distributed database management system should be configured for in-house usage and expected long-range expansion requirements. Software that performs efficiently should also be brought in house if it is economically justified.

Along with these tasks, outside CAE consultants are recommended to help guide and develop an overall CAE implementation plan. Educational programs and seminars in all aspects of CAE implementation are essential for all levels within an organization. Once CAE tools are implemented and the in-house organization structured to suit the particular CAE implementation philosophy, the outside consultants' role can be reduced to solving difficult problems.

A central group to maintain and assure commonality of methods and facilities within various departments must be formed. This group should only develop CAE capabilities and applications software when they are absolutely essential and unavailable from reputable suppliers. Because CAE is not a product or a piece of hardware but a design philosophy, corporate management must be committed to this concept and willing to expend the resources necessary to bring CAE into reality. CAE is successful only when top corporate management makes the decision and assumes a leadership role in the implementation of the CAE approach.

3.11 OPTIMIZATION AND CAD

The conventional design process is largely based on the experience and intuition of the designer. Both of these characteristics contribute to the conceptual changes in the design and/or in introducing additional specifications to the design process. Hence optimum designs are attained through a judgment call or simply by a trial-and-error approach. Therefore, the conventional design process can lead to uneconomical designs in terms of cost and time.

The optimum design function forces the designer to clearly identify a set of design variables and a cost function to be minimized subject to the constraints of the system. Typically, designers create a general configuration for which numerical values of independent variables are not fixed. Then they establish an objective function that defines the value of the design in terms of the independent variables such as

$$G = G(x_1, x_2, \ldots, x_n) \qquad (3.15)$$

Objective functions could be cost, weight, or reliability. The objective function is subject to certain constraints that arise from certain limitations or compatibility conditions of the individual variables.

The solution methods to the optimum design problems can benefit greatly by the designer's experience and intuition. In addition, the role of computers is fundamental in the optimization process because each iteration cycle may require substantial calculations. Computers can also be used to provide graphical representation of data and animation, and simulate the working of the prototype before fabrication.

3.11.1 Formulation of an Optimum Design

As stated earlier, optimization is the process of maximizing a desired quality or minimizing an undesired one. Optimization theory is a body of mathematics that deals with the problem of maxima and minima and the process of finding the maxima and minima numerically. Any design process requires formulation of the objective in terms of a problem to which a solution is required. Formulation of an optimum design requires the conversion of the verbal description of the problem into an explicitly defined mathematical statement.

There are four steps to the formulation of an optimum design:

1. Identifying the design parameters
2. Defining the design constraints
3. Defining the objective functions
4. Evaluating alternatives

3.11.2 Design Variables

The quantities or variables that define the design of a system are called design variables or design parameters. The first problem is to decide which quantities should be considered as variables. It is desirable not to increase the amount of variables as it complicates the problem. Usually direct geometric quantities define the design variables. It is also important to have all design variables independent from each other.

3.11.3 Constraints

Constraints can be defined as the limitations placed on the design. A functional design is one that satisfies all the constraints. For a constraint to be meaningful, it must be influenced by one or more variables. Constraints can be of many types. Constraint functions can be expressed either as equality or inequality constraints depending on the type of design problem. Equality constraints are also called functional constraints or constraining functions. They represent relations that must exist between the design variables:

$$\Phi_i(x_1, x_2, \ldots, x_n) = 0 \qquad (i = 1, m) \qquad (3.16)$$

where m denotes the total number of constraints.

An example of a constraint equation optimizing a volume of a cylindrical storage tank is

$$V = \pi x_1^2 x_2 \qquad (3.17)$$

where x_1 and x_2 denote the radius and the height of the tank, respectively.

Inequality constraints arise because certain variables have practical limits on their values. The inequality constraints are called regional constraints or limit equations. They are expressed as

$$\Psi_j(x_1, x_2, x_3, \ldots, x_n) < L_j$$

where $j = l, p$, with p the total number of constraints. Constraint functions having only first-order terms in design variables are called constraints. Linear programming problems have these types of constraints.

3.11.4 Evaluation

A certain criterion is needed for comparison to decide which design is optimal among several alternatives. This evaluation criterion is based on the objective function and the constraints. In a situation where there are two or more cost functions, the most important criterion is taken as the cost function and the rest treated as constraints.

There are a number of methods that could be used to solve the combined objective functions and the constraints. The solutions usually give either a unique solution or more than one solution.

A unique solution is a perfect result that is accepted as the optimized design solution. However, when there is more than one solution, an additional criterion, which is based on the company's needs, is used to judge which of the solutions should be considered as the optimal design solution. The additional criterion used to select the optimal solution could be manpower, financial, functional, or safety requirements.

Example 3.4   Design for Minimum Cost

An example of a design formulation problem for minimum cost of a rectangular storage container of a given volume to be stored between two shelves is given in Figure 3.34.

Solution   The length, L, width, W, and height, H, comprise one set of design variables for this problem. The cost function for this problem is the dollar cost of the sheet metal for the storage container. The total surface area of the sheet metal re-

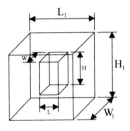

Figure 3.34   storage container.

quired for the container is

$$A = 2LH + 2HW + 2WL \qquad (3.18)$$

Now if C is the dollar cost of the sheet metal per unit area, then the cost function for the problem is given by

$$T = C(2LH + 2HW + 2WL) \qquad (3.19)$$

The volume of the tank is given by V and

$$V = LWH \qquad (3.20)$$

All three design variables are limited by the dimensions of the shelf:

$$L < L_1 \qquad W < W_1 \qquad H < H_1$$

As shown by the example, the steps that generally follow in formulation of a design problem are

1. identification of the design variables
2. selection of a cost function and developing an expression for it in terms of the design variables
3. identification of constraints and developing expressions for them in terms of design variables ∎

3.12 OPTIMIZATION METHODS

There are no standard methods for optimization in engineering design and the usefulness of a technique depends on the nature of the functions represented in the design problem. Some methods commonly used in optimization follow.

3.12.1 Optimization by Differentiation

Differential calculus is often used to determine the maxima and minima values of a function. Figure 3.35 shows a criterion function T as a function of x_1. The various types of extremes that can occur are shown, where A provides a local minima, and B a local maxima.

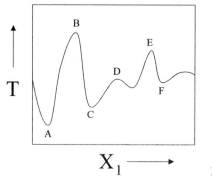

Figure 3.35 Types of extrema.

A unique property of an extreme is described by the function as it approaches its minimum or maximum. If T becomes stationary momentarily at a particular point, then T increases as it approaches E, stops increasing at E, and then decreases. These points are therefore called stationary points and satisfy the following condition

$$dT/dx_1 = 0 \tag{3.21}$$

The behavior of the curve in the neighborhood of a stationary point a is given by Taylor's expansion:

$$T(x_1) = T(a) + \frac{dT}{dx_1}\bigg|_a \frac{x_1 - a}{1!} + \frac{d^2T}{dx_1^2}\bigg|_a \frac{(x_1 - a)^2}{2!} + \cdots \tag{3.22}$$

The sign of $T(x_1) - T(a)$ is determined by examining the sign of the second derivative, neglecting higher-order terms. Thus,

$$(d^2T/dx_1^2)_a > 0$$

indicates a minimum at a,

$$(d^2T/dx_1^2)_a < 0$$

indicates a maximum at a,

$$(d^2T/dx^2)_a = 0$$

indicates that higher derivatives should be considered as no conclusion can be drawn. If the derivative is odd, the point is one of inflection.

If T is a function of two independent variables, x_1 and x_2, then it is necessary for both $\partial T/\partial x_1$ and $\partial T/\partial x_2$ to be set to zero to extract the minimum and maximum of the function.

Example 3.5   Design Optimization of a Cylindrical Tank

A design optimization problem for the minimum cost of a cylindrical tank is considered. The cylinder is closed on both ends and these closing lids cost \$6.00/m². The cylinder material costs \$12.00/m². Find the height, h, and radius, r, to minimize the cost if the volume of the cylinder is 4π m³.

Solution   The objective function in terms of cost is represented by

$$T = 6(2 \times \pi r^2) + 12(2\pi rh) \tag{3.23}$$

The functional constraint is given by the volume:

$$V = \pi r^2 h = 4\pi \ m^3 \qquad \text{or} \qquad \Psi(r, h) = r^2 h - 4 = 0 \tag{3.24}$$

This yields

$$h = 4/r^2 \tag{3.25}$$

Substituting Equation (3.25) into the objective function, we obtain

$$T = 12\pi r^2 + 24\pi rh = 12\pi r^2 + 24\pi r (4/r^2) \tag{3.26}$$

Therefore,

$$T = 12\pi r^2 + 96\pi/r \tag{3.27}$$

The objective function can now be differentiated and equated to zero. Therefore,

$$dT/dr = 24\pi r - 96\pi/r^2 = 0 \tag{3.28}$$

Yielding

$$r = 2 \wedge h = 1 \tag{3.29}$$

Because the second derivative is always positive in this case, $r = 2$ represents a relative minimum. The minimum cost is given by equation (3.23) which yields $T = \$301.44$.

Method of Lagrange Multipliers

Functional constraints are used to reduce the dimensions of the criterion function, where each constraint eliminates one variable. However, the elimination becomes difficult when the functional constraints are implicit functions of the design parameters. Lagrange multipliers provide a powerful method for finding the optima in multivariable problems involving functional constraints.

The function to be optimized is defined by augmenting the objective function by the constraints premultiplied by a variable called the Lagrange multiplier. This is given by

$$T = T_o + \sum_{j=1}^{m} \lambda_j \Psi_j \tag{3.30}$$

where T_o is the objective function, λ the undetermined multipliers, and ψ the constraints.

The optimum is obtained by differentiating with respect to the independent variables and the undetermined multipliers.

$$\frac{\partial T}{\partial X_i} = 0 \qquad \frac{\partial T}{\partial \lambda_j} = 0 \qquad (i = 1, n; \text{ and } j = 1, m) \tag{3.31}$$

∎

Example 3.6   Design Optimization of Cylindrical Tank Using Language Multipliers

Solve for the optimal design problem of Example 3.5 by the method of Lagrange multipliers.

    Solution   The objective function is

$$T_o = 6 \times 2\pi r^2 + 24\pi rh \tag{3.32}$$

The functional constraint is $\Psi(r, h) = r^2h - 4 = 0$. Hence the function to be optimized is

$$T = T_o + \lambda(r^2h - 4) \tag{3.33}$$

Taking the partial derivatives of T with respect to r, h and λ and setting them equal to zero will yield 3 equations and 3 unknowns. The solution of which gives the optimum values of r, h, λ and of course T. The partial derivatives of T_o and Ψ with respect to r, λ and h are

$$\partial T_o/\partial r = 24\pi r + 24\pi h \qquad \partial T_o/\partial h = 24\pi r$$
$$\partial \Psi \partial r = 2rh \qquad\qquad \partial \Psi/\partial h = r^2 \tag{3.34}$$
$$\partial T_o/\partial \lambda = 0 \qquad\qquad \partial \Psi/\partial \lambda = 0$$

Similarly those of T are found to be

$$\partial T/\partial r = \partial T_o/\partial r + \lambda \partial \Psi/\partial r = 0 = 24\pi(r + h) + 2\lambda rh$$
$$\partial T/\partial h = \partial T_o/\partial h + \lambda \partial \Psi/\partial h = 0 = 24\pi r + \lambda r^2 \tag{3.35}$$
$$\partial T/\partial \lambda = \partial T_o/\partial \lambda + \frac{\partial}{\partial \lambda}[\lambda(rh^2 - 4)] = rh^2 - 4 = 0$$

From the equations above, we solve for r, h and λ and get

$$r = 2, \qquad h = 1, \qquad \text{and } \lambda = -12\pi$$

The cost of the container is obtained by substituting the above values into equation (3.32).

$$T_o = 12\pi(2)^2 + 24\pi(2)(4/2^2) = 96\pi = \$301.59 \tag{3.36}$$

                                                                        ■

    Linear Programming.   There are times when the general equations of optimization take a characteristic linear form. In this case, the formulation and solution of the design problem is done by the method of linear programming.

    The linear programming method deals with objective functions of the form

$$T = \sum_i k_i x_i$$

to be maximized or minimized subject to some constraints that are also linear in x.

$$\psi_1 = a_{11}x_1 + a_{12}x_2 + \cdots + a_{1n}x_n \geq l_1$$
$$\psi_2 = a_{21}x_1 + a_{22}x_2 + \cdots + a_{2n}x_n \geq l_2$$

$$\vdots \qquad \vdots \qquad \vdots \qquad\qquad \vdots \qquad \vdots \qquad\qquad (3.37)$$

$$\psi_n = a_{n1}x_1 + a_{n2}x_2 + \cdots + a_{nn}x_n \geq l_n$$

The general linear programming consists of a set of m linear equations involving n variables. The nonnegative values of the variables that satisfy the constraint equations and maximize or minimize the linear objective function are to be found.

The linear programming approach is illustrated in the following example using two variables.

Example 3.7   Optimization of an Objective Function Using Linear Programming Techniques

An objective function is given by

$$T = 4x_1 + x_2 \qquad\qquad (3.38)$$

subject to the following constraints:

$$2x_1 + x_2 > 2$$
$$4x_1 - 3x_2 > -3$$
$$2x_1 + 3x_2 < 21 \qquad \text{(inequality constraints)} \qquad (3.39)$$
$$4x_1 - x_2 < 16$$

In addition,

$$x_1 > 0 \qquad \text{and} \qquad x_2 > 0 \qquad \text{(nonnegativity requirements)} \qquad (3.40)$$

Find the optimal point for the objective function (CT) using linear programming method.

Solution   This problem can be solved graphically, as shown in Figure 3.36.

The limiting equations are satisfied by any solution inside the shaded area. The optimization can be rewritten as

$$x_2 = T - 4x_1 \qquad\qquad (3.41)$$

The slashed lines represent this equation for different values of T. It is apparent that point D is the optimum solution with $T = 23.43$, $x_1 = 4.93$ and $x_2 = 3.71$.

The procedure in linear programming is to start at any one corner of the shaded polygon and jump to an adjacent corner having a higher value of T until no adjacent corner exists with a higher value.

Geometric Programming

Geometric programming is a nonlinear optimization technique utilizing polynomial programming developed by Duffin, Peterson, and Zener.

An example of the objective function used in geometric programming is given by

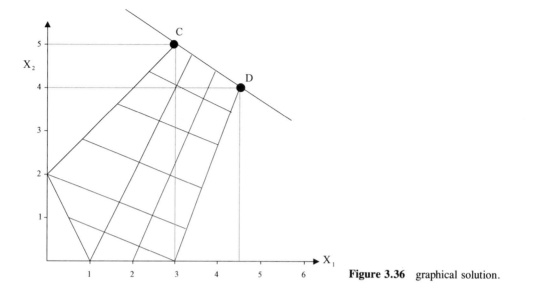

Figure 3.36 graphical solution.

$$T = x_1 + 2x_1^1 x_2 + \frac{3}{\sqrt{5}} \sqrt{x_1 x_2} + x_3^3 \qquad (3.42)$$

These objective functions take the following form:

$$T = u_1 + u_2 + \cdots + u_p \qquad (3.43)$$

Next, a function G is defined such that

$$G = \left(\frac{u_1}{s_1}\right)^{s_1} \left(\frac{u_2}{s_2}\right)^{s_2} \cdots \left(\frac{u_p}{s_p}\right)^{s_p} \qquad (3.44)$$

where the s_p's are chosen properly to minimize T.

The method uses a concept of duality similar to that used for linear programming. The dual problem is simpler to solve than the primal problem. The method is quite complex but works well on a computer and has the advantage of providing a global optimum.   ∎

Other Optimization Methods.   There are many other methods to solve an optimization problem. Some of the common solution techniques are

Search methods
  Exhaustive search
  Bisective search
  Grid search
  Random search
  Golden search
  Simplex search

Gradient methods
    Steepest descent
    Conjugate gradients
    Newton's methods
Second-derivative methods
Nonlinear programming
    Johnson's method
    Powell's method for unconstrained situations

In addition, there are other methods that could be applied to special problems.

These numerical methods can be used to solve the design problem once it is formulated. The methods are iterative and generate a sequence of design points before converging to an optimum solution. Hence these are best suited for computer implementation to exploit computer speed for beginning repetitive calculations. The software used for design optimization should have interactive facilities to enable the designer to alter the course of the design process if necessary. The software should also be able to interrupt the iterative process to inform the designer about the status of the design. There are many computer algorithms available, most of which have been written in FORTRAN.

PROBLEMS

3.1   Give, in tabular form, the best characteristics of man/machine. (The machine in this case is assumed to be the computer or CAD/CAM system.)

Problems 2–4 should be solved following the examples provided in Secs. 3.2 and 3.4.

3.2   An SAE Formula car (Figure P3.1) is to be designed by a group of students. There are two main types of restrictions, namely, dimensional and design. The two main dimensional restrictions are that the car should have a minimum wheel base of 60 inches measured from the centers of the front and rear tires while they are pointed forward. The second dimensional restriction is that the lateral dimension from the center of the left tires to that of the right tires on the front and rear axles be such that the car does not roll over if tilted to an angle of 57 degrees at a normal acceleration of 1.5 g.

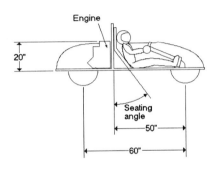

Figure P3.1   SAE formula car.

The design restrictions to ensure safety and constancy among the cars include: The engine should be any four-cycle piston engine with less than 610-cc displacement per cycle. The suspension system must incorporate shock absorbers and allow at least 2 in. of wheel travel. The roll bar to protect the driver must have a minimum outside diameter of 1.00 in., a wall thickness of 0.060 in., and be made of mild steel. The car should have a four-wheel braking system and its tire rims must be between 8 and 13 in. in diameter.

(a) To aid the students involved in the project, discuss the design process steps involved in the design of the frame and roll cage of the car, keeping in mind the previous restrictions and criteria.

(b) Provide a distinction between the conventional analysis and the FEM analysis.

3.3 Riding comfort is not a concern in the design of the SAE formula car. However, the suspension could be of importance to the performance and handling of the car. Through the design steps, describe a particular model of your choice.

3.4 Design an artificial leg for a person who has lost a leg above the knee. The artificial leg should capture as many normal movements as possible. Consider a mechanism with two links connected with the knee joint. (Follow the steps of the design process.)

3.5 Conceptualize and design an oil cooler using the engine coolant as the cooling medium for an automobile. The designed oil cooler must maintain a desired oil temperature, must withstand oil and coolant pressures without leakage, and it must not loosen due to engine vibration. The oil cooler design should also consider additional criteria such as low production cost, minimum size, adaptability to a variety of vehicles, allowing for the heating of oil during cold starts, adaptability of the cooler to the existing coolant system, and availability in kit form.

3.6 Find an optimum solution using the graphical method for the problem constraints given by

$$-2x_1 + 6x_2 < 20$$
$$2x_1 + 2x_2 < 12$$
$$2x_1 - 2x_2 < 4$$
$$2x_1 + 6x_2 > 12$$

and

$$x_1 > 0 \qquad \text{and} \qquad x_2 > 0$$

and the objective function

$$U = 2x_1 + 4x_2 = \text{maximum}$$

3.7 Formulate a design optimization problem for a cylindrical can that has a volume of 475 cm³. The height-to-diameter ratio for the can is limited between 1.5 and 3.5. The cost of the material is estimated at $3/cm².

3.8 Solve the design problem given in Problem 7 using the Lagrange multipliers optimization method.

3.9 Using a set of geometric constraints, design the hand brake shown in Figure P3.2. Also show the effect of change in one dimension on the part.

3.10 A two-jaw clutch has the dimensions shown in Figure P3.3. Design the part using a

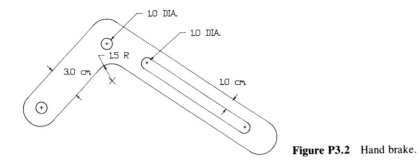

Figure P3.2 Hand brake.

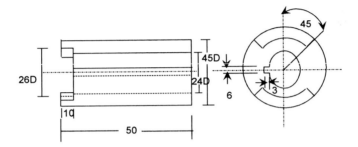

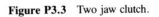

Figure P3.3 Two jaw clutch.

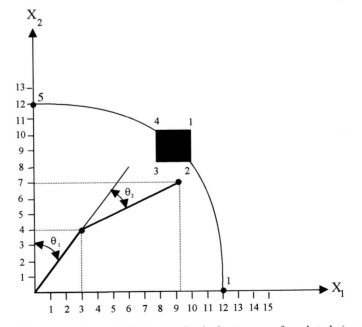

Figure P3.4 A robotic manipulator operating in the presence of an obstacle (square).

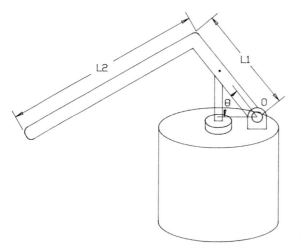

Figure P3.5 Hand pump.

parametric design system. Generate a set of equations that can incorporate any change in dimension, and redraw the part.

3.11 Figure P3.4 shows a two-arm robotic manipulator. The lengths of the arms are 5 and 7 m respectively. Determine the range of angles that can cover the quadrant working area by avoiding the square block shown. Use the variational approach.

3.12 A one-cylinder hand pump has the dimensions shown in Figure P3.5. Using the variational design approach, derive a set of equations that can be used to design the handle and the fixed joint for pumping the maximum amount of fluid with minimum hand force.

REFERENCES

3.1 *ADAMS User's Manual (Ver. 5.2)*, Mechanical Dynamics, Inc., Ann Arbor, Michigan, October 1987.

3.2 Akin, J. E., *Computer Assisted Mechanical Design*, Prentice-Hall, Englewood Cliffs, NJ, 1990.

3.3 Amirouche, F. M. L., *DYnamic Analysis of MUltibody Systems (DYAMUS), User's Guide*, Mechanical Engineering Department, University of Illinois at Chicago, 1988 and Prentice Hall, 1992.

3.4 Amirouche, F. M. L., *Dynamic Analysis of Rotorcraft Systems (DARS), Users' Guide*, Mechanical Engineering Department, University of Illinois at Chicago, 1990.

3.5 Amirouche, F. M. L., Dynamics of Multi-Body Systems, Course Notes ME 404, Mechanical Engineering Department, University of Illinois at Chicago, 1990.

3.6 Amirouche, F. M. L., Introduction to Computer-Aided Design and Manufacturing, Course Notes ME 347, Mechanical Engineering Department, University of Illinois at Chicago, 1987.

3.7 Angel, J. C., Interactive Simulation of Machinery with Friction and Impact Using DRAM, SAE Paper No. 770050, 1977.

3.8 *ANSYS Engineering Analysis System User's Manual,* (Rev. 4.3) Vols. 1 and 2, Swanson Analysis Systems, Houston, Pa., 1987.

3.9 Arora, J., *Introduction to Optimum Design,* McGraw-Hill, New York, 1989.

3.10 Bodley, C. S., Devers, A. D., Park, A. C., and Frisch, H. P., *A Digital Computer Program for the Dynamic Interaction Simulation of Controls and Structure (DISCOS),* Vols. 1 and 2, NASA Technical Paper 1219, May 1978.

3.11 Chance, M. A., Using DRAM and ADAMS Programs to Simulate Machinery, Vehicles, *Agricultural Engineering,* Warrendale, Pa., November 1978, pp. 16–18.

3.12 Chung, J. C. H., and Schussel, M. D., *Comparison of Variational and Parametric Design,* SDRC, Milford, Oh.

3.13 IDEAS, "Getting Started" Finite Element Modelling and Analysis, SDRC, Milford, Oh., 1990.

3.14 Cook, R., and Young, Y., *Advanced Mechanics of Materials,* Macuri Uan, New York, 1985.

3.15 Dantzig, G. B., *Linear Programming and Extensions,* Princeton University Press, Princeton, 1963.

3.16 Date, C. J., *An Introduction to Database Systems,* Vol. 1, 3d ed., Addison-Wesley, Reading, Ma., 1982.

3.17 Dieter, J., *Engineering Design,* McGraw-Hill, New York, 1983.

3.18 Duffin, R. J., Peterson, E. L., and Zener, C., *Geometric Programming,* John Wiley & Sons , New York, 1967.

3.19 *Dynamic Analysis of Constrained Multibody Systems (DYNACOMS),* Department of Mechanical Engineering, University of Cincinnati, 1984.

3.20 *Dynamic Analysis & Design System (DADS),* Computer Aided Design Software, Inc. (CADSi), Oakdale, Ia., 1989.

3.21 Erdman, A. G., and Sandor, G. N., *Mechanism Design Analysis and Synthesis,* Vol. 1, Prentice-Hall, Englewood Cliffs, NJ, 1990.

3.22 Frost, R. A., Ed., *Database Management Systems,* McGraw-Hill, New York, 1984.

3.23 Gavdan, Y., and Lucas, M., *Interactive Graphics in CAD,* Unipub., New York, 1984.

3.24 *An Introduction to Computer-Aided Engineering,* CAE Annual, 1982.

3.25 Lawry, M., *I-DEAS Student Guide,* SDRC, Milford, Oh., 1990.

3.26 Lemon, J. R., Tolani, S. K., and Klosterman, A. L., *Integration and Implementation of Computer-Aided Engineering and Related Manufacturing Capabilities into Mechanical Product Development Process,* Gi-Jahrestagung, FRG, October 1, 1980.

3.27 Paul, B., Analytical Dynamics of Mechanisms—A Computer Oriented Overview, *Mechanisms and Machine Theory,* Vol. 10, No. 6, 1975, pp. 481–507.

3.28 Reinholtz, G. F., Duarde, S. G., and Sanda, G. N., Kinematic Analysis of Planar Higher-Pair Mechanisms, *Mechanism and Machine Theory,* Vol. 13, No. 6, 1978, pp. 619–629.

3.29 Riley, D. R., Linkage Design Using the Linkages Package, SAE Paper No. 830801, Warrendale, Pa., 1983.

3.30 Sidall, J., *Analytical Decision Making in Engineering Design,* Prentice-Hall, Englewood Cliffs, NJ, 1972.

3.31 Sidall, J., *Optimal Engineering Design,* Marcel Dekker, New York, 1982.

3.32 Simon, H., *A Student's Introduction to Engineering Design,* Pergamon, New York, 1975.

3.33 Taraman, K., Ed., *CAD/CAM: Meeting Today's Productivity Challenge,* Prentice-Hall, Englewood Cliffs, NJ, 1982.

3.34 Teicholtz, E., *CAD/CAM Handbook,* McGraw-Hill, 1985.

3.35 Three Precision Point Synthesis of a Four-Bar Linkage: An Example Using the LINCAGES-4 Program, *Proceedings of ASME, Computer in Engineering 1988,* Vol. 2, ASME, New York, pp. 91–96.

3.36 Van Benschoten, J. R., Angus, G. D., Kormos, J. G., and Sherlock, J. E., *CAE . . . Revolution Not Evolution: Competitive Marketplace Breeds CAE,* 81-0511-CP, AIAA/ASME/ASCE/AHS, 22nd Structures, Structural Dynamics and Materials Conference, Atlanta, Ga., April 6–8, 1981.

3.37 Zener, C., *Engineering Design by Geometric Programming,* John Wiley & Sons, New York, 1971.

3.38 Zener, C., A Mathematical Aid in Optimizing Engineering Design I, *Proc. Nat. Acad. Sci. USA,* Vol. 47, No. 5, 1961, pp. 537–539.

chapter 4

Geometry Description

4.1 INTRODUCTION

Geometrical representation of objects on a CAD workstation is based on computer graphics. Computer graphics is defined as the "generation, presentation, and manipulation of models of an object and their different views with the help of a combined form of computer hardware, software and graphic devices." The integrated system is used by the designer to create, display, and store the desired database. Now the question arises: Why do we need computer graphics?

Today the computer is serving as a processing tool that can store, retrieve, manipulate, and combine information. A benefit of this technology is that it is making our work rewarding to an extent never possible before. But as the volume of information increases, another question is asked: How can information be transferred efficiently between humans and machines? We know that the computer is a machine that generates data in a numerical form that is difficult to understand and interpret by a human being. Hence, the graphical representation of the data serves as a medium between the user and the computer, enhancing the user's ability to make quick decisions. Computer graphics is a technique used to improve the communication between humans and machines. A single graph can substitute for huge tables of numbers and allow the user to interpret the quantities and characteristics at a glance. Thus, the use of such information can enhance productivity and provide for more effective problem solving.

Computer graphics strongly supports the old adage that "a picture is worth a thousand words." Through computer graphics, we can simulate and hence predict automobile collisions, the piloting of a jet plane or space shuttle, the performance of a compressor, a turbine, or a pump at different speeds and loads, and many other engineering situations. The same graphic facilities in computer-aided design allow us to generate a complete automobile body layout (see Figure 4.1), a printed circuit board, a detailed building, or any mechanical component with its corresponding drawing.

Up to this point, we have discussed computer graphics in general. Now we explore the methods used to project an image (described in terms of Cartesian coordinates) onto a graphic screen and then manipulate it (see Figure 4.2). Often, we may want to change the scale of an image to see some details more clearly. We may have to rotate an image by a certain angle to get a better view of an object or to translate an image to another location to display it in a different environment. These steps constitute geometry manipulation. These are the basic functions of computer graphics and can be accomplished by using geometric transformation techniques, which we study in this chapter. We also examine the fundamentals of mathematics for computer graphics by considering the representation and transformation of points, lines, surfaces, and objects in two- and three-dimensional planes.

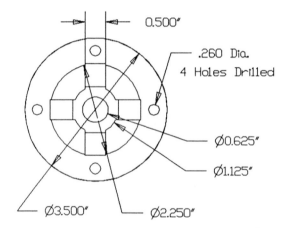

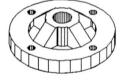

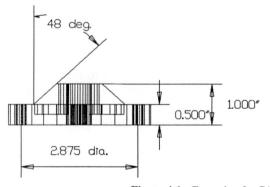

Figure 4.1 Example of a CAD layout.

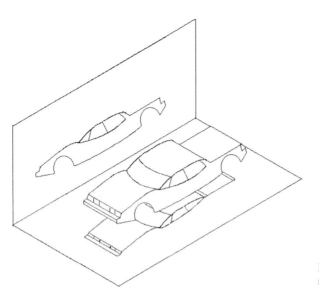

Figure 4.2 Projection of a car onto several planes.

4.2 TRANSFORMATION MATRIX

An object or a geometry can be represented by a set of points in several planes. Let us represent a set of data by a matrix called $\mathbf{C}_{\text{old}}$. We now define an operator $\mathbf{R}$ that once multiplied by $\mathbf{C}_{\text{old}}$ produces a new matrix $\mathbf{C}_{\text{new}}$.

$$\mathbf{C}_{\text{new}} = \mathbf{C}_{\text{old}}\mathbf{R} \qquad (4.1)$$

Here $\mathbf{R}$ is called a transformation matrix, which could involve rotation about a point or axis, translation to a given destination, scaling, reflecting, or mirror imaging about a plane, or a combination of all these. The basic rule in transformation is matrix multiplication. It is essential to read Equation (4.1) as "operating on $\mathbf{C}_{\text{old}}$ by $\mathbf{R}$ yields $\mathbf{C}_{\text{new}}$." The rule of thumb here is to remember that the product of two matrices exists only if the number of columns of the first matrix is equal to the number of rows of the second. (See Appendix A.)

4.3 2D TRANSFORMATION

Consider an arbitrary point given by the coordinates (x, y), as shown in Figure 4.3. Let us operate on this point by a transformation matrix $\mathbf{R}$, defined as follows:

$$[x \quad y]_{\text{new}} = [x \quad y]_{\text{old}} \begin{bmatrix} R_{11} & R_{12} \\ R_{21} & R_{22} \end{bmatrix} \qquad (4.2)$$

We note here that R_{11}, R_{12}, R_{21}, and R_{22} are scalar quantities. The coordinates of the new point, that is, x_{new} and y_{new} are given by

$$x_{\text{new}} = x_{\text{old}}R_{11} + y_{\text{old}}R_{21} \qquad (4.3)$$

$$y_{\text{new}} = x_{\text{old}}R_{12} + y_{\text{old}}R_{22} \qquad (4.4)$$

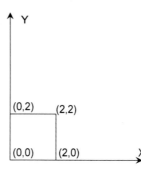

Figure 4.3 An arbitrary point with x, y, coordinates.

Now let us examine what happened to the old (x, y) coordinates. Several things could be deduced from Equations (4.3) and (4.4). We first notice that if R_{12} and R_{21} are equal to zero, then the new coordinates are simply obtained by multiplying the old coordinates by scalar quantities. This, in effect, causes a stretching of old coordinates in both x and y directions. This actually produces a scaling. On the other hand, we can let the elements of **R** be such that nothing can happen to the old coordinates. It can be seen that this is achieved by letting $R_{21} = R_{12} = 0$ and $R_{11} = R_{22} = 1$. Thus, if **R** is the identity matrix, no effect will result from the operation on the old (x, y). But suppose we let $R_{11} = R_{12} = 1$ and $R_{12} \neq R_{21} \neq 0$; then what does **R** do to the old point? The transformation matrix now causes a shear-type deformation. An illustration of this can be seen by considering the following example:

Example 4.1   2D Transformation of a Simple Geometry

Given the coordinates of the geometry as depicted by Figure 4.4, show what hap-

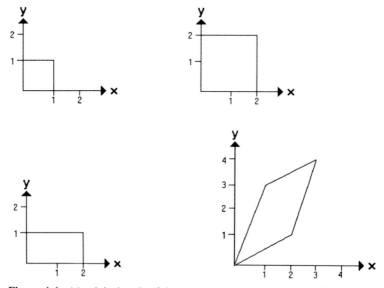

Figure 4.4 (a) original scale of the geometry, (b) overall scaling, (c) scaling in the x-direction, (d) shear type deformation.

pens to it when operated on by

(a) $\mathbf{R} = \begin{bmatrix} 2 & 0 \\ 0 & 2 \end{bmatrix}$

(b) $\mathbf{R} = \begin{bmatrix} 2 & 0 \\ 0 & 1 \end{bmatrix}$ (4.5)

(c) $\mathbf{R} = \begin{bmatrix} 1 & 3 \\ 2 & 1 \end{bmatrix}$

Solution

(a) $\begin{bmatrix} 0 & 0 \\ 0 & 1 \\ 1 & 1 \\ 1 & 0 \end{bmatrix} \begin{bmatrix} 2 & 0 \\ 0 & 2 \end{bmatrix} = \begin{bmatrix} 0 & 0 \\ 0 & 2 \\ 2 & 2 \\ 2 & 0 \end{bmatrix}$

(b) $\begin{bmatrix} 0 & 0 \\ 0 & 1 \\ 1 & 1 \\ 1 & 0 \end{bmatrix} \begin{bmatrix} 2 & 0 \\ 0 & 1 \end{bmatrix} = \begin{bmatrix} 0 & 0 \\ 0 & 1 \\ 2 & 1 \\ 2 & 0 \end{bmatrix}$

(c) $\begin{bmatrix} 0 & 0 \\ 0 & 1 \\ 1 & 1 \\ 1 & 0 \end{bmatrix} \begin{bmatrix} 1 & 3 \\ 2 & 1 \end{bmatrix} = \begin{bmatrix} 0 & 0 \\ 2 & 1 \\ 3 & 4 \\ 1 & 3 \end{bmatrix}$ ∎

It is important to study and analyze the transformation techniques in two-dimensional space, and then expand the developed concepts to three-dimensional space. Indeed, now that we have some idea about the transformation matrix and its effects, we proceed to study the 2×2 transformation matrix and its usefulness in geometry manipulation. However, it is apparent from the foregoing analysis that a 2×2 transformation matrix can cause scaling, rotation, and shear deformation.

4.4 SCALING

In 2D transformation, scaling is controlled by the magnitude of the two terms on the primary diagonal of the transformation matrix.

$$\mathbf{R} = \begin{bmatrix} R_{11} & 0 \\ 0 & R_{22} \end{bmatrix}$$ (4.6)

For matrix $\mathbf{R}$:

(a) If $R_{11} = R_{22}$, we have enlargement about the origin, or uniform scaling.
(b) If $R_{11} \neq R_{22}$, we have distortion, or nonuniform scaling. It should be noted

that the point of origin only remains unchanged during the scaling operation. If we choose **R** equal to

$$\mathbf{R} = \begin{bmatrix} 2 & 0 \\ 0 & 2 \end{bmatrix} \qquad (4.7)$$

and operate on the vertices of the object shown in Figure 4.5(a), which is the top view of a pyramid, uniform scaling takes place and an enlargement of "2 times" the original object occurs. But if the same original object is operated on by the matrix

$$\mathbf{R} = \begin{bmatrix} 1 & 0 \\ 0 & 2 \end{bmatrix} \qquad (4.8)$$

a distorted picture results [see Figures 4.5(c) and 4.5(d)], as the geometric configuration is enlarged only in the y direction, caused by nonuniform scaling.

4.4.1 General Scaling in 2D

In many cases, the geometry of a particular design in engineering and architectural drawings and some art sketches can be illustrated by a mesh or a wireframe. The configuration of a wireframe can be obtained by properly joining the lines and curves to their corresponding vertices. The global picture can then be represented by the coordinates of the vertices of the geometry given. Let us call the matrix that

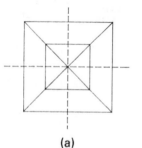

(a)

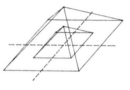

Uniform Scaling

(b)

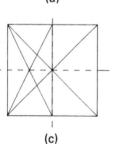

(c)

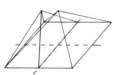

Non-Uniform Scaling

(d)

Figure 4.5 (a) uniform scaling of the top view of a pyramid, (b) A 3D illustration of part (a) (z is unchanged), (c) Nonuniform scaling of the top view of a pyramid, (d) A 3D illustration of part (c) (z is unchanged).

contains the coordinates of all vertices (or points) the configuration matrix designated by **C**; then

$$\mathbf{C} = \begin{bmatrix} x_1 & y_1 \\ x_2 & y_2 \\ x_3 & y_3 \\ \cdot & \cdot \\ \cdot & \cdot \\ \cdot & \cdot \\ x_n & y_n \end{bmatrix} \qquad (4.9)$$

where n denotes the total number of points.

Now, if matrix **C** is operated on by transformation matrix **R**, it yields

$$\mathbf{C}^* = \mathbf{CR} \qquad (4.10)$$

where **C***- is the newly resulted (transformed) configuration matrix.

An illustration of the foregoing can be seen in the following example. Let

$$\mathbf{R} = \begin{bmatrix} 2 & 0 \\ 0 & 2 \end{bmatrix}$$

And the points

$$p_1 = (x_1, y_1)$$
$$p_2 = (x_2, y_2)$$
$$p_3 = (x_3, y_3)$$
$$p_4 = (x_4, y_4)$$
$$p_5 = (x_5, y_5)$$
$$p_6 = (x_6, y_6)$$

represent the vertices of the hexagon shown in Figure 4.6. Using Equation (4.10), we can obtain the transformed hexagon shown in Figure 4.6. Note that its vertices are given by elements of matrix **C***.

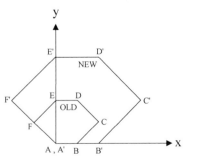

Figure 4.6 Transformation of a hexagon.

4.5 ARBITRARY ROTATION ABOUT THE ORIGIN

Consider the following x–y coordinate system. These axes are perpendicular and also form a set of orthogonal axes. If we rotate both axes counterclockwise by an angle Θ, we obtain a new set of axes, x', and y'. (see Figure 4.7).

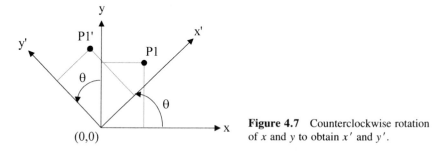

Figure 4.7 Counterclockwise rotation of x and y to obtain x' and y'.

If point P_1 has coordinates (x_1, y_1) in the x–y plane, then its new position P_1' is defined by the new coordinates (x_1', y_1') after the rotation.

We can write the relationship between the new and old coordinates as follows:

$$\left.\begin{array}{l} x_1' = x_1 \cos \Theta - y_1 \sin \Theta \\ y_1' = x_1 \sin \Theta + y_1 \cos \Theta \end{array}\right\} \tag{4.11}$$

which can be expressed in matrix form:

$$\begin{bmatrix} x_1' \\ y_1' \end{bmatrix} = \begin{bmatrix} \cos \Theta & -\sin \Theta \\ \sin \Theta & \cos \Theta \end{bmatrix} \begin{bmatrix} x_1 \\ y_1 \end{bmatrix} \tag{4.12a}$$

Writing the old coordinates in terms of the new coordinates, we use $\mathbf{R}^{-1}$.

$$\begin{bmatrix} x_1 \\ y_1 \end{bmatrix} = [\mathbf{R}^{-1}] \begin{bmatrix} x_1' \\ y_1' \end{bmatrix} \tag{4.12b}$$

Since $\mathbf{R}^{-1} = \mathbf{R}^T$, then we obtain:

$$\begin{bmatrix} x_1 \\ y_1 \end{bmatrix} = \begin{bmatrix} \cos \Theta & \sin \Theta \\ -\sin \Theta & \cos \Theta \end{bmatrix} \begin{bmatrix} x_1' \\ y_1' \end{bmatrix} \tag{4.12c}$$

Note that the left-hand side of Equations (4.12a) and (4.12b) are written with coordinates in a column type vector. Therefore, if we wish to obtain the resulting transformation matrix relating the old and new coordinates and vice versa with the coordinates in a row type vector, we need to take the transpose of both sides, which yields

$$[x \quad y] = [x' \quad y'] \begin{bmatrix} \cos \Theta & -\sin \Theta \\ \sin \Theta & \cos \Theta \end{bmatrix} \tag{4.13a}$$

$$[x' \quad y'] = [x \quad y] \begin{bmatrix} \cos \Theta & \sin \Theta \\ -\sin \Theta & \cos \Theta \end{bmatrix} \tag{4.13b}$$

We must carefully notice that in deriving the foregoing matrix equations, we rotated the x–y axes counterclockwise at an angle of rotation of Θ, which is positive. However, if the x–y axes are rotated clockwise by the same angle Θ, we consider that angle to be negative. Therefore, we put $\Theta = -\Theta$ in Equations (4.12) to (4.13). Due to trigonometric functions' properties, matrix **R** for clockwise movement is equal to $\mathbf{R}^T$ of counterclockwise movement. All other coordinates and their respective locations and matrix types (i.e., row vector or column vector type) remain the same as discussed earlier. Therefore, we can deduce the following important rule

matrix [**R**] for Θ in the clockwise direction = transpose matrix of [**R**] for Θ in the counterclockwise direction

4.5.1 Rotation by Different Angles

In cases in which the rotation of the x and y axes is done through two different angles, such as Θ_1 and Θ_2 (as shown in Figure 4.8), the relationship between the coordinates of point $P_2(x', y',)$ and $P_1(x, y)$ is

$$[x' \quad y'] = [x \quad y] \begin{bmatrix} \cos \Theta_2 & \sin \Theta_2 \\ -\sin \Theta_1 & \cos \Theta_1 \end{bmatrix} \frac{1}{\cos(\Theta_2 - \Theta_1)} \qquad (4.14)$$

It can easily be seen that for $\Theta_1 = \Theta_2$, $\cos(\Theta_2 - \Theta_1) = 1$ and equation (4.14) is equivalent to Equation (4.12a). Now that we see how the transformation matrix **R** can be used for both scaling and rotation, we can introduce the concept of concatenation.

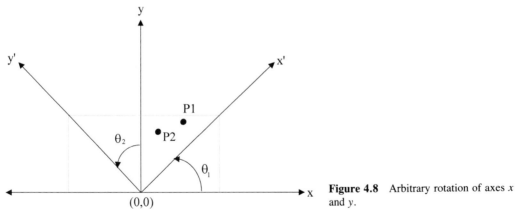

Figure 4.8 Arbitrary rotation of axes x and y.

4.6 CONCATENATION

Concatenation is defined as "the resultant transformation matrix **R** that causes more than one transformation to a configuration matrix **C**." For example, if we were to scale a set of data points, namely, **C**, and then rotate the scaled geometry in a counterclockwise direction by an angle Θ about the origin, we obtain the following:

$$\mathbf{C}_{\text{new}} = \mathbf{C}_{\text{old}}\mathbf{R}_s\mathbf{R}_r \tag{4.15}$$

where $\mathbf{R}_s$ is the scaling matrix, and $\mathbf{R}_r$ is the rotation matrix. Then we define the concatenated matrix $\mathbf{R}$ to be

$$\mathbf{R} = \mathbf{R}_s\mathbf{R}_r \tag{4.16}$$

Concatenation is a unique feature used in many CAD activities in which a certain number of transformations is to be applied to a certain geometry. The advantage is in the amount of multiplication performed to get the desired picture. In the concatenation procedure, the transformation matrix $\mathbf{R}$ is first evaluated and then stored for future use. This eliminates the need of premultiplying the individual matrices to yield the desired transformed geometry.

What remains to be studied at this point is the translation. Unlike rotation and scaling, transformation matrix $\mathbf{R}$ cannot be used for translation. Thinking ahead, one would need a transformation matrix in a concatenated form to cause not only scaling and rotation, but translation as well. What follows is an illustration of how that is achieved.

During the design process when a graphic model is being developed, the use of the combined transformation is quite common. This allows changes to be made much faster.

An example in which concatenation is required is the rotation of the geometry about an arbitrary point 0 followed by uniform scaling. Incidently, the CAD system performs only the combined scaling and rotation; translation is done separately.

4.7 2D TRANSLATION

To overcome the difficulty of causing a translation with the 2×2 transformation matrix $\mathbf{R}$, we extend the order of the matrix to 3×3. Hence, $\mathbf{R}$ becomes

$$\mathbf{R} = \begin{bmatrix} a & b & | & 0 \\ c & d & | & 0 \\ \Delta x & \Delta y & | & 1 \end{bmatrix} \tag{4.17}$$

To suit the 3×3 matrix introduced, the representation of any point (x, y) in 2D is represented by $(x, y, 1)$. This preserves the rules of operating on matrices. The third element could be regarded as an additional coordinate of the point. The translation process is achieved by

$$\mathbf{R} = \begin{bmatrix} 1 & 0 & 0 \\ 0 & 1 & 0 \\ \Delta x & \Delta y & 1 \end{bmatrix} \tag{4.18}$$

where, as seen earlier, for the case of no rotation and no scaling, the 2×2 matrix becomes the identity matrix. For instance, if a given triangle is to be translated to a different position (i.e., destination), we simply operate on its vertices (x_1, y_1), (x_2, y_2), and (x_3, y_3) by $\mathbf{R}$, where Δx and Δy take on the value of the number of units for translation of the points along x and y, respectively. That is,

$$\begin{bmatrix} x_1 & y_1 & 1 \\ x_2 & y_2 & 1 \\ x_3 & y_3 & 1 \end{bmatrix} \begin{bmatrix} 1 & 0 & 0 \\ 0 & 1 & 0 \\ \Delta x & \Delta y & 1 \end{bmatrix} = \begin{bmatrix} x_1 + \Delta x & y_1 + \Delta y & 1 \\ x_2 + \Delta x & y_2 + \Delta y & 1 \\ x_3 + \Delta x & y_3 + \Delta y & 1 \end{bmatrix} \qquad (4.19)$$

Consider the following transformation:

$$\mathbf{R}_1 = \begin{bmatrix} 1 & 0 & p \\ 0 & 1 & q \\ 0 & 0 & 1 \end{bmatrix} \qquad (4.20)$$

where p and q are two arbitrary constants.

Let us examine projection and normalization. Given the $(x, y, 1)$ point operated on by the foregoing $\mathbf{R}$, the transformed point has coordinates (x^*, y^*, H), where

$$H = px + qy + 1 \qquad (4.20a)$$

and

$$x^* = x \qquad \text{and} \qquad y^* = y \qquad (4.20b)$$

Thus, the new point (x^*, y^*) is projected onto a plane given by H (along the z axis). This yields a projection.

Normalization is achieved by making the third component representing the point (H in this case) equal to 1. To plot point (x^*, y^*, H) on the x–y plane, we divide by H to get

$$\left(\frac{x^*}{H}, \frac{y^*}{H}, 1 \right)$$

4.8 OVERALL SCALING

The overall scaling could be achieved as follows:

$$\mathbf{CR} = \mathbf{C}^* \qquad (4.21)$$

where

$$\mathbf{R} = \begin{bmatrix} 1 & 0 & 0 \\ 0 & 1 & 0 \\ 0 & 0 & s \end{bmatrix} \qquad (4.21a)$$

The overall scaling is achieved by simply setting

$$s = \frac{1}{\text{value of the desired scale}}$$ (4.22)

4.9 ROTATION ABOUT AN ARBITRARY POINT

Besides the origin point 0, it might be important in some instances to rotate the given geometry about an arbitrary point in space. If we restrict our analysis to 2D, we say that the rotation about an arbitrary point is achieved by first moving the center of the geometry to the desired point and then rotating the object. Once the rotation is performed, the transformed geometry (object) is translated back to its original position.

Example 4.2   Rotation of an Object about an Arbitrary Point in 2D

Let $\mathbf{C}$ describe an object or configuration of some geometry, where $\mathbf{C}$ is an array of data-point coordinates.

   Solution   To rotate $\mathbf{C}$ about an arbitrary point (m, n) the following transformation is performed:

$$[\mathbf{C}]\begin{bmatrix} 1 & 0 & 0 \\ 0 & 1 & 0 \\ -m & -n & 1 \end{bmatrix}\begin{bmatrix} \cos\Theta & \sin\Theta & 0 \\ -\sin\Theta & \cos\Theta & 0 \\ 0 & 0 & 1 \end{bmatrix}\begin{bmatrix} 1 & 0 & 0 \\ 0 & 1 & 0 \\ m & n & 1 \end{bmatrix} = [\mathbf{C}^*]$$ (4.23)

where $\mathbf{C}^*$ represents the rotated object about point (m, n). The foregoing equation can be written in compact form as follows:

$$[\mathbf{C}^*] = [\mathbf{C}][\mathbf{R}]$$ (4.24)

where

$$[\mathbf{R}] = \begin{bmatrix} \cos\Theta & \sin\Theta & 0 \\ -\sin\Theta & \cos\Theta & 0 \\ -m(\cos\Theta - 1) + n\sin\Theta & -m\sin\Theta - n(\cos\Theta - 1) & 1 \end{bmatrix}$$
                                                                      (4.25)

Here $[\mathbf{R}]$ is the result of the product of three matrices. $[\mathbf{R}]$ is written in a convenient form and can be used directly to perform the multiplication of three corresponding matrices. This technique is often used in CAD systems to save space and time. It can be extended for a number of other common transformations where more than one function is needed.   ∎

Example 4.3   Uniform Scaling in 2D

Find the transformation matrix that would produce rotation of the geometry about point A, as shown in Figure 4.9(a), followed by a uniform scaling of the geometry down to half its original size.

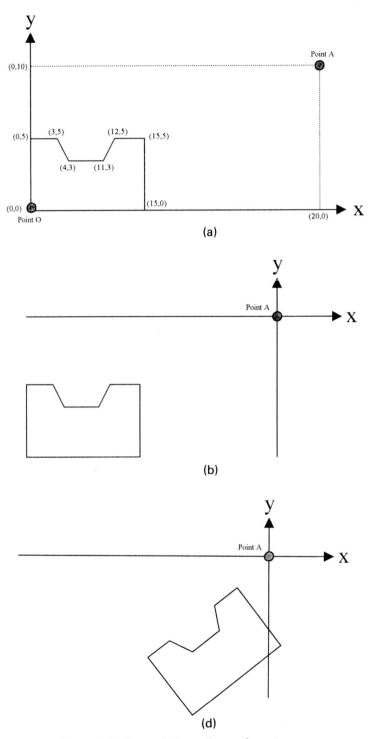

Figure 4.9 Geometrical coordinates of a part.
(a) Translation of point A to origin, (b) Rotation about z axes, (c) Translation
of point A to original position, (d) Scaling.

109

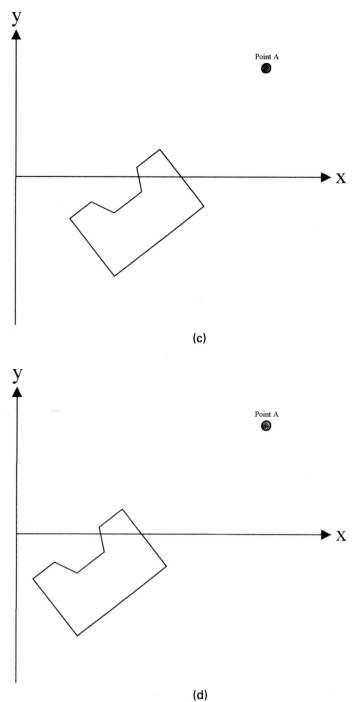

(c)

(d)

Figure 4.9 *(continued)*

Solution

Step 1: Place the points into a matrix.

Step 2: Translate point *A* to the origin, that is, -20 along the *x* axis and -10 along the *y* axis, as shown in Figure 4.9(b).

Step 3: Rotate the object 30 degrees about the *z* axis, as shown in Figure 4.9(c).

Step 4: Translate point *A* to its original position.

Step 5: Scale the object to half its original size, as shown in Figure 4.9(d). ■

4.10 TRANSLATION IN 3D

To analyze drawings and designs more accurately, it is essential that they be represented in 3D. As with the 2D transformation, the 3D representation of data points should be $[x \quad y \quad z \quad 1]$, where (x, y, z) denotes the coordinates of a point, and 1 is a "dummy" assigned to facilitate the multiplication between the vector array representing the data and the transformation matrix.

4.11 3D SCALING

As demonstrated in the 2D case, scaling is achieved through two processes: (a) local scaling by using the diagonal elements of the matrix responsible for scaling and rotation, and (b) overall scaling by using 1×1 submatrix of the transformation matrix, which is known as *s*. The two cases follow:

(a) Local Scaling:

$$\mathbf{R}_s = \begin{bmatrix} a & 0 & 0 & 0 \\ 0 & b & 0 & 0 \\ 0 & 0 & c & 0 \\ 0 & 0 & 0 & 1 \end{bmatrix} \tag{4.26}$$

(b) Overall Scaling:

$$\mathbf{R}_s = \begin{bmatrix} 1 & 0 & 0 & 0 \\ 0 & 1 & 0 & 0 \\ 0 & 0 & 1 & 0 \\ 0 & 0 & 0 & s \end{bmatrix} \tag{4.27}$$

In local scaling, if $a = b = c \neq 0$, we have uniform scaling; otherwise the transformation yields nonuniform scaling or distortion. On the other hand, in overall scaling *s* causes the desired scaling only if coordinates (x, y, z) are divided by *s*; this is the result of the normalization procedure that makes sure that all points are represented by the same format. For example, normalizing $[x^* \quad y^* \quad z^*]$, we obtain

$$\left[\frac{x^*}{s} \quad \frac{y^*}{s} \quad \frac{z^*}{s} \quad 1\right] \tag{4.28}$$

Again we have the "dummy" equal to 1. Thus, the coordinates are normalized and we have the required scaling.

To summarize, we can say that given a set of data points representing some given geometry and letting **C** represent the configuration of the geometry, then

$$\mathbf{CR}_s = \mathbf{C}^* \tag{4.29}$$

where $\mathbf{C}^*$ is a neatly scaled **C**. An illustration of this can be seen in the following:

$$\mathbf{C} = \begin{bmatrix} 0 & 0 & 0 & 1 \\ 0 & 0 & -1 & 1 \\ 2 & 0 & 0 & 1 \\ 2 & 0 & 1 & 1 \\ 0 & 1 & 0 & 1 \\ 0 & 1 & -1 & 1 \\ 2 & 1 & 0 & 1 \\ 2 & 1 & 1 & 1 \end{bmatrix} \begin{matrix} a \\ b \\ c \\ d \\ e \\ f \\ g \\ h \end{matrix} \tag{4.30}$$

Let

$$\mathbf{R}_s = \begin{bmatrix} 1 & 0 & 0 & 0 \\ 0 & 2 & 0 & 0 \\ 0 & 0 & 1 & 0 \\ 0 & 0 & 0 & 1 \end{bmatrix} \tag{4.31}$$

Then

$$\mathbf{CR} = \mathbf{C}^* \tag{4.32}$$

where $\mathbf{C}^*$ is the volume bounded by planes $a \, b \, c \, d$ and $i \, j \, k \, l$, as shown in Figure 4.10.

Quite often we need to magnify a portion of a model to work on intricate details. By traditional means, a designer would make several drawings of the object in different scales for different purposes. An architect, for example, routinely creates detailed drawings to clarify a feature that is not ordinarily visible on the original drawings. By using the CAD system, it is possible to construct a single model that can then be viewed at any level of magnification. This allows the designer to zoom in or zoom out to refine a detail close up or to look at the model as a whole. The designer can also construct a large-scale model and then zoom in on one area in order to make sure elements do not overlay or interfere with one another. Note that the zoom function on the CAD system merely alters the size of the geometry that is inspected in order to make changes. It does not change the scale at which the draw-

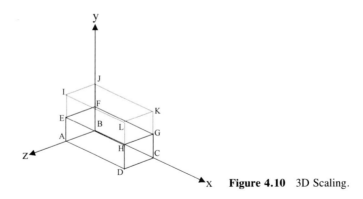

Figure 4.10   3D Scaling.

ing was created. Consequently, the original scale is that in which the drawing appears on the printed page. The matrix to describe 3D scaling transformation is given by Equation (4.26), where a, b, and c represent the scaling factors in the x, y, and z directions, respectively.

Example 4.4   Scaling of a Pyramid Object

Uniformly scale the pyramid, whose dimensions are shown in Figure 4.11(a), down to one-quarter of its original size such that any view of the pyramid can be printed on a standard $8\frac{1}{2} \times 11$-in. sheet of paper.

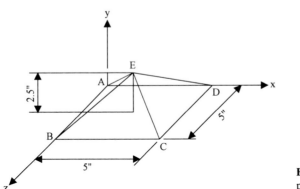

Figure 4.11   (a) A simple uniform pyramid, (b) Scaling of a pyramid.

Solution   The solution will be performed in the following two steps.

Step 1: Define the set of data points comprising the geometry (i.e., define each point that makes up the pyramid in terms of its x, y, and z coordinates)
Step 2: Multiply the set of data points by the scaling matrix.

Specifically, for our example:

Step 1: Create the geometry to contain the coordinates of pyramid (*ABCDE*), as shown in Figure 4.11(a).

We first list the coordinates of the pyramid in matrix form:

$$[C] = \begin{bmatrix} 0 & 0 & 0 & 1 \\ 0 & 0 & 20 & 1 \\ 20 & 0 & 20 & 1 \\ 20 & 0 & 0 & 1 \\ 10 & 10 & 10 & 1 \end{bmatrix}$$

Step 2: Use the scaling matrix to scale the 3D object to one-quarter of its original size [see Figure 4.11(b)].

$$\mathbf{C^*} = \mathbf{CR}_s$$

$$[C^*] = \begin{bmatrix} 0 & 0 & 0 & 1 \\ 0 & 0 & 20 & 1 \\ 20 & 0 & 20 & 1 \\ 20 & 0 & 0 & 1 \\ 10 & 10 & 10 & 1 \end{bmatrix} \begin{bmatrix} \frac{1}{4} & 0 & 0 & 0 \\ 0 & \frac{1}{4} & 0 & 0 \\ 0 & 0 & \frac{1}{4} & 0 \\ 0 & 0 & 0 & 1 \end{bmatrix} = \begin{bmatrix} 0 & 0 & 0 & 1 \\ 0 & 0 & 5 & 1 \\ 5 & 0 & 5 & 1 \\ 5 & 0 & 0 & 1 \\ 2.5 & 2.5 & 2.5 & 1 \end{bmatrix} \blacksquare$$

4.12 3D ROTATION

3D rotation of an object represented by a set of data points is given by

$$\mathbf{R}_r = \begin{bmatrix} & & & 0 \\ 3 & \times & 3 & 0 \\ & Matrix & & 0 \\ 0 & 0 & 0 & 1 \end{bmatrix} \tag{4.33}$$

where the 3×3 matrix causes the given rotation. Rotation about the x axis is obtained by

$$\mathbf{R}_x = \begin{bmatrix} 1 & 0 & 0 \\ 0 & \cos \Theta & -\sin \Theta \\ 0 & \sin \Theta & \cos \Theta \end{bmatrix} \tag{4.34}$$

where $\mathbf{R}_x$ is the result of the relationship between (x, y, z) and (x', y', z') (see Figure 4.12).

To show how the foregoing matrix $\mathbf{R}_x$ is derived, observe that

$$x = x'$$
$$y = y' \cos \Theta - z' \sin \Theta \tag{4.35}$$
$$z = z' \cos \Theta + y' \sin \Theta$$

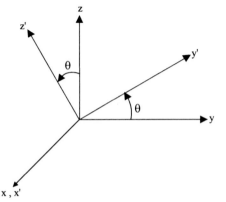

Figure 4.12 Rotation by an angle 'θ'.

Arranging and expressing these three equations in the matrix, we get

$$[x \quad y \quad z] = [x' \quad y' \quad z'] \begin{bmatrix} 1 & 0 & 0 \\ 0 & \cos \Theta & \sin \Theta \\ 0 & -\sin \Theta & \cos \Theta \end{bmatrix}$$

$$\mathbf{R} = \begin{bmatrix} 1 & 0 & 0 \\ 0 & \cos \Theta & \sin \Theta \\ 0 & -\sin \Theta & \cos \Theta \end{bmatrix}$$

and noting that rotation matrix $\mathbf{R}$ is orthogonal (i.e., transpose equals inverse),

$$\mathbf{R}^{-1} = \begin{bmatrix} 1 & 0 & 0 \\ 0 & \cos \Theta & -\sin \Theta \\ 0 & \sin \Theta & \cos \Theta \end{bmatrix} = \mathbf{R}^T \tag{4.36}$$

Therefore, the new coordinates $(x' \ y' \ z')$ can be written in terms of old coordinate $(x \ y \ z)$ as:

$$[x' \quad y' \quad z'] = [x \quad y \quad z] \begin{bmatrix} 1 & 0 & 0 \\ 0 & \cos \Theta & -\sin \Theta \\ 0 & \sin \Theta & \cos \Theta \end{bmatrix} \tag{4.37}$$

or

$$[x' \quad y' \quad z'] = [x \quad y \quad z][\mathbf{R}_x] \tag{4.38}$$

Similarly, we can obtain the transformation matrices for rotation about the y and z axes.

Rotation about the y Axis

$$\mathbf{R}_y = \begin{bmatrix} \cos \Theta & 0 & \sin \Theta \\ 0 & 1 & 0 \\ -\sin \Theta & 0 & \cos \Theta \end{bmatrix} \tag{4.39}$$

Rotation about the z Axis

$$\mathbf{R}_z = \begin{bmatrix} \cos \Theta & -\sin \Theta & 0 \\ \sin \Theta & \cos \Theta & 0 \\ 0 & 0 & 1 \end{bmatrix} \tag{4.40}$$

Rotation moves an object through a specified angle from its original orientation. For a positive angle, this direction of rotation is counterclockwise.

115

Example 4.5   Rotation in 3D Space

The box shown in Figure 4.13(a) will demonstrate rotation about an axis in 3D space. The box shown in the figure is at the initial starting point for all three rotations. The labeled points of the box listed in matrix format (see Sec. 4.3) are used with the transformation rotation matrices, Equations (4.37), (4.39), and (4.40), to obtain the new coordinates after rotation (rotations are in a counterclockwise direction in this example).

Solution   The coordinates in matrix form are

$$[\mathbf{C}] = \begin{bmatrix} A \\ B \\ C \\ D \\ E \\ F \\ G \end{bmatrix} = [X \quad Y \quad Z]$$

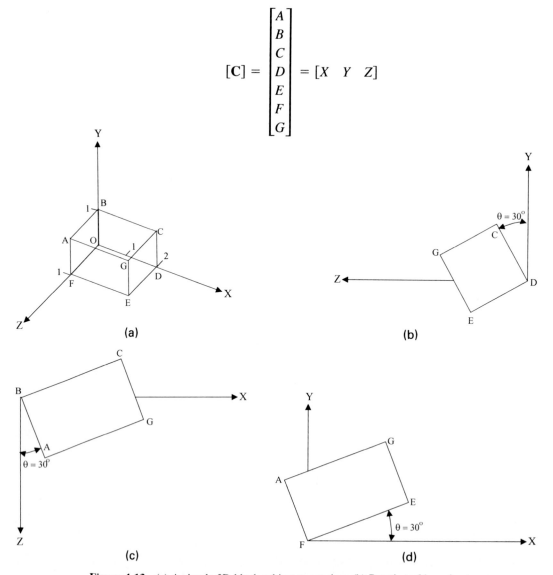

Figure 4.13   (a) A simple 3D block subject to rotation, (b) Rotation of box about x axes, (c) Rotation of box about y axes, (d) Rotation of box about z axes.

$$[\mathbf{C}] = \begin{bmatrix} 0 & 0 & 0 \\ 0 & 1 & 1 \\ 0 & 1 & 0 \\ 2 & 1 & 0 \\ 2 & 0 & 0 \\ 2 & 0 & 1 \\ 0 & 0 & 1 \\ 2 & 1 & 1 \end{bmatrix}$$

Rotation about the x Axis

Suppose we wanted to rotate the box 30 degrees about the x axis [see Figure 4.13(b)]. We would use Equation (4.32), where the transformation matrix is defined by Equation (4.37).

$$[\mathbf{C}^*] = [\mathbf{C}][\mathbf{R}_x]$$

$$[\mathbf{C}^*] = \begin{bmatrix} 0 & 0 & 0 \\ 0 & 1 & 1 \\ 0 & 1 & 0 \\ 2 & 1 & 0 \\ 2 & 0 & 0 \\ 2 & 0 & 1 \\ 0 & 0 & 1 \\ 2 & 1 & 1 \end{bmatrix} \begin{bmatrix} 1 & 0 & 0 \\ 0 & \dfrac{\sqrt{3}}{2} & -\dfrac{1}{2} \\ 0 & \dfrac{1}{2} & \dfrac{\sqrt{3}}{2} \end{bmatrix}$$

$$= \begin{bmatrix} 0 & 0 & 0 \\ 0 & \dfrac{\sqrt{3}}{2} + \dfrac{1}{2} & -\dfrac{1}{2} + \dfrac{\sqrt{3}}{2} \\ 0 & \dfrac{\sqrt{3}}{2} & -\dfrac{1}{2} \\ 2 & \dfrac{\sqrt{3}}{2} & -\dfrac{1}{2} \\ 2 & 0 & 0 \\ 2 & \dfrac{1}{2} & \dfrac{\sqrt{3}}{2} \\ 0 & \dfrac{1}{2} & \dfrac{\sqrt{3}}{2} \\ 2 & \dfrac{\sqrt{3}}{2} + \dfrac{1}{2} & \dfrac{\sqrt{3}}{2} - \dfrac{1}{2} \end{bmatrix}$$

Rotation about the y Axis

If the box is to be rotated 30 degrees about the y axis [see Figure 4.13(c)], we repeat the rotation procedure about the x axis, except we use Equation (4.39) for the rotation matrix.

$$[\mathbf{C}^*] = [\mathbf{C}][\mathbf{R}_y]$$

$$[\mathbf{C}^*] = \begin{bmatrix} 0 & 0 & 0 \\ 0 & 1 & 1 \\ 0 & 1 & 0 \\ 2 & 1 & 0 \\ 2 & 0 & 0 \\ 2 & 0 & 1 \\ 0 & 0 & 1 \\ 2 & 1 & 1 \end{bmatrix} \begin{bmatrix} \dfrac{\sqrt{3}}{2} & 0 & -\dfrac{1}{2} \\ 0 & 1 & 0 \\ \dfrac{1}{2} & 0 & \dfrac{\sqrt{3}}{2} \end{bmatrix}$$

$$= \begin{bmatrix} 0 & 0 & 0 \\ \dfrac{1}{2} & 1 & \dfrac{\sqrt{3}}{2} \\ 0 & 1 & 0 \\ \sqrt{3} & 1 & -1 \\ \sqrt{3} & 0 & -1 \\ \sqrt{3}+\dfrac{1}{2} & 0 & \dfrac{\sqrt{3}}{2} - 1 \\ \dfrac{1}{2} & 0 & \dfrac{\sqrt{3}}{2} \\ \sqrt{3}+\dfrac{1}{2} & 1 & \dfrac{\sqrt{3}}{2} - 1 \end{bmatrix}$$

Rotation about the z Axis

We repeat the procedure used before except we use Equation (4.40) as the transformation matrix for rotation about the z axis [see Figure 4.13(d)].

$$[\mathbf{C}^*] = [\mathbf{R}_z][\mathbf{C}]$$

$$[\mathbf{C}^*] = \begin{bmatrix} 0 & 0 & 0 \\ 0 & 1 & 1 \\ 0 & 1 & 0 \\ 2 & 1 & 0 \\ 2 & 0 & 0 \\ 2 & 0 & 1 \\ 0 & 0 & 1 \\ 2 & 1 & 1 \end{bmatrix} \begin{bmatrix} \dfrac{\sqrt{3}}{2} & -\dfrac{1}{2} & 0 \\ \dfrac{1}{2} & \dfrac{\sqrt{3}}{2} & 0 \\ 0 & 0 & 1 \end{bmatrix}$$

$$= \begin{bmatrix} 0 & 0 & 0 \\ \dfrac{1}{2} & \dfrac{\sqrt{3}}{2} & 1 \\ \dfrac{1}{2} & \dfrac{\sqrt{3}}{2} & 0 \\ \sqrt{3}+\dfrac{1}{2} & \dfrac{\sqrt{3}}{2}-1 & 0 \\ \sqrt{3} & -1 & 0 \\ \sqrt{3} & -1 & 1 \\ 0 & 02 & 1 \\ \sqrt{3}+\dfrac{1}{2} & \dfrac{\sqrt{3}}{2}-1 & 1 \end{bmatrix}$$

■

4.13 3D REFLECTION

Reflection is mirroring an object in space with respect to a defined plane or planes. The simplest reflections occur through a plane. Reflection about the x–y plane is given by the reflection matrix:

$$\mathbf{R}_r = \begin{bmatrix} 1 & 0 & 0 & 0 \\ 0 & 1 & 0 & 0 \\ 0 & 0 & -1 & 0 \\ 0 & 0 & 0 & 1 \end{bmatrix} \tag{4.41}$$

i.e., for reflection about x–y plane element of 3×3 identity submatrix (which is responsible for z-axis). $-\mathbf{R}_r$ is negative. Similarly, for reflection about the y–z plane, the matrix is given by

$$\mathbf{R}_r = \begin{bmatrix} -1 & 0 & 0 & 0 \\ 0 & 1 & 0 & 0 \\ 0 & 0 & 1 & 0 \\ 0 & 0 & 0 & 1 \end{bmatrix} \tag{4.42}$$

and reflection about the x–z plane is given by the matrix:

$$\mathbf{R}_r = \begin{bmatrix} 1 & 0 & 0 & 0 \\ 0 & -1 & 0 & 0 \\ 0 & 0 & 1 & 0 \\ 0 & 0 & 0 & 1 \end{bmatrix} \tag{4.43}$$

Reflection is also known as a mirror image that can be created about a specified axis/plane using the mirror option on the CAD system. It is especially convenient in terms of reducing time and effort in creating drawings.

An example of reflection is the creation of a complete model of a symmetrical model/object by drawing one section of the object and then mirroring it about a specified axis to create the remainder of the object. This technique simplifies creating models made up of symmetrical forms, such as a cast wheel. Figure 4.14 makes this concept clear.

Example 4.6   Reflection of a Block

Use reflection to simplify the creation of the block shown in Figure 4.15.

Solution   The block can be divided into four equally symmetric parts (see Figure 4.16). The entire coordinates of the block can be described using the coordinates of one-quarter of the block given by

$$
[C_1] = \begin{bmatrix} a \\ b \\ c \\ d \\ e \\ f \\ g \\ h \\ i \\ j \\ k \\ l \\ m \\ n \end{bmatrix} = \begin{bmatrix}
0 & 0 & 1 & 1 \\
\frac{1}{2} & 0 & 1 & 1 \\
\frac{1}{2} & 0 & 0 & 1 \\
0 & 0 & 0 & 1 \\
0 & \frac{1}{2} & 1 & 1 \\
\frac{1}{4} & \frac{1}{2} & 1 & 1 \\
\frac{1}{2} & \frac{1}{2} & \frac{1}{2} & 1 \\
\frac{1}{2} & \frac{1}{2} & 0 & 1 \\
0 & \frac{1}{2} & 0 & 1 \\
\frac{1}{4} & \frac{1}{2} & \frac{1}{2} & 1 \\
\frac{1}{4} & 1 & 1 & 1 \\
\frac{1}{2} & 1 & 1 & 1 \\
\frac{1}{2} & 1 & \frac{1}{2} & 1 \\
\frac{1}{4} & 1 & \frac{1}{2} & 1
\end{bmatrix}
$$

Step 1: Establish the transformation matrix to reflect the quarter block about the x–y plane (see Figure 4.17). Using the reflection equation, we have

$$
[C^*] = \mathbf{CR}_1 = \mathbf{C} \begin{bmatrix}
1 & 0 & 0 & 0 \\
0 & 1 & 0 & 0 \\
0 & 0 & -1 & 0 \\
0 & 0 & 0 & 1
\end{bmatrix}
$$

This creates the other quarter of the block. The coordinates of one-half of the block is known.

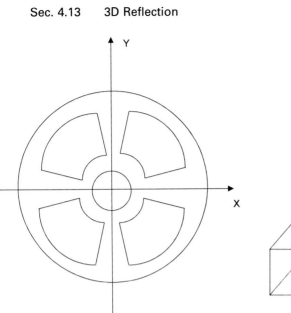

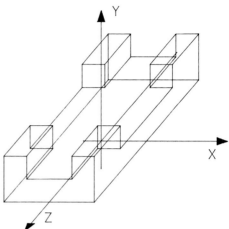

Figure 4.14   The concept of reflection.

Figure 4.15   A 3D geometry of a symmetric block.

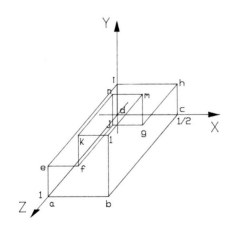

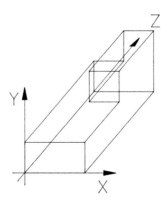

Figure 4.16   Coordinate description using a quarter portion of the block.

Figure 4.17   Quarter block obtained by reflection about the xy plane of Figure 4.16.

$$[\mathbf{C}^*] = \begin{bmatrix} 0 & 0 & -1 & 1 \\ \frac{1}{2} & 0 & -1 & 1 \\ \frac{1}{2} & 0 & 0 & 1 \\ 0 & 0 & 0 & 1 \\ 0 & \frac{1}{2} & -1 & 1 \\ \frac{1}{4} & \frac{1}{2} & -1 & 1 \\ \frac{1}{2} & \frac{1}{2} & -\frac{1}{2} & 1 \\ \frac{1}{2} & \frac{1}{2} & 0 & 1 \\ 0 & \frac{1}{2} & 0 & 1 \\ \frac{1}{4} & \frac{1}{2} & -\frac{1}{2} & 1 \\ \frac{1}{4} & 1 & -1 & 1 \\ \frac{1}{2} & 1 & -1 & 1 \\ \frac{1}{2} & 1 & -\frac{1}{2} & 1 \\ \frac{1}{4} & 1 & -\frac{1}{2} & 1 \end{bmatrix}$$

Step 2: Reflect the half portion of the block about the y–z plane (see Figure 4.18). Using the reflection equation, we have

$$[\mathbf{C}^{**}] = \mathbf{C}_a \mathbf{R}_2 = \mathbf{C} \begin{bmatrix} -1 & 0 & 0 & 0 \\ 0 & 1 & 0 & 0 \\ 0 & 0 & 1 & 0 \\ 0 & 0 & 0 & 1 \end{bmatrix}$$

where

$$[\mathbf{C}_a] = \begin{bmatrix} \mathbf{C} \\ \mathbf{C}^* \end{bmatrix}$$

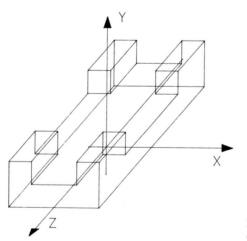

Figure 4.18 Reflection of half portion of block about the *YZ* plane.

By using the coordinate matrices **C** and **C***, the coordinates of the other half of the block are determined using this transformation matrix. The coordinates for the first half are

$$[\mathbf{C}_{\mathbf{C}}^{**}] = \begin{bmatrix} 0 & 0 & 1 & 1 \\ -\frac{1}{2} & 0 & 1 & 1 \\ -\frac{1}{2} & 0 & 0 & 1 \\ 0 & 0 & 0 & 1 \\ 0 & \frac{1}{2} & 1 & 1 \\ -\frac{1}{4} & \frac{1}{2} & 1 & 1 \\ -\frac{1}{2} & \frac{1}{2} & \frac{1}{2} & 1 \\ -\frac{1}{2} & \frac{1}{2} & 0 & 1 \\ 0 & \frac{1}{2} & 0 & 1 \\ -\frac{1}{4} & \frac{1}{2} & \frac{1}{2} & 1 \\ -\frac{1}{4} & 1 & 1 & 1 \\ \frac{1}{2} & 1 & 1 & 1 \\ -\frac{1}{2} & 1 & \frac{1}{2} & 1 \\ -\frac{1}{4} & 1 & \frac{1}{2} & 1 \end{bmatrix}$$

and the coordinates for the second half are

$$[\mathbf{C}_{\mathbf{C}*}^{**}] = \begin{bmatrix} 0 & 0 & -1 & 1 \\ -\frac{1}{2} & 0 & -1 & 1 \\ -\frac{1}{2} & 0 & 0 & 1 \\ 0 & 0 & 0 & 1 \\ 0 & \frac{1}{2} & -1 & 1 \\ -\frac{1}{4} & \frac{1}{2} & -1 & 1 \\ -\frac{1}{2} & \frac{1}{2} & -\frac{1}{2} & 1 \\ -\frac{1}{2} & \frac{1}{2} & 0 & 1 \\ 0 & \frac{1}{2} & 0 & 1 \\ -\frac{1}{4} & \frac{1}{2} & -\frac{1}{2} & 1 \\ -\frac{1}{4} & 1 & -1 & 1 \\ -\frac{1}{2} & 1 & -1 & 1 \\ -\frac{1}{2} & 1 & -\frac{1}{2} & 1 \\ -\frac{1}{4} & 1 & -\frac{1}{2} & 1 \end{bmatrix}$$

where the coordinates for the whole block (**C****) consists of

$$[\mathbf{C}^{**}] = \begin{bmatrix} \mathbf{C}_{\mathbf{C}}^{**} \\ \mathbf{C}_{\mathbf{C}*}^{**} \end{bmatrix} \qquad \blacksquare$$

4.14 3D TRANSLATION

The translation is simply given by

$$\mathbf{R}_T = \begin{bmatrix} 1 & 0 & 0 & 0 \\ 0 & 1 & 0 & 0 \\ 0 & 0 & 1 & 0 \\ \Delta x & \Delta y & \Delta z & 1 \end{bmatrix} \qquad (4.44)$$

where $\mathbf{R}_T$ represents the transformation matrix needed to translate a configuration matrix $\mathbf{C}$ to some given destination. Therefore,

$$\mathbf{C}^* = \mathbf{CR} \qquad (4.45)$$

where $\mathbf{C}^*$ is the translated configuration matrix.

Example 4.7   Translation of a Block in 3D

Using the same box of Figure 4.13 in Example 4.5, translate the box 2 units in the x direction, 1 unit in the y direction, and 1 unit in the z direction, as shown in Figure 4.19.

   Solution   Using Equation (4.44), we substitute the numerical values into the translation matrix and apply Equation (4.45) to find the new coordinates of the points after translation. We know $\Delta x = 2$, $\Delta y = 1$, and $\Delta z = 1$. The new coordinates of the box are

$$[\mathbf{C}^*] = \begin{bmatrix} 0 & 0 & 0 & 1 \\ 0 & 1 & 2 & 1 \\ 0 & 1 & 0 & 1 \\ 2 & 1 & 0 & 1 \\ 2 & 0 & 0 & 1 \\ 2 & 0 & 1 & 1 \\ 0 & 0 & 1 & 1 \end{bmatrix} \begin{bmatrix} 1 & 0 & 0 & 0 \\ 0 & 1 & 0 & 0 \\ 0 & 0 & 1 & 0 \\ 2 & 1 & 1 & 1 \end{bmatrix}$$

$$[\mathbf{C}^*] = \begin{bmatrix} 2 & 1 & 1 & 1 \\ 2 & 2 & 3 & 1 \\ 2 & 2 & 1 & 1 \\ 4 & 2 & 1 & 1 \\ 4 & 1 & 1 & 1 \\ 4 & 1 & 2 & 1 \\ 2 & 1 & 2 & 1 \end{bmatrix}$$

∎

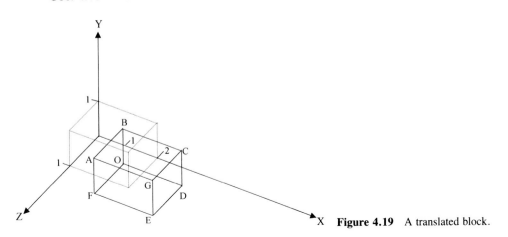

Figure 4.19   A translated block.

4.15 3D ROTATION ABOUT AN ARBITRARY AXIS

Successive rotations about the x, y, and z axes lead to a rotation about an arbitrary axis, say, l–l' shown in Figure 4.20. The rotation about this axis by an angle γ can be achieved by the following transformation matrices:

$$\mathbf{R}_r = \mathbf{R}_x^{\alpha} \mathbf{R}_y^{\beta} \mathbf{R}_z^{\gamma} \qquad (4.46)$$

where $\mathbf{R}_x^{\alpha}$, $\mathbf{R}_y^{\beta}$, and $\mathbf{R}_z^{\gamma}$ are rotation matrices about the x, y, and z axes, respectively, by the angles α, β, and γ, as shown in Figure 4.20. This representation usually has some disadvantages associated with finding the correct angles for α, β, and

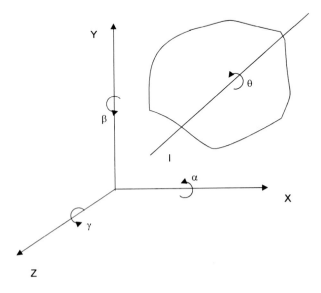

Figure 4.20   Successive rotations of x, y, and z axes by α, β, and γ.

γ to yield the proper rotation. Transformation matrix $\mathbf{R}_r$ could be achieved through a second procedure as follows:

1. The object is translated such that the origin of coordinates passes through the line
2. Rotation is accomplished
3. The object is translated back to its origin

If we concatenate the three foregoing transformation matrices, we obtain:

$$\mathbf{C}^* = \mathbf{C}\mathbf{R}_{T1}\mathbf{R}_r\mathbf{R}_{T2} \tag{4.47}$$

where

$$\mathbf{R}_{T1} = \begin{bmatrix} 1 & 0 & 0 & 0 \\ 0 & 1 & 0 & 0 \\ 0 & 0 & 1 & 0 \\ -\Delta x & -\Delta y & -\Delta z & 1 \end{bmatrix} \tag{4.48}$$

$$\mathbf{R}_{T2} = \begin{bmatrix} 1 & 0 & 0 & 0 \\ 0 & 1 & 0 & 0 \\ 0 & 0 & 1 & 0 \\ \Delta x & \Delta y & \Delta z & 1 \end{bmatrix} \tag{4.49}$$

and

$$[\mathbf{R}_r] = \begin{bmatrix} C_2 C_3 & C_1 S_3 + S_1 S_2 C_3 & S_1 S_3 - C_1 S_2 C_3 & 0 \\ -C_2 S_3 & C_1 C_3 - S_1 S_2 S_3 & S_1 C_3 + C_1 S_2 S_3 & 0 \\ S_2 & -S_1 C_2 & C_1 C_2 & 0 \\ 0 & 0 & 0 & 1 \end{bmatrix} \tag{4.50}$$

where

$$C_1 = (\cos \alpha) \qquad C_2 = (\cos \beta) \qquad C_3 = (\cos \gamma)$$

$$S_1 = (\sin \alpha) \qquad S_2 = (\sin \beta) \qquad S_3 = (\sin \gamma)$$

Example 4.8   Rotation of a Box in 3D Space

Using the box of Figure 4.13 in Example 4.5, find the new coordinates of the box if it is rotated 30 degrees about the x axis, 60 degrees about the y axis, and 90 degrees about the z axis. (Rotations are in the counterclockwise direction.) The rotations of the coordinate reference frames are illustrated in Figure 4.21. x''', y''', and z''' indicate the new coordinate system where the box resides $[\mathbf{C}^*]$.

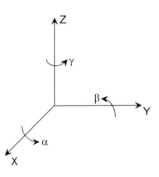

Figure 4.21 A box subjected to a combined rotation on the x, y, and z axes.

Solution Using Equations (4.32) and (4.50), we write the following

$$[\mathbf{C^*}] = [\mathbf{C}][\mathbf{R}]$$

where

$$[\mathbf{C}] = \begin{bmatrix} 0 & 0 & 0 & 1 \\ 0 & 1 & 0 & 1 \\ 0 & 1 & 1 & 1 \\ 0 & 0 & 1 & 1 \\ 2 & 1 & 0 & 1 \\ 2 & 0 & 0 & 1 \\ 2 & 0 & 1 & 1 \\ 2 & 1 & 1 & 1 \end{bmatrix}$$

and substituting $\alpha = 30°$, $\beta = 60°$, and $\gamma = 90°$, we obtain

$$[\mathbf{R}] = \begin{bmatrix} 0 & \dfrac{\sqrt{3}}{2} & \dfrac{1}{2} & 0 \\ \dfrac{1}{2} & -\dfrac{\sqrt{3}}{4} & \dfrac{3}{4} & 0 \\ \dfrac{\sqrt{3}}{2} & -\dfrac{1}{4} & \dfrac{\sqrt{3}}{4} & 0 \\ 0 & 0 & 0 & 1 \end{bmatrix}$$

$$[\mathbf{C^*}] = \begin{bmatrix} 0 & 0 & 0 & 1 \\ 0 & 1 & 0 & 1 \\ 0 & 1 & 1 & 1 \\ 2 & 1 & 0 & 1 \\ 2 & 0 & 0 & 1 \\ 2 & 0 & 1 & 1 \\ 2 & 1 & 1 & 1 \end{bmatrix} \begin{bmatrix} 0 & \dfrac{\sqrt{3}}{2} & \dfrac{1}{2} & 0 \\ \dfrac{1}{2} & -\dfrac{\sqrt{3}}{4} & \dfrac{3}{4} & 0 \\ \dfrac{\sqrt{3}}{2} & -\dfrac{1}{4} & \dfrac{\sqrt{3}}{4} & 0 \\ 0 & 0 & 0 & 1 \end{bmatrix}$$

The final answer is

$$[\mathbf{C^*}] = \begin{bmatrix} 0 & 0 & 0 & 1 \\ \dfrac{1}{2} & -\dfrac{\sqrt{3}}{4} & \dfrac{3}{4} & 1 \\ \dfrac{1}{2}+\dfrac{\sqrt{3}}{2} & -\dfrac{\sqrt{3}}{4}-\dfrac{1}{4} & \dfrac{3}{4}+\dfrac{\sqrt{3}}{4} & 1 \\ \dfrac{\sqrt{3}}{2} & -\dfrac{1}{4} & \dfrac{\sqrt{3}}{4} & 1 \\ \dfrac{1}{2} & \sqrt{3}-\dfrac{\sqrt{3}}{4} & 1+\dfrac{3}{4} & 1 \\ 0 & \sqrt{3} & 1 & 1 \\ \dfrac{\sqrt{3}}{2} & \sqrt{3}-\dfrac{1}{4} & 1+\dfrac{\sqrt{3}}{2} & 1 \\ \dfrac{1}{2}+\dfrac{\sqrt{3}}{2} & \sqrt{3}-\dfrac{1}{4}(\sqrt{3}+3) & 1+\dfrac{1}{4}(3+\sqrt{3}) & 1 \end{bmatrix} \quad \blacksquare$$

Example 4.9   Rotation and Translation of a Cube in 3D Space

Given the unit cube shown in Figure 4.22(a), find the transformation matrix required for the display of the cube shown in Figure 4.22(b).

Step 1: Place the points in matrix form.

$$[\mathbf{C}] = \begin{bmatrix} 0 & 1 & 1 & 1 \\ 1 & 1 & 1 & 1 \\ 1 & 1 & 0 & 1 \\ 0 & 1 & 0 & 1 \\ 0 & 0 & 1 & 1 \\ 1 & 0 & 1 & 1 \\ 1 & 0 & 0 & 1 \\ 0 & 0 & 0 & 1 \end{bmatrix}$$

Step 2: Rotate the cube +90 degrees about the z axis [see Figure 4.23(a)]. Using the rotation matrix,

$$[\mathbf{R}_{s1}] = \begin{bmatrix} \cos 90° & \sin 90° & 0 & 0 \\ -\sin 90° & \cos 90° & 0 & 0 \\ 0 & 0 & 1 & 0 \\ 0 & 0 & 0 & 1 \end{bmatrix}$$

Step 3: Rotate the cube +90 degrees about the x axis [see Figure 4.23(b)].

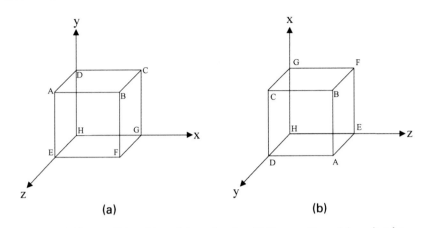

Figure 4.22   (a) Old position of the unit cube, (b) New position of the unit cube.

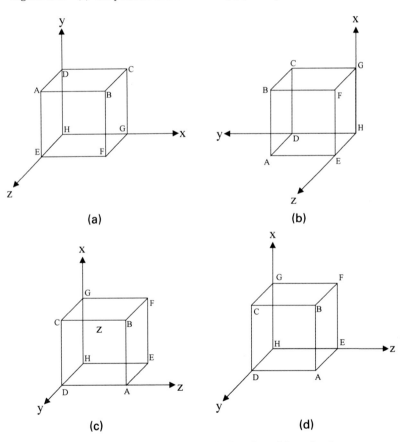

Figure 4.23   (a) Coordinates of the cube, (b) Rotation of the cube about z axes, (c) Rotation of the cube about the x axes, (d) Translation of the cube along the y axes.

Using the rotation matrix,

$$[\mathbf{R}_{s2}] = \begin{bmatrix} \cos 90° & 0 & -\sin 90° & 0 \\ 0 & 1 & 0 & 0 \\ \sin 90° & 0 & \cos 90° & 0 \\ 0 & 1 & 0 & 1 \end{bmatrix}$$

Step 4: Translate the cube along the y axis by -1 [see Figure 4.23(c)]. Using the translation matrix,

$$[\mathbf{R}_t] = \begin{bmatrix} 1 & 0 & 0 & 0 \\ 0 & 1 & 0 & 0 \\ 0 & 0 & 1 & 0 \\ 0 & 0 & -1 & 1 \end{bmatrix}$$

By combining the transformation matrices [see Figure 4.23(d)], we have

$$\mathbf{C}^* = \mathbf{C}\mathbf{R}_{s1}\,\mathbf{R}_{s2}\,\mathbf{R}_t$$

$$[\mathbf{C}^*] = \begin{bmatrix} 0 & 1 & 1 & 1 \\ 1 & 1 & 1 & 1 \\ 1 & 1 & 0 & 1 \\ 0 & 1 & 0 & 1 \\ 0 & 0 & 1 & 1 \\ 1 & 0 & 1 & 1 \\ 1 & 0 & 0 & 1 \\ 0 & 0 & 0 & 1 \end{bmatrix} \begin{bmatrix} \cos 90° & \sin 90° & 0 & 0 \\ -\sin 90° & \cos 90° & 0 & 0 \\ 0 & 0 & 1 & 0 \\ 0 & 0 & 0 & 1 \end{bmatrix}$$

$$\begin{bmatrix} \cos 90° & 0 & -\sin 90° & 0 \\ 0 & 1 & 0 & 0 \\ \sin 90° & 0 & \cos 90° & 0 \\ 0 & 0 & 0 & 1 \end{bmatrix} \begin{bmatrix} 1 & 0 & 0 & 0 \\ 0 & 1 & 0 & 0 \\ 0 & 0 & 1 & 0 \\ 0 & 0 & -1 & 1 \end{bmatrix}$$

The final answer is

$$[\mathbf{C}^*] = \begin{bmatrix} 1 & 0 & 0 & 1 \\ 1 & 1 & 0 & 1 \\ 0 & 1 & 0 & 1 \\ 0 & 0 & 0 & 1 \\ 1 & 0 & -1 & 1 \\ 1 & 1 & -1 & 1 \\ 0 & 1 & -1 & 1 \\ 0 & 0 & -1 & 1 \end{bmatrix}$$

∎

Example 4.10   Pyramid Rotation and Translation

Give the concatenated transformation matrix that would generate the new position of the object shown in Figure 4.24. (Face A given by points ABCD lies in the x–z plane with its center along the x axis.)

Note: Show the steps you wish to take before writing the transformation matrices.

The matrix of the coordinates that contains all vertices of the pyramid is

$$[\mathbf{C}] = \begin{bmatrix} A \\ B \\ C \\ D \\ E \end{bmatrix} = \begin{bmatrix} h & \dfrac{a}{2} & \dfrac{a}{2} & 1 \\[2ex] h & \dfrac{a}{2} & -\dfrac{a}{2} & 1 \\[2ex] h & -\dfrac{a}{2} & -\dfrac{a}{2} & 1 \\[2ex] h & \dfrac{a}{2} & \dfrac{a}{2} & 1 \\[2ex] 0 & 0 & 0 & 1 \end{bmatrix}$$

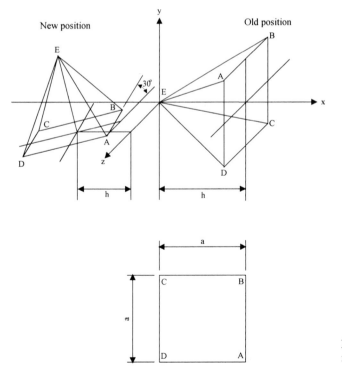

Figure 4.24   Transformation of a pyramid (old and new positions).

Solution

Step 1: Determine the matrix to translate the pyramid along the x axis by $-h$ units [see Figure 4.25(a)].

$$[C^*] = \begin{bmatrix} h & \dfrac{a}{2} & \dfrac{a}{2} & 1 \\[2mm] h & \dfrac{a}{2} & -\dfrac{a}{2} & 1 \\[2mm] h & -\dfrac{a}{2} & -\dfrac{a}{2} & 1 \\[2mm] h & -\dfrac{a}{2} & \dfrac{a}{2} & 1 \\[2mm] 0 & 0 & 0 & 1 \end{bmatrix} \begin{bmatrix} 1 & 0 & 0 & 0 \\ 0 & 1 & 0 & 0 \\ 0 & 0 & 1 & 0 \\ -h & 0 & 0 & 1 \end{bmatrix} = \begin{bmatrix} 0 & \dfrac{a}{2} & \dfrac{a}{2} & 1 \\[2mm] 0 & \dfrac{a}{2} & -\dfrac{a}{2} & 1 \\[2mm] 0 & -\dfrac{a}{2} & -\dfrac{a}{2} & 1 \\[2mm] 0 & -\dfrac{a}{2} & \dfrac{a}{2} & 1 \\[2mm] -h & 0 & 0 & 1 \end{bmatrix}$$

Step 2: Determine the matrix to rotate the object -90 degrees about the z axis [see Figure 4.25(b)].

$$[R_2] = \begin{bmatrix} \cos -90° & \sin -90° & 0 & 0 \\ -\sin -90° & \cos -90° & 0 & 0 \\ 0 & 0 & 1 & 0 \\ 0 & 0 & 0 & 1 \end{bmatrix}$$

$$[C^{**}] = [C^*][R_2]$$

$$[C^{**}] = \begin{bmatrix} \dfrac{a}{2} & 0 & \dfrac{a}{2} & 1 \\[2mm] \dfrac{a}{2} & 0 & -\dfrac{a}{2} & 1 \\[2mm] -\dfrac{a}{2} & 0 & -\dfrac{a}{2} & 1 \\[2mm] -\dfrac{a}{2} & 0 & \dfrac{a}{2} & 1 \\[2mm] 0 & h & 0 & 1 \end{bmatrix}$$

Step 3: Rotate the object $+30$ degrees about the y axis (see Figure 4.26). (This rotation generates an angle of $+30$ degrees at point A with respect to the z axis.)

$$[R_3] = \begin{bmatrix} \cos 30° & 0 & -\sin 30° & 0 \\ 0 & 1 & 0 & 0 \\ \sin 30° & 0 & \cos 30° & 0 \\ 0 & 0 & 0 & 1 \end{bmatrix}$$

$$[\mathbf{C}{***}] = [\mathbf{C}{**}][\mathbf{R_3}]$$

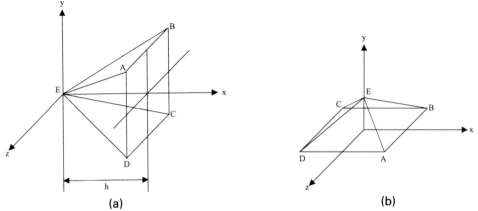

$$[\mathbf{C}{***}] = \begin{bmatrix} \dfrac{a}{2}\cos 30° + \dfrac{a}{2}\sin 30° & 0 & -\dfrac{a}{2}\sin 30° + \dfrac{a}{2}\cos 30° & 1 \\[2ex] \dfrac{a}{2}\cos 30° - \dfrac{a}{2}\sin 30° & 0 & -\dfrac{a}{2}\sin 30° - \dfrac{a}{2}\cos 30° & 1 \\[2ex] -\dfrac{a}{2}\cos 30° - \dfrac{a}{2}\sin 30° & 0 & \dfrac{a}{2}\sin 30° - \dfrac{a}{2}\cos 30° & 1 \\[2ex] -\dfrac{a}{2}\cos 30° + \dfrac{a}{2}\sin 30° & 0 & \dfrac{a}{2}\sin 30° + \dfrac{a}{2}\cos 30° & 1 \\[2ex] 0 & h & 0 & 1 \end{bmatrix}$$

Figure 4.25   (a) Translation of a pyramid along the x axes, (b) Rotation of a pyramid about the z axes.

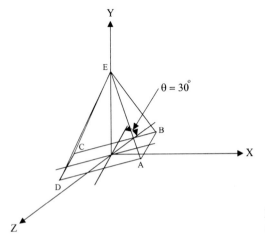

Figure 4.26   Rotation of a pyramid about the y axes.

Step 4: Translate by $-h$ along the x axis and $a/2$ units along the z axis.

$$[\mathbf{R_4}] = \begin{bmatrix} 1 & 0 & 0 & 0 \\ 0 & 1 & 0 & 0 \\ 0 & 0 & 1 & 0 \\ -h & 0 & \dfrac{a}{2} & 1 \end{bmatrix}$$

$$[\mathbf{C}^{****}] = [\mathbf{C}^{**}][\mathbf{R_4}]$$

$$[\mathbf{C}^{****}] = \begin{bmatrix} \dfrac{a}{2}\cos 30° + \dfrac{a}{2}\sin 30° - h & 0 & -\dfrac{a}{2}\sin 30° + \dfrac{a}{2}\cos 30° + \dfrac{a}{2} & 1 \\[2ex] \dfrac{a}{2}\cos 30° - \dfrac{a}{2}\sin 30° - h & 0 & -\dfrac{a}{2}\sin 30° - \dfrac{a}{2}\cos 30° + \dfrac{a}{2} & 1 \\[2ex] -\dfrac{a}{2}\cos 30° - \dfrac{a}{2}\sin 30° - h & 0 & \dfrac{a}{2}\sin 30° - \dfrac{a}{2}\cos 30° + \dfrac{a}{2} & 1 \\[2ex] -\dfrac{a}{2}\cos 30° + \dfrac{a}{2}\sin 30° - h & 0 & \dfrac{a}{2}\sin 30° + \dfrac{a}{2}\cos 30° + \dfrac{a}{2} & 1 \\[2ex] -h & h & \dfrac{a}{2} & 1 \end{bmatrix}$$

$\mathbf{C}^{****}$ represents the final set of coordinates for the new position.

$$[\mathbf{C}^{****}] = [\mathbf{C}]\,[\mathbf{R_1}]\,[\mathbf{R_2}]\,[\mathbf{R_3}]\,[\mathbf{R_4}] \qquad\blacksquare$$

4.16 3D VISUALIZATION

In engineering, we are often required to visualize an object in 3D space. There are two main techniques that yield such a representation. As is often seen on a CAD workstation, one can adapt the 2D representation. Such is the case in drafting, where absolute coordinates used are defined with the z axis normal to the screen. Hence we view the picture from it. Rotating the image by keeping the axis orthogonal is an option used for viewing and editing the graphics. On the other hand, we can work in so-called 3D space by adapting the isometric view. This option displays a 3D axis on a 2D screen to form such a view.

In what follows are the mathematical steps needed to generate the transformation matrix that takes a 3D representation of a given object and gives its 2D isometric representation. First, we discuss the representation of pictures on the screen going from 3D to 2D keeping the axes orthogonal. This is trimetric projection. All the foregoing projections fall under the category of axonometric projections.

4.17 TRIMETRIC PROJECTION

Consider a 3D picture or object represented by a set of data points. Let **C** denote such a configuration; then if we operate on **C** by **R**, we get

$$\mathbf{CR} = \mathbf{C}^* \qquad (4.51)$$

where **C*** is the trimetric projection of **C** if transformation matrix **R** causes pure rotation. Hence, the coordinate axes remain orthogonal when projected onto a 2D plane.

A projection from 3D to 2D can be made by projecting onto a $z = 0$ plane with

$$\mathbf{R} = \begin{bmatrix} 3 \times 3 & \vdots & 0 \\ Rotation & \vdots & 0 \\ matrix & \vdots & 0 \\ \hline 0 \quad 0 \quad 0 & \vdots & 1 \end{bmatrix} \begin{bmatrix} 1 & 0 & 0 & 0 \\ 0 & 1 & 0 & 0 \\ 0 & 0 & 0 & 0 \\ 0 & 0 & 0 & 1 \end{bmatrix} \qquad \text{(for } z = 0) \qquad (4.52)$$

Pure rotation is done prior to projection and matrix **R** projects the object on the x–y plane (this is done by setting the third column to 0).

Similarly, the projection onto the $z = t$ plane is obtained by

$$\mathbf{R} = \begin{bmatrix} 3 \times 3 & \vdots & 0 \\ Rotation & \vdots & 0 \\ matrix & \vdots & 0 \\ \hline 0 \quad 0 \quad 0 & \vdots & 1 \end{bmatrix} \begin{bmatrix} 1 & 0 & 0 & 0 \\ 0 & 1 & 0 & 0 \\ 0 & 0 & 0 & 0 \\ 0 & 0 & t & 1 \end{bmatrix} \qquad (4.53)$$

The transformation matrix **R** is the product of two matrices. It is obtained by first performing a simple rotation of the object if needed and then projecting it onto the corresponding 2D plane. In this case, $z = 0$ or t.

If we were to project the object onto $x = 0$ or $x = r$ plane, the projection matrix takes the following form:

$$\mathbf{R} = \begin{bmatrix} 0 & 0 & 0 & 0 \\ 0 & 1 & 0 & 0 \\ 0 & 0 & 1 & 0 \\ 0 & 0 & 0 & 1 \end{bmatrix} \qquad \text{(for } x = 0) \qquad (4.54)$$

and

$$\mathbf{R} = \begin{bmatrix} 0 & 0 & 0 & 0 \\ 0 & 1 & 0 & 0 \\ 0 & 0 & 1 & 0 \\ r & 0 & 0 & 1 \end{bmatrix} \qquad \text{(for } x = r) \qquad (4.55)$$

In a similar fashion, the projection onto the $y = 0$ or $y = s$ plane is

$$\mathbf{R} = \begin{bmatrix} 1 & 0 & 0 & 0 \\ 0 & 0 & 0 & 0 \\ 0 & 0 & 1 & 0 \\ 0 & 0 & 0 & 1 \end{bmatrix} \quad \text{(for } y = 0) \tag{4.56}$$

and

$$\mathbf{R} = \begin{bmatrix} 1 & 0 & 0 & 0 \\ 0 & 0 & 0 & 0 \\ 0 & 0 & 1 & 0 \\ 0 & s & 0 & 1 \end{bmatrix} \quad \text{(for } y = s) \tag{4.57}$$

Example 4.11   Projection on a Plane

Determine the projection of Figure 4.13 in Example 4.5 on planes (a) $x = 6$, (b) $y = 6$, and (c) $z = 6$.

Solution   The coordinates of the box (Figure 4.13) are defined by:

$$\mathbf{C} = \begin{bmatrix} 0 & 0 & 0 & 1 \\ 0 & 1 & 0 & 1 \\ 0 & 1 & 1 & 1 \\ 0 & 0 & 1 & 1 \\ 2 & 1 & 0 & 1 \\ 2 & 0 & 0 & 1 \\ 2 & 0 & 1 & 1 \\ 2 & 1 & 1 & 1 \end{bmatrix}$$

(a) The projection of the box on $x = 6$ plane (see Figure 4.27) has the following transformation matrix:

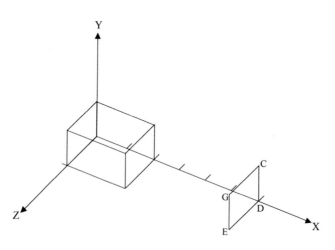

Figure 4.27   Projection on the plane ($x = 6$) of the box given by Figure 4.13 of Example 4.5.

$$[\mathbf{R}] = \begin{bmatrix} 0 & 0 & 0 & 0 \\ 0 & 1 & 0 & 0 \\ 0 & 0 & 1 & 0 \\ 6 & 0 & 0 & 1 \end{bmatrix}$$

Therefore, the coordinates for the projection are

$$[\mathbf{C}^*] = [\mathbf{C}][\mathbf{R}]$$

$$[\mathbf{C}^*] = \begin{bmatrix} 0 & 0 & 0 & 1 \\ 0 & 1 & 1 & 1 \\ 0 & 1 & 1 & 1 \\ 0 & 0 & 1 & 1 \\ 2 & 1 & 0 & 1 \\ 2 & 0 & 0 & 1 \\ 2 & 0 & 1 & 1 \\ 2 & 1 & 1 & 1 \end{bmatrix} \begin{bmatrix} 0 & 0 & 0 & 0 \\ 0 & 1 & 0 & 0 \\ 0 & 0 & 1 & 0 \\ 6 & 0 & 0 & 1 \end{bmatrix} = \begin{bmatrix} 6 & 0 & 0 & 1 \\ 6 & 1 & 2 & 1 \\ 6 & 1 & 0 & 1 \\ 6 & 0 & 1 & 1 \\ 6 & 1 & 0 & 1 \\ 6 & 0 & 0 & 1 \\ 6 & 0 & 1 & 1 \\ 6 & 1 & 1 & 1 \end{bmatrix}$$

(b) The projection of the box on the $y = 6$ plane (see Figure 4.28) has the fol-

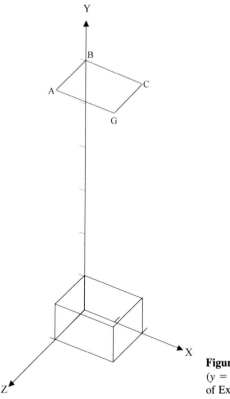

Figure 4.28 Projection on the plane ($y = 6$) of the box given by Figure 4.13 of Example 4.5.

lowing transformation matrix:

$$[\mathbf{R}] = \begin{bmatrix} 1 & 0 & 0 & 0 \\ 0 & 0 & 0 & 0 \\ 0 & 0 & 1 & 0 \\ 0 & 6 & 0 & 1 \end{bmatrix}$$

Therefore, the coordinates for the projection are

$$[\mathbf{C}^*] = [\mathbf{C}][\mathbf{R}]$$

$$[\mathbf{C}^*] = \begin{bmatrix} 0 & 0 & 0 & 1 \\ 0 & 1 & 0 & 1 \\ 0 & 1 & 1 & 1 \\ 0 & 0 & 1 & 1 \\ 2 & 1 & 0 & 1 \\ 2 & 0 & 0 & 1 \\ 2 & 0 & 1 & 1 \\ 2 & 1 & 1 & 1 \end{bmatrix} \begin{bmatrix} 1 & 0 & 0 & 0 \\ 0 & 0 & 0 & 0 \\ 0 & 0 & 1 & 0 \\ 0 & 6 & 0 & 1 \end{bmatrix} = \begin{bmatrix} 0 & 6 & 0 & 1 \\ 0 & 6 & 2 & 1 \\ 0 & 6 & 1 & 1 \\ 0 & 6 & 1 & 1 \\ 2 & 6 & 0 & 1 \\ 2 & 6 & 0 & 1 \\ 2 & 6 & 1 & 1 \\ 2 & 6 & 1 & 1 \end{bmatrix}$$

(c) The projection of the box on the $z = 6$ plane (see Figure 4.29) has the following transformation matrix:

$$[\mathbf{R}] = \begin{bmatrix} 1 & 0 & 0 & 0 \\ 0 & 1 & 0 & 0 \\ 0 & 0 & 0 & 0 \\ 0 & 0 & 6 & 1 \end{bmatrix}$$

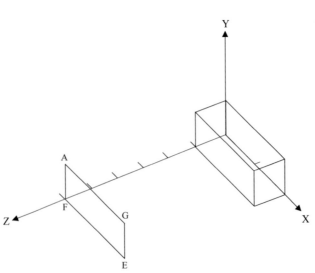

Figure 4.29 Projection on the plane $(y = 6)$ of the box given by Figure 4.13 of Example 4.5.

Therefore, the coordinates for the projection are

$$[C^*] = [C][R]$$

$$[C^*] = \begin{bmatrix} 0 & 0 & 0 & 1 \\ 0 & 1 & 0 & 1 \\ 0 & 1 & 1 & 1 \\ 0 & 0 & 1 & 1 \\ 2 & 1 & 0 & 1 \\ 2 & 0 & 0 & 1 \\ 2 & 0 & 1 & 1 \\ 2 & 1 & 1 & 1 \end{bmatrix} \begin{bmatrix} 1 & 0 & 0 & 0 \\ 0 & 1 & 0 & 0 \\ 0 & 0 & 0 & 0 \\ 0 & 0 & 6 & 1 \end{bmatrix} = \begin{bmatrix} 0 & 0 & 6 & 1 \\ 0 & 1 & 6 & 1 \\ 0 & 1 & 6 & 1 \\ 0 & 0 & 6 & 1 \\ 2 & 1 & 6 & 1 \\ 2 & 0 & 6 & 1 \\ 2 & 0 & 6 & 1 \\ 2 & 1 & 6 & 1 \end{bmatrix}$$

∎

4.18 ISOMETRIC PROJECTION

Combined rotations followed by projection from infinity form the basis for generating all axonometric projections.

We are familiar with the isometric view (see Figure 4.30). Unlike other projections, an isometric projection is obtained by equally foreshortening all three axes when going from 3D to 2D. From the point of view of CAD software development, we are interested in finding the transformation matrix **R** that yields such a projection. Observe how we first manipulate the geometry and then project it onto a 2D plane by imposing the isometric conditions. For that, we perform the following:

1. Rotate about the y axis
2. Rotate about the x axis
3. Project about the $z = 0$ plane
4. Apply the final transformation conditions of foreshortening all axes equally
5. Get the final transformation matrix to yield the isometric view

Consider a point P given by $(x \quad y \quad z \quad 1)$. Let us find the isometric projection of this point while using the previous definitions. Operating on P by Θ and ϕ, we get

$$[x \; y \; z \; 1] \begin{bmatrix} \cos\phi & 0 & -\sin\phi & 0 \\ 0 & 1 & 0 & 0 \\ \sin\phi & 0 & \cos\phi & 0 \\ 0 & 0 & 0 & 1 \end{bmatrix} \begin{bmatrix} 1 & 0 & 0 & 0 \\ 0 & \cos\Theta & \sin\Theta & 0 \\ 0 & -\sin\Theta & \cos\Theta & 0 \\ 0 & 0 & 0 & 1 \end{bmatrix} = [x^* \; y^* \; z^* \; 1]$$

where $[x^* \quad y^* \quad z^*]$ represents the coordinates of the rotated point P about the y and x axes. The concatenated transformation matrix is given by

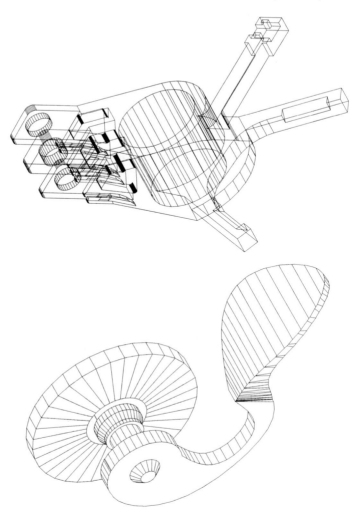

Figure 4.30   Drawings in isometric view: (top) an actuator and (bottom) a wheel handle.

$$\mathbf{R} = \begin{bmatrix} \cos\phi & \sin\phi\sin\Theta & -\sin\phi\cos\Theta & 0 \\ 0 & \cos\Theta & \sin\Theta & 0 \\ \sin\phi & -\cos\phi\sin\Theta & \cos\phi\cos\Theta & 0 \\ 0 & 0 & 0 & 1 \end{bmatrix} \quad (4.58)$$

Suppose point P denotes different unit vectors along the x, y, and z axes. Hence along x, we have $[1 \quad 0 \quad 0 \quad 1]$, which when operated on by $\mathbf{R}$ given by Equation (4.58) yields

$$[1 \quad 0 \quad 0 \quad 1][\mathbf{R}] = [x^* \quad y^* \quad z^* \quad 1] \quad (4.59)$$

where

$$x^* = \cos \phi$$
$$y^* = \sin \phi \sin \Theta \qquad (4.60)$$
$$z^* = -\sin \phi \cos \Theta$$

If we consider the unit vector along the y axis, it transforms into

$$[0 \quad 1 \quad 0 \quad 1][\mathbf{R}] = [x^* \quad y^* \quad z^* \quad 1] \qquad (4.61)$$

where

$$x^* = 0$$
$$y^* = \cos \Theta \qquad (4.62)$$
$$z^* = \sin \Theta$$

Because we are projecting onto the $z = 0$ plane, we should suppress all z components by making them equal zero. To create the isometric projection, we must foreshorten all three axes equally. One way of doing this is to equate the magnitude of the unit vectors along the x and y axes and then equate the one corresponding to the y and z axes. The latter gives the conditions of our isometric projection.

The magnitudes of the unit vectors along the x, y, and z axes after the projection are obtained from Equations (4.59) and (4.61), respectively.

$$n_x = \sqrt{(x^*)^2 + (y^*)^2 + (z^*)^2} = \sqrt{\cos^2 \Phi + \sin^2 \Phi \sin^2 \Theta}$$
$$n_y = \sqrt{(x^*)^2 + (y^*)^2 + (z^*)^2} = \sqrt{\cos^2 \Theta}$$
$$n_z = \sqrt{(x^*)^2 + (y^*)^2 + (z^*)^2} = \sqrt{\sin^2 \Phi + \cos^2 \Phi \sin^2 \Theta}$$

and then

$$n_x = n_y \Rightarrow \sin^2 \Phi = \frac{\sin^2 \Theta}{1 - \sin^2 \Theta} \qquad (4.63)$$

$$n_y = n_z \Rightarrow \sin^2 \Phi = \frac{1 - 2 \sin^2 \Theta}{1 - \sin^2 \Theta} \qquad (4.64)$$

Equations (4.63) and (4.64) form a set of two equations with two unknowns.

Using trigonometric relationships and the method of substitution, we can solve for ϕ and Θ which yield $\Theta = 35.26°$, $\Phi = 45°$. We can then conclude that given a geometry in 3D represented by $[\mathbf{C}]$, its isometric projection is obtained by premultiplying it by $\mathbf{R}$ given by Equation (4.64) with Θ and Φ being $35.26°$ and $45°$ respectively. The resulting $[\mathbf{C}^*]$ represents the projection for which we are looking.

4.19 DESCRIPTION OF CURVES AND SURFACES

Continuous objects are best represented by curves and surfaces. To yield an accurate representation that appears as real as possible, we need to find the necessary mathematical tools. We start our discussion with a description of curves and splines. Our main interest is to explain in the simplest way possible how to construct a spline; then we explore its utility in design using the CAD workstation.

The bottom line in design is to construct an accurate picture so one can learn more about its features and characteristics when it is put in a different environment.

There are two methods of fitting curves: (1) using polynomials and (2) using splines.

The first requirement is that a set of data points must exist $(x_i \quad y_i)$ (for the 2D case). The second step is to find a function y of order n that best represents the curve. Obviously, one would have to try several polynomials to achieve the desired fit. On the other hand, the methods of splines work with the basic assumption that we can pass a cubic function between any two points. By properly choosing the conditions at the end points, a smooth curve can be derived. Let us see how a cubic spline is formed.

4.19.1 Cubic Splines

A spline is a smooth curve that can be generated by computer to go through a set of data points. The mathematical spline derives from its physical counterpart—the thin elastic beam. Because the beam is supported at specified points (we call them knots), it can be shown that its deflection (assumed small) is characterized by a polynomial of order three, hence a cubic spline.

$$y(x) = \sum a_i x^{i-1} \qquad (1 < i < 4) \qquad (4.65)$$

The benefits of using cubic splines are as follows:

1. They reduce computational requirements and numerical instabilities that arise from higher-order curves.
2. They have the lowest degree space curve that allows inflection points.
3. They have the ability to twist in space.

4.19.2 Parametric Cubic Spline

Consider a set of data points described in the x–y plane by $(x_i \quad y_i)$ with $i = 1, n$. Our objective is to pass a parametric cubic spline between all these points. A parametric cubic spline is a curve that is represented as a function of one or more parameters. The parametric cubic spline equation between any two points is given in terms of a parameter t as follows:

$$s(t) = a_0 + a_1 t + a_2 t^2 + a_3 t^3 \tag{4.66}$$

with a_0, a_1, a_2, and a_3 being some constraints that are determined from the boundary conditions and the continuity and smoothness of the curve. Therefore, one can write $s(t)$ between any two given points as

$$s(t) = [x(t) \quad y(t)] \tag{4.67}$$

Our objective at this point is to evaluate the constants between each interval. Parameter t varies between zero and one when normalized ($0 \leqq t \leqq 1$); hence the function $s(t)$ can be evaluated for any value t.

The procedure for evaluating the constraints works as follows.

Consider three points, P_1, P_2, and P_3. Let the chord length between P_1 and P_2 be t_2 and the one between P_2 and P_3 be t_3. Let S_i be the parametric cubic spline between P_1 and P_2 and S_{i+1} the one between P_2 and P_3. Because $S_i(t)$ starts at P_1 and ends at P_2, the value of t should start from zero at P_1 and end with $t = t_2$ at P_2.

$$S_i(0) = a_0 \tag{4.68}$$

For an arbitrary value, for example, $t = t_2$, we have

$$S_i(t_2) = a_0 + a_1 t + a_2 t^2 + a_3 t^3 \tag{4.69}$$

Let $S_i(0)$ be denoted by S_1, then

$$S_1 = a_0 \tag{4.70}$$

Similarly, let $S_i(t_2)$ be given by S_2. Then we can write the derivatives at points P_1 and P_2 as

$$S_1' = a_1 \tag{4.71}$$

$$S_2' = a_1 + 2a_2 t_2 + 3a_3 t_2^2 \tag{4.72}$$

Our cubic spline Equation (4.66) takes the following form if we substitute the constraints a_0 and a_1 by S_1 and S_2 obtained from Equations (4.70) and (4.71), respectively.

$$S_i(t) = S_1 + S_1' t + a_2 t^2 + a_3 t^3 \tag{4.73}$$

Now we can find the expressions for a_2 and a_3 as functions of S_1, S_1', S_2, and S_2'. Using Equations (4.69) and (4.72), we get

$$a_2 = \frac{3(S_2 - S_1)}{t_2^2} - \frac{2S_1'}{t_2} - \frac{S_2'}{t_2} \tag{4.74}$$

$$a_3 = \frac{2(S_1 - S_2)}{t_2^3} + \frac{S_1'}{t_2^2} + \frac{S_2'}{t_2^2} \tag{4.75}$$

Therefore, the spline function becomes

$$S_i(t) = S_1 + S_1' + \left[\frac{3(S_2 - S_1)}{t_2^2} - \frac{2S_1'}{t_2} - \frac{S_2'}{t_2} \right] t^2 + \left[\frac{2(S_1 - S_2)}{t_2^3} + \frac{S_1'}{t_2^2} + \frac{S_2'}{t_2^2} \right] t^3$$

$$(4.76)$$

S_1' and S_2' are known. Then the equation for $S_i(t)$ is explicitly given by Equation (4.76).

In the context of computer graphics and general-purpose algorithm development, we need to ask the following questions:

1. How can we generate a solution for S_1' and S_2' for all cubic functions $S_i(t)$, $S_{i+1}(t), \ldots, S_n(t)$?
2. How do we select t, t_1, and t_2 or a given set of data points?
3. How do we assure continuity between the splines at knots $P_1, P_2, \ldots, P_n$?

In any case, the solution given by Equation (4.76) can be generalized for any two adjacent cubic segments such as $S_i(t)$ and $S_{i+1}(t)$ for $1 < i < n - 2$, where n is the number of data points. Rewriting Equation (4.76), we get

$$S_i(t) = S_i + S_i' + \left[\frac{3(S_{i+1} - S_i)}{t_2^2} - \frac{2S_i'}{t_2} - \frac{S_{i+1}'}{t_2} \right] t^2 + \left[\frac{2(S_i - S_{i+1})}{t_2^3} + \frac{S_i'}{t_2^2} + \frac{S_{i+1}'}{t_2^2} \right] t^3$$

$$(i = 1, n) \tag{4.77}$$

To answer the foregoing questions, we first notice that to assure continuity between the cubic segments, we need to compute the second derivative of $S_i(t)$ and $S_{i+1}(t)$ and equate them at their corresponding connecting points. From Equation (4.65), we obtain

$$S_i''(t) = 2a_2 + 6a_3 t \tag{4.78}$$

$$S_i''(0) = 2a_2 \tag{4.79}$$

$$S_i''(t_2) = 2a_2 + 6a_3 t_2 \tag{4.80}$$

We also know from the boundary conditions that

$$S_i''(t_2) = S_{i+1}''(0) \tag{4.81}$$

By using Equations (4.74) and (4.75), Equation (4.81) yields

$$t_i + 2S_i' + 2(t_{i+2} + t_{i+1})S_{i+1}' + t_{i+1}S_{i+2}'$$
$$= (3/t_{i+1}t_{i+2})[t_{i+1}^2(S_{i+2} - S_{i+1}) + t_{i+2}^2(S_{i+1} - S_i)] \qquad (1 \leq i \leq n - 2) \tag{4.82}$$

In matrix form, Equation (4.82) becomes

$$\begin{bmatrix} t_3 & 2(t_2 + t_3) & t_2 & 0 & 0 & \cdots & \cdots & 0 \\ 0 & t_4 & 2(t_3 + t_4) & t_3 & 0 & \cdots & \cdots & 0 \\ 0 & 0 & t_5 & 2(t_2 + t_4) & t_4 & \cdots & \cdots & 0 \\ \vdots & \vdots & \vdots & \vdots & \vdots & \cdots & \cdots & \vdots \\ 0 & 0 & \cdots & \cdots & \cdots & t_n & 2(t_n + t_{n+1}) & t_n \end{bmatrix} \begin{bmatrix} S_1' \\ S_2' \\ S_3' \\ \vdots \\ S_n' \end{bmatrix}$$

$$= \begin{bmatrix} \dfrac{3}{t_2 t_3} [t_2^2(S_3 - S_2) + t_3^2(S_2 - S_1)] \\[2ex] \dfrac{3}{t_3 t_4} [t_3^2(S_4 - S_3) + t_4^2(S_3 - S_2)] \\[2ex] \vdots \\[2ex] \dfrac{3}{t_{n-1} t_n} [t_{n-1}^2(S_n - S_{n-1}) + t_n^2(S_{n-1} - S_{n-2})] \end{bmatrix} \qquad (4.83)$$

Equation (4.83) yields $n - 2$ equations with n unknowns. On the other hand, if end points S_1' and S_n' are known, as is the case in beam deflection analysis, then the system of equations results in a consistent set of equations for which we can solve for the unknowns.

4.19.3 Boundary Conditions

Natural Spline.   Also known as relaxed conditions, they are determined by setting the second derivatives of $S(t)$ with respect to time (t) at the beginning and end to zero. Thus,

$$S''(t = 0) = 0 \qquad (4.84)$$

$$S''(t = t_n) = 0 \qquad (4.85)$$

Writing these conditions in terms of S', we get

$$S_1' + 0.5 S_2' = 1.5(S_2 - S_1)/t_2 \qquad (4.86)$$

and

$$2S_{n-1}' + 4S_n' = (6/t_n)(S_n - S_{n-1}) \qquad (4.87)$$

Adding Equations (4.86) and (4.87) to the $n - 2$ equations given by (4.83), we can solve for all the S'.

Clamped Spline.   The boundary conditions for this spline are such that the first derivatives (slopes) at $t = 0$ and $t = t_n$ are specified. Hence, they form the additional two other equations needed in Equation (4.83) to solve all S'.

4.19.4 Summary

The parametric cubic spline between any two points is constructed as follows:

1. Find the maximum cord length and determine $t_1, t_2, \ldots, t_n$.
2. Use Equation (4.83) together with the corresponding boundary conditions to solve for all the $S_1', S_2', \ldots, S_n'$.
3. Solve for the parameters that make up the parametric cubic splines using Equations (4.83), (4.84), and (4.85).

Example 4.12   Cubic Spline Connecting 3 Points

Find the cubic spline (natural spline) for the points shown in Figure 4.31.

$$P_1 = [1 \quad 2] \qquad P_2 = [2 \quad 1.5] \qquad P_3 = [3 \quad 0.5]$$

Solution   The cord lengths are

$$t_2 = \sqrt{(x_2 - x_1)^2 + (y_2 - y_1)^2}$$

$$= \sqrt{(1)^2 + (0.5)^2}$$

$$= \sqrt{1.25} = 1.118$$

and

$$t_3 = \sqrt{(x_3 - x_2)^2 + (y_3 - y_2)^2}$$

$$= \sqrt{(1)^2 + (-1)^2}$$

$$= \sqrt{2} = 1.414$$

Using the boundary conditions given by Equations (4.86) and (4.87), together with Equation (4.83), we get

$$S_1' + \frac{1}{2}S_2' = \frac{3}{2}\frac{S_2 - S_1}{t_2}$$

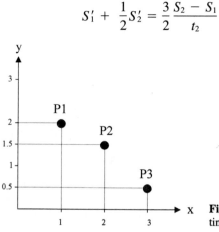

Figure 4.31   Three points used for fitting a cubic spline.

$$t_3 S_1' + 2(t_3 + t_2)S_2' + t_2 S_3' = \frac{3}{t_2 t_3}[t_2^2(S_3 - S_2) + t_3^2(S_2 - S_1)]$$

$$2S_2' + 4S_3' = \frac{6}{t_3}(S_3 - S_2)$$

Substituting values into these equations yields

$$S_1' + \frac{1}{2}S_2' = \frac{3}{2}\frac{S_2 - S_1}{t_2}$$

$$= \frac{3}{2(1.118)}(S_2 - S_1)$$

$$= 1.342(S_2 - S_1)$$

$$= 1.342[(2 - 1)\ (1.5 - 2)]$$

$$= [1.342 \ -0.671]$$

$$t_3 S_1' + 2(t_3 + t_2)S_2' + t_2 S_3' = \frac{3}{t_2 t_3}[t_2^2(S_3 - S_2) + t_3^2(S_2 - S_1)]$$

$$= \frac{3}{1.58}(1.25[(3 - 2)\ (0.5 - 1.5)]$$

$$+ 2[(2 - 1)\ (1.5 - 2)]$$

$$= 1.897[(2 + 1.25)\ (-2 - 1)]$$

$$= [4.628 \ -4.268]$$

$$2S_2' + 4S_3' = \frac{6}{t_3}(S_3 - S_2)$$

$$= 4.243[1 \ -1]$$

$$= [4.243 \ -4.243]$$

In matrix form, the foregoing equations become

$$\begin{bmatrix} 1 & 0.5 & 0 \\ 1.414 & 5.064 & 1.118 \\ 0 & 2 & 4 \end{bmatrix} \begin{bmatrix} S_1' \\ S_2' \\ S_3' \end{bmatrix} = \begin{bmatrix} 1.342 & -0.671 \\ 4.268 & -4.268 \\ 4.243 & -4.243 \end{bmatrix}$$

which can be solved as

$$\begin{bmatrix} S_1' \\ S_2' \\ S_3' \end{bmatrix} = \begin{bmatrix} 1 & 0.5 & 0 \\ 1.414 & 5.064 & 1.118 \\ 0 & 2 & 4 \end{bmatrix}^{-1} \begin{bmatrix} 1.342 & -0.671 \\ 4.268 & -4.268 \\ 4.243 & -4.243 \end{bmatrix} = \begin{bmatrix} 1.189 & -0.394 \\ 0.308 & -0.558 \\ 0.908 & -0.783 \end{bmatrix}$$

For the first segment between P_1 and P_2, we have

$$S_1(t) = a_0 + a_1t + a_2t^2 + a_3t^3$$

where

$$a_0 = P_1$$

$$a_0 = [1 \quad 2]$$

Using Equations (4.74) and (4.75), we solve for a_2 and a_3:

$$a_1 = [1.189 \quad -0.394]$$

$$a_2 = 2.4[1 \quad -0.5] - 1.789[1.189 \quad -0.191]$$

$$a_2 = \frac{3}{1.25}(S_2 - S_1) - \frac{2S_1'}{\sqrt{1.25}} - \frac{S_2'}{\sqrt{1.25}} - 0.8944[0.308 \quad -0.558]$$

$$a_2 = [-0.002 \quad 0.004]$$

$$a_3 = \frac{2}{(\sqrt{1.25})^3}(S_1 - S_2) + \frac{S_1'}{(\sqrt{1.25})^2} + \frac{S_2'}{(\sqrt{1.25})^2}$$

and

$$a_3 = 1.431[-1 \quad 0.5] + 0.8[1.189 \quad -0.394] + 0.8[0.308 \quad -0.558]$$

$$a_3 = [-0.234 \quad -0.046]$$

resulting in

$$S_1(t) = [1 \quad 2] + [1.189 \quad -0.394]t + [-0.002 \quad 0.004]t^2$$
$$+ [-0.234 \quad -0.046]t^3$$

The selection of t can be made following the assumption that

$$0 \leq \frac{t}{t_2} \leq 1$$

Hence, for some selective points

$$\frac{t}{t_2} = \frac{1}{4}, \frac{1}{2}, \frac{3}{4}$$

we get

$$S(\tfrac{1}{4}) = [1.293 \quad 1.901]$$

$$S(\tfrac{1}{2}) = [1.565 \quad 1.798]$$

$$S(\tfrac{3}{4}) = [1.792 \quad 1.687]$$

Similarly, we find the parametric cubic spline between P_2 and P_3 to be

$$S(t) = [1 \quad 2] + [0.308 \quad -0.558]t + [0.847 \quad -0.316]t^2 + [-0.099 \quad 0.032]t^3$$

Once more, choosing

$$\frac{t}{t_3} = \frac{1}{4}, \frac{1}{2}, \frac{3}{4}$$

we get

$$S\left(\tfrac{1}{4}\right) = [1.128 \quad 1.841]$$

$$S\left(\tfrac{1}{2}\right) = [1.353 \quad 1.646]$$

$$S\left(\tfrac{3}{4}\right) = [1.666 \quad 1.417]$$

The results are plotted in Figure 4.32.   ∎

4.19.5 Nonparametric Cubic Spline

A nonparametric cubic spline is defined as a curve having a function of only one parameter. Nonparametric cubic splines allow a direct variable relationship between the parameter value x and the value of the cubic spline function to be determined. This is seen from its mathematical representation:

$$S(x) = a + bx + cx^2 + dx^3 \tag{4.88}$$

From Equation (4.88), we see that the cubic spline is a function of x alone. Thus, we could say that for a given set of data points $P_1, P_2, \ldots, P_n$ defined in the interval in the domain $[x_0, x_1, \ldots, x_n]$, we need to construct the spline that passes through all these points. Let each subinterval be denoted by $[x_i, x_{i+1}]$; hence, our task is to find the cubic spline function for each one of these intervals. Once more, we must find an algorithm to solve the constants a, b, c, and d.

Consider the cubic spline that passes through the given points shown in Figure 4.33.

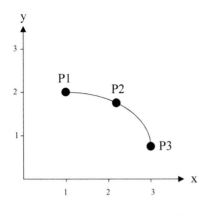

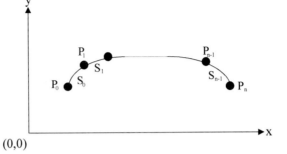

Figure 4.32 A cubic spline fitted for three given points.

Figure 4.33 The cubic spline $s(x)$ is composed of S_0, $S_1, \ldots, S_{n-1}$ cubic splines passing through n points.

Cubic spline $S(x)$ is composed of $n - 1$ cubic segment splines. Each point has an x and y value; hence, the $S(x)$ function is defined for all points. For the interval $[x_i, x_{i+1}]$, we can write

$$S_i(x_i) = y_i \tag{4.89}$$

$$S_i(x_{i+1}) = S_{i+1}(x_{i+1}) = y_{i+1} \tag{4.90}$$

By considering the smoothness and continuity of the cubic splines, the following conditions are derived:

$$S_i'(x_{i+1}) = S_{i+1}'(x_{i+1}) \tag{4.91}$$

$$S_i''(x_{i+1}) = S_{i+1}''(x_{i+1}) \tag{4.92}$$

The nonparametric cubic spline function for any interval $x_i \leq x \leq x_{i+1}$ could be expressed as

$$S_i(x) = a_i + b_i(x - x_i) + c_i(x - x_i)^2 + d_i(x - x_i)^3 \tag{4.93}$$

Its first and second derivatives are

$$S_i' = b_i + 2c_i(x - x_i) + 3d_i(x - x_i)^2 \tag{4.94}$$

$$S_i'' = 2c_i + 6d_i(x - x_i) \tag{4.95}$$

Making use of the criteria of the spline given by Equations (4.89) to (4.92), we deduce the following:

$$S_i(x_i) = a_i = y_i \tag{4.96}$$

$$S_i(x_{i+1}) = a_{i+1} = a_i + b_i h_i + c_i h_i^2 + d_i h_i^3 \tag{4.97}$$

and

$$S_i'(x_i) = b_i \tag{4.98}$$

$$S_i'(x_{i+1}) = S_{i+1}'(x_{i+1})b_{i+1} = b_i + 2c_i h_i + 3d_i h_i^2 \tag{4.99}$$

$$S_i''(x_{i+1}) = S_{i+1}''(x_{i+1}) = 2c_{i+1} = 2c_i + 6d_i h_i \tag{4.100}$$

where

$$h_i = x_{i+1} - x_i$$

Because all the a_i values are known, we can solve for b_i using Equations (4.97) and (4.100):

$$b_i = \frac{a_{i+1} - a_i}{h_i} - \frac{h_i(2c_i + c_{i+1})}{3} \tag{4.101}$$

In essence, the foregoing equation for b_i was the result of using S_i and S_{i+1}. In a similar fashion, if we use S_{i-1} and S_i, we will get

$$b_i = \frac{a_i - a_{i-1}}{h_{i-1}} - \frac{h_{i-1}(c_{i-1} + 2c_i)}{3} \tag{4.102}$$

Equations (4.102) and (4.101) result in an equation in terms of the constants c's as

$$h_{i-1}c_{i-1} + 2(h_{i-1} + h_i)c_i + h_ic_{i+1} = 3\left(\frac{a_{i+1} - a_i}{h_i} - \frac{a_i - a_{i-1}}{h_{i-1}}\right) \tag{4.103}$$

$$(i = 1, 2, \ldots, n - 1)$$

In matrix form, Equation (4.103) can be written as

$$
\begin{bmatrix}
h_0 & 2(h_0 + h_1) & h_1 & 0 & \cdots & & \cdots & 0 \\
0 & h_1 & 2(h_1 + h_2) & h_2 & \cdots & & \cdots & 0 \\
0 & 0 & h_2 & 2(h_2 + h_3) & \cdots & & \cdots & 0 \\
\vdots & \vdots & \vdots & \vdots & \cdots & & \cdots & \vdots \\
0 & 0 & 0 & \cdots & h_{n-2} & 2(h_{n-2} + h_{n-1}) & h_{n-1}
\end{bmatrix}
\begin{bmatrix}
c_0 \\ c_1 \\ c_2 \\ \vdots \\ c_n
\end{bmatrix}
$$

$$
= 3
\begin{bmatrix}
\dfrac{a_2 - a_1}{h_1} - \dfrac{a_1 - a_0}{h_0} \\
\vdots \\
\dfrac{a_n - a_{n-1}}{h_{n-1}} - \dfrac{a_{n-1} - a_{n-2}}{h_{n-2}}
\end{bmatrix}
\tag{4.104}
$$

Equation (4.104) consists of $n - 2$ equations with n unknowns; therefore, it cannot be solved. However, end points P_0 and P_n of the spline are usually known through the boundary conditions that must be supplied. By knowing c_0 and c_n, Equation (4.104) is then used to solve for the remaining c_1 through c_{n-1} values. In turn, the equation of the splines can be determined by computing the d's from Equation (4.100) followed by the b's from Equation (4.101).

4.19.6 Boundary Conditions

Natural Splines.   The boundary conditions in natural splines are found by selecting the second derivatives at both the beginning and end points of the curve to equal zero. Therefore,

$$S''(x_0) = S''(x_n) = 0 \tag{4.105}$$

which when substituted into Equation (4.100) yields

$$c_0 = c_n = 0 \tag{4.106}$$

Clamped Splines.   The clamped end conditions are determined by specifying the first derivatives (slope) at x_0 and x_n. That is,

$$S'(x_0) = f'(x_0) \tag{4.107}$$

and

$$S'(x_n) = f'(x_n) \tag{4.108}$$

where f' is a specified function. The following example illustrates the methodology employed in evaluating the nonparametric cubic splines and highlights its usefulness. Note that we only introduced the concepts of splines in a rather simplistic way, and it is left for the reader to explore further the mathematics behind this most important curve-fitting methodology.

Example 4.13   Nonparametric Spline Connecting 3 Points

Find the nonparametric cubic spline (natural spline) for the points shown in Figure 4.34.

i	x_i	y_i
0	1.0	1.0
1	1.5	2.0
2	2.5	1.75

$$h_0 = 0.5 \qquad h_1 = 1.0$$

Let us begin by stating the following: for the three points we need to generate two cubic splines S_0 and S_1

$$S_0 = a_0 + b_0(x - x_0) + c_0(x - x_0)^2 + d_0(x - x_0)^3$$

or

$$S_0 = a_0 + b_0(x - 1) + c_0(x - 1)^2 + d_0(x - 1)^3$$

and

$$S_1 = a_1 + b_1(x - 1.5) + c_1(x - 1.5) + c_1(x - 1.5)^2 + d_1(x - 1.5)$$

To solve for the constants of the two splines, we know that for $x = 1$

$$S_0 = a_0 = Y_0 = 1.0$$

and for $x = 1.5$,

$$S_1 = a_1 = Y_1 = 2.0$$

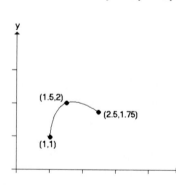

Figure 4.34 Points used for fitting a cubic spline.

From the natural boundary conditions, we have

$$S''(x = x_0) = S''(x = x_2) = 0$$

or simply

$$S_0''(x = 1) = 2c_0 = 2c_2 = 0 \quad \longrightarrow \quad c_0 = c_2 = 0$$

Now, let us use Equation (4.110) where we can write the following

$$h_0 c_0 + 2(h_0 + h_1)c_1 + h_1 c_2 = 3\left(\frac{a_2 - a_1}{h_1} - \frac{a_1 - a_0}{h_0}\right)$$

Substituting values of h_0, h_1, c_2, a_2, a_1, and a_0 in the above equation,

$$2(1.5)c_1 = 3(-0.25 - 2) \quad \longrightarrow \quad c_1 = \frac{-7.75}{2(1.5)} = -2.25$$

Now we can make use of Equations (4.107), (4.103) and (4.106) to solve for b_1, and d_1, respectively.

$$b_0 = \frac{a_1 - a_0}{h_0} - \frac{h_0(2c_0 + c_1)}{3}$$

$$b_1 = \frac{a_2 - a_1}{h_1} - \frac{h_1(2c_1 + c_2)}{3}$$

$$d_0 = (2c_1 - 2c_0 h_0)/6h_0$$

$$d_1 = (2c_2 - 2c_1 h_1)/6h_1$$

Substituting values for c_0, c_1, c_2, h_0, and h_1 in the above equations, we get

$$b_0 = 2.375 \quad \text{and} \quad d_0 = -1.5$$

$$b_1 = 1.25 \quad\quad\quad d_1 = 0.75$$

Collecting the determined values in the form of a table, we get

i	x_i	a_i	b_i	c_i	d_i
0	1	1	2.375	—	−1.5
1	1.5	2.0	1.25	−2.25	0.75
2	2.5	1.75	—	—	—

Hence the spline functions are

$$S_0 = (x) = 1 + 2.375(x - 1) - 1.5(x - 1)^3$$

$$S_1(x) = 2.0 + 1.25(x - 1.5) - 2.25(x - 1.5)^2 + 0.75(x - 1.5)$$

For verification we determine S_0 and S_1 for different values of x.

$$S_0(1) = 1.0 \quad \text{and} \quad S_1(1.5) = 2.0$$

$$S_0(1.5) = 2.0 \quad\quad\quad\quad S_1(2.5) = 1.75$$

Those of course are the values of the function y_i and they check properly.   ■

4.19.7 Bezier Curves

The shapes of Bezier curves are defined by the position of the points, and the curves may not intersect all the given points except for the endpoints. In certain circumstances where there are insufficient points or awkwardly located points, the cubic spline method may not provide a smooth curve without defining more points. Bezier curves allow the flexibility of not constraining the curve to fit through all the points. One can imagine the shape of the curve to fit in a polygon defined by a series of points.

       The mathematical basis (the weighing factor that affects the shape of the curve) of the Bezier curve is related to the Bernstein basis given by

$$J_{n,i}(t) = \begin{bmatrix} n \\ i \end{bmatrix} t^i (1 - t)^{n-1} \tag{4.109}$$

where

$$\begin{bmatrix} n \\ i \end{bmatrix} = \frac{n!}{i!(n - i)!}$$

and $n!$ is defined as

$$n! = n * (n - 1) * (n - 2) * \cdots \tag{4.110}$$

where n is the degree of the polynomial, and i is the particular vertex in the ordered set (between zero and n). The curve points are defined by

$$S(t) = \sum_{i=1}^{n} S_i J_{n,i}(t) \quad\quad (0 \leq t \leq 1) \tag{4.111}$$

where $i = 1$ to n, and the S_i contain the vector components of the various points.

       In order to construct the Bezier curve, we need to evaluate the $J_{n,i}$, which are functions of parameter t. It is seen that the maximum value of the function $J_{n,i}$ occurs at $t = i/n$ and is given by

$$J_{n,i}\left(\frac{i}{n}\right) = \binom{n}{i} \frac{i^i (n - i)(n - i)}{n^n} \tag{4.112}$$

The following example illustrates the Bezier curve method of curve fitting.

Example 4.14   Bezier Curve Through Given Points

For the position vectors given:

$$P_0 = \begin{bmatrix} 0 & 1 \end{bmatrix} \quad\quad P_1 = \begin{bmatrix} 2 & 5 \end{bmatrix}$$

$$P_2 = [4 \quad 5] \qquad P_3 = [6 \quad 1]$$

Find the Bezier curve space that passes through these points.

Solution We note that the four points form the Bezier polygon. Because we have four defined vertices, then $n = 3$. Using Equation (4.109), we evaluate the J function, where

$$J_{3,0}(t) = (1)t^0(1 - t)^3 = (1 - t)^3$$

$$J_{3,1}(t) = 3(1 - t)^2$$

$$J_{3,2}(t) = 3t^2(1 - t)$$

$$J_{3,3}(t) = t^3$$

Therefore,

$$S(t) = P_0 J_{3,0} + P_1 J_{3,1} + P_2 J_{3,2} + P_3 J_{3,3}$$

For various values of t, the coefficients for the Bezier curve are found in Table 4.1.

TABLE 4.1 EVALUATION OF THE BEZIER FUNCTION $J_{3,i}$ (i = 0, 1, 2, 3, 4) IN TERMS OF PARAMETER t.

t	$J_{3,0}$	$J_{3,1}$	$J_{3,2}$	$J_{3,3}$
0	1	0	0	0
0.15	0.614	0.325	0.0574	0.0034
0.35	0.275	0.444	0.239	0.043
0.5	0.125	0.375	0.375	0.125
0.65	0.043	0.239	0.444	0.275
0.85	0.0034	0.0574	0.325	0.614
1	0	0	0	1

The resulting $S(t)$ function is then found as

$$S(0) = [0 \quad 1] \qquad\qquad S(0.15) = [0.9 \quad 2.529]$$

$$S(0.35) = [2.102 \quad 3.733] \qquad S(0.5) = [3 \quad 4]$$

$$S(0.65) = [3.904 \quad 3.733] \qquad S(0.85) = [5.099 \quad 2.529]$$

$$S(1) = [6 \quad 1]$$

The results are plotted in Figure 4.35.   ∎

4.20 SURFACE CREATION

Surface creation is instrumental in visualizing objects in space. It allows the user to work with a more concrete look that shows the outer shape of the object. This enhances the design aspects of the problem and sets the stage for decisions on how to manufacture the components of the part.

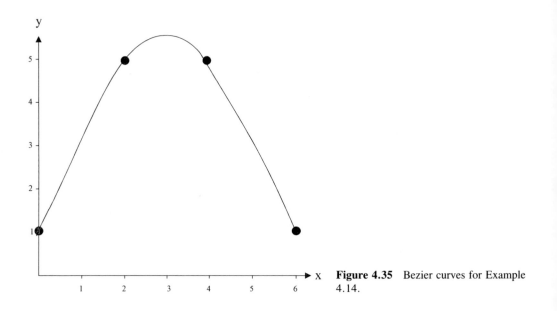

Figure 4.35 Bezier curves for Example 4.14.

Surface generation depends on the techniques used to fit the appropriate curves between the given boundaries. A major problem in surface fitting is defining the visual criteria for the design at hand. Therefore, selecting the appropriate method for engineering applications is essential to a finer and more visually acceptable design. The methods should allow certain flexibility in modifying the curve fitting for better interpolation.

Some of the methods in surface fitting include the following.

4.20.1 Plane Surface

A plane surface is defined by four curves or lines that connect four corners. By using a CAD system, a plane is created by specifying three points.

4.20.2 Ruled Surface

Also called lofted surface, a ruled surface is simple and fundamental to surface design. It is defined as follows: Given two space parametric curves c_1 and c_2, a curve S is defined that contains both curves as opposite boundary curves. (An interpolation is then carried out between c_1 and c_2; see Figure 4.36.)

4.20.3 Rectangular Surface

A rectangular surface is bounded by four curves (see Figure 4.37). The plane surface is a special case. Ruled surfaces could be obtained from a rectangular surface.

4.20.4 Surface of Revolution

A surface of revolution is formed when a curve is rotated about an axis. The angle of rotation can be controlled; a full rotation is used to obtain the surface in Figure 4.38. A grid can then be used for better visualization. Other surface creations include the Bezier surface and the B-spline surface.

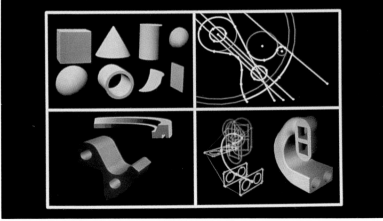

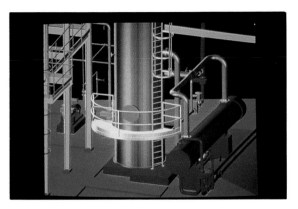

Screen display of complex model on an RS/6000

Graphics capabilities and computer-aided design

Power visualization on a CAD workstation

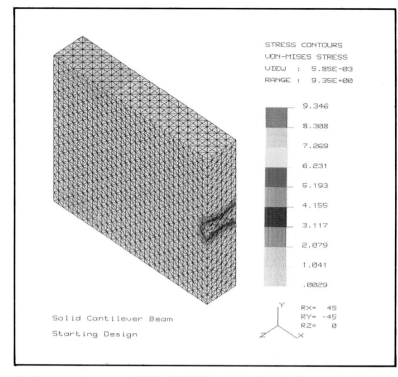

Optimum design using NISA SHAPE program (initial design) *Courtesy of EMRC, Troy, MI*

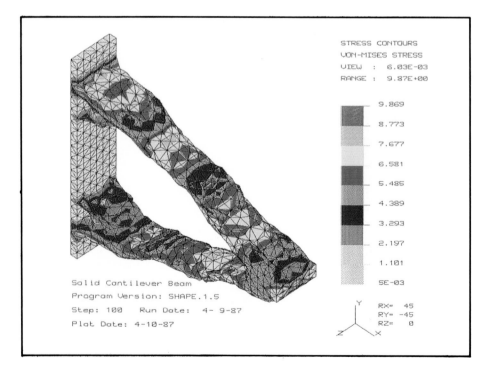

Optimum design using NISA SHAPE program (final design) *Courtesy of EMRC, Troy, MI*

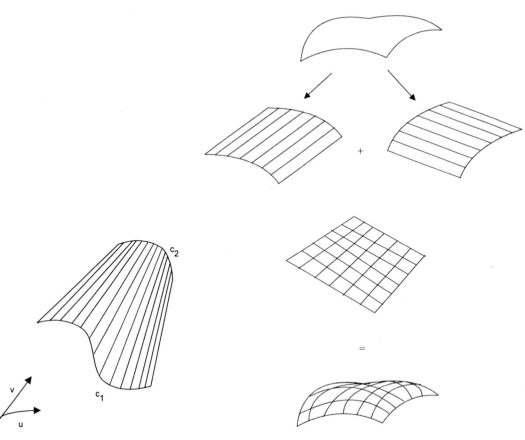

Figure 4.36 Ruled surfaces: given two arbitrary curves C_1 and C_2, a surface is fitted between them using linear interpolation.

Figure 4.37 A rectangular surface is bounded by four curves.

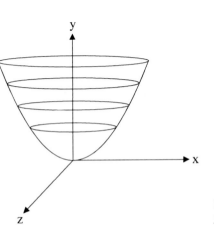

Figure 4.38 A ruled parabola about the y axes.

PROBLEMS

4.1 See the original shape and position of the cube shown in Figure P4.1.

    (a) Find the configuration matrix **C** that represents the geometry.

    (b) Use uniform scaling (with respect to the origin) to magnify the object to two times its original size.

4.2 Find the position of the vertices of the square shown in Figure P4.2 when rotated +45 degrees (CCW).

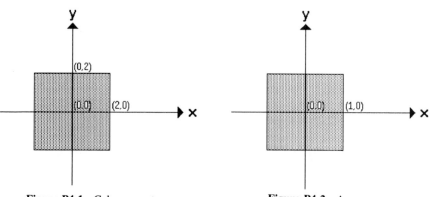

         Figure P4.1 Cube geometry.   **Figure P4.2** A square.

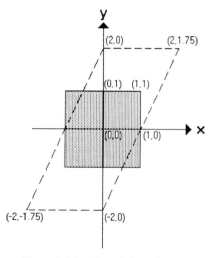

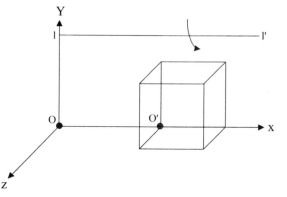

Figure P4.3 Shear deformation of a square.   **Figure P4.4** Rotation of a unit cube.

4.3 Using the same square of Problem 2, find the transformation matrix that produces the shear deformation shown by the dashed lines in Figure P4.3.

4.4 Find the transformation needed to rotate the unit cube shown in Figure P4.4 about $l–l'$ in a clockwise fashion by 30°. Point O' lies on the x axis, and $l–l'$ is at distance m from the x axis, and passes through the y axis. If the cube were positioned such that O' passes through O, what changes in **R** would we expect?

4.5 We would like to obtain an isometric view of an object (Figure P4.5) given in a Cartesian frame. In order to determine the desired transformation matrix, we performed the following manipulation of the object:
   (i) Rotated the object about the z axis clockwise by an angle γ
   (ii) Rotated the object about the x axis counterclockwise by an angle α
   (iii) Projected the object onto the $y = 0$ plane.
   Find the transformation matrix **R** that yields the isometric view.

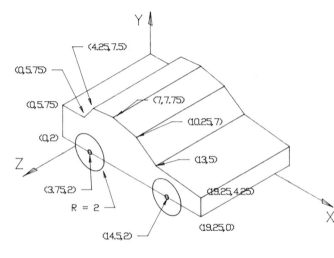

The (x,y) coordinate shown are on the Z = 12.25 plane,
(x,y) coordinate on plane Z = 0 are the same.

Figure P4.5 Coordinates and isometric view of a geometry.

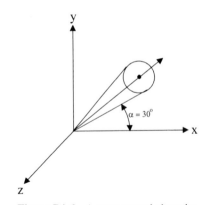

Figure P4.6 A cone rotated about its center line.

4.6 The cone shown in Figure P4.6 is to be rotated about the center line by 30 degrees (CCW). Find the transformation **R** to produce the rotation. If the center axis of the cone lies in the x–y plane and passes through 0, is there an alternative solution that would yield the same **R** as before?

4.7 A strange object was found in the fields of Cincinnati and must be moved to a research center. Given the information in Figure P4.7, determine the set of transformation matrices needed to move the object to the research center.

4.8 Automated robots, used by Widgets, Inc., operate by use of transformation matrices to move the widgets along the production line. Given a schematic of the path (Figure P4.8) through which the widget must go, determine the transformation matrices that can make this possible.

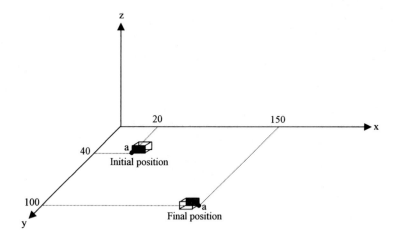

Figure P4.7 Initial and final positions of an object.

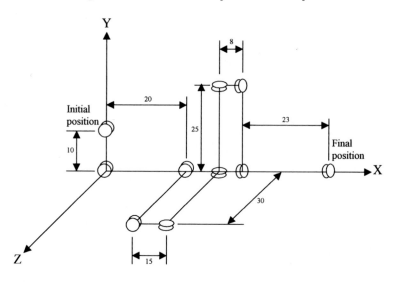

Figure P4.8 Schematic view of a path followed by robots.

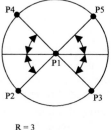

R = 3
P1 IS THE CENTER

4.9 To draw the mechanical part shown in Figure P4.9, we need to use several transformation matrices. Suppose the only information we have is that the part is symmetric and there exist the three points, P_1, P_2, and P_3. Show how the complete geometry could be obtained based on the given information. (Check your answer on a CAD system.)

4.10 Give the concatenated transformation matrix that would generate the new position of the object in Figure P4.10 (face *eijg* in the original position lies in the *x–y* plane). Note: Show all the steps you want to take before writing the transformation matrices.

4.11 Given the dimensions of a tile design (Figure P4.11) that must be enlarged two times its original size, you must do the following:

(i) Label all points that outline the part (24 points minimum).

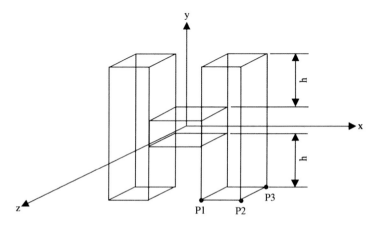

Figure P4.9 Geometric description of a mechanical part.

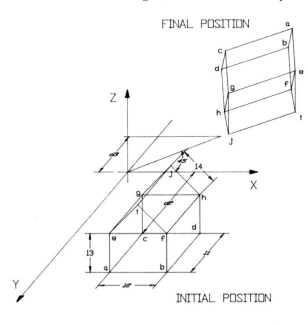

Figure P4.10 Transformation of a geometry.

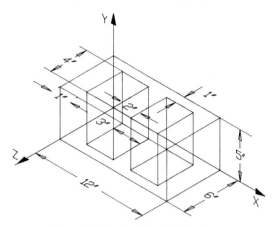

Figure P4.11 Scaling of a block.

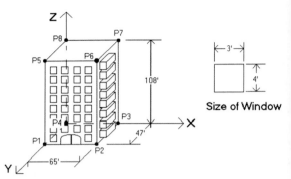

Figure P4.12 Scaling of a high rise building.

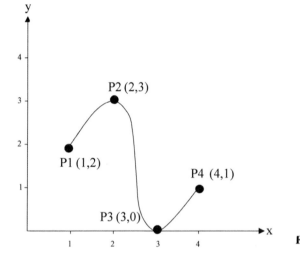

Figure P4.13 Parametric cubic spline.

(ii) Identify the coordinates of each point and place into matrix form.

(iii) Perform the overall scaling and show new coordinates of these points.

4.12 The height of the high-rise building (Figure P4.12) is too short. Given the eight points and dimensions of the building, perform scaling (nonuniform scaling) to double the building's height. How are the size of the windows affected by the scaling transformation matrix?

4.13 For the data points shown in Figure P4.13, find the parametric cubic spline function satisfying the natural spline boundary conditions.

4.14 Use the data from Problem 13 to generate the nonparametric cubic spline function for the same boundary conditions.

4.15 Generate the Bezier spline curve for the data points given by Figure P4.13.

4.16 Compare the three solutions given by Problems 13, 14, and 15 and draw your conclusions.

LABORATORY PROJECTS

The following set of problems are to be drawn using a CAD workstation. If a CAD workstation is unavailable (or 3D conceptualization is not possible), select points on the object and apply the appropriate transformation matrix to determine the new position in space.

In all projects, considerable leeway is given for you to work comfortably at your own pace and level of understanding. Give all the information on what you did to solve each set and the references (axes, planes, etc.) used to solve each problem.

1. Check the answers of Problems 9, 10, 11, and 12 using your CAD workstation.

2. *Gear Support*
    (a) Given the dimensions of the gear support in Figure P4.14(a), perform the following (assume the *x*–*y* plane):

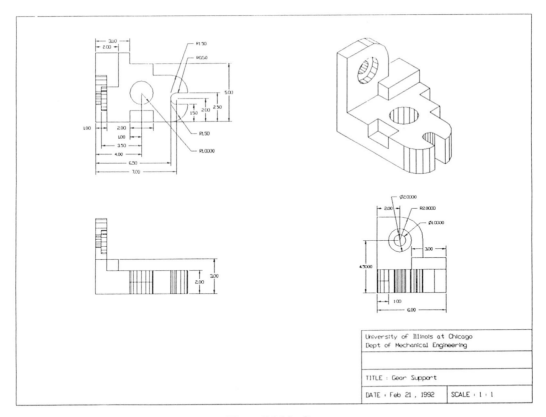

Figure P4.14 Gear support.

(i) Double the size of this part.

(ii) Move this drawing 3 units in the x direction and 4 units in the y direction.

(iii) Rotate it 45 degrees about the z axis (assume the same coordinate system used in the examples).

(b) Figure P4.14(b) defines the dimensions of the gear support in 3D space. Create an isometric view for this part.

3. *Slide Bracket Design.* Figure P4.15 describes the design of a slide bracket. In this project:

(a) Recreate the part shown on your CAD system.

(b) Scale the size of this part by a factor of 1.5.

(c) After Steps (i) and (ii), find the isometric view of this part.

(d) Find the reflection of this part with respect to the x–z plane.

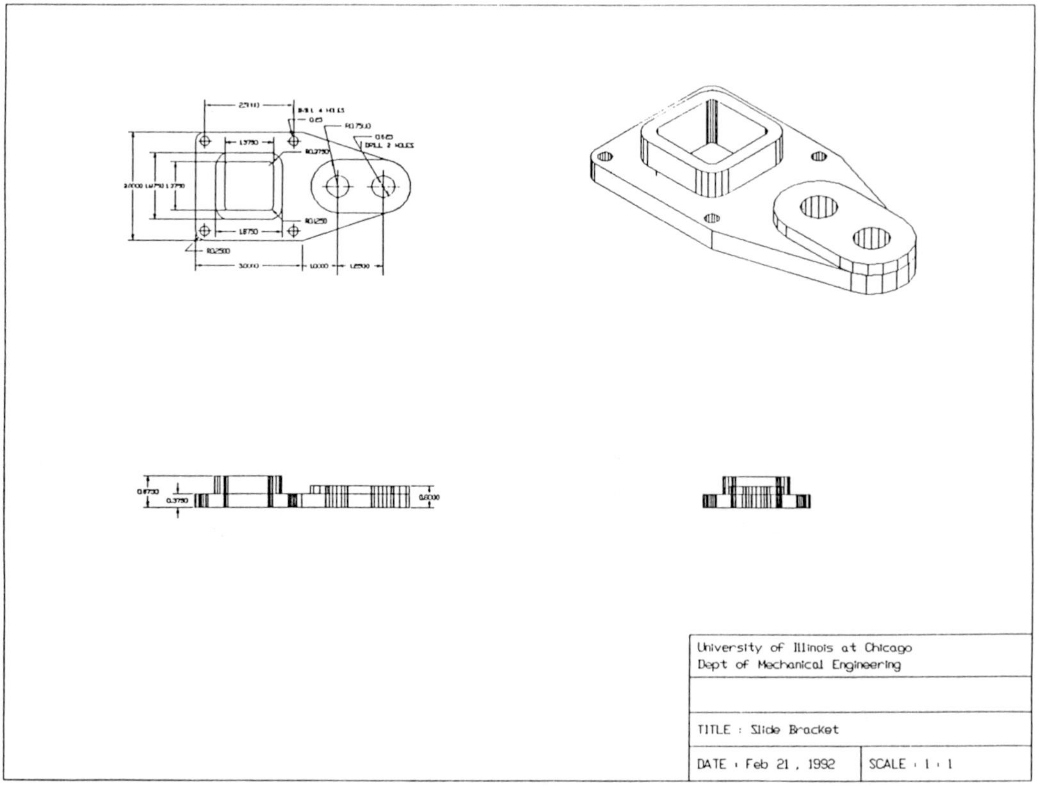

Figure P4.15 Slide bracket: Front view, Top view.

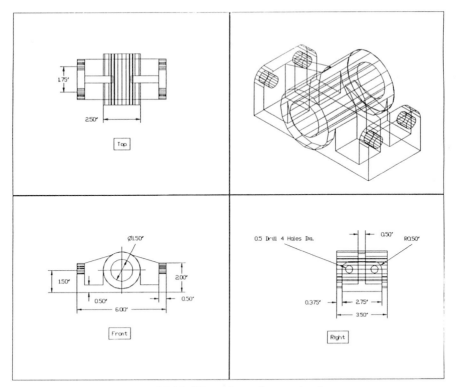

Figure P4.16   Three views of a truss bearing.

4. *Truss Bearing.* The truss bearing shown in Figure P4.16 is symmetric about the x–y plane.
   (a) Draw half of this part and reflect the other half.
   (b) Translate the truss bearing 5 units in the x direction.
   (c) Find all the views shown including the isometric view of the part.

5. *Slide Bracket.* Given the slide bracket shown in Figure P4.17, create the isometric view found in Figure 4.30. (Hint: provide your own dimension to the part.)

6. *Turbine Blade.* A complete surface description of a turbine blade is given in Figure P4.18. Reproduce the part views on your CAD system. Provide the complete dimensions of the part.

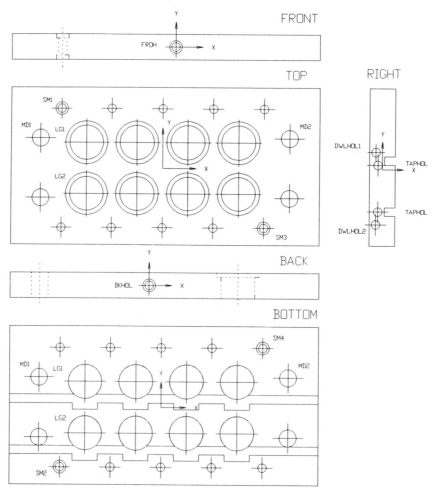

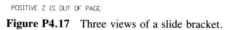
POSITIVE Z IS OUT OF PAGE

Figure P4.17   Three views of a slide bracket.

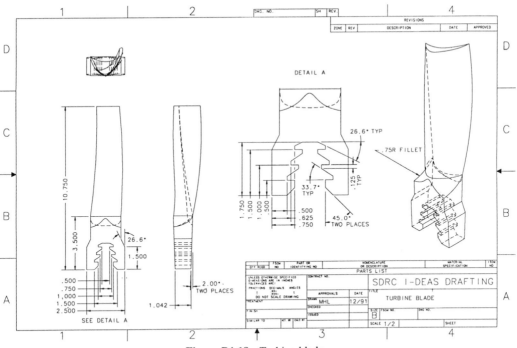

Figure P4.18   Turbine blade.

REFERENCES

4.1 Amirouche, F. M. L., Introduction to Computer-Aided Design and Manufacturing, Course Notes ME 347, Mechanical Engineering Department, University of Illinois at Chicago, 1990.

4.2 Amirouche, F. M. L., Introduction to Computer-Aided Design and Manufacturing, Laboratory Notes ME 347, Mechanical Engineering Department, University of Illinois at Chicago, 1987.

4.3 Bronson, R., *Matrix Methods—An Introduction,* Academic Press, New York, 1970.

4.4 Farin, G., *Curves and Surfaces for Computer Aided Geometric Design—A Practical Guide,* Academic Press, New York, 1988.

4.5 Lancaster, P., and Salkauska, K., *Curve and Surface Fitting—An Introduction,* Academic Press, New York, 1986.

4.6 Rodgers, D. F., and Adams, J. A., *Mathematical Elements for Computer Graphics,* McGraw-Hill, New York, 1976.

chapter 5

Solid Modeling

5.1 INTRODUCTION

The most common methods used to represent an object in computer-aided design systems are wireframe, surface modeling, and solid modeling.

Wireframe models are relatively simple to construct. They are at the heart of any CAD system and they are especially well suited for drafting. Although wireframe models provide accurate information about the location of a surface discontinuity on a part, they usually do not provide a complete description of the part. Surface modeling is a creation of a surface, or profile, through a series of points, curves, and/or lines. It allows for more complex shapes that otherwise could not be created by solid modeling. Surface modeling is usually used in conjunction with solid modeling to create a part in CAD for analysis.

Several disparate strands of research led to the development of computer programs for the representation and manipulation of solid objects. One of these was an approach to the design of mechanical parts by treating them as combinations of simple building blocks such as cubes and cylinders. Such programs are known as solid modelers or volume modelers, and can hold the complete unambiguous representation of geometries of a wide range of solid objects. The completeness of information contained in a solid model allows the automatic production of realistic images of a particular shape and assists in the automation of the process of interference checking.

A solid modeling system is one that provides a complete, unambiguous description of solid objects. Solid model data can be used as partial input data for analysis programs like finite-element. The output of the analysis can be represented on the solid model with centers of different colors. Once the solid object is created, one can rotate, shade, or even section the object to show interior details. Solid objects can also be combined with the other parts stored in the database to form a complex assembly of the part whose design has to be carried out. Furthermore, the solid model not only depicts the interior properties such as size and shape, but depicts interior properties such as mass as well.

5.2 CONSTRUCTION TECHNIQUES

Solid modeling mathematical algorithms require a certain manipulation of geometry to obtain the desired shape. There are several techniques used for the construction and editing of solid objects. Some are quite promising for future developments and others are currently in use and quite popular. These techniques include

1. Boolean operation
2. Sweeping
3. Automated filleting and chamfering
4. Tweaking
5. Fleshing out of wireframe and projections

None of these techniques seems to be adequate by itself, so the ideal solid model system should support several of them. A common feature of the techniques considered in this section is the ability to do a number of modifications with minimum user input. For example, one Boolean operation might do the work of several dozen drafting operations of the type used in traditional CAD systems.

5.2.1 Boolean Operation

Theoretic Boolean operations of intersection, union, and difference provide a useful method of constructing complex objects from simple primitives. Figure 5.1 illustrates three Boolean operations.

These operations are "regularized" in some way to guarantee that valid input always produces valid output. This prevents the conversion of unrealistic features such as dangling faces and edges. Some systems that rely upon boundary representation internally still allow the use of Boolean operation for input. Other systems support only special limited types of Boolean operations. For example, they do not support general union operations, but allow for the joining of two objects that have disjointed interiors that meet in a common face. Even in systems that do not support general union operations, it is useful to provide gluing as a special case because it requires little computation. Boolean operations applied to two different objects are illustrated in Figure 5.2.

Constructive solid geometry representations are often stored internally as binary trees. The system user, however, can apply the union operation to a sequence

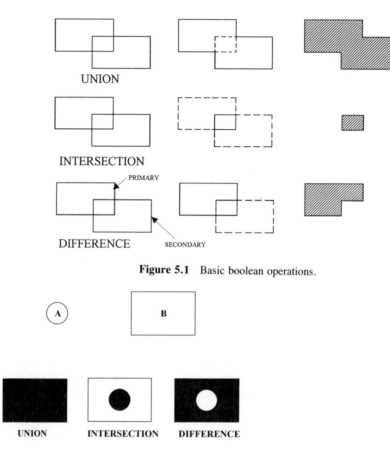

Figure 5.1 Basic boolean operations.

UNION   INTERSECTION   DIFFERENCE

Figure 5.2 Boolean operations (2D objects).

A - SECONDARY OBJECT   B - PRIMARY OBJECT

of objects in one step or subtract several objects from a given object simultaneously. Certain systems use a stack-oriented approach to Boolean arithmetic. A new object created is pushed on top of the stack and Boolean operations are applied to the top two objects of the stack. This mode of operation is extremely flexible.

Boolean operations form a very natural constructive technique, particularly, the Boolean operation of subtraction, which is natural to people with experience in material removal processes. The object being subtracted can be thought of as the volume swept out by a cutting tool. Similarly, the union operation is analogous to bounding processes such as welding and gluing.

5.2.2 Sweeping

In a sweep operation, an object (i.e, a generator) is moved along a curve (i.e, a trajectory) in order to sweep out a new object. Figure 5.3(a) illustrates a simple exam-

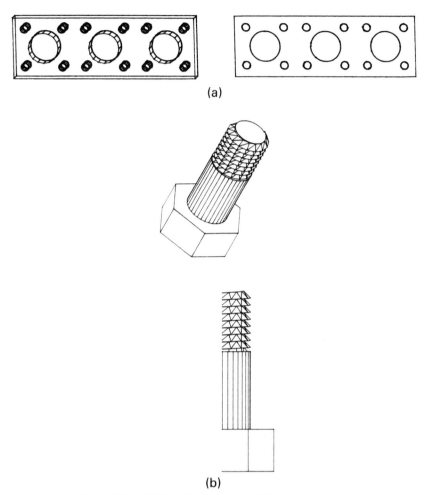

(a)

(b)

Figure 5.3   (a) Transitional sweep, (b) Rotational sweep.

ple in which a face representing a cross section is swept along a linear trajectory in order to create the object. The generator can be a curve, a face, or a solid object, whereas the trajectory can only be a curve or a strip of curves. The path geometry and the curves of the edges of the face operated on determine the surface geometry of the generated lateral faces. The edge curves of the lateral faces can be determined either from the path swept out by the vertices or by finding the intersections of surfaces of lateral faces.

Sweeping is a very convenient input technique. For many objects, most of the construction can be performed with just a few sweep operations. For example, intruded or projected parts can be easily modeled using sweep operations in which the trajectory is a straight line, as in the construction of tabulated cylinders. Also, curved parts can be modeled using sweep operations in which the trajectory is a circle lying in a plane perpendicular to the center line. A turned part, modeled using a rotational sweep, is shown in Figure 5.3(b).

5.2.3 Automated Filleting and Chambering

In a system employing only a boundary representation, linear edges whose vertices are trihedral can often be filleted fairly easily. The edge is identified and a fillet radius is specified. The system can create a cylindrical face with its four edges and then it automatically modifies all adjoining faces and edges (Figure 5.4). Similar functions can be devised for chambering. The algorithms are very similar, but only planar faces should be created.

In constructive solid geometry based systems, chambering and filleting are usually accomplished using Boolean operations. Sometimes special primitives are created to facilitate this operation.

5.2.4 Tweaking

Most interactions with any design tool are making small adjustments to an existing shape. Boolean operations are expensive for this purpose. An example of an operation that adjusts the geometry of the face is tweaking.

Tweaking is an editing operation in which a face of an object is moved in some way. The "tweaked" face and the faces adjacent to it are then adjusted to maintain the integrity of the object. The best way to perform this adjustment is to recompute the intersection of these faces, where the intersection curves become the new common boundaries. For example, in Figure 5.5, the two upper faces of the base of the object have been tweaked slightly upward.

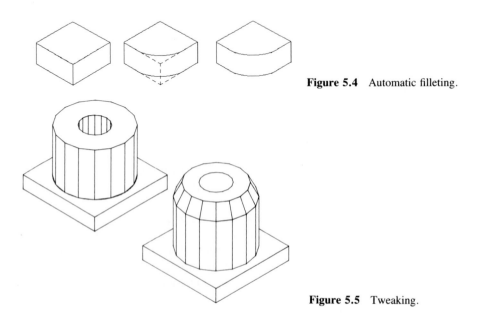

Figure 5.4   Automatic filleting.

Figure 5.5   Tweaking.

5.2.5 Fleshing Out Wireframes and Projections

In this method, an entire wireframe model is constructed and then surfaces are patched on using the wireframe's geometry to define the shape and position of the surfaces. Because many current users of CAD/CAM systems have extensive archives of wireframe system models, it is important that the method of "fleshing out" wireframes works in an automated fashion without user intervention. Algorithms have been developed to perform this function for unambiguous, planar-faced objects. For 3D objects, heuristic algorithms are emerging that assist the user by automatically inserting surfaces. Also, algorithms that flesh out collections of 2D orthographic projects have been developed that are beneficial in certain applications.

5.3 REPRESENTATION SCHEMES

Most solid modeling systems can create, modify, and inspect 3D solid objects. There are a number of methods that can be used for representing such models in a computer. They can be classified as

1. Instantiation
2. Boundary representation
3. Constructive solid geometry
4. Cellular decomposition

5.3.1 Instantiation

Instantiation is a traditional method of creating geometry. The usefulness of this technique depends on the range of primitives that is available, and the number and types of values that can be specified at the time of instantiation.

In a contemporary system, the basic set of primitives includes arbitrarily orientable blocks, cylinders, cones, and spheres. For the user, these can be supplemented with convenient primitives such as wedges, fillets, and truncated cones. Figure 5.6 illustrates some of the system-supplied primitives. Convenient primitives do not contain any new surface types; therefore, they have to be described. On the other hand, these primitives are very useful and are usually simple for the system developer to implement.

More sophisticated CAD systems allow the end user to enter the primary dimension features of primitives by defining parameterized objects. Essentially, the user writes a procedure that describes the structure of the new primitive and then the parameters needed are specified when the geometry is instantiated. These parameters include orientation and location, an overall scale factor, independent size parameters (e.g., inner diameter and wall thickness of a pipe), feature form parameters (e.g., whether a bolt should have a square or a hexagonal head), and an enumeration feature parameter (e.g., how many holes there should be in a bolt circle or a

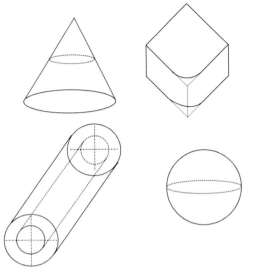

Figure 5.6 Convenient primitives.

cover plate). A generic cover plate is shown in Figure 5.7 in which the user can employ the technique of newly developed primitives to create the part. This is much faster in developing solid objects as compared to conventional system-supplied primitives.

Table 5.1 gives a set of primitives commonly used in systems.

In addition to base primitives, some systems can create user-defined primitives; that is, they can equip users with software to create their own set of primitives, in addition to those already defined by the system. The language used to define new primitives has enough information power that it might be possible to encode design rules within its definitions. For example, in Figure 5.7, we might write a generic definition in which only the diameter and the thickness of the plate need to be specified at the instantiation time. The number and size of holes needed in one bolt circle would then be computed internally. A sophisticated "family of parts" of this sort is supported by the user programming languages that accompany many commercial turn-key systems.

5.3.2 Boundary Representation

Boundary representation is a scheme wherein the objects are defined by their enclosing surfaces or boundaries. This technique consists of listing all faces, vertices, and edges of an object.

Once the entity is comprised, its appropriate surfaces are then swept through space in such a way as to create the desired depths of each surface, thus creating the finished modeled representation. Mathematically, the so-called B-REP solid model is created by taking an array of data points for a given view to define the edges, faces, and vertices. Once all the points from all the views are defined and stored in

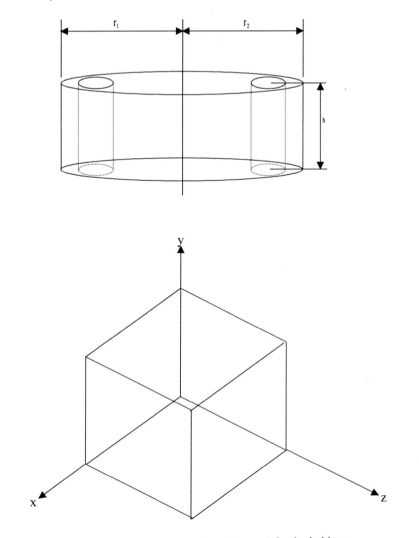

Figure 5.7 Geometry creation with user defined primitives.

TABLE 5.1 BASE PRIMITIVES

IBM CATIA	Hewlett-Packard ME 30
Cuboid (box)	Cube
Prism	Block
Pyramid	Prism
Pipe (cylinder)	Cylinder
Cone	Cone
Sphere	Sphere
Torus	Torus

the computer's memory, they are then joined appropriately to form the 3D entity. Once the entity is comprised, the computer can be instructed to use basic transformation matrices to bring out the finished solid model. The B-REP concept is demonstrated in Figure 5.8.

To interact with the B-REP modelers, the designer needs certain operating tools that assist in constructing and/or modifying the design with relative ease. Some of these operating techniques include the Boolean and sweeping operations.

Boolean operations provide a useful facility for combining and constructing solids in a B-REP modeler. They are operations that act on two boundaries and combine them into one or more new boundaries. Basic Boolean operations such as union, intersection, or difference can be used to combine different parts, resulting in a desired shape.

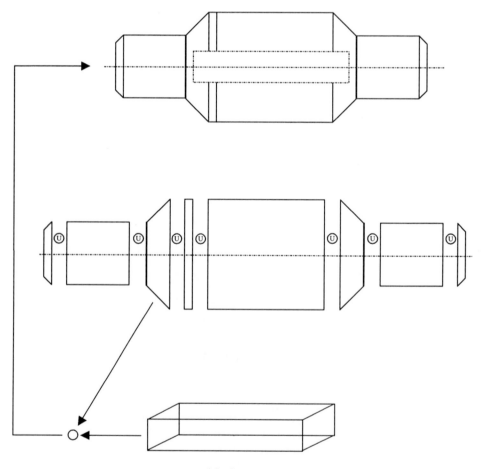

block

Figure 5.8 Boundary representation.

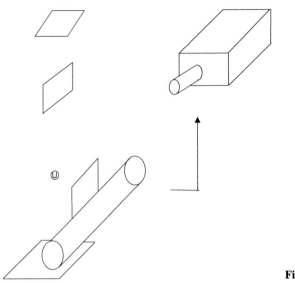

Figure 5.8   (*continued*)

Prismatic and translational objects can be created by sweeping and swinging types of operations. Sweeping takes place along the cross section of the object, whereas the swinging operations are used for rotationally symmetric objects. Figure 5.9 illustrates these two operations.

5.3.3 Constructive Solid Geometry

A constructive representation (C-REP) is a treelike structure wherein the leaves are simple primitive objects such as blocks, cones, and cylinders, and the nodes represent Boolean operations. Each node shows the set of operations that should be applied to the two subsolids below it on the tree.

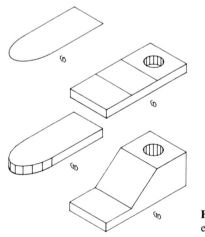

Figure 5.9   Sweeping and swinging operations.

C-REP is based on the principle that any complex part can be designed by adding or subtracting basic shapes such as cubes, cylinders, and cones by putting them in appropriate positions. A simple example of basic Boolean operations such as union, difference, and intersection is given in Figure 5.10.

The constructive solid geometry representation of a solid is very compact and can be generated quickly when two solids are combined by a set of operations. Figure 5.11 gives an idealization of C-REP representation.

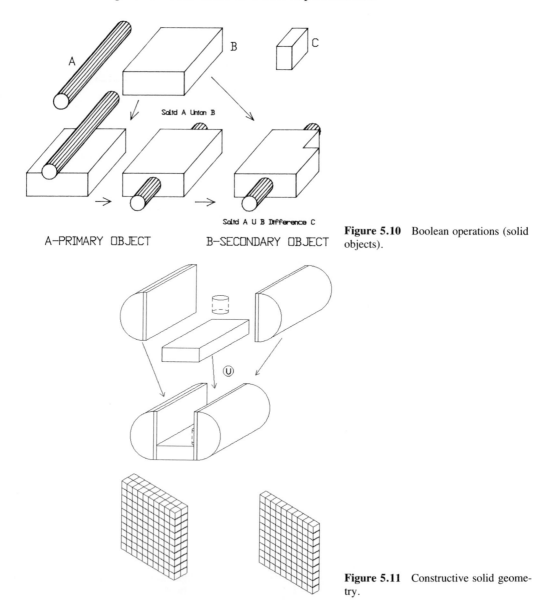

Figure 5.10 Boolean operations (solid objects).

Figure 5.11 Constructive solid geometry.

Each of the two approaches just discussed has its relative advantages and disadvantages. The C-REP method usually has a significant procedural advantage in the initial tabulation of the model. It is relatively easy to construct a solid model out of regular solid primitives by adding, subtracting, and intersecting components. As a result of the building-block approach, the C-REP method has a more compact file in its database.

One of the biggest advantages of the B-REP system is its capability to construct unusual shapes that would not be possible with the available repertoire of C-REP systems. This is exemplified by aircraft fuselages, swing shapes, and automobile body styling.

A B-REP scheme uses faces, edges, and vertices to define an object. As a result, the 2D shapes of the object are assembled to form the component. This in turn requires more storage but less computational time to reconstruct the image. On the other hand, the C-REP is a scheme wherein solid shapes are combined to form a part, which requires less storage but more computation. What follows are two examples to demonstrate further the utility of the C-REP and B-REP of solids.

Example 5.1   Construction of a Wrench

Using boundary representation, construct the part shown in Figure 5.12.

Solution   The basic Boolean operation, union ($\cup$), intersection ($\cap$), and difference ($-$) are used to construct the part. This is shown in Figure 5.13.   ■

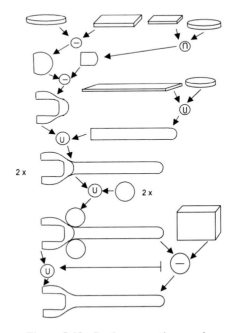

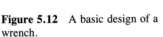

Figure 5.12   A basic design of a wrench.

Figure 5.13   Boolean operations on the wrench.

Example 5.2   Construction of a Solid Model

Using constructive solid geometry representation, construct the solid model shown in Fig. 5.14.

   Solution   Similar to B-REP, the Boolean operations are carried out on solid objects to get the final model. Figure 5.15 gives a clear picture of the operations and the completed model.   ∎

5.3.4 Cellular Decomposition

A solid object can be represented by dividing its volume into smaller volumes or cells. Thus, cells need not be cubic or identical in shape. Cellular decomposition produces an approximate representation of the object because some cells will be partly in one object grid and others will be discarded. As a result of this, "empty spaces" are created.

   This problem can be removed by using cell shapes of varying sizes so that they can conform to the object boundary. But further complications take place in describing complex sculptured cell shapes when computation becomes expensive. Depend-

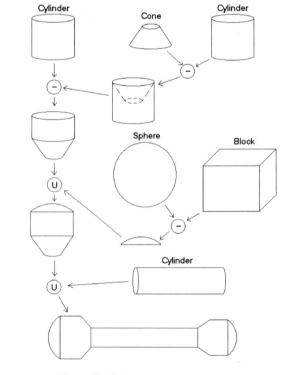

Figure 5.14   A solid model.

Figure 5.15   Boolean operations on the solid model.

ing on whether the cell is outside, entirely inside, or partially inside the object, it can be classified as empty, full, or partial.

There are various types of sides used in cellular decomposition. Two of the most common ones follow.

Simple Regular Grid.   This type of grid is produced by dividing the given space into a number of regular cells. These cells generally are cubes in the 3D case and squares in the 2D case. Figure 5.16 gives a clear picture of this type of grid.

Regular grid representation requires more storage. In order to improve the resolution of representation, the cell size has to be reduced. Thus, a storage problem is created, which, in turn, produces poor resolution.

Octree Adaptive Grid.   The octree encoding recursively subdivides the cubic modeling space into eight octants until homogeneous cells are obtained. They can be subclassified as follows.

Classical Octree Encoding. The following recursive procedure is usually performed when the octree representation of a 3D object is described. We start with a cube that represents the whole modeling space. If the object contained in it is too complex, the cube is classified as a grey node and is divided into eight octants in the order shown in Figure 5.17. The procedure is repeated recursively until a white or black node is obtained or the minimal size of octants is reached. A white node is completely outside the object, whereas a black one is completely inside.

The octree can be stored as a classical tree with eight pointers per node, or by using the parenthesize linear notation, as shown in Figure 5.18. Every code of a grey node is followed by the codes of its eight sons.

When 3D objects are represented by means of octree, Boolean operations are

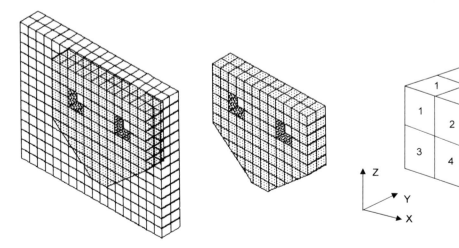

Figure 5.16 Regular grid.

Figure 5.17 Classical octree representation.

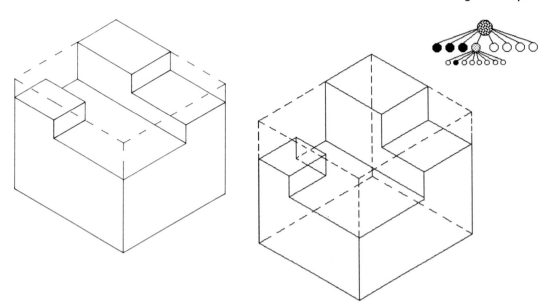

Figure 5.18 Parenthesize linear representation.

also very simple. The two great advantages that prevent the use of classical octrees as a representative scheme in modeling systems are

1. octree encoding of the solid yields minimum size nodes over the complete boundary and so the obtained octree is too large in most cases
2. once the Boolean operations have been performed, the algorithm for the computation of the boundaries from the octree becomes very complex

Exact Octree Encoding. In this octree representation system, in addition to the classical node types—white, black, and grey—we have face, edge, and vertex nodes. Consider the polyhedral shown in Figure 5.19. The nodes are defined as follows.

Face node: The node that contains a piece of the polyhedral faces.
Edge node: The node formed at the intersection of two neighboring faces.
Vertex node: The node at the intersection of the face and edge of the object.

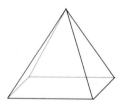

Figure 5.19 Octree encoding.

TABLE 5.2 DESCRIPTION OF NODES

Code	Description
00	White node
01	Black node
100	Grey node
101	Face node: In this case, following the code, there is a pointer to the corresponding equation.
110	Edge node: The code is followed by two equation pointers and a bit indicating whether the edge is convex or not.
111	Vertex node

In the parenthesize linear representation of the octree, all nodes require only two or three digits for their representation. Table 5.2 describes such nodes.

5.4 APPLICATIONS OF SOLID MODELING

Solid models often resemble surface models or wireframe models with hidden lines removed. However, the major difference could be assessed in the severe limitations wireframes have when used as mathematical tool models to represent the parts needed. For instance, in modeling, parts need to exhibit certain properties that are essential to the design. Properties of part models are useful in predicting the weight, moment of inertia, and volume of finished products. Solid models represent a more accurate picture of the parts being designed. This is especially true for complex geometries.

A model created by surface elements can be clearly shown as a solid model by removing the hidden lines. However, these surface models do not represent the actual solid object because they contain no information on what lies in the interior of the part. Surface models when used in conjunction with engineering analysis programs such as the finite-element method, which requires properties such as weight, volume, and moment of inertia, usually need a secondary program to compute these properties. Solid models are recorded in the computer mathematically as volumes bounded by surfaces rather than structures. Hence, it is possible to calculate the inertia properties of objects and visually display cross sections of parts to reveal the internal details that are often required for engineering analysis.

For example, consider a cube whose wireframe representation consists of points and lines (in contrast, the solid model of the cube is represented by a 3D object that contains a volume). If the volume of the wireframe model is to be calculated, then a formula for a cube is used. For complex shapes, it would be difficult to calculate volumes for each shape because the programmer would have to know the shape of the part in advance in order to use the appropriate formula. The advantage of using a solid model is that the volume of any complex shape can be calculated by dividing one face of the solid into a rectangular grid and tracing the rectangles back through the solid until they reach the back edge of the model.

Furthermore, solid modeling enables us to set up an entire manufacturing process that can be simulated for real-time interference monitoring. Numerically controlled programs in combination with solid modeling can play a major role in optimizing the machining processes. This, in turn, increases the quality of products.

The finite-element method is applicable in several types of analyses. The most common is static analysis, which solves for deflections, strains, and stresses in a structure under a constant set of applied loads. Wireframe models were used for creating a geometry and carrying out analysis on it. Recent trends in FEA include a detailed stress analysis on a solid model rather than on a wireframe model. This new technology has been developed by PDA, wherein the use of a solid model is done to carry out the analysis.

PROBLEMS

5.1 (a) Create drawings showing the effect of Boolean operations on the models given by Figures P5.1(a) and P5.1(b).

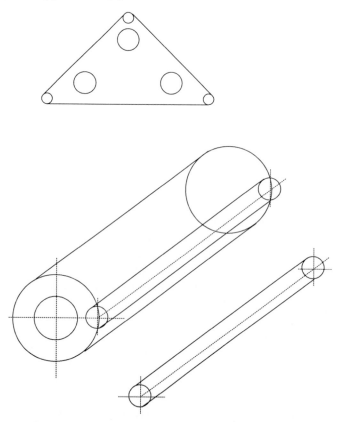

Figure P5.1   (a) Triangular model, (b) Cylindrical model.

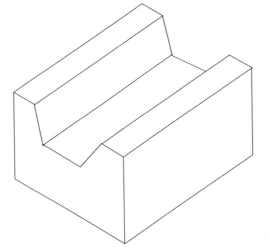

Figure P5.2   A solid model.

(**b**) Using your computer workstation, recreate the sketches made in answering part (a).

5.2 (**a**) Following the procedures outlined in Sec. 5.2.2, show the effect of sweeping on the mechanical model shown in Figure P5.2 along the *x* and *y* directions.

(**b**) Create the final part determined in the first half of this problem by using a CAD system.

5.3 Making use of a graphical representation, show the effect of chambering and filleting on the model shown in Figure P5.2.

5.4 (**a**) Using boundary representation, construct the bevel gear assembly shown in Figure P5.3.

(**b**) Given the bit brace shown in Figure P5.4, use boundary representation to create the part.

(**c**) Make a 3D drawing of the gear assembly and brace using your CAD system.

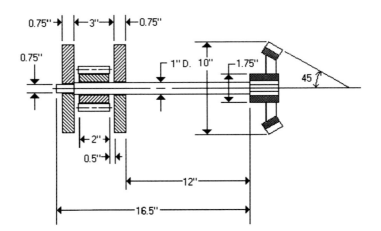

Figure P5.3   Bevel gear assembly.

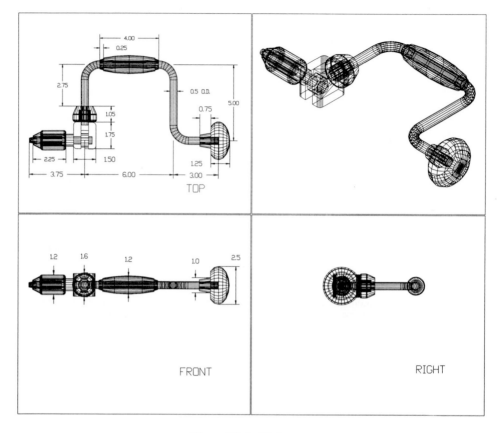

Figure P5.4   Bit brace.

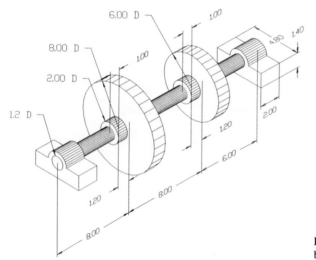

Figure P5.5   Shaft and bearing assembly.

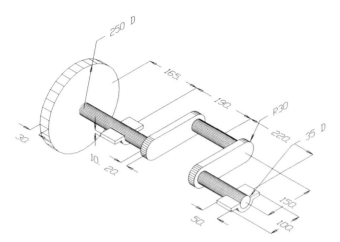

Figure P5.6 Flywheel and crankshaft assembly.

5.5 (a) Figure P5.5a illustrates the shaft mounted on bearings *A* and *D*, with pulleys attached at points *B* and *C*. Construct this assembly using C-REP.

(b) Figure P5.6 illustrates the crankshaft and flywheel assembly for a one-cylinder compressor. Using C-REP, create the system.

(c) Create the final part determined in parts (a) and (b) using your CAD system.

REFERENCES

5.1 Allen, G., An Introduction to Solid Modeling, *Computer Graphics World*, November 1982, pp. 32–36, 81–87.

5.2 Besant, C. B., and Lui, C. W. K., *Computer-Aided Design and Manufacture*, John Wiley & Sons, New York, 1986.

5.3 Faun, I. D., and Pratt, M. J., *Computational Geometry for Design and Manufacture*, Halstead Press, New York, 1979.

5.4 Meagher, D. J., A New Mathematics for Solid Processing, *Computer Graphics World*, October 1984, pp. 75–87.

5.5 Rooney, J., and Steadman, P., *Principles of Computer-Aided Design*, Pitman Publishing, London, 1987.

5.6 Sharpe, R. J., Thomas, P. J., and Thorne, R. W., Constructive Geometry in Three-Dimensions for Computer-Aided Design, *Journal of Mechanical Design*, Vol. 104, October 1982, pp. 813–816.

5.7 Teicholz, E., *Computer-Aided Design and Manufacturing Handbook*, McGraw-Hill, New York, 1985.

chapter 6

Finite-Element Method and Computer-Aided Design (CAD)

6.1 INTRODUCTION

The finite-element method (FEM), praised by many engineers as the best thing to happen since computers, is essentially a technique that discretizes a given physical or mathematical problem into smaller fundamental parts called elements. Then an analysis of the element is conducted using the required mathematics. Finally, the solution to the problem as a whole is obtained through an assembly procedure of the individual solutions of the elements. Hence, complex problems can be tackled by dividing the problem into smaller and simpler problems that can be solved by using existing mathematical tools. These finite-element techniques have been used in many fields of engineering and science. General-purpose codes have been developed, many of which are quite interactive and user-friendly to those who need not necessarily know the in-depth details of FEM. Engineering students and practicing engineers mostly use these codes.

Intricate geometries of mechanical components need huge amounts of data to describe completely the discretized finite-element model. Accuracy of data is also of prime importance, as the main processing errors would otherwise go undetected. The role of a CAD workstation is to provide the means of graphically displaying the huge data for visual inspection and quick review of the analysis. Finite-element programs have two types of data: the *input* required to run the program and the *generated output* that describes the behavior of the system under the assumed conditions. To further enhance communication between the user and the machine in which a particular finite-element program resides, many vendors of CAD software are developing pre- and postprocessors that allow the user to graphically visualize their input and output (see Figures 6.1 and 6.2). Therefore, CAD workstations equipped

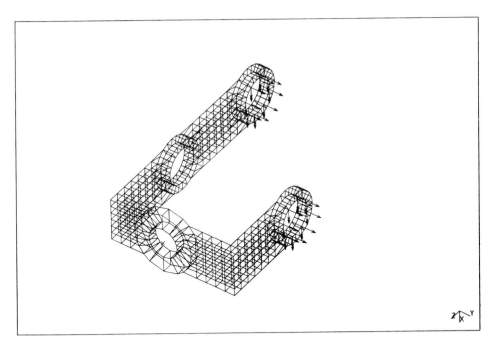

Figure 6.1 Automatic mesh generation with surfaces and solids.

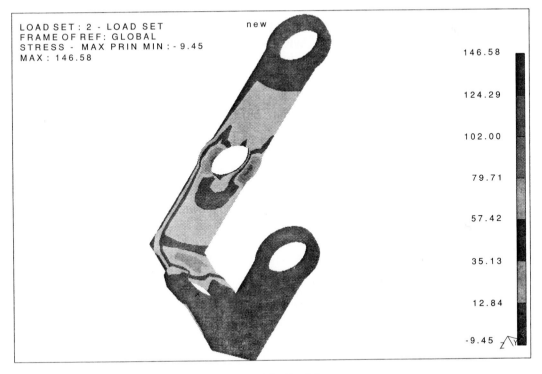

LOAD SET : 2 - LOAD SET
FRAME OF REF: GLOBAL
STRESS - MAX PRIN MIN : - 9.45
MAX : 146.58

new

146.58

124.29

102.00

79.71

57.42

35.13

12.84

-9.45

Figure 6.2 Von-Mises stress.

with such software assist the user to interact with finite-element programs, thus minimizing the time required to learn how to use the FEM program. Most importantly, the graphics capability of CAD workstations provides the user the means of visual display of huge amounts of outputs, making the interpretation faster and more convenient.

This chapter introduces the basics of the finite-element method. Step-by-step examples are provided to guide the reader through problem solving.

6.2 BASIC CONCEPTS IN THE FINITE-ELEMENT METHOD (FEM)

Consider an element of a continuum as shown in Figure 6.3. Let the element be represented by a small cube. The nodal points are defined as the end points of the edges of the cube, which are eight in this case.

All the elements are connected through the nodal points. Any deformation of the body caused by external loads or temperatures induces certain displacements at the nodes. In general, the displacements are the unknowns and are related to the external loads or temperatures through a mathematical relationship of the form

$$f^e = k^e u^e + f^e_{add} \tag{6.1}$$

where k^e (e being the element) is the local element stiffness, f^e is the external forces applied at each element, u^e represents the nodal displacements for the element, and f^e_{add} represents the additional forces. These additional forces could be a result of surface traction or of the material being initially under stress. For the moment, we will assume them to be zero. Hence, Equation (6.1) reduces to

$$f^e = k^e u^e \tag{6.2}$$

It is important at times to express this equation using the relationship between stresses and strains:

$$\sigma^e = s^e u^e \tag{6.3}$$

where σ^e is the element stress matrix, and s^e is the constitutive relationship connecting u^e and σ^e. From Equation (6.2), we can see that if f^e and k^e are known, u^e can be evaluated. Similarly, if u^e and k^e are known, we can compute f^e. The finite-element method's most basic function is to automatically generate the local stiffness

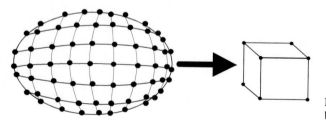

Figure 6.3 A general discretization of a body into finite elements.

matrix knowing the element type and the properties of the material of the element. Several types of elements that are available in the finite-element library are given in Figure 6.4. The well-known general-purpose FEM packages like NASTRAN and ANSYS each provide an element library. These codes and others can select any of these elements with the proper number of nodes. Also, the nodal loads can be specified at various nodes based on the boundary conditions. By using the options of the pre- and postprocessor offered by the FEM code, a CAD workstation with graphical capabilities can visualize the graphical display of the discretized components before executing the main FEM process. Thus, it is important at this stage to understand the basic mathematics involved in finite-element formulations.

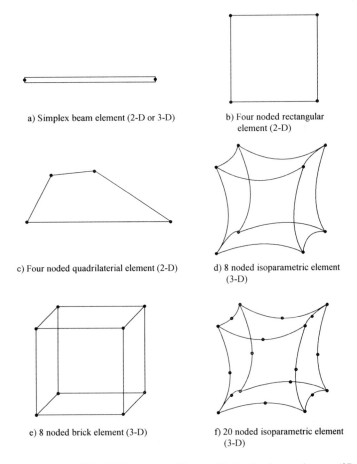

a) Simplex beam element (2-D or 3-D)

b) Four noded rectangular element (2-D)

c) Four noded quadrilaterial element (2-D)

d) 8 noded isoparametric element (3-D)

e) 8 noded brick element (3-D)

f) 20 noded isoparametric element (3-D)

Figure 6.4   A simplified finite-element library: (a) simplex beam element (2D or 3D), (b) four-node rectangular element (2D), (c) four-node quadrilateral element (2D), (d) eight-node isoparametric element (2D), (e) eight-node brick element (3D), and (f) 20-node isoparametric element (3D).

6.3 FEM AND CAD APPLICATIONS

In FEM, the structure is discretized into a number of elements forming what is known as a "mesh." Using CAD graphical capabilities, one can generate the complete mesh interactively through the use of a preprocessor designed to prepare the input for the existing FEM programs. At times, it is required to utilize different types of elements in order to suit the geometry of the component, which in many cases is irregular.

Depending on the geometry of the component under analysis, the number of elements ranges from a few to a very large number. A complicated geometry using a large number of elements increases the nodal degrees of freedom quite rapidly, easily going up to a couple of thousand in certain cases. As discussed earlier, the assembled global stiffness matrix would have to be multiplied by the nodal displacement vector, subsequently resulting in thousands of linear simultaneous equations, whose solution can only be carried out by mainframe and supercomputers.

A savings in execution time can be achieved through the development of efficient algorithms and experience with FEM codes. As a general rule, the areas of stress concentration or stress raisers should be discretized with finer meshes for detailed analysis of that region. For example, if two connected pipes (Figure. 6.5) are being studied, then the area near the joint will have to be discretized with finer

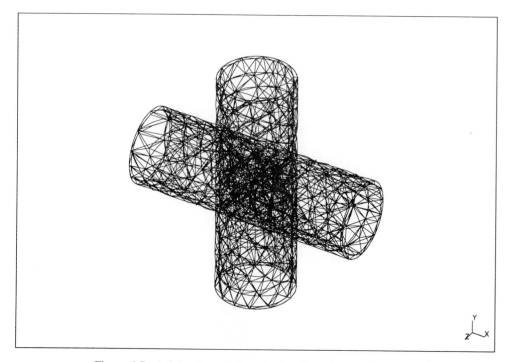

Figure 6.5 A finite-element discretization of two intersecting pipes.

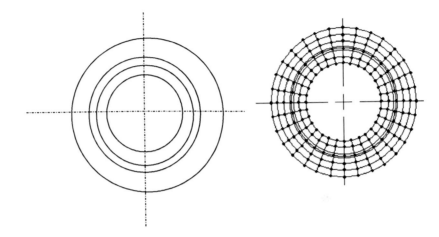

Figure 6.6   A wireframe and finite-element representation of a hole in a cylindrical plate.

meshes to understand the stress distribution in that location. Or consider a hole inside some component (Figure 6.6), which requires a similar detailed mesh around the hole because of the stress concentration.

There is no hard or fast rule in selecting the appropriate number of elements when using FEM. It is purely judgment to arrive at the right number of elements that will give the approximate results in the desired range of accuracy. However, accuracy is best achieved by learning through simulation of examples that have analytical solutions.

The FEM technique is introduced in the next sections through the study of a simple structure like a truss by performing its force and stress analyses.

6.4 TRUSS ANALYSIS USING THE FINITE-ELEMENT METHOD

Trusses are typical structures in which the finite-element method can be best illustrated. We know that FEM relies on (a) discretizing the finite element of the system, (b) developing the mathematical relationships between the forces and displacements, stresses and strains, etc., for a given element, and (c) formulating the general problem through an assembly procedure of all the elements to solve the given problem. The steps for the truss application follow.

6.4.1 Local Stiffness Matrix

Consider an element of an arbitrary truss, as shown in Figure 6.7. It is subjected to either tension or compression, as is the case for all the truss elements. Let us label the element's ends 1 and 2, and, consequently, call the corresponding forces f_1 and f_2.

Figure 6.7 One-dimensional truss element subject to tension.

We also know from static analysis that for the element to be in a state of equilibrium, then

$$f_1 + f_2 = 0 \tag{6.4}$$

which simply says that the forces at both ends are equal and opposite in direction. This is true for both tension and compression of the element. Using Hooke's law, we can write the force displacement relation as

$$u = f_{1,2}\frac{L}{AE} \tag{6.5}$$

or

$$f_{1,2} = ku \tag{6.6}$$

where $k = AE/L$ is the stiffness constant when the element is under tension or compression. Note that $f_{1,2}$ denotes either f_1 or f_2. The relative displacement between the nodal points of this truss element can be written as

$$u = u_2 - u_1 \tag{6.7}$$

where u_1 and u_2 are the displacements at ends 1 and 2, respectively. We also refer to ends 1 and 2 as nodes 1 and 2 of the truss element.

Using Equation (6.6), we can write

$$f_1 = ku_1 - ku_2 \tag{6.8}$$

and

$$f_2 = -ku_1 + ku_2 \tag{6.9}$$

Using matrix notation, we write Equations (6.8) and (6.9) in combined form as

$$\begin{bmatrix} f_1 \\ f_2 \end{bmatrix} = \begin{bmatrix} k & -k \\ -k & k \end{bmatrix}\begin{bmatrix} u_1 \\ u_2 \end{bmatrix} \tag{6.10}$$

or simply

$$\{\mathbf{f}\} = [\mathbf{k}]\{\mathbf{u}\} \tag{6.11}$$

where

$$\{\mathbf{f}\} = \begin{Bmatrix} f_1 \\ f_2 \end{Bmatrix} = \text{the nodal force vector for the element}$$

$$\{\mathbf{u}\} = \begin{Bmatrix} u_1 \\ u_2 \end{Bmatrix} = \text{the nodal displacement vector}$$

and

$$[\mathbf{k}] = \begin{bmatrix} k & -k \\ -k & k \end{bmatrix} = \text{the element stiffness matrix}$$

Thus, Equation (6.11) shows that the nodal displacements and nodal forces are related by the element (local) stiffness matrix. As the orientation and loadings of various elements in the structure (a truss in this case) vary from each other, we need to develop the local stiffness that will apply to any element orientation.

In the sequel, a more general local stiffness (2D) will be developed. A uniform system for symbol notation will be adopted that is crucial for easy reading and understanding and subsequent computer implementation.

Let us consider an orientation of a truss element, as shown in Figure 6.8. For $\Theta = 0$, we developed a relationship between the forces and the displacements given by Equation (6.10), where $\mathbf{v}$ is a unit vector along the line of action of the forces.

Because we have to express all forces (tension or compression) in the global axes (x, y) given by the fixed frame R, we define the following:

$$\begin{aligned} f_{1x} &= f_1 \cos \Theta \\ f_{1y} &= f_1 \sin \Theta \end{aligned} \tag{6.12}$$

$$\begin{aligned} f_{2x} &= f_2 \cos \Theta \\ f_{2y} &= f_2 \sin \Theta \end{aligned} \tag{6.13}$$

Given that the relative displacement u is along the unit vector $\bar{\mathbf{v}}$, then

$$u = (\bar{u}_2 - \bar{u}_1) \cdot \bar{\mathbf{v}} \tag{6.14}$$

where

$$\bar{\mathbf{v}} = (\cos \Theta)\mathbf{i} + (\sin \Theta)\mathbf{j} \tag{6.15}$$

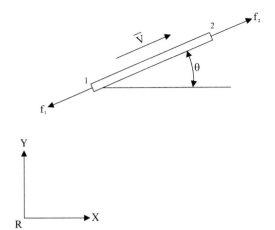

Figure 6.8 Arbitrary orientation of a truss element in tension.

and

$$\bar{u}_1 = u_{1x}\mathbf{i} + u_{1y}\mathbf{j}$$
$$\bar{u}_2 = u_{2x}\mathbf{i} + u_{2y}\mathbf{j}$$

$$(6.16)$$

then by substitution of Equations (6.16) and (6.15) into Equation (6.14) and making use of Equations (6.6), (6.12), and (6.13), we obtain

$$f_{1x} = (k \cos^2 \Theta)u_{1x} + (k \sin \Theta \cos \Theta)u_{1y} - (k \cos^2 \Theta)u_{2x}$$
$$- (k \sin \Theta \cos \Theta)u_{2y}$$

$$(6.17)$$

$$f_{1y} = (k \sin \Theta \cos \Theta)u_{1x} + (k \sin^2 \Theta)u_{1y}$$
$$- (k \sin \Theta \cos \Theta)u_{2x} - (k \sin^2 \Theta)u_{2y}$$

$$(6.18)$$

$$f_{2x} = (-k \cos^2 \Theta)u_{1x} - (k \sin \Theta \cos \Theta)u_{1y} + (k \cos^2 \Theta)u_{2x}$$
$$+ (k \sin \Theta \cos \Theta)u_{2y}$$

$$(6.19)$$

$$f_{2y} = (k \sin \Theta \cos \Theta)u_{2x} - (k \sin^2 \Theta)u_{2y}$$
$$+ (k \sin \Theta \cos \Theta)u_{2x} + (k \sin^2 \Theta)u_{2y}$$

$$(6.20)$$

Writing Equations (6.17) through (6.20) in matrix form yields

$$\begin{bmatrix} f_{1x} \\ f_{1y} \\ f_{2x} \\ f_{2y} \end{bmatrix} = k \begin{bmatrix} c^2 & sc & -c^2 & -sc \\ sc & s^2 & -sc & -s^2 \\ -c^2 & -sc & c^2 & sc \\ -sc & -s^2 & sc & s^2 \end{bmatrix} \begin{bmatrix} u_{1x} \\ u_{1y} \\ u_{2x} \\ u_{2y} \end{bmatrix}$$

$$(6.21)$$

where s and c are abbreviations for $\sin \Theta$ and $\cos \Theta$, respectively, and k is the stiffness constant. We can write Equation (6.21) in more compact form as

$$[\mathbf{f}] = [\mathbf{k}][\mathbf{u}]$$

$$(6.22)$$

where

$$[\mathbf{f}] = \begin{bmatrix} f_{1x} \\ f_{1y} \\ f_{2x} \\ f_{2y} \end{bmatrix} \quad \text{and} \quad [\mathbf{u}] = \begin{bmatrix} u_{1x} \\ u_{1y} \\ u_{2x} \\ u_{2y} \end{bmatrix}$$

$$(6.23)$$

and

$$[\mathbf{k}] = \frac{AE}{L} \begin{bmatrix} c^2 & sc & -c^2 & -sc \\ sc & s^2 & -sc & -s^2 \\ -c^2 & -sc & c^2 & sc \\ -sc & -s^2 & sc & s^2 \end{bmatrix}$$

$$(6.24)$$

For $\Theta = 0$, the truss element reduces to the one shown in Figure 6.7 and the local stiffness matrix is simply

$$[\mathbf{k}] = \frac{AE}{L} \begin{bmatrix} 1 & 0 & -1 & 0 \\ 0 & 0 & 0 & 0 \\ -1 & 0 & 1 & 0 \\ 0 & 0 & 0 & 0 \end{bmatrix} \qquad (6.25)$$

which checks with Equation (6.11). Note how the zero rows and columns are simply used to expand the local stiffness matrix given by Equation (6.11) to account for the zero forces and displacements along the y axis.

6.4.2 Properties of the Local Stiffness Matrix

First, we observe that the local stiffness matrix is symmetric and that its coefficients are functions of $\cos \Theta$ and $\sin \Theta$. In addition, let the local stiffness be partitioned as follows:

$$[\mathbf{k}] = \begin{bmatrix} c^2 & sc & -c^2 & -sc \\ sc & s^2 & -sc & -s^2 \\ -c^2 & -sc & c^2 & sc \\ -sc & -s^2 & sc & s^2 \end{bmatrix} = \begin{bmatrix} ① & ② \\ ③ & ④ \end{bmatrix} \qquad (6.25a)$$

where we can see that the partitioned matrices 1, 2, 3, and 4 are such that

$$① = ④$$
$$② = ③ \qquad (6.25b)$$

and

$$① = (-②)$$

It is evident from the partition and Equation (6.25b) that to build the local stiffness, we only need to know submatrix 1, and then submatrix 2 is obtained by premultiplying 1 by -1; 3 and 4 are then obtained from 2 and 1, respectively.

6.5 GLOBAL STIFFNESS MATRIX

The global stiffness matrix relates the global forces (external forces) and the global displacements (displacements associated with each joint). We developed the local stiffness matrix for an arbitrary element of the truss; what remains is to assemble all the local stiffness matrices associated with the truss elements. Later it will be apparent in our analysis that the efficiency of the computer program is greatly dependent on the technique developed to formulate the global stiffness matrix. The classical approach for a truss is to take a free-body diagram of each joint and, using the equilibrium equations, group all the equations together and isolate the global stiffness matrix (see Huston and Passerelo, *Finite Element Methods, an Introduction*). This approach is tedious and requires a large computational effort from the computer. The method that is illustrated in what follows to obtain the global stiffness matrix is one that Huston and Passerelo developed. It shows how the building of the global stiffness matrix can be done by a simple strategy in which connectivity tables are used to identify the truss elements and their joints. The method is as follows.

Step 1.   Consider an arbitrary truss, as shown in Figure 6.9. First, label the truss elements and joints in an arbitrary fashion, as shown in Figure 6.10. There are five joints (1, 2, . . . , 5) and seven elements ([1], [2], . . . , [7]).

Step 2.   We proceed to develop three tables that basically store geometrical information about the truss. Table 6.1 has the truss-joint/matrix-column matching, where the column numbers are developed by pairs starting from 1, 2.

Table 6.2 identifies the connecting joints to all the elements of the truss.

Using Tables 6.1 and 6.2, we construct Table 6.3, which will be used to assemble the global matrix.

To show how Table 6.3 is constructed, consider truss element 1. From Table 6.2, we read the connecting joints to element 1, which are 1 and 2; with these joint numbers, we use Table 6.1 to extract the corresponding column numbers, which are 1, 2 and 3, 4. Therefore, in Table 6.3 number 1 (referring to the element number),

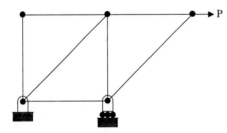

Figure 6.9   A two-dimensional truss.

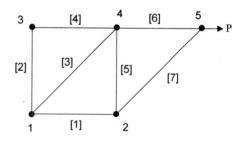

Figure 6.10   Labeling of joints and elements for a 2D truss.

TABLE 6.1   TRUSS-JOINT/MATRIX-COLUMN MATRIX

Joint	Column numbers	
1	1	2
2	3	4
3	5	6
4	7	8
5	9	10

TABLE 6.2   ELEMENTS VS. JOINT NUMBERS

	Joint numbers	
Truss element e	N_1	N_2
1	1	2
2	1	3
3	1	4
4	3	4
5	2	5
6	4	5
7	2	4

TABLE 6.3   TRUSS ELEMENTS VS. k_{ij}

i, j from k_{ij}^e	Truss elements, e						
	1	2	3	4	5	6	7
1	1	1	1	5	3	7	3
2	2	2	2	6	4	8	4
3	3	5	7	7	9	9	7
4	4	6	8	8	10	10	8

we insert the values 1, 2, 3, and 4, as shown. We repeat the procedure for the remaining elements 2 to 7. Table 6.3 plays an important role in identifying the location where the local stiffness matrix terms will be inserted in the global matrix.

For the whole truss system, we write the equation relating the global forces and displacements:

$$\{F\} = [K]\{U\} \tag{6.26}$$

where

$$\{F\} = \begin{bmatrix} F_{1x} \\ F_{1y} \\ F_{2x} \\ F_{2y} \\ F_{3x} \\ F_{3y} \\ F_{4x} \\ F_{4y} \\ F_{5x} \\ F_{5y} \end{bmatrix} \quad \text{and} \quad \{U\} = \begin{bmatrix} U_{1x} \\ U_{1y} \\ U_{2x} \\ U_{2y} \\ U_{3x} \\ U_{3y} \\ U_{4x} \\ U_{4y} \\ U_{5x} \\ U_{5y} \end{bmatrix} \tag{6.27}$$

and

$$[K] = \begin{bmatrix} K_{1,1} & K_{1,2} & K_{1,3} & \cdots & K_{1,10} \\ K_{2,1} & K_{2,2} & K_{2,3} & \cdots & K_{2,10} \\ \vdots & \vdots & \vdots & \vdots & \vdots \\ K_{10,1} & K_{10,2} & K_{10,3} & \cdots & K_{10,10} \end{bmatrix} \tag{6.28}$$

Note that the size of the global stiffness matrix $[K]$ is 10 by 10. This is equal to the number of nodal points (joints in this case) in the truss multiplied by the degrees of freedom permitted at each node (2 for the planar truss shown).

Thus, the $[K]$ in Equation (6.28) is the assembled global stiffness matrix obtained from the assembly of individual element stiffness matrices, that is,

$$f_i^e = k_{ij}^e u_j \qquad (e = 1, \ldots, \text{number of elements}; \ i, j = 1, 4) \tag{6.29}$$

where k_{ij}^e is the local element stiffness matrix and is given by Equation (6.24).

For $\Theta = 0$, k_{ij}^1 is given by Equation (6.25).

For $\Theta = 90$, k_{ij}^2 is

$$k_{ij}^2 = \frac{AE}{L} \begin{bmatrix} 0 & 0 & 0 & 0 \\ 0 & 1 & 0 & -1 \\ 0 & 0 & 0 & 0 \\ 0 & -1 & 0 & 1 \end{bmatrix} \tag{6.30}$$

In order to construct the global stiffness matrix, first evaluate all the local element stiffness matrices. Then Table 6.3 is used to transfer the terms from the local stiffness matrices to the locations in the global stiffness matrix.

For example, consider element 1 from Table 6.3. The element column identifies the location in the global stiffness matrix of its local stiffness. The variation by pair of the column numbers identifies the i, j entries of the local stiffness matrix in the global stiffness matrix, K_{ij}. For example, the column numbers for element 1 basically correspond to the column and row numbers in the global stiffness matrix. The elements of the local stiffness matrix for element 1 when transferred to the location in the assembled global stiffness matrix looks like

$$\mathbf{K}^1 = \begin{bmatrix} k_{11}^1 & k_{12}^1 & k_{13}^1 & k_{14}^1 & 0 & 0 & 0 & 0 & 0 & 0 \\ k_{21}^1 & k_{22}^1 & k_{23}^1 & k_{24}^1 & 0 & 0 & 0 & 0 & 0 & 0 \\ k_{31}^1 & k_{32}^1 & k_{33}^1 & k_{34}^1 & 0 & 0 & 0 & 0 & 0 & 0 \\ k_{41}^1 & k_{42}^1 & k_{43}^1 & k_{44}^1 & 0 & 0 & 0 & 0 & 0 & 0 \\ 5 & 0 & 0 & 0 & 0 & 0 & 0 & 0 & 0 & 0 \\ 0 & 0 & 0 & 0 & 0 & 0 & 0 & 0 & 0 & 0 \\ 0 & 0 & 0 & 0 & 0 & 0 & 0 & 0 & 0 & 0 \\ 0 & 0 & 0 & 0 & 0 & 0 & 0 & 0 & 0 & 0 \\ 0 & 0 & 0 & 0 & 0 & 0 & 0 & 0 & 0 & 0 \\ 0 & 0 & 0 & 0 & 0 & 0 & 0 & 0 & 0 & 0 \end{bmatrix} \tag{6.31}$$

For element 2, we read the row and column entries, which are 1, 2, 5, and 6, from Table 6.3. Hence, its contribution to the global stiffness is given by

$$K^2 = \begin{bmatrix} k_{11}^2 & k_{12}^2 & 0 & 0 & k_{13}^2 & k_{14}^2 & 0 & 0 & 0 & 0 \\ k_{21}^2 & k_{22}^2 & 0 & 0 & k_{23}^2 & k_{24}^2 & 0 & 0 & 0 & 0 \\ 0 & 0 & 0 & 0 & 0 & 0 & 0 & 0 & 0 & 0 \\ 0 & 0 & 0 & 0 & 0 & 0 & 0 & 0 & 0 & 0 \\ k_{31}^2 & k_{32}^2 & 0 & 0 & k_{33}^2 & k_{34}^2 & 0 & 0 & 0 & 0 \\ k_{41}^2 & k_{42}^2 & 0 & 0 & k_{43}^2 & k_{44}^2 & 0 & 0 & 0 & 0 \\ 0 & 0 & 0 & 0 & 0 & 0 & 0 & 0 & 0 & 0 \\ 0 & 0 & 0 & 0 & 0 & 0 & 0 & 0 & 0 & 0 \\ 0 & 0 & 0 & 0 & 0 & 0 & 0 & 0 & 0 & 0 \\ 0 & 0 & 0 & 0 & 0 & 0 & 0 & 0 & 0 & 0 \end{bmatrix} \tag{6.32}$$

For element 7, we get

$$K^7 = \begin{bmatrix} 0 & 0 & 0 & 0 & 0 & 0 & 0 & 0 & 0 & 0 \\ 0 & 0 & 0 & 0 & 0 & 0 & 0 & 0 & 0 & 0 \\ 0 & 0 & k^7_{11} & k^7_{14} & 0 & 0 & k^7_{13} & k^7_{14} & 0 & 0 \\ 0 & 0 & k^7_{21} & k^7_{22} & 0 & 0 & k^7_{23} & k^7_{24} & 0 & 0 \\ 0 & 0 & 0 & 0 & 0 & 0 & 0 & 0 & 0 & 0 \\ 0 & 0 & 0 & 0 & 0 & 0 & 0 & 0 & 0 & 0 \\ 0 & 0 & k^7_{31} & k^7_{32} & 0 & 0 & k^7_{33} & k^7_{34} & 0 & 0 \\ 0 & 0 & k^7_{41} & k^7_{42} & 0 & 0 & k^8_{43} & k^7_{44} & 0 & 0 \\ 0 & 0 & 0 & 0 & 0 & 0 & 0 & 0 & 0 & 0 \\ 0 & 0 & 0 & 0 & 0 & 0 & 0 & 0 & 0 & 0 \end{bmatrix} \qquad (6.33)$$

Once all the elements are completed and their local stiffness matrices are inserted into the global stiffness matrix K, the general global matrix of the system is then obtained by adding all the entries in different locations if they are more than one.

$$K_{ij} = K^1_{ij} + K^2_{ij} + K^3_{ij} + \cdots K^7_{ij} \qquad (6.34)$$

The global stiffness is found to be

	1	2	3	4	5	6	7	8	9	10
1	$k^1_{11} + k^2_{11}$ $+ k^3_{11}$	$k^1_{12} + k^2_{12}$ $+ k^3_{12}$	k^1_{13}	k^1_{14}	k^2_{13}	k^2_{14}	k^3_{13}	k^3_{14}	0	0
2	$k^1_{21} + k^2_{21}$ $+ k^3_{21}$	$k^1_{22} + k^2_{22}$ $+ k^3_{22}$	k^1_{23}	k^1_{24}	k^2_{23}	k^2_{24}	k^3_{23}	k^3_{24}	0	0
3	k^1_{31}	k^1_{32}	$k^1_{33} + k^5_{11}$ $+ k^7_{11}$	$k^1_{34} + k^5_{12}$ $+ k^7_{12}$	0	0	k^7_{13}	k^7_{14}	k^5_{13}	k^5_{14}
4	k^1_{41}	k^1_{42}	$k^1_{43} + k^5_{21}$ $+ k^7_{21}$	$k^1_{44} + k^5_{22}$ $+ k^7_{22}$	0	0	k^7_{23}	k^7_{24}	k^5_{23}	k^5_{24}
5	k^2_{31}	k^2_{32}	0	0	$k^2_{33} + k^4_{11}$	$k^2_{34} + k^4_{12}$	k^4_{13}	k^4_{14}	0	0
6	k^2_{41}	k^2_{42}	0	0	$k^2_{43} + k^4_{21}$	$k^2_{44} + k^4_{22}$	k^4_{23}	k^4_{24}	0	0
7	k^3_{31}	k^3_{32}	k^7_{31}	k^7_{32}	k^4_{31}	k^4_{32}	$k^3_{33} + k^4_{33}$ $+ k^6_{11}$ $+ k^7_{33}$	$k^3_{34} + k^4_{34}$ $+ k^6_{12}$ $+ k^7_{34}$	k^6_{13}	k^6_{14}
8	k^3_{41}	k^3_{42}	k^7_{41}	k^7_{42}	k^4_{41}	k^4_{42}	$k^3_{43} + k^4_{43}$ $+ k^6_{21}$ $+ k^7_{43}$	$k^3_{44} + k^4_{44}$ $+ k^6_{22}$ $+ k^7_{44}$	k^6_{13}	k^6_{24}
9	c	0	k^5_{31}	k^5_{32}	0	0	k^6_{31}	k^6_{32}	$k^5_{33} + k^6_{33}$	$k^5_{34} + k^6_{34}$
10	0	0	k^5_{41}	k^5_{42}	0	0	k^6_{41}	k^6_{42}	$k^5_{43} + k^6_{43}$	$k^5_{44} + k^6_{44}$

$K = $

The above outlined procedure for developing the global stiffness matrix could be automated using computer coding.

6.6 SOLUTION OF THE TRUSS PROBLEM

As stated earlier, the global force and displacement vectors are related through the global stiffness matrix:

$$[\mathbf{F}] = [\mathbf{K}][\mathbf{U}] \qquad (6.35)$$

After the development of $[\mathbf{K}]$, the global stiffness matrix, the identification of boundary forces and displacements is important. These are to be substituted into the $[\mathbf{F}]$ and $[\mathbf{U}]$ vectors.

For the truss shown in Figure 6.10, the reaction forces at joint 1 in the x and y directions are R_{1x} and R_{1y}, respectively. The reaction at joint 2 is only in the y direction as it is the roller joint, that is, R_{2y}. Also, force P acts as an external force in the x direction at joint 5.

Thus,

$$
\begin{aligned}
F_{1x} &= R_{1x} \\
F_{1y} &= R_{1y} \\
F_{2y} &= R_{2y} \\
F_{5x} &= P
\end{aligned}
\qquad (6.36)
$$

Except for these, all other forces are equal to zero.

Substituting these values into force vector $[\mathbf{F}]$, we get

$$
[\mathbf{F}] =
\begin{bmatrix}
R_{1x} \\
R_{1y} \\
0 \\
R_{2y} \\
0 \\
0 \\
0 \\
0 \\
P \\
0
\end{bmatrix}
\qquad (6.37)
$$

Similarly, the displacement boundary condition can be identified, where

$$
\begin{aligned}
U_{1x} &= 0 \\
U_{1y} &= 0 \\
U_{2y} &= 0
\end{aligned}
\qquad (6.38)
$$

All others are nonzero. Substituting into displacement vector [**U**], we get

$$[\mathbf{U}] = \begin{bmatrix} 0 \\ 0 \\ U_{2x} \\ 0 \\ U_{3x} \\ U_{3y} \\ U_{4x} \\ U_{4y} \\ U_{5x} \\ U_{5y} \end{bmatrix} \tag{6.39}$$

Substituting [**F**] and [**U**] from Equations (6.37) and (6.39) into Equation (6.26), we obtain

$$\begin{bmatrix} R_{1x} \\ R_{1y} \\ 0 \\ R_{2y} \\ 0 \\ 0 \\ 0 \\ 0 \\ P \\ 0 \end{bmatrix} = \begin{bmatrix} K_{11} & K_{12} & \cdots & K_{1,10} \\ K_{21} & K_{22} & \cdots & K_{2,10} \\ \vdots & \vdots & & \\ \vdots & \vdots & & \\ \vdots & \vdots & & \\ \vdots & \vdots & & \\ \vdots & \vdots & & \\ \vdots & \vdots & & \\ \vdots & \vdots & & \\ K_{10,1} & K_{10,2} & \cdots & K_{10,10} \end{bmatrix} \begin{bmatrix} 0 \\ 0 \\ U_{2x} \\ 0 \\ U_{3x} \\ U_{3y} \\ U_{4x} \\ U_{4y} \\ U_{5x} \\ U_{5y} \end{bmatrix} \tag{6.40}$$

   Note how in Equation (6.40) the unknowns are in the global force array as well as in the joint displacement vector. A typical strategy to solve such a problem in which the unknowns are on both sides of the equation is to solve for the U's first by partitioning the matrices such that the force vector is completely in terms of the known forces. The partitioning is done by eliminating the first, second, and fourth rows and columns, ultimately eliminating the reaction forces. The resulting equation is

$$
\begin{bmatrix} 0 \\ 0 \\ 0 \\ 0 \\ 0 \\ P \\ 0 \end{bmatrix} = [\mathbf{K'}] \begin{bmatrix} U_{2x} \\ U_{3x} \\ U_{3y} \\ U_{4x} \\ U_{4y} \\ U_{5x} \\ U_{5y} \end{bmatrix} \tag{6.41}
$$

where $[\mathbf{K'}]$ is the new stiffness matrix resulting from the global stiffness after eliminating the rows and columns corresponding to the zero displacements. Equation (6.41) constitutes a set of seven equations and seven unknowns, which can be solved using the Gaussian elimination method, Cramer's rule (see Appendix A), or simply the inverse of $[\mathbf{K'}]$ as

$$
\begin{bmatrix} U_{2x} \\ U_{3x} \\ U_{3y} \\ U_{4x} \\ U_{4y} \\ U_{5x} \\ U_{5y} \end{bmatrix} = [\mathbf{K'}]^{-1} \begin{bmatrix} 0 \\ 0 \\ 0 \\ 0 \\ 0 \\ P \\ 0 \end{bmatrix} \tag{6.42}
$$

Once the equations are solved for the displacements, reactions R_{1x}, R_{1y}, and R_{2y} can be evaluated by premultiplying the corresponding terms of $[\mathbf{K}]$ and $[\mathbf{U}]$ in Equation (6.40). The solutions are

$$
R_{1x} = -P
$$

$$
R_{1y} = -\frac{Pb}{a} \tag{6.43}
$$

$$
R_{2y} = \frac{Pb}{a}
$$

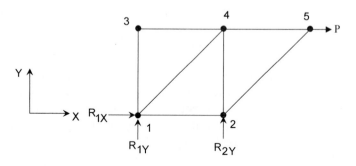

Figure 6.11 A simple freebody diagram of a 2D truss subject to loading.

The answers obtained from the FEM analysis as described before can be checked by simply taking the free-body diagram for the truss as shown in Figure 6.11.

Writing the equilibrium equations

$$\sum F_x = 0 \qquad \sum F_y = 0 \qquad \sum M = 0 \qquad (6.44a)$$

we get

$$\sum F_x = R_{1x} + P = 0 \Rightarrow R_{1x} = -P$$

$$\sum F_y = R_{1y} + R_{2y} = 0 \Rightarrow R_{1y} = -R_{2y} \qquad (6.44b)$$

$$\sum M_0 = R_{2y}a - Pb = 0 \Rightarrow R_{2y} = \frac{Pb}{a}$$

which checks with the FEM solution.

6.7 EVALUATION OF THE LOCAL FORCES

The internal forces are those that are either compressing or putting the truss elements in tension. To find the components of the forces acting at each end, we use the previously computed global displacements and local stiffness matrix.

From Equation (6.21), we have

$$\begin{bmatrix} f^e_{1x} \\ f^e_{1y} \\ f^e_{2x} \\ f^e_{2y} \end{bmatrix} = \frac{AE}{1} \begin{bmatrix} c^2_e & s_e c_e & -c^2_e & -s_e c_e \\ s_e c_e & s^2_e & -s_e c_e & -s^2_e \\ -c^2_e & -s_e c_e & c^2_e & s_e c_e \\ -s_e c_e & -s^2_e & s_e c_e & s^2_e \end{bmatrix} \begin{bmatrix} u^e_{1x} \\ u^e_{1y} \\ u^e_{2x} \\ u^e_{2y} \end{bmatrix} \qquad (6.45)$$

The stiffness matrix in this equation (for the particular element at hand) is known. The nodal displacements are also known from the global displacement vector as explained in what follows.

Let the local displacement be written as u^e_{ij}, where e is the element number of the truss, i denotes either end 1 or end 2 of the element, and j assigns the direction x or y to the end displacements. Assuming that all elements of the truss undergo the same displacement at each joint, we then write the following.

For joint 1:

$$U_{1x} = u^1_{1x} = u^2_{1x} = u^3_{1x}$$
$$U_{1y} = u^1_{1y} = u^2_{1y} = u^3_{1y} \qquad (6.46)$$

For joint 2:

$$U_{2x} = u_{2x}^1 = u_{1x}^5 = u_{1x}^7$$
$$U_{2y} = u_{2y}^1 = u_{1y}^5 = u_{1y}^7 \tag{6.47}$$

For joint 3:

$$U_{3x} = u_{2x}^2 = u_{1x}^4$$
$$U_{3y} = u_{2y}^2 = u_{1y}^4 \tag{6.48}$$

For joint 4:

$$U_{4x} = u_{2x}^3 = u_{2x}^4 = u_{1x}^6 = u_{2x}^7$$
$$U_{4y} = u_{2y}^3 = u_{2y}^4 = u_{1y}^6 = u_{2x}^7 \tag{6.49}$$

For joint 5:

$$U_{5x} = u_{2x}^5 = u_{2x}^6$$
$$U_{5y} = u_{2y}^5 = u_{2y}^6 \tag{6.50}$$

The nodal displacements for any particular element can be found from the relationships between the global displacements and the local displacement by using Equations (6.46) to (6.50). Subsequent substitution of these values for a particular element in Equation (6.45) and multiplying by the corresponding stiffness matrix terms yield the nodal forces. The signs of these forces indicate whether the member is in tension or compression.

A complete program based on the previously outlined finite-element procedure for 2D trusses is given in Appendix B. The reader is urged to use it to analyze a variety of trusses. The program is written to highlight the simplicity of the method discussed in solving 2D finite-element trusses. Therefore, it is limited to determined trusses, with concentrated forces acting at the joints. Indeed, it can easily be extended to handle concentrated loads and inclined supports. These could serve as projects to readers with advance knowledge of truss analysis.

Example 6.1   Analysis of a Three-Element Truss

Use the finite-element method to solve for the truss shown in Figure 6.12.

(a) Find the global stiffness matrix.
(b) Solve for the reaction forces.
(c) Solve for the member forces and determine whether a truss element is in tension or compression.

Solution   The first step in our analysis is to label the truss for the joint numbers and link numbers, as shown in the figure. The second step is to compute the local stiffness matrices for each member using Equation (6.45), which gives

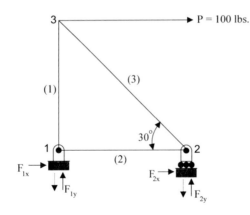

Figure 6.12   A three-element truss subject to loading.

$$[\mathbf{k}_{ij}^1] = \frac{A_1 E}{L_1} \begin{bmatrix} 0 & 0 & 0 & 0 \\ 0 & 1 & 0 & -1 \\ 0 & 0 & 0 & 0 \\ 0 & -1 & 0 & 1 \end{bmatrix} \tag{6.51}$$

$$[\mathbf{k}_{ij}^2] = \frac{A_2 E}{L_2} \begin{bmatrix} 1 & 0 & -1 & 0 \\ 0 & 0 & 0 & 0 \\ -1 & 0 & 1 & 0 \\ 0 & 0 & 0 & 0 \end{bmatrix} \tag{6.52}$$

$$[\mathbf{k}_{ij}^3] = \frac{A_3 E}{4L_3} \begin{bmatrix} 3 & -\sqrt{3} & -3 & \sqrt{3} \\ -\sqrt{3} & 1 & \sqrt{3} & -1 \\ -3 & \sqrt{3} & 3 & -\sqrt{3} \\ \sqrt{3} & -1 & -\sqrt{3} & 1 \end{bmatrix} \tag{6.53}$$

where A_1, A_2, A_3 and L_1, L_2, L_3 are the areas of cross section and lengths of the members of the truss, respectively, and E is the Young's modulus of elasticity.

For the sake of simplicity, let us assume

$$A_1 = A_2 = A_3 = A$$

and $L_1 = l$, such that

$$L_2 = l\sqrt{3}$$

$$L_3 = 2l$$

Now let us construct Tables 6.4 to 6.6 (see earlier Tables 6.1 to 6.3) which help in arriving at the global stiffness matrix **K**.

Using the local stiffness matrices and transferring the entries with the help of Table 6.6, we can arrive at the global stiffness matrix:

TABLE 6.4 TRUSS-JOINT/MATRIX-COLUMN MATRIX

Joint number	Column numbers	
1	1	2
2	3	4
3	5	6

TABLE 6.5 ELEMENT AND JOINT CONNECTIONS

	Joint numbers	
Truss elements, e	N_1	N_2
1	1	3
2	1	2
3	2	3

TABLE 6.6 CONTRIBUTION TO **K** FROM K_{ij}^e

	Truss elements, e		
i, j from k_{ij}^e	1	2	3
1	1	1	3
2	2	2	4
3	5	3	5
4	6	4	6

$$\frac{AE}{l}\begin{bmatrix} \dfrac{1}{\sqrt{3}} & 0 & -\dfrac{1}{\sqrt{3}} & 0 & 0 & 0 \\ 0 & 1 & 0 & 0 & 0 & -1 \\ -\dfrac{1}{\sqrt{3}} & 0 & \dfrac{8+3\sqrt{3}}{8\sqrt{3}} & -\dfrac{\sqrt{3}}{8} & -\dfrac{3}{8} & \dfrac{\sqrt{3}}{8} \\ 0 & 0 & -\dfrac{\sqrt{3}}{8} & \dfrac{1}{8} & \dfrac{\sqrt{3}}{8} & -\dfrac{1}{8} \\ 0 & 0 & -\dfrac{3}{8} & \dfrac{\sqrt{3}}{8} & \dfrac{3}{8} & -\dfrac{\sqrt{3}}{8} \\ 0 & -1 & \dfrac{\sqrt{3}}{8} & -\dfrac{1}{8} & -\dfrac{\sqrt{3}}{8} & \dfrac{9}{8} \end{bmatrix}\begin{bmatrix} U_{1x} \\ U_{1y} \\ U_{2x} \\ U_{2y} \\ U_{3x} \\ U_{3y} \end{bmatrix} = \begin{bmatrix} F_{1x} \\ F_{1y} \\ 0 \\ F_{2y} \\ P \\ 0 \end{bmatrix} \qquad (6.54)$$

Zeros in the force vector indicate that the forces in the x and y directions at joints 2 and 3 are zeros because of the roller and free joint, respectively.

Applying the displacement boundary conditions, $U_{1x} = 0$, $U_{1y} = 0$, $U_{2y} = 0$, and eliminating the corresponding rows and columns, we get

$$\begin{bmatrix} 0.952 & -0.375 & 0.2165 \\ -0.375 & 0.375 & -0.2165 \\ 0.2165 & -0.2165 & 1.125 \end{bmatrix}\begin{bmatrix} U_{2x} \\ U_{3x} \\ U_{3y} \end{bmatrix} = \begin{bmatrix} 0 \\ 100 \\ 0 \end{bmatrix} \qquad (6.55)$$

Solving for the unknowns, we obtain

$$U_{2x} = 173.31 \frac{l}{AE}$$

$$U_{3x} = 473.13 \frac{l}{AE} \tag{6.56}$$

$$U_{3y} = 57.57 \frac{l}{AE}$$

The reaction forces can thus be computed using Equation (6.43) as

$$F_{1x} = \left(\frac{1}{\sqrt{3}} U_{1x} - \frac{1}{\sqrt{3}} U_{2y} \right) \frac{AE}{l} = -100.0 \text{ lb}$$

$$F_{1y} = (1 \cdot U_{1y} - 1 \cdot U_{3y}) \frac{AE}{l} = -57.57 \text{ lb} \tag{6.57}$$

$$F_{2y} = \left(-\frac{\sqrt{3}}{8} U_{2x} + \frac{\sqrt{3}}{8} U_{3x} - \frac{1}{8} U_{3y} \right) = 57.71 \text{ lb} \tag{6.57a}$$

These results can be verified using the free-body diagram of the truss (Figure 6.12):

$$\sum F_x = 0 \qquad \sum F_y = 0 \qquad \text{and} \qquad \sum M = 0$$

$\sum F_x = 0$ gives $F_{1x} + 100.0 = 0$, that is, $F_{1x} = -100.0$ lb

$$\tag{6.57b}$$

$\sum F_y = 0$ gives $F_{1y} + F_{2y} = 0$, that is, $F_{1y} = -F_{2y}$

$\sum M = 0$ gives $pl - F_{2y} \sqrt{3} \, l = 0.0$, that is, $F_{2y} = \begin{cases} +57.73 \\ -F_{1y} \end{cases}$

Therefore, members 1 and 3 are in tension, whereas member 2 is in compression.

The member forces are obtained from the local element force-displacement relationship:

$$\begin{Bmatrix} f_{1x}^e \\ f_{1y}^e \\ f_{2x}^e \\ f_{2y}^e \end{Bmatrix} = \frac{AE}{l} \begin{bmatrix} c^2 & sc & -c^2 & -sc \\ sc & s^2 & -sc & -s^2 \\ -c^2 & -sc & c^2 & sc \\ -sc & -s^2 & sc & s^2 \end{bmatrix} \begin{Bmatrix} u_{1x}^e \\ u_{1y}^e \\ u_{2x}^e \\ u_{2y}^e \end{Bmatrix} \tag{6.57c}$$

The global and local displacements at each joint are related as follows:

$$U_{1x} = u_{1x}^1 = 0$$
$$U_{1y} = u_{1y}^1 = 0$$
$$U_{3x} = u_{2x}^1$$
$$U_{3y} = u_{2y}^1$$

(6.57d)

Using the local stiffness already computed and given by Equations (6.51) to (6.53), we obtain element

$$\begin{Bmatrix} f_{1x}^1 \\ f_{1y}^1 \\ f_{2x}^1 \\ f_{2y}^1 \end{Bmatrix} = \frac{AE}{l} \begin{bmatrix} 0 & 0 & 0 & 0 \\ 0 & 1 & 0 & -1 \\ 0 & 0 & 0 & 0 \\ 0 & -1 & 0 & 1 \end{bmatrix} \begin{Bmatrix} 0 \\ 0 \\ U_{3x} \\ U_{3y} \end{Bmatrix}$$

(6.57e)

$$\Rightarrow f_{1y}^1 = -\left(\frac{AE}{l}\right) U_{3x} = -\left(\frac{AE}{l}\right) 473.3 \frac{l}{AE} = -473.3 \text{ lb}$$

$$f_{2y}^1 = \left(\frac{AE}{l}\right) U_{3y} = 473.3 \text{ lb}$$

(6.57f)

The forces acting on element 1 clearly show that it is in tension as predicted. Similarly, we can obtain the magnitude of the forces and their directions for elements 2 and 3.

$$F_{1x} = F_{2x} = 0 \qquad \blacksquare$$

6.8 HEAT CONDUCTION ANALYSIS AND FEM

Now we apply the finite-element method to the solution of heat flow in some simple one-dimensional steady-state heat conduction systems. Several physical shapes fall into the one-dimensional analysis such as spherical and cylindrical systems in which the temperature of the body is a function only of radial distance. Consider the straight bar of Figure 6.13(a). Heat flows across the end surfaces. Heat is also assumed to be generated internally by a heat source at a rate f per unit volume. The

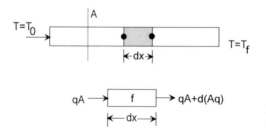

Figure 6.13 A bar with constant cross section (a typical element is shown).

temperature varies only with x, and we suppose to formulate a finite-element technique that would yield the temperature $T = T(x)$ in the steady-state condition.

In steady-state conditions, the net rate of heat flow into any differential element is zero. We know that for heat conduction analysis, the Fourier heat conduction equation is

$$q = -\mathrm{K}\frac{dT}{dx} \tag{6.58}$$

This equation states that the heat flux q in direction x is proportional to the gradient of temperature in direction x. The conductivity constant is K.

From the differential element in Fig. 6.13(b), we can write the heat flux balance:

$$qA + fA\, dx - [qA + d(Aq)] = 0 \tag{6.59}$$

or simply

$$qA + fA\, dx - \left[qA + \frac{dq}{dx}\, dx\, A \right] = 0 \tag{6.60}$$

which reduces to

$$\frac{dq}{dx} = f \tag{6.61}$$

Substituting Equation (6.58) into Equation (6.61), we get the governing differential equation for the temperature:

$$\kappa \frac{d^2T}{dx^2} = -f \tag{6.62}$$

The boundary conditions are

$$T = T_0 \text{ at } x = 0 \qquad \text{and} \qquad T = T_f \text{ at } x = L$$

6.8.1 Finite-Element Formulation

We first develop the following functional I as

$$I = \int \left[\kappa A \frac{d^2T}{dx^2} + fA \right] T\, dx \tag{6.63}$$

which yields Equation (6.62) for $dI = 0$ using the standard manipulation of calculus of variations. Equation (6.63) could be expressed further in two parts, I_1 and I_2, as

$$I = \int \underbrace{\frac{d}{dx}\left[A\kappa \frac{dT}{dx} \right] T\, dx}_{I_1} + \int \underbrace{fAT\, dx}_{I_2} \tag{6.64}$$

Integrating I_1 by parts, we get

$$I_1 = TA\kappa \frac{dT}{dx}\bigg|_0^L - \int_0^L \frac{dT}{dx} A\kappa \frac{dT}{dx} dx \tag{6.65}$$

If we assume that the boundary conditions are such that $T(0) = T(L) = 0$, then the functional I becomes

$$I = -\int \frac{dT}{dx} A\kappa \frac{dT}{dx} dx + \int fAT \, dx \tag{6.66}$$

We have an expression for I ready to use if $T = T(x)$ has an explicit form that can be substituted into the equation so that we can carry on the integration.

Next, consider the functional I_e for an element rather than for the structure:

$$I_e = -\int_{x_1}^{x_2} \frac{dT}{dx} A\kappa \frac{dT}{dx} dx + \int_{x_1}^{x_2} fAT \, dx \tag{6.67}$$

For that, let us find an expression for T. Assume a linear interpolation for the temperature between x_1 and x_2. A representation of the temperature in shown in Figure 6.14.

$$T = ax + b \tag{6.68}$$

At each node, we can write the temperature as

$$T_1 = ax_1 + b$$
$$T_2 = ax_2 + b \tag{6.69}$$

from which we can solve for a and b:

$$a = \frac{T_2 - T_1}{L_e} \quad \text{and} \quad b = T_1 - \frac{T_2 - T_1}{L_e}x_1 \tag{6.70}$$

where L_e denotes the length of the element. Substituting the values of a and b into Equation (6.68), we get an expression for T as

$$T = T_1 N_1 + T_2 N_2 \tag{6.71}$$

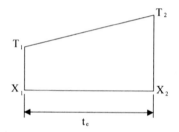

Figure 6.14 A representation of the temperature between two nodal points.

where

$$N_1 = \frac{x_2 - x}{L_e} \quad \text{and} \quad N_2 = \frac{x - x_1}{L_e} \tag{6.72}$$

The latter are known as shape functions.

In matrix form, from Equation (6.71), the temperature can be expressed as

$$T = [T_1 \quad T_2]\begin{bmatrix} N_1 \\ N_2 \end{bmatrix} \tag{6.73}$$

and its derivative takes on the following form:

$$\frac{dT}{dx} = [T_1 \quad T_2]\begin{bmatrix} \dfrac{dN_1}{dx} \\ \dfrac{dN_2}{dx} \end{bmatrix} \tag{6.74}$$

with

$$\frac{dN_1}{dx} = -\frac{1}{L_e} \quad \text{and} \quad \frac{dN_2}{dx} = \frac{1}{L_e} \tag{6.75}$$

The functional I_e then becomes

$$I_e = \int_{x_1}^{x_2} [T_1 \quad T_2]\begin{bmatrix} \dfrac{dN_1}{dx} \\ \dfrac{dN_2}{dx} \end{bmatrix} A\kappa \begin{bmatrix} \dfrac{dN_1}{dx} & \dfrac{dN_2}{dx} \end{bmatrix}\begin{bmatrix} T_1 \\ T_2 \end{bmatrix} dx$$

$$+ \int_{x_1}^{x_2} fA[T_1 \quad T_2]\begin{bmatrix} N_1 \\ N_2 \end{bmatrix} dx \tag{6.76}$$

Next, writing the steady-state condition for an element, we get

$$\left\{\frac{\partial I_e}{\partial T_e}\right\} = \{O\} \tag{6.77}$$

which yields

$$\frac{\kappa A}{L_e}\begin{bmatrix} 1 & -1 \\ -1 & 1 \end{bmatrix}\begin{bmatrix} T_1 \\ T_2 \end{bmatrix} = \frac{fAL_e}{2}\begin{bmatrix} 1 \\ 1 \end{bmatrix} \tag{6.78}$$

or simply

$$[K]\{T\} = \{F\} \tag{6.79}$$

where

$$\{\mathbf{T}\} = \begin{bmatrix} T_1 \\ T_2 \end{bmatrix} \qquad \{\mathbf{F}\} = \begin{bmatrix} \dfrac{fAL_e}{2} \\ \dfrac{fAL_e}{2} \end{bmatrix} \tag{6.80}$$

and

$$[\mathbf{k}] = \frac{\kappa A}{L_e} \begin{bmatrix} 1 & -1 \\ -1 & 1 \end{bmatrix} \tag{6.81}$$

Note how $[\mathbf{k}]$ is analogous to a local stiffness matrix (we refer to it as the conductivity matrix), how $\{\mathbf{T}\}$ is analogous to nodal displacements, and how $\{\mathbf{F}\}$ is analogous to nodal forces. With this in mind, we can use a table analogous to Table 6.3 in the analysis of trusses to develop the connectivity relations between elements. The latter will assist us in the formulation of the global stiffness matrix and the heat source array. The global problem can be stated as

$$[\mathbf{K}]\{\mathbf{T}\} = \{\mathbf{F}\} \tag{6.82}$$

where $[\mathbf{K}]$ is the global conductivity matrix (equivalent to the global stiffness), $\{\mathbf{T}\}$ the nodal temperatures, and $\{\mathbf{F}\}$ the heat source contribution. The formulation of $[\mathbf{K}]$ and $\{\mathbf{F}\}$ could be done as shown in the following example.

Example 6.2   Heat Conduction Analysis of a Two-Element Rod

Let us divide our system into two elements with three nodes, as shown in Figure 6.15. In the development of the connectivity table (Table 6.7), we list the node numbers under each element.

First, we note that the global connectivity matrix $\mathbf{K}$ is a 3×3 matrix. The contribution of the conductivity matrices for elements 1 and 2 are

$$[K_{ij}^1] = \frac{\kappa A}{L_e} \begin{bmatrix} 1 & -1 & 0 \\ -1 & 1 & 0 \\ 0 & 0 & 0 \end{bmatrix} \tag{6.83}$$

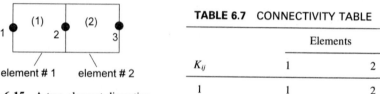

Figure 6.15 A two-element discretization of the rod.

TABLE 6.7 CONNECTIVITY TABLE

	Elements	
K_{ij}	1	2
1	1	2
2	2	3

and

$$[K_{ij}^2] = \frac{\kappa A}{L_e}\begin{bmatrix} 0 & 0 & 0 \\ 0 & 1 & -1 \\ 0 & -1 & 1 \end{bmatrix} \tag{6.84}$$

Note how in these local conductivity matrices the zero row and column correspond to the node that is not part of the element in question. The global conductivity matrix is then obtained by summation:

$$\mathbf{K} = [K_{ij}^1] + [K_{ij}^2] \tag{6.85}$$

or

$$\mathbf{K} = \frac{\kappa A}{L_e}\begin{bmatrix} 1 & -1 & 0 \\ -1 & 2 & -1 \\ 0 & -1 & 1 \end{bmatrix} \tag{6.86}$$

Similarly, the global force vector is obtained by adding the two local force vectors:

$$[\mathbf{F}] = \frac{fAL_e}{2}\begin{Bmatrix} 1 \\ 1 \\ 0 \end{Bmatrix} + \frac{fAL_e}{2}\begin{Bmatrix} 0 \\ 1 \\ 1 \end{Bmatrix} = \frac{fAL_e}{2}\begin{Bmatrix} 1 \\ 2 \\ 1 \end{Bmatrix} \tag{6.87}$$

Thus, combining Equations (6.86) and (6.87) and writing in the form of Equation (6.82), we get

$$\frac{\kappa A}{L_e}\begin{bmatrix} 1 & -1 & 0 \\ -1 & 2 & -1 \\ 0 & -1 & 1 \end{bmatrix}\begin{bmatrix} T_1 \\ T_2 \\ T_3 \end{bmatrix} = \frac{fAL_e}{2}\begin{bmatrix} 1 \\ 2 \\ 1 \end{bmatrix} \tag{6.88}$$

Applying the boundary conditions

$$T_1(x = 0) = 0 \qquad \text{and} \qquad T_3(x = L) = 0$$

Equation (6.88) becomes

$$\frac{\kappa A}{L_e}\begin{bmatrix} 1 & -1 & 0 \\ -1 & 2 & -1 \\ 0 & -1 & 1 \end{bmatrix}\begin{bmatrix} 0 \\ T_2 \\ 0 \end{bmatrix} = \begin{bmatrix} \dfrac{fAL_e}{2} \\ fAL_e \\ \dfrac{fAL_e}{2} \end{bmatrix} \tag{6.89}$$

which reduces to

$$T_2 = \frac{1}{2}\frac{fL_e^2}{\kappa} = \frac{1}{8}\frac{fL_e^2}{\kappa} \tag{6.90}$$

For simplicity, let

$$F = 1 \ \Omega/\text{m}^3 \qquad \kappa = 1 \ \Omega/\text{m} = {}^\circ\text{K} \qquad L = 1 \ \text{m}$$

Then

$$T_2 = \frac{1}{8} = 0.125{}^\circ\text{K} \tag{6.91}$$

Integrating Equation (6.62), we get an explicit solution of the temperature distribution for the assumed boundary conditions:

$$T(x) = \frac{fL}{2\kappa}\left(x - \frac{x^2}{L}\right) \tag{6.92}$$

where $T(x = \frac{1}{2}) = 0.125{}^\circ\text{K}$ checks exactly with our finite-element solution given by Equation (6.91). ∎

6.9 FORMULATION OF GLOBAL STIFFNESS MATRIX FOR *N* ELEMENTS

The concept of global conductivity matrix $[\mathbf{K}]$ in Equation (6.85) is exactly the same as the global stiffness matrix that was discussed in Section (6.5). $\{\mathbf{T}\}$ and $\{\mathbf{F}\}$ now represent the nodal temperature vector and the heat source contribution vector, respectively, instead of the nodal displacement and the nodal force vectors as described by Equation (6.37). Table 6.3 will be helpful in the formulation of the global conductivity matrix.

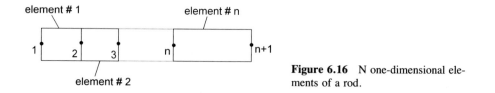

Figure 6.16 N one-dimensional elements of a rod.

Let us consider a body discretized into N one-dimensional elements, as shown in Figure 6.16. Let the boundary conditions be such that

$$T_1 = T_{N+1} = 0 \tag{6.93}$$

The connectivity table (Table 6.8) shows that the global conductivity matrix is of the order $(N + 1) \times (N + 1)$. The ascending order of elements helps the global K to have a predictable bandwidth.

By following the steps discussed in Sec. 6.5 and using the table information for inserting the local stiffness terms to the global matrix from Table 6.8, the global problem takes the following form:

TABLE 6.8 CONNECTIVITY TABLE AND
CONTRIBUTION TO *K* FROM k_{ij}^e

i, j from k_{ij}^e	Elements, *e*			
	1	2	3	*N*
1	1	2	3	*N*
2	2	3	4	*N* + 1

$$N\begin{bmatrix} 1 & -1 & 0 & & & & 0 \\ -1 & 1+1 & -1 & & & & \\ 0 & -1 & 1+1 & -1 & \cdots & & 0 \\ \vdots & \vdots & \vdots & \vdots & \ddots & & \vdots \\ & & & -1 & 1+1 & -1 \\ 0 & & & & 0 & -1 & 1 \end{bmatrix}\begin{bmatrix} T_1 \\ T_2 \\ T_3 \\ \vdots \\ T_{N+1} \end{bmatrix} = \begin{bmatrix} \dfrac{1}{2N} \\ \dfrac{1}{2N}+\dfrac{1}{2N} \\ \dfrac{1}{2N}+\dfrac{1}{2N} \\ \vdots \\ \dfrac{1}{2N} \end{bmatrix} \tag{6.94}$$

where *F* is assumed 1 for simplicity. By applying the boundary conditions, the problem reduces to

$$\begin{bmatrix} 2 & -1 & 0 & & & & 0 \\ -1 & 2 & -1 & & & & \\ 0 & -1 & 2 & -1 & \cdots & & 0 \\ \vdots & \vdots & \vdots & \vdots & & \ddots & \vdots \\ & & & -1 & 2 & & -1 \\ & & & 0 & -1 & & 2 \end{bmatrix}\begin{bmatrix} T_2 \\ T_3 \\ \vdots \\ T_{N-1} \\ T_N \end{bmatrix} = \frac{1}{N^2}\begin{bmatrix} 1 \\ 1 \\ 1 \\ \vdots \\ 1 \\ 1 \end{bmatrix} \tag{6.95}$$

Example 6.3   Heat Conduction Analysis of a Five-Element Rod

For the one-dimensional heat transfer problem given

$$\frac{d^2T}{dx^2} = -10 \qquad A = 1 \qquad (0 \le x \le 1 \text{ with } T(0) = 0)$$

find the temperature at *x* = 0.2, 0.4, 0.6, 0.8, and 1.0 using FEM (see Figure 6.17).

Solution The boundary conditions are $T_1 = T_6 = 0$. The connectivity table is

K_{ij}	1	2	3	4	5
1	1	2	3	4	5
2	2	3	4	5	6

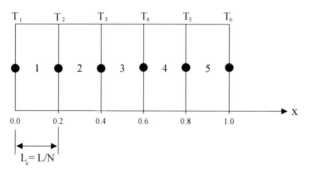

Figure 6.17 A five-element discretization of a heat conduction rod.

Each element has an element conductivity matrix $\mathbf{K}^e$ of the form:

$$\mathbf{K}^e = \frac{\kappa A}{L_e}\begin{bmatrix} 1 & -1 \\ -1 & 1 \end{bmatrix} \tag{6.96}$$

Substituting

$$A = 1 \qquad L_e = \frac{L}{N} = \frac{1}{5} = 0.2$$

and assuming $\kappa = 1$, then

$$\mathbf{K}^e = 5\begin{bmatrix} 1 & -1 \\ -1 & 1 \end{bmatrix} \tag{6.97}$$

Using the connectivity table, we expand the local matrices $\mathbf{K}_s^e$ to an order of 5×5, and the global matrix $[\mathbf{K}]$ is obtained by summation:

$$\mathbf{K} = k^1 + k^2 + k^3 + k^4 + k^5 \tag{6.97a}$$

The following global matrix can be formed:

$$[\mathbf{K}] = 5\begin{bmatrix} 1 & -1 & 0 & 0 & 0 & 0 \\ -1 & 2 & -1 & 0 & 0 & 0 \\ 0 & -1 & 2 & -1 & 0 & 0 \\ 0 & 0 & -1 & 2 & -1 & 0 \\ 0 & 0 & 0 & -1 & 2 & -1 \\ 0 & 0 & 0 & 0 & -1 & 1 \end{bmatrix} \tag{6.98}$$

By applying the boundary conditions, the global temperature vector becomes

$$\{\mathbf{T}\} = \begin{bmatrix} 0 \\ T_2 \\ T_3 \\ T_4 \\ T_5 \\ 0 \end{bmatrix} \tag{6.99}$$

The forcing vector for an element is shown to be

$$\mathbf{F}^e = \frac{fAL_e}{2}\begin{bmatrix} 1 \\ 1 \end{bmatrix}$$

where f is the heat generation per unit volume and is obtained from the relation

$$\kappa \frac{d^2 T}{dx^2} = -f \tag{6.100}$$

Substituting $\kappa = 1$ and $d^2T/dx^2 = -10$ yields $f = 10$. Substituting into $\mathbf{F}^e$ those values, we get

$$\mathbf{F}^e = \begin{bmatrix} 1 \\ 1 \end{bmatrix}$$

Assembling the global forcing vector using the connectivity table yields

$$\mathbf{F} = \begin{bmatrix} 1 \\ 1+1 \\ 1+1 \\ 1+1 \\ 1+1 \\ 1 \end{bmatrix} = \begin{bmatrix} 1 \\ 2 \\ 2 \\ 2 \\ 2 \\ 1 \end{bmatrix} \tag{6.101}$$

Using the relation $[\mathbf{K}]\{\mathbf{T}\} = \{\mathbf{F}\}$, we write

$$5\begin{bmatrix} 1 & -1 & 0 & 0 & 0 & 0 \\ -1 & 2 & -1 & 0 & 0 & 0 \\ 0 & -1 & 2 & -1 & 0 & 0 \\ 0 & 0 & -1 & 2 & -1 & 0 \\ 0 & 0 & 0 & -1 & 2 & -1 \\ 0 & 0 & 0 & 0 & -1 & 1 \end{bmatrix}\begin{bmatrix} 0 \\ T_2 \\ T_3 \\ T_4 \\ T_5 \\ 0 \end{bmatrix} = \begin{bmatrix} 1 \\ 2 \\ 2 \\ 2 \\ 2 \\ 1 \end{bmatrix} \tag{6.102}$$

By deleting the first and last rows together with their corresponding columns, Equation (6.102) becomes

$$\begin{bmatrix} 2 & -1 & 0 & 0 \\ -1 & 2 & -1 & 0 \\ 0 & -1 & 2 & -1 \\ 0 & 0 & -1 & 2 \end{bmatrix}\begin{bmatrix} T_2 \\ T_3 \\ T_4 \\ T_5 \end{bmatrix} = \begin{bmatrix} 0.4 \\ 0.4 \\ 0.4 \\ 0.4 \end{bmatrix} \tag{6.103}$$

Note that $T_2 = T_5$ and $T_3 = T_4$. From symmetry, we can solve Equation (6.103) very easily. The solutions are as follows:

$$\begin{bmatrix} T_1 \\ T_2 \\ T_3 \\ T_4 \\ T_5 \\ T_6 \end{bmatrix} = \begin{bmatrix} 0 \\ 0.8 \\ 1.2 \\ 1.2 \\ 0.8 \\ 0 \end{bmatrix} \qquad (6.104)$$

■

6.10 2D HEAT CONDUCTION ANALYSIS

In a similar fashion, the finite-element method can be used to analyze the 2D and 3D heat conduction problems. Let us examine the 2D case and bear in mind that, first, we need to develop the element temperature relationship and then expand it to the global problem.

The heat conduction problem is formulated by a variational boundary value problem as

$$\delta I = 0 \qquad (6.105)$$

where

$$I = \tfrac{1}{2} \int_\Omega [\kappa (\nabla T)^2 + 2fT] \, d\Omega \qquad (6.106)$$

and where k = thermal conductivity, which we assume constant
$\quad\ f$ = heat source
$\quad\ \nabla T = [\partial T/\partial x \quad \partial T/\partial y]^T$
$\quad\ (\nabla T)^2 = \nabla T \cdot \nabla T;$ "$\cdot$" denotes the dot product
$\quad\ \Omega$ = domain of interest

If domain Ω is divided into N elements, as shown in Figure 6.18, then

$$I = \sum_{e=1}^{N} I^e \qquad (6.107)$$

where

$$I^e = \tfrac{1}{2} \int_e [\kappa (\nabla T^e)^2 + 2f^e T^e] \, d\Omega \qquad (6.108)$$

Let us consider the triangular element shown in Figure 6.19. The local representation of the temperature can be expressed as

$$T(x, y) = T_1 N_1 + T_2 N_2 + T_3 N_3 \qquad (6.109)$$

where $N_i(x, y)$ ($i = 1, 2, 3$) are the shape functions given by

$$N_i^e = a_i^e + b_i^e x + c_i^e y \qquad (6.110)$$

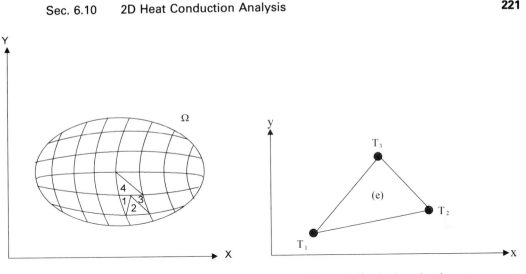

Figure 6.18 Finite-element discretization of the domain.

Figure 6.19 A triangular element.

The shape functions must satisfy the following conditions:

1. $N_i^e(x, y)$ are linear in both x and y.
2. $N_i^e(x, y)$ have the value 1 at node i and zero at other nodes.
3. $N_i^e(x, y)$ are zero at all points in Ω, except those of $N_i^e(x, y)$ can be written as

$$N_i(x, y) = [a_i \quad b_i \quad c_i] \begin{bmatrix} 1 \\ x \\ y \end{bmatrix} \tag{6.111}$$

and for the three nodes of the triangular element, we can write

$$\begin{bmatrix} N_1 \\ N_2 \\ N_3 \end{bmatrix} = \begin{bmatrix} a_1 & b_1 & c_1 \\ a_2 & b_2 & c_2 \\ a_3 & b_3 & c_3 \end{bmatrix} \begin{bmatrix} 1 \\ x \\ y \end{bmatrix} \tag{6.112}$$

For node 1, following condition 1, Equation (6.112) yields

$$N_1 = 1 = a_1 + b_1 x_1 + c_1 y_1$$

$$N_2 = 0 = a_1 + b_1 x_2 + c_1 y_2 \tag{6.113}$$

$$N_3 = 0 = a_1 + b_1 x_3 + c_1 y_3$$

which can be written in matrix form as

$$\begin{bmatrix} 1 \\ 0 \\ 0 \end{bmatrix} = [\mathbf{A}] \begin{bmatrix} a_1 \\ b_1 \\ c_1 \end{bmatrix} \tag{6.114}$$

where

$$[\mathbf{A}] = \begin{bmatrix} 1 & x_1 & y_1 \\ 1 & x_2 & y_2 \\ 1 & x_3 & y_3 \end{bmatrix} \tag{6.115}$$

Solving for coefficients a, b, and c, we get

$$\begin{bmatrix} a_1 \\ b_1 \\ c_1 \end{bmatrix} = \begin{bmatrix} 1 & x_1 & y_1 \\ 1 & x_2 & y_2 \\ 1 & x_3 & y_3 \end{bmatrix}^{-1} \begin{bmatrix} 1 \\ 0 \\ 0 \end{bmatrix} = [\mathbf{A}]^{-1} \begin{bmatrix} 1 \\ 0 \\ 0 \end{bmatrix} \tag{6.116}$$

Similarly, for the interpolation functions N_2 and N_3, we get

$$\begin{bmatrix} a_2 \\ b_2 \\ c_2 \end{bmatrix} = [\mathbf{A}]^{-1} \begin{bmatrix} 0 \\ 1 \\ 0 \end{bmatrix} \quad \text{and} \quad \begin{bmatrix} a_3 \\ b_3 \\ c_3 \end{bmatrix} = [\mathbf{A}]^{-1} \begin{bmatrix} 0 \\ 0 \\ 1 \end{bmatrix} \tag{6.117}$$

The inverse of matrix $\mathbf{A}$ is

$$[\mathbf{A}]^{-1} = \frac{1}{2a} \begin{bmatrix} (x_2 y_3 - x_3 y_2) & (y_2 - y_3) & (x_3 - x_2) \\ (x_3 y_1 - x_1 y_3) & (y_3 - y_1) & (x_1 - x_3) \\ (x_1 y_2 - x_2 y_1) & (y_1 - y_2) & (x_2 - x_1) \end{bmatrix} \tag{6.118}$$

where a is the area of the triangle. By combining Equations (6.107), (6.108), and (6.103), the inverse of $\mathbf{A}$ is

$$[\mathbf{A}]^{-1} = \begin{bmatrix} a_1 & b_1 & c_1 \\ a_2 & b_2 & c_2 \\ a_3 & b_3 & c_3 \end{bmatrix} \tag{6.119}$$

Then the triangle element functions can be written in a more general form:

$$\{\mathbf{N}^e\} = \begin{bmatrix} N_1 \\ N_2 \\ N_3 \end{bmatrix} = [\mathbf{A}]^{-1} \begin{bmatrix} 1 \\ x \\ y \end{bmatrix} \tag{6.120}$$

where

$$N_1 = \frac{1}{2a}[(x_2 y_3 - x_3 y_2) + x(y_2 - y_3) + y(x_3 - x_2)]$$

$$N_2 = \frac{1}{2a}[(x_3 y_1 - x_1 y_3) + x(y_3 - y_1) + y(x_1 - x_3)] \tag{6.121}$$

$$N_3 = \frac{1}{2a}[(x_1 y_2 - x_2 y_1) + x(y_1 - y_2) + y(x_2 - x_1)]$$

6.10.1 Element Conductivity Matrix

From Equation (6.108),

$$I^e = \tfrac{1}{2} \int_e \left[\underbrace{\kappa^e (\nabla T)^2}_{I_2^e} + \underbrace{f^e T^e}_{I_2^e} \right] d\Omega \qquad (6.122)$$

The temperature at the nodes of the triangle element is

$$T(x, y) = T_1 N_1 + T_2 N_2 + T_3 N_3 \qquad (6.123)$$

From Equation (6.121), we define

$$\frac{\partial N_i}{\partial x} = b_1 \qquad \text{and} \qquad \frac{\partial N_i}{\partial y} = c_i \qquad (6.124)$$

Hence, we can write the gradient of the temperature as

$$\nabla T = \begin{bmatrix} \dfrac{\partial T}{\partial x} \\[2mm] \dfrac{\partial T}{\partial y} \end{bmatrix} = \begin{bmatrix} \dfrac{\partial N_1}{\partial x} & \dfrac{\partial N_2}{\partial x} & \dfrac{\partial N_3}{\partial x} \\[2mm] \dfrac{\partial N_1}{\partial y} & \dfrac{\partial N_2}{\partial y} & \dfrac{\partial N_3}{\partial y} \end{bmatrix} \begin{bmatrix} T_1 \\ T_2 \\ T_3 \end{bmatrix} \qquad (6.125)$$

which, expressed in compact form, yields

$$\Delta T = \mathbf{B T} \qquad (6.125a)$$

where

$$\mathbf{B} = \begin{bmatrix} b_1 & b_2 & b_3 \\ c_1 & c_2 & c_3 \end{bmatrix} \qquad \text{and} \qquad \mathbf{T} = \begin{bmatrix} T_1 \\ T_2 \\ T_3 \end{bmatrix} \qquad (6.126)$$

Note how the coefficients of $\mathbf{B}$ are obtained from the partial derivatives of the shape functions given by Equation (6.124).

Now we can define $(\nabla T)^2$ needed in Equation (6.122).

$$(\nabla T)^2 = \begin{bmatrix} \dfrac{\partial T}{\partial x} & \dfrac{\partial T}{\partial y} \end{bmatrix} \begin{bmatrix} \dfrac{\partial T}{\partial x} \\[2mm] \dfrac{\partial T}{\partial y} \end{bmatrix} \qquad (6.127)$$

For a given element, this equation can be expressed as

$$[\nabla T^e]^2 = \{\mathbf{T}^e\}^T [\mathbf{B}^e]^T [\mathbf{B}^e] \{\mathbf{T}^e\} \qquad (6.127a)$$

This yields

$$I_1^e = \tfrac{1}{2} \kappa \int_e \{\mathbf{T}^e\}^T [\mathbf{B}^e]^T [\mathbf{B}^e] \{\mathbf{T}^e\} \, d\Omega \qquad (6.128)$$

Because $[\mathbf{B}]$ and $[\mathbf{T}]$ are constant matrices, Equation (6.128) reduces to

$$I_1^e = \tfrac{1}{2}\kappa \{\mathbf{T}^e\}^T[\mathbf{B}^e]^T[\mathbf{B}^e]\{\mathbf{T}^e\} \int_e d\Omega \qquad (6.129)$$

or simply

$$I_1^e = \tfrac{1}{2}\{\mathbf{T}^e\}^T[\mathbf{k}^e]\{\mathbf{T}^e\} \qquad (6.130)$$

where $[\mathbf{k}^e]$ denotes the element conductivity matrix:

$$[\mathbf{k}^e] = \kappa a[\mathbf{B}^e]^T[\mathbf{B}^e] \qquad (6.131)$$

which takes the final form

$$[\mathbf{k}^e] = \kappa a \begin{bmatrix} (b_1^2 + c_1^2) & (b_1b_2 + c_1c_2) & (b_1b_3 + c_1c_3) \\ (b_2b_1 + c_2c_1) & (b_2^2 + c_2^2) & (b_2b_3 + c_2c_3) \\ (b_3b_1 + c_3c_1) & (b_3b_2 + c_3c_2) & (b_3^2 + c_3^2) \end{bmatrix} \qquad (6.132)$$

and $a = \int_e d\Omega$ is the area of the triangular element.

6.10.2 Element-Forcing Function

To complete the integration of Equation (6.122), we need to evaluate the second term, I_2^e

$$I_2^e = \int_e f^e T^e \, d\Omega \qquad (6.133)$$

As was done with temperature, the heat source f can be expressed in a similar fashion:

$$f = f_1 N_1 + f_2 N_2 + f_3 N_3 = \begin{bmatrix} f_1 & f_2 & f_3 \end{bmatrix} \begin{bmatrix} N_1 \\ N_2 \\ N_3 \end{bmatrix} \qquad (6.134)$$

For an arbitrary element, this equation can be written in compact matrix form:

$$f^e = \{\mathbf{f}^e\}^T\{\mathbf{N}^e\} \qquad (6.135)$$

Recall that

$$T = T_1 N_1 + T_2 N_2 + T_3 N_3 = \begin{bmatrix} N_1 & N_2 & N_3 \end{bmatrix} \begin{bmatrix} T_1 \\ T_2 \\ T_3 \end{bmatrix} \qquad (6.136)$$

or

$$T^e = \{\mathbf{N}^e\}^T\{\mathbf{T}^e\} \qquad (6.137)$$

Therefore, I_2^e after substitution becomes

$$I_2^e = \int_e \{\mathbf{f}^e\}^T\{\mathbf{N}^e\}\{\mathbf{N}^e\}^T\{\mathbf{T}^e\} \, d\Omega = \{\mathbf{g}^e\}^T\{\mathbf{T}^e\} \qquad (6.138)$$

where

$$\{\mathbf{g}^e\}^T = \{\mathbf{f}^e\}^T \int_e \{\mathbf{N}^e\}\{\mathbf{N}^e\}^T \, d\Omega \qquad (6.139)$$

The integrand $\{\mathbf{N}^e\}\{\mathbf{N}^e\}^T$ yields

$$\{\mathbf{N}^e\}\{\mathbf{N}^e\}^T = [\mathbf{A}]^{-1} \begin{bmatrix} 1 \\ x \\ y \end{bmatrix} \begin{bmatrix} 1 & x & y \end{bmatrix} [\mathbf{A}^T]^{-1} = [\mathbf{A}]^{-1} \begin{bmatrix} 1 & x & y \\ x & x^2 & xy \\ y & xy & y^2 \end{bmatrix} [\mathbf{A}^T]^{-1} \qquad (6.140)$$

Note that $[\mathbf{A}]$, given by Equation (6.115), is a constant matrix therefore, the integral of $\{\mathbf{g}\}$ depends only on the matrix with variables x and y. Integrating each element of the matrix is rather tedious and long. An alternative is to use a method developed by Eisenberg and Malvern.

From this method, we have the following statement of the integral:

$$\int_e N_1^m N_2^n N_3^p \, d\Omega = \frac{m! \, n! \, p!}{(m + n + p + 2)!} \, 2a \qquad (6.141)$$

$$\{\mathbf{g}^e\} = \left[\int_e \{\mathbf{N}^e\}\{\mathbf{N}^e\}^T \, d\Omega \right] \{\mathbf{f}^e\} \qquad (6.142)$$

Hence,

$$\{\mathbf{g}^e\} = \left\{ \int_e \begin{bmatrix} N_1^2 & N_1 N_2 & N_1 N_3 \\ N_2 N_1 & N_2^2 & N_2 N_3 \\ N_3 N_1 & N_3 N_2 & N_3^2 \end{bmatrix} d\Omega \right\} \{\mathbf{f}^e\} \qquad (6.143)$$

which yields

$$\{\mathbf{g}^e\} = \frac{a}{12} \begin{bmatrix} 2 & 1 & 1 \\ 1 & 2 & 1 \\ 1 & 1 & 2 \end{bmatrix} \{\mathbf{f}^e\} \qquad (6.144)$$

The element integral of the variational formulation is broken into two parts:

$$I^e = I_1^e + I_2^e \qquad (6.145)$$

which simplifies to

$$I^e = \tfrac{1}{2} \{\mathbf{T}^e\}^T [\mathbf{k}^e]\{\mathbf{T}^e\} + \{\mathbf{g}^e\}^T \{\mathbf{T}^e\} \qquad (6.146)$$

The "global integral" over the domain Ω of the entire body becomes

$$I = \sum_{e=1}^{N} I^e = \sum_{e=1}^{N} \{ \tfrac{1}{2} \{\mathbf{T}^e\}^T [\mathbf{k}^e]\{\mathbf{T}^e\} + \{\mathbf{g}^e\}^T \{\mathbf{T}^e\} \} \qquad (6.147)$$

or

$$I = \tfrac{1}{2} \{\mathbf{T}\}^T \left[\sum_{3=1}^{N} [\mathbf{k}^e] \right] \{\mathbf{T}\} - \left[\sum_{e=1}^{N} \{\mathbf{F}^e\}^T \right] \{\mathbf{T}\} \qquad (6.148)$$

where

$$\{\mathbf{F}^e\}^T = -\{\mathbf{g}^e\}^T$$

and

$$\{\mathbf{T}\} = [T_1 T_2 \cdots T_n]^T$$

Hence,

$$I = \tfrac{1}{2}\{\mathbf{T}\}^T[\mathbf{k}]\{\mathbf{T}\} - \{\mathbf{F}\}^T\{\mathbf{T}\} \tag{6.149}$$

where the global conductivity matrix is defined by

$$[\mathbf{k}] = \sum_{e=1}^{N} [\mathbf{k}^e] \tag{6.150}$$

and the global forcing function (equivalent to the global force in the analysis of a truss) is

$$\{\mathbf{F}\} = \sum_{e=1}^{N} \{\mathbf{F}^e\} \tag{6.151}$$

The variation $\delta I = 0$ is equivalent to

$$\frac{\partial I}{\partial T_i} = 0 \qquad (i = 1, \ldots, n) \tag{6.152}$$

Applying Equation (6.152) to Equation (6.149) gives the global equation governing the temperature distribution and the heat source:

$$[\mathbf{k}]\{\mathbf{T}\} = \{\mathbf{F}\} \tag{6.153}$$

This equation is similar to our FEM application to the truss and the one-dimensional heat flow problems.

The analysis of 2D heat conduction problems can be done by using the FEM procedures developed herein. One proceeds by identifying the element shape functions and then evaluating the local conductivity (stiffness) matrices. The global [**K**] is then assembled using Equation (6.150). The element forcing function is computed using Equation (6.144) and then global array {**F**} is assembled according to Equation (6.151).

Example 6.4   Temperature Distribution on a Square Plate

For the square plate shown in Figure 6.20, find element matrices [**B**^{e}] and [**k**^{e}] and solve for all the element conductivity matrices. Find the temperature distribution at all of the nodes shown for the boundary conditions given.

Solution   There are four types of elements, as shown in Figure 6.21. The area of each triangular element is $a = 1/8$.

Figure 6.22 shows the temperature distribution along the x and y axis for the

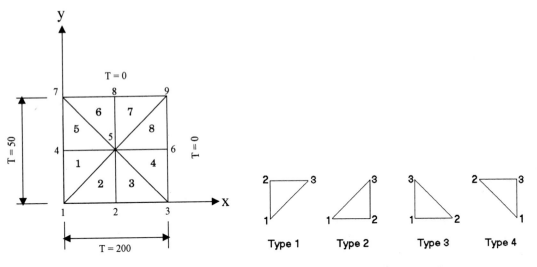

Figure 6.20 A square plate.

Figure 6.21 Triangular elements.

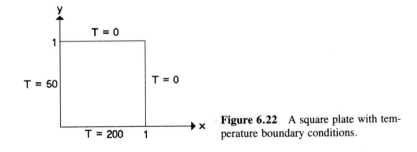

Figure 6.22 A square plate with temperature boundary conditions.

plate. Matrices $[\mathbf{B}^e]$ for each type of element are obtained from

$$[\mathbf{B}^e] = \frac{1}{2a} \begin{bmatrix} (y_2 - y_3) & (y_3 - y_1) & (y_1 - y_2) \\ (x_3 - x_2) & (x_1 - x_3) & (x_2 - x_1) \end{bmatrix} \tag{6.154}$$

which gives

$$[\mathbf{B}^1] = \begin{bmatrix} 0 & 2 & -2 \\ 2 & -2 & 0 \end{bmatrix} \tag{6.155}$$

$$[\mathbf{B}^2] = \begin{bmatrix} -2 & 2 & 0 \\ 0 & -2 & 2 \end{bmatrix} \tag{6.156}$$

$$[\mathbf{B}^3] = \begin{bmatrix} -2 & 2 & 0 \\ -2 & 0 & 2 \end{bmatrix} \tag{6.157}$$

$$[\mathbf{B}^4] = \begin{bmatrix} 0 & 2 & -2 \\ 2 & 0 & -2 \end{bmatrix} \tag{6.158}$$

The element conductivity matrices

$$[\mathbf{k}^e] = ka\ [\mathbf{B}^e]^T[\mathbf{B}^e]$$

are obtained from Equation (6.131):

$$[\mathbf{k}^1] = [k^2] = \frac{k}{8}\begin{bmatrix} 4 & -4 & 0 \\ -4 & 8 & -4 \\ 0 & -4 & 4 \end{bmatrix} \tag{6.159}$$

$$[\mathbf{k}^3] = \frac{k}{8}\begin{bmatrix} 8 & -4 & -4 \\ -4 & 4 & 0 \\ -4 & 0 & 4 \end{bmatrix} \tag{6.160}$$

$$[\mathbf{k}^4] = \frac{k}{8}\begin{bmatrix} 4 & 0 & -4 \\ 0 & 4 & -4 \\ -4 & -4 & 8 \end{bmatrix} \tag{6.161}$$

The relationship between elements and nodes is described by Table 6.9. From the boundary conditions, we get

$$\{\mathbf{T}\} = \begin{bmatrix} T_1 \\ T_2 \\ T_3 \\ T_4 \\ T_5 \\ T_6 \\ T_7 \\ T_8 \\ T_9 \end{bmatrix} = \begin{bmatrix} 125 \\ 200 \\ 100 \\ 50 \\ T_5 \\ 0 \\ 25 \\ 0 \\ 0 \end{bmatrix} \tag{6.162}$$

where T_5 is the only unknown. Hence, from the global equation $kT = f$, we obtain

$$\sum_{i=1}^{9} k_{5i}T_i = F_5 \tag{6.163}$$

Because there is no heat source, F_5 is zero. From the relationship between $[\mathbf{k}^e]$ and

TABLE 6.9   CONNECTIVITY RELATIONS OF ELEMENTS AND NODES

Nodes	Elements							
	1	2	3	4	5	6	7	8
1	1	1	2	3	4	5	5	5
2	4	2	3	5	5	7	8	6
3	5	5	5	6	7	8	9	9

the triangles, we can easily deduce the following

$$[k_{ij}^e] = \frac{\kappa}{8} \begin{cases} (4 + 4) & \text{for } i = j \text{ and } Li = 90° \\ 4 & \text{for } i = j \text{ and } Li \neq 90° \\ -4 & \text{for } i \neq j \text{ and nonhypotenuse} \\ 0 & \text{for } i \neq j \text{ and hypotenuse} \end{cases} \qquad (6.164)$$

From this equation, k_{5i} is

$$k_{5i} = \frac{\kappa}{8} \begin{bmatrix} 0 \\ -8 \\ 0 \\ -8 \\ 32 \\ -8 \\ 0 \\ -8 \\ 0 \end{bmatrix} \qquad (6.165)$$

Then from Equations (6.162), (6.165), and (6.163), we get

$$T_5 = 62.5 \qquad (6.166)$$

∎

Example 6.5   Steady State Heat Conduction

Find the temperature distribution for steady-state heat conduction in a square domain, as shown in Figure 6.23, with

$$T(0, y) = 10 \qquad \text{and} \qquad T(1, y) = T(x, 0) = T(x, 1) = 0$$

$$(0 \leq x \leq 1; 0 \leq y \leq 1)$$

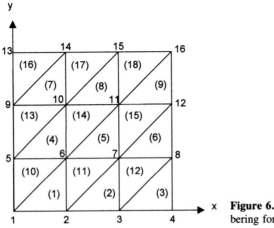

Figure 6.23   Node and element numbering for the finite-element model.

The boundary value for this problem is given by

$$\frac{\partial^2 T}{\partial x^2} + \frac{\partial^2 T}{\partial y^2} = 0 \tag{6.167}$$

Solution   This solution differs from the previous example in two respects: (1) there are only two types of elements used and (2) we doubled the number of elements to learn more about the temperature inside the plate. As shown in Figure 6.23, we divide this domain into 18 elements. There are two different types of triangles in the model (see Figure 6.24). The method of numbering the elements and nodes is arbitrary. However, one has to do it systematically so as to obtain matrices that require less storage space in the computer. Once the global conductivity matrix [**K**] is formulated its bandwidth will be checked to see whether its final form is mathematically sound. Let us proceed in the solution of this problem by identifying the element types and computing their corresponding [**B**] and [**k**] matrices.

The areas of the two triangles are the same

$$a = \left(\frac{1}{2}\right)\left(\frac{1}{3}\right)\left(\frac{1}{3}\right) = \frac{1}{18}$$

For an arbitrary triangular element, we have

$$[\mathbf{B}^e] = \frac{1}{2a} \begin{bmatrix} (y_2 - y_3) & (y_3 - y_1) & (y_1 - y_2) \\ (x_3 - x_2) & (x_1 - x_3) & (x_2 - x_1) \end{bmatrix}$$

For a type 1 element, [**B**¹] becomes

$$\mathbf{B}^1 = g = \begin{bmatrix} -\frac{1}{3} & \frac{1}{3} & 0 \\ 0 & -\frac{1}{3} & \frac{1}{3} \end{bmatrix} = \begin{bmatrix} -3 & 3 & 0 \\ 0 & -3 & 3 \end{bmatrix} \tag{6.168}$$

For a type 2 element,

$$[\mathbf{B}^e] = g \begin{bmatrix} 0 & \frac{1}{3} & -\frac{1}{3} \\ -\frac{1}{3} & 0 & \frac{1}{3} \end{bmatrix} = \begin{bmatrix} 0 & 3 & -3 \\ -3 & 0 & 3 \end{bmatrix} \tag{6.169}$$

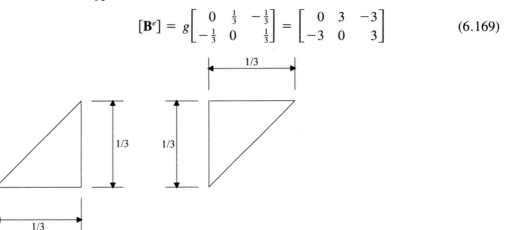

TYPE 1   TYPE 2

Figure 6.24   Element types for the finite-element model.

The conductivity matrix is given by

$$[\mathbf{k}^e] = \kappa a [\mathbf{B}^e]^T [\mathbf{B}^e]$$

For a type 1 element,

$$[\mathbf{k}^e] = \frac{\kappa}{18} \begin{bmatrix} 9 & -9 & 0 \\ -9 & 18 & -9 \\ 0 & -9 & 9 \end{bmatrix} \qquad (6.170)$$

For a type 2 element,

$$[\mathbf{k}^e] = \frac{\kappa}{18} \begin{bmatrix} 9 & 0 & -9 \\ 0 & 9 & -9 \\ -9 & -9 & 18 \end{bmatrix} \qquad (6.171)$$

The relationship between elements and nodes is given in Table 6.10.

Assembling the element conductivity matrices yields the global conductivity matrix:

$$\mathbf{K} = [\mathbf{k}^1] + [\mathbf{k}^2] + [\mathbf{k}^3] + \cdots + [\mathbf{k}^{18}] \qquad (6.172)$$

As in Example 6.4, from Figure 6.24 and Equations (6.170) and (6.171), we can deduce the element conductivity relations:

$$[\mathbf{k}_{ij}^e] = \frac{\kappa}{18} \begin{cases} (9+9) & \text{for } i = j \text{ and } \angle i = 90° \\ 9 & \text{for } i = j \text{ and } \angle i \neq 90° \\ -9 & \text{for } i \neq j \text{ and nonhypotenuse} \\ 0 & \text{for } i \neq j \text{ and hypotenuse} \end{cases} \qquad (6.173)$$

Then equation (6.172) takes the following form

$$\mathbf{K} = k \begin{bmatrix} 1 \\ -1/2 & 2 \\ 0 & -1/2 & 2 \\ 0 & 0 & -1/2 & 1 \\ -1/2 & 0 & 0 & 0 & 2 \\ & -1 & 0 & 0 & -1 & 4 \\ & & -1 & 0 & 0 & -1 & 4 \\ & & & -1/2 & 0 & 0 & -1 & 2 \\ & & & & -1/2 & 0 & 0 & 0 & 2 \\ & & & & & -1 & 0 & 0 & -1 & 4 \\ & & & & & & -1 & 0 & 0 & -1 & 4 \\ & & & & & & & -1/2 & 0 & 0 & -1 & 2 \\ & & & & & & & & -1/2 & 0 & 0 & 0 & 1 \\ & & & & & & & & & -1 & 0 & 0 & -1/2 & 2 \\ & & & & & & & & & & -1 & 0 & 0 & -1/2 & 2 \\ & & & & & & & & & & & -1/2 & 0 & 0 & -1/2 & 1 \end{bmatrix} \quad \blacksquare$$

$$(6.174)$$

TABLE 6.10   CONNECTIVITY RELATIONS OF ELEMENTS AND NODES

Nodes	Elements					
	1	2	3	4	$\cdots$	18
1	1	2	3	5	$\cdots$	11
2	2	3	4	6	$\cdots$	15
3	6	7	8	10	$\cdots$	16

Boundary Conditions

$$T_1 = T_{13} = \frac{1}{2}(10 + 0) = 5 \qquad \text{and} \qquad T_5 = T_9 = 10$$

and that

$$T_2 = T_3 = T_4 = T_8 = T_{12} = T_{14} = T_{15} = T_{16} = 0$$

Therefore, the unknown nodal temperatures are T_6, T_7, T_{10}, and T_{11}. Note that the heat source f is zero thus the system of equation becomes

$$[\mathbf{k}]\{T\} = 0 \tag{6.175}$$

where

$$\{T\} = [5 \quad 0 \quad 0 \quad 0 \quad 10 \quad T_6 \quad T_7 \quad 0 \quad 10 \quad T_{10} \quad T_{11} \quad 0 \quad 5 \quad 0 \quad 0 \quad 0]^T$$

Using the boundary conditions on the global system, we obtain the equations for the unknown nodal temperatures

$$4T_6 - T_7 - T_{10} = 10$$
$$-T_6 + 4T_7 - T_{11} = 0$$
$$-T_7 - T_{10} + 4T_{11} = 0 \tag{6.176}$$
$$-T_6 + 4T_{10} - T_{11} = 10$$

From the property of symmetry of the system, we know $T_6 = T_{10}$ and $T_7 = T_{11}$. The solution is as follows

$$T_6 = T_{10} = \frac{15}{4} = 3.75 \tag{6.177}$$

and

$$T_7 = T_{11} = \frac{5}{4} = 1.25$$

6.11 FEM AND OPTIMIZATION

In order to survive in today's competitive industrial/scientific world, the products will have to have the following characteristic features:

1. Low cost
2. High built-in reliability of performance
3. Limited time frame for design/manufacture

The first factor is usually achieved by minimizing the volume/mass/weight of the structure component, whereas the second factor would need the various constraints defined in the problem statement to be satisfied in the process of design. The third factor emphasizes the reduction of the overall time for bringing the product into the market by using proper computational tools/manufacturing techniques, which will complete the process at higher speeds.

In recent times, state-of-the-art structural optimization algorithms and design sensitivity analysis methods have come into existence, which cover the first two points mentioned above to a considerable extent. The third point could be brought into control by utilizing a combination of hardwares and softwares. The concepts of inherent vector and concurrent processing made possible by the recent advances in the computer architecture would assist in the design and analysis stage as well as in the numerical control machines, Group Technology and CIM architectures discussed in the latter chapters. This technology will definitely be a key to the speed of the manufacturing process.

The structural optimization process deals with a systematic procedure of manipulating the design variables that describe the structural system while simultaneously satisfying prescribed limits on the structural response.

The design variables for a component could include volume or mass or weight, minimizing which, would reduce the cost. These design variables can be grouped and linked in many ways and fixed in certain regions of the structural system. This is needed for uniformity of structure and in creating a symmetrical design under unsymmetrical loading conditions. Prescribed limits on the response of the structure may refer to nodal displacements and element stresses under static loading as well as eigenvalues for free vibration (natural frequencies) and/or for stability (buckling load factors).

Finite-element discretization is a powerful tool used for the optimization of design of machine components. This method of analysis breaks up the complex geometry of the structure into a large number of "finite elements" whose response to applied stresses and constraints can be well approximated with simple functions. The accuracy of results in this type of analysis is a strong function of the manner in which the structure is subdivided into finite elements. Hence it is seen that there are three major operations integrated into the procedure of structural optimization.

These are:

1. **Finite-Element Analysis**
2. **Design Sensitivity Analysis**
3. **Optimization Algorithm**

A number of powerful and versatile programs have been developed that can treat large scale structural design problems.

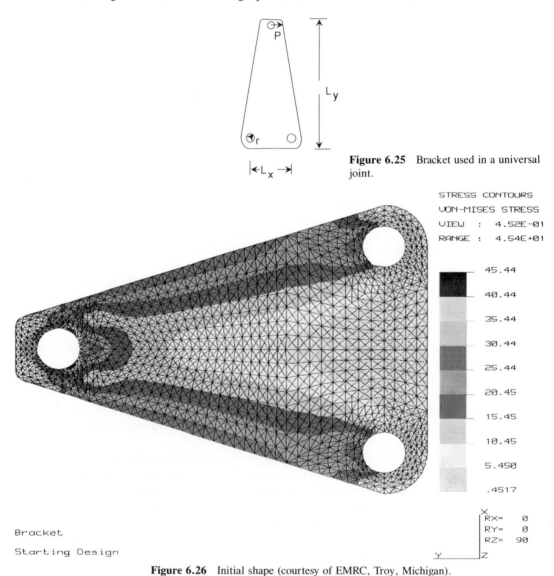

Figure 6.25   Bracket used in a universal joint.

Figure 6.26   Initial shape (courtesy of EMRC, Troy, Michigan).

Let us discuss an example of design optimization applied to the solid cantilever structure shown in Figure 6.24. This example is extracted from EMRC publication [12]. A software package called SHAPE developed by EMRC was used for this purpose and makes use of a technique presented in reference [13]. The cantilever is loaded at mid-height at the right end. Due to the symmetry and anti-symmetry conditions, only one quarter was modeled with 7680 tetrahedra and 2244 nodes (6732 d.o.f.). Using consistent units, the constraints for the problem are $L_x = L_y = 16$, $L_z = 3$, $E = 3.0 \times 10^4$, $u = 0.3$, $p = 2$ ($7p = 14$), Von-Mises stress < 10 (all elements).

One layer of the displacement elements was frozen at the fixed end, which means the node displacements of the elements on that side were zero as they are subject to no change in the process. The package adopts an iterative procedure to arrive at the final optimized design. At the end of each iteration, the design variables are compared with the prescribed limits (constraints). Based on the need/requirement subsequent to this comparison, new boundaries may be created as appropriate by removal of the material from inside the system. The finite-element mesh of the structure is sufficient to model the boundaries by parametric curves.

The changes in the shape and the stress at various stages during shape optimization are shown in Figures 6.25 through 6.28. The final material volume is

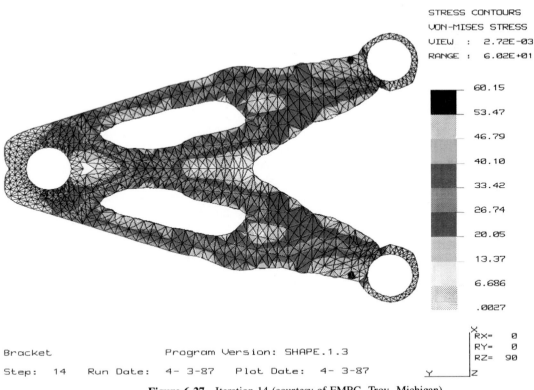

Figure 6.27 Iteration 14 (courtesy of EMRC, Troy, Michigan).

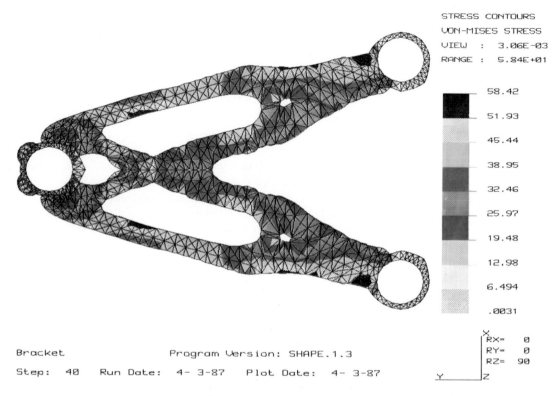

STRESS CONTOURS
VON-MISES STRESS
VIEW : 3.06E-03
RANGE : 5.84E+01

58.42
51.93
45.44
38.95
32.46
25.97
19.48
12.98
6.494
.0031

Bracket   Program Version: SHAPE.1.3

Step: 40   Run Date: 4- 3-87   Plot Date: 4- 3-87

X
RX=   0
RY=   0
RZ=   90
Y   Z

Figure 6.28   Iteration 40 (courtesy of EMRC, Troy, Michigan).

140.4 compared to the initial design material volume of 768.0, indicating a savings of nearly 82% in terms of material.

As reported in the description of the software SHAPE a NISA II product of EMRC [12]. The combination of the finite-element method, optimization techniques, and graphics enables the designer/engineer to obtain optimum designs in real time releasing him or her from the exhaustive time one spends in arriving at such a conclusion. This is a perfect example, once done, that shows how CAD and engineers could be blended together to form the ultimate CAD system, drawing from the best capabilities of each.

Let us consider another design optimization example taken again from reference [12] using the finite-element discretization procedure.

The design of a bracket used in an automotive universal joint is to be optimized. The bracket shown in Figure 6.25 is loaded by a force P applied towards the right at the middle of the top bolt bole. The periphery of the bottom two bolt holes is restricted against translation in the x and y directions.

For the process of design optimization, only half of the system needs to be modeled because of the condition of anti-symmetry. The modeled half was 1619 elements and 881 nodes (1762 nodes). One layer of elements around each bolt hole is frozen because of the support and load conditions. The width of material beyond

A bicycle drawn on RS/6000 workstation
Reprinted by permission of International Business Machines Corporation

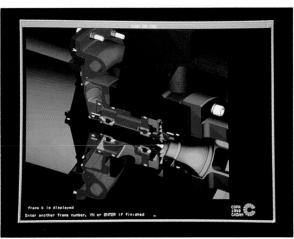

A cross-sectional view of a solid model using CADAM *Reprinted by permission of International Business Machines Corporation*

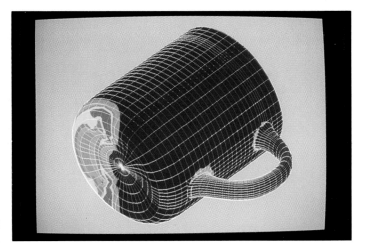

Heat transfer analysis of a mug using FEM
Courtesy of Algor, Inc.

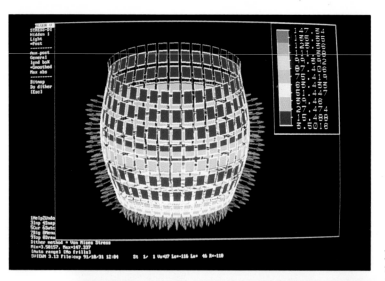

Nonlinear pressure vessel analysis using FEM *Courtesy of Algor, Inc.*

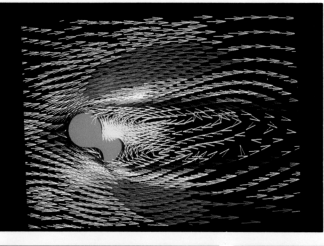

Display of fluid flow analysis on a CAD workstation *Courtesy of Algor, Inc.*

A French horn model displaying reflection, surface, and solid modeling capabilities using I-DEAS *Courtesy of Tennessee Technological University. Pictures prepared by Bob Mabrey.*

Wire frame and sectional solid modeling of a chuck using CATIA *Reprinted by permission of International Business Machines Corporation*

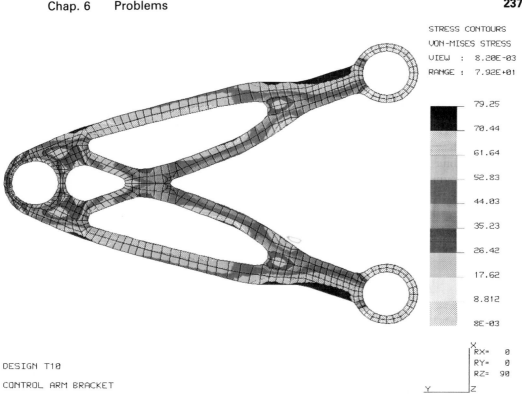

STRESS CONTOURS

VON-MISES STRESS

VIEW :   8.20E-03

RANGE :   7.92E+01

- 79.25
- 70.44
- 61.64
- 52.83
- 44.03
- 35.23
- 26.42
- 17.62
- 8.812
- 8E-03

RX=   0
RY=   0
RZ=   90

DESIGN T10

CONTROL ARM BRACKET

Figure 6.29 Final shape (courtesy of EMRC, Troy, Michigan).

this layer is arbitrarily assigned for the initial design. Using consistent units, the constants for the problem are $L_x = 10$, $L_y = 15$, $t = 0.3$ $r = 1.0$, $E = 2.074 \times 10^4$, $D = 0.3$, $P = 15$, and Von-Mises stress < 80 (all elements).

Figures 6.26 through 6.29 illustrate the changes in shape and stress during the shape optimization process. The final design (Figure 6.29) is about 68% lighter than the original design based on material volumes of 48.07.

PROBLEMS

6.1 For the plane truss shown in Figure P6.1, derive the global stiffness matrix knowing that joint 1 is a roller, joint 2 is fixed, and each bar has the same material properties E and A. Define the boundary conditions for each joint and solve for the nodal displacements and reaction forces. (Assume $A = |x|$ in^2, $a = 6$ ft, $E = 30 \times 10^6$ psi.)

6.2 **(a)** Use the truss finite-element program given in Appendix B to check the answers to Problem 1.

   (b) Find the axial forces in the three bars and determine whether each bar is in tension or compression.

   (Assume $E = 30 \times 10^6$ psi and $A = |x|$ in^2 for all truss elements.)

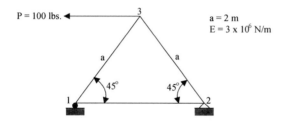

P = 100 lbs.

a = 2 m
E = 3 x 10⁶ N/m

Figure P6.1 Plane truss subjected to a load.

6.3 Find the incidence matrices relating the global displacement and the local displacement for elements 1, 2, and 3 in Problem 1 [use Equation (6.39)].

$$
\begin{bmatrix} U_{1x} \\ U_{1y} \\ \vdots \\ U_{nx} \\ U_{ny} \end{bmatrix} = [\wedge] \begin{bmatrix} u^e_{1x} \\ u^e_{1y} \\ u^e_{2x} \\ u^e_{2y} \end{bmatrix}
$$

where n is the number of joints.

6.4 Use the incidence matrices approach developed in Problem 3 to write an equation relating the local forces of element 2 to the global forces of the truss in Problem 1.

6.5 Use the 2D truss finite-element program given in Appendix B to solve for the trusses in Figure P6.2.

6.6 A thin rod 100 cm long with a 1 cm² cross-sectional area has a temperature distribution given by

$$
\frac{d^2T}{d^2} = -10.0 \qquad (0 \le x \le 100.0)
$$

with boundary conditions

$$
T(0) = 10°C \qquad \text{and} \qquad T(100) = 0°C
$$

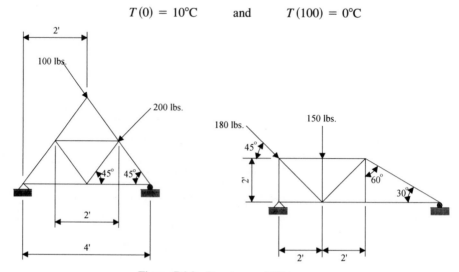

Figure P6.2 Two types of 2D trusses.

Using one-dimensional finite elements, compute the temperature at the middle point of the rod ($x = 50$ cm) when the rod is discretized (a) using two elements, and (b) using four elements.

Compare the finite-element solution with the one obtained by integrating the governing differential equation.

6.7 A thin metallic plate 100 cm $\times$ 100 cm $\times$ 1 cm is discretized using three-noded 2D triangular elements, as shown in Figure P6.3. The boundary conditions at the various edges of the plate are also shown in the figure. Find the following:
   (a) The local conductivity matrix for each element.
   (b) The contribution to the global conductivity matrix from all local conductivity matrices of elements 1, 2, 3, and 4.
   (c) The temperature at the mid node, node 5.

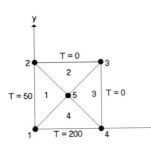

Figure P6.3   A metallic plate.

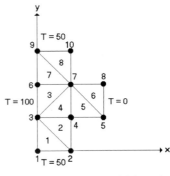

Figure P6.4   A plate with boundary conditions and nodes.

6.8 The boundary conditions and discretization of a plate are shown in Figure P6.4.
   (a) Write the various tables needed for the solution process.
   (b) Find the incidence matrix relating the local and global nodal temperatures.
   (c) Write the local and global heat source contribution vectors.
   (d) Assemble the global nodal temperature matrix.
   (e) Write the final equations after imposing the boundary conditions.

6.9 Write a pre- and postprocessor to generate graphics for the FEM 2D truss program given in Appendix B.

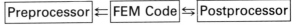

The preprocessor prepares the input and the postprocessor displays the output.

6.9 Why is the finite-element method important in the analysis of physical problems such as heat transfer and stress analysis? What are its advantages compared to other numerical techniques?

6.10 Why is selection of elements important in finite-element analysis? How does one select the appropriate elements for creating a mesh in FEM?

REFERENCES

6.1 Akin, J., Ed., *Finite Element Analysis for Undergraduates,* Academic Press, Orlando, FL 1986.

6.2 *ANSYS Engineering Analysis System,* Swanson Analysis Systems, Inc., Houston, Pennsylvania, 1983.

6.3 Burnett, D. S., *Finite Element Analysis: From Concepts to Applications,* Addison-Wesley, Reading, MA, 1987.

6.4 Huston, R. L., and Passerello, C. E., *Finite Element Methods, an Introduction,* Marcel Dekker, New York, 1984.

6.5 Kenneth, H., *Finite Element Methods for Engineers,* John Wiley & Sons, New York, 1975.

6.6 Martin, H. C., and Carey, G. F., *Introduction to Finite Element Analysis: Theory and Applications,* McGraw-Hill, New York, 1973.

6.7 Reddy, J. N., *An Introduction to the Finite Element Method,* McGraw-Hill, New York, 1984.

6.8 Rockey, K. C., *The Finite Element Method: A Basic Introduction,* John Wiley & Sons, New York, 1975.

6.9 Stasa, F. L., *Applied Finite Element Analysis for Engineers, HRW Series in Mechanical Engineering,* CBS College Publishing, New York, 1985.

6.10 Timoshenko, S. D., and Goodier, *Theory of Elasticity,* McGraw-Hill, New York, 1969, 1970.

6.11 Zienkiewcz, O. C., and Taylor, R. L., *The Finite Element Method,* McGraw-Hill, New York, 1989.

6.12 Engineering Mechanics Research Corp., Software Products pamphlets on Finite Elements, 1991, Troy, Mich.

6.13 SHAPE NISOPT Publication EMRC, Troy, Mich., 1991.

chapter 7

Applications
of CAD/CAM Technology

7.1 INTRODUCTION

Interactive computer graphics can be applied to various areas of science and technology in which drawings are an essential part for presenting ideas to another person. Its possible applications cover a wide range, which is shown in the following examples.

7.2 CAD/CAM AND THE AEROSPACE INDUSTRY

Computer technology plays a large part in the aircraft industry, training pilots, lessening flight crew workloads, and speeding up aircraft production.

In aircraft development and production, CAD/CAM has made many contributions. Northrop Corporation developed a new 3D computer graphics system to develop the B-2 stealth bomber. The system has a large database that can be accessed by the Air Force, Northrop, and the project's subcontractors. This allows coordination between the individual groups.

Computer graphics eases the design of the complex shapes the B-2 requires for its stealth role of being invisible to radar. Also, the fit of parts manufactured from the details in the computer database fit together much better than they would otherwise. Northrop cites a 6 : 1 reduction in first-time part-fit problems and expects a 40% decrease in the development time of parts from design to manufacture.

CAD/CAM also greatly aided in the development of a home-built plane called the Prescott Pusher. Except for the initial sketches, the aircraft was totally designed on a McDonnell Douglas CAD/CAM system. The computer was used in designing and testing the entire aircraft. It took eighteen months to go from preliminary design to a flying prototype.

Another particular advantage of CAD/CAM applied to the Prescott Pusher plane was the design and manufacture of parts. Since it is a kit plane, being built by amateurs in their garages in some cases, parts that fit together well are a definite plus. The parts in this kit fit together well, being cut precisely by computer controlled machine tools to specification supplied by a CAD system. (See Chapter 8 for more on this subject.)

When the aircraft was first flown, the only adjustments needed were in the tail incidence, which was off by a couple of degrees, and the size of the elevator trim tab. Flight tests confirmed all of the other computer and wind tunnel predictions.

Computer graphics is also used in pilot training. Today, many airlines use large simulators to familiarize new crew members to their aircraft. These simulators are large units mounted on movable stands connected to hydraulic cylinders. The insides of the simulators are identical to that particular aircraft, with all instrumentation and controls. Computer graphics, integrated with hydraulic controls, shows flight crews their simulated flights out the cockpit window. The hydraulics moves the entire simulator, coordinating control inputs, so that the crews inside actually feel as if they are flying. In these simulators, crews can practice various emergency situations, such as engine failure and cabin decompression. Many airlines now also use these simulators regularly to check seasoned crews, as well as to train new ones.

The military also uses simulators to train pilots. Because many military frontline fighters have only one seat, pilots are trained in elaborate simulators that show other aircraft as well as terrain. Combat situations and formation flying can be practiced without endangering the pilots or the multimillion dollar aircraft. These simulators are programmed to be so like the real aircraft that when pilots enter the real aircraft, they are well prepared.

Computer technology has also lowered flight crew workloads in large aircraft. The new Boeing 747-400 has a cockpit that has eliminated the need for a flight engineer. Onboard computers allowed elimination of the entire flight engineer's panel, making data available to the pilot and co-pilot through CRTs mounted on their instrument panel (Figure 7.1). Many of the aircraft's systems are monitored by the computers so that the flight crew can concentrate on flying. Six large CRTs display whatever instrumentation the crew wants by request using a keyboard. Flight instruments, flight path and navigation data, and engine and system instrumentation can all be punched up and combined on the various CRTs.

Simulators are used to train crews of new aircraft before they receive any actual flight time in the real planes.

7.2.1 CAD and EFIS/CFPD Display

In recent years, there have been numerous breakthroughs in better presenting computer graphics images on a screen. Updating from a CGA (color graphics adapter) to an EGA (enhanced graphics adapter) can be done in a matter of minutes. The use of

Figure 7.1   Cockpit of the Boeing 747-400 (courtesy of Boeing Co., Seattle, WA).

this technology in simulators to train motorists and aircraft pilots saves thousands of dollars.

The effectiveness of such simulators is questionable, but a new technology, known as EFIS/CFPD displays, which are much more useful and interactive than the latest generation of simulators, is developing.

What are EFIS/CFPD displays? The abbreviation stands for electronic flight instrument system and command flight path display. They are a form of computer graphics that helps the aircraft pilot fly in almost any condition. They virtually eliminate pilot error in bad weather, low-level flying, and navigation.

The main computer is connected to a very sophisticated navigation system that utilizes radar and satellites to pinpoint exactly the aircraft location. At the pilot's discretion, the computer displays graphics in the form of rectangles, for example, that define the correct path the aircraft is to take. These graphics are displayed on the cockpit window in much the same way as the heads-up display (HUD) now employed in fighter aircraft, and also in some automobiles, allowing the pilot to read aircraft speed, engine rpm, and other engine parameters without looking at the instrument panel. All the pilot has to do is to fly the plane within these rectangles on the cockpit window. This is vastly superior to the current instrument landing system (ILS), which only partially aids the pilot and can only be used during landings. Such a system can virtually ensure no chance of drifting off course.

Many more contributions of computer technology are being made to the aviation industry. There is no limit to the extent that computers can help in this field.

7.3 NAVIGATION COMPUTER FOR AUTOMOBILES

As highways become more crowded, traffic researchers are looking to develop sophisticated computer-controlled navigation systems. Current navigation systems only pinpoint a vehicle on a map display and leave it up to the driver to decide which route to take.

A new generation of navigation systems, however, will determine the best route to take based on current traffic and road conditions. A great deal of research is being carried out to develop these navigation systems whose basic goals are to improve mobility and transportation productivity, enhance safety, maximize the use of existing transportation facilities and energy resources, and protect the environment.

A navigation system is made up of a number of components. A database on a compact disk provides mapping of the metropolitan- and highway-level information for the region. The map includes all streets, roads, and highways. Information can be obtained in at least three different ways that are currently being tested.

The first system uses onboard sensors, such as wheel-rotation counters and a magnetic compass, to send data to a computer that determines how far and in what direction the car has traveled. This dead reckoned position is improved upon using a computationally intensive "map-matching" algorithm. Graphical driving directions are displayed on a dash-mounted screen that can also present magnified maps. The driver uses a keypad to enter desired destinations and other commands to the onboard computer. Equipped with knowledge of the location of the car and the destination, the system's software can plot an efficient route and display directions on the screen.

Another system being tested uses satellites to receive information. An onboard computer analyzes signals from three to four satellites and then displays the vehicle's altitude, longitude, speed, and direction, all superimposed on a map.

A third approach to vehicle navigation uses infrared transmitters located on roadside or on traffic signals to tell the vehicle its location and give route and traffic data. A central facility computes the routes and transmits them to the cars via infrared beacons. The car in turn signals its destination in order to updata traffic information.

In the United States, such a navigation system is called the intelligent vehicle highway system (IVHS). One of the navigation systems being tested is the Pathfinder system, an in-vehicle motorist information and road navigation system sponsored by

Caltrans, FHWA (Federal Highway Administration), and General Motors Corporation. This is a driver information system that informs motorists of existing traffic congestion. The hardware includes a processor, voice synthesis equipment, modem, radio, and an Etak Inc., navigation device called the TravelPilot. This is a navigational system made by Etak that displays electronic road maps. The driver enters a desired destination and it appears on the map display. Map data are stored on compact disk located in the vehicle. A separate computer collects and sorts congestion data received by radio from the central computer systems. The display device is shown in Figure 7.2.

Another project, being developed for the Orlando, Florida, area, is a cooperative and shared-cost partnership of General Motors, FHWA, the American Automobile Association (AAA), the Florida Department of Transportation, and the City of Orlando called TravTek.

The TravTek system, consisting of a video screen, two microcomputers, a voice synthesizer, and radio for data communications, is to be installed in about 75 general-use GM rental cars and 25 vehicles used by local drivers. Upon selection of a destination, the TravTek processor uses travel time to determine the best routes and uses both graphics displays and synthesized voice to guide the drivers. The traffic

Figure 7.2 Travel pilot display used in the pathfinder system (courtesy of Etak, Inc.).

management center combines and sorts traffic-related information from a variety of sources. From this data, information on accidents, travel times, and affected routes is estimated and transmitted to the vehicles. The in-vehicle processor then determines if the driver's route is affected and calculates a new routing if necessary and informs the driver that a revised route is available. An LCD display screen in a car is shown in Figure 7.3.

Europe and Japan are also moving forward with major automobile navigation projects. The Program for European Traffic with Highest Efficiency and Unprecedented Safety (PROMETHEUS) is a consortium launched by the European Community. Dedicated Road Infrastructure for Vehicle Safety (DRIVE) is another program launched in Europe, focusing on road infrastructure. These programs have generated experimental projects in West Berlin and London. The Leit-und Informations Systems Berlin (LISB) connects about 500 cars with route-guidance information over approximately 3000 km of roads, 4500 intersections, and 1300 traffic signals in West Berlin. The vehicles send and receive data from 250 roadside infrared proximity beacons at a rate of 8 kilobytes per second.

London's Autoguide navigation system, also based on the LISB, enables the driver to enter a destination using a handheld remote device. The car's processor communicates with a central control through infrared signals and beacons. A dashboard-mounted device tells the driver the number of kilometers left in the trip, whether to turn or go straight, and the proximity of intersections.

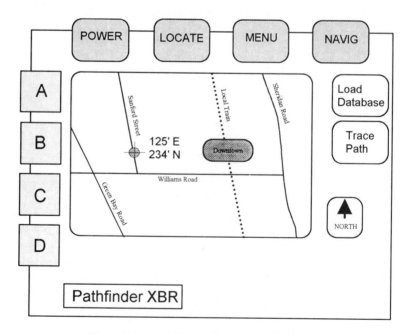

Figure 7.3 An LCD display screen model in a car.

7.4 DYNAMIC ANALYSIS AND COMPUTER SIMULATION OF MECHANICAL SYSTEMS

Advances in computer system hardware and the proliferation of computers in the engineering environment have allowed multibody dynamics to become a total engineering solution. It is possible to view the performance of a vehicle or mechanical system before an expensive prototype is built. Benefits include the reduction of engineering and testing costs, simulation and animation of results, and shortening of overall time to market.

Dynamic analysis of multibody systems is used to understand the movement of individual parts within a complex assembly and the forces they endure when the assembly interacts with its environment. These assemblies include suspension systems, aircraft landing gear, robotic manipulators, and construction and agricultural machinery.

Because systems are now lightweight and are operating at higher speeds, inclusion of elastic deformations of the flexible bodies in the multibody system in conjunction with large-scale nonlinear rigid body displacements gains paramount importance. The result is a multidisciplinary representation of mechanical systems.

Based on these concepts, a number of CAD codes has been developed, with suitable pre- and postprocessors to ease the input data preparation and output data interpretation. These codes not only help in carrying out design analysis, but also provide graphics capabilities, to visualize and predict the system's motion.

The capabilities of these codes include the following:

1. Dynamic Analysis: Computes the position, velocities, reaction forces, and acceleration of each body at various time intervals.
2. Kinematic Analysis: Calculates the motion of various bodies in the mechanisms, disregarding mass and force.
3. Static Analysis: Computes the static equilibrium position and potential energy.
4. Assembly Analysis: Configures and reviews joint and connection constraints between bodies.

Computer-aided simulation programs such as ADAMS, DYAMUS (Dynamic Analysis of Multibody Systems), and DADS (Dynamic Analysis & Design System) are capable of 3D dynamic analysis and are used to evaluate the handling and maneuverability of several engineering applications including three-wheeled all-terrain vehicles (ATVs).

These programs simulate the complex interaction of ATVs' mechanical and control systems by measuring vehicle response without the skill of expert riders (i.e., riders lean in response to terrain changes). It was found, among other data, that at speeds above 7.5 mph, the ATVs rolled over a turning radius of 20 ft. Thus, the safety of the machine was brought into question for novice riders, and three-wheeled ATVs were taken off the market.

In general, then, dynamic simulation programs can model mechanical systems such as ATV by automating the creation and solution of the generalized equations of motion and constraint. If the system requires algebraic, digital, hydraulic, or other controls, the DADS (Multibody Dynamics Code) solution procedure allows the coupling of the mechanical and control systems. The program can represent the complex interactions between the controls and the controlled variables.

The simulation model of the three wheeled ATV is of interest not only in the study of the vehicle response, but also in the evaluation of a rider's steering and throttling responses. (See Figure 7.4) [5].

Also, other vehicles could be evaluated and their performance categorized, thus giving the public further criteria and data involved in determining a vehicle purchase.

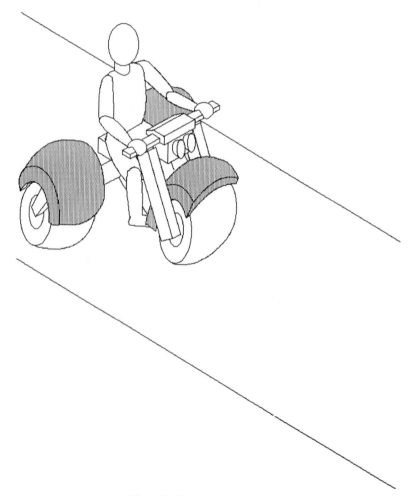

Figure 7.4 A three wheel ATV.

A more useful application of multibody dynamic codes would be in the design process. If the vehicle does not perform to the specifications required, changes can be automatically made in the computer design and the dynamic simulation performed. In this manner, an optimum design can be made at a cost much less than that required to build several prototypes for testing. In addition we need to build in a significant safety factor because the computer simulation results are only as good as the programmer's expertise. If several key data are missing, the output could be erroneous and misleading. Thus, these simulations must be thoroughly tested and well understood by the designer.

There are several programs available today that are designed for the dynamic analysis of multibody/mechanical systems. TREETOPS, ADAMS, and DYAMUS are designed to handle complex mechanical articulated structures such as robotic arms, space structures and maneuvers, mechanisms, and biosystem applications.

7.5 CAD/CAM AND ELECTRICAL NETWORK DESIGN

Computer-aided design plays a major role in the fabrication of integrated circuit chips (ICs). The process is in three parts: circuit design, process design, and mask design. Each part depends on the others because the data used are to some extent common to all three.

Circuit design includes placement and connections between transistors, sensors, hides, etc. Without CAD, this task requires many draftspeople, and because the circuits are so small and highly detailed, any mistakes or modifications often results in redrawing the entire circuit. With CAD, an interactive program is used with data about the individual circuit elements already in memory. The circuit can be drawn on a CRT terminal and stored for later examination, analysis, or modification. The circuit can be tested by computer and logical flaws found and corrected before a single silicon chip is produced.

Process design is making the chip itself. Parts of the chip must be exposed to high-temperature high-pressure gas consisting of the dopant molecules. There is also a certain amount of time to be taken to regulate the amount of doping. A CAD system can use the information about proper semiconductors and correlate the pressure, temperature, and time of exposure to ensure proper manufacture. This takes the place of extensive calculations, guess work, and trial-and-error methods.

Mask design is used in making the glass masks of the chip. The masks show the locations of similar elements, which are stacked one atop another, until the chip is finished. This requires precise positioning of the elements in the different masks. One advantage of a CAD system is to ensure proper alignment and positioning of the masks and their elements with one another.

Using manual techniques, IC design can only produce about 20 to 30 transistors per chip (see Figure 7.5). Using today's modern CAD systems, this number jumps to hundreds and even thousands of transistors per chip. As ICs become more complex and CAD systems become more powerful, we can have millions of transistors on a single chip.

Figure 7.5   The 33 Mhz i486 Microprocessor chip (courtesy of Intel Corp.).

7.6 INTEGRATION OF CAD/CAM TO THE DESIGN OF SPORTS EQUIPMENT

The increasing interest of today's athletes to improve performance and set new records has prompted many to resort to modern technology. By investigating variations in body motion and equipment, the sports world has been able to optimize the athlete's performance. CAD systems have contributed to new advances, especially in the design of sports equipment. As with any application where CAD is useful, many factors are taken into design consideration, including weather conditions, mobility, and safety.

The design of a competitive rowboat, for example, is a good challenge for a CAD system. The challenge in designing an efficient and stable rowboat consists of maximizing the propulsion generated by the rower and the oars while minimizing the retarding hydrodynamic and aerodynamic drag (see Figure 7.6). These must be accomplished while staying within the restrictions placed on the particular competition. Aerodynamic forces account for approximately 12% of the total drag, but this drag can be reduced by streamlining the oars and the oar riggers that support the

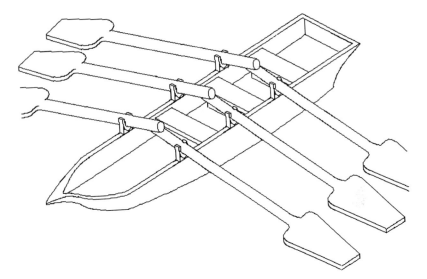

Figure 7.6   Typical rowboat. (Note the stream lined riggers body shape.)

oars. The aerodynamic drag can be reduced about 9% by streamlining. The rest of this drag can be reduced by the athlete wearing special clothing. Hydrodynamic drag, however, is not as simple to reduce. The shearing action of the boat's hull as it travels through the water creates a viscous drag. The problem is complicated further because as the boat travels at higher speed, greater pressure distributions are experienced by the hull due to surface waves. In order to gain speed, this force must be overcome. From fluid mechanics, we recognize that the shape of the boat determines the magnitude of these forces. A careful design incorporates all these concepts.

A flowchart of how this analysis is performed is shown in Figure 7.7. One quickly realizes that in order to perform this analysis, many computations must be carried out. This is why using a CAD system is so helpful. Ideally, we want to combine the physical restrictions and the technicalities of the competition. Then when factors such as wave conditions, weight distribution, and propulsion strength are applied to the force equations, a design can be generated. This method of taking a mediocre boat design and subtracting or adding curves under the condition of improving the boat's mobility gives the optimum design.

Increasingly, manufacturers of high-speed boats, fishing boats, and pleasure crafts are turning to CAD/CAM. Companies are using interactive graphics systems to develop new boats in significantly less time (see Figure 7.8). Preliminary hull lines are digitized into the CAD system as B-spline curves. The computer automatically interpolates a blended surface between preliminary curves completing the hull surface model. The CAD system is also used to model structural members and for laying out other components and equipment. Three-dimensional modeling not only

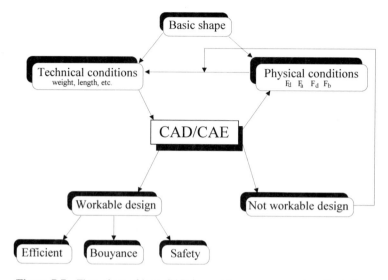

Figure 7.7   Flow chart of how CAD is used to generate a series of solutions.

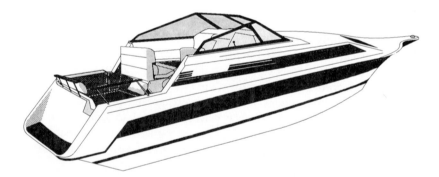

Figure 7.8   A sports yacht model designed using CAD/CAM.

simplifies the process of creating molds for the fiberglass hulls, but also helps program numerically controlled wood routers when interfaced with CAM software.

NC programming capabilities also boost efficiency in the manufacture of other components, including stringers and bulkheads that support the hull. Profiles from the CAD models are extracted for these members and used to automatically create tool paths for the wood routers in the manufacturing plant.

The capabilities of CAD systems have also been exploited in the design of diverse sports equipment. The wide range of activities engaged in by today's outdoorsmen, from windsurfing to mountain-biking and skiing to kayaking, created a need for a reliable means of transporting the equipment such as a rooftop carrier.

Major suppliers of sport racks are turning to CAD/CAM systems to aid the design and manufacture of racks. For example, Yakima, a supplier of sports racks [4], turned to a CAD system to help speed the design and manufacture of their carriers. Yakima designers slashed the design process from one year to six months using Anvil-5000 software from Manufacturing & Consulting Services, Inc. running on Unix-based workstations from Sun Microsystems.

Tennis rackets are one of the most intensely analyzed pieces of sporting equipment (see Figure 7.9). Ellipse Sports Companies uses extensive finite-element analysis on racket designs to understand what happens to the racket and player when the ball hits the strings. A nonlinear model of the strings to include the effects of string size and tension in the analysis are also being analyzed.

Based on measurements of racket mode shapes and forces transmitted to wrist and elbow, tennis racket manufacturers can produce a racket forged from a hybrid of graphite and other composites. This combination is said to be several times more effective in damping vibration and absorbing shock than conventional materials used in rackets.

No less important is the role of CAD in the design of exercise equipment. For example, companies employ a computer generated 3D model of a man to put their

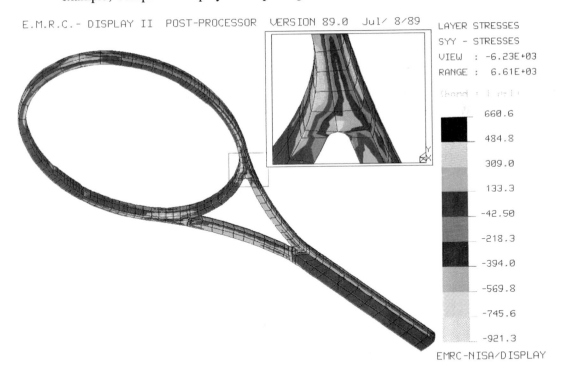

E.M.R.C.- DISPLAY II POST-PROCESSOR VERSION 89.0 Jul⁄ 8⁄89

LAYER STRESSES
SYY - STRESSES
VIEW : -6.23E+03
RANGE : 6.61E+03

(band : 1 of 1)

660.6
484.8
309.0
133.3
-42.50
-218.3
-394.0
-569.8
-745.6
-921.3

EMRC-NISA⁄DISPLAY

TENNIS RACKET WITH CORRECTED FIBER ORIENTATION FOR IDRA=0

TENNIS RACQUET

Figure 7.9 A tennis racket designed using CAD/CAM (courtesy of EMRC, Troy, Michigan).

exercise equipment through its paces even before a machine is built (see Figure 7-10). The designers use the model to analyze the motion of people during exercise and build a machine around them. Model sizes and proportion are changed quickly, using macros to ensure that the equipment is suitable for people of different body make-up.

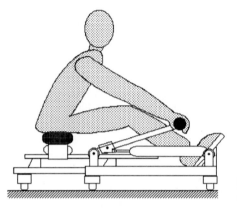

Figure 7.10 Human body modelling equipment for exercise.

The interaction of the human body with exercise machines can be simulated using CAD/CAE. The purpose is to optimize the design for better human fitness and safety. Usually a human model is created on the CAD system and then placed on the proposed machine. The computer provides information such as center of gravity, axis of rotation, and specific gravity of every part. It also indicates where and how to counterbalance rotating parts so the strength curve is not adversely affected. As a result of the use of CAD, companies are able to reduce the lead time for bringing new machines to the market.

The use of advanced aerospace materials and computer-aided design is finding wider use in the field of sports, recreation, and exercise equipment.

7.7 STRUCTURAL DESIGN AND CAD/CAM

Structural engineering is the art and science of designing cost-efficient support structures and is one of the most natural applications for CAD.

CAD provides the structural engineer with all the tools needed to generate and revise structural concepts or models, to define and redefine applied loads and structural attributes, and to control the design and analysis cycles. The engineer can assert creativity in design because all the tools are integrated in one system and no restrictions are applied on the sequence of actions.

The majority of CAD packages are divided into three principal sections: pre-processing, analysis, and post-processing. In pre-processing, the engineer uses functions to model the geometry and loading of trusses or frames, etc. In analysis, the displacements, forces, and reactions are determined using finite-element methods. In post-processing, the engineer uses functions to review the analysis results and its design members and connections. All three sections and functions within them are integrated using a network of menus and specially programmed keys.

With the advent of CAD and the ability to interface with precise non-linear inelastic analysis packages, clear understanding of frame response is possible. With the capacity of CAD packages doing simulation, the structural engineer has the ability to make decisions regarding the apportionment of materials throughout the framing system. A typical frame problem being analyzed on the computer is illustrated in Figure 7.11. Most CAD packages allow the structural engineer to perform static, limit, and dynamic structural analysis of structures composed of beams and shells.

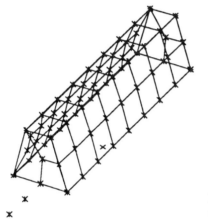

Figure 7.11 Frame analyzed on the computer.

The structural engineering of multi-story buildings is a complex task. With the use of CAD workstations the engineer can create the initial framing system design through the CAD program and then verify the structural integrity using associative finite-element analysis packages and the n update the optimized members in the CAD database. Thus, hundreds of hours of data entry are reduced as well as many costly data entry errors avoided.

Some of the programs can combine all types of structural materials used in the building into a single 3-D model, eliminating the need to create separate models for each material type. The 3-D model can enable analysis to be carried out with fewer errors and can capture a better analytical response.

Thus it seems that the benefits CAD offers a structural designer are as follows:

1. Productivity increase and faster response time.
2. Reduction in design errors and increase in consistencies in design drawings.
3. Improvements in quality control of the design.
4. Reduction of total cost.

REFERENCES

7.1 Computer System Design Reflects B-2's Complexity, *Aviation Week,* Nov. 28, 1988, pp. 26–27.

7.2 New Design, Production Tools Will Play a Key Role in B-2 Cost, *Aviation Week,* Dec. 5, 1988, pp. 18–21.

7.3 Smart Cars and Highways Go Global, IEEE, *Spectrum,* May 1991, pp. 26–36.

7.4 Beercheck, R. C., Recreation Equipment: Engineering the Competitive Edge, *Machine Design,* June 7, 1990, pp. 58–63.

7.5 Buxton, J. L. et al., The Travelpilot: A Second-Generation Automotive Navigation System, *IEEE Transactions on Vehicular Technology,* vol. 40 no. 1, Feb. 1991, pp. 41–44.

7.6 Crosheck, J., and Ford, M., Simulation Takes Three Wheeler for a Spin, *Mechanical Engineering,* Nov. 1988, pp. 48–51.

7.7 Nobbe, T. A., Giving Cars a Mind of Their Own, *Machine Design,* June 21, 1990, pp. 56–59.

7.8 Zavoli, W. B., A Vehicle Tracking and Monitoring System Including Digital Dispatch and Driver Guidance, *Proceedings of the National Technical Meeting,* Institute of Navigation, Jan. 23–26, 1989, San Mateo, Calif., pp. 35–39.

chapter 8

Computer-Aided Manufacturing

8.1 INTRODUCTION

In the past, when a particular design of a mechanical part was completed, its corresponding blueprints were given to the manufacturing department's process engineer. The engineer devised a processing plan to machine the part to its final stage. The specific information on the blueprint constituted the database.

In design, the CAD system provides the ultimate tool for the designer to geometrically conceptualize, analyze, and optimize the design. As in the design process, the CAD/CAM system assists the engineer in all aspects of manufacturing. One of the biggest advantages of this technology is the CAD's provision of the database of the part to be produced, eliminating blueprints and manual data transfer. The process engineer can graphically test the machining process by simulating it on the screen and interactively modifying it to obtain the optimum process plan. With computers and computer graphics, we can go from the initial design step to making a product using one integrated system (Figure 8.1). The integrity of design and manufacturing is achieved through access to the common database.

Figure 8.1 Integration of the database in design and manufacturing.

8.2 NUMERICAL-CONTROL MACHINING

Manufacturing industries continue to evolve by constantly upgrading and automating their processes. The manufacturing revolution, however, started after World War II. It began in 1952 when the Massachusetts Institute of Technology (MIT) first demonstrated the programmability or numerical control of a machine for a project sponsored by the U.S. Air Force, which was known as the NC machine. The concept was based on a machine-readable numerical code. Among the advantages of an NC machine is its capability of storing complicated sequences of machining operations and retrieving them for use.

8.2.1 Programming Languages and NC Systems

In 1955, a group of researchers at MIT developed a computer program (Automatically Programmed Tool, APT) that could assist in preparing NC tapes for all kinds of NC systems. Aerospace companies were the major users because the early version of APT was designed for mainframes and was used mostly for 3D and multiaxis profiling. Because of the requirements of APT software, other NC programs were developed as alternatives, adding extra functions to the process and easing down the mainframe requirement, which was expensive to small industries. Those programs, structured in a similar fashion to APT, included ADAPT, EXAPT, IFAPT, MINIAPT, NELAPT, and CORPACT II. Today, APT is the most used NC program around the world, and it has been standardized in the United States since 1974. Some of the advantages of APT programming languages are that they (a) simplify NC programming, (b) simplify tape preparation, and (c) reduce programming time.
Advantages of the NC machine include:

1. Reduces nonchip making time (i.e., reduces the unit cost of production).
2. Provides fixed resolution: accuracy and repeatability are relatively constant, which yields a high-quality product.
3. Allows production flexibility (setup time) and materials handling.
4. Eliminates machining time studies (the programs dictate this).
5. Is suitable for small lot sizes.
6. Reduces operator decision making.
7. Reduces scrap.
8. Simplifies inspection.

Disadvantages of the NC machine include:

1. Requires high initial costs.
2. Needs critical part location.
3. Provides no operator feedback.
4. Requires trained programmers.

The Electronic Industrial Association (EIA) defines the NC machine as "a system in which actions are controlled by the direct insertion of numerical data at some point. The system must automatically interpret at least some portion of the data."

8.2.2 NC Configuration

A numerical-control machine consists of three distinct parts, as shown in Figure 8.2: (1) data input, (2) control unit, and (3) the machine tool to be controlled.

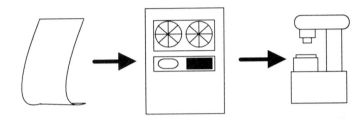

Data input   Control unit   Machine tool

Figure 8.2   NC system configuration.

Data Input.   The data input, also called a program of instructions, is recorded and stored by several methods for the NC machine. These methods include

- punched tape
- punched cards
- magnetic tape
- remote computer storage
- floppy disks
- control unit memory system

The most common data input device is the punched tape (Figure 8.3), which is manually mounted on the control unit device. The device reads the tape instructions and executes a set of commands that moves the machine tool. The punched tape consists of eight columns of punched holes within the 1-inch width of the tape. The holes are in a certain format to transmit data to the control unit. The tape is divided into blocks, which constitute one set of instructions. The block usually gives commands for movement along the x, y, and z axes, including the speed of the spindle (if drilling is required), tool change, feed rate, and coolant start and stop. Each NC system has different capabilities and hence the programmer has to check the available functions for programming. Special NC punched tape readers are used (Figure 8.4) to generate complete program instructions. The programmer requires knowledge of machining and must be trained for NC programming. The programmer's most important assets include the ability to read drawings (blueprints) and to devise a process plan on which operation is to be performed first. Efficient programs are those that require less time for execution and provide the optimum machining sequence of operations. It should be pointed out that control units can be programmed directly by an operator. This is known as manual data input (MDI).

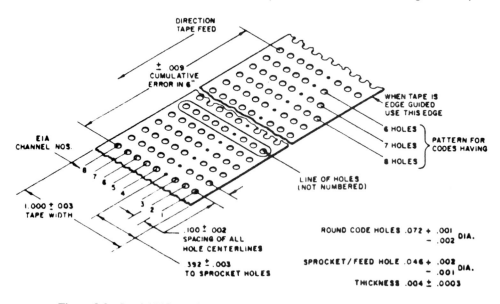

Figure 8.3 Special NC punch tape (courtesy of Cincinnati Milacron, Cincinnati, Ohio).

Figure 8.4 Punched tape reader (courtesy of Cincinnati Milacron, Cincinnati, Ohio).

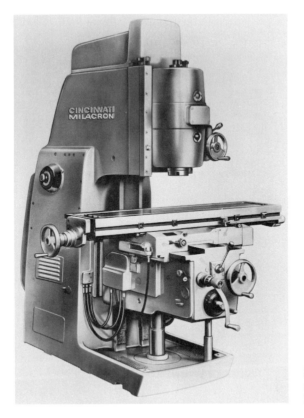

Figure 8.5 Conventional vertical milling machine (courtesy of Cincinnati, Milacron, Cincinnati, Ohio).

Control Unit.   The machine control unit plays the role of the central processing unit (CPU) of a computer. The conventional NC machine (Figure 8.5) has a tape reader that converts information from the tape to commands that are sent to the machine tool through pulses of electric energy. The proper controls are activated, causing the machine tool to perform the machining process automatically. The NC control unit, therefore, converts instructions from the input medium to a set of instructions for the machine. The control unit has a control panel or console that controls its operation (Figure 8.6). The panel is usually handled by a skilled operator.

Machine Tool (Controlled Equipment).   This is the part that does the actual drilling, cutting, and taping. The machine tool is part of the NC system and responds to commands generated by the part program.

Some of the main features of the machine tool include low friction between moving parts, and fast response time (accurate) through antibacklash components.

The machine tool's motion is controlled by servo drives (Figure 8.7). Servo drives have ratings of 1/6 to 50 horsepower (hp). The average machines are usually between 1/3 to 5 hp. Servo drives have a feed rate control between 0 and

Figure 8.6 NC control unit (Acramatic 950, courtesy of Cincinnati, Milacron, Cincinnati, Ohio).

500 in./min., resolutions (command increments) between 0.0001 and 0.001 in., and accuracies of 0.000025 to 0.01 in. Servo drives can be classified as follows:

- electric:
  ac motor-line contactors
  ac motor-magnetic clutches
  2- or 3-phase ac servo motors
  dc motor generators
  stepping motors
- hydraulic
- pneumatic

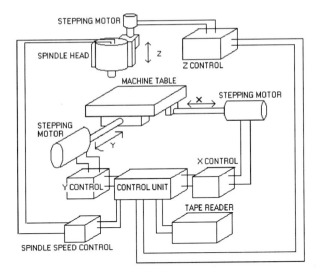

Figure 8.7   Servo mechanism.

Servo drives are

- tolerant to tool cutting forces
- insensitive to load mass inertias (stiffness)
- insensitive to running friction forces
- linear to a high degree

In NC systems, the machine tool is equipped with transducers for feedback information (Figure 8.8). This information is usually in the forms of displacement and velocity, which are sent directly to the controller for verification.

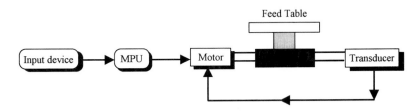

Figure 8.8   Typical NC single axes configuration.

8.3 NC AXES DEFINITIONS

The key concept in an NC system is interpreting the command by the machine tool and executing its precise motion in a given set of reference frames (x, y, and z axes). The machine tool motions are generally described in x–y–z Cartesian space.

Both the workpiece and the tool positions must be known at all times. There are two basic axis systems used for executing a motion: (a) incremental positioning, and (b) absolute positioning.

In programming NC systems, the operator has the option of either using incremental positioning to move from one position to another by simply taking the last position as the zero position or using absolute positioning in which all locations on a part are given with respect to a fixed reference frame known as the home base. Consider the four-hole plate shown in Figure 8.9. If we take the lower left-hand corner of the plate to be the origin in the x–y–z frame, then the positions of P_1, P_2, P_3, and P_4 can be given in two ways:

Incremental positioning	Absolute positioning
$P_1: x = 1.0, y = 1.0$	$P_1: x = 1.0, y = 1.0$
$P_2: x = 0.0, y = 2.0$	$P_2: x = 1.0, y = 3.0$
$P_3: x = 2.0, y = 0.0$	$P_3: x = 3.0, y = 3.0$
$P_4: x = 0.0, y = -2.0$	$P_4: x = 3.0, y = 1.0$

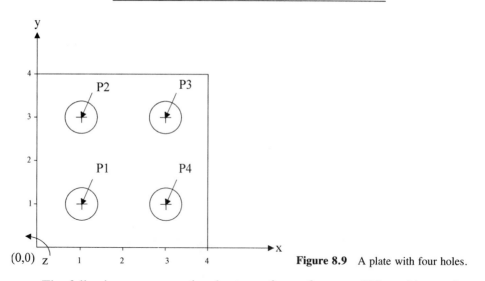

Figure 8.9   A plate with four holes.

The following are conventional setups of axes for some NC machine tools:

1. **Coordinate system for a lathe (Figure 8.10):** X axis is the axis rectangular to the turning axis; z axis is the axis parallel to the turning axis; $+z$ movement is the movement of the longitudinal slide away from the headstock; $-z$ movement is the movement of the longitudinal slide in the direction of the headstock; $+x$ movement: see the figure; and $-x$ movement: see the figure.
2. Axis system for a vertical mill (Figure 8.11).
3. Axis system for a horizontal boring mill (Figure 8.12).
4. Axis system for a vertical turret lathe (Figure 8.13).

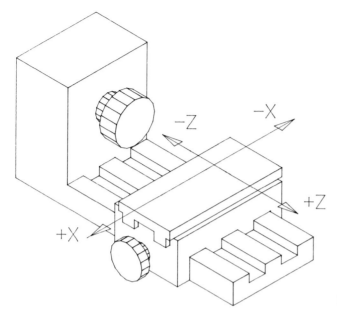

Figure 8.10   Lathe coordinate systems.

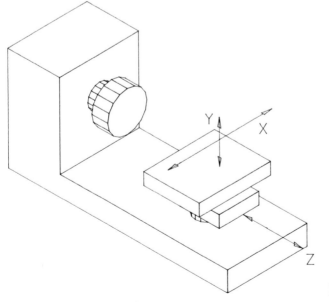

Figure 8.11   Vertical Mill.

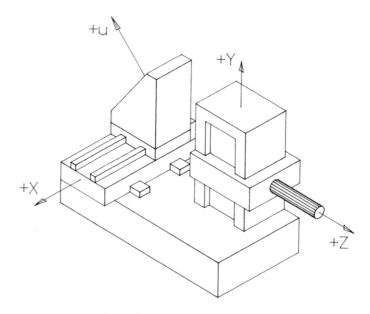

Figure 8.12   Horizontal Boring Mill.

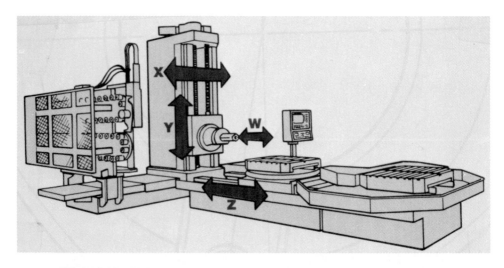

Figure 8.13   CNC Machining Center (T-Bar Horizontal Spindle CNC machining center, courtesy of Cincinnati, Milacron, Cincinnati, Ohio).

8.4 MOTION CONTROL

There are two basic controls used in a machining process. The first controls the travel direction and distance of the cutting tool and is known as point-to-point (PTP) and the other controls the cutting tool over contours and is known as contouring.

8.4.1 Point-to-Point (PTP) Motion Control

In the point-to-point operation, we are only concerned about the positioning of the tool at the right location relative to the workpiece so the process can begin. For instance, in drilling holes, the motion of the tool from a drilled hole to another position in which a hole is to be drilled is not important and therefore need not be precisely controlled. However, when the tool reaches its final destination (programmed position), the machine moves the drill a finite distance (increment) in the direction in which the hole is to be created and then retracts it (see Figure 8.14). Once that is achieved, the table is moved so that the position of the next hole to be drilled is under the tool. This procedure usually continues until all the drilling is complete.

Motion control based on PTP is the simplest of them all; hence, an NC machine with such a controller is the least expensive. Simple operations, where the motion is controlled in only one direction, are typified by milling slots.

8.4.2 Contouring

The machining of curved surfaces is more complex than the one described by PTP. It requires the control of tool velocities along two or three axes. These velocities are constantly being checked through feedback so that the desired path to be machined is achieved. For example, if the tool is moving along a path (see Figure 8.15), then V_x and V_y are the velocities along the x and y axes, respectively, to be controlled (see

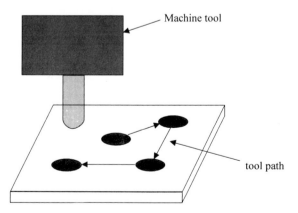

Figure 8.14   Point-to-point (PTP) motion control.

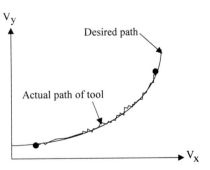

Figure 8.15   Contouring cutting path.

Figure 8.16). Examples of such machine tools are milling machines, turning machines, flame cutters, welders, and grinders.

The accuracy of such machines is usually referred to as tolerance. There are two types of tolerance: inside tolerance (Figure 8.17) and outside tolerance (Figure 8.18).

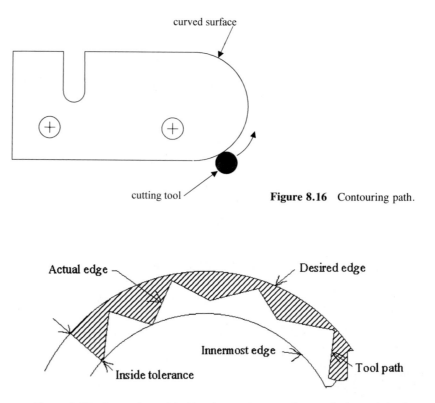

Figure 8.16   Contouring path.

Figure 8.17   Comparison of inside tolerance between the actual edge and the desired cutting edge.

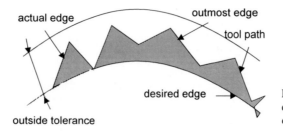

Figure 8.18   Comparison of outside tolerance between the actual edge and the desired cutting edge.

8.5 CNC AND DNC MACHINES

8.5.1 Computer Numerical Control (CNC) Unit

Most NC machines are equipped with CNC controllers (Figure 8.19), which have a variety of features. Some of these features are standard and others can be added on depending on the needs of the customer. The CNC configuration replaces the control unit with a dedicated microcomputer. The microcomputer adds a new dimension to the capability of the NC system in terms of programming, memory, and built-in diagnostics. An illustration of a CNC computer-based configuration is given by Figure 8.20.

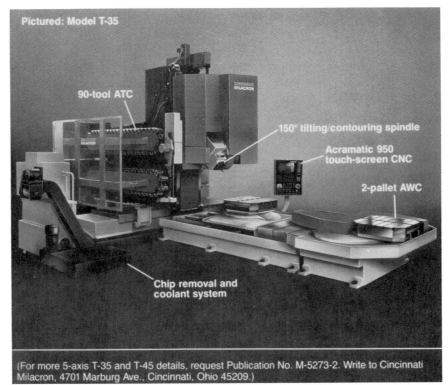

Pictured: Model T-35

90-tool ATC

150° tilting/contouring spindle

Acramatic 950 touch-screen CNC

2-pallet AWC

Chip removal and coolant system

(For more 5-axis T-35 and T-45 details, request Publication No. M-5273-2. Write to Cincinnati Milacron, 4701 Marburg Ave., Cincinnati, Ohio 45209.)

Figure 8.19 NC machine with a built-in CNC controller (a T30 Horizontal Spindle CNC machining center, courtesy of Cincinnati, Milacron, Cincinnati, Ohio).

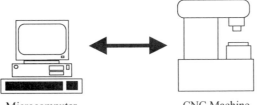

Microcomputer   CNC Machine

Figure 8.20 A CNC computer-based configuration.

The characteristics and advantages of CNC control units are as follows:

1. The CRT character display allows reviewing and editing of NC programs when needed.
2. The graphical display of the cutter path allows checking the machining processes before they are actually performed. Additional hardware and software might be needed for simulation of the cutter.
3. The NC program is read only once. Once the information is stored in the computer, it can be easily recalled for further use without having to reread the tape as in NC systems. This feature saves time and adds flexibility to the programmer's editing skills.
4. The computer interface allows exchanging information between different units through integrated systems; hence, a CNC can communicate with other units such as robots and machine tools.
5. The CNC controller allows accurate positioning. Today's CNC has a position repeatability of 0.4×10^{-4} to 0.8×10^{-8} inches, a maximum spindle speed of 4000 to 8000 rpm, and a feed rate of 197 to 590 in./min.
6. The CNC controller has advanced software features that allow more functions to be added for better machining.

8.5.2 Direct Numerical Control (DNC)

Direct numerical control (DNC) is a manufacturing system that uses a main (host) computer to control several machines simultaneously (Figure 8.21). The direct connection between the main computer and the machines allows for quick information exchange in real time.

The basic configuration of a DNC system is as follows:

1. Main computer
2. Minicomputers
3. Communication lines
4. Machine tools

The main computer retrieves the data on the part to be machined from either its own data storage unit or from an outside source. It then sends the commands to the NC machines to produce the desired part. The host computer controls all the operating conditions of the machine and allows data to be manipulated locally by an NC processor when needed.

In some DNC systems, a minicomputer local to each NC machine can be inserted to relieve the main computer from certain operations. A computer hierarchy can be developed by installing additional computers (less powerful computers, called satellites) between the NC machine tools and the host so as to

Main Computer (HOST)

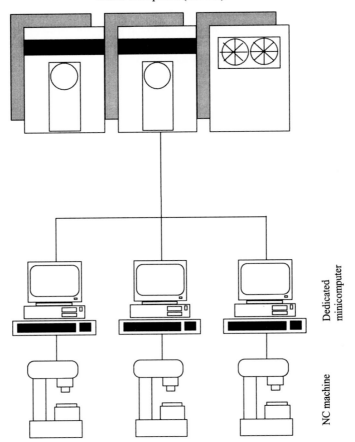

Figure 8.21   DNC configuration.

1. facilitate the speed of the entire system
2. handle large computer files
3. expand the number of machine tools used
4. decrease the computing time and increase quality

The communication line is a two-way system. The computer can send information to the machine and the machine can in turn request information from the computer to complete the job.

Communication between the computer and the machines is done through a controller that is efficient in the import and export of information. Each NC machine is equipped with a controller, known as the machine-control unit (MCU), which receives and executes instructions from the computer. The MCU also provides feedback to the main computer as to its present status and condition.

The advantages of DNC machines include the following:

- Eliminate problems with paper tapes.
- Provide optional links with CAD systems.
- Increase efficiency due to information response from the machines.
- Allow modification and savings (of cost) by reprogramming rather than hardware overhaul.
- Provide better housekeeping and maintenance records on machine usage and inventory of finished parts.
- Generate instant reports on the status of the NC machines and their corresponding processes.
- In a satellite network, allow immediate changes on NC information to be made in the branch affected (on the shop floor).

DNC allows more versatility than the other systems and is less likely to become obsolete.

8.6 ECONOMICS OF NUMERICAL CONTROL

The economics of machine tools plays an important part in any manufacturing activity. A part can be manufactured on many different machine tools, but certain factors render some machines unacceptable. Economics has a major role in the selection of the correct machine for a particular job. In many cases, a few simple pieces can be machined by a skilled machinist in less time and at a lower cost on a general-purpose conventional machine than on an NC machine, which requires programming and or setting up routines for an automated machine tool. However, with intricate parts, even one piece can be done more economically on an NC machine. Once the programming is done, additional parts can be machined at a very low cost per piece within a shorter time.

Some of the factors that are considered in selecting NC machines include the following:

- NC machines cost 1.5 to 5 times more than conventional machines of the same size.
- Maintenance requires trained, skilled personnel. Experienced programmers are required to program NC machines.
- Idle time is minimum, fatigue is nonexistent, there are fewer rejects, human mistakes are avoided, and all planning is carried out before a job is started on NC machines. All these are cost factors. A study by one manufacturer showed

NC machines have a cutting time of 80% against less than 25% cutting time on conventional machines.

- Tool life is greater in NC machines because speed and depth of cut as initially set are continuously maintained.
- There is at least a 25% reduction in scrap and rework using NC machines.
- There is a 20 to 25% reduction in material handling.
- There is a 30 to 40% reduction in inspection and quality control time.
- The floor space area required is less: a single NC machine can replace several conventional machines because multiple operations can be performed on NC machines.
- Tooling costs, storage costs, and setup costs for intricate parts are considerably less in NC machines.

The University of Michigan carried out a study of 356 companies employing 4648 NC machines that showed the average savings and productivity gains from NC compared to conventional machine tools (see Ref. 8.12). Productivity gains were more impressive than time savings. For example, consider that the time taken to produce a part on an NC machine is 40% of that required on a conventional machine; thus, there is a 60% savings in time. If the conventional machine takes 1 h to make one part, the NC machine can make the part in 24 min and produce 2.5 parts per hour, resulting in an increase in productivity of 150%. However, NC machines cannot compete with fixed-program special-purpose machines to produce large quantities of pieces. On the other hand, NC machines can supplement special machines in certain aspects. NC machines can be part of a flexible process that produces large numbers of different parts but not a large number of any one part at one time.

Example 8.1   Comparison Between Conventional Milling and NC Machines

The evaluation of the economics of machining a part on both a conventional milling machine and NC machine is to be carried out.

The conventional milling machine costs $45,000. The machine produces 20 parts per hour. The annual maintenance cost of the machine is $2,600. The labor cost for the conventional machine is $12.50/h and other labor-associated overhead rates amount to 25%. The NC machine costs $115,000 and is capable of producing 55 parts per hour. The annual maintenance costs amount to $5,400. The labor cost and overhead for operating this machine amounts to one-third that of the conventional milling machine.

Determine the minimum number of parts required to be produced to make the choice of the NC machines more profitable to the company.

Solution   The total cost for the conventional milling machine (T_C) is

$$T_C = \$45,000 + \$2,600 + \frac{\$12.50/h \times (1 + 25\%)}{55 \text{ parts/h}} \times Q$$

where Q is the number of parts produced. Therefore,

$$T_C = \$47,600 + 0.28Q \tag{8.1}$$

The total cost for the NC machine (T_{NC}) is

$$T_{NC} = \$115,000 \times \$5,400 + \frac{\$12.50/\text{hr} \times (1 + 25\%) \times 1/3}{55 \text{ parts/h}} \times Q$$

$$T_{NC} = \$120,400 + 0.09Q \tag{8.2}$$

Solving Equations (8.1) and (8.2) gives the value of the minimum number of parts that are required to make the NC machine more profitable.

$$-1 \times T_C = -\$47,600 - 0.28Q$$
$$\underline{T_{NC} = \$120,400 + 0.09Q}$$
$$0 = \$72,800/\text{year} - 0.19Q$$

$$Q = 383,158 \text{ parts/year} \qquad\blacksquare$$

PROBLEMS

8.1 Discuss the benefits of PTP motion control over contouring with regard to inside and outside tolerances.

8.2 What kind of job requires a DNC machining system? Give an example of a part that can be machined on both a CNC and DNC system. Justify the choice of the system.

8.3 Describe the location of points P_1 to P_5 in Figure P8.1 using: (a) absolute positioning, and (b) incremental positioning.

8.4 Describe the location of points P_1 to P_4 in Figure P8.2 using: (a) absolute positioning, and (b) incremental positioning.

8.5 A part is to be machined on a conventional production machine. It can also be machined on the company's automated NC machine. What is the minimum number of parts required to be produced to make the company consider using the NC machine?

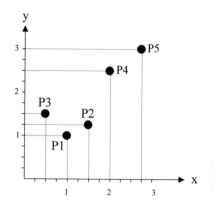

Figure P8.1 Location of points using absolute positioning, incremental positioning.

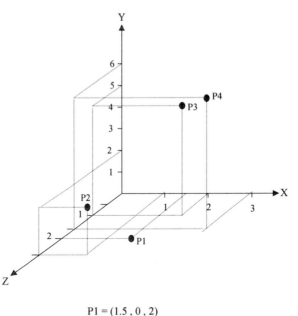

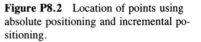

P1 = (1.5 , 0 , 2)
P2 = (1 , 3 , 2.5)
P3 = (2 , 5 , 1)
P4 = (3 , 6 , 1.5)

Figure P8.2 Location of points using absolute positioning and incremental positioning.

The part has a cycle time of 6 h/piece at a rate of $25/h on the conventional production machine. Two hundred h are required to design and make a jig and fixture for the part in the tool room. Cycle time for the part on the automated machine is 3.5 h/piece at $60/h. Sixty-five h are required at $20/h to write the program and 1 h is needed at $50/h to load the program in the computer.

The tool room rate (for both machines) is $15/h.

Also graphically compare the costs of NC and conventional machines.

8.6 A job can be set up on a standard jig boring machine in 1.5 h. Each piece takes 6 h for boring. If the job is set up on a tape-controlled jig boring machine, 3 h goes into programming. Each part can be bored in 5 h. The labor rate for the standard jig milling machine is $25/h and $80/h for the NC borer. Other costs amount to $18/h for both. When is the numerically controlled machine justified?

REFERENCES

8.1 Blauk, L. T., and Tarquin, A. J., *Engineering Economy,* 2d ed., McGraw-Hill, New York, 1983.

8.2 Buckerfield, S. T., Continuous Numerical Control of Machine Tools, *Control,* Vol. 3, June/July 1960, pp. 90–98.

8.3 Childs, J. J., *Principles of Numerical Control,* Industrial Press, New York, 1965.

8.4 Evans, J. T., and Kelling, L. V., Inside the Mark Century Numerical Control, *Control Eng.,* Vol. 10, May 1963, pp. 112–118.

8.5 Haringx, J. A., A Numerically Controlled Contour Milling Machine, *Philips Technical Review,* Vol. 24, September 1963, pp. 299–331.

8.6 Harrington, J., *Computer Integrated Manufacturing,* Industrial Press, New York, 1973.

8.7 Koren, Y., Shani, A., and Ben-Uri, Numerical Control of a Lathe, *IEEE Trans. Ind. Elec. Ind. Gen. App.,* Vol. 6, No. 2, March 1970, pp. 175–179.

8.8 Modern Machine Shop, *1986 NC/CAM Guidebook,* Gardner Publications, Cincinnati, 1986.

8.9 Olesten, N. O., *Numerical Control,* John Wiley & Sons, New York, 1970.

8.10 Smith, D. N., NC for Profit and Productivity, *Amer. Mach.,* Oct. 16, 1972, p. 68.

8.11 Taft, C. K., Lutz, F. N., and Mazoh, M., Dynamic Accuracy in Numerical Control Systems, *Tool Manuf. Eng.,* Part 1, May 1967, pp. 18–20; Part 2, June 1967, pp. 80–83.

8.12 Thuesen, G. J., and Fabrycky, W., *Engineering Economy,* 6th ed., Prentice-Hall, Englewood Cliffs, NJ, 1984.

chapter 9

Geometry Description by Programming

9.1 INTRODUCTION

Geometry creation by programming requires listing and executing all the entity statements that comprise the object(s). This option, which is available through CAD/CAM software packages, is an alternative to interactive programs such as AUTOCAD, CADKEY, UNIGRAPHICS, and CADAM. Its function is based on writing the entire "program" to draw the desired object. In the case of a manually drawn object, we have to label it and write its corresponding CAD program to reproduce it. This enables us to save and alter the drawing when needed. CAD's programming language bypasses the interactive mode and tells the computer exactly what to draw and where to locate the entity without equipment errors such as a tolerance difference when using a joystick.

The benefits of using geometry description by programming are similar to those of computer programming using a high-level language. They include the following:

1. Use of variable names. (The entity itself can be changed by modifying the values of the variables instead of erasing the entity and creating another one in its place.)
2. Creation of subroutines where repeated drawing of the same object is necessary.
3. Easier control of entity assignment through variable names (such as in common blocks, where subroutines are used).

4. Easy interaction with analysis software. Geometry creation through programming forms the basis for the pre- and postprocessor developments in CAD/CAM software packages such as finite-element analysis and computerized machining. (See Chapter 10.)

9.2. GEOMETRY STATEMENTS

The geometry statements consist of creating entities such as points, lines, circles, planes, cylinders, ellipses, cones, and spheres. There are a number of methods to create each of these entities. The programmer is urged to learn, as with any other programming language, to build a strategy on how to create a geometry of a particular part to be machined. Previously known or created entities can be used intelligently to build the design. The structure of the geometry statement is as follows:

$$\frac{\text{variable name}}{\text{of the entity}} = \frac{\text{function name}}{\text{of the entity}} \Big/ \text{function description}$$

In some circumstances in which the information cannot be exactly described, such as the desired point of the two points indicated when a line intersects a circle, a modifier is incorporated to best describe the entity with respect to the absolute coordinates and other entities. Figure 9.1 illustrates the modifier description in the *x–y* plane. The following abbreviations are used in geometry statements:

INTERC: intersection
TANTO: tangent to
ATANGL: at an angle of
PERPTO: perpendicular to
PARLEL: parallel to

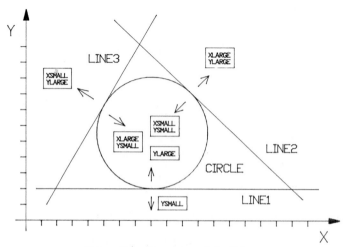

Figure 9.1　Illustration of the object.

The following sections give general descriptions of geometry statements available in most CAD packages. They form the basis for APT programming in machining.

9.2.1 Point Definitions

Point creation is the most common one. Points are usually needed for the creation of other entities. Once a point is created, it can be used by simply referring to its variable name. Note that the computer processes the entities in the sequence in which the program is written. If a geometry statement incorporates another entity, the referenced entity must be previously defined or the processor will terminate the program. There are a number of possible ways to create points and they are fully described in what follows.

1. *Absolute coordinates:* Express the Cartesian coordinates of the location of the point with respect to the absolute coordinate (Figure 9.2).

$$PT = POINT / X, Y, Z$$

(If Z is zero, the z component could be omitted from the statement.)

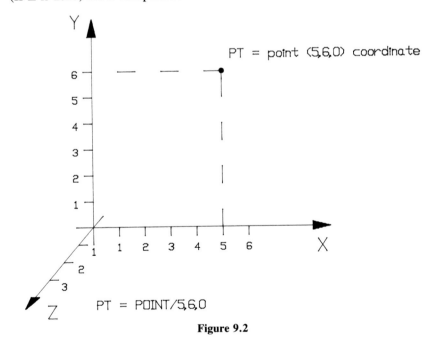

Figure 9.2

2. *Intersection of two lines:* Two lines intersect at a point (Figure 9.3) that is defined as

$$PT = POINT / INTOF, LINE1, LINE2$$

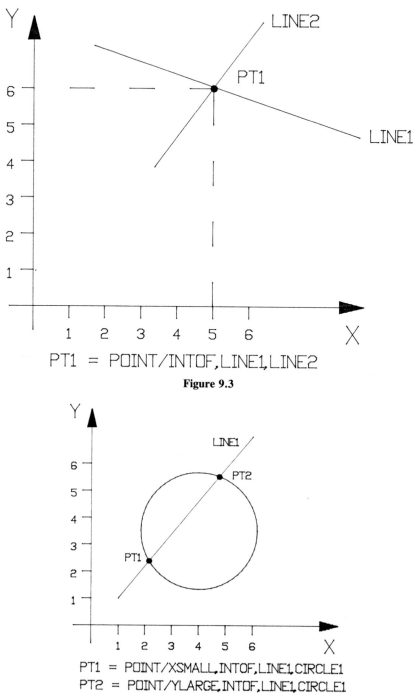

PT1 = POINT/INTOF,LINE1,LINE2

Figure 9.3

PT1 = POINT/XSMALL,INTOF,LINE1,CIRCLE1
PT2 = POINT/YLARGE,INTOF,LINE1,CIRCLE1

Figure 9.4

3. *Intersection of a line and a circle:* Because a line intersects a circle at two points (Figure 9.4), a modifier is needed to differentiate between the two. For example, if XSMALL is used, the computer compares the *x* coordinates of the two points and uses the one with the smallest value. The same applies for the comparison of the *y* and *z* coordinates.

PT = POINT / MODIFIER, INTOF, LINE, CIRCLE

The modifier options are {XLARGE, XSMALL, YLARGE, YSMALL}.

4. *Intersection of two circles:* This option generates two points (Figure 9.5); hence, we need a modifier to select the one we need.

PT = POINT / MODIFIER, INTOF, C1, C2

The modifier options are {XLARGE, XSMALL, YLARGE, YSMALL}.

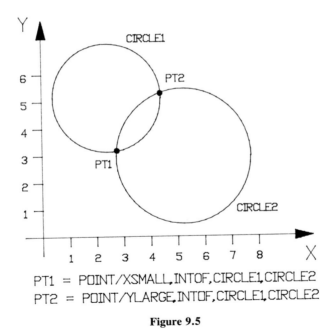

PT1 = POINT/XSMALL,INTOF,CIRCLE1,CIRCLE2
PT2 = POINT/YLARGE,INTOF,CIRCLE1,CIRCLE2

Figure 9.5

5. *Point resulting from an imaginary line making an angle (θ) with repect to the X axis and tangent to a circle:* The angle is described in degrees and is positive in the counterclockwise direction starting from the X axis (Figure 9.6).

PT = POINT / CIRCLE, ATANGL (angle in degrees)

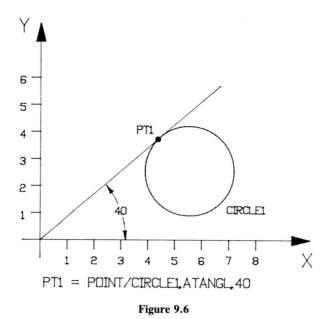

PT1 = POINT/CIRCLE1,ATANGL,40

Figure 9.6

6. *Point at the center of a circle:* To use the center point of a circle (Figure 9.7), the following definition is used:

PT = POINT / CENTER, CIRCLE

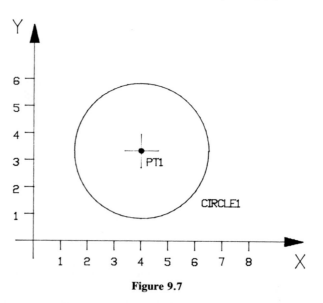

Figure 9.7

7. *Intersection of a line and a cone:* As with a point at the intersection of a line and a circle, a modifier is needed to select the desired point (Figure 9.8).

PT = POINT / MODIFIER, INTOF, LINE, CONE

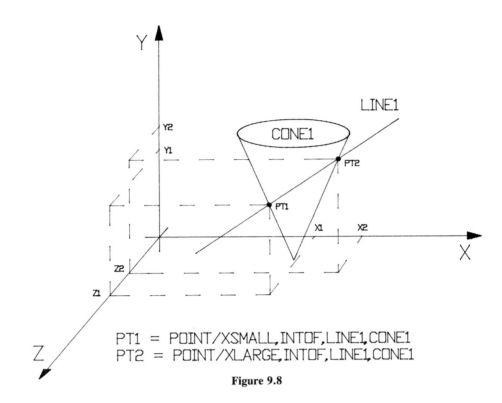

$$PT1 = POINT/XSMALL, INTOF, LINE1, CONE1$$
$$PT2 = POINT/XLARGE, INTOF, LINE1, CONE1$$

Figure 9.8

8. *Intersection of three planes:* Three planes intersect at a point (Figure 9.9).

$$PT = POINT / INTOF, PLANE1, PLANE2, PLANE3$$

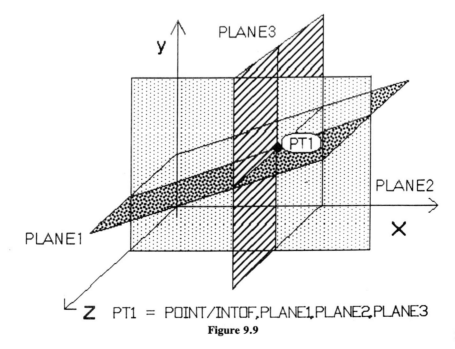

$$PT1 = POINT/INTOF, PLANE1, PLANE2, PLANE3$$

Figure 9.9

9. *Polar coordinates:* Using the x–y, y–z, and z–x planes, we can define points and circumference of a circle using the radius and the angle of rotation (Figure 9.10).

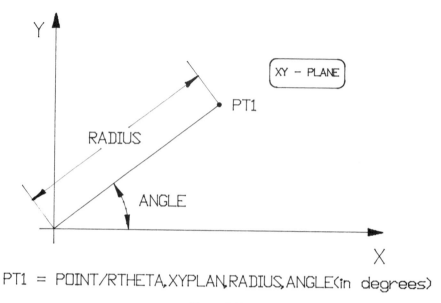

$$PT1 = POINT/RTHETA, XYPLAN, RADIUS, ANGLE(in\ degrees)$$

Figure 9.10

$$PT = POINT\ /\ RTHETA,\ XYPLAN,\ RADIUS,\ ANGLE\ (in\ degrees)$$
$$PT = POINT\ /\ RTHETA,\ YZPLAN,\ RADIUS,\ ANGLE\ (in\ degrees)$$
$$PT = POINT\ /\ RTHETA,\ ZXPLAN,\ RADIUS,\ ANGLE\ (in\ degrees)$$

where

$$XYPLAN = x\text{–}y\ plane$$
$$YZPLAN = y\text{–}z\ plane$$
$$ZXPLAN = z\text{–}x\ plane$$

10. *Intersection of a line and a tabulated cylinder:*

$$PT = POINT\ /\ INTOF,\ LINE,\ TABCYL,\ TABC1$$

The point of reference should be near the desired intersection point. The best choice is the nearest point in the tabulated cylinder definition (Figure 9.11).

11. *Point as the Nth location of a pattern:* A set of points in a pattern type can be stored under one name. (Figure 9.12). Any point in the pattern can then be selected by referring to its position (see Sec. 9.2.7).

$$PT = POINT\ /\ PATTERN,\ N$$

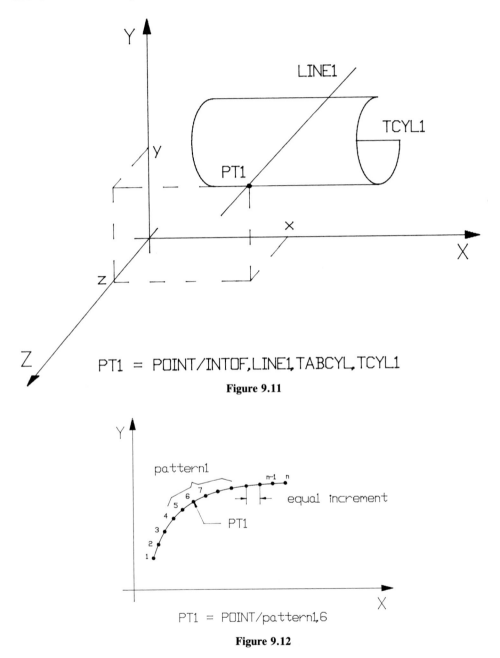

PT1 = POINT/INTOF,LINE1,TABCYL,TCYL1

Figure 9.11

PT1 = POINT/pattern1,6

Figure 9.12

9.2.2 Line Definitions

The description of a line can either be a segment between the absolute coordinates or a continuous line throughout the defined limit of the work space available. It can be determined by several methods. The following list of statements is used in the line description.

1. *Line through two points:* This statement describes a segment by defining its endpoints (Figure 9.13). The endpoints can be given by previously defined points or simply by their coordinates.

$$LIN = LINE / X1, Y1, Z1, X2, Y2, Z2$$

or

$$LIN = LINE / PT1, PT2$$

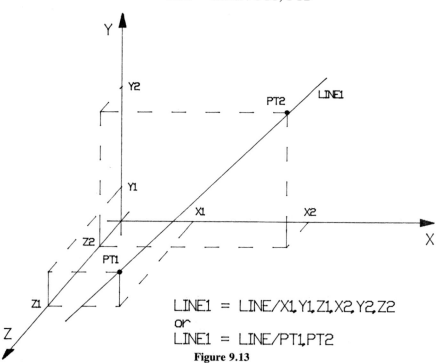

LINE1 = LINE/X1,Y1,Z1,X2,Y2,Z2
or
LINE1 = LINE/PT1,PT2

Figure 9.13

2. *Line through a point and tangent to a circle:* There are two lines that can be drawn from a point and tangent to a circle (Figure 9.14).

$$LIN = LINE / POINT, MODIFIER, TANTO, CIRCLE$$

where MODIFIER is {RIGHT or LEFT}. Select RIGHT and LEFT by viewing the circle from the point.

3. *A line tangent to two circles:*

$$LIN = LINE / MODIFIER, TANTO, CIRCLE2, MODIFIER, TANTO,$$
$$CIRCLE2$$

The options of this modifier are {RIGHT or LEFT} (Figure 9.15). The first cir-

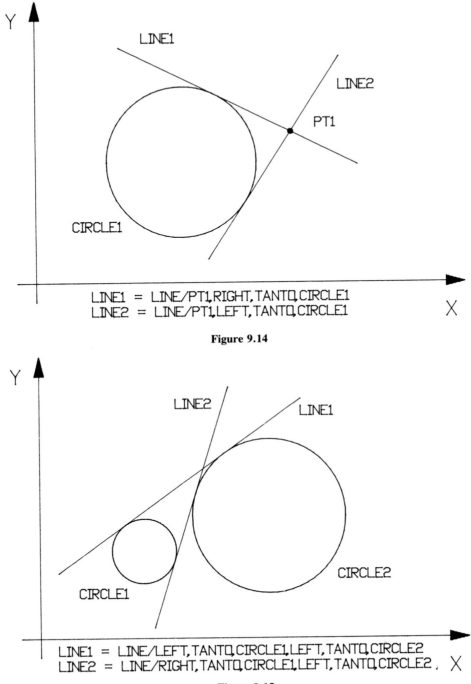

LINE1 = LINE/PT1,RIGHT,TANTO,CIRCLE1
LINE2 = LINE/PT1,LEFT,TANTO,CIRCLE1

Figure 9.14

LINE1 = LINE/LEFT,TANTO,CIRCLE1,LEFT,TANTO,CIRCLE2
LINE2 = LINE/RIGHT,TANTO,CIRCLE1,LEFT,TANTO,CIRCLE2

Figure 9.15

cle serves as the circle from which you view the second one; the modifier then is selected appropriately.

4. *A line through a point making an angle with the x or y axis:*

$$\text{LIN} = \text{LINE} / \text{PT1, ATANGL (in degrees), AXIS}$$

Note that the *x* axis is assumed if nothing is omitted from the statement. (See Figure 9.16.)

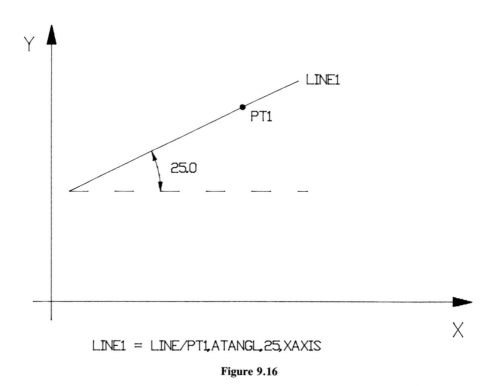

LINE1 = LINE/PT1,ATANGL,25,XAXIS

Figure 9.16

5. *A line through a point and having a slope with respect to the x and y axes:*

$$\text{LIN} = \text{LINE} / \text{POINT, SLOPE, NUMERICAL VALUE}$$

The slope is with respect to the axis chosen (Figure 9.17). (The *x* axis assumed as before.)

6. *A line on the x or y axis on the x–y plane:* See Figure 9.18.

$$\text{LIN} = \text{LINE} / \text{XAXIS}$$

$$\text{LIN} = \text{LINE} / \text{YAXIS}$$

Note: The options could be the *x* axis (or *z* axis) for the *x–z* plane and the *y* axis (or *z* axis) for the *y–z* plane.

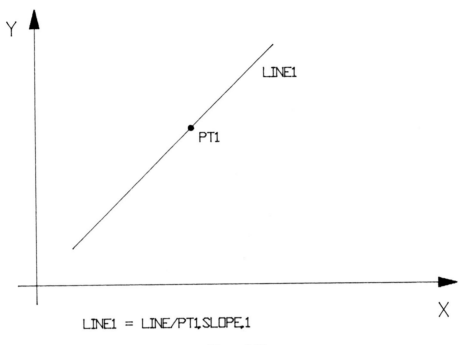

Figure 9.17

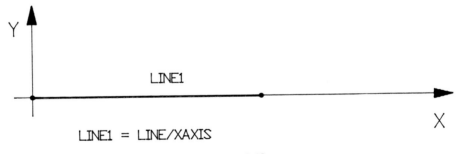

Figure 9.18

7. *A line through a point with a slope respective to another line*: See Figure 9.19.

LIN = LINE / POINT, SLOPE, NUMERICAL VALUE, LINE

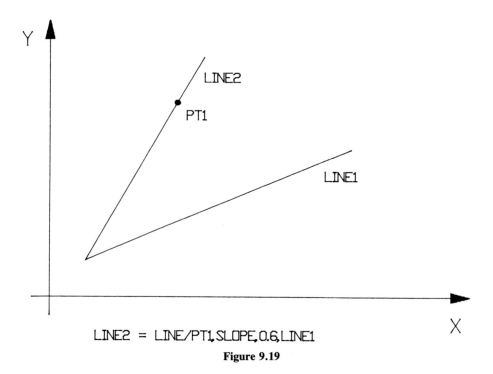

LINE2 = LINE/PT1,SLOPE,0.6,LINE1

Figure 9.19

8. *A line through a point making an angle with another line:* See Figure 9.20.

LIN = LINE / POINT, ATANGL, ANGLE (in degrees), LINE

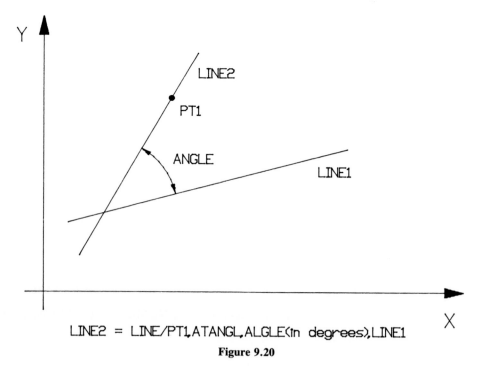

LINE2 = LINE/PT1,ATANGL,ALGLE(in degrees),LINE1

Figure 9.20

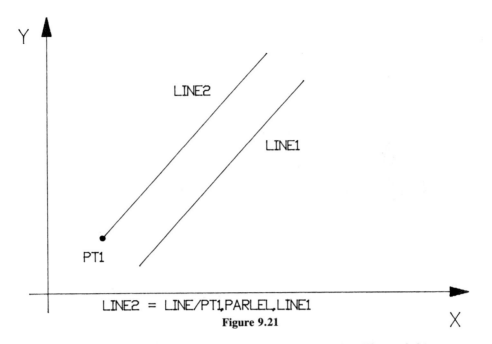

LINE2 = LINE/PT1,PARLEL,LINE1

Figure 9.21

9. *A line through a point and parallel to another line:* See Figure 9.21.

LIN = LINE / POINT, PARLEL, LINE

10. *A line through a point and perpendicular to another line:* See Figure 9.22.

LIN = LINE / POINT, PERPTO, LINE

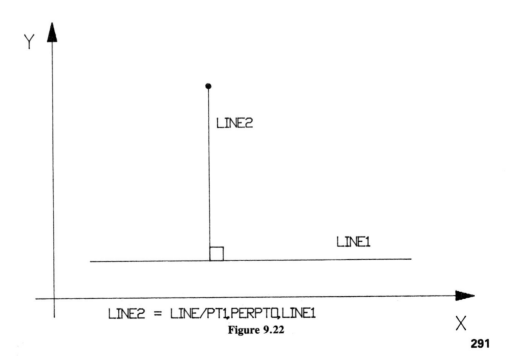

LINE2 = LINE/PT1,PERPTO,LINE1

Figure 9.22

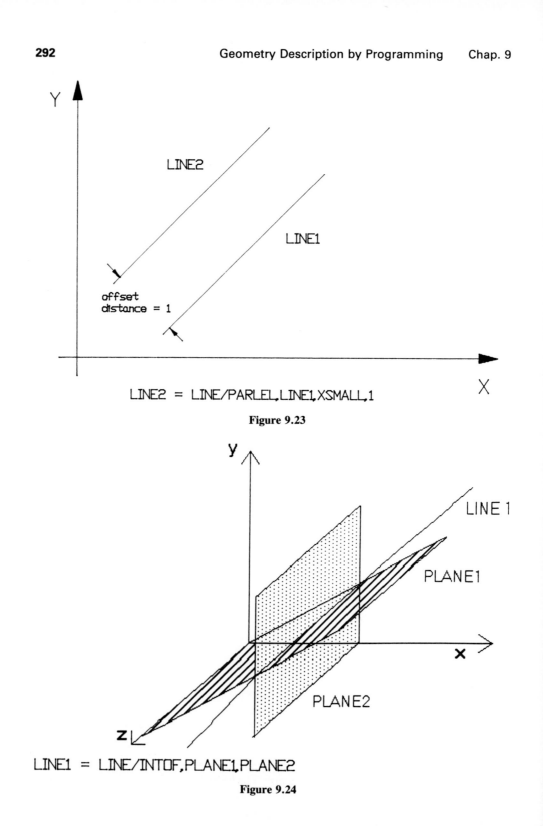

LINE2 = LINE/PARLEL,LINE1,XSMALL,1

Figure 9.23

LINE1 = LINE/INTOF,PLANE1,PLANE2

Figure 9.24

11. *A line parallel to another line given the offset distance:* See Figure 9.23.

> LIN = LINE / PARLEL, LINE, MODIFIER, OFFSET VALUE

The modifier options are {XSMALL, XLARGE, YSMALL, YLARGE, ZSMALL, ZLARGE}.

12. *A line given by the intersection of two planes:* See Figure 9.24.

> LIN = LINE / INTOF, PLANE1, PLANE2

13. *A line using the slope–intercept equation:* See Figure 9.25.

> LIN = LINE / SLOPE, SLOPE VALUE, INTERC, MODIFIER, d

where the slope value is y/x. The modifier options are {XAXIS, YAXIS}, and d is the corresponding intercept value on the selected axis (i.e., modifier).

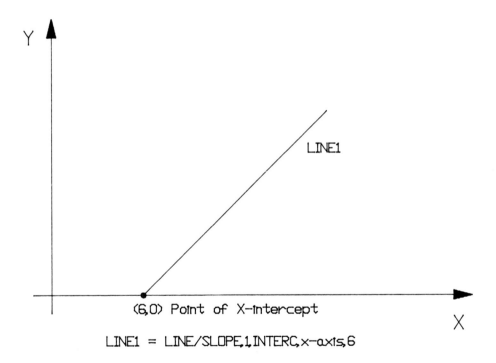

LINE1 = LINE/SLOPE,1,INTERC,x-axis,6

Figure 9.25

14. *A line formed by an angle and a coordinate intercept*: See Figure 9.26.

LIN = LINE / ATANGL, DEGREES, INTERC, MODIFIER, d

The modifier options are {XAXIS, YAXIS}, and d is the corresponding inter-cept value on the selected axis (i.e., modifier).

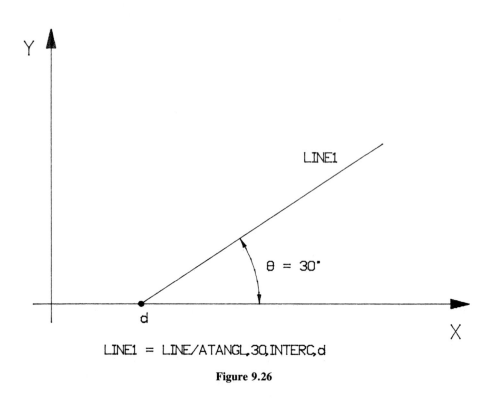

LINE1 = LINE/ATANGL,30,INTERC,d

Figure 9.26

15. *A line in the x–y plane passing through a point and tangent to a tabulated cyl-inder:*

LIN = LINE / POINT, TANTO, TABCYL

The point is defined to be the next closest to the tabulated cylinder (Figure 9.27).

16. *A line through a point and perpendicular to a tabulated cylinder:*

LIN = LINE / POINT, PERPTO, TABCYL

The point is defined to be the closest to an actual point on the tabulated cylin-der (Figure 9.28).

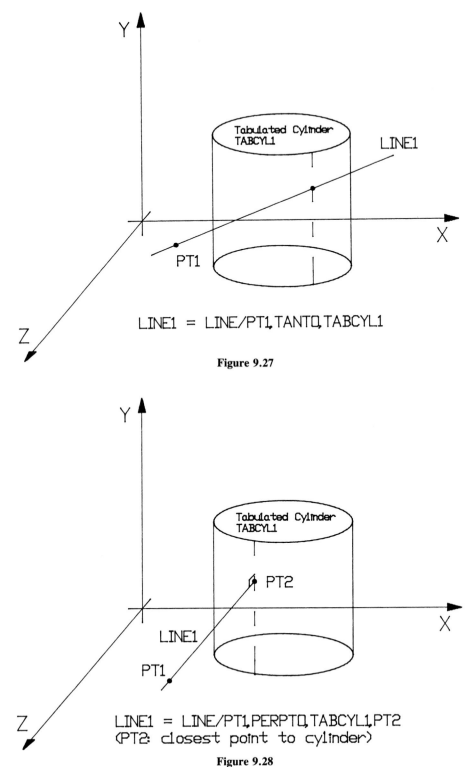

LINE1 = LINE/PT1,TANTO,TABCYL1

Figure 9.27

LINE1 = LINE/PT1,PERPTO,TABCYL1,PT2
(PT2: closest point to cylinder)

Figure 9.28

Example 9.1   Geometry Description Using Points and Lines Commands

Give the geometry description of the object shown in Figure 9.29 using the various options available.

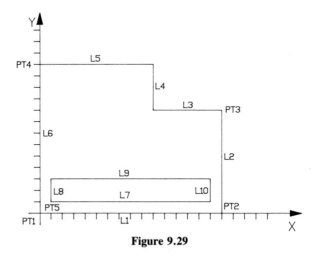

Figure 9.29

Solution

```
 PT1 = POINT / 0,0
 PT2 = POINT / 16,0
 PT3 = POINT / 16,9
 PT4 = POINT / 0,13
LIN1 = LINE / PT1, PT2
LIN2 = LINE / PT3, PERPTO, LIN1
LIN3 = LINE / (POINT / 10,9), PT3
LIN4 = LINE / (POINT / 10,13), PERPTO, LIN3
LIN5 = LINE / PT4, PERPTO, LIN4
LIN6 = LINE / PT1, PT4
LIN7 = LINE / (POINT / 1,1), (POINT / 15,1)
LIN8 = LINE / (POINT / 1,3), PERPTO, LIN7
LIN9 = LINE / PARLEL, LIN7, YLARGE, 2
LIN10 = LINE / PARLEL, LIN8, XLARGE, 14                                    ■
```

Example 9.2   Geometry Statements Using Slope Option

Using the ATANG and slope options in creating L1 and L2 and RTHETA for creating PT2, give the geometrical statements that define the part described in Figure 9.30.

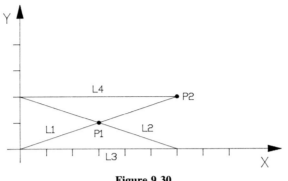

Figure 9.30

Solution

L1 = LINE / SLOPE, (1/3), INTERC, XAXIS, 0
L2 = LINE / ATANGL, 150, INTERC, XAXIS, 6
L3 = LINE / XAXIS
L4 = LINE / PARLEL, L3, YLARGE, 2
P1 = POINT / INTOF, L1, L2
P2 = POINT / RTHETA, XYPLAN, 2, ARCTAN (1/3)   ■

Example 9.3   Use of Additional Features in APT to Create a Geometry

In this example, we want to incorporate additional features to create the geometry given in Figure 9.31. L4 and L5 have to be created first before point PT2 can be defined.

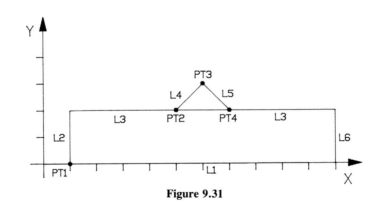

Figure 9.31

Solution

PT1 = POINT / 1,0
L1 = LINE / PT1, SLOPE, 0

L2 = LINE / PT1, SLOPE, 90
L3 = LINE / PARLEL, L1, YLARGE, 2
L4 = LINE / (POINT / 5, 2), SLOPE, 1, L3
L5 = LINE / (POINT / 6, 3), ATANGL, 270, L4
L6 = LINE / (POINT / 11,0), PERPTO, L3
(or L6 = LINE / PARLEL, L2, XLARGE, 10)
PT2 = POINT / INTOF, L4, L3

9.2.3 Planes

A plane requires at least three points to describe it. The following are the options available to describe a plane.

1. *Through the coefficients of its plane equation:* $ax + by + cz - d = 0$. See Figure 9.32.

$$PL = PLANE / a, b, c, d$$

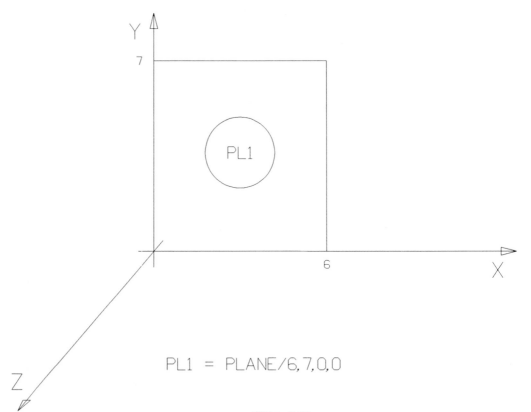

PL1 = PLANE/6, 7, 0, 0

Figure 9.32

2. *By three points:* See Figure 9.33.

$$PL = PLANE / POINT1, POINT2, POINT3$$

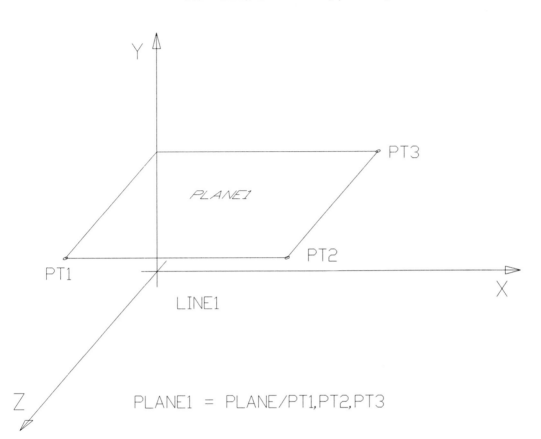

PLANE1 = PLANE/PT1,PT2,PT3

Figure 9.33

3. *A plane that passes through a point and is parallel to another plane:* See Figure 9.34.

PL = PLANE / POINT, PARLEL, P12

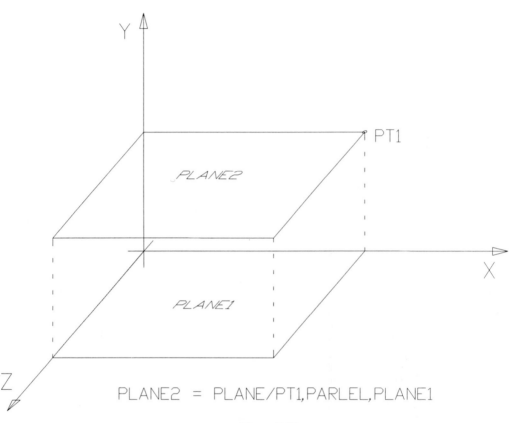

PLANE2 = PLANE/PT1,PARLEL,PLANE1

Figure 9.34

4. *A plane parallel to another plane at a certain distance away:* See Figure 9.35.

PL = PLANE / PARLEL, P12, MODIFIER, NUMERICAL VALUE

The modifier options are {XSMALL, XLARGE, YSMALL, YLARGE, ZSMALL, ZLARGE}.

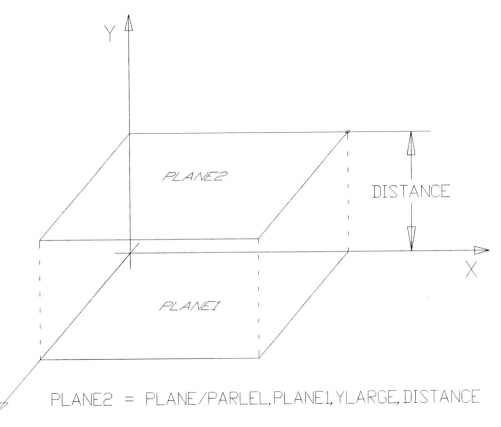

PLANE2 = PLANE/PARLEL,PLANE1,YLARGE,DISTANCE

Figure 9.35

5. *A plane that passes through a point and is perpendicular to a given vector:* See
Figure 9.36.

$$PL = PLANE / POINT, PERPTO, VECTOR1$$

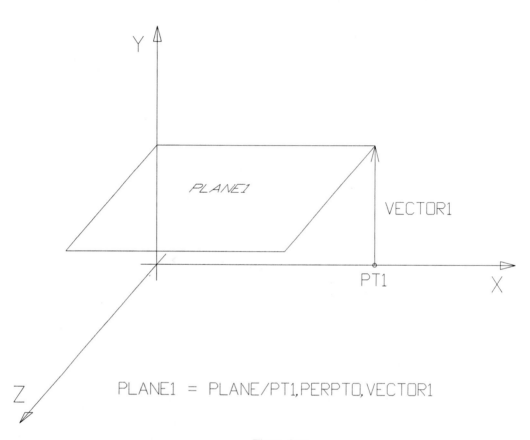

PLANE1 = PLANE/PT1,PERPTO,VECTOR1

Figure 9.36

6. *A plane that passes through two points and is perpendicular to another plane:*
See Figure 9.37.

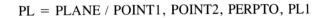

PL = PLANE / POINT1, POINT2, PERPTO, PL1

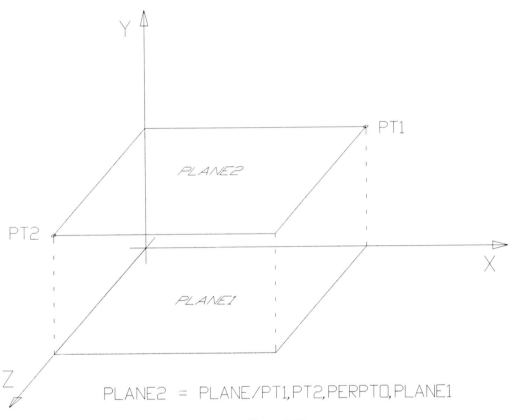

PLANE2 = PLANE/PT1,PT2,PERPTO,PLANE1

Figure 9.37

7. *A plane perpendicular to two planes and through a point:* See Figure 9.38.

PL = PLANE / POINT, PERPTO, Pl1, Pl2

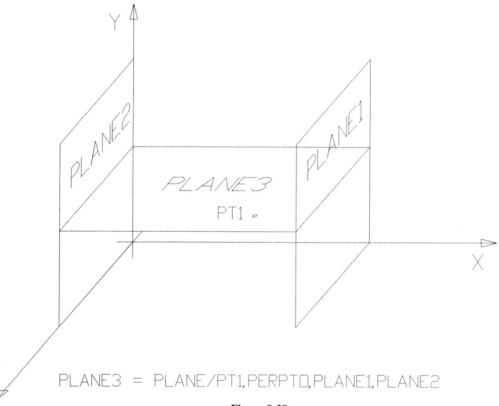

PLANE3 = PLANE/PT1,PERPTO,PLANE1,PLANE2

Figure 9.38

Example 9.4   Geometry Statements to Generate Planes

In this example, we are asked to write the geometry statements to generate the planes that form the profile of the cube shown in Figure 9.39.

Solution

PT1 = POINT / 0,0,0
PT2 = POINT / 5,5,0
PT3 = POINT / 5,0,5
PL1 = PLANE / PT1, (POINT / 5,0,0), PT3
PL2 = PLANE / PARLEL, PL1, YLARGE, 5
PL3 = PLANE / PT2, PT3, PERPTO, PL1
PL4 = PLANE / PARLEL, PL3, XSMALL, 5

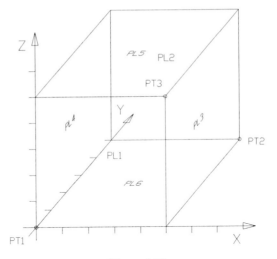

Figure 9.39

PL5 = PLANE / (POINT / 0,0,5), (POINT / 5,5,5), PERPTO, PL4
PL6 = PLANE / PARLEL, PL5, ZSMALL, 5   ■

Example 9.5   Geometry Statements Using Different Plane Options

In a fashion similar to Example 9.4, the profile of the part shown in Figure 9.40 is
generated using further plane option statements.

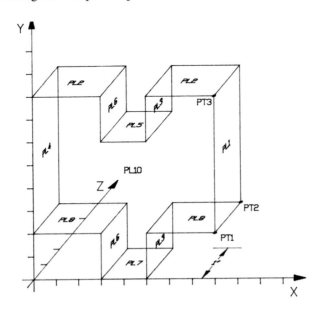

Figure 9.40

Solution

PT1 = POINT / 8,2,0
PT2 = POINT / 8,2,−1
PT3 = POINT / 8,8,0
PL1 = PLANE / PT1, PT2, PT3
PL4 = PLANE / PARLEL, PL1, XSMALL, 8
PL3 = PLANE / PARLEL, PL1, XSMALL, 3
PL6 = PLANE / PARLEL, PL1, XSMALL, 5
PL8 = PLANE / PT1, PT2, PERPTO, PL1
PL2 = PLANE / PARLEL, PL8, YLARGE, 6
PL5 = PLANE / PARLEL, PL8, YLARGE, 4
PL10 = PLANE / PT1, PT3, PERPTO, PL8
PL9 = PLANE / PARLEL, PL10, ZSMALL, 1
PL7 = PLANE / PARLEL, PL8, YSMALL, 2   ■

9.2.4 Circles

The mathematical description of a circle requires the center and radius to be given. The following circle statements incorporate the various methods of creating a circle.

1. *A circle described by a center and a radius:* See Figure 9.41.

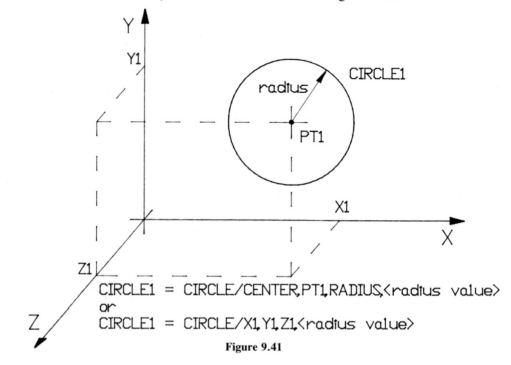

CIRCLE1 = CIRCLE/CENTER,PT1,RADIUS,<radius value>
or
CIRCLE1 = CIRCLE/X1,Y1,Z1,<radius value>

Figure 9.41

C = CIRCLE / CENTER, POINT1, RADIUS, RADIUS VALUE

or

C = CIRCLE / X, Y, Z, RADIUS VALUE

2. *A circle described by its center point and tangent to a line:* See Figure 9.42.

C = CIRCLE / CENTER, POINT, TANTO, LINE

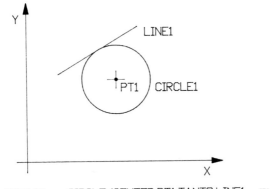

CIRCLE1 = CIRCLE/CENTER,PT1,TANTO,LINE1   **Figure 9.42**

3. *A circle described by its center point and a point on its circumference:* See Figure 9.43.

C = CIRCLE / CENTER, POINT1 (center point), POINT2

(circumference point)

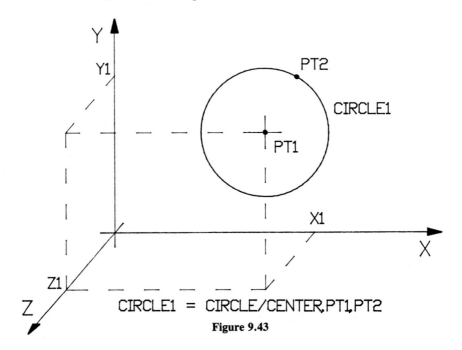

CIRCLE1 = CIRCLE/CENTER,PT1,PT2

Figure 9.43

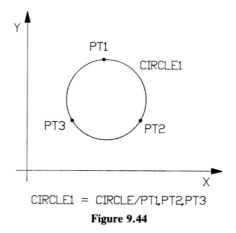

CIRCLE1 = CIRCLE/PT1,PT2,PT3

Figure 9.44

4. *A circle described by three points on its circumference:* See Figure 9.44.

C = CIRCLE / POINT1, POINT2, POINT3

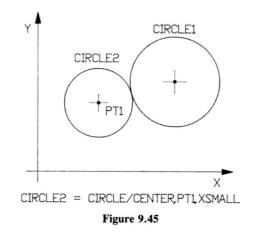

CIRCLE2 = CIRCLE/CENTER,PT1,XSMALL

Figure 9.45

5. *A circle described by a center point and a tangent to another circle:* See Figure 9.45.

C = CIRCLE / CENTER, POINT1, MODIFIER

The modifier options are {LARGE or SMALL}.

6. *A circle described by a radius and two intersecting lines:* See Figure 9.46.

C = CIRCLE / MODIFIER, LINE1, MODIFIER, LINE2, RADIUS VALUE

7. *A circle specified by a given radius tangent to a line and passing through a point:* See Figure 9.47.

C = CIRCLE / TANTO, LINE, MODIFIER, POINT,

RADIUS, RADIUS VALUE

The modifier options are {XLARGE, XSMALL, YLARGE, YSMALL, ZLARGE, ZSMALL}.

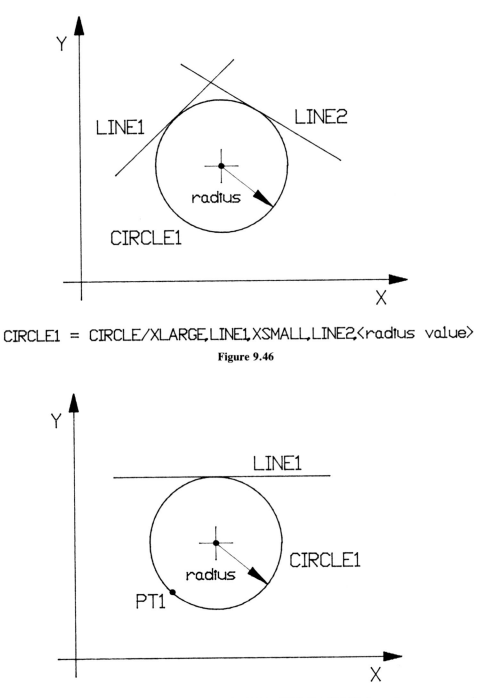

CIRCLE1 = CIRCLE/XLARGE,LINE1,XSMALL,LINE2,<radius value>

Figure 9.46

CIRCLE1 = CIRCLE/TANTO,LINE1,XSMALL,PT1,RADIUS,<radius value>

Figure 9.47

8. *A circle specified by a given radius tangent to a line and another circle:* See Figure 9.48.

    C = CIRCLE / MODIFIER, LINE1, MODIFIER, IN/OUT, C2, RADIUS, RADIUS VALUE

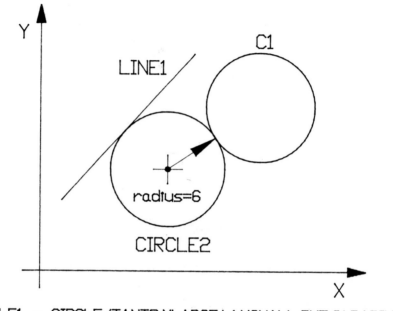

CIRCLE1 = CIRCLE/TANTO, XLARGE, L1, YSMALL, OUT, C1, RADIUS, 6

Figure 9.48

9. *A circle described by a radius and a tangent to two circles:* See Figure 9.49.

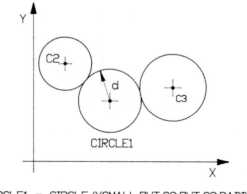

CIRCLE1 = CIRCLE/YSMALL, OUT, C2, OUT, C3, RADIUS, d

Figure 9.49

$$C = CIRCLE / MODIFIER, IN/OUT, C2, IN/OUT, C3,$$

$$RADIUS, RADIUS VALUE$$

10. *A circle with a given radius tangent to a line and a tabulated cylinder:* See Figure 9.50.

$$C = CIRCLE / TANTO, LINE1, MODIFIER, TABCYL, MODIFIER,$$

$$POINT (closest point), RADIUS, RADIUS VALUE$$

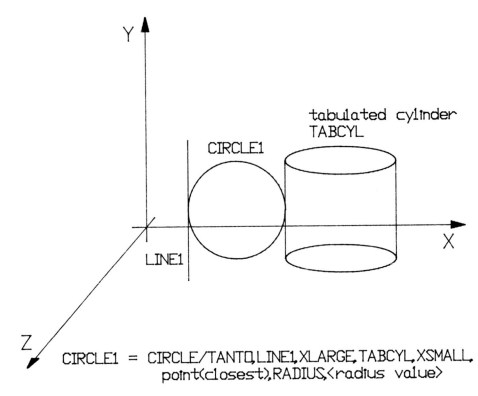

CIRCLE1 = CIRCLE/TANTO,LINE1,XLARGE,TABCYL,XSMALL, point(closest),RADIUS,<radius value>

Figure 9.50

Example 9.6   Description of Contours

A typical mechanical part is shown in Figure 9.51. What are the APT geometry statements that make up its contour? (Note: Avoid creating too many points.)

Solution

$$PT1 = POINT / 0,0$$
$$PT2 = POINT / 16,0$$
$$PT3 = POINT / 16,9$$
$$PT4 = POINT / 0,13$$

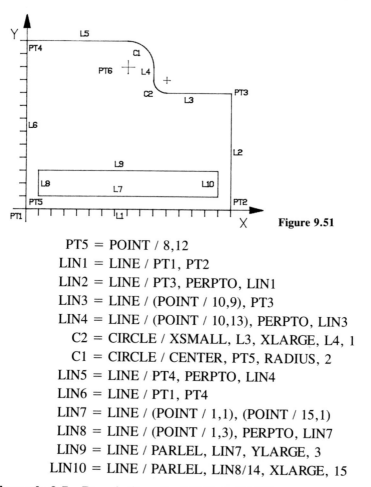

Figure 9.51

$$PT5 = POINT / 8,12$$
$$LIN1 = LINE / PT1, PT2$$
$$LIN2 = LINE / PT3, PERPTO, LIN1$$
$$LIN3 = LINE / (POINT / 10,9), PT3$$
$$LIN4 = LINE / (POINT / 10,13), PERPTO, LIN3$$
$$C2 = CIRCLE / XSMALL, L3, XLARGE, L4, 1$$
$$C1 = CIRCLE / CENTER, PT5, RADIUS, 2$$
$$LIN5 = LINE / PT4, PERPTO, LIN4$$
$$LIN6 = LINE / PT1, PT4$$
$$LIN7 = LINE / (POINT / 1,1), (POINT / 15,1)$$
$$LIN8 = LINE / (POINT / 1,3), PERPTO, LIN7$$
$$LIN9 = LINE / PARLEL, LIN7, YLARGE, 3$$
$$LIN10 = LINE / PARLEL, LIN8/14, XLARGE, 15$$

∎

Example 9.7   Description of a 2D Cam Profile

The mechanical part shown in Figure 9.52 is composed of a large circle tangent to a smaller circle and a line. The complete part forms a device needed for a cam profile. We are asked to generate the geometry statements to draw the 2D picture.

Solution

$$PT1 = POINT / 0,0$$
$$PT2 = POINT / 15,0$$
$$L1 = LINE / PT1, PT2$$
$$L2 = LINE / SLOPE, 0.8, INTERC, XAXIS, 15$$
$$C1 = CIRCLE / PT1, RADIUS, 20.396$$
$$L3 = LINE / YAXIS$$
$$C2 = CIRCLE / TANTO, L3, XLARGE, IN, C1$$

∎

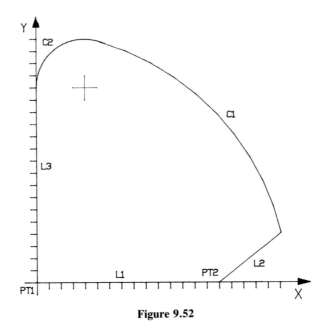

Figure 9.52

Example 9.8   Geometry Statements to Draw a Gasket

Given the profile of the gasket shown in Figure 9.53, use the geometry statements to draw the profile of the part. Use only a few points to generate this part.

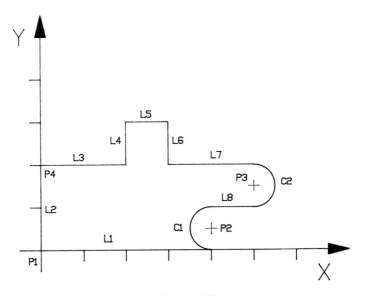

Figure 9.53

Solution

P1 = POINT / 0,0
P2 = POINT / 4,0.5
P3 = POINT / 5,2.5
P4 = POINT / 0,2
C1 = CIRCLE / CENTER, P2, RADIUS, 0.5
L1 = LINE / P1, RIGHT, TANTO, C1
L2 = LINE / P4, PERPTO, L1
L3 = LINE / P4, PARLEL, L1
L4 = LINE / (POINT / 2,3), PERPTO, L3
L5 = LINE / PARLEL, L1, YLARGE, 3
L6 = LINE / PARLEL, L4, XLARGE, 1
L7 = LINE / PARLEL, L1, YLARGE, 2
L8 = LINE / (POINT / 5,1), RIGHT, TANTO, C1
C2 = CIRCLE / TANTO, L7, YSMALL, (POINT / 5.5,1.5),
        RADIUS, 0.5

9.2.5 Cylinders

The description of a cylinder requires the radius, center, and height. As with the circle, there are mathematical equivalents that can be used to describe the cylinder.

1. *A cylinder described by an axis point, axis vector, and its radius:* See Figure 9.54.

CY = CYLINDER / x, y, z, a, b, c, RADIUS VALUE

2. *A cylinder described using point coordinates, a unit vector in the axis direction, and its radius:* See Figure 9.55

CY = CYLINDER / POINT, VECTOR, RADIUS

3. *Tabulated cylinder:* There is another option in cylinder generation known as the tabulated cylinder. A tabulated cylinder is a surface generated by moving a line along a space curve so that it is always parallel to a given line. Two methods used to generate tabulated cylinders are described below.

(a) First method

TC = TABCYL / MODIFIER1, MODIFIER2, [,TRFORM, M}, DATA

This is shown in Figure 9.56.

The options for MODIFIER1 are

{NOX, NOY, NOZ, RTHETA, THETAR}

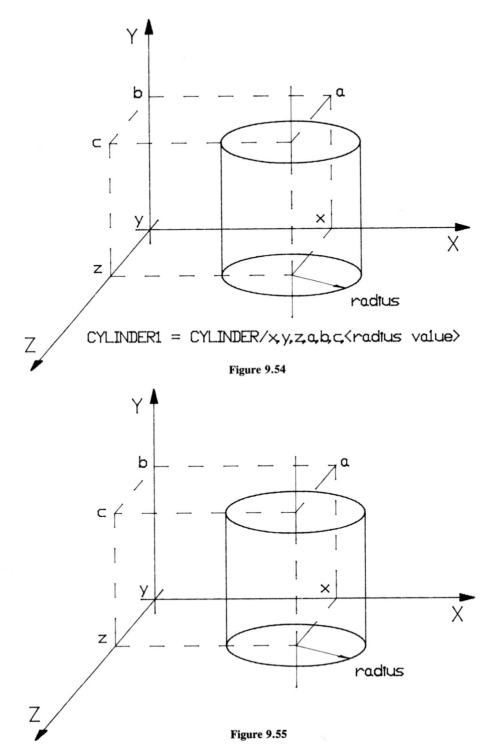

CYLINDER1 = CYLINDER/x,y,z,a,b,c,<radius value>

Figure 9.54

Figure 9.55

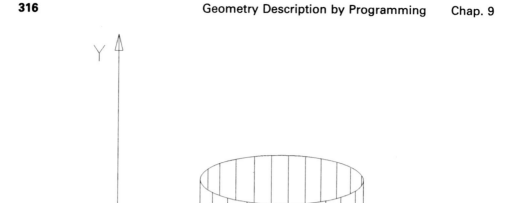

$$TC = TABCYL/modifier1, modifier2, TRFORM, data$$

Figure 9.56

NOX defines the tabulated cylinder parallel to the x axis. All "data" points are entered as y–z coordinates.

NOY defines the tabulated cylinder parallel to the y axis. All "data" points are entered as x–z coordinates.

NOZ, RTHETA, and THETAR define the tabulated cylinder parallel to the z axis. All "data" points are entered as x–y coordinates. RTHETA and THETAR are in polar coordinates.

The options for MODIFIER2 are

{SPLINE, PTSLOP, PTNORM}

SPLINE is used when data are entered as points with the slope or angle at selected given points. The minimum number of data is 3.

PTSLOP is used when data are input as points and slopes (i.e., x_1, y_1, s_1, . . . , x_n, y_n, s_n).

PTNORM is used when data are to be input as points with normals measured counterclockwise from the x axis (i.e., x_1, y_1, z_1, . . . , x_n, y_n, z_n).

TRFORM translates cylinder data into another coordinate system defined by matrix **M.**

For example, one can define the following tabulated cylinder using

$$TC = TABCYL / NOZ, SPLINE, TRFORM, M, x_1, y_1, x_2, y_2, \ldots x_n, y_n$$

This is illustrated by Figure 9.57.

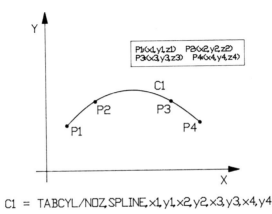

$$C1 = TABCYL/NOZ, SPLINE, x_1, y_1, x_2, y_2, x_3, y_3, x_4, y_4$$

Figure 9.57

(b) Second method

$$TC = TABCYL / NOZ, \begin{Bmatrix} TWOPT \\ FOURPT \end{Bmatrix} M, x_1, y_1, x_2, y_2, \text{slope,}$$

$$s_2, x_3, y_3, x_4, \text{NORMAL}, N_4$$

TWOPT is used when slopes or normals are only defined at selected points. (FOURPT defines a series of curves passing through four points with discontinuous slopes.)

4. RULED SURFACES: They are surfaces generated by straight lines called rulings joining similar points on two space curves. They are permitted only on some surfaces (e.g., line, plane, circle, cylinder).

Ruled Surface is given by a surface and three points on a plane that cuts it. (See Figure 9.58.)

RLSURF = RLDSRF / surface1, p1, p2, p3, surface2, p21, p22, p23..and so on

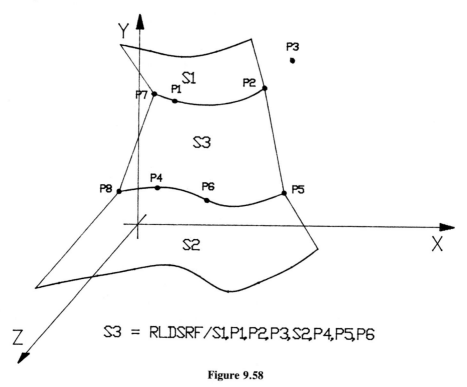

$$S3 = RLDSRF/S1,P1,P2,P3,S2,P4,P5,P6$$

Figure 9.58

Example 9.9   Geometry Statements for Torque Handle

The torque handle device of Figure 9.59 is composed of two shafts mounted on the offset center of the larger cylinder. Give the geometry statements that define it.

Solution

```
 PT1 = POINT / 0,0,0
 PT2 = POINT / 0,1,3
 PT3 = POINT / 0,-2,0
VEC1 = VECTOR / 0, 0, 3
VEC2 = VECTOR / (-1/3), TIMES, VEC1
CYL1 = CYLINDER / 0,0,0,0,0,3,3
CYL2 = CYLINDER / PT2, VEC1, 2
CYL3 = CYLINDER / PT3, VEC2, 1
```

■

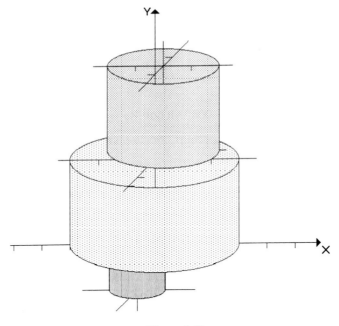

Figure 9.59

9.2.6 Additional Geometry Statements

The following geometry statements are used in more complex objects. They are all basically described by their mathematical equation using the needed input values or values derived from other information.

Ellipse. An ellipse is created by giving the values in the order of center point, the semimajor axis, the semiminor axis, and the angle the major axis makes with the center (Figure 9.60).

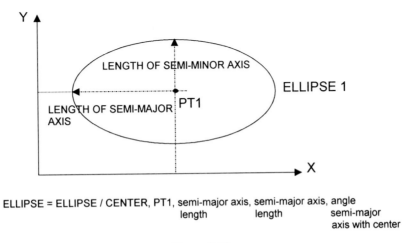

Figure 9.60

For example if we let

$$a = \text{length of semimajor axis}$$

$$b = \text{length of semiminor axis}$$

$$\Theta = \text{angle (in degrees)}$$

then

EL = ELLIPSE / CENTER, POINT, a, b, Θ

Hyperbola.   See Figure 9.61. A self-contained explanation for defining a hyperbola is given below:

HYP = HYPERB / CENTER, POINT, length of half transverse axis, length of half conjugate axis, angle that transverse axis makes with the x axis

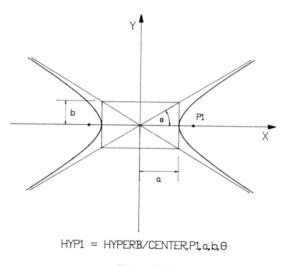

HYP1 = HYPERB/CENTER,P1,a,b,θ

Figure 9.61

Cones.   A cone is defined by its vertex located at (x, y, z) and its center line being parallel to a vector defined by (a, b, c). See Figure 9.62.

CN = CONE / CANON, x, y, z, a, b, c, cos Θ

or

Another option for generating a cone makes use of a vector fixed to a given point with an angle of inclination.

CN = CONE / POINT, VECTOR, Θ

where set $\{x, y, z\}$ represents the vertex coordinates, set $\{a, b, c\}$ represents the unit vector in the axis direction of the cone, and Θ is the half angle of the cone.

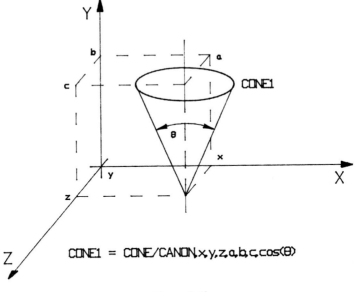

$$CONE1 = CONE/CANON, x, y, z, a, b, c, \cos(\theta)$$

Figure 9.62

Vectors

1. *Vector description by Cartesian coordinates:* See Figure 9.63.

$$VECTOR1 = VECTOR / \Delta x, \Delta y, \Delta z$$

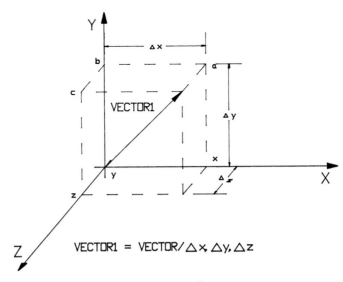

$$VECTOR1 = VECTOR/ \Delta x, \Delta y, \Delta z$$

Figure 9.63

2. *Vector description is described by two points:* See Figure 9.64.

$$V = VECTOR / POINT1, POINT2$$

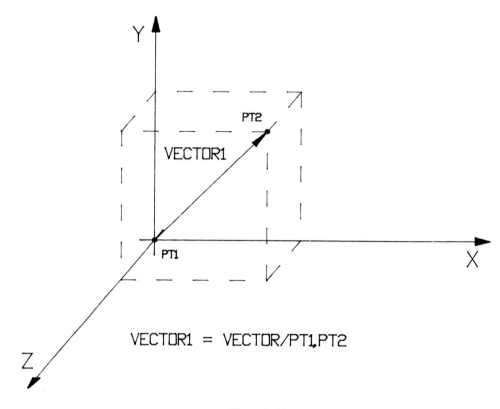

VECTOR1 = VECTOR/PT1,PT2

Figure 9.64

3. *Vector direction that is perpendicular to a specified plane:* See Figure 9.65.

$$V = VECTOR / PERPTO, PLANE, MODIFIER$$

The modifier options are {POSX, POSY, POSZ}

4. *Magnification of a vector by multiplying it by a scalar value:* See Figure 9.66.

$$V = VECTOR / SCALAR VALUE, TIMES, V2$$

5. *The cross product of two vectors V_1 and V_2.*

$$V = VECTOR / V_1, cross, V_2$$

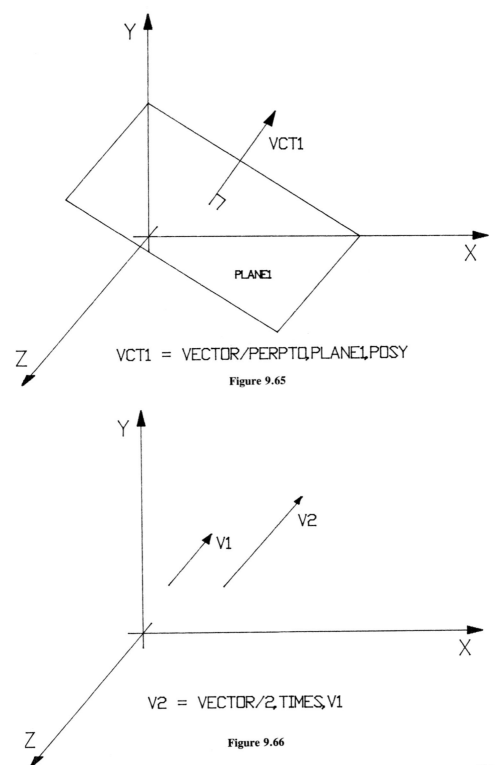

VCT1 = VECTOR/PERPTO,PLANE1,POSY

Figure 9.65

V2 = VECTOR/2,TIMES,V1

Figure 9.66

Example 9.10   Cone/Cylinder Geometry Object

A cone mounted on top of a cylinder, as shown in Figure 9.67, is to be drawn using geometry statements.

Solution 1

CYL1 = CYLINDER / 0,0,0,0,0,4,2
  CN1 = CONE / CANON 0,0,$(4 + 2\sqrt{3})$,0,0,4,30

Solution 2

  PT1 = POINT / 0,0,0
VEC1 = VECTOR / 0,0,4
CYL1 = CYLINDER / PT1, VEC1, 2
  CN1 = CONE / CANON 0,0,$(4 + 2\sqrt{3})$,0,0,4,30   ∎

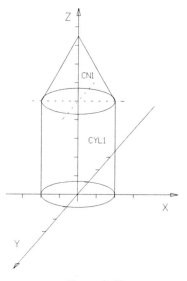

Figure 9.67

9.3 PATTERNS

The pattern statement allows specifying a series of points within two points either in a linear path or in a description of an arc. Although this statement is more suitable with computerized machining (see Chapter 10), it can create a single entity made up of a combination of entities.

9.3.1 Linear Patterns

1. *Creating points within a linear path:* The path is described by a starting point, ending point, and the total number of points (Figure 9.68).

PAT = PATTERN / LINEAR, PT1, PT2, NUMBER OF POINTS

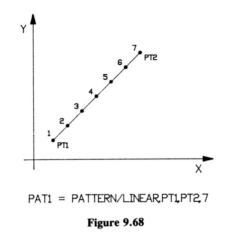

PAT1 = PATTERN/LINEAR, PT1, PT2, 7

Figure 9.68

2. *Creating a series of points within a linear path:* The path is defined by the starting point, the vector direction of the linear path, the number of desired increments, and the distance between each increment (Figure 9.69).

PAT = PATTERN / LINEAR, PT1, V1, INCR,

NUMBER OF INCREMENTS, AT, *d*

where *d* is the incremental distance.

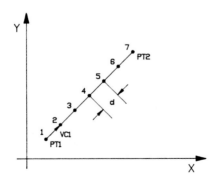

PAT1 = PATTERN/LINEAR, PT1, VC1, 6, AT, d

Figure 9.69

3. *Creating a series of points in a linear path:* The path is defined by the starting point, the vector direction of the linear path, and the increment entities (Figure 9.70).

PAT = PATTERN / LINEAR, PT1, VC1, INCR, INC#1, . . . , INC#n

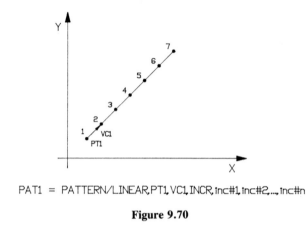

PAT1 = PATTERN/LINEAR,PT1,VC1,INCR,inc#1,inc#2,...,inc#n

Figure 9.70

9.3.2 Arc Patterns

The abbreviations of the modifiers used in arc patterns are

CLW: Clockwise direction
CCLW: Counterclockwise direction

1. *Creating an arc pattern by describing a circle:* The circle is defined by starting and end angles and the number of equally spaced points along the circumference (Figure 9.71).

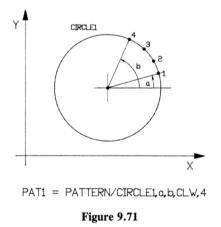

PAT1 = PATTERN/CIRCLE1,a,b,CLW,4

Figure 9.71

PAT = PATTERN / ARC, CIRCLE, a, b, CLW (or CCLW),

NUMBER OF POINTS

The angles are measured positive clockwise from the *x* axis.

2. *Creating an arc pattern for a nonuniform pattern:* The pattern is specified by indicating the circle, the start angle (with respect to the *x* axis), the direction of angle measurement, and the individual angles (Figure 9.72).

PAT = PATTERN / ARC, CIRCLE, START ANGLE,

CLW, INCR, Θ, a, b, c, d

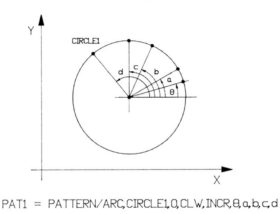

Figure 9.72

PROBLEMS

9.1 Use the 2D geometrical statements to describe the center guide shown in Figure P9.1.

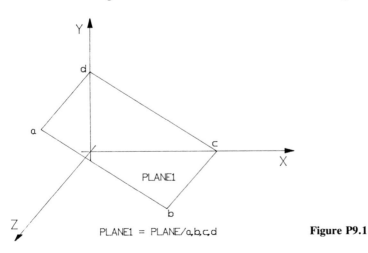

PLANE1 = PLANE/a,b,c,d   **Figure P9.1**

9.2 Create the 2D geometry of the space gage given in Figure P9.2 using points and lines of the geometry statements. (Use at least four different line statement options in your geometry description.)

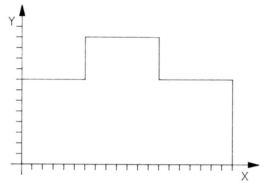

Figure P9.2

9.3 Describe the 2D representation of the guide block shown in Figure P9.3 using the several methods listed in this chapter. Try to solve this problem without creating any point entities.

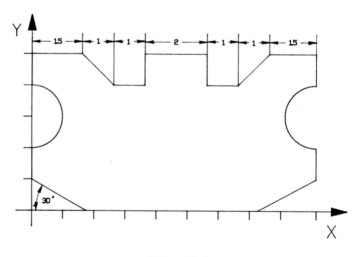

Figure P9.3

9.4 Create a 3D geometry description of the sector separator having a 1/2-in. thickness, as shown in Figure P9.4. (Note: Some geometry descriptions that are correct in 2D space may be incorrect in 3D space. For example, circles actually can be cylinders in 3D space.)

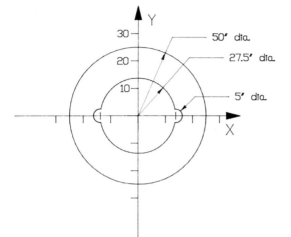

Figure P9.4

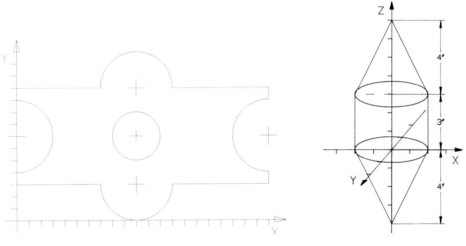

Figure P9.5   **Figure P9.6**

9.5 Describe the jigsaw piece shown in Figure P9.5. The outer circular contours have a 3-in. radius. The inside circle has a 2-in. radius. The marked units are in inches. The total length is 20 inches and the height is 14 inches.

9.6 The plug bar in Figure P9.6 is composed of two cones mounted on both ends of a cylinder. The cylinder and the cones share the same center axis. Use geometry description to describe the bar. Given a 3-in. radius for the cylinder and a 4-in. height for each cone, determine the half-angle value.

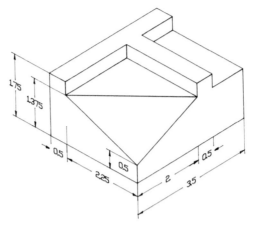

Figure P9.7

9.7 Give the 3D geometrical description of the cam block of Figure P9.7. Use a modifier to link an entity with another if possible (e.g., parallel to and perpendicular to).

9.8 Give the geometrical description of the angling V guide shown in Figure P9.8.

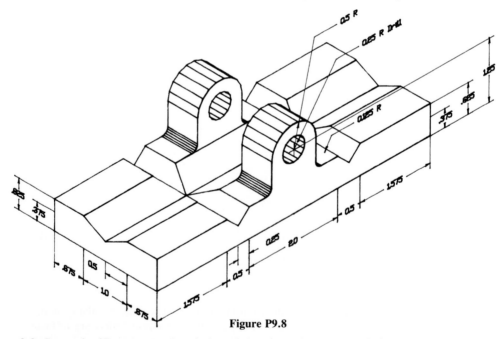

Figure P9.8

9.9 Create the 2D geometry description of the arc guide shown in Figure P9.9. The first description is to give the location of the curves and circles using absolute coordinates to define the center and location of the holes. The second description is to use polar coordinates to specify the holes of the arc guide using the same point (which is to be used as a reference point).

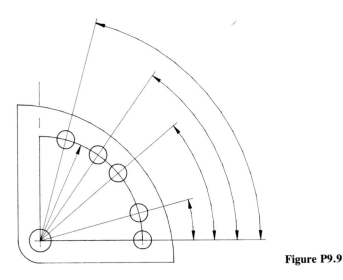

Figure P9.9

REFERENCES

9.1 Barnhill, R. E., and Riesenfeld, R. F. (Eds.), *Computer-Aided Geometric Design*, Academic Press, New York, 1974.

9.2 Besant, C. B., and Lui, C. W. K., *Computer-Aided Design and Manufacture*, 3d ed., Ellis Horwood, Chichester, U.K., 1986.

9.3 Bezier, P., *Numerical Control: Mathematics and Applications*, trans. by A. R. Forrest and A. F. Pankhurst, Wiley, London, 1972.

9.4 Brown, S. A., Drayton, C. E., and Mittman, B., "A Description of the APT Language," *Commun. ACM*, Vol. 6, No. 11, Nov. 1963.

9.5 Chang, Choa-Hwa, and Melkanoff, Michel A., *NC Machine Programming*, Prentice-Hall, Englewood Cliffs, N.J., 1989.

9.6 Groover, M. P., and Zimmers, E. W., *CAD/CAM: Computer-Aided Design and Manufacturing*, Prentice-Hall, Englewood Cliffs, N.J., 1984.

9.7 IBM Manual SH20-1413-3: APT-AC NC Processor: Operations Guide, 4th ed., IBM Corp., Rye Brook, N.Y., 1985.

9.8 IBM Manual SH20-2095-6: CADAM APT Interface, IBM Corp., Rye Brook, N.Y., 1989.

9.9 IBM Manual SH20-6640-0: APT-AC NC Processor-Advanced Functions: Program Reference Manual, 1st ed., IBM Corp., Rye Brook, N.Y., 1983.

9.10 ITT Research Institute: "APT Part Programming," McGraw-Hill Book Company, New York, 1967.

9.11 Kelly, R. S., "The Production Man's Guide to APT-ADAPT," *Am. Mach.*, Vol. 97, June 22, 1969.

9.12 Kishel, C. J., and Howe, R. E. (Eds.), "Introduction to numerical control in manufacturing," American Society of Tool and Manufacturing Engineers, Dearborn, Michigan, 1969.

9.13 Mortenson, M. E., *Geometric Modelling*, John Wiley & Sons, New York, 1985.

9.14 Pressman, R., *Numerical Control and Computer-Aided Manufacturing*, John Wiley & Sons, New York, 1977.

chapter 10

NC Part Programming

10.1 INTRODUCTION

There are two methods to program NC machines: (1) manual programming, and (2) computer-assisted programming. These methods are introduced along with some examples illustrating how the programming and actual machining are performed. First, the basic concepts in manual programming are discussed. Second, the computer-assisted approach is illustrated through the use of APT programming. Finally, the aspects of automating a manufacturing process are presented. Before we discuss the structure of the programs, it is important to note that NC tape carries the NC programming languages. Although NC tape is required by most NC machines, integrated systems involving CAD/CAM workstations and high-level languages are being introduced in which an NC program can be tested and executed directly from the CAD workstation without a punched tape. This level of computer sophistication requires changes at both the hardware and software levels (Figure 10.1).

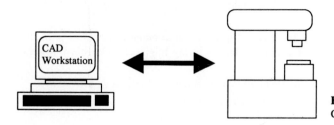

Figure 10.1 Direct interaction between CAD and the machine tool.

10.2 MANUAL PROGRAMMING

Manual programs consist of a set of instructions generated on a punched tape according to certain formats to instruct the machine tool how to machine a part. The format depends on the design of the controller; however, the instructions are given in sets of blocks. Each block is equivalent to a statement in programming and is composed of words such as G01, G03, XO, Y10, and Z3.2.

To communicate with the NC machine, the words in the blocks must be specified according to several available formats.

Fixed Sequential.   This is the first type of format employed and it is based on a fixed set of sequential words that must be used, even if the state of certain words does not change. For instance, if the y axis is kept constant, provisions for the y coordinate still must be provided.

Block Address.   In this format, a block code is specified at the machine that defines the words that are going to be used in that particular command. Those words that are not used are kept unchanged. The block address is characterized by its compact form in programming because its code replaces the usual sequence of words such as the one required by the fixed sequential format. A typical block address format is shown in Table 10.1.

TABLE 10.1   BLOCK ADDRESS FORMAT

Tab Sequential.   This is a modified fixed sequential format in which a TAB is inserted before and after each word and each block ends by an EOB (end of a block). Unchanged words are omitted from the block, and a block can be terminated by the EOB whenever all the words needed to describe the instructions are given. See Figure 10.2.

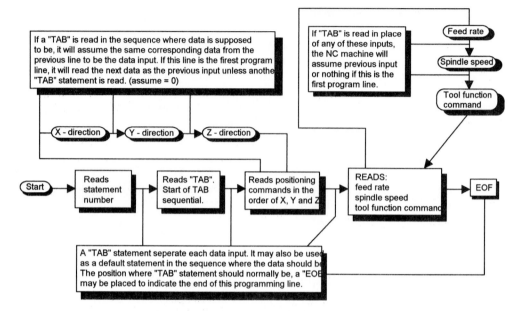

Figure 10.2   Tab sequential format.

Word Address.   Currently, this is the most used block format by CNC controller systems. It is composed of words that describe an address (identifier) and a number that specifies its content. A typical NC block takes the form

$$N \_, G \_, X \_, Y \_, I \_, J \_, K \_, F \_, S \_, T \_, M \_$$

where N: identification number
     G: preparatory command
     X: x axis
     Y: y axis
     Z: x axis
     I, J, K: coordinate values of an arc center
     F: feed rate
     S: spindle speed
     T: tool number
     M: miscellaneous functions

For example,

$$NO1 \ GO2 \ X1500 \ Y2000 \ F4 \ S400 \ T10 \ MO3$$

Omitted words are assumed to be zero or as previously defined.

10.2.1 Motion Commands

There are three types of motion commands CNC controllers can have, which follow.

Rapid Positioning.   This motion is used for point-to-point operations and is defined by a G00 code followed by the coordinates of the next tool position; for example,

$$G00 \ X1000 \ Y2000 \ Z1500$$

which means that the tool is to be moved from its residence to the next point, given by X = 1.0, Y = 2.0, and Z = 1.5 (in. or mm) if absolute coordinates are used. If not 1.0, 2.0 and 1.5 refer to the increments along the x, y, and z axes, respectively, if incremental positioning is used. Keep in mind, as mentioned earlier, in the rapid transverse mode, the path on how to move from one point to another is not important.

Linear Interpolation.   This is achieved by the G01 command. In linear interpolation, the G01 command is preceded by the X, Y, and Z coordinates and the feed rate by which it executes its motion. For example,

$$G01 \ X1000 \ Y2000 \ Z1500 \ F3.0$$

defines the next position the tool is to move to with a feed rate of 3 in./mm (or mm/mm) using linear interpolation. The control for linear interpolation is based on the fact that simultaneous speeds are given to the x, y, and the z axes to achieve a linear function. In most cases, linear interpolation is required for only one plane: x–y, y–z, or x–z. For the latter case, the coordinates for the axis perpendicular to the plane of the tool motion do not have to be specified.

Circular Interpolation.   Most CNC machines that perform contouring are equipped with a circular interpolation type of motion controller. The G function defining this motion is G02. For arcs of 90 degrees in one plane (x–y, x–z, or y–z), clockwise motion is achieved by

$$G02 \ X1000 \ Y1500 \ F3$$

where X and Y coordinates define the end point for the arc (Figure 10.3).

Counterclockwise motion is achieved by G03.

For arcs less than 90 degrees within a quadrant, motion is accomplished by additional codes given by I, J, K, and R, such as G02 or G03 followed by the plane-of-motion coordinates X, Y, I, and J, followed by radius R, and then feed rate F., I., and J denote the incremental coordinates from the center of the circle to the initial tool position (Figure 10.4). For example,

$$G02 \ X1000 \ Y2000 \ I0200 \ J0200 \ R1000 \ F3$$

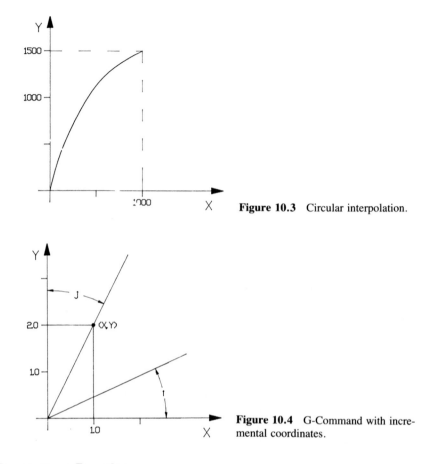

Figure 10.3 Circular interpolation.

Figure 10.4 G-Command with incremental coordinates.

10.2.2 Preparatory Function

G Function. There are two types of G codes:

1. *One-Shot G Code.* This G code is only effective within the block where it is specified.
2. *Nodal G Code.* This code is effective until another G code of the same group is specified.

G92 Reference Offset Point. For example,

$$G92 \ X2000 \ Y1000 \ Z\text{-}1000$$

where X, Y, and Z denote the coordinates from the workpiece's zero point to the cutter. Table 10.2–10.4 provide a selected list of common M functions, tool commands, and preparatory G functions used in machining.

TABLE 10.2   M FUNCTIONS

M01	Program stop
	Optional stop (depends on the control panel button)
M02	End of program
M03	Start spindle rotation (CW)
M04	Start spindle rotation (CCW)
M05	Stop spindle
M06	Tool changes
M08	Coolant on
M09	Coolant off
M11	Tool change
M98	Go to subroutine
M99	Return from subroutine

TABLE 10.3   PREPARATORY G FUNCTIONS IN MILLING

G00	Positioning rapid traverse
G01	Linear interpolation
G02	Circular interpolation CW
G03	Circular interpolation CCW
G17	x–y plane selection
G18	z–x plane selection
G19	y–z plane selection
G20	Inch data input
G21	Metric data input
G28	Return to reference point
G29	Return from reference point
G41	Cutter diameter compensation left
G42	Cutter diameter compensation right
G43	Tool length compensation (positive)
G44	Tool length compensation (negative)
G84	Tapping cycle
G86	Boring cycle
G90	Absolute input
G91	Incremental input

TABLE 10.4   PREPARATORY G FUNCTIONS IN TURNING

G00	Rapid traverse
G01	Linear interpolation
G02	Circular interpolation (CW)
G03	Circular interpolation (CCW)
G20	Input data in inches
G21	Input data in metric
G28	Return to reference point
G29	Return from reference point
G32	Thread cutting
G36	Automatic tool compensation
G70	Finishing cycle
G71	Stock removal
G96	Constant surface speed control
G98	Feed per minute
G99	Feed per revolution

Example 10.1   Manual Programming and Machining of a Sheet Metal Board

Using the word address method, write a program to instruct the machine tool to cut the sample sheet metal part. The CAM picture of this part is shown in Figure 10.5. (This example was furnished by Shelly Bosserman, Motorola Inc., Mechanical Engineering Technology Group.)

Solution   In writing this program, we must take several milling passes in order to obtain the final finished part. An abbreviated typical program is used. We emphasize the use commands and machining techniques rather than the extensive list of coordinate values where the tool must be positioned or travel on.

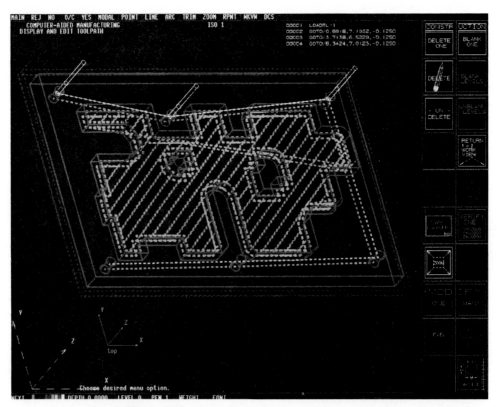

Figure 10.5 Tool path for the given geometry.

Note: The use of the "$$" symbol is not part of the syntax for this program. It is used for comments.

```
PARTNOTP0001
TOOL LIST
T1 = cdrill
T2 = .250drill
T3 = .250endmill
T4 = .500endmill

N1G70G75
N2T1M6
N2M08
N3G0X.6918Y7.1932Z.1S1850M03
N3G81X.6918Y7.1932Z.225F10.
N4X3.7138Y6.5229
$$ The M05 command turns off the spindle and the M09 command is
$$ used to turn off the coolant (M08 turns on coolant) for changing
$$ the tool. A rough outline of this part is to be cut by the
```

$$ cutting drill. The T1 and M6 commands instruct the machine tool
$$ to select cutting drill T1. The M03 command starts the spindle
$$ at a rate of 1850 rpm (S1850) and a feed rate of 10 inches per
$$ second (F10.).
N8X.7876Y2.3624
N8M09
N8M05
N9G80
N10T2M6
N10M08
N3G0X.6918Y7.1932Z.1S1650M03
N3G81X.6918Y7.1932Z.475Z.150Z.05F10.
$$ This segment of the program gives the instructions to drill five
$$ 0.25-in. diameter holes by the machine tool. The M6 command
$$ instructs the machine tool to select cutting drill T2. The M03
$$ command starts the spindle at a rate of 1650 rpm (S1650) and a
$$ feed rate of 10 inches per second (F10.).
N8X.7876Y2.3624
N8M09
N8M05
N17G80
N18T3M6
N18M08
N19G0X1.3958Y6.3806Z.1S2200M03
N20G1Z-.1875F5.
N21X1.6854Y6.6702F10.
N22X2.0266
$$
$$ The M6 command instructs the tool change. Tool T3 has been
$$ called to begin the first milling pass to form the outline of
$$ the sample part. The G1 command activates the linear
$$ interpolation control for a series of points for straight-line
$$ milling. The M05 command turns the spindle off and the M09
$$ command turns off the coolant (M08 turns on the coolant) for
$$ changing the tool.
N97G17G2X3.2439Y5.2258I3.6294J5.2282
N98G1Y5.4605
N99X3.4035
$$
$$ A G17 command tells the machine tool to work only in the X-Y
$$ plane. The G2 command tells the machine tool to cut a curve (or
$$ arc) by defining the coordinate values of the center of an arc
$$ by X and Y and the major and minor axes by I and J. (Remember K
$$ is omitted because we are working in the 2D X-Y plane.) Another
$$ G1 command is used to call for straight-line milling. Actually,
$$ G1 instructs the linear interpolation of a series of points.
$$
N114X3.6272Y4.84

N115G2X3. 2439Y5. 222I3. 6301J5. 2262

N116G1Y5. 4605

N117X3. 4035

$$

$$ Several curves exist in this sample part design. The foregoing
$$ G2 command is used for a path of an arc (curve) to be created
$$ by defining the coordinate values of the center of an arc by X
$$ and Y and the major and minor axes by I and J. The straight-line
$$ milling is resumed by the G1 command. This method is repeated
$$ several times for all defined path points until the final
$$ (desired) geometry is achieved. The spindle speed and feed rates
$$ are adjusted accordingly for the proper finish.
$$

N209Y6. 3806Z. 1S2200M03

N210G1Z-. 1875F5.

N211X1. 6854Y6. 6702F10.

$$

N1369Y5. 1263

N1370X8. 4515

N1371Z. 1F20.

N1372T4M6

N1373G0X-. 0413Y7. 9371Z. 1S1350M03

N1374G1Z-. 25F5.

N1375X9. 2139F10.

N1376Y1. 6718

$$

$$ The final tool change is made for a finer milling tool piece.
$$ This process is used to give the desired areas a better finish.
$$ The M2 command indicates the end of the program.
$$

N1389Z. 1F20.

N1390M09

N1390M05

N1391M2

E

10.3 APT PROGRAMMING LANGUAGE

APT (Automated Programming Tool) is a programming language that allows geometrical data together with cutter motion statements to be specified for NC machines. APT is a computer program and a programming language (see Chapter 9). As stated in Chapter 8, it is designed so that NC machines can be automatically programmed to execute complex geometrical contours, hence increasing machining-process capabilities.

The APT program is composed of four parts:

1. APT part program
2. APT processor
3. APT postprocessor
4. Auxiliary statements

The APT part program defines the geometry statements of the workpiece and the tool-motion statements. It makes up about 70% of the APT program.

The APT processor creates a file called the cutter location data, referred to as CL-DATA.

The APT postprocessor translates the CL-DATA into a specific numerical code for an NC machine to produce the NC tape.

Statements for tool identification, tolerances, and other special functions are considered auxiliary statements and must be supplied separately.

The APT language consists of a set of statements that direct the computer to produce instructions for machine tools. Those statements, like any other computer language, are formed by words, symbols, numbers, punctuation, and statement labels. The words are strings of alphanumeric characters (one to six characters) that either define or create an entity, or a computer type of operation. The words are main words or auxiliary words or modifiers. We discuss the APT words and symbols in more detail in the next section.

10.4 APT PROGRAMMING STATEMENTS

The structure of the APT program is similar in many ways to FORTRAN. In the discussion that follows, we describe all APT functions required in programming.

10.4.1 Declaration Statements

All variables used in an APT program must be declared by name and data type. There are four different types of variable declaration: data, entity, number, and string. Except for data, all the other declarations require a list of names to be used as variables to represent the data type.

The following is a brief description of the declaration statements.

Data: Data assigns an initial numerical or character value to a number-type or string-type variable. The format is

DATA / NAME, VALUE

where the name must belong to a declared type, number or string, and have an assigned value (of the same type).

Entity: The entity declaration statement assigns the variable to represent an entity in the CAD's geometry statement. One can declare an array to be of the entity type. Depending on the type of computer and compiler, assignment NAME[0] could be possible. The general format of an entity declaration is

ENTITY / NAME1, NAME2, . . . , NAMEN

Number: The number declaration identifies the list of variable names that are assigned only numerical values. As with entities, arrays can be declared as number-type variables. The general format is

NUMBER / NAME1, NAME2, . . . , NAMEN

String: The string declaration statement is used for variable names to contain only character-value data. As with entities, arrays can be used as string-type variables. The general format is

STRING / NAME1, NAME2, . . . , NAMEN

For example,

```
ENTITY / CIR1, CIR2, LINE[23], SED
NUMBER / DIA[10], HEIGHT
STRING / SIDE1,  SIDE2,  FACE[4]
DATA / SIDE1, PAINT, GREEN
DATA / DIA[2], 5
```

This example identified 43 elements (3 arrays with 37 elements total and 6 variables) and assigned 3 elements with initial values.

In the foregoing example, the first statement declares that CIR1, CIR2, array LINE[23], and SED are entities. The latter will be defined in the geometry statement of the APT program. The second statement declares that array DIA[10] and HEIGHT are to be assigned only numerical values. The string declaration statement defines variable names that will be assigned character values. The data statement assigns initial values to variables. For example, the last statement in array DIA[2] is assigned the value of 5.

10.4.2 Geometry Statements

Once all variable names have been declared, one can assign entities and values as necessary to create the object. This part of the program tells the computer the space (and shape) that the object occupies. Example 10.2, which follows, is a further illustration of the geometry description, but refer to Chapter 9 for all definitions of geometry statements.

Example 10.2   Three Dimensional Profile of a Mechanical Part

Write the combination of geometry statements necessary to draw the part in Figure 10.6.

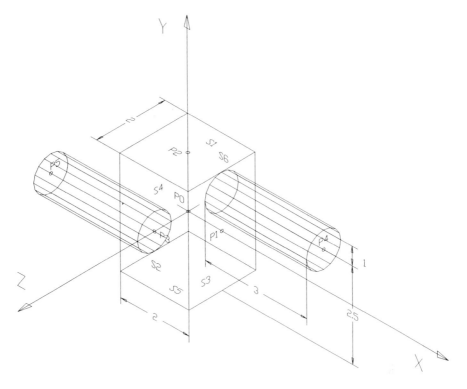

Figure 10.6   Typical example showing the combination of geometry statements.

Solution

P0 = POINT / 0,0,0
P1 = POINT / 1,0,0
P2 = POINT / 0,3,0
P3 = POINT / 0,0,1
P4 = POINT / 4,2,0
P5 = POINT / − 4, − 2,0
XYPLN = PLANE / P0, P1, P2
YZPLN = PLANE / P0, P2, P3
ZXPLN = PLANE / P0, PERPTO, XYPLN, YZPLN
S1 = PLANE / P2, PARLEL, ZXPLN
S2 = PLANE / P3, PARLEL, XYPLN
S3 = PLANE / P1, PARLEL, YZPLN
S4 = PLANE / PARLEL, S3, XSMALL, 2.0
S5 = PLANE / PARLEL, S1, YSMALL, 6.0
S6 = PLANE / PARLEL, S2, ZSMALL, 2.0
CY1VCT = VECTOR / 1,0,0
CY2VCT = VECTOR / − 1,0,0, or CY2VCT = VECTOR / − 1,TIMES,

```
CY1VCT
CY1 = CYLNDR / P4, CY1VCT, 1
CY2 = CYLNDR / P5, CY2VCT, 1
ENDC1 = PLANE / P4, PARLEL, S3
ENDC2 = PLANE / P5, PARLEL, ENDC1
```
■

10.4.3 Motion Statements

The part to be machined is geometrically identified by its entities (points, lines, circles, etc.) that make up its database. This serves as a basis for guiding the tool around the desired contour.

There are two types of motion statements, namely, (a) point-to-point (PTP), and (b) contouring.

Point-to-Point (PTP) Motion Statements. Point-to-point statements are used to move the tool from one location to another to perform operations such as drilling, taping, and reaming.

This tool-movement operation relies on a simple control algorithm and has the least expensive features available in NC machine tools. The format for the PTP statements is

- FROM / SYMBOL OF A POINT
- GOTO / SYMBOL OF A POINT
- GODLTA / INCREMENTS ALONG THE X, Y, AND Z AXES

In the foregoing commands, we can specify the feed rate and the vector denoting the axis cutter. The latter options are usually omitted and the feed rate could be defined as a separate statement to avoid confusion. This explicit format of the PTP motion commands is given by

1. FROM / POINT, vector denoting axis of cutter, FEED RATE
2. GOTO / POINT, vector denoting axis of cutter, FEED RATE
3. GODLTA / $\Delta x, \Delta y, \Delta z$, FEEDRATE

A simplified version is

1. FROM / POINT
2. GOTO / POINT
3. GODLTA / $\Delta x, \Delta y, \Delta z$

Example 10.3   Drilling

We are to drill three holes using the same tool (Figure 10.7). Point P0 is the target point where the tool is at rest. The program can be written in two ways: (1) define

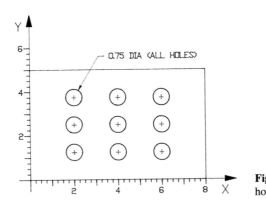

Figure 10.7 Typical plate with drilled holes.

the points of drilling through the geometry statements and (2) proceed directly by identifying the points in the PTP commands. Use the second option for the solution.

Solution

```
FROM / P0
GOTO / 2.0,1.25
GODLTA / 0.0,0.0,-1.0
GODLTA / 0.0,0.0,1.0
GOTO / 4.0,1.25
GODLTA / 0.0,0.0,-1.0
GODLTA / 0.0,0.0,1.0
GOTO / 6.0,1.25
GODLTA / 0.0,0.0,-1.0
GODLTA / 0.0,0.0,1.0
GOTO / P0
```

The GODLTA / $0,0,(+/-)1.0$ guides the tool along the z direction; hence, it performs the drilling. Prior to the motion statements, the feed rate, spindle speed, and tool diameter must be specified in order to complete the process. These are introduced in the auxiliary statements. Note that the z components in the drilling command should be greater than the thickness in order to assure perfect drilling at the bottom. This is essentially a good practice to clean up the chips at the edges. Therefore, proper clearances between the workpiece and the table are needed.

Contouring. Contouring is the most complex motion in machining. In order to guide a tool in 3D space, APT requires that the tool once moved from a given location or residence is to be positioned with respect to three surfaces. These surfaces are the drive surface, part surface, and check surface (Figure 10.8). There are several ways of positioning the tool with respect to these surfaces. The modifiers ON, TO, PAST, and TANTO are used to appropriately select the desired position. The GO statement used to position the tool with respect to the three surfaces is defined

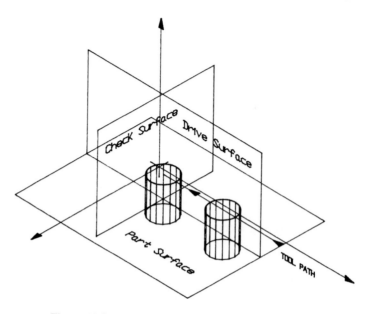

Figure 10.8   3-D view of surfaces in contouring motion.

as follows:

<pre>
        TO   DRIVE   TO   PART   TO
   GO / PAST, SURFACE, PAST, SURFACE, PAST, CHECK SURFACE
        ON   ON   ON
</pre>

The surfaces are defined as follows:

Check Surface:
- Creates starting and stopping points for cutter movement. It defines a surface with respect to which the tool must stop.
- Adds a constraint to motion along the drive surface and part surface.

Part Surface:
- Is the bottom surface that remains in contact with the cutter.
- Controls depth of cut.

Drive Surface:
- Is the surface that guides the cutter tangentially to perform the desired motion.

Once the tool is positioned with respect to the corner of the workpiece, we need a set of commands to tell it which way to proceed. There are six motion commands that allow the tool to move with respect to the predefined geometry of the

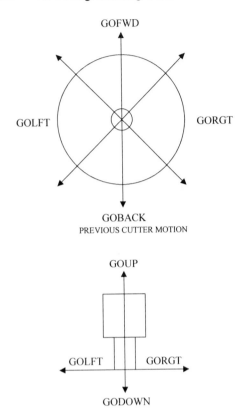

Figure 10.9 Illustrates how the tool command can be selected. Any deviation from the line of motion by a small angle (2°) is considered a right or left motion.

workpiece (Figure 10.9). The structure of each command is as follows:

MOTION COMMAND/ DRIVE SURFACE, MODIFIER, CHECK SURFACE

where the motion commands are

{GORGT, GOLFT, GOUP, GODWN, GOFWD, GOBACK}

which are defined as follows:

GORGT: Go right
GOUP: Go up
GOFWD: Go forward
GOLFT: Go left
GODWN: Go down
GOBACK: Go back

and the modifier options are {TO, ON, PAST, TANTO}. The modifiers play a major role in CNC machining as they provide the essential information of where and how

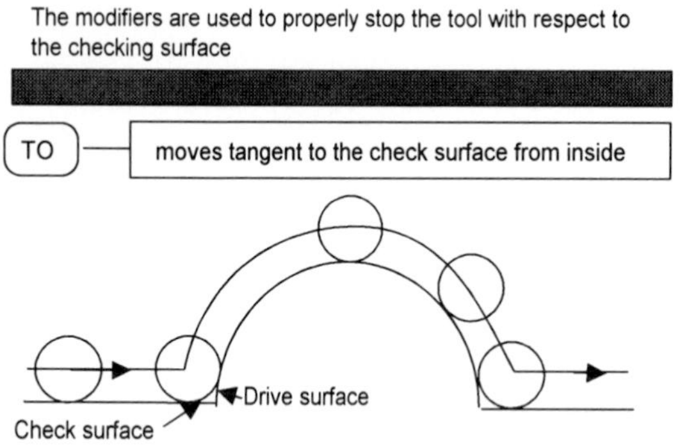

The modifiers are used to properly stop the tool with respect to the checking surface

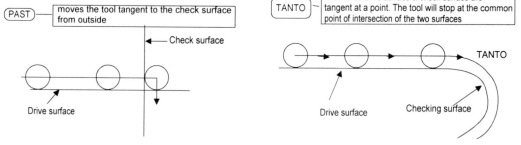

TO — moves tangent to the check surface from inside

Drive surface

Check surface

Figure 10.10   'TO' modifier.

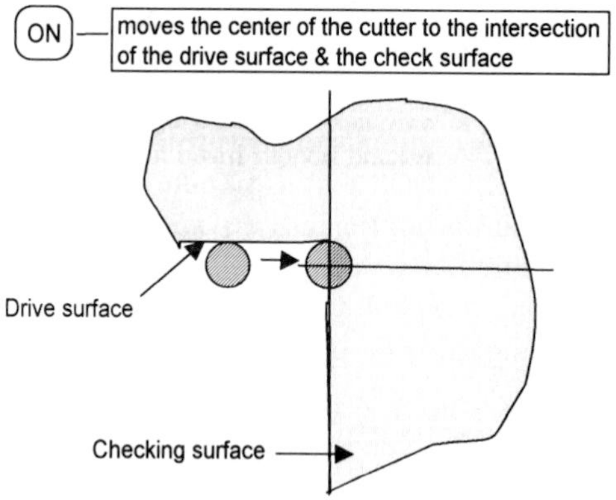

ON — moves the center of the cutter to the intersection of the drive surface & the check surface

Drive surface

Checking surface

Figure 10.11   'ON' modifier.

PAST — moves the tool tangent to the check surface from outside

Check surface

Drive surface

Figure 10.12   'PAST' modifier.

TANTO — used when drive surface & check surface are tangent at a point. The tool will stop at the common point of intersection of the two surfaces

TANTO

Drive surface   Checking surface

Figure 10.13   'TANTO' modifier.

the tool is to be positioned with respect to the check surface at the end of each motion command. Figures 10.10–10.13 illustrate the position of the tool for different modifiers.

The selection of the appropriate cutter-motion command is done by assuming that one is always riding on the tool. The following examples illustrate the use of the motion commands and the selection of the modifiers.

In addition to positioning the tool with respect to three surfaces, there are two additional options that require either one or two surfaces:

1. *Single-Surface Positioning:* A simplified GO statement that uses a single surface (driving surface) is

$$\text{GO / } \begin{matrix} \text{TO} \\ \text{PAST,} \\ \text{ON} \end{matrix} \quad \begin{matrix} \text{DRIVE} \\ \text{SURFACE} \end{matrix}$$

2. *Two-Surface Positioning:* In this case, only the drive surface and the part sur-

face are needed to position the tool.

$$
\text{GO / } \begin{matrix} \text{TO} \\ \text{PAST,} \\ \text{ON} \end{matrix} \quad \begin{matrix} \text{DRIVE} \\ \text{SURFACE,} \end{matrix} \quad \begin{matrix} \text{TO} \\ \text{PAST,} \\ \text{ON} \end{matrix} \quad \begin{matrix} \text{PART} \\ \text{SURFACE} \end{matrix}
$$

Example 10.4   Tool Commands for Machining

Given the name of each entity of the part shown in Figure 10.14, write the proper motion statements to machine this part.

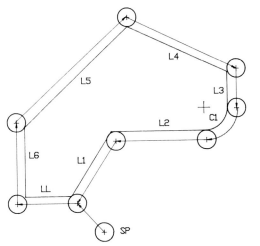

Figure 10.14 Layout of a part to be machined.

Solution   (This part resides on the plane called PLN.)

```
FROM / SP
GO / TO, L1, TO, PLN, ON, LL
GORGT / L1, TO, L2
GORGT / L2, TANTO, C1
GOFWD / C1, TANTO, L3
GOFWD / L3, PAST, L4
GOLFT / L4, PAST, L5
GOLFT / L5, PAST, L6
GOLFT / L6, PAST, LL
GOLFT / LL, PAST, L1
GOTO / SP
```

■

Example 10.5   Tool Motion Statements

Tool motion is indicated by the path shown in Figure 10.15. Write the proper motion statements to machine the part.

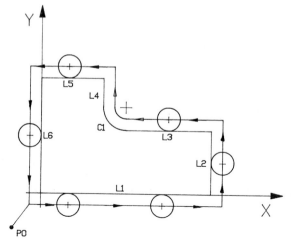

Figure 10.15   Tool motion.

Solution   (Assume that the part lies on plane PL1.)

FROM / P0
GO / TO, L1, TO, PL1, TO, L6
GORGT / L1, PAST, L2
GOLFT / L2, PAST, L3
GOLFT / L3, TANTO, C1
GOFWD / C1, TO, L4
GOFWD / L4, PAST, L5
GOLFT / L5, PAST, L6
GOLFT / L6, PAST, L1
GOTO / P0   ∎

10.4.4 Postprocessor and Auxiliary Statements in APT

Before the actual commands for machining begins, there must be a set of instructions to turn certain functions on and off by computer. Such functions include the spindle speed and feed rate, when the coolant is to be turned on and off, and the kind of tolerances and processors needed to be activated. The following are some of the postprocessor statements used in APT.

   Feed Rate

FEDRAT / NUMERICAL VALUE

For example,

FEDRAT / 5

The cutter removes the stock at a rate of 5 inches per minute. (The units are defined by either the NC machine or the program.)

Spindle Speed

SPINDL / NUMERICAL VALUE

For example,

SPINDL / 500

The spindle speed is set at the rate of 500 rpm.

Outside Tolerance

OUTTOL / NUMERICAL VALUE

For example,

OUTTOL / 0.00

Inside Tolerance

INTOL / NUMERICAL VALUE

For example,

INTOL / 0.005

Both Inside and Outside Tolerances

TOL / NUMERICAL VALUE

See Chapter 8 for tolerance measurement definitions.

Defining Diameter of the Cutter

CUTTER / DIAMETER OF THE CUTTER

For example,

CUTTER / 2,0

or

CUTTER / 2

Note: Cutters come in different sizes and shapes. The foregoing statement assumes that the end mill has a flat bottom with a given diameter. Other auxiliary statements are needed to complete the APT programming language. They include the following:

PARTNO: Defines the first statement in APT and should be preceded by a title or a name.

CLPRNT: Initiates a printout of the program.

COOLNT: Indicates the characteristic output of the coolant.

The statement for the coolant command is

COOLNT / MODIFIER

The options of the modifier are {ON, OFF, FLOOD, MIST, TAPKUL}.

Example 10.6   A Complete APT Program

Use the ATANG and slope options to create L1 and L2 and RTHETA to create PT2. Give the geometrical statements that define and machine the part described in Figure 10.16.

Solution

```
MACHIN / MILL
S1 = POINT /  − 1, − 1,3
L1 = LINE / SLOPE, (1/3), INTERC, XAXIS, 0
L2 =  LINE / ATANGL, 150, INTERC, XAXIS, 6
L4 = LINE / XAXIS
L3 = LINE / PARLEL, L4, YLARGE, 2
P1 = POINT / INTOF, L1, L4
P2 = POINT / INTOF, L1, L2
P3 = POINT / INTOF, L2, L3
P4 = POINT / RTHETA, XYPLAN, 2, 10, 30
P5 = POINT / L2, L4
PL = PLANE / P1, P2, P3
CUTTER / 6
TOLER / 0.005
SPINDL / 300
COOLNT / MIST
FEDRAT / 300
FROM / S1
GO / TO, L1, TO, PL, TO, L4
GOFWD / L1, TO, L2
GOLFT / L2, PAST, L3
GORGT / L3, PAST, L1
GORGT / 1, TO, L2
GOLFT / L2, PAST, L4
GORGT / L4, PAST, L1
GOTO / S1
COOLNT / OFF
END
FINI
```

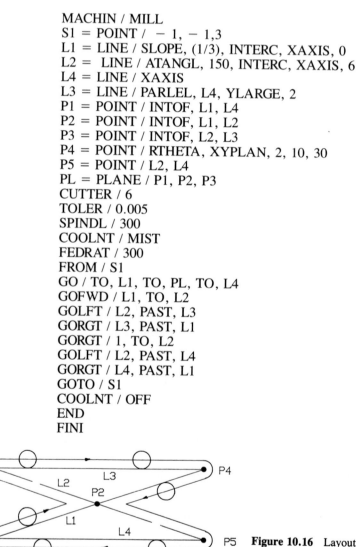

Figure 10.16   Layout of a part displaying tool motion.

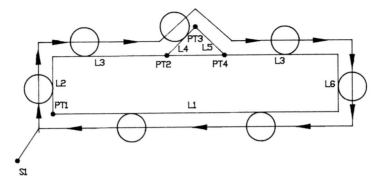

Figure 10.17 Layout of a part displaying tool motion.

Example 10.7 A Complete APT Program

We want to incorporate additional features to create the geometry given in Figure 10.17. L4 and L5 have to be created first before point PT2 can be defined. Write the geometrical and APT statements to machine this part.

Solution

```
MACHIN / MILL
S1 = POINT / 0,0,3
PT1 = POINT / 1,0
L1 = LINE / PT1, SLOPE, 0
L2 = LINE / PT1, SLOPE, 90
L3 = LINE / PARLEL, L1, YLARGE, 2
L4 = LINE / (POINT / 4,2), SLOPE, 1, L3
L5 = LINE / (POINT / 6,4), ATANGL, 270, L4
L6 = LINE / (POINT / 10,0), PERPTO, L3
PT2 = POINT / INTOF, L3, L4
PT3 = POINT / INTOF, L4, L5
PT4 = POINT / INTOF, L5, L3
PL = PLANE / PT1, PT2, PT3
CUTTER / 60
TOLER / 0.1
SPINDL / 200
COOLNT / ON
FEDRAT / 20
FROM / S1
GO / TO, L1, TO, PL, TO, L2
GOFWD / PT1, PAST, L3
GORGT / L3, TO, PT2
GOLFT / PT2, TO, PT3
GORGT / PT3, TO, PT4
GORGT / PT4, PAST, L6
GOBACK / L6, PAST, L1
```

GOLFT / L1, TO, PT1
COOLNT / OFF
END
FINI   ▪

10.5 MACRO STATEMENTS

In machining, it is customary to make more than one pass to accomplish the desired dimension of a workpiece. The reasons, which vary from one case to another, include the following:

1. Extend the life of the cutting tool to save cost.
2. It is physically impossible to cut the amount of stock in one pass.
3. Unable to achieve the desired cutting finish.
4. Extend the life of the machinery.
5. There is a hazardous cutting environment due to friction heat, etc.

Name = MACRO / ⟨list of parameters⟩
.
.
.
TERMAC
CALL name / ⟨list of parameters⟩

APT has macro statements that can be conveniently used when certain motion commands are repeated. The macro statement that acts as a subroutine can be called from the main program and, for example, consists of the following statements:

.
.
.
DRILL = MACRO/ DIA
CUTTER / DIA
GODLTA / 0,0, − 1.0
GODLTA / 0, 0,1.0
TERMAC
.
.
.
CALL DRILL / DIA = 0.5
CALL DRILL / DIA = 0.6
.
.
.

In the foregoing, we show how parameter DIA assigned to the cutter takes on different values each time CALL statements are executed.

We can have more than one variable in the parameter list, and that will depend on the problem at hand.

For example, if we require that the first drill be done at a feed rate of 1 in./min and the second at 0.5 in./min, the previous statements take on the following form:

```
         .
         .
         .
DRILL = MACRO / V, DIA
FEDRAT / V
CUTTER / DIA
GODLTA / 0,0, − 1.0
GODLTA / 0,0, + 1.0
FEDRAT / OFF
TERMAC
         .
         .
         .
CALL DRILL / V = 1, DIA = 0.5
CALL DRILL / V = 0.5, DIA = 0.6
         .
         .
         .
```

In a macro statement, we can call another macro. For instance,

```
DRILL = MACRO / V, DIA
FEDRAT / V
CUTTER / DIA
COOLANT / ON
GODLTA / 0,0, − 1.0
GODLTA / 0,0, + 1.0
FEDRAT / OFF
COOLANT / OFF
CALL MOVEX
TERMAC
         .
         .
         .
MOVEX = MACRO
GODLTA / dx, 0, 0
TERMAC
         .
         .
         .
CALL DRILL / V = 1, DIA = 0.5
```

In the foregoing, statements with variables that change with each CALL have their values assigned through the parameters list. A macro statement does not have to have a parameter list such as shown with the macro MOVEX. Further examples follow to demonstrate the usefulness of macro statements in contouring as well as in point-to-point machining.

Note: Care must be taken to correctly match the corresponding list of parameters to properly execute the CNC machine.

Example 10.8   The Use of MACROS in APT

We are required to drill nine holes on a plate 1 in. thick, as shown in Figure 10.18. The diameter of each hole is 0.75 in. Use the macro statements in APT to write the motion statements. The feed rate is 0.5 in./min and the spindle speed is 400 rpm.

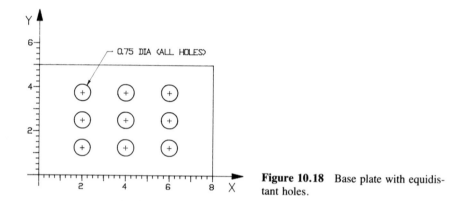

Figure 10.18   Base plate with equidistant holes.

Solution

$$ THE DRILL MACRO IS USED FOR DRILLING HOLES.
    DRILL = MACRO
    COOLNT / ON
$$ A RAPID MOTION RATE IS DEFINED BY THE STATEMENT
    "RAPID".
$$ THE TWO STATEMENTS BELOW CALL THE TOOL TO RAPIDLY
    MOVE
$$ DOWN AND 1" IN THE Z-DIRECTION.
$$ A SEMICOLON IS A STATEMENT THAT IMPLIES A NEW
    STATEMENT
$$ IS CONTINUED ON THE SAME LINE.
    RAPID; GODLTA / 0.0,0.0, − 1.0
    RAPID; GODLTA / 0.0,0.0,1.0
    COOLNT / OFF
    TERMAC
$$ THE MACRO NAMED "ROW" MOVES THE TOOL HORIZONTALLY
    IN THE
    X-DIRECTION BY AN INCREMENT OF 2" AND CALLS THE
$$ MACRO NAMED "DRILL".

```
        MACRO = ROW
        GODLTA / 2.0,0.0,0.0
        CALL / DRILL
        GODLTA / 2.0,0.0,0.0
        CALL / DRILL
        GODLTA / 2.0,0.0,0.0
        CALL / DRILL
        TERMAC
        FEDRAT / 0.5
        SPINDL / 400
        FROM / 0.0,0.0,0.0
        GOTO / 0.0,1.25
        CALL / ROW
  $$ MOVES THE TOOL UP TO THE NEXT ROW
        GODLTA / 0.0,1.25,0.0
        CALL / ROW
  $$ MOVES THE TOOL TO THE THIRD ROW
        GODLTA /  − 6.0,0.0,0.0
        CALL / ROW
        GOTO / 0.0,0.0,0.0
        END
        FINI
```

■

Example 10.9   Control of Stock Removal Using MACROs

Macro statements can be used to control the amount of stock removal during a single pass. Write the complete APT program to utilize the option mentioned before for machining the small tab shown in Figure 10.19. Assume the cutting diameter of the tool is 0.50 in. and the amount of stock to be removed is such that after the first pass, there is 0.1 in. of stock left.

Solution

$$P0 = POINT / 0, - 2,0$$
$$P1 = POINT / 0.312,0.312,0$$
$$P2 = POINT / 4,1,0$$

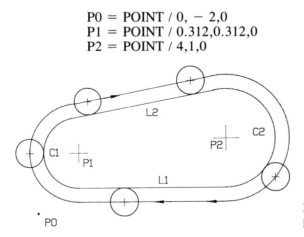

Figure 10.19 Tool motion profile for a part with contours.

```
C1 = CIRCLE / CENTER, P1, RADIUS, 0.312
C2 = CIRCLE / CENTER, P2, RADIUS, 1
L1 = LINE / RIGHT, TANTO, C2, RIGHT, TANTO, C1
L2 = LINE / LEFT, TANTO, C2, LEFT, TANTO, C1
PL1 = PLANE / P0, P1, P2
```
$$ THE FOLLOWING STATEMENT CREATES A MACRO
STATEMENT
$$ CALLED "MILL" THAT ALSO INCLUDES A VARIABLE "DIA"
$$ THAT MUST BE SPECIFIED WHEN CALLING THIS MACRO.
```
MILL = MACRO / DIA
CUTTER / DIA
FROM / P0
GOTO / L1, TO, PL1, TO, C2
GORGT /L1, PAST, C1
GOFWD / C1, PAST, L2
GOFWD / L2, PAST, C2
GOFWD / C2, PAST, L1
GOTO / P0
TERMAC
```
$$ THE FOLLOWING "DIA" VALUES TAKE INTO ACCOUNT THE
$$ DIAMETER OF THE TOOL AND THE AMOUNT OF STOCK TO
BE
$$ REMOVED.
```
CALL MILL / DIA = 0.70
END
FINI
```

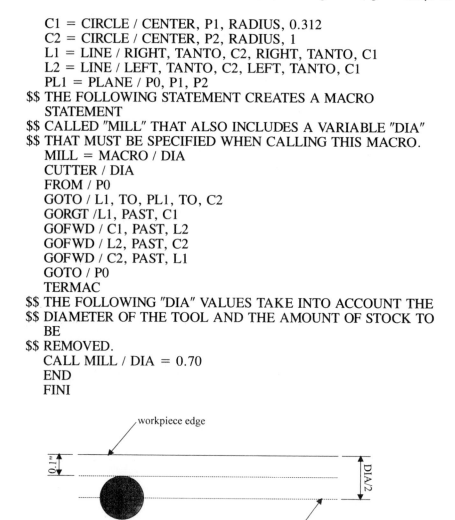

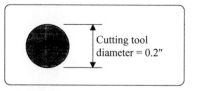

Figure 10.20   Tool position with respect to driving surface (workspace edge).

Note: The cutter diameter is measured using the center line of the tool and the workpiece edge (drive surface), as shown in Figure 10.20. This is useful because the tool can be positioned with respect to the workpiece by simply controlling the cutter diameter.

We should also note that the actual tool is selected using a statement called TURRET.   ∎

Example 10.10   A Complete APT Program for Milling Process

The part outline of Figure 10.21 is to be milled in three passes with the same tool. The tool diameter is 0.75 in. The first cut is to leave 0.1 in. of stock and the second leaves 0.05 in. of stock on the part outline. The third pass takes the part to size. Write the complete APT program using the following information:

Inside and outside tolerances = 0.001 in.

Feed rate = 3 in./min

Speed = 400 rpm

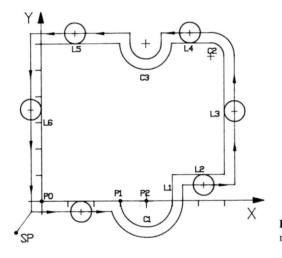

Figure 10.21   Part geometry and tool motion profile.

Solution

SP = POINT / − 1, − 1
P0 = POINT / 0,0
P1 = POINT / 3,0
P2 = POINT / 4,0
C1 = CIRCLE / CENTER, P2, RADIUS, 1 {OR C=CIRCLE / CENTER, P2, P1}
L0 = LINE / P0, P1
L1 = LINE / (POINT / 5,1), LEFT, TANGENT, C1
L2 = LINE / (POINT / 7,1), PERPTO, L1
C2 = CIRCLE / CENTER, (POINT / 6.5,5.5), RADIUS, 0.5
L3 = LINE / (POINT / 7,1), RIGHT, TANGENT, C1

```
L4 = LINE / (POINT / 5,6), LEFT, TANGENT, C2
C3 = CIRCLE / CENTER, (POINT / 4,6), (POINT / 3,6)
L5 = LINE / (POINT / 0,6), (POINT / 3,6)
L6 = LINE / P0, PERPTO, L5
PL1 = PLANE / P0, P1, P2
MILL = MACRO / DIA
CUTTER / DIA
GORGT / L0, TO, C1
GORGT / C1, TO, L2
GORGT / L2, PAST, L3
GOLFT / L3, TANTO, C2
GOFWD / C2, TANTO, L4
GOFWD / L4, PAST, C3
GOLFT / C3, PAST, L5
GOLFT / L5, PAST, L6
GOLFT / L6, PAST, L0
TERMAC
FROM / SP
GO / TO, L0, TO, PL1, TO, L6
COOLNT / ON
FEDRAT = 3
SPINDL = 400
CALL MILL / DIA = 0.95
CALL MILL / DIA = 0.85
CALL MILL / DIA = 0.75
COOLNT / OFF
END
FINI
```

Example 10.11   A Drilling Operation

Write the APT program to drill all the holes on the part shown in Figure 10.22 if a vertical press is used. The depth of the holes is 0.5 in., and all holes are equidistant.

Let the initial target holes be located at P0 located on the y axis. The parameters used for the drilling are

Feed rate = 2.5 in./min

Speed = 800 rpm

The parameters used for reaming are

Feed rate = 4.0 in./min

Speed = 500 rpm

Note: The drilling has to be done by repositioning the part such that the motion is only in the y direction.

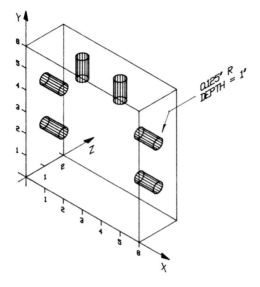

Figure 10.22   3-D view of a cubic part with side holes.

Solution

```
DRILL = MACRO
GODLTA / 0, − 0.5,0
GODLTA / 0,0.5,0
TERMAC
P0 = POINT / 0,7,0
P1 = POINT / 0.5,6,0
FEDRAT = 2.5
SPINDL = 800
FROM / P0
GOTO / P1
GODLTA / 2, 0, 0
CALL DRILL
GODLTA / 2, 0, 0
CALL DRILL
GOTO / P0
```
$$ Reposition the plate to drill side B. Rotate about the
$$ X axis followed by a translation along the Z axis.
```
FROM / P0
GOTO / P1
GODLTA / 0,0,2
CALL DRILL
GODLTA / 0,0,2
CALL DRILL
GOTO / P0
```
$$ Reposition the plate to drill side C. Rotate about
$$ the X axis by 180 degrees followed by a translation.

```
FROM / P0
GOTO / P1
GODLTA / 0,0,2
CALL DRILL
GODLTA / 0,0,2
CALL DRILL
GOTO / P0
```
$$ Repeat the whole program with the feed rate and spindle
$$ speed at FEDRAT = 4 and SPINDL = 500
```
END
FINI
```
■

10.6 ADDITIONAL CUTTER-POSITIONING COMMANDS

Cutter Relationship with the Part Surface

TLOWPS: Tool on PS (bottom center of the tool is on the surface).

TLOFPS: Tool off PS (usually means the tool is tangent to PS at some other point).

Cutter Relationship with the Drive Surface

TLLFT: Place the tool tangent to the drive surface on the left-hand side looking from the tool toward the direction of motion.

TLRGT: Same as TLLFT but the tool is on the right.

TLON: End of the tool is on the surface.

The tool must have a position and orientation before movement. An initial point where the tool starts and ends must be given. The tool can be manipulated by the following:

1. *Position:* The processor receives the starting point from the FROM command:

FROM / ST   {ST is the starting point}

This should always be the first motion command; it defines the current cutter.

2. *Direction:* The INDIRV or INDIRP commands may precede the GO statement to help directional capabilities, but the tool must conform to the tolerance restrictions of the drive surface and part surface.

- From point-to-point commands, GOTO and GODLTA.
- From an INDIRV command,

INDIRV / VECTOR

which means in the direction of the vector that points toward the forward tool direction.

- From an INDIRP command,
  INDIRP / POINT
  which is a vector from the current position to the point that defines the forward cutter direction.

The INDIRP command always requires FROM and GO commands to start.

One can use a GOTO statement along with PATTERN (Chapter 9, Sec. 9.3) to position the tool. The GOTO statement is illustrated here through the use of patterns together with the modifiers OMIT, CONST, INVERS, RETAIN, and AVOID. The GOTO statement is used to direct the tool path along a path defined by a pattern. The structure of the GOTO statement is as follows:

GOTO / PATTERN, MODIFIER

The modifiers are as follows:

OMIT, N1, . . . , NN: Omits points N1, . . . , NN of the pattern (see Figure 10.23).

RETAIN, N1, . . . , NN: Only keeps the points between N1, . . . , NN (see Figure 10.24).

AVOID, VERTICAL DISPLACEMENT, N1, . . . , NN: Puts a vertical displacement between listed points and the next point in the sequence (see Figure 10.25).

INVERS: Motion occurs in the reverse pattern order (see Figure 10.26).

CONST: Used to specify pattern numbers by index order not output order.

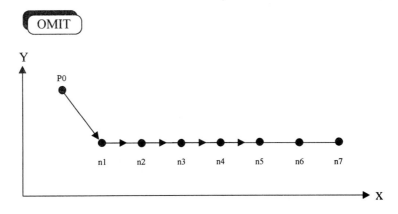

GOTO / PATTERN , OMIT , n5 , n7

Figure 10.23

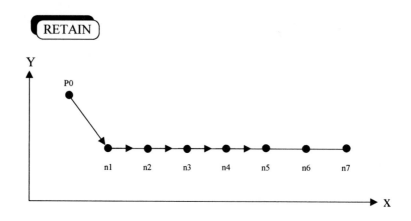

GOTO / PATTERN , RETAIN , n2 , n5

Figure 10.24

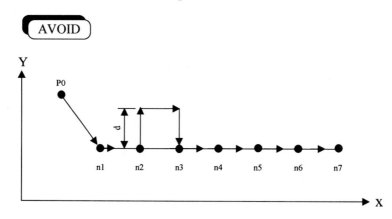

GOTO / PATTERN , AVOID , n2 , n3

Figure 10.25

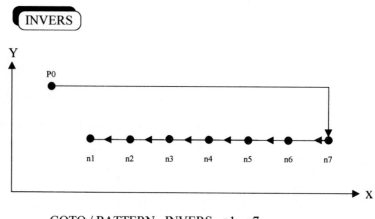

GOTO / PATTERN , INVERS , n1 , n7

Figure 10.26

10.7 APT STRUCTURE

The overall structure of APT can be described as follows:

PARTNO {Specification of the part number and/or the name}
MACHIN / {selection of the processor for machining such as
               PTP or contouring}

  .
  .   {Geometry description of the part}
  .

  .
  .   {Machining specifications (cutter tolerances,
  .   coolant, feed rate, spindle speed)}

  .
  .   {Motion statements}
  .

  .
  .   {Instructions to turn things off (coolant, spindle)}
  .

END
FINI

Note that the APT program must be written such that the beginning and end statements are included. The definitions for the rest of the statements must conform to the following:

1. Start at column 7. Columns 1 to 6 are used for referencing statements such as DO LOOPS.
2. "$$", the double dollar sign, is used for comment statements.
3. All words must be in capital letters. APT has its own spelling and commands that must be followed.
4. Macro statements must precede the call statements and be placed at the beginning of the program.
5. A continuation card is defined by using a dollar sign ($).
6. Cutter motion commands are written from the viewpoint of the programmer guiding the cutter.
7. For debugging purposes, use convenient names to describe the geometrical entities.

10.8 ADDITIONAL FEATURES IN APT PART GEOMETRY

10.8.1 Arrays In APT

RESERV / A, 50:   Reserves 50 locations in array A, each of which is indexed by a
                  subscript

name: A(1), A(2), . . . , A(50)

extent: First use of A(?) defines its type (surface or scalar)

Subscripts can be shown by symbols or expressions, but must be within extent inclusive and are truncated in the case of functions.

Subscripts can be inclusive of the form A(x, thru, y, dec⟨inc⟩z), where x is the first element, y is the last, and z is the increment between. When using "inc", x is the starting element. When using "dec", y is the starting element.

10.8.2 Matrix Definitions

Matrices are used for changing the geometry position in space with the introduction of coordinate rotations, translations, and scaling.

1. Matrix defined by coefficients:

$$M = \text{MATRIX} / a_{11}, a_{22}, . . . , a_{34}$$

2. Matrix defined by translation:

$$M = \text{MATRIX} / \text{TRANSL}, x, y, z$$

where x, y, z are translation distances.

3. Matrix defined by rotation about an axis:

$$M = \text{MATRIX} / \text{XY ROT, ANGLE IN DEGREES}$$
$$\text{yz ROT}$$
$$\text{zx ROT}$$

where positive rotation is from + axis looking toward the origin.

4. Matrix defined as a scale factor:

$$M = \text{MATRIX} / \text{SCALE}, s$$

where s is the scale factor.

5. Matrix defined as a mirror image in one or more coordinate planes:

$$M = \text{MATRIX} / \text{MIRROR, XY plan, XY plan, XY plan}$$
$$\text{YZ plan, YZ plan, YZ plan}$$
$$\text{ZX plan, ZX plan, ZX plan}$$

6. Matrix defined as a mirror about a line or plane:

$$M = \text{MATRIX/MIRROR, LINE (or PLANE)}$$

7. Matrix defined by translation of a coordinate system by two vectors and a point:

$$M = \text{MATRIX/POINT, V1, V2}$$

where V2 lies in the *x–y* plane.

8. Matrix as an inverse:

$$M = \text{MATRIX} / \text{INVERSE, MATRIX}$$

which inverts any transformation matrix.

10.8.3 Combining Matrices

As shown combination of two matrices are given in order,

$$M = \text{MATRIX} / \text{M1, M2}$$

where order is from right to left with exceptions for translation.

REFSYS: Translates the local coordinate system into the base coordinate system.

REFSYS/MATRIX: Begins the transformation.

REFSYS/NOMORE: Cancels the transformation and returns to the base coordinate system.

In a part program, those objects that were used under REFSYS are changed each time they are encountered outside a REFSYSTEM.

Example 10.12   Positioning the Part for Machining Using the MATRIX Command.

Using the conditions of Example 10.11, write the matrices in the APT program to machine the same part (Figure 10.27).

Solution

```
PARTNO BLOCK
P0 = POINT / 0,6,0
P1 = POINT / 2,6,0.5
P2 = POINT / 4,6,0.5
$$ THE MACRO NAMED "DRILL" IS TO MAKE
$$ TWO HOLES OF 0.5" DEPTH.
DRILL = MACRO
FROM / P0
GOTO / P1
GODLTA / 0, − 0.5,0
GODLTA / 0,0.5,0
GOTO / P2
GODLTA / 0, − 0.5,0
GODLTA / 0, − 0.5,0
GOTO / P0
TERMAC
$$ THE FOLLOWING MACRO CALLED "TRANS" TRANSLATES THE
$$ REFERENCE COORDINATE OF THE MACHINE TO REPEAT
$$ THE MACHINING ON SIDES A, B, AND C.
TRANS = MACRO
```

$$ THIS FIRST CALL MACRO STATEMENT IS TO MACHINE SIDE A
    CALL / DRILL
$$ THE FOLLOWING STATEMENT WILL MACHINE SIDE B.
$$ THE MATRIX STATEMENT WILL:
$$ (1) TRANSLATE THE BASE COORDINATE SYSTEM 3" TO THE LEFT
$$ ON THE X AXIS AND DOWN 3" ALONG THE Y AXIS.
$$ (2) ROTATE THE MATRIX 90 DEGREES ABOUT THE Z AXIS.
$$ (3) TRANSLATE THE MATRIX 3" TO THE RIGHT
$$ ON THE X AXIS AND UP 3" ALONG THE Y AXIS.
    MAT1 = MATRIX / TRANSL, − 3, − 3,0, XYROT, 90, TRANSL,
    3,3,0
$$ THE FOLLOWING STATEMENT REDEFINES THE BASE
    COORDINATE
$$ SYSTEM WITH THAT DESCRIBED IN MATRIX "MAT1".
    REFSYS / MAT1
    CALL / DRILL
$$ THE FOLLOWING STATEMENT WILL MACHINE SIDE C.
$$ THE MATRIX STATEMENT WILL:
$$ (1) TRANSLATE THE BASE COORDINATE SYSTEM 3" TO THE LEFT
$$ ON THE X AXIS AND DOWN 3" ALONG THE Y AXIS.
$$ (2) ROTATE THE MATRIX -180 DEGREES ABOUT THE Z AXIS.
$$ (3) TRANSLATE THE MATRIX 3" TO THE RIGHT
$$ ON THE X AXIS AND UP 3" ALONG THE Y AXIS.
    MAT2 = MATRIX / TRANSL, − 3, − 3,0, XYROT, − 180, TRANSL,
    3,3,0
$$ THE FOLLOWING STATEMENT REDEFINES THE BASE
    COORDINATE
$$ SYSTEM WITH THAT DESCRIBED IN MATRIX "MAT2".
    REFSYS / MAT2
    CALL / DRILL
    REFSYS / MAT1
    TERMAC
$$ THIS STATEMENT CALLS FOR THE TOOL (NAMED "T1") THAT CAN
$$ BE USED WITH THE DESIRED FEED RATE AND SPINDLE SPEED.
$$ <FOR DRILLING>
    TURRET / T1
    SPINDL / 800
    FEDRAT / 2.5
    CUTTER / 0.125
    SPINDL / ON
    CALL / TRANS
    SPINDL / OFF
$$ THIS STATEMENT CALLS FOR THE TOOL (NAMED "T2") THAT CAN
$$ BE USED WITH THE DESIRED FEED RATE AND SPINDLE SPEED.
$$ <FOR REAMING>
    TURRET / T2
    SPINDL / 500
    FEDRAT / 4.0
    CUTTER / 0.125

```
SPINDL / ON
CALL / TRANS
SPINDL / OFF
END
FINI
```

10.8.4 Additional Features in APT

What follows are additional features used in APT programming.

Functions in APT.   The output of each function is single-valued and can be used to form arithmetic expressions.

Nested Definitions.   Anything can be nested except TABCYL, POLCON, and RDLSRF, which can have symbols attached.

Loop Structures.   APT allows loop statements to perform repetitive tasks. They can be used in repeated drawings and/or numerical manipulation. The format is similar to the DO LOOP format in FORTRAN.

$$DO \ L1; \ a, \ n, \ i \quad \{Starting \ statement \ of \ the \ LOOP\}$$

$$. \qquad\qquad \{Content \ of \ the \ LOOP\}$$

$$L1: \qquad\qquad \{Repeating \ label \ (end \ of \ LOOP)\}$$

where L1 is the label for the loop, "a" is the initial starting value, "n" is the end value that stops the loop, and "i" is the increment value from "a" to "n".

The increment value is assumed to be 1 if no "i" value is indicated.

Example 10.13   Drilling a Nested Set of Points

Create a loop structure using point-to-point statements to drill the series of holes shown in Figure 10.27.

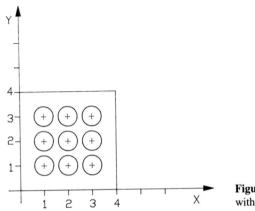

Figure 10.27 Part layout of a plate with symmetric holes.

Solution

```
PARTNO TEST PART NO1
MACHIN / DRILL
$$ THE FOLLOWING IS THE CREATION OF A MACRO STATEMENT TO
    DRILL
$$ 2" DEPTH HOLES.
DRL = MACRO
FEDRAT / 0.75
COOLNT / ON
GODLTA / 0, − 2,0
GODLTA / 0,2,0
COOLNT / OFF
TERMAC
DX = 0
DY = 0
DO L1; 1, 3
        DX = DX + 1
        DO L2; 1, 3
                DY = DY + 1
                GOTO/ DX, DY, 0
                CALL/ DRILL
        L2:
L1:
END
FINI
```

10.9 APT PROGRAMMING DESIGN

The following sections provide a rather comprehensive view of APT programming. The programming ranges from a simple to a complex design, where the constraints have been considered. The goal is to provide a series of designs and APT programs that can conceptualize the design and machining processes.

   With reference to the foregoing constraints, they are considerations that must be placed in the process of machining the workpiece to yield the properly dimensioned finished product. The following must be considered: the material to be machined; the sequence, path, and setting (for the amount of tolerance allowed, if coolant is needed to prevent the tool from yielding an improper cut due to heat generated from friction, etc.); the correct setting of the tool(s) to conform to proper machining codes set by industry; etc.

10.9.1 Car Battery Terminal (Screw-Type)

This is a simple design that involves a basic APT program using a simple machining technique.

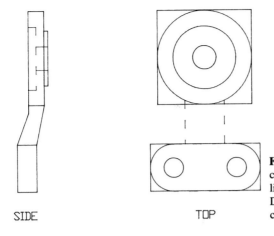

Figure 10.28 Side and top view of a car battery terminal (screw type). Solid lines indicate borders for the coated part. Dotted linear indicate borders after machining.

SIDE   TOP

The part is manufactured in a two-step process. The process involves first casting it into a rough general shape and then machining it into the final product (Figure 10.28).

During the machining of the part, it is necessary to put plates underneath it to keep it flat. For example, while the top part is machined, a 0.1875-in. (3/16-in.) plate must be placed under the lower end of the part. Likewise, when the bottom surface is machined, a 0.245-in. plate must be placed under the top end of the part (Figure 10.29).

Lead has been chosen as the material for the part for the following reasons:

- It is inexpensive.
- It conducts electricity well.
- It can be easily cast and machined because of its softness.
- The scrap produced in machining can be returned to the melt for casting, resulting in almost no waste of material.
- No chemical reaction occurs between the battery contact and the terminal because the contacts on most batteries are also made of lead.

The APT program that follows defines and machines the part. Each of the views shown on the labeled APT diagram (Figure 10.30) has entities that can be machined with the part facing only as it appears in the diagram. This means that it is necessary to rotate the part to complete the machining. Because the machine coordinate system does not rotate when the part is rotated, each view must redefine the part's entities in the machine's coordinate system. For this reason, the coordinate system drawn on each view of the APT diagram is defined with an x and y direction (the z direction is assumed to go into the page). This puts each view into the proper coordinate system.

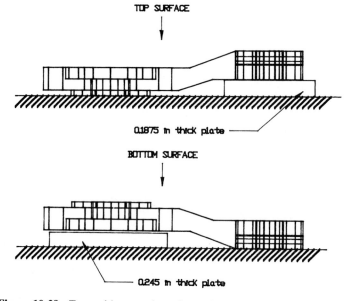

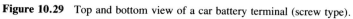

Figure 10.29   Top and bottom view of a car battery terminal (screw type).

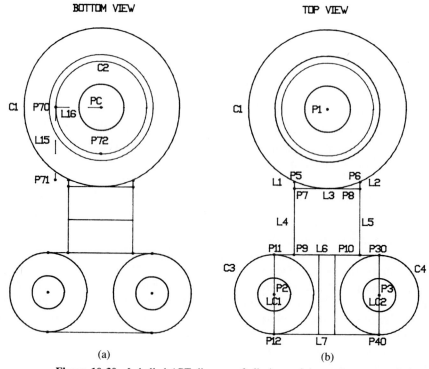

Figure 10.30   Labelled APT diagram of all views of the car battery terminal.

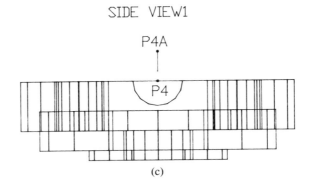

SIDE VIEW1

P4A

P4

(c)

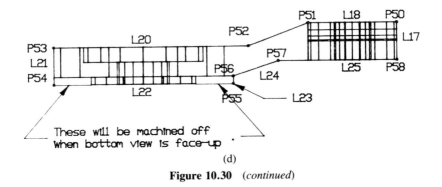

SIDE VIEW 2

These will be machined off
when bottom view is face-up

(d)

Figure 10.30   (*continued*)

APT Program

```
$$ This program creates a screw-type battery terminal.
PSET = POINT / -1,-1, 0
$$ The tolerance can be the same for the whole part
$$ because it does not actually have to fit into any other part.
$$TOLER/0.01
$$
$$ Entities defined on top view.
P1 = POINT / 0.71875,1.71875,0.3175
P2 = POINT / 0.3125,0.3125,0.5625
P3 = POINT / 1.125,0.3125,0.5625
P5 = POINT / 0.46875,1.1802,0.3175
```

```
P6 = POINT / 0.96875, 1.1802, 0.3175
P7 = POINT / 0.46875, 1.125, 0.3175
P8 = POINT / 0.96875, 1.125, 0.3175
P9 = POINT / 0.46875, 0.625, 0.5625
P10 = POINT / 0.96875, 0.625, 0.5625
P11 = POINT / 0.3125, 0.3125, 0.5625
P12 = POINT / 0.3125, 0, 0.5625
C1 = CIRCLE / CENTER, P1, RADIUS, 0.59375
C3 = CIRCLE / CENTER, P2, RADIUS, 0.3125
C4 = CIRCLE / RADIUS, P3, RADIUS, 0.3175
L1 = LINE / P5, P7
L2 = LINE / P6, P8
L3 = LINE / P7, P8
L4 = LINE / P7, P9
L5 = LINE / P8, P10
L6 = LINE / P11, LEFT, TANTO, C4
L7 = LINE / P12, RIGHT, TANTO, C4
$$ The following are various points, lines, and planes
$$ created to help cut the shape on the top view.
$$ They are not actually part of the shape.
PL1 = PLANE / P2, P3, P9
PL2 = PLANE / PARLEL, PL1, ZSMALL, 0.5625
LC1 = LINE / P11, P12
P30 = POINT / 1.125, 0.625, 0.5625
P40 = POINT / 1.125, 0, 0.5625
LC2 = LINE / P30, P40
$$
$$ This takes care of drilling the holes.
CUTTER / 0.3125
FROM / PSET
GO / TO, P2
SPINDL / ON
GODLTA / 0, 0, -0.375
GODLTA / 0, 0, 0.375
SPINDL / OFF
GO / TO, P3
SPINDL / ON
GODLTA / 0, 0, -0.375
GODLTA / 0, 0, 0.375
SPINDL / OFF
CUTTER / 0.375
GO / TO, P1
SPINDL / ON
GODLTA / 0, 0, -0.3175
GODLTA / 0, 0, 0.3175
SPINDL / OFF
CUTTER / 0.8125
```

```
SPINDL / ON
GODLTA / 0, 0, -0. 125
GODLTA / 0, 0, 0. 375
SPINDL / OFF
GO / TO, PSET
CUTTER / 0. 25
CALL / TOPOUT
CUTTER / 0. 125
CALL / TOPOUT
END
```
$$ The part must now be turned and clamped in on its side.
$$ This defines the outer edge for the part when it is
$$ clamped by L17 and L21 (on side view 2).
```
P58 = POINT / 0. 1875, 0, 1. 4375
P50 = POINT / 0. 5625, 0, 1. 4375
P51 = POINT / 0. 5625, 0, 625. 4375
P52 = POINT / 0. 3175, 1. 125, 1. 4375
P53 = POINT / 0. 3175, 2. 3125, 1. 4375
P53A = POINT / 0. 3175, 2. 3125, 0
P54 = POINT / 0, 2. 3125, 1. 4375
P54A = POINT / 0, 2. 3175, 0
P55 = POINT / 0, 1. 125, 1. 4375
P56 = POINT / 0. 625, 1. 125, 1. 4375
P57 = POINT / 0. 1875, 0. 875, 1. 4375
L17 = LINE / P50, P58
L18 = LINE / P50, P51
L19 = LINE / P51, 52
L20 = LINE / P52, 53
L21 = LINE / P53, 54
L21A = LINE / P54A, P54
L21B = LINE / P53A, P53
L21C = LINE / P54A, P53A
L22 = LINE / P54, P55
L23 = LINE / P55, P56
L24 = LINE / P56, P57
L25 = LINE / P57, P58
PL3 = PLANE / P58, P50, P51
PL4 = PLANE / PARLEL, PL3, ZSMALL, 1. 4375
$$
```
$$ This is where the outer edges for the part
$$ in side view 2 get machined.
```
CUTTER / 0. 25
GO / TO, L17, TO, PL4, TO, L25
SPINDL / ON
GOLFT / L25, TO, L24
GOLFT / L24, TO, L23
GOLFT / L23, PAST, L22
```

```
GORGT / L22, PAST, L21
$$ To avoid hitting the clamp, the cutter must be raised.
GOUP / L22, PAST, L21
GORGT / L21, PAST, L20
GODOWN / L20, TO, L21C
GORGT / L20, TO, L19
GOLFT / L19, PAST, L18
GORGT / L18, PAST, L17
$$ Raise bit so it will not be broken.
GODLTA / 0, 0, 1.4375
GORGT / L17, PAST, L25
SPINDL / OFF
GOTO / PSET
END
$$
$$ This part must now be turned upside down.
$$ This defines the bottom-view entities.
PC = POINT / 0.71875, 1.71875, 0.5625
C2 = CIRCLE / CENTER, PC, 0.375
P70 = POINT / 0.3435, 1.71875, 0.5625
P71 = POINT / 0.3435, 1.34375, 0.5
P72 = POINT / 0.71875, 1.34375, 0.5
PL9 = PLANE / P70, P71, P72
L15 = LINE / P70, P71
L16 = LINE / P70, PC
$$
$$ This defines the motion statements for the bottom-view
$$ machining. The outer edges were machined when the top view was
$$ machined. Therefore, the only machining necessary here is for
$$ circle C2.
CUTTER / 0.25
GO / TO, L15, TO, PL9, TO, L16
GOFWD / C2, P70
SPINDL / OFF
GOTO / PSET
END
$$
$$ The part must now be clamped so that side view 1 is
$$ facing up. This defines the entities for side view 1.
P4A = POINT / 0.7185, 0.8125, 1.6875
P4 = POINT / 0.7185, 0.8125, 0
$$
$$ This is the machining for side view 1. Because the part is
$$ made of lead, which is fairly soft, a cutter can be used
$$ to make the half circle.
CUTTER / 0.25
GOTO / P4A
```

```
SPINDL / ON
GODLTA / 0, -0.25, 0
GODLTA / 0, 0, 0.625
SPINDL / OFF
GOTO / PSET
STOP
FINI
$$
$$ This is the macro for cutting the outer edges on the top
$$ and bottom views.
TOPOUT = MACRO /
GO / TO, L7, TO, PL2, TO, LC1
SPINDL / ON
GORGT / L7, ON, LC2
GOFWD / C4, ON, LC2
GOFWD / L5, PAST, L3
GOFWD / L2, TANTO, C1
GOFWD / C1, TO, L1
GOFWD / L1, PAST, L3
GOFWD / L4, TO, L6
GORGT / L6, ON, LC1
GOFWD / C1, ON, LC1
SPINDL / OFF
GO / TO, PSET
TERMAC
```

10.9.2 Support Bracket for a Printed
Circuit Board

This APT program involves machining plastic to create the product. It is slightly more complex because several more machining passes must be made (controlled by the APT program).

The function of this part is to securely hold and support a printed circuit board. It is part of a desktop control console, such as found in security offices.

There are two circuit board supports per unit, which includes a housing molded of structural foam plastic and several other injection-molded parts. The housing has four molded-in capturing pockets (Figure 10.31) into which the circuit board support is inserted. These pockets prevent movement in the x and/or y direction. The printed circuit board is placed between the supports and four locating ribs and four locating slots are used to hold the board. Note that the circuit board supports themselves are prevented from moving in the z direction by another part of the assembly that is not shown in the figure. Also, the two 3-mm holes are for possible future use and serve no purpose at this time. Figure 10.32 shows the isometric and front view of the bracket, respectively.

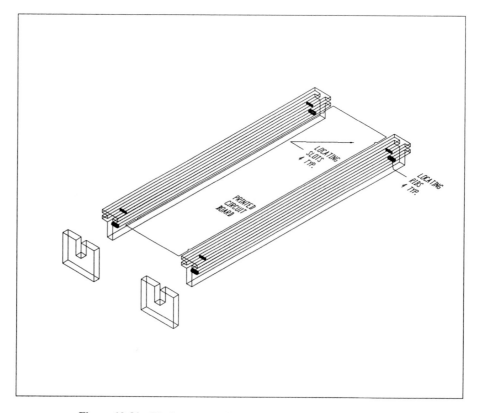

Figure 10.31 Final geometry description of the car battery terminal.

Machining the Part.   To machine the part, assume the following:

1. The material to be used has not been selected, but is assumed to be a material such as glass-filled nylon.
2. Because the material we are machining is a thermoplatic, which could heat up and clog the cutting area, we must specify the appropriate coolant and machining conditions.
3. Although the part is not an appearance item and surface finish is not critical, the methods of holding and positioning the part during machining are carefully selected to prevent damage to the part.
4. The plastic part to be machined has dimensions, in millimeters, of $x = 8.0$, $y = 19.86$, and $z = 338.0$.

APT Program

```
P0 = POINT / 0.0, 0.0, -8.0      $ SET POINT $
P1 = POINT / 2.0, 19.65, -5.35
```

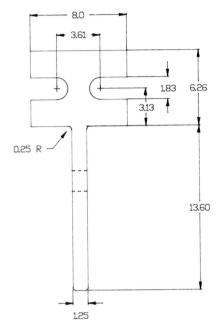

Figure 10.32 Support bracket for printed circuit board.

P2 = POINT / 340.0, 19.65, -5.35
P3 = POINT / 2.0, 2.0, -5.35
P4 = POINT / 340.0, 2.0, -5.35
P5 = POINT / 14.5, 19.65, -5.35
P6 = POINT / 14.5, 17.82, -5.35
P7 = POINT / 16.5, 19.65, -5.35
P8 = POINT / 16.5, 17.82, -5.35
P9 = POINT / 325.5, 19.65, -5.35
P10 = POINT / 325.5, 17.82, -5.35
P11 = POINT / 325.5, 19.65, -5.35
P12 = POINT / 327.5, 17.82, -5.35
P13 = POINT / 12.0, 10.3, -8.0
P14 = POINT / 2.0, 15.6, -5.35
P15 = POINT / 340.0, 15.6, -5.35
P16 = POINT / 330.0, 10.3, -8.0
L1 = LINE / P1, P3
L2 = LINE / P1, P5
L3 = LINE / P2, P4
L4 = LINE / P11, P2
L5 = LINE / P5, P6
L6 = LINE / P7, P8
L7 = LINE / P9, P10
L8 = LINE / P11, P12
L9 = LINE / P14, P15
L10 = LINE / P3, P4
L11 = LINE / P3, P14

Figure 10.33 Front view of printed circuit board support bracket.

```
L12 = LINE / P15, P4
L13 = LINE / P1, P2
PL1 = PLANE / P1, P2, P3      $ PART SURFACE $
MILL-SLOT = MACRO
FROM / PO
GO / TO, L2, TO, PL1, TO, L1
GOLFT / L2, TO, L5
GODLTA / 0.0, 0.0, -2.65   $ (-) SIGN DUE TO COORD. SYSTEM $
GODLTA / 2.0, 0.0, 0.0
GODLTA / 0.0, 0.0, 2.65
GOFWD / L9, TO, L7
GODLTA / 0.0, 0.0, -2.65
GODLTA / 2.0, 0.0, 0.0
GODLTA / 0.0, 0.0, 2.65
GOFWD / L4, PAST, L3
TERMAC


$$ REMARK - SET THE MACHINING CONDITIONS.
          - CUTTER IS A BALL END MILL.


CUTTER / 1.82
TOLER / 0.1
SPINDL / 2000, CLW
FEDRAT / 20
COOLNT / ON
SPINDL / ON


$$ REMARK - MOTION STATEMENTS TO MACHINE A SLOT ON ONE SIDE OF THE
    PART.


CALL MILL-SLOT
GOTO / PO
COOLNT / OFF
SPINDL / OFF


$$ REMARK - CHANGE TOOL TO DRILL TWO HOLES.


MACHIN / DRILL, 01
CUTTER / 3.0
SPINDL / 2000, CLW
COOLNT / ON
SPINDL / ON
```

$$ REMARK - MOTION STATEMENTS TO DRILL TWO HOLES.

```
FROM / PO
GOTO / P13
GODLTA / 0.0, 0.0, 8.0
GODLTA / 0.0, 0.0, -8.0
GOTO / P16
GODLTA / 0.0, 0.0, 8.0
GODLTA / 0.0, 0.0, -8.0
GOTO / PO
COOLNT / OFF
SPINDL / OFF
```

$$ REMARK - CHANGE TOOL TO MILL BOTTOM FLANGE.

```
MACHIN / MILL, 02
CUTTER / 13.6
FEDRAT / 15
SPINDL / 2200, CLW
COOLNT / ON
SPINDL / ON
```

$$ REMARK - MOTION STATEMENTS TO MILL BOTTOM FLANGE.

```
FROM / PO
GO / TO, L9, TO, PL1, TO, L11
GOLFT / L9, TO, L12
GOTO / PO
COOLNT / OFF
SPINDL / OFF
```

$$ REMARK - THIS MILLING COULD HAVE BEEN DONE IN TWO CUTS, ONE
$$ ROUGH CUT AND ONE TO BRING IT TO SIZE.
$$ - THE PART MUST BE TURNED OVER AND RECLAMPED. NOTE THAT
$$ SOME KIND OF SHIMMING IS NECESSARY BEFORE MACHINING THE SECOND
$$ SIDE.

```
MACHIN / DRILL, 01
CUTTER / 1.82
SPINDL / 2000, CLW
FEDRAT / 20
```

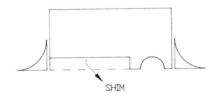

SHIM

Figure 10.34 Machining of the circuit board slot on the side with part supports shown on both sides.

```
COOLNT / ON
SPINDL / ON

$$ REMARK - MOTION STATEMENTS TO MACHINE A SLOT ON THE SECOND SIDE
$$ OF THE PART.

CALL MILL-SLOT
GOTO / PO
COOLNT / OFF
SPINDL / OFF

$$ REMARK - CHANGE TOOL TO MILL BOTTOM FLANGE.

MACHIN / MILL, 02
CUTTER / 13.6
FEDRAT / 15
SPINDL / 2200, CLW
COOLNT / ON
SPINDL / ON

$$ REMARK - MOTION STATEMENTS TO MILL BOTTOM FLANGE.

FROM / PO
GO / TO, L9, TO, PL1, TO, L11
GOLFT / L9, TO, L12
GOTO / PO
COOLNT / OFF
SPINDL / OFF

$$ REMARK - THIS MILLING COULD HAVE BEEN DONE IN TWO CUTS, ONE
$$ ROUGH CUT AND ONE TO BRING IT TO SIZE.

FINI
```

PROBLEMS

The following is to be assumed if not specified in the problem statement:
> Feed rate = 0.785 in./min
> Coolant = on (mist)
> Tolerance = ±0.01 in. (for both inside and outside)
> Cutter = diameter of the hole
> Spindle = 500 rpm

10.1 Given the geometrical description of a mounting plate found in Example 9.6 in Chapter 9, incorporate the description into an APT program to machine it. Assume the thickness of the mounting plate is $\frac{1}{2}$ in.

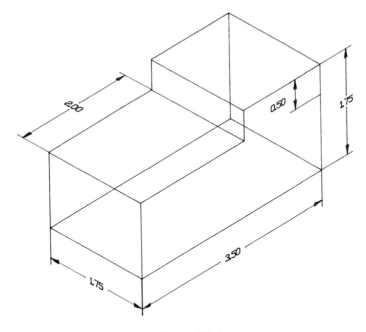

Figure P10.1

10.2 Using the geometrical description in Example 10.1, try to incorporate it into an APT program (some modification may be necessary) to machine this part.

10.3 Use APT programming to machine the bracket blank shown in Figure P10.1. Include the geometrical description of this part in the program. The feed rate is 0.987 in./s. Coolant is not necessary in machining this part. The tolerance is ±0.001 in.

10.4 Create the APT program to machine the part described in Example 9.4 in Chapter 9. The feed rate is 0.500 in./min, the inside tolerance is ±0.005 in., the outside tolerance is ±0.05 in., and the spindle speed of the drill is 345 rpm.

10.5 Using the geometry description given in Example 9.5 in Chapter 9, write the complete APT program to manufacture the part. Let the tool begin from a starting point and return to the starting point after the machining is done. The feed rate is 1.112 in./s, the coolant is on, and the inside and outside tolerances are ±0.0005 in.

10.6 Write a macro routine to machine the pattern shown in Figure P10.2. The coolant, the inside and outside tolerances, and the spindle speed should be set to the same specifications as the main body of the APT program. Let the coolant specification be blank at this point. These macro statements will be called later in another program and the adjustments will be made later.

10.7 An APT program must be written to create the alignment disk shown in Figure P10.3. A geometry description must be written first to describe the part. Use Cartesian coordinates to describe the location of the holes to be drilled. Make sure a starting point is specified (see Problem 10.3). The feed rate is 0.675 in./s, the coolant is on, the cutter is 0.625 in., the inside tolerance is ±0.0001 in., and the outside tolerance is ±0.05 in.

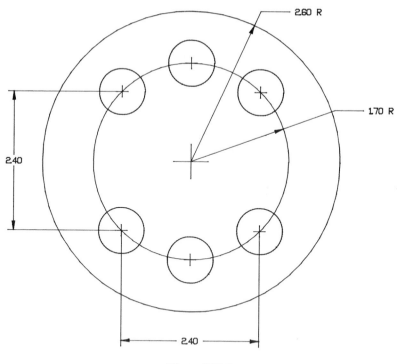

Figure P10.2

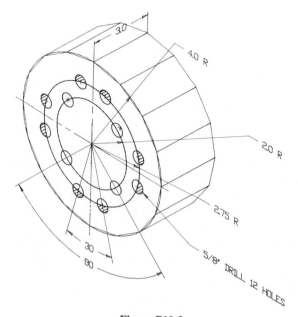

Figure P10.3

Up to now, the problems involved "one-pass" routines to cut the part. We now consider cases where several passes must be made.

10.8 Given a rectangular blank with sides of 25 in. and a thickness of $\frac{3}{4}$ in., create macro routines to machine the part. The tool removes a layer of 0.125 in. per pass. Several passes must be made and the use of macro statements will simplify the programming necessary to machine the part.

10.9 A rectangular workpiece of dimensions 4.0 in. in length, 1.75 in. in height, and 2.0 in. in thickness must be machined until it resembles the guide block as shown in Figure P10.4. Create and use macro routines in an APT program to produce it. The tool removes at the rate of 0.125 in. per pass. The feed rate is 0.432 in./min, the outside tolerance is 0.05 in., and the coolant is on.

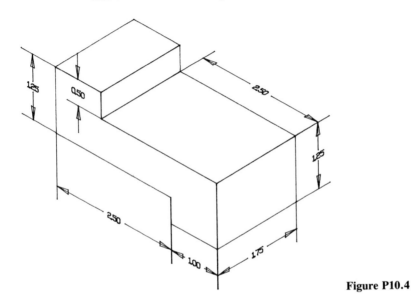

Figure P10.4

10.10 Use macro routines to machine the bench stop shown in Figure P10.4. Start with the geometrical description of the part. The workpiece is a square piece of aluminum with side lengths of 3 in. The tool removes stock at the rate of 0.05 in. per pass. The feed rate is 0.655 in./s, the coolant is off, and the outside tolerance is 0.025 in.

10.11 Write the program to machine the gage block shown in Figure P10.5 out of a rectangular piece of stock with the dimensions of 4 in. in length, 2 in. in height, and 2 in. in thickness. The stock is removed at the rate of 0.1 in. per pass. Macro routines are suggested in areas where multiple passes are necessary.

10.12 The cam block described in Problem 9.7 is to be created out of a spherical piece of plastic with a radius of 6 in. The stock is removed at the rate of 0.1 in. per pass. Coolant is not necessary, the outside tolerance is ±0.0125 in., and the feed rate is 0.545 in./min. Write the necessary APT program to machine the part.

10.13 A rectangular piece of iron of dimensions 3.75 in. in length, 1.5 in. in height, and 2.2 in. in depth is to be machined into the V-slide stop shown in Figure P10.6. The

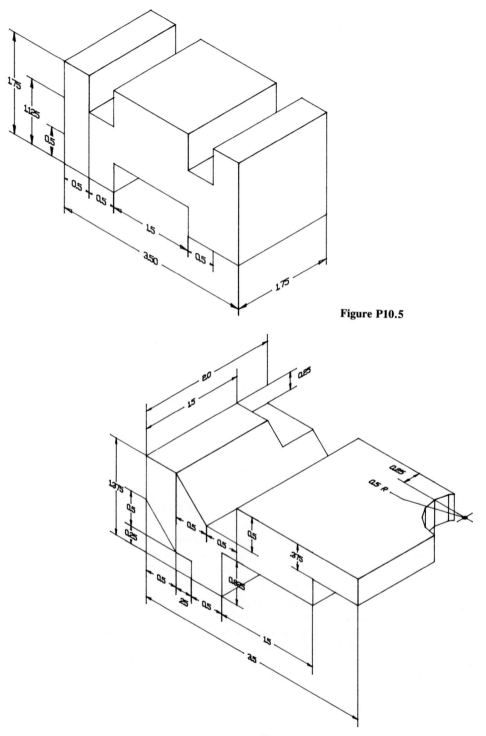

Figure P10.5

Figure P10.6

rate of removal of stock is 0.01 in. per pass. Write the APT program to produce the proposed part. (Identify the necessary machining steps before writing the program.)

REFERENCES

10.1 Besant, C. B., and Lui, C. W. K., *Computer-Aided Design and Manufacture,* 3d ed., Ellis Horwood, Chichester, UK, 1986.

10.2 Bezier, P., *Numerical Control: Mathematics and Applications,* A. R. Forrest and A. F. Pankhurst., trans., John Wiley & Sons, London, 1972.

10.3 Brown, S. A., Drayton, C. E., and Mittman, B., A Description of the APT Language, *Commun. ACM,* Vol. 6, No. 11, November 1963.

10.4 Hyodo, Y., HAPT-3D: A Programming System for Numerical Control, In: *Computer Languages for Numerical Control,* J. Hatvany, ed., North-Holland, Amsterdam, 1973.

10.5 IBM Corp., *IBM Manual SH20-1413-3: APT-AC NC Processor: Operations Guide,* 4th ed., Rye Brook, NY, 1985.

10.6 IBM Corp., *IBM Manual SH20-2095-6: CADAM APT Interface Installation Guide,* 7th ed., Rye Brook, NY, 1985.

10.7 IBM Corp., *IBM Manual SH20-6640-0: APT-AC NC Processor-Advanced Functions: Program Reference Manual,* 1st ed., Rye Brook, NY, 1983.

10.8 ITT Research Institute, *APT Part Programming,* McGraw-Hill, New York, 1967.

10.9 Kelly, R. S., The Production Man's Guide to APT-ADAPT, *Am. Mach.,* Vol. 97, June 22, 1969.

10.10 Koren, Y., Design Concepts of a CNC System, *Proc. IEEE Ind. App. Soc.,* 10th Annual Meeting, Atlanta, Oct. 1975, pp. 275–282.

10.11 McWaters, J. F., *NC User's Guide to the International Computer Programs,* McGraw-Hill, London, 1968.

10.12 Middleditch, A. E., Design Criteria for Multi-axis Closed Loop Computer Numerical Control Systems, *Trans. ASME, J. Dyn. Sys., Meas. Contr.,* Vol. 96, No. 1, March 1974, pp. 36–40.

10.13 Parkinson, A., An Automatic NC Data Generation Facility for the BUILD Solid Modeling System, In: *Proceedings of the 16th CIRP International Seminar on Manufacturing Systems,* Tokyo, 1984.

10.14 Parkinson, A., The Use of Solid Models in BUILD as a Database for NC Machining, In: *Software for Discrete Manufacturing,* J. P. Crestin and J. F. McWaters, eds., North-Holland, Amsterdam, 1986.

10.15 Texas Instruments, *TM990-Introduction to Microprocessors, Hardware and Software,* Dallas, 1979.

10.16 Willete, E. J., The Computer's Role in Numerical Control, *Manuf. Eng.,* September 1977, pp. 36–37.

chapter 11

Industrial Robotics

A robot is a reprogrammable, multifunctional manipulator designed to move material, parts, tools or specialized devices through variable programmed motions for the performance of a variety of tasks.

The Robot Institute of America

11.1 INTRODUCTION

In today's highly competitive markets, more and more companies are pressed to deliver quality products at low prices. To meet such a challenge, a number of companies are turning to computer-based automation and computer-integrated manufacturing. The high costs associated with conventional manufacturing techniques and their task limitations have opened the door for the use of robots.

Historically, robots have fascinated many of us because of their capabilities to emulate human beings. Although our perceptions of robots are still far from being realistic, we are beginning to feel their impact on industrial technology, especially in the field of space exploration.

The concept of a robot can be traced back to ancient Egypt, but its industrial utility began in the 1950s when teleoperators were developed to handle radioactive materials. These were the so-called master–slave manipulators in which an operator used the master and, through a window, saw how the slave manipulator duplicated the task.

It was not until the early 1960s that the first industrial robot was built in the United States. The initial use of robots was hampered by economics and hardware.

The robot operational cost was in the range of $9 an hour compared to the average hourly wage of a worker at that time of about $5 an hour. In addition, the technology was limited to a few applications.

In the mid-1970s, robots were used in a wider range of applications. This was due in particular to the development of microprocessors. Robots began increasingly to be used in manufacturing operations. Furthermore, there was an increased aware-

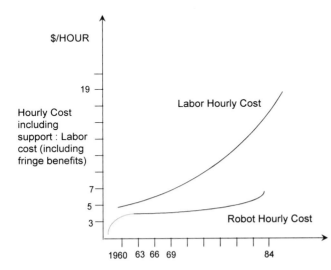

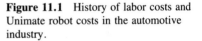

Figure 11.1   History of labor costs and Unimate robot costs in the automotive industry.

ness that for well-defined repetitive operations, robots could outperform human operators.

In the 1980s, workers' hourly wages increased to about $20 an hour, whereas the hourly wages of operating robots didn't change much (Figure 11.1).

Robots became more sophisticated and reliable, factors that have driven a number of industrial sectors to implement them in their manufacturing operations. The automotive industry accounts for about 55% of the robots in operation in the United States. They are used in the assembly line and perform a variety of tasks usually done by skilled operators. The tasks range from pick and place, welding and pointing, to the placement of engine blocks into cars. Today's manufacturing cells are designed around the capabilities of robot speed and reach and they are becoming an essential element of manufacturing processes. The benefits robots offer are numerous and include:

- Increased productivity
- Reduced labor costs
- Effective equipment utilization
- Utilization in hazardous environments
- Improved quality

- Handsome returns on investment
- Improved flexibility
- Short lead times
- Improved competitive positions

The primary applications for industrial robots in the United States are in manufacturing areas of automobiles and electrical machinery where welding and material handling are the primary tasks. In addition, robots are increasingly being used for die casting, investment casting, forging, press work, spray painting and surface treatment, foundries, plastic molding, and loading and unloading of machine tools.

In this chapter, the basic concepts of different robot configurations are presented, together with the programs, features, and different options they possess.

11.2 CONFIGURATION OF A ROBOT

The basic components of a robot are the manipulator, the controller, and the power supply. Today's robots come with additional options such as minicomputers or microcomputers as storage and control devices and external sensors such as digital vision, force sensors, transducers, tactile sensors, and effectors.

11.2.1 The Manipulator

The manipulator consists of "arm" and "wrist," both of which are mounted on a support stand. The workspace, or volume of the robot, is the volume in which the arm and wrist subassembly unit can travel at any point. Mechanically, robot manipulators can be classified into the following types.

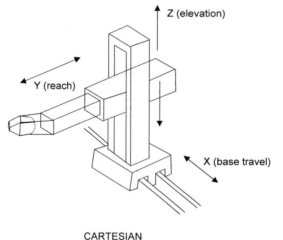

CARTESIAN

Figure 11.2 Robot in a cartesian coordinate system.

Rectangular or Cartesian Robots.   For these robots, all motions are done in translation along three linear orthogonal axes (Figure 11.2). This type of robot is referred to as the "pick and place" robot. The base axis of the Cartesian system can be extended to enlarge the working volume of the robot.

Cylindrical Robots.   These robots consist of two linear orthogonal translations and a base rotation (Figure 11.3). The base rotary motion can provide rapid positioning. The maximum and minimum reach of the horizontal axis determine the maximum and minimum workspace of the robot.

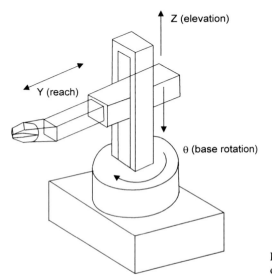

Figure 11.3 Robot in a cylindrical co-ordinate system.

Spherical Robots.   Spherical robots have two rotations and one translation (Figure 11.4). They have the lowest weight and shortest joint travel for most robots. The linear axis forms the radius of the workspace (sphere).

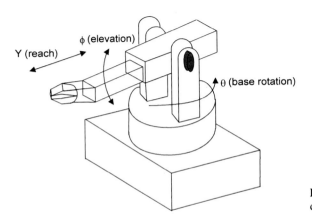

Figure 11.4 Robot in a spherical coordinate system.

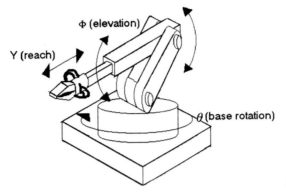

Figure 11.5   Robot with revolute joints.

Revolute or Articulated Robots.   These robots use a series of rotary motions similar to those performed by human arms (Figure 11.5). They have the flexibility to reach under or over an object.

11.2.2 The Controller

The control unit is the "brains of the robot." The basic function of the controller is to direct the motion of the end effector in terms of position and orientation. It works in a fashion similar to the control unit in an NC machine. Thus, robots can also be classified by their method of control.

The control unit is equipped with different controllers to perform point-to-point operations or continuous path motion. The most common controllers found in industrial robotic systems are as follows.

Point-to-Point (PTP) Robots.   Also known as nonservo robots, they are used mostly in pick-and-place operations. The controller sends signals to the manipulator actuators and controls, which in turn articulate the manipulator's arms to perform the desired task. The control unit's functions include the conversion of secondary programs into machine language to generate the appropriate pulses to drive the motors. PTP robots have fewer than six degrees of freedom and are capable of stopping at several different programmed positions although their path between the programmed points cannot be specified. The advantages of these robots include speed of operation, accuracy, and reliability. The drawback is the limited tasks they can perform.

Continuous-Path Controlled Robots.   Also known as "walk-through" continuous-path robots, they emulate a human operator in performing such operations as painting and welding. The controlled path is achieved by the human operator's hand leading the end effector through the desired path, which is stored as digitized information in the computer (Figure 11.6).

The generated program when played back gives the same motion. Hence, in programming the operator's hand motion, the path and the speed of execution are essentially defined. One last note on the walk-through method and why the end ef-

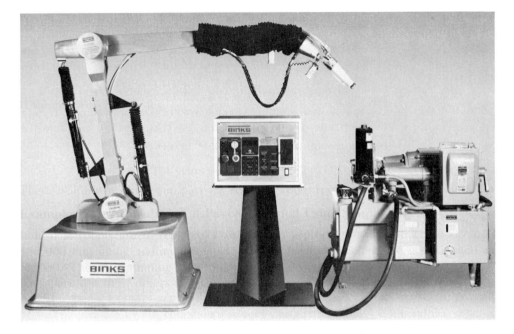

Figure 11.6 Components of a walk-through robot (courtesy of Binks Manufacturing Company).

fector must be manually driven to create the desired path of motion. Essentially, tasks like welding vary from one application to another and programming them efficiently is expensive. Hence, duplicating an experienced welder is faster and more economical.

The point-to-point motion controller is based on an open loop and the controlled robot utilizes the closed loop type of feedback controller. The latter requires more tooling and hence is the most expensive option a robot can have.

Controlled-Path Robots.   These robots have the most sophisticated level of motion control. Given a few intermediate points, a smooth path is generated by the computer using mathematical tools such as cubic splines. They generally have six degrees of freedom and are capable of straight-line and arc interpolated motion and continuous paths.

11.2.3 The Power Supply

There are three types of power sources: electric, pneumatic, and hydraulic. The characteristics of each are discussed in the following.

Electric Drives.   Direct-current (dc) servo and stepper motors are the two main types of electric drives used in robotic applications. These dc motors can provide high torques in small volumes and they are precise, clean, and reliable. The torque produced is proportional to the magnitude and direction of current flow in the rotating armature. The electrical energy is converted to mechanical energy.

As costs decrease and technological improvements take place, dc servo motors will be the principal drives for robotic applications.

The dc stepper motors are driven by sequence of electric pulses and the number of pulses directly controls the portion of the motor in an open-loop fashion. These motors are used for less sophisticated robotic applications. They are larger than servo motors and have limited performance capabilities.

The advantages of electric drives include

- low cost
- reduced floor space
- high accuracy and repeatability
- easy maintenance

Pneumatic Drives. These are the simplest to design and cost less than other drives. However, they are used in less sophisticated robotic applications like pick-and-place and quick assembly operations. Because air is easily compressible, these robots are difficult to position and control. Hence, they have low accuracy and poor repeatability.

The advantages of pneumatic drives include

- low operating cost
- low maintenance
- quick assembly

Hydraulic Drives. These were the primary sources of power in earlier robots. They have the greatest strength because they produce the greatest power in the smallest volume. However, they are very noisy, take up a large space, and have high maintenance costs.

The advantages of hydraulic drives include

- high speed
- highest power-to-weight ratio
- design simplicity
- good physical strength

11.3 PROGRAMMING ROBOTS

The controller is the part of the robot that initiates and terminates the motion of the manipulator. It stores position and sequence data in memory and communicates with the outside world.

There are two ways of programming the controller to accomplish these functions: on-line programming and off-line programming.

11.3.1 On-Line Programming

The process of programming the controller by on-line programming is known as "teaching" the robot. The process of teaching involves reaching, editing, and replaying the desired path. In the teaching mode, the robot is manually led through a desired sequence of motions by the operator. The movement information and other necessary data are recorded by the controller as the robot is guided through the desired sequence. On-line programming can be carried out by two techniques: manual teaching and lead-through programming.

Manual Teaching.   This is normally done by means of a portable hand-held programming unit that contains a number of buttons and joysticks used to direct the controller in moving the robot to different locations. Subsequently every move is saved in memory so that a file of motion is created that can be replayed by the robot (Figure 11.7). Manual teaching is used to program nonservo robots.

Figure 11.7   The use of a teach box in manual programming of the PUMA robot (courtesy of Staubli & Unimation).

Lead-Through Programming.   In this technique, the operator grasps the manipulator and leads it through the tasks or motions, simultaneously recording the positions (Figure 11.8). Lead-through programming is used for operations such as spray painting, arc welding, and other complex motion trajectories.

Lead-through programming is the most widely used method to program a robot. It is the most natural way of programming the controller to make the robot perform required tasks. During the programming, the speed of the robot can be controlled, enabling the programming to be carried out safely. At the same time, the operator can coordinate the robot's motion with other equipment with which the robot has to interact. This type of programming does not require special skills and can be performed with ease and speed. Repetitive program sequences can be stored in memory for future recall. The only disadvantage is the loss of valuable production time while programming is being carried out. Lead-through programming is used with point-to-point servo robots.

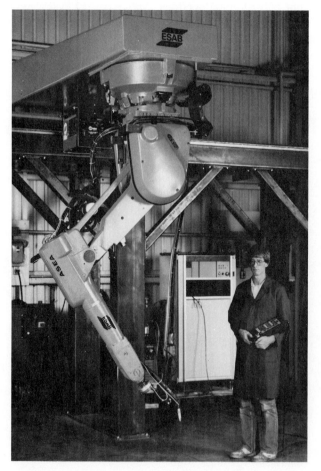

Figure 11.8 Lead-through programming (courtesy of ESAB Automation).

11.3.2 Off-Line Programming

Programming a robot by programming languages does not require the robot's participation. The major benefit of explicit programming languages is that external data such as sensor feedback can easily be used. Programming languages reduce robot downtime and make the interface with other machines simpler.

Currently, considerable research is going on in off-line programming methods and their implementation. The increased sophistication in controllers, sensors. and other hardware makes off-line programming even more feasible. Unlike on-line programming, the off-line method requires the programmer to have some knowledge in programming and in the design of the robotic sensor-based motion strategies. It is apparent that some difficulties arise when developing a generalized programming system adaptable to all robotic systems.

Some off-line programming systems currently in use are VAL, SIGLA, GEOMAP, ROBEX, RAPT, CATIA, AL, ANIMATE/PLACE, GRASP, and AUTO PASS.

11.4 PROGRAMMING LANGUAGES

The programming of NC machines led to a higher-level programming language used for robot motive controls. The first robot-level programming language was developed at the Massachusetts Institute of Technology (MIT) by Ernst in 1961 and was called the "Mechanical Hand Interpreter," or MHI. It is modeled around guarded moves, that is, the hand moves until a sensor detects a particular situation. A program contains commands like "move" to indicate direction and speed, "until" to test a sensor, "if continue" to continue the program if desired conditions are met, and "of goto" to indicate logical branching.

Silver in 1973 developed the nest program called MINI at MIT. This language was an extension of LISP; however, the major limitation of this language was its inability to control robotic joints dependently.

WAVE was another general-purpose programming language developed by Paul in 1977 at the Stanford Artificial Intelligence Laboratory. It was modeled using the assembly language POP-10 and it had the ability to specify the robotic joint and hand compliance.

Further research in software for robotic control resulted in languages such as VAL, developed by Shimano and Unimation Inc. in 1980 and 1983, and EMILY, ML, and AML developed at IBM in 1979. Recently, AMML/E was developed, which is based on AML and is for IBM PCs or compatibles.

All the robotic programming languages can be classified under a five-level classification scheme based on the abilities of their problem-solving methodologies. Table 11.1 illustrates such classification levels of robotic programming languages. The functions of a Level 4 structured programming language are shown in Figure 11.9.

TABLE 11.1 HUMAN INTELLIGENCE LEVELS OF
ROBOTIC PROGRAMMING LANGUAGES

Level 5	Task-oriented level	AUTOPASS, LAMA
Level 4	Structured programming level	AL, AML, HELP, RAPT, RAIL, PAL ROBEX, MCL, MAPEX
Level 3	Primitive-motion level	AML/E, EMILY, RCL, RPL, PRBE, SIGLE, VAL, ANORAD
Level 2	Point-to-point level	T3, FUNKY
Level 1	Microcomputer level	

The heart of a structured programming language is its logic in the form of program control. The impression of robot intelligence is created by the combination of program control with various functions. In the Level 4 language, the user provides each robot task with a control algorithm executed by the robot controller.

Level 5 is the ideal level because it virtually eliminates all the tedious programming steps concerned with the details of a particular task. This level of programming relies on vision sensors and built-in artificial-intelligence functions. It is still at the research level and robots equipped with such programs are not commercially available.

The major difference among these programming languages is their level of sophistication in detecting and using external sensor information. The more sophisticated languages can interface with a variety of external sensors and are capable of updating the position of stored precision points based on various sensory inputs.

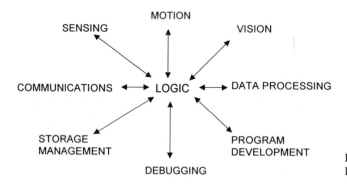

Figure 11.9 Program control using logic.

Thus, more sophisticated languages allow continual robot performance in the presence of uncertainty and environmental changes.

Let us illustrate a typical robot operation that has been programmed in VAL, a well-known commercial language. VAL closely resembles the BASIC computer language and it is a user friendly interpreted language that can handle most of today's robotic applications.

Example 11.1   VAL Program to Move Objects

The following program called PALLET is used to sequentially move nine objects from a 3-row, 3-column pallet to a location called MACH. The program is composed of two points, the main program and a subroutine SUB. As with any program, all variables must be defined prior to execution.

```
.PROGRAM PALLET
1.   SET HOLE = CORNER
2.   SETI COL = 0
100  SETI ROW = 0
200  GOSUB PALLET.SUB
5.   SHIFT HOLE BY 50.00, 0.00,0.00
6.   SET I ROW = ROW + 1
7.   IF ROW LT 3 THEN 200
8.   SHIFT HOLE BY −150.00, 50.00, 0.00
9.   SET I COL = COL + 1
10.  IF COL LT 3 THEN 100
.END
PROGRAM PALLET.SUB
1.   OPEN I 0.00
2.   APPROS HOLE, 100.00
3.   MOVES HOLE,
4.   CLOSEI 0.00
5.   DEPART 50.00
6.   APPROS MACH,50.00
7.   MOVES MACH,
8.   OPENI 0.00
9.   DEPART 50.00
10.  RETURN 0
.END                                                ∎
```

In this program, the specific corner and MACH locations represent two precise points that can be identified by a lead-through operation prior to task execution. The numerical distances are specified in millimeters and the I associated with SETI, OPENI, and CLOSEI commands denotes an immediate operation. APPROS denotes a straight-line approach to position the gripper 100 mm directly above each object prior to a straight-line move to the object (MOVES HOLE). Subsequently, the grasp function is defined by CLOSEI 0.00. The implementation of this program on a PUMA 560 robot takes less than 1 min to complete, depending on the distance between MACH and CORNER and the selected speed.

Example 11.2   **A Peg-in-Hole Insertion Program in AML**

To illustrate the procedure of programming a robot, a program written in AML language for peg insertion in a hole is given below.

```
PICKUP:SUBR(PART
DATA,TRIES);
     MOVE(GRIPPER
DIAMETER(PART–DATA)+0.2);
     MOVE(<1,2,3>,XYZ–POSITION(PART–DATA) +<0,0,1>);
     TRY
PICKUP(PART
DATA,TRIES);
     END;
TRY–PICKUP:SUBR(PART–DATA,TRIES);
     IF TRIES LT 1 THEN RETURN('NO PART');
     DMOVE(3,-1.0);
     IF GRASP(DIAMETER(PART–DATA)='NO PART'
     THEN TRY–PICKUP(PART–DATA,TRIES-1);
     END;
GRASP:SUBR(DIAMETER,F);
     FMONS:NEW APPLY ($MONITOR,PINCH–FORCE(F));
     MOVE (GRIPPER,0,FMONS)
     RETURN (IF QPOSITION–(GRIPPER)LE DIAMETER/2
          THEN 'NO PART'
          ELSE 'PART');
     END;
INSERT: SUBR(PART–DATA,HOLE);
     FMONS: NEW APPLY (SMONITOR, TIP–FORCE(LANDING–
     FORCE));
     MOVE(<1,2,3>,HOLE + <0,0,25>);
     DMOVE(3,-1.0.FMONS);
     IF QMONITOR(FMONS) = 1
     THEN RETURN ('NO HOLE');
     MOVE(3HOLE(3) + PART–LENGTH(PART–DATA));
     END;
PART–IN–HOLE:SUBR(PART–DATA,HOLE);
     PICKUP (PART–DATA,2.);
     INSERT (PART–DATA,HOLE);
     END;                                                    ■
```

This program was written for an IBM 7565 robotic manipulator just for testing the six degrees-of-freedom motion as well as the grip-motion and speed sensors. It moves the robot to seven different kinematic attitudes and sets the distance between the jaws of the gripper and its speed (Figure 11.10).

AML allows the user to specify motion in the joint-variable space and to specify motion in Cartesian space. The MOVE command indicates the destination frame to which the arm should move. In AML, the aggregates of the form ⟨speed,

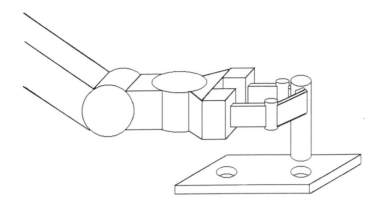

Figure 11.10   Insertion of a peg in a hole by a robot.

acceleration, deceleration⟩ are added to the MOVE statement to specify speed, acceleration, and deceleration, respectively, of the robot. The predefined variable GRIPPER indicates the gripper that can be programmed to move to a certain opening. The primitive MONITOR is specified in the motion commands to detect asychronous events. The programmer specifies the sensors to monitor and specifies when they are to be triggered and motion halted. The syntax for MONITOR is MONITOR (sensors, test type, limit1, limit2).

11.5 SENSORY SYSTEM OF A ROBOT

Sensors are for the most part used to add a degree of intelligence to robots. Without sensors, robots are unable to respond to any change in their working environment. For example, with a sensor, a robot used in a pick-and-place operation always tends to pick the desired object even if the object is moved to a different location. Serious collision problems can occur if an obstacle appears in the path of the robot gripper. These are some of the concerns of programming a robot to perform a certain task.

Robots equipped with an array of sensors possess a certain degree of artificial intelligence that allows them to operate in a changing environment by making real-time decisions that can change their course of action. The real-time decisions are based on information received from the sensors. Such robots are called intelligent robots.

The sensory system of the robot monitors and interprets the events in the working environment. The feedback received from the environment enables the robot to react in an orderly fashion so as to comply with its objectives. A data-acquisition system uses data from the sensors to feed back into the robot-control algorithm, which in turn activates the actuators to drive the robot. Monitoring joint positions, velocities, acceleration, and gripper force is carried out by the interval measurement devices and sensors through special algorithms. A robotic gripper with built-in sensors is shown in Figure 11.11.

Figure 11.11 A robotic grippe with built-in sensor (courtesy of Center for Engineering Design, University of Utah).

11.5.1 Classification of Robotic Sensors

Robotic sensors can be broadly classified into two groups: internal and external sensors.

Internal Sensors. Internal sensors establish their configuration in their own set of coordinate axes. They measure movement, speed, acceleration, and stress. Movement sensors are of different types, either rectilinear (translational) or angular (rotational).

External Sensors. External sensors allow the robot to position itself relative to its environment. They are classified as contact and noncontact sensors. Contact sensors can be further divided into tactile and force-torque sensors. A simple tactile sensor is a microswitch that senses the presence of barriers, obstacles, and surfaces beyond which the robot is not permitted to move. Thus, tactile sensors can be used to avoid collisions, to signal the robot system that a target was reached, or to measure object dimensions during inspection. External sensors are used for approximation, touch, geometry, vision, and safety. They usually consist of the following sensors:

- Tactile (touch) sensors
- Proximity detectors
- Force feedback devices
- Vision sensors

Tactile sensors can also be subclassified into touch sensors and stress sensors. Stress tactile sensors produce a signal indicating magnitude and distribution of contact forces and touch sensors produce a binary output signal. However, tactile sensors do not indicate the presence of objects until they come in contact with the object.

Force and torque sensors are located between the end effector and the last joint of the wrist; they measure the force and torque components by sensing deflections of the sensing element.

Force sensors generally consist of piezoelectric transducers or strain gages mounted on the compliant sections of the manipulator's end effector. They measure three components of force and three components of torque acting between the gripper and the object being held. A six-axis wrist sensor is shown in Figure 11.12. It consists of strain gages mounted on elastic beams. Strain gages are low cost, high resolution, and have a high degree of reliability. The SRI sensor has eight elastic beams of which four are parallel to the Z axis and are labeled V_{x+}, V_{y+}, V_{x-}, and V_{y-}. The other four beams are perpendicular to the Z axis and are labeled W_{x+}, W_{y+}, W_{x-}, and W_{y-}. Two foil strain gages, R_1 and R_2, are mounted on each of the eight beams to respond to the compressive or tensile strains generated along the axis of the beam. On beams V_{x+} and V_{x-}, gages are placed on the two faces perpendicular to the y direction. On beams V_{y+} and V_{y-}, gages are placed on the face perpendicular to the x direction. On beams W_{x+}, W_{y+}, and W_{x-}, the gages are placed perpendicular to the z direction. The two strain groups, R_1 and R_2, are connected to a potentiometer circuit, whose output voltage is given by the name of its beam. When a peg-hole insertion task is applied, the voltages proportional to three force and three torque components acting on the wrist are given by the following linear combinations:

$$F_x \propto V_{y+} + V_{y-} \tag{11.1}$$

$$F_y \propto V_{x+} + V_{x-} \tag{11.2}$$

$$F_z \propto W_{x+} + W_{x-} + W_{y+} + W_{y-} \tag{11.3}$$

$$M_x \propto W_{y+} - W_{y-} \tag{11.4}$$

$$M_y \propto -W_{x+} + W_{x-} \tag{11.5}$$

$$M_z \propto V_{x+} - V_{x-} - V_{y+} + V_{y-} \tag{11.6}$$

Now, these six components of the force and torque are sent to the computer for processing. The computer then generates six correction signals that are sent as

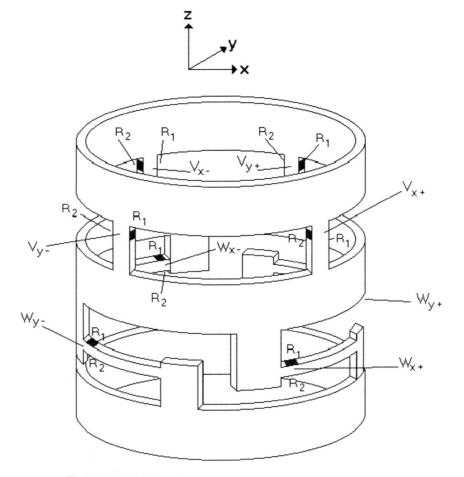

Figure 11.12 A six axis sensor based on design by SRI International.

references to the six corresponding joints. The manipulator then moves the peg based on these signals toward the center of the hole in order to insert the peg into the hole. It is essential to have a certain degree of compliance between the grasped peg (object) and the end of the robot's wrist. When passive devices are employed, such as a Remote Center Compliance device (RCC), the compliance is provided by the device itself. With active devices, the mechanical flexibility of the wrist plays the same role.

11.5.2 Vision Systems

Vision systems typically use a number of video cameras linked to vision processors that are capable of digitizing and processing the acquired digital information. The vision processor analyzes the image and defines the object. The major applications of vision systems are in assembly processes, quality control, part classification, and inspection. These systems are capable of screening parts not meeting specifications; they can also detect the presence and absence of a part.

A typical robotic vision system has a video camera that is interfaced with the vision computer through a video buffer called a frame grabber and a visual information preprocessor (Figure 11.13). The video signal is sent to a TV monitor and is displayed continuously for analysis. The preprocessor stores the useful information and hence reduces processing time. Upon instruction, a frozen frame from the camera is scanned row by row and the corresponding output signal is stored in the frame grabber in digital form. This digitized image is transferred to the vision computer in parallel bytes for image processing. Some of the cameras available today are the Image Orthicon Tube, Vicicon Tube, Plumbicon Tube, Charge-Coupled Device (CCD), and Image Dissector Tube.

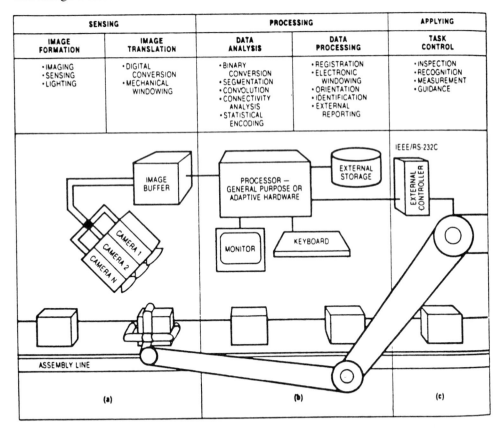

Figure 11.13 Three parts of the machine vision process. For an assembly line robot, for example, there is (a) sensor consisting of a camera and translator, (b) an image-data processor to perform both analysis and processing, and (c) an external controller for application development (courtesy of Pattern Processing Technologies Inc.).

11.5.3 Other Sensors

A range sensor/detector can provide precise measurement of the distance between the object and the sensor itself. A range detector measures the distance from a reference point, on the sensor itself, and a point on the object using the principle of beam triangulation. The distance is measured by measuring the time taken for the last beam to reach the object and back again. The triangular principle that is used is shown in Figure 11.14.

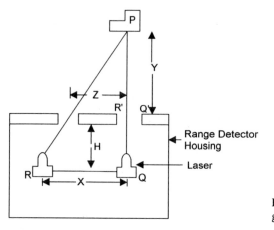

Figure 11.14 Principle of beam triangulation.

The sensor consists of a light source and an array of light-sensitive elements. These photosensors are scanned to detect the one having the maximum output signal. If x_i is the distance of the ith light detector, then by using the two similar triangles, it can be shown that

$$Y = \frac{ZH}{X_i - Z}$$

where Y is the distance of the object from the range detector.

11.6 FUNDAMENTALS OF GRIPPER DESIGN

The end effector of a robotic manipulator is connected to the end link through the wrist. In most gripper designs, the wrist is equipped with three possible rotations. These motions along the rotary axis are called roll, pitch, and yaw. A wrist with the three rotary motions is shown in Figure 11.15. Roll is defined as rotation in a plane perpendicular to the end of the arm, pitch is rotation in the vertical plane, and yaw is rotation in the horizontal plane.

Various parameters have to be considered to design a wrist. The design requirements also depend greatly on the application of the robot.

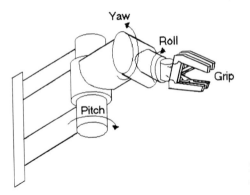

Figure 11.15 Details of robotic wrist articulation.

A wrist is usually designed as a low-power, high-torque type of device. Because the wrist does not move far enough and fast enough, power requirements are low. However, forces and moments transmitted through the wrist can be nearly as large as those transmitted through the robotic arm. Physical control, which can be electronic, pneumatic, hydraulic, or mechanical, is also an important aspect in designing grippers and manipulators. Pneumatics was the major method of physical control for powering manipulators and grippers in early robots. Now, with advances in microprocessor technology, electronic control has become more feasible and affordable. Mathematical algorithms were developed in parallel to predict and finally generate the optimum control mechanism for driving the manipulators and grippers. The ability of a gripper to grasp parts in a stable manner in space and to provide feedback on the amount of force that is being applied on the object is a major consideration for certain robot tasks. Feedback is provided through sensors.

The most common robot applications are pick and place, welding, and spray painting. These applications usually do not require great emphasis on the interaction between the objects and the robot end effectors, or grippers. Therefore, sensing is limited to simple feedback measuring the end-effector position with the loop of operation. A primary concern in the design and control of grippers for complex tasks is the constant monitoring of the force stimuli during the course of a particular motion. Therefore, the ability of a robotic manipulator to react to contact forces and tactile stimuli defines its so-called compliance. As technology evolves, more complex manufacturing processes will be done by robotic manipulators equipped with sensors that allow a certain controllability of its compliance to account for external contact forces that are unaccounted for. Generally, compliance is either passive or programmed into the robot-control system. The passive one is inherent from the robot's structure such as its material properties.

It is essential to determine the mechanism responsible for compliant motion. Compliant motion is attained by deriving the proper mathematical relationships between the forces interacting between the robot and its contacting environment. Once these contact forces are established, predictions of the robot's response can be analyzed. Usually, it is assumed that contact forces cause local deformation at the points of contact; hence, relationships between forces and displacements can be established. If we assume that the deformation is denoted by u, then

$$f = \mathbf{k}u \qquad (11.7)$$

represents the linear relationship between the contact forces f and displacements u through the stiffness matrix $\mathbf{k}$. The inverse of $\mathbf{k}$ is the mechanical compliance matrix, say, $\mathbf{c}$. Hence,

$$u = \mathbf{c}f \qquad (11.8)$$

Using sensors, we can determine f, and knowing the mechanical compliance $\mathbf{c}$, we can compute u, which in turn can be used to readjust the position of the gripper (end effector).

The versatility of the human hand is unattainable in robot gripper design. The precision by which the hand can perform certain tasks like inserting a pen into a hollow and the handling of fragile objects is one that we would like to achieve in gripper design. Those tasks that qualify as simple and require minimum effort by humans are more complicated and require much more sophisticated motion control from robots.

Precision and flexibility of the gripper can become conflicting requirements although both are desirable. Multijoined fingers of a mechanical hand give it an enor-

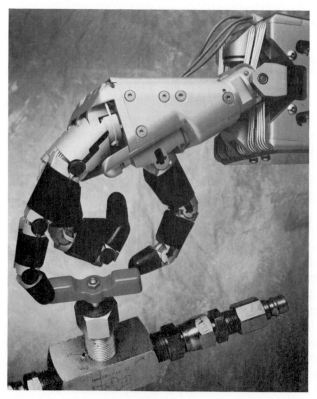

Figure 11.16 Utah MIT hand (courtesy of Center for Engineering Design, University of Utah).

mous flexibility for manipulating objects. However, controlling the motion of such a system is yet to be fully exploited.

Most of the active hands built to date have anthropomorphic designs with several jointed fingers. However, fingers sometimes are not required to manipulate grasped objects. Nonanthropomorphic mechanical hands (grippers) can manipulate objects in up to five degrees of freedom using rotating belts. The advantage of fingers in a hand seems to be less for manipulation than for grasping. Fingers are open kinematic chains, like manipulator arms, that form closed loops when grasping or holding. Unlike manipulators, which can have mounted actuators and motors to perform their articulation, fingers are usually small and require smaller and more precise motors. Most of the current hand design relies on cables and pulleys driven by actuator motors mounted on the arm (Figure 11.16).

11.7 POSITIONING A ROBOT IN SPACE

Consider a three-link planar manipulator, as shown in Figure 11.17, with three revolute joints at O_1, O_2, and O_3. The local axes are defined as those associated with each link. They form a set of orthogonal axes; for simplicity in the figure, the x_i ($i = 1, 2, 3$) ordinates are along the control axis of each link. Each local axis is fixed to the particular link and moves with it as it articulates. On the other hand, the global axes x, y, and z are defined as the base references fixed in an inertia frame.

We want to describe the position of each link and the end point of the terminal link in most cases with respect to the global reference frame. Recall from Chapter 4 that transformation matrices were used to describe the relationship between manipu-

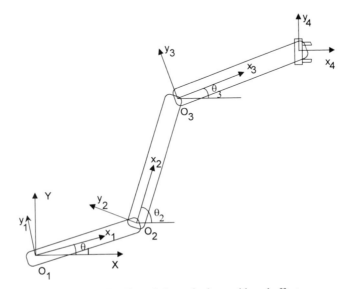

Figure 11.17   Three link manipulator with end effector.

lated objects. In this context of robotic motion, we will use them to relate points described in the local axes to the global one. For instance, point O_2 in the local axes (x, y, z) is defined by $(l, 0, 0)$, whereas in the global frame, its components are $(l_1 \cos \theta, l_1 \sin \theta, 0)$. It is obvious that a rotation about the z axis of the local axes (x_1, y_1, z_1) clockwise by θ_1 will make it coincide with the global axes x, y, and z. We can then write the following:

$$[l_1 \cos \Theta_1 \quad l_1 \sin \Theta_1 \quad 0] = [l_1 \quad 0 \quad 0] \begin{bmatrix} \cos \Theta_1 & \sin \Theta_1 & 0 \\ -\sin \Theta_1 & \cos \Theta_1 & 0 \\ 0 & 0 & 1 \end{bmatrix} \qquad (11.9)$$

$\underbrace{\qquad\qquad\qquad\qquad\qquad}_{\substack{\text{Position in the} \\ \text{global frame}}}$ $\underbrace{\qquad\qquad}_{\substack{\text{Position in the} \\ \text{local frame}}}$

In compact form, this relationship is expressed as

$$^{1}P\mathbf{R} = {}^{G}P \qquad (11.10)$$

where ^{1}P denotes the position of a point in the local axes, here chosen to be the origin of link 2 (O_2), and ^{G}P represents the point position in the global frame.

Similarly, we can write relationships between any local axis describing the position of the robot links and the global frame.

Example 11.3   Transformation Between Local and Global Axes for a Three-Link Manipulator

Give the transformation matrix that relates the position of the end point of link 3 between its local and global axes of the three-link manipulator in Figure 11.18.

Solution   From Equation (11.10), we write

$$^{3}P\mathbf{R} = {}^{G}P_3$$

where $\mathbf{R}$ is the transformation matrix relating the position of link 3 in local coordi-

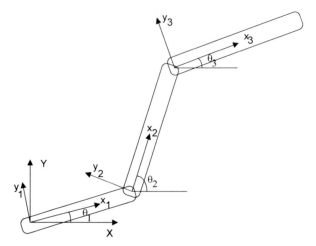

Figure 11.18   Three link manipulator.

nates (x_3, y_3, z_3) and global coordinates. We should also note that its global components are measured from point O_2. Hence, we need to add the previous components of link 2 and link 1 to form the actual position of link 3 in the global frame.

The latter is given by

$$^Gp = {}^1p + {}^2p + {}^3p \tag{11.11}$$

or

$$^Gp = [l_1 \quad 0 \quad 0] \begin{bmatrix} \cos\Theta_1 & \sin\Theta_1 & 0 \\ -\sin\Theta_1 & \cos\Theta_1 & 0 \\ 0 & 0 & 1 \end{bmatrix} + [l_2 \quad 0 \quad 0] \begin{bmatrix} \cos\Theta_2 & \sin\Theta_2 & 0 \\ -\sin\Theta_2 & \cos\Theta_2 & 0 \\ 0 & 0 & 1 \end{bmatrix}$$

$$+ [l_3 \quad 0 \quad 0] \begin{bmatrix} \cos\Theta_3 & \sin\Theta_3 & 0 \\ -\sin\Theta_3 & \cos\Theta_3 & 0 \\ 0 & 0 & 1 \end{bmatrix} \tag{11.12}$$

Assuming that all links are of the same length l, we obtain

$$^Gp = [l(\cos\theta_1 + \cos\theta_2 + \cos\theta_3), \ l(\sin\theta_1 + \sin\theta_2 + \sin\theta_3), \ 0] \tag{11.13}$$

∎

Example 11.4   Placement of a Metal Block in a Small Area

A metal block with a curved opposite edge is to be positioned properly so it can be inserted in a storage area, as shown in Figure 11.19. Give the rotation(s) required by the robot link to assure its insertion.

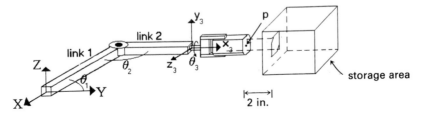

Figure 11.19   Positioning of a block by a 2 link manipulator.

Solution   A rotation of the end effector alone by 90° about the x_3 axis suffices to position the object with respect to the hole of the storage area.   ∎

Example 11.5   Geometric Positioning of the End-Effector

In Example 11.4, if the dimensions of the object block are given such that the width and the height are about 1 and 3 in., respectively, what instructions should be given to make sure that the forward motion will keep the metal block in the direction of the hole?

Solution   The motion must be such that the position of point p remains invariant along the y_3 and z_3 axes and moves by an increment of at least 2 in. along the

x_3 axis. This could be accomplished by setting the velocity components (v_x, v_y, v_z) of point p as follows:

$$v_x = \text{constant}$$

$$v_y = 0$$

$$v_z = 0$$

The velocity components are found by first deriving an expression for point p in the global frame:

$$^Gp = [(l_1 \cos \theta_1 + l_2 \cos \theta_2 + r \cos \theta_2), (l_1 \sin \theta_1 + l_2 \sin \theta_2 + r \sin \theta_2), 0]$$

$$\text{(11.14)}$$

l_1, l_2, and r are positions in the total frames of line 1, link 2, and the metal block, respectively.

Then, from the above two equations it follows that

$$v_x = (d/dt)(l_1 \cos \theta_1 + l_2 \cos \theta_2 + r \cos \theta_2) \qquad \text{(11.15)}$$

$$v_y = (d/dt)(l_1 \sin \theta_1 + l_2 \sin \theta_2 + r \sin \theta_2) \qquad \text{(11.16)}$$

$$v_z = 0 \qquad \text{(11.17)}$$

These equations yield

$$v_x = -[l_1 \sin \Theta_1 + (l_2 + r) \sin \Theta_2] \begin{bmatrix} \dot{\Theta}_1 \\ \dot{\Theta}_2 \end{bmatrix} \qquad \text{(11.18)}$$

$$v_y = [l_1 \sin \Theta_1 + (l_2 + r) \sin \Theta_2] \begin{bmatrix} \dot{\Theta}_1 \\ \dot{\Theta}_2 \end{bmatrix} \qquad \text{(11.19)}$$

$$v_z = 0 \qquad \text{(11.20)}$$

Following the conditions set on the motion of point p, Equations (11.18) to (11.20) are solved for $\dot{\theta}_1$, $\dot{\theta}_2$, θ_1, and θ_2 as functions of time using an integrator. (The assumptions are $v_z = v_y = 0$ and $v_x = \text{const.}$) The results are rather important, because they provide information needed on how the actuators and motors used to drive the robot links are going to perform. ∎

11.8 DEFINING THE WORKSPACE OF A ROBOT

The workspace of a robot manipulator is an important design criterion used to determine the optimum structural configuration of a robot. The workspace is defined as the volume or space the robot occupies given its joint constraints. The workspace is also defined as an envelope bounding its minimum and maximum reach.

There are two basic approaches to the workspace problem:

1. Given the structure of a robot, what constitutes the workspace?
2. Given the workspace, what should the robot's structure be?

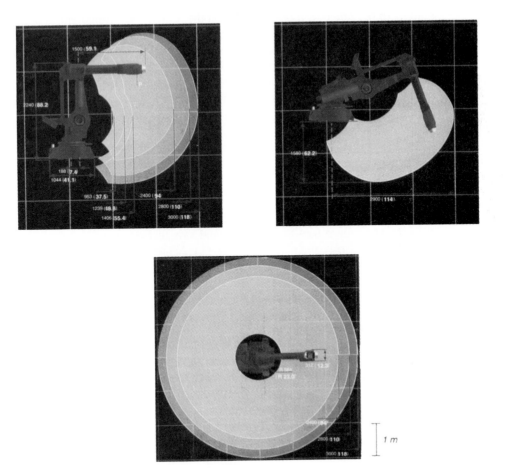

Figure 11.20   Work envelope of a robot (courtesy of ABB robotics, Inc.).

In the first approach, robot parameters, such as link lengths, joint constraints, and loads, are known. Hence, the accessible region where the robot can operate can easily be found by using a CAD system (Figure 11.20).

The second approach is more complex because the robot structure is not known, but the accessible regions are defined. This problem involves a synthesis and an optimization of the parameters chosen to define the robot. These parameters usually involve joint constraints and link lengths.

11.8.1 Accessible Region

The workspace of a robot is an important criterion for evaluating the manipulator as the volume within which every point can be reached by the hand or end effector (gripper). The workspace also defines the working area of the robot. Due to the limitations of the range of motion placed on the joints, the manipulator's operational capacity is restricted to a well-defined region.

The workspace of a robot can be understood through the analysis of its accessible regions. Consider a simple two-link planar manipulator with revolute joints as shown in Figure 11.21. The x, y coordinates of the end of the second link (x, y) represent the position of the hand and are given by

$$x = l_1 \sin \theta_1 + l_2 \sin(\theta_1 + \theta_2) \tag{11.21}$$

$$y = l_1 \cos \theta_1 + l_2 \cos(\theta_1 + \theta_2) \tag{11.22}$$

Squaring and adding these equations, we obtain

$$x^2 + y^2 = l_1^2 + l_2^2 + 2l_1 l_2 \cos \theta_2 \tag{11.23}$$

which represents an equation of a circle (where only θ_2 is present) with a radius given by the square root of the right-hand side of Equation (11.23).

We can also reorganize Equations (11.21) and (11.22) and get

$$(x - l_1 \sin \theta_1)^2 + (y - l_1 \cos \theta_1)^2 = l_2^2 \tag{11.24}$$

which yields another representation of the circle with θ_1 only and a radius given by l_2.

In the analysis of the workspace, one would solve for θ_1 and θ_2 given the coordinates (x, y) of a point using Equations (11.21) and (11.22), respectively. (This can be done with the assumption that links l_1 and l_2 are known.) As a matter of fact, we can derive expressions for θ_1 and θ_2, expanding Equations (11.23) and (11.24),

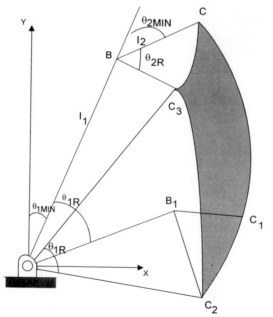

Figure 11.21 Two link workspace.

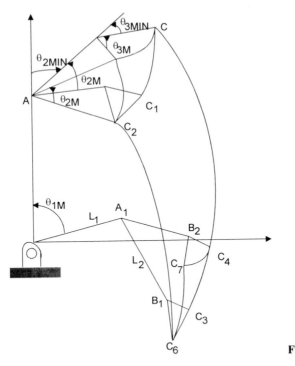

Figure 11.22 Three link workspace.

which gives

$$\Theta_1 = \cos^{-1} \frac{y}{\sqrt{x^2 + y^2}} - \cos^{-1} \frac{x^2 + y^2 + l_1^2 - l_2^2}{2l_1\sqrt{x^2 + y^2}} \tag{11.25}$$

$$\Theta_2 = \cos^{-1} \frac{x^2 + y^2 - l_1^2 - l_2^2}{2l_1 l_2} \tag{11.26}$$

We should note that Equations (11.9) and (11.10) serve as a basis for determining the boundary of the work area by simply setting one angle to its minimum value and rotating the other through its range of values, and vice versa. Figures 11.21 and 11.22 show the construction of the work area for two- and three-link robots.

11.9 ROBOTS AND COMPUTER-AIDED DESIGN

There is an increasing trend to incorporate robots into the computer-aided design process in order to obtain maximum efficiency. This trend has immense benefits both in design and manufacturing.

The maximum efficiency from a robot can be availed if it could be task programmed directly from a supervisory control via a hardware interface in the flexible manufacturing cell. This is possible because of the ability of rapid changeover of work-cell activities with a minimum disruption of productive time.

Supportive software for the hardware interface would have a protocol to confirm that the robot is in a condition to receive a program before program downloading begins. On completion of the download, the software must confirm the status of data transmission, which would among other things confirm if the data were received correctly.

With the development of new languages and techniques such as off-line programming, a robot can be directly programmed after completing the computer-aided design process. Most computer-aided design and solid modeling software available have the ability to develop programs to enable programming a robot.

However, to effectively program a robot off line, a CAD and/or CAM database is required. A CAD database provides information related to part geometry and a CAM database provides machine and tool information. The available database has to be in most cases enhanced as it requires clearance and interference-checking data and information such as weight, center of gravity, surface features, surface quality, and gripper constraints.

Not only can robot productivity be enhanced by the inclusion of robots in the CAD process, but complex tasks can be simulated, analyzed, and refined with computer assistance for optimal performance.

Simulation of a robot task on the computer screen avoids building expensive prototypes and allows testing and safety from hazardous environments. All tasks are simulated on the screen and robot paths can be checked and optimized with computer-aided programs to verify clearances, and the interaction of machines,

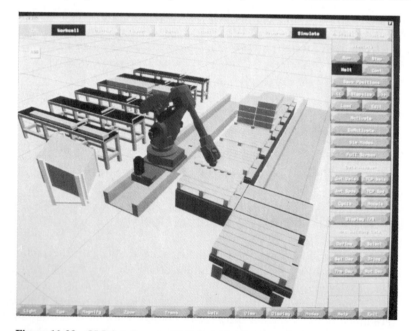

Figure 11.23 OLP/S software used for reach analysis, cycle time and to create the robot program (courtesy of ABB robotics, Inc.).

tools, and workpieces can be tested in the manufacturing cell. There are programs like OLP/S (Figure 11.23) that are used to assist managers to appropriately select the robot type and placement that best optimize task and productivity.

The robot task itself can be designed with computer-aided simulation. The simulation also allows the system programmer to test the procedures and concepts without tying up the work cell.

In an industrial environment, it is quite unlikely that a robot will function independently as a pure stand-alone device. Grouping of machine tools in various work cells is done in any manufacturing arrangement. The machine tools are interconnected by a workpiece transport system. Also included is a secondary transport system incorporating one or more robots. Each robot is assigned the task of moving workpieces to and between machines. Figure 11.24 is a schematic diagram of one such arrangement.

The entire system depicted in the figure is controlled by computer programs designed specifically for robotic applications. Usually, a central computer processes all instructions to one system and continually monitors the system during operations. A computer system of this nature is designed and operated as a hierarchial structure.

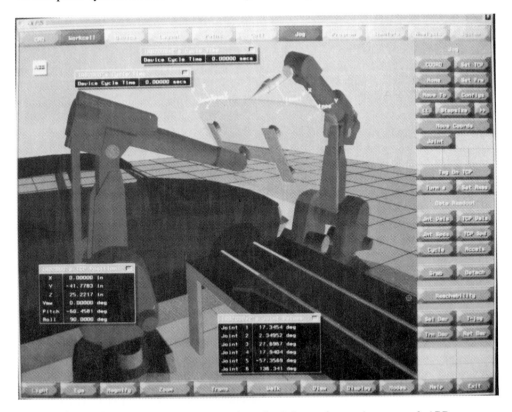

Figure 11.24 Off-line programming simulation software (courtesy of ABB robotics, Inc.).

A typical three-level hierarchy employs a top-level supervisory computer to handle general managerial functions, desk scheduling, coordination of machines, and material flow and fault management; it employs an intermediate-level host computer to generate desired trajectories, tool speeds, feed rates, and other reference signals for low-level controllers; and it employs a set of low-level computers or hardware controllers for direct digit control.

PROBLEMS

11.1 A decision has to be made on the type of robot needed to move a plate from position 1 to position 2 in such a way that face B is positioned normal to the vertical axis (Figure P11.1).

11.2 **(a)** Justify the answer to Problem 1 by giving the concatenated transformation matrices to two different type of robots that could accomplish the same task.

    (b) Use your computer or workstation to justify the answer to Problem 1.

11.3 The planar two-arm robot is to be used for painting the wall shown in Figure P11.2.
        If the paint gun is located at point A as shown,

    (a) find an expression for the tip velocity.

    (b) If the vertical speeds are given by Figure P11.3, give the expressions for Θ_1 and Θ_2 to control tip A at such speeds.

    (c) Use the results from parts (a) and (b) on your computer or workstation to yield some output of the robot motion.

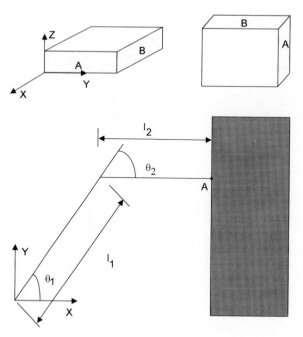

Figure P11.1   Positioning of a plate.

Figure P11.2   Two link robot used for spraying a wall.

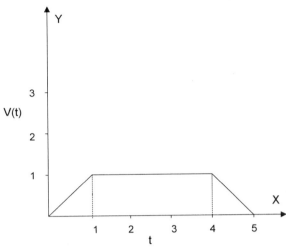

Figure P11.3 Velocity vs. time graph.

11.4 (a) For Problem 1, give the transformation matrices needed to manipulate the plate so it will be positioned as desired.

(b) Using the workstation with any appropriate application software or self-created program, determine the correct method(s) to manipulate the plate to any desired position.

11.5 For Example 11.1, a pick-and-place robot is used to carry out the operation. Explain the basic differences between the AVAL programming language and those of APT motion statements.

11.6 For a robot equipped with a wrist that has the yaw, pick, and roll capabilities, give an industrial application to justify its use.

11.7 Two industrial robots are needed to collaborate on a particular task.

(a) What is the optimum volume that the two robots will occupy?

(b) What are the ranges of the revolute joint angles to assure that the endpoints of the terminal links will reach the object shown?

REFERENCES

11.1 Amirouche, F. M. L., and Tushar, V., Accessible Regions and Synthesis of Two-Arm Robots, *J. Rob. Automat.*, 1989.

11.2 Ardayfio, D., *Fundamentals of Robotics*, Marcel Dekker, New York, 1987.

11.3 Asfahl, C. R., *Robots and Manufacturing Automation*, John Wiley & Sons, New York, 1985.

11.4 Coiffet, P., and Chirouze, M., *An Introduction to Robot Technology*, McGraw-Hill, New York, 1983.

11.5 Craig, J. J., *Adaptive Control of Mechanical Manipulators*, Addison-Wesley, Reading, Ma., 1955.

11.6 Cutkosky, M. R., *Robotic Grasping and Fine Manipulation*, Kluwer Academic, Boston, 1985.

11.7 Duffy, J., *Analysis of Mechanisms and Robot Manipulators*, John Wiley & Sons, New York, 1980.

11.8 Durrant-Whyte, H. F., *Integration Coordination and Control of Multi-Sensor Robot Systems*, Kluwer Academic, Boston, 1987.

11.9 Hall, E. L., and Hall, B. C., *Robotics—A User-Friendly Introduction*, Holt, Rinehart and Winston, New York, 1985.

11.10 Koren, Y., *Robotics for Engineers*, McGraw-Hill, New York, 1985.

11.11 Lee, M., *Intelligent Robotics*, Open University Press and Halstead Press, New York, 1989.

11.12 Minsky, M., *Robotics*, Omni Press, Anchor Press/Doubleday, Garden City, New York, 1985.

11.13 Murata, H., Kinematic Design for Articulated Robot Arm, *Engineering Faculty (Japan),* No. 22, 1976, pp. 83–92.

11.14 Paul, R. P., *Robot Manipulators: Matrices, Programming and Control*, The MIT Press, Cambridge, Mass., 1981.

11.15 Pugh, A., *Robot Sensors, Vol. 2—Tactile and Non-Vision*, IFS (Publications) Ltd., Bedford, UK, 1986.

11.16 Rooks, B., *Developments in Robotics 1983,* IFS Publications, Kempston, Bedford, UK, 1983.

11.17 Shahinpoor, M., *A Robot Engineering Textbook*, Harper and Row, New York, 1987.

11.18 Simons, G., *Is Man a Robot?,* John Wiley & Sons, New York, 1986.

11.19 Tsai, Y. C., and Soni, A. M., Accessible Regions and Synthesis of Robot Arms, *ASME J. Mech. Design,* 1981, pp. 803–811.

11.20 Unimation Inc., *Users Guide to VAL: A Robot Programming and Control System*, Version 12, Unimation, Danbury, Conn., 1980.

11.21 Vukobrakovic, M., *Applied Dynamics of Manipulation Robots*, Springer-Verlag, Berlin, 1989.

11.22 Young, D. C. H., and Lee, T. W., On the Workspace of Mechanical Manipulators, *Trans. AMSE, J. Mech., Transm. Autom. Design,* Vol. 105, No. 5, 1983, pp. 63–69.

chapter 12

Robot Economics

12.1 INTRODUCTION

Prior to the purchase of a robot system, it is important to consider its area of application, its need, the long-range plans, objectives of the company, and especially the social impact robots are going to have on the displacement of workers, if it occurs. The introduction of robots is justifiable when it is possible to increase productivity, improve product quality, and reduce production costs.

An economic justification for the use of robots in manufacturing can be measured by the short- and long-term profitability robots can provide. Profitability of any manufacturing operation is determined by the overall production costs. Thus, besides the purchase cost of robots, all other auxiliary equipment and tooling costs have to be considered. Furthermore, the cost of maintenance and periodic overhaul, operating power, depreciation, special tooling, and installation have to be determined.

Robots, like any other machinery, have competitive prices. The cost usually varies from $5,000 to $350,000. Selecting the robot for the application at hand requires information such as load, speed, accuracy, repeatability, power supply, programming, and size. Traditionally, purchasing robots could be done by either paying cash or obtaining a loan from an appropriate institution. These loans come with an annual interest rate that can be quantified on an hourly basis. All plant equipment depreciates over a period of time due to wear and tear. An annual depreciation factor is then applied to such equipment, which can also be computed on an hourly basis. The cost of the power supply for the robot system and the cost of its maintenance can also be quantified on an hourly basis. In addition to regular maintenance, a robot system might need a complete overhaul requiring a temporary shutdown. To realistically estimate the total cost of a robot system on an hourly basis, all these costs have to be determined and added up. Note that the hourly cost of the robot system will be compared with that of manual labor.

The comparison of hourly costs between manual labor and a robot system was carried out by Unimation Inc. in 1981 for a Unimate robot applied in the automotive industry. The various costs for the robot are listed in Table 12.1.

TABLE 12.1 HOURLY COST ESTIMATE OF A UNIMATE ROBOT

Price of Unimate robot	$50,000
Cost of installation	$12,000
Interest rate	15%

Cost on a two-shift basis in 1981($/h)	
Depreciation	1.56
Interest payment	1.10
Installation cost	0.80
Power	0.40
Overhaul (two)	0.40
Maintenance	1.15
Total cost of robot	5.41

At the time of this survey, the gross hourly wage rate of a worker was around $20/h in the automotive industry. Thus, the robot is cheaper. Even if we considered a depreciation period of 5 years, the robot cost was only $8/h. Logically, if a robot is used for two shifts, then its hourly cost will be significantly cheaper than the manual labor. In the late 1980's and early 1990's the prices of robots dropped and so did the interest rates. This became even more attractive to industries.

There are several other factors justifying the application of industrial robots besides economics. These include:

1. Safety and protection for workers who used to be exposed to high temperatures, such as foundries in steel mills, and radiation and toxic waste in hazardous environments.

2. Increased productivity, especially if the robots operate much faster than humans.

3. Improved quality because robots perform at constant accuracy and the inherent fatigue factor of humans is eliminated.

4. Flexibility because robots can be programmed to perform different tasks. Although this is one function where humans are far superior, robots can possess some degree of flexibility.

The social impact of robots is another consideration we have to look at before implementation. Union representatives should be included in the discussion from the very beginning so that the inherent benefits of robots are known. This is mainly a suggestion because each company operates differently.

12.2 ECONOMIC JUSTIFICATION

The economic feasibility of robots can be evaluated from the viewpoints of a payback period and return on investment.

The following are the variables that pertain to the payback and return on investment equations:

P: Payback period (years)
I: Total cost of robot and accessories
L: Annual direct labor cost savings
M: Annual material cost savings
E: Annual maintenance cost and operating cost of robot
T: Investment tax credit (available from government as an incentive for robot technology implantation)
t: Tax rate
q: Production rate coefficient
D: Annual depreciation

12.2.1 Payback Period

The equation for the payback period is

$$P = \frac{I - T}{(L + M - E)(1 - T) + D \times t} \tag{12.1}$$

The annual savings result from labor cost savings and material cost savings. A simpler form of Equation (12.1) used as a rule of thumb is

$$P = \frac{I}{L - E} \tag{12.2}$$

In this equation, I is the total cost of the robot system.

Example 12.1   Payback Returns for a T³ Robot

If the total capital investment to purchase a Cincinnati T³ robot is $75,000 and the cost of labor is estimated at $20/h for the same task (including benefits), find the payback return for one and two shifts if the maintenance cost of the robot is $2.00/h.

Solution   The following assumptions are made:

One shift = 8 h
Number of working days/year = 250

For a single shift, using Equation (12.2), we get

$$P = \frac{75,000}{20(250 \times 8) - 2.0(250 \times 8)} = 2.08 \text{ years}$$

For two shifts, we obtain

$$P = \frac{75,000}{20(250 \times 16) - 2.0(250 \times 16)} = 1.04 \text{ years}$$

One can easily see that if the robot is scheduled to work at least 16 h, then the payback return is only 1.04 years. By management standards, this is a reasonable investment.   ■

12.2.2 Production Rate Payback Formula

In the foregoing simple formula, the performance in terms of speed is assumed to be the same for both robots and the humans being displaced. Depending on how fast or slow a robot can perform the desired task, we can estimate the payback return to decrease or increase. To take into consideration the rate of robot speed, the following equation is used:

$$P \frac{I}{L - E \pm q(L + z)} \tag{12.3}$$

This equation also considers savings resulting from increased productivity. The tax rate is assumed to be negligible.

Example 12.2   Payback Return Using Production Rate Payback Formula

The following data are given for purchasing a particular robot:

    I: $75,000
    L: $20.00/h is taken over 250 days with one or two shifts
    E: $2.00/h is taken over the same period as L
    z: $45,000, or 15% of the total capital cost, which is $300,000
    q: either 20% faster or 20% slower than a human operator

Find the payback return for either q assuming a single shift of operation.

    Solution   For a single shift, we obtain

$$L = 20(250 \times 8) = \$40,000$$

$$E = 2.0(250 \times 8) = \$4,000$$

Assuming the robot is 20% slower, using Equation (12.3), we get

$$P = \frac{75,000}{40,000 - 4,000 - 0.2(40,000 + 45,000)}$$

$$= 3.95 \text{ years}$$

If the robot is 20% faster,

$$P = \frac{75,000}{40,000 - 4,000 + 0.2(40,000 + 45,000)}$$

$$= 1.4 \text{ years}$$

There is a drastic change in payback return if robot speed is taken into account. ∎

Example 12.3   Calculation of Payback Period Using Simple Formula

Industrial robots are to replace 12 workers in a production line. Each robot costs $80,000, including tooling. Annual maintenance for each robot is estimated at $5,000. The programming cost for the whole system is $18,000. What is the payback period if the workers are paid $32,000/year including fringe benefits?

Solution

$$\text{Total investment} = \$80,000 \times 5 = \$400,000$$

$$\text{Maintenance and programming cost/year} = \$5,000 \times 5 + \$18,000$$

$$= \$43,000$$

$$\text{Labor savings/year} = \$32,000 \times 12 = \$384,000$$

The payback period, using Equation (12.3), is

$$P = \frac{400,000}{384,000 - 43,000} = 1.17 \text{ years}$$

We were not given the rate of production of the robot being purchased versus the human labor, and by assuming single-shift replacement, the simple formula was used.

∎

12.3 JUSTIFICATION OF ROBOT IMPLEMENTATION

The principal justification for robotic application in a manufacturing operation can be carried out by studying the economics of the process. The following steps can determine the possibility of integrating a robot into the manufacturing process.

1. *Survey*. The first step is to determine the number and types of robotic applications in a manufacturing operation.
2. *Screen*. Each potential robot application is then analyzed for its economics and task limitations. The following factors are considered for the economics:

- number of shifts per day
- numbers of setups per week
- major equipment to be moved
- number of persons to be replaced

Factors considered for task limitations:

- simple repetitive operations
- visual inspection
- part weight
- part location and orientation suitable for a robot
- cycle time greater than 5 seconds
- speed and accuracy
- reach

3. *Company Need and Priority*. Before purchasing a robot, the company's needs must be clearly stated as to whether a robot should be purchased. One approach is to look for other alternatives within the company to perform the job. An elaborate study provides an insight into the company's need and priorities.

4. *System Development*. To minimize the risks of implementation, suitable trials should be arranged to determine appropriate toolings, workplace layout, and cycle time for the proposed application. This is a critical step. Any problems that might occur can then be addressed and corrected before a purchase is made. In addition, demonstrations and tests by various vendors should be explored to learn more about the manufacturing processes performed by the robot.

5. *Economic Feasibility*. The economic feasibility can be carried out by the payback period, return on investment (ROI), discounted rate of return (DCRR), and cash flow.

The following example gives an illustration of the economic study that is usually performed.

Example 12.4   Comparison of Production Costs of Manual System Versus Proposed Robotic System

A firm anticipating major sales increases is contemplating a $1.4 million capital investment in a system of 11 robotic paint sprayers with associated automatic spray-line conveyor equipment to replace a manual spray line employing 14 skilled painters.

The existing manual system produces 90 units/h and achieves a daily operation time of 6 h/day, employing spray-painting personnel for a full 8-h shift including breaks, line servicing, and maintenance. The average cost of a human operator including fringe benefits is \$20/h. Additional cost due to maintenance for the manual system is \$400/month.

The new robotic spray line simultaneously operates 11 robotic paint sprayers and achieves a production rate of 150 units/h of operation working an 8-h shift per day. The total cost of the robot system is \$0.8 million/year. The cost of operating the system is \$85/h of which the maintenance costs of the robot are \$1.3/h for one shift and \$1.5/h for two shifts.

Compare the unit production costs of the manual system versus the proposed robotic system. Also find the payback period for the robotic system.

Solution

Manual Spraying

The hourly labor cost is

$$\text{Labor cost/h} = \frac{\text{no. workers} \times \text{wage/h} \times \text{no. hours/day}}{\text{operation time/day}}$$

$$= \frac{\text{wage/h} \times \text{no. hours/day}}{\text{operation time/day}} \tag{12.4}$$

which yields

$$\text{Labor cost/h} = \frac{14 \times 20 \times 8}{6} = \$373.3/\text{h} \tag{12.5}$$

$$\text{Maintenance cost/h} = \frac{\text{Maintenance cost/month} \times 12 \text{ months/year}}{50 \text{ weeks/year} \times 5 \text{ days/week} \times \text{operation time/day}}$$

which gives

$$\text{Maintenance cost/h} = \frac{400 \times 12}{50 \times 5 \times 6} = \$3.2/\text{h}$$

The production rate is 90 units/h. The unit cost is then defined as:

$$\text{Unit cost} = \frac{\text{hourly production cost}}{\text{production rate}} \tag{12.6}$$

or

$$\text{Unit cost} = \frac{376.5}{90} = \$4.2/\text{unit}$$

Robotic Spraying

$$\text{Production cost/h} = \text{operating cost/h} + \text{total robot system cost/h} \tag{12.7}$$

$$\text{Total robot system cost/h} = \frac{800,000}{50 \text{ weeks} \times 5 \text{ days/week} \times 8 \text{ h/day}} = \$400/\text{h}$$

$$\tag{12.8}$$

We find

$$\text{Production cost/h} = \$400/\text{h} + \$85/\text{h} = \$485/\text{h}$$

We know that

$$\text{Production rate} = 150 \text{ units/h}$$

Therefore,

$$\text{Unit cost} = \frac{\text{production cost/h}}{\text{production rate/h}} \qquad (12.9)$$

which yields

$$\text{Unit cost} = \frac{\$485/\text{h}}{150 \text{ units/h}} = \$3.2/\text{unit}$$

Thus, the difference in unit cost per component is

$$\text{Difference in unit cost} = \text{manual} - \text{robot system}$$

$$= 4.2 - 3.2 = \$1.0/\text{unit}$$

To compute the payback return, we use Equation (12.2), where I is the total investment (robot and accessories), L is the annual labor savings, and E is the expense of robot upkeep/year.

Using the values

$$I = \$1,400,000$$

$$E = \$1.40/\text{h} \times 50 \text{ weeks/year} \times 5 \text{ days/week} \times 8 \text{ h/day} = \$2600/\text{h}$$

Hence,

$$L/\text{h} = \text{robot system cost/h} - \text{operation labor cost/h}$$

$$= \$400/\text{h} - \$373.31/\text{h} = \$26.69/\text{h}$$

Annual labor savings are

$$L = \frac{L}{\text{h}} \times \frac{50 \text{ weeks}}{\text{year}} \times \frac{5 \text{ days}}{\text{week}} \times \frac{8 \text{ h}}{\text{day}} \qquad (12.10)$$

Hence,

$$L = \$53,400.00$$

Using Equation (12.2),

$$P = \frac{I}{L - E}$$

we get

$$P = \frac{140,000}{53,400 - 2600} = 2.75 \text{ years}$$

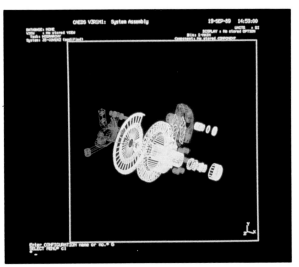

Assembly of different components of a mechanical part using CAEDS *Reprinted by permission of International Business Machines Corporation*

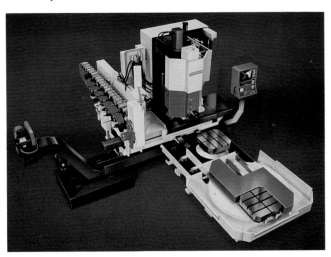

A CNC machining center
Courtesy of ABB Robotics Inc.

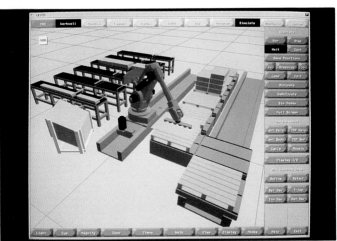

OLP/S software used for reach analysis, cycle time, and programming of robots *Courtesy of ABB Robotics Inc.*

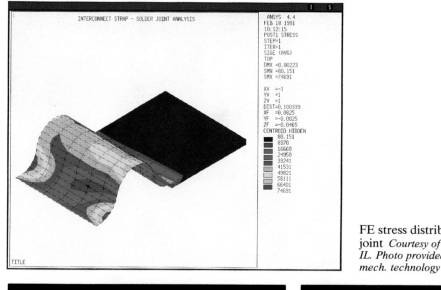

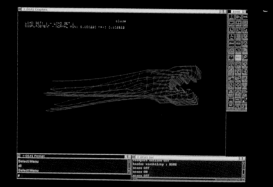

FE stress distribution of a strap-solder joint *Courtesy of Motorola Inc., Schaumberg, IL. Photo provided by Sherry Bosserman, mech. technology group.*

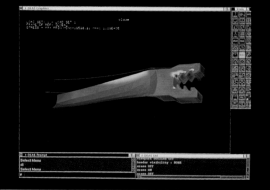

Wireframe of a turbine blade using I-DEAS *Courtesy of SDRC, Milford, OH*

Solid model of a turbine blade using I-DEAS *Courtesy of SDRC, Milford, OH*

Cockpit of a Boeing 747/400 *Courtesy of Boeing Co., Seattle, WA*

The payback return is based on the simple equation and assuming only one shift. The robot system yields a savings of $1.0/unit, which translates into a significant savings per year. To make a decision based on this analysis, one would argue that 2.75 years in payback return is high, but if we anticipate to use the robots for two shifts, then its implementation is definitely justifiable.   ■

Example 12.5   Production Per Unit Costs for a Robotic Spray System Operating on Two Shifts

Reevaluate the production cost per unit for both the proposed robotic paint spray system and the current manual system on the basis of a two-shift operation for each. Assume a 10% shift differential for all operator personnel costs associated with the second shift. Also find the payback period for this particular case.

Solution

Manual System

The following items are given:

$$\text{Operation labor cost/h (one shift)} = \$373.3/\text{h}$$

$$\text{Maintenance cost/h} = \$3.2/\text{h}$$

Considering a 10% increase in operator costs for two shifts, we get Equation (12.11):

Operator labor cost/h (two shifts)

$$= \text{labor cost (one shift)} + \text{labor cost (one shift)} \times 1.10 \qquad (12.11)$$

Hence,

$$\text{Average operator cost/h} = \frac{\$373.3/\text{h} + \$373.3/\text{h} \times 1.10}{2}$$

$$= \$391.96/\text{h}$$

$$\text{Average production cost/h} = \$391.96/\text{h} + \$3.20/\text{h} = \$395.16/\text{h}$$

Now, we define the unit cost to be

$$\text{Unit cost} = \frac{\$395.16/\text{h}}{90 \text{ units/h}} = \$4.4/\text{unit}$$

Robotic System

$$\text{Total robot system cost/h (two shifts)} = \frac{\text{production cost/h}}{2} \text{ (one shift)}$$

$$= \frac{\$400/\text{h}}{2} = \$200.00/\text{h}$$

The operation cost is determined as

$$\text{Operating cost/h} = \frac{\$85/h + \$85/h \times 1.10}{2} = \$89.25/h$$

The production cost is equal to the sum of the total cost of the robot system and the operation cost. Hence,

$$\text{Production cost/h} = \$200/h + \$89.25/h = \$289.25/h$$

$$\text{Production rate} = 150 \text{ units/h}$$

The unit cost is then obtained:

$$\text{Unit cost} = \frac{\$289.25/h}{150 \text{ units/h}} = \$1.92/\text{unit}$$

The new payback period for the two shifts can be obtained using the single formula, Equation (12.2):

$$P = \frac{I}{L - E}$$

where

$$I = \$140,000$$

$$E = \$1.3 \times 50 \times 8 \times 5 \times 2 = \$5200/\text{year (two shifts)}$$

Hence,

$$\frac{L}{h} = \$400/h - \frac{\$373.2 \times 2}{2}h = \$26.7/h$$

$$L \text{ (two shifts)} = \$26.70 \times 50 \times 5 \times 8 \times 2$$

$$= \$53,400 \times 2 = \$106,800.00$$

$$P = \frac{140,000}{160,800 - 5,200} = 1.3 \text{ years}$$

As expected, the payback period was reduced significantly to 1.3 years. Hence, from the economic viewpoint, it is profitable to go along with the project. What is more important is the unit cost savings of $2.48 if the robotic system is adopted.   ∎

12.4 ROBOT APPLICATIONS

With the advent of microprocessors and controls, the technology of robotics is advancing in all areas of industrial and space applications. Robots are especially being used in areas such as welding, painting and finishing, machine loading, material handling, machining, and assembling.

12.4.1 Welding

Welding is the area of largest application for robots. They are being used in assembly lines for automobile and truck manufacturing (Figure 12.1). Spot welding is the essential application for those robots; however, robots are now increasingly being used in arc-welding applications.

In welding applications, workers are exposed to certain risks that make their jobs undesirable. For instance, they have to wear protective clothing to move heavy equipment, which renders the job difficult and limits their flexibility.

Other reasons for using robots in welding are the quality, product uniformity, and reliability attained by their use.

Spot welding is an autogenous process in which two pieces of metal are joined at certain points. There are four major parameters that affect the quality of welded spots:

1. duration of the current supplied
2. magnitude of the electric current
3. pressure provided by the electrodes
4. material and thickness of the metal to be welded

Figure 12.1 Industrial robots are changing manufacturing methods. An IRB 6000 robot performs spot weld operations at Ford (courtesy of ABB robotics, Inc.).

The first three parameters must be appropriately selected to suit the thickness and type of welded material. These parameters are usually set and maintained throughout the process in a robotic welding system. Thus, under repetitive production conditions, high-quality welds are produced. Spot-welding robots are mounted on assembly lines that produce between 50 and 90 cars per hour. Work is performed while the car bodies are continuously moving on conveyors. Most of the work done by robots in the automotive industry is that of respotting, which is repetitive welding by several robots to the body of the automobile. These robots are under computer control, which signals the arrival of a particular body style and automatically causes the robot to switch to the appropriate task program in its memory.

Spot welding utilizes a point-to-point type of control. Because of the complicated shapes of automobile bodies, spot-welding robots utilize six axes of motion and are designed to carry a heavy gun.

Arc welding, on the other hand, is a relatively difficult task to perform by robots. The electrode has to follow a continuous programmed path while maintaining a constant distance from the ream. Arc-welding robots require five axes of mo-

Figure 12.2 An IRB 5000 robot used for spraying adhesive on interiors of commercial aircraft (courtesy of ABB Robotics, Inc.).

tion, although in certain applications, four axes are adequate. They are designed to carry a lighter gun and move at constant speed along a continuous path.

12.4.2 Painting and Finishing

Robots were used in painting at an early stage in the automobile industry due to hazardous working conditions resulting from toxic fumes. Of the various painting techniques, robots are largely used for spray painting (Figure 12.2).

Skilled human operators guide the robot through the painting task to develop the necessary database for the robot to repeat the task. Once the optimum program is attained, the robot is then used in spray-painting operations with consistency unattainable by human operators.

A spray-painting robot has to have a high level of manipulator dexterity, a compact wrist, a large working volume for a small-base manipulator, a small payload, low accuracy, and repeatability. The high mechanical dexterity of the hand is essential to enable it to reach the less accessible areas of the inside of the automobile. This is why spray-painting robots have at least six degrees of freedom. Because of the restricted space in spray booths, a spray-painting robot must occupy a small amount of floor space and also be able to reach the middle of the spray booth. A compact wrist enables the robot spray gun to penetrate narrow spaces. Because spray guns are lightweight, robots handle light payloads. Repeatability and resolution are not critical for spray-painting robots as each location of the endpoints is not critical.

Programming the spray-painting robot is done by a lead-through technique in which a skilled painter leads the robot through the required painting path, which is stored and played back by the robot.

12.4.3 Machine Loading

Robots are used for machine loading to provide workers relief and safety from handling heavy loads such as loading heavy jobs on punch presses, milling machines, forging machines, and iron-casting machines (see Figure 12.3). Thus, robots help to increase industrial safety standards.

Assemblies.   Speed, efficiency, reliability, and accuracy are the favorable criteria motivating applications of robots for assembly. Industrial robots do not make errors to which humans are susceptible, like errors of omission and substitution.

Robots are used for assembly of small products like electric switches, electric motors, engine assembly in the automotive industry, and the electronic industry. An assembly robot system is usually very sophisticated and has a variety of tactile and/or visual feedback loops to enable the robot to monitor the results. Tactile force sensors are mounted on the robot's hand to indicate when a part is misaligned and when to back up and try again. The visual and tactile sensors also allow the use of the robot for quality control. The robot senses a defective assembly and signals for corrective action.

Figure 12.3 An IRB 3000 robot used for picking cylinder heads and rotating them prior to loading them on the indexing table (courtesy of ABB Robotics, Inc.).

Assembly robots can operate in any coordinate system: Cartesian, spherical, cylindrical, or articulated. Certain tasks only require vertical assembly motions such as the assembly of printed circuit boards. For such applications, a four-axis robot is sufficient, whose arm has two articulated motions and whose wrist has a linear vertical displacement and a roll movement. Such a robot can pick up parts located on the horizontal plane, bring them to the assembly location, orient them with the roll motion of the wrist, and insert them in a vertical motion.

There are certain difficulties in applying robots to assembly. Part preparation with the right orientation is needed and the mating of parts is difficult due to close dimensional tolerances. However, new product designs have been developed to overcome these difficulties.

Machining. Of the various machining processes available, drilling is the only one in which robots have been successfully applied. Robots have also been applied to deburring metal parts (removal of ridges or rough edges left on metal by machine tools).

Robots are applied to drilling processes in the aircraft industry. Because a large number of holes have to be drilled in aircraft with close tolerances, the repeatability criterion of robots is the biggest advantage they have in this application. The robot is programmed using the manual teaching method for drilling applications.

Robots perform deburring in two ways. If the part is lightweight, then the robot picks it up and brings it to the deburring tool; however, for heavy parts, the robot welds the tool and brings it to the workpiece. These robots are either adaptive robots or programmable servo-controlled robots. Robots are also used for grinding purposes, typically in automobile plants. They are also used to dispense urethane on windshields and backlite openings. (Figure 12.4)

Figure 12.4   Two IRB 2000 robots used to dispense urethane on windshields of cars (courtesy of ABB Robotics, Inc.).

12.5 SELECTION AND IMPLEMENTATION OF ROBOTS

The selection and implementation of robots are performed through four phases:

1. *Planning*. This phase requires an evaluation of the nature of the production operations(s) for which the robots are being considered and a determination that robots are justifiable.
2. *Application*. A detailed study of the robot application is conducted and a specific application along with a specific robot are selected. Some requirements for the application are analyzed, such as layout requirements, workplace modifications, and robot accessories required.
3. *Installation*. This phase covers the time from the preparatory work performed on the workplace through the installation and startup of the robot.
4. *Integration*. Once the robot has begun operation, an ongoing process is required to ensure that it continues to perform its job in an effective manner.

The various steps involved in the four phases are highlighted in Table 12.2.

TABLE 12.2   THE PROCESS LAYOUT

Phase 1	Organize the team project Define the objectives Conduct an economic analysis
Phase 2	Select the initial application Select the robot Select the initial application requirement
Phase 3	Prepare for installation Install and start up
Phase 4	Monitor performance Upgrade for new developments and applications

PROBLEMS

12.1 A firm is planning to buy a robot system for its manufacturing plant that is expected to cost $88,000. The manual labor cost for the task required at present is $22/h. The maintenance and operating costs for the robot system is $2.00/h. Justify the purchase of the robot system based on the simple formula of payback return for one and two shifts.

12.2 The union is trying to keep management from purchasing a robot. If the decision is based on the payback return and that the value of $P = 3$ years is not a feasible purchase to make that happen, what should the labor cost be if the robot and maintenance costs are taken from Problem 1?

12.3 At what rate should the robots function (Problem 1) in order for the payback return to be 1.2 years for both one and two shifts?

12.4 The capital cost of a spray-painting plant using robots is $400,000. $120,000 is the total cost of the robot and accessories, $25.00/h is the labor cost savings, and there is a 20% return on the total capital cost of the plant by utilizing the robot system. The maintenance cost of the robot is estimated at $4500/year. Find the payback return based on the production-rate equation if the robots are assumed to be 25% faster.

12.5 **(a)** Is our estimated value of a 20% return on the capital cost low or high in decreasing the payback return for the robotic system proposed in Problem 4?

(b) At what return rate could the payback period be kept below 1.6 years?

12.6 An automobile manufacturing plant is considering a $1.6 million investment for a robotic welding system that would use 18 robots. At present, 22 workers produce 45 units/h and the actual working time is 6 h out of an 8-h shift. The workers are paid $21.0/h including benefits. The monthly maintenance cost of the manual system is $600.00.

The robotic system has a production rate of 95 units/h in an 8-h shift. The annual cost of the robot system is $1 million. The operating cost is $95/h and of this the maintenance cost is $4.00/h for one shift and $4.50/h for two shifts.

Compare the unit production costs of the manual welding system to the proposed system utilizing robots for one shift. Also find the payback period for the new system.

12.7 The management of an automobile company wants to compare the unit costs for parts for the manual and robot systems when two shifts are utilized. Assume a 12% differential for all personnel costs associated with the second shift. Find the payback period for this particular case.

REFERENCES

12.1 Ardayfio, D. D., *Fundamentals of Robotics,* Marcel Dekker, New York, 1987.

12.2 Bein, G., and Hackwood, S., *Recent Advances in Robotics,* John Wiley & Sons, New York, 1985.

12.3 Cutkosky, M. R., *Robotic Grasping and Fine Manipulation,* Kluwer Academic, Boston, 1985.

12.4 IBM Corporation, *IBM Robot System: AML, Reference Manual,* SC34-0410-1; *IBM Robot System/1: AML, Concepts and User's Guide,* 1st ed., SC34-0411-0; *IBM Robot System/1: General Information Manual and User's Guide,* 3rd ed., 0180-2, IBM Corporation, Boca Raton, Fla., 1981, 1982.

12.5 Koren, Y., *Robotics for Engineers,* McGraw-Hill, New York, 1985.

12.6 McDonnell Douglas, Inc., *Robotic System for Aerospace Batch Manufacturing, Task B—High Level Language User Manual,* Tech. Rept. AFML-JR-79-4202, Wright Patterson Air Force Base, Oh., 1981.

12.7 Paul, R. P., *Robot Manipulators—Mathematical Programming and Control,* The MIT Press, Cambridge, Ma., 1983.

12.8 Rosenburg, J., *A History of Numerical Control, 1949–1972: The Technical Development, Transfer to Industry and Assimilation,* Report No. IS1-RR-72-3, U.S.C. Information Sciences Institute, Marina Del Ray, Ca., 1972.

12.9 Shahinpoor, M., *A Robot Engineering Textbook*, University of New Mexico Press, Albuquerque, 1984.

12.10 Unimation, Inc., *User's Guide to VAL, Version 12*, Unimation, Inc., Danbury, Ct., 1980.

12.11 Unimation, Inc., *User's Guide to VAL-II, Part 1: Control from the System Terminal, Version X2; Part 2: Communication with a Supervisory System, Version X2; Part 3: Real Time Path Control, Version X2*, Unimation, Inc., Danbury, Ct., 1983.

12.12 Unimation, Inc., *VAL Univision Supplement, Version 13, VSNO*, 2nd ed., Unimation, Inc., Danbury, Ct., 1981.

12.13 Vukobratovic, M., and Stokic, D., One Engineering Concept of Control of Manipulators, *Trans. ASME, J. Dyn. Syst. Meas. Cont.*, Vol. 103, No. 2, 1981, pp. 119–125.

12.14 Wichman, M. W., *The Use of Optical Feedback in Computer Control of an Arm*, Stanford Artificial Intelligence Laboratory, Stanford University, Stanford, Ca., 1987.

12.15 Wolovich, W. A., *Robotics: Basic Analysis and Design*, Holt, Rinehart and Winston, New York, 1987.

12.16 Yang, D. C. H., and Lee, T. W., On the Workspace of Mechanical Manipulators, *Trans. ASME, J. Mech., Transm. Autom. Des.*, Vol. 105, No. 5, pp. 63–69.

chapter 13

Group Technology

13.1 INTRODUCTION

Group technology is a method used to optimize manufacturing processes in an orderly fashion. Its main objective is to form a database of similar parts, design, and processes and use it to establish a common procedure for designing and manufacturing those parts. The parts grouped together form a "part family." This family is usually based on similarities in design, such as shape, or processes, such as milling and drilling operations. The benefits of this method include efficient plant floor ordering and increased production, resulting in a great cost savings brought about by proper planning and measures that avoid duplicating existing designs. Group technology is best achieved using a CAD/CAM system, taking advantage of its CPU and graphics capabilities.

The assignment of numbers, classification, and coding to parts is highly beneficial in the initial stages of a design. These are fundamental to the success of group technology. To avoid the expense that a new design requires in time and effort from engineers, and the cost for setup, and assuming a similar part exists within the company inventory, group technology allows finding and retrieving the exact part. Making the necessary modifications results in the desired design, saving the company time and money.

The part classification and coding system is also applied in computer-aided process planning and it involves the automatic generation of a process plan to manufacture the part. The process route sheet is developed by recognizing specific attributes of a part and relating them to the corresponding manufacturing operations.

Part numbering is an important aspect in today's design and production. The design department uses part numbers as identification numbers for design retrieval. The manufacturing department uses them as references on documents such as process plans, production schedules, bill of materials, and cost estimates. The sales department uses them on invoices. No manufacturing or engineering organization is effective without an accurate and well-structured part numbering system.

Part numbering systems are of two types: (1) for individual components; and (2) for products and subassemblies. The numbering system used for individual components carries information helpful in manufacturing the part. All parts with similar manufacturing processes are gathered in a one-part family. This results in manufacturing advantages such as reduction in setup time and inventory. The numbering system for products and subassemblies requires a different method of classification and it does not carry most of the information used in coding individual components. In what follows are descriptions of parts classification and coding systems and the common software available.

13.2 PART CLASSIFICATION AND CODING

The method mostly used in classification and coding is usually based on a primary and secondary code. The primary code identifies the part and the secondary code carries additional information useful in other sectors of the organization. The primary code is an address behind which the secondary code is stored. The primary code carries only the permanent attributes, such as shape, size, and material, which are decided when the part is designed. The details of production are not basic or permanent attributes. They form the secondary code and help in the interpretation of the design. The design is only partially implied by the shape of the component, which can change as product demand alters or production technology is improved. Thus, the primary code is more important for identification purposes.

13.2.1 Part Families

The part classification and coding system is concerned with identifying the similarities between parts and relating them to a coding system. In part classification, parts that are similar in shape and that have similar manufacturing operations form a so-called "family of parts." The advantages are

1. reduced setup times
2. lower in-process inventories
3. better scheduling
4. improved tool control
5. use of standard process plans

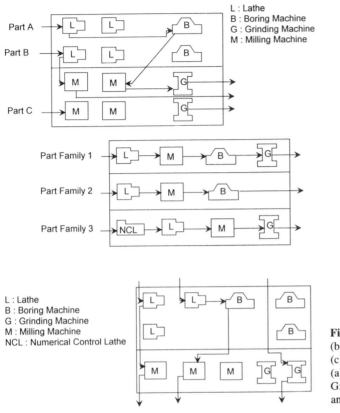

Figure 13.1 (a) Product layout
(b) Group technology flow line
(c) Group technology layout. For parts
(a) to (c), L:lathe; B:boring machine;
G:grinding machine; M:milling machine;
and NCL:numerical-control lathe.

These advantages are illustrated by the two layouts for the same product in Figure 13.1. Work handling time, lead times, setup times, and in-process times are all reduced by using the group technology layout.

13.2.2 Design Retrieval

An effective design-retrieval system is very important to an engineering department with a large inventory of drawings. A designer faced with the task of developing a new design has either to start from scratch or to pull an existing drawing from the file and make necessary changes to conform to the requirements of the new part. Finding a similar design can be quite difficult and time-consuming. So the designer may decide that it is easier to start from scratch to develop the new part, resulting in increased drafting and engineering costs. With an effective design-retrieval system, duplication can be avoided, but that requires an a priori form of coding and classification system.

13.2.3 Coding System Structure

A large number of classification systems exists whose code digit lengths range from 2 to 20 or more. The actual number of digits used only partially indicates the information carried by a particular system. Thus, it is the structure of the code and the attributes it carries that provide the information.

There are basically three forms of classification system structures used for coding:

1. monocodes (hierarchial codes)
2. polycodes (attributes of fixed-significance codes)
3. hybrid codes (mixed monocodes/polycodes)

Monocodes.   The monocodes or hierarchial codes use a treelike structure. The code is obtained through a step-by-step procedure of choosing values from a series of coding charts. Each successive value chosen leads to a different coding chart. Monocodes are difficult to construct, but they provide a detailed analysis of the nature of the classified item. Monocodes are best suited for classifiying parts with a limited number of digits. This type of system is ideally suited to the identification and retrieval of similar designs.

Polycodes.   A polycode is a code in which each digit is independent of all others. Thus, each digit carries self-contained information about the part. Polycodes are easier to construct and modify as needed. They are generally preferred for parts whose information is liable to change. One of the drawbacks is the limited information the code digits can carry; hence, polycodes are longer. On the other hand, polycodes allow for the convenient identification of specific part attributes, which is helpful in identifying parts with similar processing operations.

Hybrid Coding System.   Most classification and coding systems used in industry are a combination of monocode and polycode systems, combining the advantages of the two. These systems have some digits arranged hierarchically and others fixed, indicating the presence of a particular attribute. Usually, the first and the second digit divide the population of items into the main subgroups as in a monocode system. Then each subgroup has its own attribute code or series of fixed-significance digits. This system is best suited for both design and manufacturing processes.

13.2.4 Different Types of Codes

Codes can also be classified as (a) universal codes and (b) tailor-made codes.

Universal Codes.   A considerable amount of effort and research has been devoted to coding. A universal code is basically an all-purpose software code that can be adapted to a wide range of applications. These programs are long and require considerable data for input. The universal codes are well received by companies with large inventories as they can take advantage of their versatility in applying them to both design and manufacturing operations. An example of a universal code is the Dewey decimal classification system, which is used in libraries around the world.

Tailor-Made Codes.   These codes are designed to meet a company's particular need. They are usually an in-house development that proves to be very effective because it is designed around the company structure to perform a specific task. Tailor-made codes are the future for small companies and for those that find large-scale programs expensive and cannot use them to their full potential. They usually run on personal computers and are easy to manipulate. Information flows rapidly and response is immediate. The initial cost associated with tailor-made programs is high, yet their benefits are overwhelming once implemented.

13.2.5 Existing Code Systems

There are a number of component classification and coding systems that have been developed for both design and production rationalization. These systems aid in the selection of families of parts and minimize the search for parts with similar processing requirements. What follows are commercial software codes used for classification.

VUOSO Classification System.   This system uses four digits, three of which are arranged hierarchically to classify the part's shape, including size and proportions, and the fourth digit defines the material. The VUOSO system codes rotational parts with more detail than nonrotational parts. Thus, companies with a large number of nonrotational parts find this system to be disadvantageous.

BRISCH System.   This code uses four to six digits as a primary code. A series of secondary polycodes can be added to cover additional classification requirements. The code number is obtained in a step-by-step procedure through a series of coding charts. A serial number is then added for the unique identification of the part. Because this code is hierarchial, the selection of specific features from various groups is difficult. BRISCH is suited for design retrieval and shape reduction.

PARTS Analog System.   Similar to the BRISCH system, this hierarchical type of code is designed to fill the client's requirements. The code is usually made up of four to six digits.

Opitz Classification System.   This system was developed by H. Opitz of Aachen Tech University, Germany. Its basic code consists of nine digits; however, it can be expanded by four more. The first five digits, called the "form code," identify the production operation type and sequence. The last four digits are called the "supplementary code." The extra four digits, A, B, C, and D, called the "secondary code," identify the production operation type and sequence.

The structure of the primary code is such that each of the first five digits can represent the basic shape, component class, rotational surface machining, plane surface machining, auxiliary holes, gear teeth, and forming. The five digits can represent the primary, secondary, and auxiliary shapes of the part. The four digits in the supplementary code classify the size, material, original material form, and the tolerance of the part. The first digit of the supplementary code represents the major dimension (either length or diameter). The component size can then be determined by using the dimension ratio specified in the geometry. The dimension ratio specified is from 0.8 to 80.0. Dimension ratios less than 0.8 in. and greater than 80 in. are represented by a 0 and a 9, respectively. The second, third, and fourth digits represent the material type, raw material shape, and the accuracy, respectively. The addition of a serial number to the code makes the system suitable for the identification of parts for design retrieval, provided that the distribution of parts is similar to that present in the code structure. The Opitz code system for rotational parts is illustrated in Figures 13.2 and 13.3.

CODE System.   The CODE system, developed by Manufacturing Data Systems, Inc. (MDSI), has an eight-digit code similar to the Opitz system. However, it has a mixed code structure in which each digit is represented by a hexadecimal value. The hexadecimal numbers allow more information to be represented with the same number of digits. The first six digits describe the shape of the part by considering its basic form and subsidiary features. The seventh and eighth digits provide the dimensions of the part. The structure of the CODE system is shown in Figure 13.4. The Code system contains form and dimensional information. Size information is described more completely because one can assign more digits to auxiliary shapes. The system was originally developed for design-retrieval purposes; however, it can be used for other production applications as well.

As an example, let us code the part shown in Figure 13.5 using the Opitz classification system and the Code system.

OPITZ CLASSIFICATION SYSTEM (REFER TO FIGURE 13.2)

Because the overall length-to-diameter ratio, L/D, is 2.57, the first digit is 1.

The part is stepped on one end and has threads, so the second digit is 2.

There is no hole or breakthrough present, hence the third digit is 0.

There is no surface machining and there are no auxiliary holes present, so the fourth and fifth digits are 0.

The whole Opitz code for the part is 12000.

CODE SYSTEM:

The basic shape of the part is cylindrical, so the first digit is 1.

Concentric parts or diameters are present, which when compared to Figure 13.3 gives the second digit as 4.

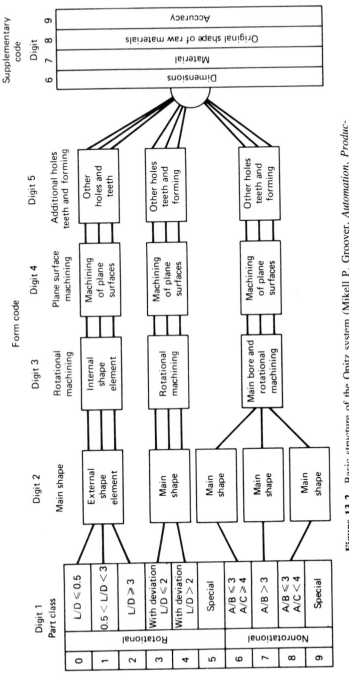

Figure 13.2 Basic structure of the Opitz system (Mikell P. Groover, *Automation, Production Systems and Computer-Integrated Manufacturing*, 1987, p. 440. Reprinted by permission of Prentice Hall, Englewood Cliffs, New Jersey).

Digit 1									
Part class									
	Rotational parts						Nonrotational parts		
0	1	2	3	4	5	6	7	8	9
$L/D \leqslant 0.5$	$0.5 < L/D < 3$	$L/D \geqslant 3$							

Digit 2									
External shape, external shape elements									
Smooth, no shape elements	Smooth or stepped to one end			Stepped to both ends					
0	1	2	3	4	5	6	7	8	9
Smooth, no shape elements	No shape elements	Thread	Functional groove	No shape elements	Thread	Functional groove	Functional cone	Operating thread	All others

Digit 3									
Internal shape, internal shape elements									
No hole, no breakthrough	Smooth or stepped to one end			Stepped to both ends					
0	1	2	3	4	5	6	7	8	9
No hole, no breakthrough	No shape elements	Thread	Functional groove	No shape elements	Thread	Functional groove	Functional cone	Operating thread	All others

Digit 4									
Plane surface machining									
0	1	2	3	4	5	6	7	8	9
No surface machining	Surface plane and/or curved in one direction, external	External plane surface related by graduation around a circle	External groove and/or slot	External spline (polygon)	External plane surface and/or slot, external spline	Internal plane surface and/or slot	Internal spline (polygon)	Internal and external polygon, groove and/or slot	All others

Digit 5									
Auxiliary holes and gear teeth									
No gear teeth						With gear teeth			
0	1	2	3	4	5	6	7	8	9
No auxiliary hole	Axial, not on pitch circle diameter	Axial on pitch circle diameter	Radial, not on pitch circle diameter	Axial and/or radial and/or other direction	Axial and/or radial on PCD and/or other directions	Spur gear teeth	Bevel gear teeth	Other gear teeth	All others

Figure 13.3 Form code (digits 1 through 5) for rotational parts in the Opitz system (Mikell P. Groover, *Automation, Production Systems and Computer-Integrated Manufacturing*, 1987, p. 441. Reprinted by permission of Prentice Hall, Englewood Cliffs, New Jersey).

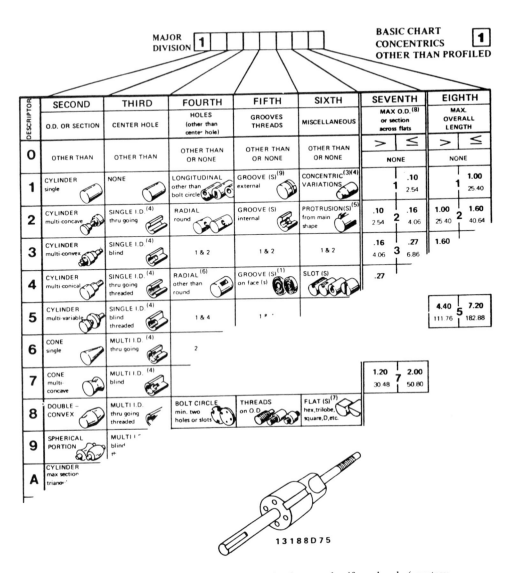

Figure 13.4 A partial CODE system showing how to classify and code (courtesy of Schlumberger CAD/CAM).

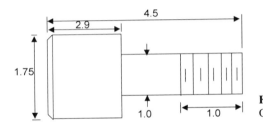

Figure 13.5 Coding of a part using Optiz and CODE systems.

There are no center holes, so the third digit is 1.

There are no auxiliary holes present, so the fourth digit is 0.

There are threads present on one end, so the fifth digit is 8.

There are no flats, slots or protrusions present, so the sixth digit is 0.

The last two digits of the code are used to define overall dimensions. The outer diameter falls within the range of 1.2 and 2 in. (O.D. = 1.75 in.), so the seventh digit is 7. The eighth digit classifies the overall length, which in this case falls between 4.4 to 7.2 in., so the eighth digit is 5.

The code of this part using the Code system shown in Figure 13.3 is then 14108075.

MICLASS System. The MICLASS system was developed by TNO (The Netherlands Organization for Applied Scientific Research) of Holland and is currently maintained in the United States by the Organization for Industrial Research. The MICLASS classification system ranges from 12 to 30 digits. The first 12 digits are universal and can be applied to any part. Up to 18 additional digits can be used for data that are specific to the particular company. These supplemental digits provide the flexibility to accommodate broad applications. For example, lot size, cost data, and operation sequence are included in the 18 supplemental digits.

The MICLASS system can help automate and standardize a number of design, production, and management functions, including standardization of engineering drawings, retrieval of drawings according to classification number, standardization of process routing, selection of parts for processing a particular group of machine tools, and automated process planning. The MICLASS system has been adapted in many U.S. industries, and several other application programs such as MIPLAN and MULTICAPP variant process planning systems are available. The MICLASS code

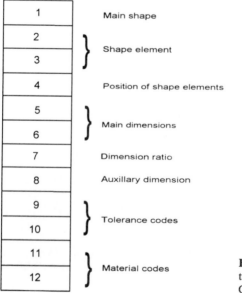

1	Main shape
2	Shape element
3	
4	Position of shape elements
5	Main dimensions
6	
7	Dimension ratio
8	Auxillary dimension
9	Tolerance codes
10	
11	Material codes
12	

Figure 13.6 The MICLASS code structure (courtesy of International Techne Group Incorporated).

```
RUN $MICLAS

    MICLAS  VERSION 2.0


ENTER THE CLASSIFICATION ROUTE (1 TO 9) >1

3 MAIN DIMENSIONS (WHEN ROT. PART D,L AND 0) >2.9375,2,0

   DEVIATION OF ROTATIONAL FORM >NO

   CONCENTRIC SPIRAL GROOVES >NO

TURNING ON OUTERCONTOUR (EXCEPT ENDFACES) >YES

   SPECIAL GROOVES OR CONE(S) OR PROFILE(S)  ON OUTERCONTOUR >NO

   ALL MACH. EXT. DIAM. AND ROT. FACES VISIBLE FROM ONE END
   (EXC. ENDFACES + GROOVE(S) >YES

TURNING ON INNERCONTOUR >YES

   INTERNAL SPECIAL GROOVES OR CONE(S) OR PROFILE(S) >NO

   ALL INT.DIA. + ROT.FACES VISIBLE FROM 1 END(EXC. GROOVES >YES

ALL DIA. + ROT.FACES VISIBLE FROM ONE END (EXCL. ENDFACES >YES

ECC. HOLING AND/OR FACING AND/OR SLOTTING >YES

   ON INNERFORM AND/OR FACES (INC. ENDFACES) >YES

   ON OUTERFORM >NO

ONLY ENCLOSED INTERNAL SLOTS >NO

ECC. MACHINING ONLY ONE SENSE >Y

   ONLY HOLES ON A BOLTCIRCLE (AT LEAST 3 HOLES) >YES

FORM-OR THREADING TOLERANCE >NO

DIAM. OR ROT. FACE ROUGHNESS LESS THAN 33 RU (MICRO-INCHES) >YES

   SMALLEST POSITIONING TOL. FIELD >.016

   SMALLEST LENGTHTOL. FIELD >.0313



CLASS.NR.= 1271 3231 3100 0000 0000 0000 0000 00
*******************************************************


DIGIT TO CHANGE >
CONTINUE [Y/N]>N
TTO  --  STOP
>
```

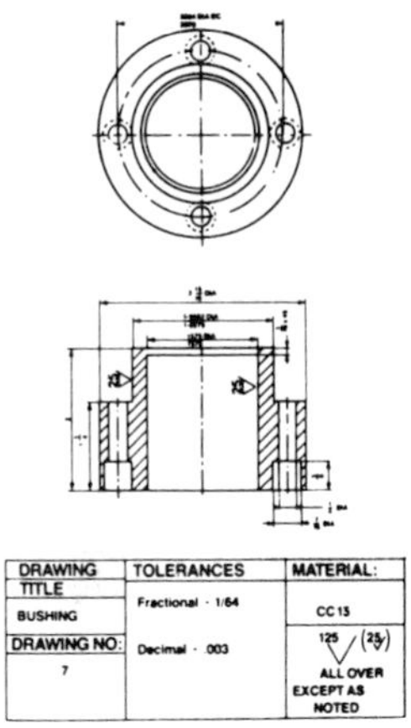

Drawing of Part

Figure 13.7 Coding session of MICLASS (courtesy of International Techne Group Incorporated).

structure is shown in Figure 13.6. An example of coding a part using the MICLASS system is described in Figure 13.7.

DCLASS Systems. The DCLASS system was developed by Del Allen, Brigham Young University, and is a decision-making and classification system. It is a tree-structured system that generates codes for components, materials, processes, machines, and tools. Each branch of the system represents a condition in which a code is formed at the junction of each branch. The complete code is obtained by taking multiple passes in the decision tree. For the components, an eight-digit code is used. Digits 1, 2, and 3 represent its basic shape; digit 4 represents the form; digit 5 represents the size; digit 6 represents the tolerance; and the last two digits (7 and 8) represent the material of the component. (Figure 13.8).

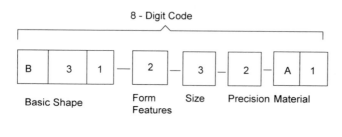

PART FAMILY CODE

Figure 13.8 A sample of DCLASS code representation.

13.3 A PROPOSED CLASSIFICATION SYSTEM

A classification and coding system developed and applicable to a manufacturing firm dealing in dies, tools, presses, and other related equipment is presented.

The structure of the proposed coding system is based on a hybrid or mixed code construction. The aims of the proposed system is product identification and design retrieval. A monocode is not suitable due to the large amount of information shared by a variety of products. A polycode structure is also not suited for this classification because of its restrictions on the numbering system itself. In a polycode structure, each digit carries information that is totally independent from the others. In this application, the commonly shared information by different products makes use of a polycode system prohibitive. In essence, for this application, the hybrid system or mixed-code structure is the optimum classification system.

The data are classified into different categories and classes utilizing most of the documented information. The proposed method of classification and coding utilizes a 12-digit code used for information retrieval and design simplification. This system provides coding for designed and purchased assemblies, products and raw materials, and has the capability to accommodate individual components and other miscellaneous items.

Component classification is done by shape or function and the shape feature is taken into account when individual components are grouped together by their manufacturing similarities. But classification of a product by its shape is almost impossible. When it comes to grouping products, usually classification by function is preferred. The proposed system brings similar items together by classifying them by function.

The code is a numerical code of constant length and is divided into two groups of six digits each:

$$\underbrace{XXXXXX}-\underbrace{XXXXXX}$$
General Code   Specific Code

The first group, the "general code," classifies the part into its major categories and subclasses. The second group, the "specific code," is tailored by user requirements to give additional information related to a certain product or assembly.

13.3.1 General Code

The breakdown of the general code is as follows:

AA BC DD

The first digit (AA) has 10 possible values, the second and third digits (B and C) are combined to give 99 possible subclasses of each item classified, and the last digit (DD) in the general code has 10 possible values. The general code gives a general description of the part, the type of operation it performs, and other specifications that uniquely identify the product.

13.3.2 Specific Code

The remaining half of the system, the specific code, carries specific information about a certain range of products. The breakdown of the specific code is as follows:

XX X X X X

The specific code gives us a more detailed description about a part by classifying it into subclasses. Some parts do not need all 12 digits. The extra digits are reserved for possible future expansion of the company line of products.

13.3.3 Method Used for the Proposed Classification System

The first step taken in designing the proposed classification system is to break down all the company's components or parts into eight major design classes as follows:

1. designed piece parts
2. designed assemblies
3. designed products
4. purchased piece parts
5. purchased assemblies
6. purchased products
7. raw material
8. miscellaneous

   Classification of Design Classes.   Each design divides each component into an assembly product or raw material and identifies whether the components are designed or purchased. Simultaneously, those components are divided into three classes: individual piece parts, products, or assemblies. This division is beneficial for family grouping and retrieval purposes. Each design class is then broken down into subclasses. Figure 13.9 illustrates this classification. The method utilizes digits two and three for this subclassification. Each design class is again subclassified into different types of products and assemblies like presses, special machines, feeders,

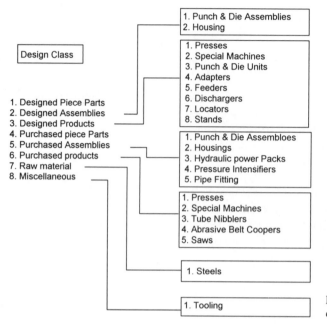

Figure 13.9 Subdivision of a design class into subclasses.

punch and die units, dischargers, etc. Thus, all similar equipment can be grouped at the initial stage, making it easier to identify their class. The subclasses are progressively subdivided into subsubclasses to form classes of items that are similar in design.

Figure 13.10 shows a code for a designed assembly and shows the general and specific codes, giving the type of information carried for one assembly that is designed and marketed by a particular company.

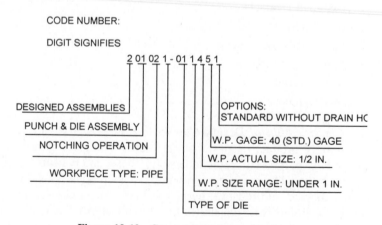

Figure 13.10 Construction of a proposed code.

13.4 WORK CELLS

Group technology can be defined as a technique of identifying and bringing together similar parts in a production process in order to utilize the inherent economy of flow production methods. In other words, when using group technology, the machines are grouped to produce a family of similar parts. Each group has the necessary machines to produce the family of similar parts. However, a certain part might not require the use of every machine. Such a system is most effective when a coding and classification system is used.

In work cells, machine layout is based on component flow, and a component enters and terminates at that cell location. Each work cell in effect can be regarded as a manufacturing unit. The number of machines in the work cell depends on the part family that is going to be manufactured. A work cell can have only one machine supported by the required tooling and fixtures. For example, a nut and bolt is made on a single lathe machine. A work cell can have a group of machines supported by either manual or mechanized material handling. Part families with a large number of parts can be manufactured by a flexible manufacturing system (FMS), which consists of automated processing stations connected by a fully integrated material handling system. An FMS employing four T-30 machining centers, each with a 2-position automatic work changer and a 90-tool automatic tool changer is shown in Figure 13.11. The system also includes automated material and tool handling systems, an automated wash station, a coordinate measuring machine for in-process inspection, and a milacron 10-station AWC for part queuing.

Figure 13.11   An FMS cell (courtesy Cincinnati Milacron, Cincinnati, Ohio).

There are a few problems arising from work cells:

1. If the mix of the workpieces requires change, then the machine layout of the work cell must also be changed.
2. Because the work cell contains several different types of machines, the supervisor must be an expert in several different machining techniques.
3. Because the machine operator is typically not an expert on several different types of machines, transfer from one machine to another can be a problem.
4. The flow of the work cell must be designed around the most complex workpiece machining route. Overloading or underloading of a single machine may occur, resulting in an uneven work balance.

13.4.1 Types of Work Cells

Work cells are of four basic types.

1. single machine work cells
2. group machine cells utilizing manual material handling
3. group machine cells utilizing semiintegrated material handling
4. flexible manufacturing systems

All four types can exist together in one factory and result from the analysis of data carried out by either part-coding or production-flow analysis.

The design of a work cell can be based on the composite-part concept or the key-machine concept.

The composite-part concept groups work at a single machine tool and designs tooling to increase productivity by reducing idle time caused by the need for resetting between batches.

When a group of components is similar in shape, size, or manufacturing requirements, then a single composite component can be formed that has all the features of the individual components. Pooling and sequencing of machines are based on the composite component. Unrequired operations and tools for certain individual parts are simply dropped. Setup times can be reduced by up to 50% and floor-to-floor process times by about 40%. We should note that the concept of work cells and flexible manufacturing systems assumes that all individual components have two basic characteristics in common:

1. similar holding or clamping requirements
2. similar surfaces for machining

The key-machine concept designs work cells so that the most expensive and important machines have the highest utilization, whereas the less important have the lowest. The expensive machines are called "key machines" and the other machines are called "supporting machines." The aim is to operate key machines at maximum output at all times. In the case of supporting machines, it is important to maximize utilization of labor rather than equipment.

13.4.2 Arrangement of Machines in a Work Cell

A simple method to decide on the arrangement of machines, developed by Hollier and described by Wild, uses From–To charts and is illustrated in the following example.

Example 13.1   Arrangement of Machines Using From–To Charts

Five machines constitute a group technology work cell. The From–To data for the machine is

Machines			To		
From	1	2	3	4	5
1	0	10	80	0	0
2	0	0	0	85	0
3	0	0	0	0	0
4	70	0	20	0	0
5	0	75	0	20	0

(a) Determine the most logical sequence arrangement of the machines for the data given using the To–From ratio.

(b) Where do the parts enter and exit the cell? How many parts are in each place?

Solution   (a) The first step is to develop a From–To chart from the data given by summing up the "From" and "To" trips for each machine:

Machines			To			
From	1	2	3	4	5	"From" sums
1	0	10	80	0	0	90
2	0	0	0	85	0	85
3	0	0	0	0	0	0
4	70	0	20	0	0	90
5	0	75	0	20	0	95
"To" Sums	70	85	100	105	0	

The second step is to calculate the To–From ratio for each machine by calculating the ratio of the "To" and "From" sums for each machine:

Machines	To	From	To–From ratio
1	70	90	0.77
2	85	85	1
3	100	0	∞
4	105	90	1.16
5	0	95	0

Now the machines are arranged in the increasing order of To–From ratios. This concept allows machines with low To–From ratios to receive work from fewer machines and distribute it to more machines. Thus, the arrangement of machines in the work cell would be as follows:

$$5 \longrightarrow 1 \longrightarrow 2 \longrightarrow 4 \longrightarrow 3$$

We then can specify the To and From parts for each machine in the arrangement found in the first step (Figure 13.12).

(b) To determine where the parts enter and leave the work cell, we need to equate the number of parts entering the work cell at specific machines to the number of parts leaving the work cell from all machines. Thus, it is seen that 95 parts enter the work cell at machine 5, 20 parts enter at machine 1, 100 parts leave at machine 3, and 15 parts leave at machine 4 (Figure 13.13). ∎

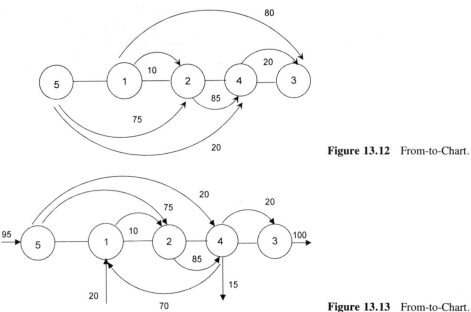

Figure 13.12 From-to-Chart.

Figure 13.13 From-to-Chart.

Let us consider a few more examples of work cells. They further illustrate how the work cells function independently. The solution provided might not be the optimum one but rather one in which the manufacturing process is described within a work cell function.

Example 13.2   Work Cell for Circuit Board Support

The work cell for a circuit board support contains one drill press; two end ball mills, with a cutter diameter of 1.82 mm; and two horizontal slab mills, with a cutter diameter of 13.6 mm, as shown in Figure 13.14.

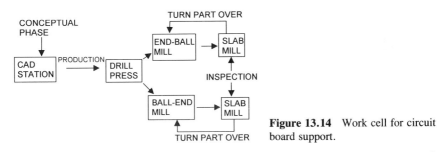

Figure 13.14   Work cell for circuit board support.

The proposed work cell shown is very simple and there are several ways that it could have been constructed. In this work cell, no tool changes are required; however, the workpiece must pass through each mill twice. The factors determining the structure of the work cell are not discussed here.   ■

Example 13.3   Work Cell for Manufacturing Castings

The work cell illustrated in Figure 13.15 is used for manufacturing castings. The manufacturing process starts on conveyor 1, where the molds for the casted parts are placed at equal distances from each other. This conveyor is controlled by a CAD/CAM machine because it starts and stops at various intervals so that the molds can end up directly beneath the molten lead valve. The valve is then opened by a CAD/CAM machine command to fill the mold. Next, the robot takes the last mold from conveyor 1 and removes the casted part from inside it. The part is then placed on the machining table in the proper position to enable the top of the part to be machined. While the top of the part is being machined, the robot brings the empty mold back to the beginning of conveyor 1 so that it can be used again. When the robot returns to the machining table, it proceeds to flip the part when required by the APT program. Between each repositioning of the part, the robot sweeps and scraps the lead onto conveyor 2. This conveyor carries the scrap lead back to the vat, where it can be remelted and used again. When the machining is complete, the robot places the part onto conveyor 3 (refer to Figure 13.13), where the finished products are turned out. The robot then grabs the next mold and repeats the process.

It is not necessary for the CAD/CAM machine to control conveyors 2 or 3 because they run constantly. The only precaution that is taken is to make the length of conveyor 1 long enough to ensure that the casted parts have cooled enough to be machined. This involves doing a study on the length of time that is required to machine each part. The intervals at which conveyor 1 is turned off and on equal the machin-

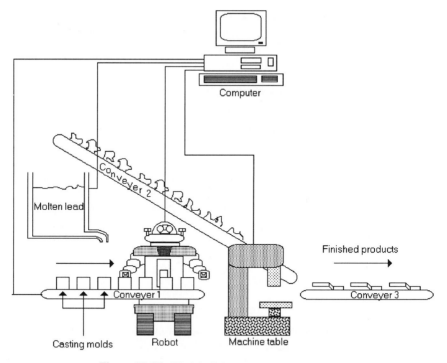

Figure 13.15   Work cell for manufacturing castings.

ing time. From the machining and cooling times required for the casted parts, the length of conveyor 1 can be determined.   ∎

Examples 13.2 and 13.3 show how an independent work cell is used for the manufacture of similar parts.

13.5 COMPUTERIZED CODING AND INFORMATION RETRIEVAL

Once part classification and other processes are completed, the information has to be stored in the computer so that it can be retrieved at a later stage. A computerized coding procedure retrieves the necessary parts by interacting with the program through a selection of items on the displayed menu.

13.5.1 Coding Parts

Part-coding tables can be used to generate part numbers. However, if this procedure is automated, considerable savings in time and money can result. One can add information about the part after generating the code number; the database is automatically modified and updated.

13.5.2 Information Retrieval

One can retrieve information about a specific component or group of components in whichever manner suitable. To obtain a general description of the part, the part code can be entered to retrieve information from the database. For a group of machines like feeders and presses, we can retrieve information about the numbers of units sold, their costs, etc.

The following illustrates how information is retrieved for a company manufacturing dies and tools. Suppose we want to retrieve information about all the different types of four post presses available at the company. In order to search for a component, we choose number 2 from the main program menu displayed in Figure 13.16.

```
                      ** PART NUMBERING SYSTEM **
_____

                    PROGRAM MENU
                    _____


              1.    PART CODING
              2.    INFORMATION RETRIEVAL
              3.    INFORMATION CORRECTION




_____

    Type 'E' to End
                    ENTER YOUR CHOICE:
```

Figure 13.16   Program menu for computerized coding and information search.

Information-Retrieval Menu.   The information-retrieval menu displayed in Figure 13.17 gives four options. There are two ways of searching for a part using the interactive search scheme or the part code number. The other two options provide a sorted printout of either all the parts or a specific product.

Interactive-Search Method.   By using the outlined procedure, this method helps us to group items of similar type and to get a list of a particular product. We pick up the choices from the menu; at a particular level, we can select option L, listing, to get information about a particular product. From the menu displayed in Figure 13.14, we pick option 1 to carry out an interactive search; the new menu displayed in Figure 13.18 gives the design class. We are now asked to pick a choice to narrow our search to a specific component. The choice is "designed products," option 3, because we are searching for a designed press. This displays another menu, shown in Figure 13.19, that contains all major designed products. Presently there

```
                         ** PART NUMBERING SYSTEM **
────────────────────────────────────────────────────────────────────


                    INFORMATION RETRIEVAL MENU
                    ─────────────────────────────


                    1.    INTERACTIVE SEARCH FOR PART
                    2.    SEARCH BY CODE NUMBER
                    3.    SORT PART BY CODE NUMBER
                    4.    SPECIFIC PART PRINTOUT MENU




────────────────────────────────────────────────────────────────────

Type 'E' to End
Type 'P' for Program Menu

                    ENTER YOUR CHOICE:
```

Figure 13.17   Information retrieval menu.

```
                         ** PART NUMBERING SYSTEM **
────────────────────────────────────────────────────────────────────


          This menu gives us the list of design classes in which
          all VOGEL products have been classified. To begin search
          pick the choices from menu to narrow down your search
          to a specific component.
                         1.    Designed Place Parts
                         2.    Designed Assemblies
                         3.    Designed Products
                         4.    Purchased Piece Parts
                         5.    Purchased Assemblies
                         6.    Purchased Products
                         7.    Raw Materials
                         8.    Miscellaneous


────────────────────────────────────────────────────────────────────

Type 'M' for Main Menu
Type 'E' to End
Type 'P' for Prev. Menu

                    ENTER YOUR CHOICE:
```

Figure 13.18   Search menu displaying a list of design classes.

are eight options available (other products could be introduced to the menu when the need arises). From the designed products menu, we select presses, option 1. The next menu displays four options (Figure 13.20) that subclassify the presses by their source of power, namely, hydraulic, pneumatic, mechanical, or manual. Because we are searching for a press in the hydraulic category, we choose option 1. The menu displayed in Figure 13.21 classifies hydraulic presses by their operation type given by eight different classes.

```
                        ** PART NUMBERING SYSTEM **
_____


        You want to search for DESIGNED PRODUCTS. Designed products
        have been further classified into the following categories.
        Select the option which matches your requirements:


                1.   Presses
                2.   Special Machines
                3.   Punch and Die Units
                4.   Adapters
                5.   Feeders
                6.   Dischargers
                7.   Locators
                8.   Stands

_____

Type 'M' for Main Menu
Type 'E' to End
Type 'P' for Prev. Menu

            ENTER YOUR CHOICE:
```

Figure 13.19 Search menu displaying a list of design products operations.

```
                        ** PART NUMBERING SYSTEM **
_____


        Your choice was PRESSES. Presses have been further classified
        by source of power.
        Select your option:


                1.   HYDRAULIC
                2.   PNEUMATIC
                3.   MECHANICAL
                4.   MANUAL




_____

Type 'M' for Main Menu
Type 'E' to End
Type 'P' for Prev. Menu
            ENTER YOUR CHOICE:
```

Figure 13.20 Search menu displaying a list of different modes of power available for presses.

In this case, our choice is the first class; we select option 1 (i.e., hydraulic press) for multipurpose operation. This gives us the menu shown in Figure 13.22. There are four choices available and we pick option 1 for four-post three-platen presses. This leads us to the menu listing four-post three-platen presses classified by tonnage, as shown in Figure 13.23. Now we enter "L" for a complete listing; the computer program in turn will ask if we want a list of all four-post three-platen

```
                         ** PART NUMBERING SYSTEM **
    _____

        Your choice was Hydraulic presses. Hydraulic presses are
        further classified by the type of operation they perform.
        Select your option:


                        1.    MULTIPURPOSE
                        2.    NOTCHING/SLOTTING
                        3.    PIERCING
                        4.    CUTTING
                        5.    BENDING
                        6.    REDUCING
                        7.    ENDFORMING (MULTIPURPOSE)
                        8.    HYDROFORMING

    _____

Type 'M' for Main Menu
Type 'E' to End
Type 'P' for Prev. Menu

                    ENTER YOUR CHOICE:
```

Figure 13.21 Search menu displaying a list of different press operations.

```
                         ** PART NUMBERING SYSTEM **
    _____

        Hydraulic presses for multipurpose operation are
        further classified into the following types.
        Select your option:


                    1.    FOUR POST THREE PLATEN PRESS
                    2.    BENCH ARC HYDRAULIC PRESS
                    3.    57000 SERIES HYDRAULIC PRODUCTION PRESSES
                    4.    VOGEL CAGE STYLE HYDRAULIC POWER UNITS




    _____

Type 'M' for Main Menu
Type 'E' to End
Type 'P' for Prev. Menu

                    ENTER YOUR CHOICE:
```

Figure 13.22 Search menu displaying different types of multi purpose hydraulic presses.

```
                          ** PART NUMBERING SYSTEM **
_____


         Four post three platen presses are available in
         following tonnage. Select your option:


                      1.    10  TONS
                      2.    15  TONS
                      3.    25  TONS




_____

    Type 'M' for Main Menu                    TYPE 'L' FOR LISTING
    Type 'E' to End
    Type 'P' for Prev. Menu
                      ENTER YOUR CHOICE:
```

Figure 13.23 Search menu displaying the tonnage of four past three platen presses.

presses or a specific one. If we need a list of all presses with 10-ton capacity, we enter 1. This display of information, shown in Figure 13.24, gives the particulars of the class, source of power, a list of all the four-post three-platen presses of 10-ton capacity, and additional information like bed length, width, and stroke. From here we can either get a hard copy or exit and go to the main menu.

The interactive search for a part can be modified in many different ways, depending upon the nature of information needed and the extent by which the information is available through the database.

Search by Code Number.   If we need to retrieve information from the computer's database, we can also use the part number as the entry key. For this we have to choose option 2 from the interactive-search menu, which takes us to the routine that searches for a part by its code number.

Selecting option 2, we then enter the part code. The computer then searches for the part in its database. If a part number exists, it brings up and displays all its information on the screen. Otherwise, it displays a message that says the part does not exist.

Sorting Parts by Code Number.   The third option available in the information-retrieval menu, displayed in Figure 13.17, is the sorting of parts by code number. Presently, it prints out a sorted list of all the coded parts with a two-line description, giving a brief summary of the part.

```
DESIGN CLASS:        DESIGNED PRODUCTS    FAMILY CODE: 301011-0100000
UNIT PRICE:          PRESSES              _____
OPERATION TYPE:      MULTIPURPOSE
SOURCE OF POWER:     HYDRAULIC
TYPE OF PRESS:       FOUR POST THREE PLATEN PRESS
```

PART CODE	TONNAGE	LENGTH	WIDTH	STROKE	PRICE	U-SOLD
301011-011110	10 TONS	12 IN	12 IN	8	5675.00	10
301011-011120	10 TONS	12 IN	16 IN	8	6095.00	11
301011-011130	10 TONS	12 IN	20 IN	8	6445.00	13
301011-011230	10 TONS	18 IN	20 IN	8	6495.00	20
301011-011240	10 TONS	18 IN	24 IN	8	6795.00	15
301011-011250	10 TONS	18 IN	28 IN	8	7165.00	12
301011-011340	10 TONS	24 IN	24 IN	8	6995.00	14
301011-011350	10 TONS	24 IN	28 IN	8	7395.00	16
301011-011360	10 TONS	24 IN	32 IN	8	7835.00	13

```
Type 'M' for Main Menu
Type 'E' to End
                    ENTER YOUR CHOICE:
```

Figure 13.24   Listing of all 10 ton four past three platen presses.

Specific Part-Listing Menu. The last option of the information-retrieval menu is the printed list of information of a specific component. For example, it can print out a sorted list of all designed and purchased punch and die assemblies. It also gives a brief description of the component with its code number. This option is useful when searching for punch and die assemblies of a particular size or type.

Information-Correction Routine. The last option in the computerized information-storage and retrieval systems program menu is the information-correction option. This helps in updating the database of all the parts.

13.6 BENEFITS OF GROUP TECHNOLOGY

Some of the benefits of classification, coding, and information retrieval are as follows.

Simplification. The use of group technology helps in reducing the occurrence of similar designs in a variety of ways. It minimizes duplication in manufacturing and enables the manufacturing engineer to better control existing inventory.

Identification. Once the system is learned, one can get a general description of a part by knowing its code number.

Reduction in the Cost of Design.   If a suitable design already exists, the unnecessary creation of a new one is usually prevented by classification. If a new design has to be created, an approximate code number can be searched. The final design is then achieved through the simple modification of an existing one. This reduces design cost. Group technology also promotes standardization in design.

Material Handling.   There is an efficient flow of materials through the shop and reduction in idle time by applying the principles of group technology.

Storage and Inventory Control.   Because all similar items have nearly related code numbers, the raw materials or individual components can be stored in code-number sequence, thus eliminating the need for bin numbers. Manufacturing lead times and work-in-process times are drastically reduced because of reduced setup times and more efficient material handling. In-process inventories can be reduced by 50% and throughput time by as much as 60% by the use of group technology.

Reduction in Tooling Cost.   In computer-aided design and computer-aided manufacturing, one of the major tasks involves geometry description of the part in question. The identification of the entities that describe the mechanical part serves as a basis for generating corresponding manufacturing processes and tooling programs. The classification and coding systems help identify those parts whose manufacturing processes are already defined.

Reduction in Cost Estimates.   By estimating the records of items with similar code numbers made in the past, the cost estimates can be made for new designs by interpolating from the actual costs of the old ones. Alternatively, the actual costs can be used to check the calculated estimates.

PROBLEMS

13.1 (a) Give two examples that form a part family for the automobile industry.

(b) What type of process-planning technique must be used to develop a process plan for machining a new part using an existing computer database of route sheets?

13.2 Using Figures 13.2 and 13.3, develop a form code using the Opitz system for the part shown in Figure P13.1.

13.3 Develop the form code for the same part shown in Figure P13.1 using the Code classification system.

13.4 Using Figures 13.6 and 13.8, generate codes using the MICLASS and DCLASS coding systems. Describe the similarities between the codes and their major differences.

13.5 Four machines consist of a work cell. The From–To chart for these machines on which 60 parts are processed follows:

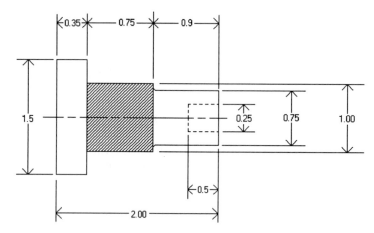

Figure P13.1 Form code for a robot.

Machines	To			
From	1	2	3	4
1	0	10	0	30
2	30	0	0	25
3	20	30	0	0
4	10	0	0	0

Fifty parts enter machine 3 and 15 enter machine 2; 45 parts leave machine 4 and 20 parts leave machine 1. Determine the logical machine arrangement and suggest a feasible layout.

13.6 In Problem 5, the numbers of parts traveling from machines 1 and 4 and from machines 2 and 3 are exchanged. How would this change the machine arrangement and machine layout?

13.7 Develop the form code for the rotational part given in Figure P13.2 using the Opitz and Code classification systems.

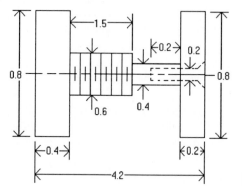

Figure P13.2 A rotational part.

REFERENCES

13.1 Allen, D. K., *Classification and Coding Theory and Application,* Monograph No. 2, Computer-Aided Manufacturing Laboratory, Brigham Young University, Provo, Utah, 1979.

13.2 Allen, D. K., Generative process planning using the DCLASS Information System, Monograph No. 4, Computer-Aided Manufacturing Laboratory, Brigham Young University, Provo, Utah, 1979.

13.3 Brankamp, K., Objectives, Layout and Possibilities of the OPITZ Workpiece Classification System, *Proc. Group Technology International Seminar,* International Center for Advanced Technical and Vocational Training, Turin, 1970.

13.4 Burbridge, J. L., *Group Technology in the Engineering Industry,* Mechanical Engineering Publications Ltd., London, 1979.

13.5 Burbridge, J. L., *The Introduction of Group Technology,* John Wiley & Sons, New York, 1975.

13.6 Burbridge, J. L., Production Flow Analysis, *The Production Engineers,* April/May 1971.

13.7 Chang, T. C., and Wysk, R. A., *An Introduction to Automated Process Planning Systems,* Prentice Hall, Englewood Cliffs, NJ, 1985.

13.8 Dautzig, G. B., *Linear Programming and Extensions,* Princeton University Press, Princeton, 1963.

13.9 Dedworth, D. D., and Bailey, J. E., *Integrated Production Control Systems,* John Wiley & Sons, New York, 1982.

13.10 Edwards, G. A. B., *Readings in Group Technology,* Machinery Publishing, London, 1971.

13.11 Gallagher, C., and Knight, W., *Group Technology,* London, Butterworth, 1973.

13.12 El Gomayel, J., and Abou-Zeid, M. R., "Piece Part Coding and the Optimization of Process Planning," North American Metalworking Research Conference, May 1975.

13.13 Groover, M. P., *Automation, Production Systems and Computer Integrated Manufacturing,* Prentice Hall, Englewood Cliffs, New Jersey, 1980.

13.14 Groover, M. P., and Zimmer, E. W., *CAD/CAM,* Prentice Hall, Englewood Cliffs, NJ, 1984.

13.15 Haan, R. A., Group Technology Coding and Classification Applied in NC Part Programming, *Proc. 14th Numerical Control Society Annual Meeting and Technical Conference,* Pittsburgh, March 1977.

13.16 Ham, I., "Introduction to Group Technology" Technical Report MMR 76-03, Society of Manufacturing Engineers, Dearborn, Mich., 1976.

13.17 Ham, I., Hitomi, K., and Yoshida, T., *Group Technology,* Kluwer-Miijhogg Publishing, Boston, 1985.

13.18 Hartley, J., FMS at Work, IFS Publications Ltd., Kempston, Bedford, U.K, 1984.

13.19 Hitomi, K., *Manufacturing System Engineering,* Taylor and Francis, London, 1979.

13.20 Houtzeel, A., Classification & Coding, Group Technology & Computer Assisted Process Planning, TNO, Organization for Industrial Research, Inc., Waltham, MA.

13.21 Hyde, W. F., *Improving Productivity by Classification, Coding, and Data Base Standardization,* Marcel Dekker, New York, 1981.

13.22 Kakino, Y. F., Oba, F., Meriwaki, T., and Iwata, K., A new method of parts description for Computer-Aided Production Planning; Advances in Computer-Aided Manufacturing, Elsevier North-Holland, New York, 1977.

13.23 Kerry, T. M., Integrating N.C. Programming with Machining and Group Technology, *Proc. 12th Numerical Control Society Annual Meeting and Technical Conference,* 1975, pp. 149–162.

13.24 King, J. R., Machine-Component Group Formation in Group Technology: Review and Extension, *Intl. J. Prod. Res.,* Vol. 20, No. 2, 1982, pp. 117–133.

13.25 Opitz, H., *A Classification to Describe Workpieces,* Pergamon, Oxford, 1970.

13.26 Organization for Industrial Research, MICLSS MIgroup, MIPLAN, MIGRAPHICS (marketing brochure), Waltham, Ma.

13.27 Orlidiy, J., *Material Requirements Planning,* McGraw-Hill, New York, 1975.

13.28 Schaffer, G., GT via Automated Process Planning, *American Machinist,* May 1980, pp. 119–122.

13.29 Scheck, D. E., New direction in process planning, SME Technical paper, series MM75-908, for meeting, Ft. Lauderdale, Fla., February 1975.

13.30 Stauffer, R. N., The Rewards of Classification and Coding, *Manuf. Eng.,* May 1979, pp. 48–52.

13.31 Woodward, J., *Industrial Organization—Theory and Practice,* Oxford University Press, Oxford, 1965.

chapter 14

Computer-Integrated Manufacturing

14.1 INTRODUCTION

The competitiveness of the United States has been steadily eroded by manufacturing challenges over the past two decades. Individual companies that have adapted to the changing technological environment have fared well; however, there is much more to be done before the United States can regain its manufacturing leadership (Tables 14.1 and 14.2).

Management, labor, and government all share responsibility for the changing face of U.S. industry. It can be safely assumed that the effectiveness of design and production functions in supporting the overall business strategy is a major determinant in the competitiveness of U.S. industry. The United States has the means to regain its manufacturing leadership.

New technologies like computer-integrated manufacturing (CIM) permit manufacturers to implement strategies and objectives to increase productivity. CIM deals with the integration of manufacturing activities and support facilities using computers. The advent of powerful low-price computers has made it practical for communications to take place between different industries. Computers used in manufacturing not only contribute to decision making, but also in the control of production and shipment of products. Integrating these computers through common databases can radically change the running of a company. CIM allows decision makers to access data on all relevant computers, enabling them to make better decisions. Further, decisions can be implemented with greater speed and their effects can be carefully monitored. The concept of CIM is taking full control over manufacturing processes through a single information source. Full control implies control over the direct manufacturing process, support systems, business practices, and enterprise goals.

TABLE 14.1   CAPITAL INVESTMENT AS PERCENTAGE OF OUTPUT[a]
IN MANUFACTURING, SELECTED COUNTRIES, 1965–1982

Period	France	West Germany	Japan	United Kingdom	United States
1965–1982	15.1	12.8[b]	21.2	13.6	10.5
1965–1973	16.5	14.3	25.3	14.3	10.0
1974–1982	13.6	11.2[c]	17.1	13.0	11.1

[a] Fixed capital & output measured in constant dollars.
[b] 1965–1981.
[c] 1974–1981.
Source: Unpublished data obtained from U.S. Bureau of Labor Statistics, 1985.

TABLE 14.2   OUTPUT PER HOUR IN MANUFACTURING, AVERAGE ANNUAL
PERCENT CHANGE

Country	1960–1973	1973–1983	1989–1990
Canada	4.7	1.8	2.7
France	6.5	4.6	1.1
West Germany	5.7	3.7	3.4
Japan	10.5	6.8	3.7
United Kingdom	4.3	2.4	0.8
United States	3.4	1.8	2.5

Source: U.S. Bureau of Labor Statistics, 1991.

14.2 CIM OBJECTIVES

CIM allows enterprises to meet higher levels of objectives that are unattainable with partially computerized industries. The objectives are as follows:

1. Develop quality products at competitive prices.
2. Integrate and control design and manufacturing operations.
3. Manage finances.
4. Increase sales by controlling product demands.

Once more, the feasibility of integrating information of all the enterprise functions is only possible through a computer network designed to meet the specifics and goals of the enterprise. Computerized industries will have two choices in the future. First, custom design the CIM computer architecture to meet the company's demand and, second, develop a standard CIM architecture for a variety of different enterprises. Because CIM is still new, its implementation requires restructuring enterprise functions and computer-controlled decision making. Communication will rely mostly on computer interaction with a database that is accessible to all CIM functions. When implemented properly, CIM can realize the enterprise goals. To see how that is possible, we now examine the major areas of CIM:

- Marketing
- Engineering design
- Research and development
- Manufacturing operations
- Financial planning

The benefits that result from the implementation of CIM extend into each functional area of the manufacturing enterprise.

Marketing.   Gathering information from customers is key to future product development. To satisfy customer needs, we need a credible database, which is only possible through CIM technology, to help manage customer demands and prompt responses to inquiries and to assist companies in accurately predicting sales projections.

Engineering Design.   The benefits of CIM are similar to those of computer-aided design (CAD); however, the speed of designing products is faster due to the enormous database available that includes current and historical product information.

Research and Development (R&D).   The benefits of integrating manufacturing functions result in a broader knowledge of past and present product performance. This knowledge enables R&D departments to assess future product development that best utilizes company resources to increase sales. The R&D function is to keep a company competitive by responding in a timely manner with newly developed products. CIM allows the enterprise to adapt quickly to market changes and provides the ultimate guidelines to future product development.

Manufacturing Operations.   The advantages of CIM are also similar to those of computer-aided manufacturing (CAM) as stated in Chapter 8. However, CIM adds a new dimension to process planning, plant operations, and resources by providing a database to manage all these operations. The resources and information available through CIM allows more realistic scheduling of manufacturing operations, resulting in shorter production times and customer satisfaction. This is possible in part due to the floor organization and the computer network serving the enterprise.

Financial Planning.   CIM offers better product cost tracking, more accurate financial projections, and improved cash flow for business management activities such as managing manufacturing finance and accounting and developing enterprise directives and financial plans.

Thus, benefits of CIM are

1. quick release of new products
2. shorter delivery times
3. more realistic inventories
4. shorter production planning
5. reduced lead times
6. improved product quality
7. increased responsiveness and competitiveness

The main CIM objective is to strengthen the relationship between the supplier and the customer. It assists the supplier to plan production and deliveries more efficiently and provides the customer with the benefits of shorter order delivery time and quality products at a reasonable cost.

The benefits of CIM presented are conceptual in nature and are idealistic, serving more as goals than as guidelines. What is at the heart of CIM is the modeling of the enterprise and the restructuring of the organization to meet those goals. Restructuring requires the careful study and implementation of a plan that has the full support of management and a well-trained team of professionals.

14.3 THE ENTERPRISE AND PRODUCT MODELING

CIM technology is based on an enterprise model that integrates all operations and functional management into a network to optimize productivity and profitability. The traditional enterprise is divided into several departments that are in most cases separate entities operating on their own. The lack of data sharing results in duplicative work, waste of time, and high expenses. To eliminate unnecessary and redundant work, the new enterprise model relies on its functions to work in harmony. Figure 14.1 illustrates the functions involved and their integration.

One of the objectives of CIM is organizing the manufacturing operation processes and machine tools to optimize the quality and efficiency or durability of the product. In other words, CIM designs work cells suited for company needs. This can only be done if the database provided is such that all interfaces are present; hence, the product is directed at all stages by computer. Feedback identifies product status and decides on concurrent operations. In the event that something goes wrong, the computer should be equipped with the best alternatives to proceed with manufacturing.

Essentially, the enterprise models the product around its CIM structure to benefit from computer-controlled process planning and manufacturing. It is often helpful to develop simple intuitive models describing the subsystem elements and their relationships. This visualization allows a better understanding of complex sys-

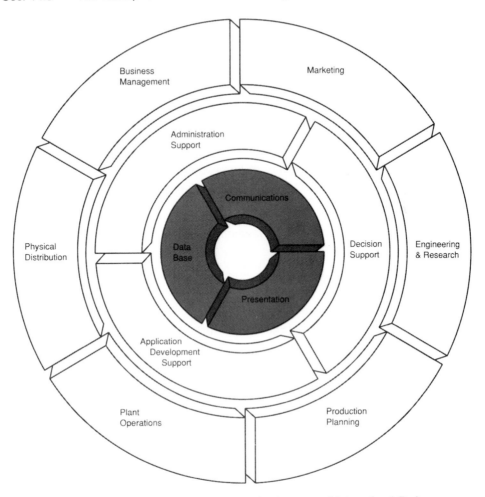

Figure 14.1 Functions of a CIM enterprise (courtesy of International Business Machines Corporation).

tems on a heuristic basis. However, it is necessary to develop more detailed system models to improve communication and learning and to study system performance.

There are broadly three types of models for viewing manufacturing systems: (a) physical models, (b) functional models, and (c) organizational models.

Physical Models.   Physical models describe the visible aspects of a manufacturing enterprise. They are classified into those involving material transformation, such as manufacturing equipment and operators, and those involving hardware for information flow and system control, such as computers and operators. Subsystems are defined in terms of hardware units and the movement of material through the system.

Functional Models. Functional models describe the manufacturing system in terms of the functions it performs. It is important to define system functions and then relate them to each other. Functional models are classified into those that describe the material transformation processes achieved by the product equipment and those that describe information flow through the system.

Organizational Models. Organizational models describe the manufacturing system in terms of the organizational relationships that exist among the people in the system. They are used to consider how informal organizations relate to one another and to overall manufacturing system activities.

Simple models are also used in all areas of a manufacturing organization to decide on the physical management of equipment, describe a process, or plan a reorganization. More formal system models can provide an in-depth system understanding, but can also mislead if the limitations of the models are not kept in mind.

14.4 CIM ARCHITECTURE

CIM architecture is a framework providing a structure of computer hardware and software with appropriate interfaces for computer systems in manufacturing enterprises to integrate information and business processes. Some of the interfaces are provided by international standards and others are determined by suppliers of hardware and software. CIM architecture can provide a consistent base for integrating the enterprise's product, processes, and business data. It defines the structure of the hardware, software, and services required to support the enterprise's complete requirements.

CIM architecture has considerable advantages in enabling a system to adapt to new business opportunities and changing technology. A proper architecture is essential to effective management and use of computer systems.

Communication is a critical aspect of the CIM architecture, because the present industrial environment, with its wide range of computer systems, makes it difficult for people and machines to communicate with each other because they format data differently. Communication has to be highly integrated to extend beyond individual areas throughout the entire enterprise and to customers and suppliers. A typical communication network in the CIM environment is shown in Figure 14.2.

In a CIM environment, local areas such as shop floors share data without passing through the central computer. The agreement that a local area network (LAN) is needed on the shop floor mainly enhances CIM environment data communication. The LAN on the shop floor has extra functions not needed in the office environment; hence, it is known as industrial LAN, or ILAN. ILANs provide a common communication system that allows suitably configured terminals and computers to be easily plugged in and disconnected. Because data are sent from one point on the network directly to another node, the switching and load-balancing functions of the central computer are avoided.

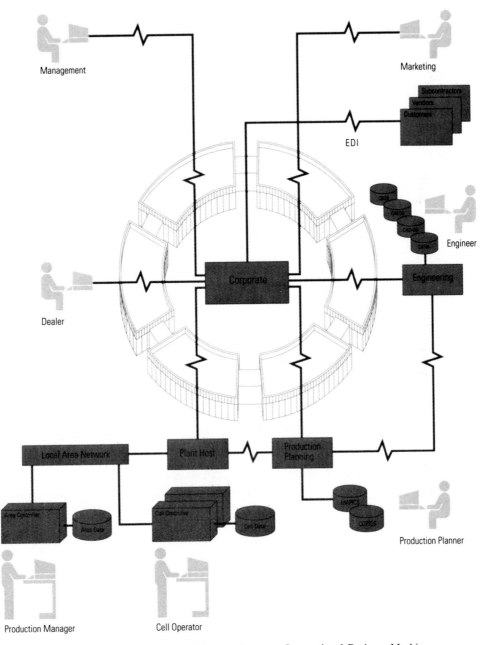

Figure 14.2   Communication Network (courtesy International Business Machines Corporation).

LAN technology allows resource sharing of printers and disks so that printing costs can be reduced and common files maintained. High reliability and serviceability are provided by the flexibility of LANs. Vertical communication to mainframe computers and horizontal communication to other networks are provided by gateways, routers, and bridges.

The major mechanism to connect different computers is by using international standards. Software is an important integration tool. Common operating systems are being developed for different computers. International standards are needed if different computer systems are to be connected. These standards are agreed to formally by organizations that are independent of computer manufacturers and competing nations. For example, the International Organization for Standardization (ISO) works through committees of representatives of the national standards organization of each participating country. These, in turn, are formed by representative industrial organizations within each country and not by individual companies. Physically, a standard is a document giving detailed specifications of hardware and software protocols. ISO standards usually begin as working papers that are published as draft proposals when agreed to by the appropriate ISO working group. In practice, many hardware and software products have become standards by virtue of their wide use and acceptance. Many suppliers of computer systems have their own proprietary interface products that may not be adapted as international standards because of constantly rising costs and the fear of loss of control. There are standards emerging that integrate these different proprietary systems, such as the OSI and MAP models.

14.4.1 Open Systems Interconnection (OSI)

The OSI reference model provides a seven-layer communication architecture that divides the complex functions needed to interface many different computer systems for different applications. Separate functions such as controlling the physical connection or providing an interface for user programs can be performed by different hardware and software. The OSI reference model is shown in Figure 14.3. Layers 1 to 4 transmit data from system to system without error, and layers 5 to 7 interpret the data stream and present it to the user within these layers. OSI provides a selection of standards for different communication purposes.

The application layer is the interface between OSI and the applications that use it. Standards are concerned with data exchanges and the sources provided such as remote file manipulation, distributed processing, message transfers, and manufacturing messages. The presentation layer selects the syntax used for data transfer. Syntax is precisely defined within OSI as a special language that ensures common representation between different manufacturers. The session layer provides facilities to manage and coordinate the dialogue between the application processes, including restarting a dialogue if there has been a temporary communication failure.

The transport layer provides reliable transfer of bit streams between end systems. Five classes of protocol are defined depending on the quality of service required by the upper layers. The network layer sets up the communication path be-

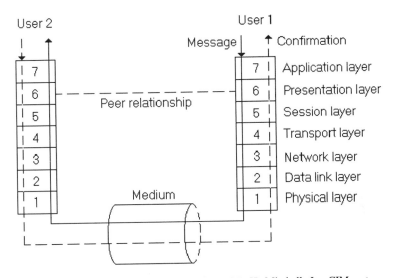

Figure 14.3   OSI Reference Model (courtesy of F. H. Mitchell, Jr., CIM systems: An Introduction to Computer-Integrated Manufacturing, 1991, pg. 360. Reprinted by permission of Prentice Hall, Englewood Cliffs, New Jersey).

tween nodes. The connection is established for the duration of the communication. The data link layer transmits the bit streams through the physical medium. It is divided into the new sublayers, logical link control, and medium access control. The physical layer activates the mechanical and electrical operations of the network.

The selection of standards within the different layers can be changed by the relevant ISO committee, that is, new standards can be added to the OSI reference model increasing the choice of standards available.

14.4.2 Manufacturing Automation Protocol (MAP)

General Motors initiated work on MAP in 1982 to prevent problems of linking shop floor computers. The objective was to establish one set of LAN protocols for communication between intelligent devices such as computer-controlled machine tools, engineering work stations, process controllers, factory floor terminals, and control rooms.

MAP is an implementation of the OSI model, that is, a set of standards is selected from the OSI model. MAP also requires defining some functions not available within OSI. This enables continuation of work without developing new standards. Another function of MAP, called manufacturing message specification (MMS), assists programming in a manufacturing environment. MMS was developed by an Electronics Industries Association (EIA) committee and it defines protocols for network services such as device status and control, program load, job queuing, and journal management. The functions of MMS affect application design and reduce the application programming required to install MAP systems.

14.5 COMPUTER-AIDED PROCESS PLANNING

Process planning defines the sequence of operations that a part has to undergo during manufacture.

When developed manually, the sequence of manufacturing operations is listed on a route sheet, which also identifies the machines to be used for the processes. Additional manufacturing information like cutting speed, feed, and depth of cut are also listed. The primary disadvantage of the manual process planning is inconsistency. For example, a family of different routes of manufacturing sequences might be specified for a part instead of a single route. This is mainly due to different planners specifying different routes for the same part. To avoid overlapping and confusion, one must use computers.

Computer-aided process planning (CAPP) devises a route sheet for any part. There are two types of computer-aided process planning: retrieval-type CAPP, and generative-type CAPP.

14.5.1 Retrieval-Type CAPP

In retrieval-type CAPP, standard process plans for each part family are stored within the computer and called up whenever required. If a new part comes in, then the existing database is searched for a similar process plan that can be modified. Hence, this type of process planning is also referred to as variant process planning.

The process followed during retrieval process planning is illustrated in Figure 14.4. To retrieve a part route sheet or process plan, the part code number is entered into the computer. The process planning program then searches the part family list-

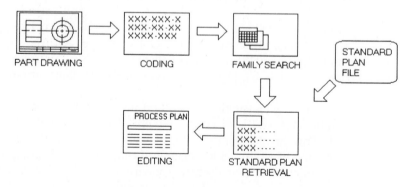

Figure 14.4 Variant process planning.

ing to determine if a part family exists. If the part family exists, then the machine sorting and operation sequences are retrieved from the computer and displayed. If no part family is found, then the standard operation sequence is displayed, which can be edited and modified to make it compatible with the new part.

14.5.2 Generative-Type CAPP

In generative process planning, a new process plan is created every time, using a set of algorithms based on general rules about manufacturing routes. The input to the system is in the form of a detailed description of the part to be manufactured, including its geometric description and material specifications.

In a generative planning system, process plans are created from the information available in a manufacturing database without human intervention. Technological and logistical decisions are made by the computer using a set of algorithms to achieve a viable manufacturing plan. However, knowledge of manufacturing must be captured and encoded into efficient software. Other planning functions such as machine selection, tool selection, and process optimization can also be incorporated into the program. Thus, the system can synthesize the design of a manufacturing process. However, present generative CAPP systems fall short of the ideal and are limited to small manufacturing processes. Human intervention is also often utilized during decision making. Hence, generative process planning is used for a less complete system. Systems with built-in decision logic are often called generative process planning systems.

Implementation of generative process planning requires the following:

1. The logic of process planning has to be identified and captured.
2. The part to be produced must be defined in a 3D model or GT code, that is, a computer-compatible format.
3. The logic of process planning and part description must be incorporated into a unified manufacturing database.

Some of the advantages of generative process planning are the ability to generate consistent process plans rapidly, the possibility of planning new components with relative ease, and the potential of interfacing with an automated manufacturing facility to provide detailed control information.

14.5.3 Popular Process Planning Systems

Most process planning systems are of the retrieval type, such as CAPP, MIPLAN, MITURN, MIAPP, ACUDATA/UNIVATION, CINTURN, COMCAPPV, etc. Some of the generative systems are CPPP, AUTAP, APPAS, GENPLAN, and CAR. Brief descriptions of the popular process planning systems follow.

CAM-I CAPP. The CAM-I automated process planning system (CAPP) is widely used. It was developed by McDonnell Douglas Automation Company under contract from CAM-I and was first released in 1976. CAPP is a database management system written in ANSI standard FORTRAN and it provides a structure for a database, retrieval logic, and interactive editing capability. The coding scheme for part classification and the output format are added by the user.

A graphical description of the CAM-I process planning system is shown in Figure 14.5. The system is operated via an interactive computer terminal. The system contains a standard process plan and a sequence of operation codes for each family in an operation plan file. Standard plans and operation plans are developed for each installation as they are a function of the machines, procedures, and expertise of individual companies. The parts are coded and classified into families outside the CAPP system using the group technology code of 36 alphanumeric characters. There are four major steps followed in the creation of a process plan:

1. The planned part is attributed to a particular group technology part family.
2. The header information, such as part numbers, materials, part name, and revision, which can identify a process plan, is input.
3. The routing (operation sequence) of the part is specified.
4. The text describing the work performed at each operation is created.

The plan is then stored and can be printed and edited as desired.

CAPP allows the user to use an existing group technology system in the process plan search, requiring minimum modification by the user during system implementation.

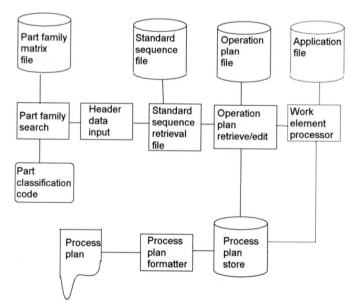

Figure 14.5 CAM-I process plan (courtesy of CAM-I, Inc., Arlington, Texas).

MIPLAN and MultiCAPP.   MIPLAN and MultiCAPP were developed in conjunction with the Organization for Industrial Research, Inc. Both are variant systems using the MICLASS coding system for part description. Process plans are retrieved based on part code, part number, family matrix, and code range. Part code input results in retrieval of similar parts and each process plan displayed can be subsequently edited by the user.

AUTAP.   AUTAP, one of the most complete planning systems, is capable of material selection, process selection, process sequencing, machine tool selection, tool selection, and part program generation.

AUTAP has its own part description language. It uses primitives similar to a constructive solid geometry language to construct a part.

The AUTAP system is illustrated in Figure 14.6, which shows the description of a rotational component. The component is divided into three entities starting from the left. The codes starting with "1" describe the first entity, consisting of a cylinder, a straight chamfer, and a fillet chamfer each assigned a unique description. Thus, any shape and information can be represented. Currently, AUTAP can plan rotational and sheet metal parts.

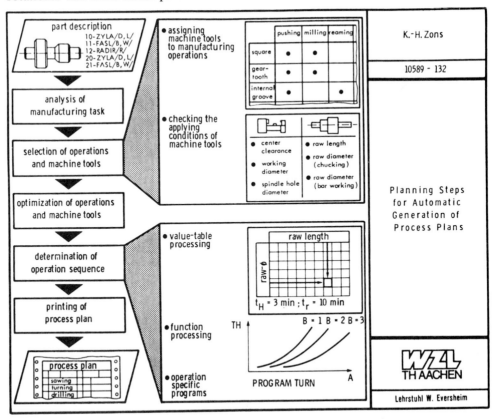

Figure 14.6 AUTAP systems (courtesy of Computer-Aided Manufacturing Laboratory, Technical University of Aachen, Germany).

APPAS and CAD/CAM.   APPAS (automated process planning and selection) is a generative system for detailed process selection. CAD/CAM interfaces with APPAS using a CAD "front end" approach and decision table logic for process selection. APPAS is unique in its surface description of a part. It describes the detailed information of each machined surface by a special code. A single machined surface is usually defined by a data string of 30 to 40 attributes and process selection is controlled by a built-in process tree. The system is capable of selecting multiple passes and processes for designated machined surfaces. The details of APPAS include selection of feed rate, cutting speed, length and diameter of the tool, number of teeth, or depth of cut for each tool pass. CAD/CAM provides an interactive graphics interface in which components can be modeled graphically and edited interactively.

CPPP.   CPPP (computerized production process planning) was developed by United Technologies Research Center partially under U.S. Army funding and was primarily developed for planning cylindrical parts. The system generates a summary of operations and detailed operation sheets required for production. CPPP utilizes a comprehensive component concept in which the composite component can be an imaginary component containing all features of components in one part family.

Components of an entire family can be planned by building a process model that contains the solution for every feature (Figure 14.7). COPPL is a special language used to describe a process model for CPPP. Development of a process model is necessary for every part family; hence, it is most suitable for applications having few part families, with each family member having some variation.

14.6 PLANNING AND CONTROL WITHIN CIM

Planning is the process of organizing material and component availability to optimize the use of productive capacity in a manufacturing organization.

14.6.1 Material Requirements Planning

Material requirements planning (MRP) is a planning method that handles ordering and scheduling of inventories such as raw materials, subassemblies, and component parts. It identifies the individual components and subassemblies that make up each end product and indicates the required quantities and when to order them. The detailed information is obtained from the master production schedule, which is prepared by the MRP process. The structure of the MRP system is shown in Figure 14.8.

The planning system is comprised of

1. the master production schedule
2. the bill of materials file
3. the inventory status file
4. MRP software

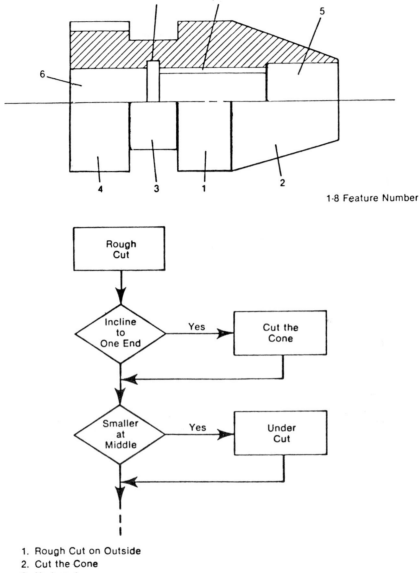

1-8 Feature Number

1. Rough Cut on Outside
2. Cut the Cone
3. Undercut
4. Cut External Thread
5. Drill Hole From LHS
6. Drill Hole From RHS
7. Recessing the Groove
8. Internal Threading
9. Part Off

Figure 14.7 Computer Production Process Planning (Tien-Chien Chang/Richard A. Wysk. *An introduction to Automated Process Planning Systems,* © 1985, p. 181. Reprinted by permission of Prentice Hall, Englewood Cliffs, New Jersey.

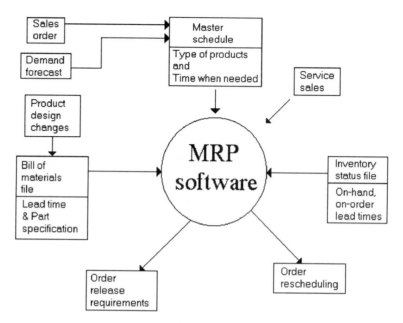

Figure 14.8 MRP system.

The master production schedule is based on an accurate forecast of demand for the firm's products along with the estimate of the firm's production capacity. It indicates the final products to be produced, their number, and the time they are to be ready for customer delivery.

Product demand influencing the master production schedule is of three types: actual customer orders, forecasted demand from past orders, or demand of individual components from the service departments.

The bill of materials file specifies the composition of a finished product and outlines its structure in terms of component parts and subassemblies. This information is required to manufacture the end products listed in the master production schedule.

The inventory status file provides data on how much inventory is in stock. It contains a record of the actual inventory level, lead time, ordered inventory, and back-order inventory.

The master production schedule, bill of materials file, and inventory status file are used as inputs for the material requirements planning package. The software processes the information in these files to calculate the net requirements for each period of the planning cycle.

After computing the requirements for each new material and component, MRP plans the time when work must commence for each product. It does this by considering the ordering lead time and the manufacturing lead time for the required product. Ordering lead time is the time required from the initiation of the purchase order to the actual receipt of the item from the supplier. Manufacturing lead time is the time required to manufacture a component part. It includes processing time, idle time, and material handling time.

Some of the benefits of MRP are

1. low inventory levels
2. avoiding possible delays
3. expediting and deexpediting orders
4. use as a long-term planning tool

14.6.2 Manufacturing Resource Planning

Manufacturing resource planning (MRP II) is a progressive evolution of material requirements planning. Priority planning is now incorporated into MRP to determine not only what part is required, but also when it is needed. Thus, MRP can deal with urgent jobs by increasing their priority and expediting them ahead of schedule.

MRP II combines material requirements planning with production planning and control function and the financial system of the company.

MRP II covers all aspects of the company business, which include sales, production, engineering, inventories, and accounting. It uses financial data as a common medium for the operations of each independent department. Through the common medium, various departments can work together and company management can obtain necessary information. MRP II can be used also as a simulator to consider alternative production plans and management decisions, enabling the company to examine probable outcomes.

14.7 CAPACITY PLANNING

The process of evaluating the feasibility of a manufacturing plan considering production constraints such as labor and equipment is known as capacity planning. The planned production orders from MRP are tentative manufacturing plans because capacity might not exist to make all of the desired products. Capacity planning entails a detailed evaluation of the feasibility of the MRP results. The basic information required for capacity planning are

1. planned orders from MRP
2. in-process orders
3. routing sheet
4. facilities information
5. labor availability
6. subroutine potential

The process of evaluating capacity requirements of a tentative manufacturing plan begins with the due dates of each order. Each order is back scheduled from the due date to determine when a particular work center is utilized using bills of material, routings, and lead times. The capacity requirements are available after carrying out the same procedure for all orders. These requirements are constantly compared with available infrastructure, which can change due to breakdown of machines or "overloaded" conditions. Certain problems can be avoided by shifting sequence of orders, expediting, subcontracting, and reusing manufacturing plans.

14.8 DATABASE MANAGEMENT SYSTEMS

A database is a collection of interrelated data, stored so as to be efficiently available for creation, update, and deletion by as many remote and local users as the applications require. There are two main types of databases: hierarchical and relational.

14.8.1 Hierarchical Databases

In a hierarchical structure, data records are related in a treelike manner. Starting at the root of the tree, each record has a one-to-many relationship to its branches. A parent record can have several child records, but a child record can have only one parent record (as seen in Figure 14.9).

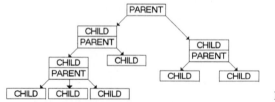

Figure 14.9 Hierarchial records.

Hierarchical database systems, or preferred-path database management systems, are most suited to the well-structured, static data of business such as item data, orders, costs, etc.

14.8.2 Relational Databases

Data are stored as a collection of tables composed of rows and columns. Rows and columns in the table need not be in any special order, making it easy to add data. Data relationships are established by queries and data are located through row-by-row searches, making relational databases more flexible. They are better suited in less structured situations in which many unanticipated queries might be made. A typical relational database is shown in Figure 14.10.

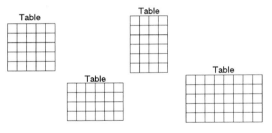

Figure 14.10   Relational database.

14.8.3 Database Management

Database management determines how data are defined, stored, and related, and who has access to that data. Database management is critical in today's environment because there are many different databases, formats, and storage and access techniques. Database management defines and recovers the location of data created and used by the enterprise's business functions that are not accessible by current standards. It also means enabling users to get the data they have used without knowing where it is located.

The accuracy of data is the user's responsibility because the computer system cannot rigorously check the data provided. Hence, continual measures should be taken to assure the data's integrity. Security has to be built into the database software, the operating system, and the communication software. Different levels of security are needed, distinguishing between access to data, update of data, creation of new records, and deletion of data. Management of databases can be assisted by use of a "data dictionary." The dictionary contains information about data fields and records, such as which programs access and update items and which departments have responsibility for the accuracy of the data.

14.9 CIM IMPLEMENTATION

For CIM to be successfully implemented, the parts to be manufactured must have certain common characteristics, allowing them to be grouped into part families. Aggregate production suitable for CIM applications ranges from 1,000 to 100,000 parts yearly, but specific processes and process times determine the profitability of a CIM system. CIM is the only technology that can be used in the intermediate volume range. Compared to stand-alone NC machine tools, robots, and work cells, a CIM system has many interconnected components, consisting of a computerized control system with its carts, pallets, shuttles, robots, and computerized control and production planning systems.

To ensure long-term benefits of CIM companywide, planning and implementation of CIM is necessary. The first step in obtaining a coordinated CIM effort is to set up long-term business goals. While moving down the corporate ladder, these goals have to be embodied into the goals and objectives of the functional areas. It is also necessary to understand and document the operation of the business. Documentation of business operations and information flows are carried out by business process modeling and data modeling, which show how the decisions, information, and products generated in one function impact other functional areas. Additional models help document the strategic direction of process operations and information flows.

For CIM to be implemented, it is necessary to develop a plan for transforming present operations to meet the business objectives. To establish a transition plan to move from the present environment to the planned one, it is necessary to identify changes, priorities, and dependencies of the changes between the two model versions and organize these changes into an implementation subset.

Changes in process operations should be distributed over several implementations. The application and data plan establishes steps for data integration and new application development. An organization plan defines gradual shifts in responsibilities of the people in the organization, and a resource plan organizes the changes in utilization of manufacturing and testing equipment, utilities, support, and information systems. The information system plan stages the implementation of processors, networks, databases, and input/output access to users and plant equipment.

Staff should be provided with ample information, education, and training to motivate them for CIM. Formal courses are available; however, most of them do not deal with the complex problems of implementing and integrating CIM technologies into the business. Training is required to upgrade the skills of the people directly involved.

To ensure that CIM is not viewed as a threat, additional incentives should be provided to compensate for the changes and it should be ensured that career paths will be readjusted. CIM effects the management of the company and, in particular, there is increased interaction of the technical function, the immediate availability of information provided by the computer.

Any kind of automation brings up the question of loss of jobs and has a negative impact on people. CIM typically creates new jobs that tend to be highly skilled, jobs like planning staff, computer hardware and software specialists, training specialists, and preventative maintenance. This results in new hirings, redeploying staff, and also a lot of training and education. It is essential that change in jobs brings about job enrichment instead of the reverse. A number of lower-skilled jobs, however, like low-level expediters, warehouse attendants, material handlers, and machine operators are lost.

14.10 COSTS ASSOCIATED WITH CIM IMPLEMENTATION

Initial costs involved in CIM implementation include expenditures in application engineering, equipment procurement, site preparation, actual installation, and operation costs. The cost of CIM includes machine tools, robots, material handling systems, computer hardware and software, interface accessories, terminals, spare parts, and special tools. Included in this cost are hazard barriers, intrusion detection devices, and other safety equipment associated with the installation. Tooling costs for special-purpose devices such as end effectors for robots, adaptor plates, part feeders, orienters, special power tools, fixtures, and positioning devices are considered during CIM implementation.

Modifications of machinery and facilities that are required to accommodate a CIM installation are considered rearrangement expenses. These include relocation of machines, auxiliary equipment, rerouting of conveyors, chip handling systems, and changes to operator interface panels. Provision of utilities such as compressed air, electrical power, and cooling water that were not previously required is also in this area.

Training programs for CIM system operators and personnel responsible for system maintenance, which are provided in advance of installation, are considered an initial cost. In addition, the cost of retraining employees displaced by the CIM system to qualify them for job reassignment and the cost of transferring displaced personnel to other jobs are also included. Cost of product changes is also chargeable to initial costs.

After installation of the CIM system, there is an additional cost incurred during programming startup and debugging. Interferences with production, scrapping of parts, overtime to make up for production losses, damaged or scrapped parts, and repairs to equipment damaged by program errors are other unforeseen expenses experienced with the launching of the system.

REFERENCES

14.1   Belby, W., and Collier, P., *New Directions Through CAD/CAM*, Society of Manufacturing Engineers, Dearborn, Mich., 1986.

14.2   Chang, T. C., and Wysk, R. A., *An Introduction to Automated Process Planning Systems*, Prentice Hall, Englewood Cliffs, NJ, 1985.

14.3   Compton, W. D., *Design and Analysis of Integrated Manufacturing Systems*, National Academy of Engineering, Washington, D. C., 1988.

14.4   Crowley, O. R., Let's Discuss CAD/CAM Integration, *Modern Machine Shop*, December 1984.

14.5   Ham, I., Hitomi, K., and Yoshida, T., *Group Technology*, Kluwer-Nijhoff Publishing, Boston, 1985.

14.6   Harrington, J., Jr., Computer Integrated Manufacturing, Robert E. Krieger Publishing, New York, 1979.

14.7   Hirsch, B., and Artis-Dato, M., *ESPRIT CIM, Design, Engineering, Management and Control of Production Systems*, North-Holland, Amsterdam, 1987.

14.8   Hunt, V. D., *Computer Integrated Manufacturing Handbook*, Chapman and Hall, New York, 1989.

14.9   IBM Corp., *Computer Integrated Manufacturing*, New York, 1989.

14.10 Lenz, J. E., *Flexible Manufacturing: Benefits for the Low-Inventory Factory*, Marcel Dekker, New York, 1988.

14.11 Mitchell, F. H., Jr., *CIM Systems: An Introduction to Computer-Integrated Manufacturing*, Prentice Hall, Englewood Cliffs, NJ, 1991.

14.12 Rembold, U., and Dillman, R., eds., *Computer-Aided Design and Manufacturing: Methods and Tools*, Springer-Verlag, New York, 1986.

14.13 Thompson, V., and Graffe, U., *CIM—A Manufacturing Paradigm*, National Research Council Report DM-C06, 1987.

14.14 Weatherall, A., *Computer Integrated Manufacturing from Fundamentals to Implementations*, Butterworth, London, 1988.

14.15 Zgorzelski, M., *Computer Integrated Manufacturing: Trends, Problems, Strategies*, Society of Automotive Engineers, Warrendale, PA, 1986.

chapter 15

Implementation of a CAD/CAM System

15.1 INTRODUCTION

The ever-increasing demand for quality products and lower prices has manufacturers turning to the new technology offered by computer-aided design and computer-aided manufacturing. The successful implementation of CAD/CAM relies on the basic principle of planning. Those manufacturers who have done their homework have seen a dramatic increase in quality products made and, in turn, have built a smooth-running operation to keep a competitive edge in the market. On the other hand, there have been manufacturers who rushed into integrating CAD/CAM technology before fully understanding their needs and who suffered serious setbacks, thus losing their competitive edge. It is essential, therefore, that "planning" be a major step before implementing CAD/CAM.

15.2 MISCONCEPTIONS ABOUT CAD/CAM

The following are some misconceptions about CAD/CAM:

1. It is an overnight success.
2. It provides magical solutions.
3. It allows a quick fix to existing problems.
4. It allows for the easy transfer of data between systems.
5. It dissolves bureaucracy and eliminates paperwork.
6. It has user-friendly software.

Salespeople tend to present CAD/CAM as the key to overnight success. This is not the case. When hidden costs surface and problems arise, management realizes that the cost of maintaining and operating a CAD/CAM system has not been fully understood. CAD/CAM technology cannot solve personnel and equipment problems nor can it make problems disappear. On the contrary, computer technology, if not used properly, can magnify problems and even produce faulty designs faster than humans. Users have experienced difficulty integrating different hardware components. In many cases, data does not transfer easily and additional work is needed. The most challenging problem of implementing CAD/CAM technology is to convince those managers that their company has not been making profits for years without so-called "fancy computers." The dissolution of paperwork threatens the managers' authority and territorial status. To think that information can be shared by all departments through a database brings fear to workers as well as managers, and fosters opposition to the full integration of CAD/CAM into the company (Figure 15.1).

Rules-Based Engineering

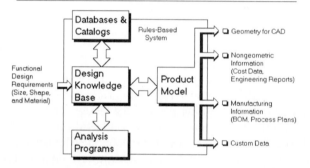

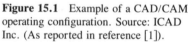

Figure 15.1 Example of a CAD/CAM operating configuration. Source: ICAD Inc. (As reported in reference [1]).

15.3 LOOKING FOR A SYSTEM

When purchasing a CAD/CAM system, the following must be considered:

1. Reason for purchase
2. Expectations from the system
3. Adjustments before and after implemention
4. Goals

It is important when planning the purchase of a CAD/CAM system that the manufacturer determine some specific reasons for the purchase. The ultimate goal of a CAD/CAM system is to provide high-quality products at low cost and that means reducing lead time in production. This is the most compelling reason for a manufacturer to implement a CAD/CAM system. For instance, if the purpose of purchasing a computer system is to improve drafting capabilities so faster layouts are produced, it is important to point out that in most cases drafting only represents 1% of the total operating cost. This alone does not economically justify a CAD/CAM system.

15.4 PRACTICAL BENEFITS

Reducing Errors in Design.   In addition to the accuracy provided by a CAD/CAM system, errors in design can be minimized if data are exchanged and transmitted via the computer network rather than the usual approach of copying, tapes, creating from scratch, etc.

Enhancing Design Using Integrated Analysis.   This function is yet to be fully utilized by all manufacturers and should be part of planning.

Graphic Simulation.   The manufacturing process can be simulated graphically to minimize errors and reduce operating costs. Graphics play a major role in checking the NC part programming, checking clearances between different parts by simply merging them on the screen, helping select product colors, and most of all in allowing the user to instantly modify the existing design.

Technological Necessity.   To stay competitive, manufacturers need to produce quality products at a competitive price. Foreign countries are becoming more and more aggressive and are determined to do what it takes to stay active in a shrinking world market. Japan has combined two very important ingredients essential to economic success: computer technology and a dedicated, skilled labor force. Japan has stayed ahead by constantly improving the quality of its products and keeping its prices competitive. In addition, it has developed a system to service and maintain its products. South American and Asian countries are providing the cheapest labor imaginable. In doing so, they have attracted a large number of businesses. Western Europe is entering a new phase by developing a European market whose main goal is to compete against Japan and the United States. To survive this harsh competition, manufacturers are planning ahead and CAD/CAM technology is becoming more of a necessity than an option.
    In addition to the practical benefits a CAD/CAM system offers, its successful performance yields.

1. shorter product cycle
2. integration of engineering functions such as design, analysis, and manufacturing
3. increased design productivity
4. shorter lead times
5. efficient planning and quality control
6. better control of manufacturing processes

7. reduced manufacturing costs

8. competitive pricing of products

15.5 COSTS

There are basically two kinds of systems to select when deciding to purchase a CAD/CAM system: turn-key systems and standard systems.

Turn-key Systems. These systems are usually designed by certain vendors so that the hardware, software, and operating system are integrated to function in the most efficient way. This usually creates a proprietary problem in which the user is committed to one vendor for better or for worse. Turn-key systems are not standard and therefore do not interface with other hardware nor do they support software other than theirs.

Standard Systems. These systems are based on popular operating systems such as DOS, UNIX, or VMS, therefore allowing the use of a multitude of software. The users have the choice of selecting the appropriate hardware and software.

The cost of a CAD/CAM system is divided into three categories: hardware, software, and training.

Figures 15.2 and 15.3 illustrate the purchasing cost and the annual cost for stand-alone PC, mini-, and mainframe systems.

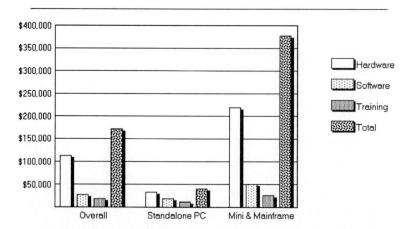

Figure 15.2 Purchasing cost of CAD/CAM system Source: PMSJ CADD Application and User Survey (As reported in reference [1]).

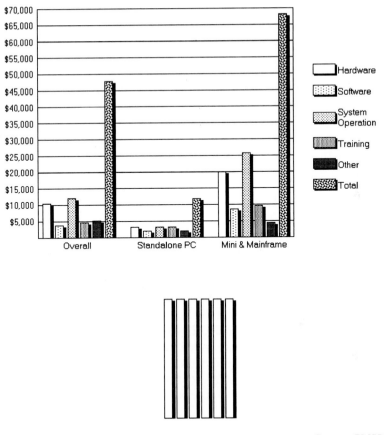

Figure 15.3 Annual operating costs of a CAD/CAM system. Source: PMSJ CADD Application and User Survey (As reported in reference [1]).

15.6 SELECTING A VENDOR

The first step in implementing a CAD/CAM system requires the formation of a committee. The committee's task is as follows:

1. Gather specific information on what the CAD/CAM system is to accomplish. This helps vendors with their proposals. The information should include:
   - Number of design engineers
   - Number of draftspersons
   - Number of NC programmers
   - Number of shifts each department works
   - Current overtime in design and drafting

- Percent of time spent generating new drawings
- Percent of the time revising drawings
- Types of NC equipment at present
- CAD/CAM systems already in use
- Competititor's use of CAD/CAM systems
- Other useful information

2. **Request proposals from vendors.** This is a normal procedure in which vendors propose the most convenient system configuration for your needs, based on the information you have gathered and provided, along with an estimate of costs.

15.7 TESTING THE SYSTEM

It is becoming standard practice to evaluate equipment by having the vendor run some of your applications. This demonstration enables you to determine the limitations, speed, labor required, and any important interfaces needed. The demonstration must be very close if not identical to the one you intend to purchase. You need to keep in mind that the people giving the demonstration are usually highly skilled technicians and do not reflect the skills of your workers.

When buying a CAD/CAM system, training is essential right from the start. Many vendors provide short courses, ranging from an introduction, system operation, and drafting to advanced courses in finite elements and manufacturing. Buyers must be aware of the importance of training and decide whether on- or off-site training is needed. This enhances company productivity and maintains long-term goals.

15.8 THE CAD/CAM MARKET

The CAD/CAM market has long been dominated by the turn-key suppliers. Today's market is evolving around a complicated network of vendors serving an ever-increasing market of users. With the advances of microprocessor technology, low-cost "open" systems are becoming more and more popular. There are three types of CAD/CAM vendors specializing in selling hardware, software, and hardware/software.

New technological advancements in hardware have opened the door to new users. What used to be a problem that could only be solved on a mainframe has migrated to the PC and workstation. The new class of hardware and its lower prices attract a large number of new users (Figure 15.4). There is an awareness by many users about CAD/CAM technology and its limitations. The limitations have made users very selective and many turn to a custom-designed CAD/CAM system.

The future market will be greatly influenced by the power of the computer. CAD/CAM systems will be established as part of engineering departments, and thereby those departments will play a much larger function in the company.

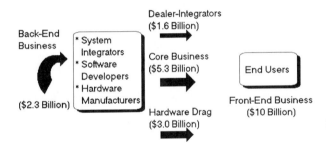

Figure 15.4 The CAD/CAM Market
Source: Daratech, Inc., Cambridge, MA.

The PC will become a vital computing power, redefining the use of mainframes and other workstations (Figure 15.5). Vector processing and parallel processing will play a major role in the next generation of CAD/CAM systems designed for real-time simulation and animation purposes.

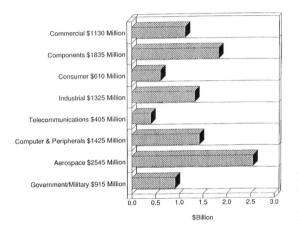

Figure 15.5 U.S. market for Computer Graphics workstations, by end users, 1990. Source: Frost and Sullivan, Inc. Report #A2356.

REFERENCES

15.1 Berliner, C., and Brimson, J., *Cost Management for Today's Advanced Manufacturing: The CAM-I Conceptual Design,* Harvard Business School Press, Boston, 1988.

15.2 CADD Application and User Study, *Professional Services Management,* Practice Management Associates, Newton, Ma., 1989.

15.3 *CAD/CAM CAE: Survey Review and Buyer's Guide,* Datatech, Cambridge, Ma.

15.4 *The Competitive Benefits of 3D Computing,* SGI, Calif., 1989.

15.5 *Cost Accounting for Factory Automation,* National Association of Accountants, NJ, 1987.

15.6   Krouse, J., Mills, R., Beckert, B., and Potter, C., CAD/CAM Planning Guide '89, *Industry Week,* July 17, 1989, pp. 1–63.

15.7   *The MCAD Evaluator,* Dataquest, San Jose, Ca., 1989.

15.8   Medland, A. J., and Burnett, P., *CAD/CAM in Practice,* John Wiley, New York, 1986.

15.9   Taraman, K., *CAD/CAM Meeting Today's Productivity Challenge,* Prentice Hall, Englewood Cliffs, NJ, 1982.

15.10 The U.S. Market for Computer Graphics Workstations, Frost and Sullivan, Inc., (A2356), New York, 1990.

Glossary

Absolute coordinates. The values of coordinates x, y, and z with respect to the origin of the coordinate system.

AC. Adaptive control: a system that controls the feed rate of an NC machine. Feedback sensors used by the machine-control unit optimize the feed and speed of the NC machine.

ALGOL. ALGorithmic Orientated Language.

Algorithm. (a) Description or outline of an exact procedure or computation routine. (b) A procedure based on results obtained by executing a series of logical step-by-step instructions.

Alphanumeric keyboard. A typewriter keyboard by which the user inputs data into a system.

ALU. Arithmetic and logic unit: the unit of the computing system that performs arithmetic operations.

APT. Automated programming tool.

APT processor. The function of the computer that can translate the part program into a tape image.

Argument. An independent variable.

ASCII. American Standard Code for Information Exchange.

Attribute. Any characteristic of a display item such as color, line style, intensity level, or detectability.

Automation.   Implementation of a process or routine by automatic means.

Axis.   A general direction of relative location or motion.

Batch.   A term for a large set of data stored by cards.

Batch processing.   (a) A method by which items to be processed are sorted into groups before processing. (b) A method that ensures that a set of computer programs is executed before the next program is started.

BAUD.   Signaling bits per second; 1 baud = 1 bits/s. It is an expression of serial data transmission bit rate.

Binary.   A numerical notation using base-2 numbers.

Binary code.   A code that uses only two distinct characters, usually, 0 and 1.

Bit.   A binary digit. It is a basic element used by digital computers to electronically use binary 0 and 1.

BPI.   Bits per inch.

B-spline.   Basic spline: it is defined by a polygon. The curve approximates the polygon.

Buffer.   A storage area that receives and subsequently releases transient data.

Byte.   A term that indicates a measurable segment of consecutive binary digits.

CAD.   Computer-aided design.

CAD/CAM.   Computer-aided design and computer-aided manufacturing.

CADE.   Computer-aided design and engineering.

CADM.   Computer-aided design and manufacturing.

CADT.   Computer-aided design and technology.

CAM.   Computer-aided manufacturing.

Card punch.   A device that stores information on cards to represent special characters, letters, and numbers.

Card recorder.   A device that reads and translates the holes in punched cards into machine codes.

Cartesian coordinate system.   A coordinate system whose axes or dimensions are three intersecting perpendicular straight lines where the origin is at the intersection.

Cathode-ray tube.   An electron tube that projects electron beams onto a phosphor-coated display screen, producing luminous spots.

Character.   A numeral, letter, or other linguistic, mathematical, or logic symbol.

Chip. A small piece of semiconductor material on which electronic components are formed.

CLDATA. Centerline data: geometric coordinates for offsetting a part outline.

Clearance. The minimum distance by which the tool avoids the part on a noncutting file.

CNC. Computer numerical control.

Code. A system of organized information that is understood and executed by a computer, control system, etc.

Compiler. A computer program that operates on symbolic input data to produce machine instructions.

Coordinates. An ordered set of data values (absolute or relative) that specifies a location in space.

CPU. Central processing unit: the basic memory and logic of a computer.

CRT. Cathode-ray tube.

Cutter path. A defined combination of vectors and retract trajectories for controlled movements of the cutting tool.

Cylindrical coordinate system. A coordinate system consisting of two linear dimensions and one angular dimension.

Data. A representation of facts, concepts, or instructions.

Data tablet. A flat surfaced graphic input device used with a stylus or puck.

Default. Assumed values of a data set when the characteristics are not specified.

Depth. Depth of cut: this is an option that allows the user to define the height of material to be removed.

Device driver. Software that converts device-independent graphic commands into device-specific display.

Digital. Information and values expressed in discrete terms.

Digitizer. A data tablet that generates coordinate data from visual data by use of a puck or stylus.

Dimensioning. Measuring distances on CAD/CAM systems.

Disk. A random-access storage device used by computers to store data.

Display. A visual representation of data.

DNC. Direct numerical control.

Dot matrix. A two-dimensional array of dots in a defined pattern.

Dragging. A technique of moving display items by interactively translating them along a path defined by a graphic input device.

DVST. Direct view storage tube.

Edit. To change the form or format of data.

Element. Any basic geometric figure that can be mathematically defined in space.

Endpoint. Either of the points that mark the ends of a line, curve, etc.

EOB. End of block.

EOF. End of file.

Family. A type of machine tool. All machine tools of the same type are said to be in the same family.

Feed rate. Rate of movement of a tool.

FEM. Finite-element model: a mathematical model of a continuous object that divides the object into an array of discrete elements for the purpose of simulated analysis.

File. A set of related blocks of data treated as a unit.

Fillet. A convex curve or surface that connects two adjacent curves or surfaces.

Fixed sequential format. An NC tape format in which each word in the format is identified by its position. Each word must be repeated despite being repeated from a previous block.

Flatbed plotter. A plotter that draws a display on a flat display plotter where the plotting head moves (draws).

Function key. A key or switch that is given a specific function to be executed when pressed.

Function keyboard. An input device that consists of a number of function keys for an interactive display console.

Geometric model. A graphical, logical, or mathematical representation of shape and spatially related elements.

Geometric modeling. A computer system that integrates the application of geometric modeling in a unified process.

Graphic input device. Any hardware that provides graphic input by the user.

Graphics. The visual presentation of data by image generation and manipulation.

Group technology. A concept based on standardization of tooling, part grouping, and the design of universal tools to accommodate as broad a spectrum of parts as possible.

Hard copy. A copy of a display on a permanent medium.

Hardware. The physical components of a computer system.

Hexadecimal. A numbering system using base 16.

High-level language. A programming language that resembles English-like algorithms such that the user can better program the computer. The HLL is compiled and translated to machine code.

Host computer. Primary or mainframe computer.

Image. A view of an object.

Incremental plotter. A plotter that produces a display, moving the plotting head in discrete steps and positioned to specific display locations.

Incremental vector. A vector defined by a relative component and an absolute component.

Input. The transfer of information using a medium to a computer.

Interactive graphics. A method that allows users to dynamically modify the display.

Interactive mode. A method of operation that allows on-line man–machine communication.

Interface. A medium that two or more separate elements can join.

I/O. Input/output: general terms used for equipment with the ability to communicate with a computer.

Joystick. A graphic input device composed of a movable stick to control the position of a cursor.

Keyboard. A graphic input device that allows the user to enter key-driven values such as letters, numbers, or other values.

Keypunch. A keyboard-controlled device used in programming that allows users to program data via punching holes in a card.

Knot points. The defining points of a spline.

Language. A defined group of symbols for interpretation and application.

Layer. Partition of a part.

Layout. A completed CAD/CAM display drawn to scale.

Library. A collection of files accessible to users.

Light pen. A graphic input device that defines position by detecting light generation on a CRT within a limited area.

Linear interpolation. A method of contouring curved shapes by a series of straight-line segments.

Line segments. A portion of a line bounded by two endpoints.

Line type. Attributes of a line that define whether it is solid, dashed, dotted, etc.

Logoff. A required sequence of commands to end a session.

Logon. A required sequence of commands to begin a session.

Machining. The cutting away of the surface of a workpiece by power-driven machinery.

Magnetic disk. A flat circular plate with a magnetic surface on which data can be stored by selective magnetization.

Magnetic tape. Tape with a magnetic surface on which data can be stored by selective magnetization.

Manufacturing cell. National Bureau of Standards Hierarchical Control System (Level 1 and 2) composed of a robot, tools, and automatic riveter.

Mapping function. A method that converts an image defined in one coordinate system to another.

MCU. Machine-control unit: a control unit that translates tape image instructions into a format recognizable to a machine tool.

Menu. A list of options that displays the functions available to the user at that particular point in operation.

Mirror. In two dimensions, the effect produced by rotating the object 180° about an axis in space.

Model. The representation of an object in world coordinates.

Modem. Modulator/demodulator: an I/O device that converts digital signals to/from telephone line transmission.

Mouse. A hand-held graphic input device that controls the position of the cursor by movement.

NC. Numerical control: automatically controlled machine tool.

Node. The intersection of two or more interconnections.

Object. An item on display that is created with respect to world coordinates.

Octal. A number system using base 8.

Offset. The difference between the established length and the actual length of the tool.

Optimize.   The process of obtaining the most efficient balance of options and hardware available.

Origin.   Reference point where all coordinates are zero.

Output.   Processed information yielded from a computer.

Parameter.   A set of characteristics that have corresponding defined values.

Part program.   A source code to generate an NC object program to control an NC machine.

Peripheral.   Auxiliary equipment used for I/O from a computer.

Pixel.   Smallest displayable picture element in a raster scan display.

Point to point.   Also known as positioning or contouring, it is a method of controlling the movement of the tool. The machining is independent to the placement of the tool in the workpiece.

Polar coordinates.   A coordinate system defined by the length of a radius vector and the angle this vector makes with a reference line.

Postprocessor.   A computer program that converts a generalized output into an acceptable format for an application program or hardware.

Precision.   A defined degree of discrimination in which values are expressed.

Program.   A plan for solving a problem.

Quadrant.   A quarter of the Cartesian coordinate system.

RAM.   Random-access memory: a read–write memory that can access any information stored in this memory in about the same time.

Rapid.   A setting used to define the positioning rate for noncutting motion.

Raster scan.   A method for video display using the process of line-by-line sweep on the display surface.

Read.   To receive information and/or data from a source.

Rectangular coordinates.   A coordinate system that consists of two or more perpendicular axes.

Refresh.   The process of repetition of a drawing on the display screen.

Resolution.   The number of raster units or plotter stop size.

Robot.   A programmable mechanical device that automatically performs a task of manipulation or locomotion.

ROM.   Read-only memory: a memory source that contains data or information that cannot be altered.

Scale. Transformation of an object to a desired size or shape by modifying coordinates.

Servomechanism. An amplifier. It can change a low-energy source signal into one of higher energy.

Slope. In the x–y plane, it is the ratio of the change in y over the change in x between two points on a line.

Soft copy. An electronic output display in a video format.

Software. Any medium of storage of programs, data, etc. associated with computers.

Solid modeling. A method of modeling that incorporates the solid characteristics into the database.

Source code. A computer program written using a high-level language.

Spline. A smooth curve shaped by a series of consecutive given points.

Step response. The time response of a tool or machine as a result of an instant change in input.

Stopping motor. A bidirectional permanent magnet motor that turns in measured steps.

Storage tube. A CRT with the ability to retain information displayed on its screen for an extended amount of time.

Subroutine. A sequenced series of instructions, information, and/or data in a program that can be repeatedly executed by other programs.

Tablet. A flat-surfaced graphic input used in conjunction with a stylus used for two-dimensional input.

Tab sequential format. A tape format that substitutes a tab code for a given program work when the character is identical to the preceding work.

Terminal. An I/O device, composed of a display, keyboard, and other hardware, that transmits and receives information with a mainframe computer.

Tool axis. An axis defined by a vector from the tool end and pointing into the tool.

Tool path. The defined path the cutting tool travels during machining.

Track ball. A graphic input device that uses a ball to control the position of the cursor.

Transformation function. A function that employs rotation, scaling, translation, or projection to modify a display.

Transformation matrix. A matrix that when multiplied with an existing coordinate matrix yields the desired transformation function.

Translate. To reposition a display item into another location.

Turn-key system. A computer system complete with hardware and software that can be used upon delivery by the supplier.

User file. A file that contains all necessary information for a job used in conjunction with an application software program.

Vector. A directed line segment.

Vertex. A topological entity formed by the intersection of edges and faces.

View plane. A projection plane to display a 3D view on a 2D surface.

View point. The point of reference of a field of view.

WCS. Work coordinate system: a coordinate system for use in construction, verification, etc.

Wireframe model. A data model that represents the outline of a 3D object by a series of line segments.

Word. A byte in a computer.

Word length. The measure of the number of characters that make up a word.

appendix A

Matrices

A.1 DEFINITION

A matrix consists of a set of numbers or elements arranged in rows and columns as in double-entry tabular form. A typical matrix is

$$\mathbf{A} = \begin{bmatrix} a_{11} & a_{12} & \cdots & a_{1n} \\ a_{21} & a_{22} & \cdots & a_{2n} \\ \cdot & \cdot & \cdot & \cdot \\ \cdot & \cdot & \cdot & \cdot \\ \cdot & \cdot & \cdot & \cdot \\ a_{m1} & a_{m2} & \cdots & a_{mn} \end{bmatrix} \tag{A.1}$$

where m indicates the number of rows, and n the number of columns.

A.2 NOTATION AND PRINCIPAL TYPES OF MATRICES

A.2.1 Order of a Matrix

A matrix having m number of rows and n number of columns is said to be of the order m by n, conveniently written as $m \times n$. However, $m \times n$ can also be called the dimension or size of a matrix. For example,

$$\mathbf{A} = \begin{bmatrix} 3 & 2 & 4 & 5 \\ 5 & 1 & 2 & -7 \\ 6 & 4 & -1 & -8 \end{bmatrix} \tag{A.2}$$

Matrix **A** is said to be of the order 3×4, where $m = 3$ indicates the number of rows, and $n = 4$ the number of columns.

A.2.2 Row Matrix

In an $m \times n$ matrix, if $m = 1$, it is called a row matrix. For example,

$$\mathbf{B} = \begin{bmatrix} 1 & 2 & 3 \end{bmatrix} \tag{A.3}$$

Matrix **B** is a row matrix.

A.2.3 Column Matrix

In an $m \times n$ matrix, if $n = 1$, it is called a column matrix. For example,

$$\mathbf{C} = \begin{bmatrix} 4 \\ -5 \\ 7 \end{bmatrix} \tag{A.4}$$

Matrix **C** is a column matrix.

A.2.4 Rectangular and Square Matrices

In an $m \times n$ matrix, if the number of rows is not equal to the number of columns, that is, $m \neq n$, then it is a rectangular matrix. On the other hand, if the number of rows is equal to the number of columns, that is, $m = n$, it is a square matrix. For example,

$$\mathbf{D} = \begin{bmatrix} 4 & 3 & 5 & 6 \\ -9 & 6 & -8 & 4 \\ 4 & -1 & 0 & -5 \end{bmatrix} \quad \text{and} \quad \mathbf{E} = \begin{bmatrix} 4 & -3 & -1 \\ -2 & 0 & 6 \\ 0 & 4 & 4 \end{bmatrix} \tag{A.5}$$

Matrix **D** is a rectangular matrix and matrix **E** is a square matrix.

A.2.5 Identity Matrix

The unity or identity matrix is a square matrix in which the diagonal elements are ones and all other elements are zeros. For example,

$$\mathbf{I} = \begin{bmatrix} 1 & 0 & 0 \\ 0 & 1 & 0 \\ 0 & 0 & 1 \end{bmatrix} \tag{A.6}$$

Matrix **I** is an identity matrix.

A.2.6 Null Matrix

The null or zero matrix is a matrix in which all the elements are zeros. The dimension of the null matrix is defined according to the dimension of the adjacent matrices. The notation for the null matrix is $\mathbf{G} = \mathbf{0}$ or $\mathbf{G} = 0$.

A.2.7 Transpose of a Matrix

Let $\mathbf{A}$ be a matrix of the order $m \times n$. When the rows and columns are interchanged, the resultant matrix is called the transpose matrix of $\mathbf{A}$. The transpose matrix of $\mathbf{A}$ is denoted by $\mathbf{A}^T$. For example,

$$\mathbf{A} = \begin{bmatrix} 1 & 2 & 3 \\ 4 & 5 & 6 \\ 7 & 8 & 9 \end{bmatrix} \quad \text{and} \quad \mathbf{A}^T = \begin{bmatrix} 1 & 4 & 7 \\ 2 & 5 & 8 \\ 3 & 6 & 9 \end{bmatrix} \tag{A.7}$$

A.2.8 Inverse of a Matrix

The inverse of the matrix $\mathbf{A}$ is written as $\mathbf{A}^{-1}$, satisfying the following relationship:

$$\mathbf{A}\mathbf{A}^{-1} = \mathbf{A}^{-1}\mathbf{A} = \mathbf{I} \tag{A.8}$$

This relationship means that the product of $\mathbf{A}$ by its inverse yields the identity matrix $\mathbf{I}$.

A.2.9 Orthogonal Matrix

The matrix is said to be orthogonal when its transpose is equal to its inverse. A matrix $\mathbf{A}$ is said to be orthogonal if the following relationship is satisfied:

$$\mathbf{A}\mathbf{A}^{-1} = \mathbf{A}\mathbf{A}^T = \mathbf{I} \tag{A.9}$$

where $\mathbf{I}$ is the identity matrix.

A.2.10 Minors, Cofactors, and Adjoints

Consider the matrix

$$\mathbf{A} = \begin{bmatrix} a_{11} & a_{12} & a_{13} \\ a_{21} & a_{22} & a_{23} \\ a_{31} & a_{32} & a_{33} \end{bmatrix} \tag{A.10}$$

The determinant obtained by deleting the ith row and the jth column of matrix $\mathbf{A}$ is called the minor of element a_{ij} and is represented as $\mathbf{M}_{ij}$.

The cofactor of element a_{ij} is denoted as $\mathbf{A}_{ij}$. The cofactor $\mathbf{A}_{ij}$ is defined as

$$\mathbf{A}_{ij} = (-1)^{i+j}\mathbf{M}_{ij} \tag{A.11}$$

The adjoint matrix of **A** is the transpose of the matrix formed by the cofactors of all the elements a_{ij} of matrix **A**. The adjoint of **A** is represented by $\tilde{\mathbf{A}}$.

$$\tilde{\mathbf{A}} = [\tilde{\mathbf{A}}_{ij}] = \begin{bmatrix} \tilde{\mathbf{A}}_{11} & \tilde{\mathbf{A}}_{12} & \tilde{\mathbf{A}}_{13} \\ \tilde{\mathbf{A}}_{21} & \tilde{\mathbf{A}}_{22} & \tilde{\mathbf{A}}_{23} \\ \tilde{\mathbf{A}}_{31} & \tilde{\mathbf{A}}_{32} & \tilde{\mathbf{A}}_{33} \end{bmatrix} = \begin{bmatrix} \mathbf{A}_{11} & \mathbf{A}_{21} & \mathbf{A}_{31} \\ \mathbf{A}_{12} & \mathbf{A}_{22} & \mathbf{A}_{32} \\ \mathbf{A}_{13} & \mathbf{A}_{23} & \mathbf{A}_{33} \end{bmatrix} \qquad (A.12)$$

From this equation, it is apparent that the adjoint of **A** is the transpose of the matrix of cofactors of **A**. For example: For the given matrix **A**, find its adjoint matrix.

$$\mathbf{A} = \begin{bmatrix} 2 & 2 & 1 \\ 1 & 3 & 3 \\ 2 & -1 & -2 \end{bmatrix}$$

The minors of matrix **A** are

$$\mathbf{M}_{11} = \begin{vmatrix} 3 & 3 \\ -1 & -2 \end{vmatrix} = -3 \qquad \mathbf{M}_{12} = \begin{vmatrix} 1 & 3 \\ 2 & -2 \end{vmatrix} = -8$$

$$\mathbf{M}_{13} = \begin{vmatrix} 1 & 3 \\ 2 & -1 \end{vmatrix} = -7 \qquad \mathbf{M}_{21} = \begin{vmatrix} 2 & 1 \\ -1 & -2 \end{vmatrix} = -3$$

$$\mathbf{M}_{22} = \begin{vmatrix} 2 & 1 \\ 2 & -2 \end{vmatrix} = -6 \qquad \mathbf{M}_{23} = \begin{vmatrix} 2 & 2 \\ 2 & -1 \end{vmatrix} = -6$$

$$\mathbf{M}_{31} = \begin{vmatrix} 2 & 1 \\ 3 & 3 \end{vmatrix} = 3 \qquad \mathbf{M}_{32} = \begin{vmatrix} 2 & 1 \\ 1 & 3 \end{vmatrix} = 5$$

$$\mathbf{M}_{33} = \begin{vmatrix} 2 & 2 \\ 1 & 3 \end{vmatrix} = 4$$

The cofactors are

$$\mathbf{A}_{11} = (-1)^2 \cdot (-3) = -3 \qquad \mathbf{A}_{12} = (-1)^3 \cdot (-8) = 8 \qquad \mathbf{A}_{13} = (-1)^4 \cdot (-7) = -7$$

$$\mathbf{A}_{21} = (-1)^3 \cdot (-3) = 3 \qquad \mathbf{A}_{22} = (-1)^4 \cdot (-6) = -6 \qquad \mathbf{A}_{23} = (-1)^5 \cdot (-6) = 6$$

$$\mathbf{A}_{31} = (-1)^4 \cdot (3) = 3 \qquad \mathbf{A}_{32} = (-1)^5 \cdot (5) = -5 \qquad \mathbf{A}_{33} = (-1)^6 \cdot (4) = 4$$

The cofactor matrix is

$$\mathbf{A}_{ij} = \begin{bmatrix} -3 & 8 & -7 \\ 3 & -6 & 6 \\ 3 & -5 & 4 \end{bmatrix}$$

And the adjoint matrix is

$$\tilde{\mathbf{A}} = \begin{bmatrix} -3 & 3 & 3 \\ 8 & -6 & -5 \\ -7 & 6 & 4 \end{bmatrix}$$

A.2.11 Symmetric Matrix

Matrix $\mathbf{A}$ is said to be symmetric when it is equal to its transpose matrix, that is, $\mathbf{A} = \mathbf{A}^T$. For example,

$$\mathbf{A} = \begin{bmatrix} 1 & 2 & 3 \\ 2 & 6 & 5 \\ 3 & 5 & 6 \end{bmatrix} \Rightarrow \mathbf{A}^T = \mathbf{A}$$

Matrix $\mathbf{A}$ can also be written as

$$\mathbf{A} = \begin{bmatrix} 1 & 2 & 3 \\ & 6 & 5 \\ symm & & 6 \end{bmatrix}$$

A.2.12 Skew Symmetric Matrix

The skew symmetric matrix is a matrix in which the diagonal elements are zeros and the rest are such that $a_{ij} = -a_{ij}$. For example,

$$\mathbf{A} = \begin{bmatrix} 0 & -3 & 2 \\ 3 & 0 & -1 \\ -2 & 1 & 0 \end{bmatrix}$$

where $a_{12} = -a_{21}$, etc.

A.2.13 Trace of a Matrix

The trace of a square matrix $\mathbf{A}$ is the sum of all the elements in the main diagonal. For example,

$$\mathbf{A} = \begin{bmatrix} 2 & 3 & 4 \\ 5 & 6 & 7 \\ 8 & 9 & 0 \end{bmatrix}$$

Then the trace of the matrix is defined as $tr(\mathbf{A}) = 2 + 6 + 0 = 8$.

A.3 DETERMINANTS

The determinant of matrix $\mathbf{A}$ is denoted by the following symbols: $|\mathbf{A}|$, $|a_{ij}|$, or det $\mathbf{A}$.

The determinant can be evaluated using Laplace's expansion:

$$\det \mathbf{A} = \sum_j a_{ij} \gamma_{ij} \qquad (i = 1, 2, \ldots, n)$$

where γ_{ij} denotes the cofactor corresponding to a_{ij}. Then the determinant for a 2×2 matrix is $|\mathbf{A}| = a_{11}a_{22} - a_{12}a_{21}$. The following illustrates the application of Laplace's expansion to a 2×2 matrix.

Given $\mathbf{A} = \begin{bmatrix} 1 & 2 \\ 3 & 4 \end{bmatrix}$, find its determinant.

$$|\mathbf{A}| = (1)(4) - (3)(2) = 4 - 6 = -2$$

By applying Laplace's expansion, the determinant for a 3×3 matrix is found as follows: Let

$$\mathbf{A} = \begin{bmatrix} a_{11} & a_{12} & a_{13} \\ a_{21} & a_{22} & a_{23} \\ a_{31} & a_{32} & a_{33} \end{bmatrix}$$

then

$$\det \mathbf{A} = a_{11} \begin{vmatrix} a_{22} & a_{23} \\ a_{32} & a_{33} \end{vmatrix} - a_{12} \begin{vmatrix} a_{21} & a_{23} \\ a_{31} & a_{33} \end{vmatrix} + a_{13} \begin{vmatrix} a_{21} & a_{22} \\ a_{31} & a_{32} \end{vmatrix}$$

For example,

$$\mathbf{A} = \begin{bmatrix} 2 & 1 & 4 \\ 1 & 0 & 6 \\ 2 & 3 & 0 \end{bmatrix}$$

Then

$$|\mathbf{A}| = \begin{vmatrix} 2 & 1 & 4 \\ 1 & 0 & 6 \\ 2 & 3 & 0 \end{vmatrix} = (2) \cdot \begin{vmatrix} 0 & 6 \\ 3 & 0 \end{vmatrix} - (1) \cdot \begin{vmatrix} 1 & 6 \\ 2 & 0 \end{vmatrix} + (4) \cdot \begin{vmatrix} 1 & 0 \\ 2 & 3 \end{vmatrix}$$

$$= (2)(-18) - (1)(-12) + (4)(3) = -36 + 12 + 12 = -12$$

A.3.1 Properties of Determinants

1. The value of det $\mathbf{A}$ remains the same regardless of the row or column chosen to find it.
2. If any two rows or columns are the same, the relevant determinant obtained is equal to zero.
3. If two parallel lines of the matrix are interchanged, the sign of the determinant of that matrix changes but not its magnitude.
4. If any row or column of a matrix is zero, the value of the determinant is zero.

A.3.2 Singularity of a Matrix

A matrix is said to be singular if the value of its determinant is equal to zero.

A.4 MATRIX PARTITIONING

If some rows and/or columns of a matrix are deleted, then the remaining array is called a submatrix of the original matrix. A matrix can be considered a submatrix of itself. For example,

$$\mathbf{A} = \left[\begin{array}{cc|c} 1 & 2 & 1 \\ 4 & 6 & 9 \\ \hline 2 & 5 & 9 \end{array}\right] = \left[\begin{array}{cc} \mathbf{A}_{11} & \mathbf{A}_{12} \\ \mathbf{A}_{21} & \mathbf{A}_{22} \end{array}\right]$$

where

$$\mathbf{A}_{11} = \begin{bmatrix} 1 & 2 \\ 4 & 6 \end{bmatrix} \qquad \mathbf{A}_{12} = \begin{bmatrix} 1 \\ 9 \end{bmatrix}$$

$$\mathbf{A}_{21} = \begin{bmatrix} 2 & 5 \end{bmatrix} \qquad \mathbf{A}_{22} = \begin{bmatrix} 9 \end{bmatrix}$$

A.5 MATRIX OPERATIONS

A.5.1 Addition

Given two matrices, $\mathbf{A} = [a_{ij}]$ and $\mathbf{B} = [b_{ij}]$, the sum is defined as

$$\mathbf{A} + \mathbf{B} = [a_{ij} + b_{ij}]$$

For example,

$$\mathbf{A} = \begin{bmatrix} 2 & 2 \\ 6 & 9 \end{bmatrix} \qquad \mathbf{B} = \begin{bmatrix} 3 & 1 \\ 1 & 0 \end{bmatrix}$$

$$\mathbf{A} + \mathbf{B} = \begin{bmatrix} 2+3 & 2+1 \\ 6+1 & 9+0 \end{bmatrix} = \begin{bmatrix} 5 & 3 \\ 7 & 9 \end{bmatrix}$$

A.5.2 Subtraction

Given two matrices, $\mathbf{C} = [C_{ij}]$ and $\mathbf{D} = [D_{ij}]$, then the difference matrix $\mathbf{E}$ is given by

$$\mathbf{E} = \mathbf{C} - \mathbf{D} = [C_{ij} - D_{ij}]$$

For example,

$$\mathbf{C} = \begin{bmatrix} 4 & 3 \\ 2 & 1 \end{bmatrix} \qquad \mathbf{D} = \begin{bmatrix} 5 & 6 \\ 4 & 5 \end{bmatrix}$$

Then

$$E = C - D = \begin{bmatrix} 4 & 3 \\ 2 & 1 \end{bmatrix} - \begin{bmatrix} 5 & 6 \\ 4 & 5 \end{bmatrix}$$

$$E = \begin{bmatrix} -1 & -3 \\ -2 & -4 \end{bmatrix}$$

A.5.3 Multiplication

Scalar Multiplication.   Given matrix $A = [a_{ij}]$, and a scalar α, then

$$\alpha A = \alpha[a_{ij}]$$

For example,

$$A = \begin{bmatrix} 2 & 4 \\ 5 & 6 \end{bmatrix} \quad \text{and} \quad \alpha = 3$$

$$\alpha A = \begin{bmatrix} 6 & 12 \\ 15 & 18 \end{bmatrix}$$

Matrix Multiplication.   Let A be a $m \times \rho$ matrix and B a $\rho \times n$ matrix. The product $C = AB$ is a $m \times n$ matrix and each element C_{ij} of matrix C is obtained by multiplying the correspondent elements of the ith row of A by those of the jth column of matrix B, adding the products. The multiplication of any two matrices exists only if the number of columns of the first matrix is equal to the number of rows of the second matrix. For example,

$$A = \begin{bmatrix} 2 & 4 \\ 4 & 3 \end{bmatrix}_{2\times2} \quad B = \begin{bmatrix} 3 \\ 1 \end{bmatrix}_{2\times1}$$

Thus,

$$C = A \cdot B = \begin{bmatrix} 2 & 4 \\ 4 & 3 \end{bmatrix}\begin{bmatrix} 3 \\ 1 \end{bmatrix}$$

$$= \begin{bmatrix} (2 \cdot 3) + (4 \cdot 1) \\ (4 \cdot 3) + (3 \cdot 1) \end{bmatrix}$$

$$= \begin{bmatrix} 10 \\ 15 \end{bmatrix}_{2\times1}$$

A.6   COMMUTATIVE, DISTRIBUTIVE, AND ASSOCIATIVE LAWS

A.6.1 Commutative Law

$$A + B = B + A \tag{A.13a}$$

$$\alpha A = A \cdot \alpha \quad \text{(for any scalar } \alpha) \tag{A.13b}$$

A.6.2 Distributive Law

$$\alpha(\mathbf{A} + \mathbf{B}) = \alpha\mathbf{A} + \alpha\mathbf{B} \tag{A.14a}$$

$$\mathbf{A}(\mathbf{B} + \mathbf{C}) = \mathbf{AB} + \mathbf{AC} \tag{A.14b}$$

$$(\mathbf{A} + \mathbf{B})\mathbf{C} = \mathbf{AC} + \mathbf{BC} \tag{A.14c}$$

A.6.3 Associative Law

$$(\mathbf{A} + \mathbf{B}) + \mathbf{C} = \mathbf{A} + (\mathbf{B} + \mathbf{C}) \tag{A.15a}$$

$$(\mathbf{AB})\mathbf{C} = \mathbf{A}(\mathbf{BC}) \tag{A.15b}$$

A.7 METHOD TO FIND THE INVERSE OF A MATRIX

A.7.1 Inverse of a 2 × 2 Matrix

Given the matrix

$$\mathbf{A} = \begin{bmatrix} a_{11} & a_{12} \\ a_{21} & a_{22} \end{bmatrix}$$

Step 1: The determinant of matrix $\mathbf{A}$ is given by

$$|\mathbf{A}| = a_{11}a_{22} - a_{21}a_{12}$$

Step 2: By interchanging the positions of the elements in the main diagonal and changing the algebraic sign of the remaining elements, the resultant matrix is

$$\mathbf{B} = \begin{bmatrix} a_{22} & -a_{12} \\ -a_{21} & a_{11} \end{bmatrix}$$

Step 3: The inverse matrix of $\mathbf{A}$ is obtained by dividing all the elements of matrix $\mathbf{B}$ by the determinant value of matrix $\mathbf{A}$, which yields

$$\mathbf{A}^{-1} = \frac{1}{a_{11}a_{22} - a_{12}a_{21}} \begin{bmatrix} a_{22} & -a_{12} \\ -a_{21} & a_{11} \end{bmatrix}$$

For example,

$$\mathbf{A} = \begin{bmatrix} 2 & 3 \\ 4 & 5 \end{bmatrix}$$

$$|\mathbf{A}| = 10 - 12 = -2$$

$$\mathbf{B} = \begin{bmatrix} 5 & -3 \\ -4 & 2 \end{bmatrix}$$

Thus,

$$\mathbf{A}^{-1} = \frac{1}{-2}\begin{bmatrix} 5 & -3 \\ -4 & 2 \end{bmatrix}$$

Finally,

$$\mathbf{A}^{-1} = \begin{bmatrix} -2.5 & 1.5 \\ 2.0 & -1.0 \end{bmatrix}$$

A.7.2 Inverse of a 3 × 3 Matrix

Given the matrix

$$\mathbf{A} = \begin{bmatrix} a_{11} & a_{12} & a_{13} \\ a_{21} & a_{22} & a_{23} \\ a_{31} & a_{32} & a_{33} \end{bmatrix}$$

Step 1: The determinant of matrix **A** is defined by

$$|\mathbf{A}| = |a_{11}(a_{22}a_{33} - a_{32}a_{23}) - a_{12}(a_{21}a_{33} - a_{31}a_{23}) + a_{13}(a_{21}a_{32} - a_{31}a_{22})|$$

Step 2: Find the adjoint matrix of **A** (Sec. A.2.10), which is denoted by **B**.
Step 3: The inverse matrix of **A** is obtained by dividing all the elements of matrix **B** by $|\mathbf{A}|$:

$$\mathbf{A}^{-1} = \frac{1}{|\mathbf{A}|}\begin{bmatrix} b_{11} & b_{12} & b_{13} \\ b_{21} & b_{22} & b_{23} \\ b_{31} & b_{32} & b_{33} \end{bmatrix}$$

For example, given

$$\mathbf{A} = \begin{bmatrix} 1 & 1 & 4 \\ 2 & 1 & 3 \\ 1 & 0 & 2 \end{bmatrix}$$

Following step 1,

$$|\mathbf{A}| = (1)(2 - 0) - (1)(4 - 3) + (4)4(0 - 1)$$
$$= 2 - 1 - 4$$
$$= -3$$

Following step 2,

$$\mathbf{M}_{11} = \begin{vmatrix} 1 & 3 \\ 0 & 2 \end{vmatrix} = 2 \qquad \mathbf{M}_{12} = \begin{vmatrix} 2 & 3 \\ 1 & 2 \end{vmatrix} = 1$$

$$\mathbf{M}_{13} = \begin{vmatrix} 2 & 1 \\ 1 & 0 \end{vmatrix} = -1 \qquad \mathbf{M}_{21} = \begin{vmatrix} 1 & 4 \\ 0 & 2 \end{vmatrix} = 2$$

$$M_{22} = \begin{vmatrix} 1 & 4 \\ 1 & 2 \end{vmatrix} = -2 \qquad M_{23} = \begin{vmatrix} 1 & 1 \\ 1 & 0 \end{vmatrix} = -1$$

$$M_{31} = \begin{vmatrix} 1 & 4 \\ 1 & 3 \end{vmatrix} = -1 \qquad M_{32} = \begin{vmatrix} 1 & 4 \\ 2 & 3 \end{vmatrix} = -5$$

$$M_{33} = \begin{vmatrix} 1 & 1 \\ 2 & 1 \end{vmatrix} = -1$$

The cofactor matrix $\mathbf{B}^T$ is then given by

$$\mathbf{B}^T = \begin{bmatrix} M_{11} & -M_{12} & M_{13} \\ -M_{21} & M_{22} & -M_{23} \\ M_{31} & -M_{32} & M_{33} \end{bmatrix}$$

which can be

$$\mathbf{B}^T = \begin{bmatrix} 2 & -1 & -1 \\ -2 & -2 & 1 \\ -1 & 5 & -1 \end{bmatrix}$$

yielding

$$\mathbf{B} = \begin{bmatrix} 2 & -2 & -1 \\ -1 & -2 & 5 \\ -1 & 1 & -1 \end{bmatrix}$$

Following step 3: By dividing all the elements of **B** by the determinant of matrix **A**, the following is obtained:

$$\mathbf{A}^{-1} = \frac{1}{-3} = \begin{bmatrix} 2 & -2 & -1 \\ -1 & -2 & 5 \\ -1 & 1 & -1 \end{bmatrix} = \begin{bmatrix} -\frac{2}{3} & \frac{2}{3} & \frac{1}{3} \\ \frac{1}{3} & \frac{2}{3} & -\frac{5}{3} \\ \frac{1}{3} & -\frac{1}{3} & \frac{1}{3} \end{bmatrix}$$

which is the inverse matrix of **A**.

A.8 SOLUTION OF SIMULTANEOUS LINEAR EQUATIONS

There are several methods in solving simultaneous equations. Cramer's rule is one of the simplest approaches to solve a set of n equations with n unknowns, especially if n is small. Thus, consider two equations having two unknowns, x and y:

$$2x - 3y = 5$$
$$x + y = 5$$

These equations rewritten in matrix form yield

$$\begin{bmatrix} 2 & -3 \\ 1 & 1 \end{bmatrix}\begin{bmatrix} x \\ y \end{bmatrix} = \begin{bmatrix} 5 \\ 5 \end{bmatrix}$$
$$\qquad \mathbf{A} \qquad\qquad \mathbf{B}$$

Using Cramer's rule, we solve for x and y as follows:

$$x = \frac{\begin{vmatrix} 5 & -3 \\ 5 & 1 \end{vmatrix}}{\det A}$$

$$x = \frac{\begin{vmatrix} 5 & -3 \\ 5 & 1 \end{vmatrix}}{\begin{vmatrix} 2 & -3 \\ 1 & 1 \end{vmatrix}} = \frac{20}{5} = 4$$

The matrix in the numerator is obtained be deleting the first column of **A** and replacing it with the vector matrix **B**. Similarly, in solving for y, the second column of **A** is replaced with vector **B**. Therefore,

$$y = \frac{\begin{vmatrix} 2 & 5 \\ 1 & 5 \end{vmatrix}}{\det \mathbf{A}} = \frac{\begin{vmatrix} 2 & 5 \\ 1 & 5 \end{vmatrix}}{\begin{vmatrix} 2 & -3 \\ 1 & 1 \end{vmatrix}} = \frac{5}{5} = 1$$

Then the solution is $x = 4$ and $y = 1$.

An example for the solution of three equations with three unknowns using Cramer's rule is shown next.

Given:

$$\begin{aligned} 2x + 2y + z &= 1 \\ x + 3y + 3z &= 4 \\ 2x - y - 2z &= -2 \end{aligned}$$

These equations can be rewritten in matrix form as

$$\begin{bmatrix} 2 & 2 & 1 \\ 1 & 3 & 3 \\ 2 & -1 & -2 \end{bmatrix}\begin{bmatrix} x \\ y \\ z \end{bmatrix} = \begin{bmatrix} 1 \\ 4 \\ -2 \end{bmatrix}$$

Then, applying Cramer's rule,

$$
x = \frac{\begin{vmatrix} 1 & 2 & 1 \\ 4 & 3 & 3 \\ -2 & -1 & -2 \end{vmatrix}}{\begin{vmatrix} 2 & 2 & 1 \\ 1 & 3 & 3 \\ 2 & -1 & -2 \end{vmatrix}}
$$

$$
= \frac{(1)\begin{vmatrix} 3 & 3 \\ -1 & -2 \end{vmatrix} - (2)\begin{vmatrix} 4 & 3 \\ -2 & -2 \end{vmatrix} + (1)\begin{vmatrix} 4 & 3 \\ -2 & -1 \end{vmatrix}}{(2)\begin{vmatrix} 3 & 3 \\ -1 & -2 \end{vmatrix} - (2)\begin{vmatrix} 1 & 3 \\ 2 & -2 \end{vmatrix} + (1)\begin{vmatrix} 1 & 3 \\ 2 & -1 \end{vmatrix}}
$$

$$
= \frac{(1)(-6+3) - (2)(-8+6) + (1)(-4+6)}{(2)(-6+3) - (2)(-2-6) + (1)(-1-6)} = \frac{-3+4+2}{-6+16-7} = 1
$$

$$
y = \frac{\begin{vmatrix} 2 & 1 & 1 \\ 1 & 4 & 3 \\ 2 & -2 & -2 \end{vmatrix}}{\begin{vmatrix} 2 & 2 & 1 \\ 1 & 3 & 3 \\ 2 & -1 & -2 \end{vmatrix}}
$$

$$
= \frac{(2)\begin{vmatrix} 4 & 3 \\ -2 & -2 \end{vmatrix} - (1)\begin{vmatrix} 1 & 3 \\ 2 & -2 \end{vmatrix} + (1)\begin{vmatrix} 1 & 4 \\ 2 & -2 \end{vmatrix}}{3}
$$

$$
= \frac{(2)(-8+6) - (1)(-2-6) + (1)(-2-8)}{3} = \frac{-4+8-10}{3} = -2
$$

$$z = \frac{\begin{vmatrix} 2 & 2 & 1 \\ 1 & 3 & 4 \\ 2 & -1 & -2 \end{vmatrix}}{\begin{vmatrix} 2 & 2 & 1 \\ 1 & 3 & 3 \\ 2 & -1 & -2 \end{vmatrix}}$$

$$= \frac{(2)(-6 + 4) - (2)(-2 - 8) + (1)(-1 - 6)}{3} = 3$$

Therefore, $x = 1$, $y = -2$, and $z = 3$.

appendix B

Finite-Element Method Program for 2D Truss Analysis

This finite-element program is based on the procedure outlined in Chapter 6. It is designed as an exercise tool to help the reader understand the development of large-scale FORTRAN finite-element programs. The input data to the program are described in what follows.

First, the truss is labeled in terms of elements and joints. Depending on the size of the problem, the dimension statements in the program might be modified.

Second, we identify the joints where we have rollers or pin joints. This allows us to define the number of constraints, which is simply the number of zero displacements (see how boundary conditions are handled in Chapter 6). Now we proceed with the first input data.

READ (5,*) NE, NJ NCONST, NFRC

where NE $\leq$ 7, NJ $\leq$ 5, and NCONST $\leq$ 3 are the defaults established by the program, and are defined as follows:

NE: number of elements
NJ: number of joints
NCONST: number of constraints (zero displacements)
NFRC: number of forces acting at each joint, expressed in terms of components along the x and y axes

READ (5,*) N1, N2

Enter the joint numbers at both ends of each element. N_1 should correspond to the smallest value of the two. Repeat this statement for all elements.

$$\text{READ } (5,*) \text{ CK, THETA}$$

where

CK: corresponds to the constant (AE/l)
THETA: orientation of the element (in degrees)

This READ statement is repeated for all elements.
The fourth set of data contains the information of the number of concentrated forces. Thus, this set of data are read NFRC times by the instruction:

$$\text{READ } (5,*) \text{ NFC, FRC}$$

where

NFC: the position number associated with the external applied force at each joint in the global force array
FRC: the value of the force

The last set of data contains the degree-of-freedom number associated with zero displacements. The amount of information is determined by the input variable NCONST.

$$\text{READ } (5,*) \text{ N(I)}$$

Example B.1   A sample input to a 2D Finite-Element Truss.
This example shows how to form the necessary input dots to solve a 2D finite-element truss.

Solution   What follows is a description of the values assigned to the variables coming from the READ statements. Following the labeling proposed on the figure and the geometrical data given.

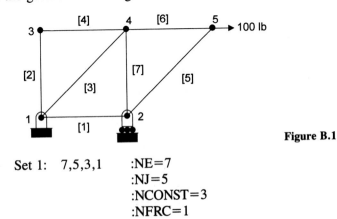

Figure B.1

Set 1:   7,5,3,1   :NE=7
                      :NJ=5
                      :NCONST=3
                      :NFRC=1

		Joints of element
Set 2:	1,2	no. 1
	1,3	no. 2
	1,4	no. 3
	3,4	no. 4
	2,5	no. 5
	4,5	no. 6
	2,4	no. 7

Set 3:	10.,0.	:These are the values of the local stiffness constants
	10.,90.	:$[CK_i = (A_iE_i)/l_i]$, and the inclination angle,
	10.,45.	:from the initial node to the final node,
	10.,0.	:of each element. (Here we assumed CK = 10 for all
	10.,45.	:elements)
	10.,0.	
	10.,90.	

| Set 4: | 9,100 | :Degree-of-freedom number and force value. |

Set 5:	4	:Degree-of-freedom number for displacement
	2	:constraints read in an ascending order.
	1	

The degree of freedom number corresponds to the force/displacement array element number. For instance F(9) degrees of freedom is 9.

The following FORTRAN program evaluates all the local stiffness matrices and then assembles the global stiffness matrices. For the boundary conditions, it partitions the general equation $F = KU$ and solves for the displacements and reaction forces, respectively. The local forces are then evaluated to determine whether they are in compression or tension. It is left as an exercise to the reader to modify the output formats in any desirable fashion. Hence, the write statements could be suppressed or added when appropriate.

```
      DIMENSION TABLE1(5,3),TABLE2(7,3),TABLE3(4,7),STM(7,4,4),
     +GSM(10,10),A(10,11),N(3)
      INTEGER TABLE1,TABLE2,TABLE3

C  ********************************************************************
C
C      THIS PROGRAM ENABLES YOU TO ANALYZE A 2D TRUSS
C
C      FIRST, YOU HAVE TO CHANGE THE DIMENSIONS OF THE ARRAYS TO SUIT
C      THE TRUSS YOU HAVE CHOSEN. THE DIMENSIONS ARE GIVEN BELOW:
C
C          NUMBER OF JOINTS        = NJ
C          NUMBER OF ELEMENTS      = NE
```

```
C            NUMBER OF CONSTRAINTS      = NCONST
C
C                  TABLE1(NJ,3)
C                  TABLE2(NE,3)
C                  TABLE3(4,NE)
C                  STM(NE,4,4)
C                  GSM(2*NJ,2*NJ)
C                  A(2*NJ,(2*NJ+1))
C                  N(NCONST)
C
C
C      THE FOLLOWING INPUTS ARE NEEDED FOR THIS DATA SUPPLIED TO THE PROGRAM
C            1- NUMBER OF ELEMENTS
C            2- NUMBER OF JOINTS
C            3- NUMBER OF CONSTRAINTS (ZERO DISPLACEMENTS)
C            4- NUMBER OF APPLIED FORCES
C            5- THE END NODE NUMBERS FOR EACH ELEMENT IN ORDER (N1,N2)
C            6- THE STIFFNESS OF EACH ELEMENT {AE/L} AND ITS INCLINATION
C            7- THE EXTERNAL FORCE NUMBER AND ITS MAGNITUDE
C            8- THE JOINT NUMBERS WITH ZERO DISPLACEMENT IN DESCENDING
C               DESCENDING ORDER
C
C ********************************************************************

      READ (5,*) NE,NJ,NCONST,NFRC
      N2J=2*NJ
      NCL=N2J+1
      WRITE(6,1000)NE,NJ,NCONST,NFRC
 1000 FORMAT('1',5X,'NUM OF ELEMENTS->',I3,5X,'NUM OF JOINTS->',I3,
     +5X,'NUM OF CONSTR-->',I3,5X,'NUM OF FORCES',I3,//)
C
C
      NROW=N2J-NCONST
      NC=NCL-NCONST
C
      CALL JOCLUM(NJ,TABLE1)
C
      DO 5 I=1,NJ
      WRITE (6,1700)  (TABLE1(I,J),J=1,3)
 1700 FORMAT (5X,3(I3,2X),2X,'1')
    5 CONTINUE
C
C
      CALL ELMJNT(NE,TABLE2)
C
      DO 10 I=1,NE
      WRITE(6,1800)(TABLE2(I,J),J=1,3)
 1800 FORMAT (5X,3(I3,2X),2X,'2')
```

```
   10 CONTINUE
C
C
      CALL INMATX (NE, NJ, TABLE1, TABLE2, TABLE3)
C
C
      DO 20 I=1, 4
      WRITE (6, 1900) (TABLE3 (I, J), J=1, 7)
 1900 FORMAT (5X, 7 (I3, 5X))
   20 CONTINUE
C
       CALL ESTIFN (NE, STM)
C      WRITE (6, 3000)
C 3000 FORMAT ('1')
C
       CALL GLOBAL (STM, NE, TABLE3, N2J, GSM)
C
C
      DO 55 I=1, N2J
C     WRITE (6, 2000) (GSM (I, J), J=1, 10)
 2000 FORMAT (5X, 10 (F12.2, 3X), 'GSM', /)
   55 CONTINUE
C
      CALL COEMTX (GSM, N2J, NCL, A, NFRC)
C
C
C
      CALL REDUCE (A, N2J, NCL, NCONST, N)
C
C
      DO 65 I=1, N2J
C     WRITE (6, 2100) (A (I, J), J=1, 11)
 2100 FORMAT (5X, 11 (F9.5, 2X), /)
   65 CONTINUE
C
      CALL FLIM (A, N2J, NCL, N2J)
C
C
      DO 80 I=1, N2J
      WRITE (6, 2200) (A (I, J), J=1, 11)
 2200 FORMAT (2X, 11 (F12.2, 2X), /)
   80 CONTINUE
C
      CALL RESULT (A, N2J, NCL, N, NCONST)
C
      STOP
      END
C
C
```

```
      SUBROUTINE JOCLUM(NJ,TABLE1)
      DIMENSION TABLE1(NJ,3)
      INTEGER TABLE1
C *************************************************************
C
C TABLE1 IS THE ELEMENT-JOINT IDENTIFICATION TABLE. IT GIVES THE MATRIX
C COLUMN NUMBERS CORRESPONDING TO THE TRUSS JOINT.
C
C    TABLE1(I,1) ----> JOINT NUMBER
C    TABLE1(I,2) ----> FIRST COLUMN NUMBER
C    TABLE1(I,3) ----> SECOND COLUMN NUMBER
C            NJ  ----> NUMBER OF JOINTS
C
C *************************************************************
      DO 10 I=1,NJ
      TABLE1(I,1)=I
      TABLE1(I,2)=2*I-1
      TABLE1(I,3)=2*I
   10 CONTINUE
      RETURN
      END
C
C

      SUBROUTINE ELMJNT(NE, TAB.52)
      DIMENSION TABLE2(NE,3)
      INTEGER TABLE2
C *************************************************************
C
C   THIS ROUTINE READS THE END NODE NUMBERS OF EACH ELEMENT AND CREATES
C   A MATRIX. IT REQUIRES END NODE NUMBERS AS INPUT IN THE ORDER OF THE
C   ELEMENTS
C
C    N1 ---> NODE NUMBER AT ONE END
C    N2 ---> NODE NUMBER AT OPPOSITE END
C    NE ---> NUMBER OF ELEMENTS
C


C *************************************************************
C     DO 5 I=1,NE
      TABLE2(I,1)=I
      READ (5,*) N1,N2
      TABLE2(I,2)=N1
      TABLE2(I,3)=N2
    5 CONTINUE
      RETURN
      END
C
C
```

```
      SUBROUTINE INMATX(NE,NJ,TABLE1,TABLE2,TABLE3)
      DIMENSION TABLE1(NJ,3),TABLE2(NE,3),TABLE3(4,NE)
      INTEGER TABLE1,TABLE2,TABLE3
C ********************************************************************
C
C   IN TABLE3 EACH COLUMN GIVES THE COLUMN NUMBERS CORRESPONDING TO EACH
C   ROW OF THE INCIDENCE MATRIX WHERE A '1' IS FOUND FOR EACH ELEMENT
C   FOR EACH ELEMENT. WE HAVE A 4XNE MATRIX.
C   ** THIS IS AN EFFICIENT WAY OF STORING SPARSE MATRICES **
C
C ********************************************************************
      DO 5 I=1,NE
C
C   THIS TABLE IS CONSTRUCTED USING THE FIRST TWO TABLES-
C
      TABLE3(1,I)=TABLE1(TABLE2(I,2),2)
      TABLE3(2,I)=TABLE1(TABLE2(I,2),3)
      TABLE3(3,I)=TABLE1(TABLE2(I,3),2)
      TABLE3(4,I)=TABLE1(TABLE2(I,3),3)
    5 CONTINUE
      RETURN
      END
C
      SUBROUTINE ESTIFN(NE,STM)
      DIMENSION STM(NE,4,4)
C ********************************************************************
C
C   THIS MATRIX GIVES THE STIFFNESS OF AN INCLINED ELEMENT IN THE
C   FOLLOWING FORM:
C
C        |  C**2      SC      -C**2     -SC    |
C        |  SC        S**2    -SC       -S**2  |
C        |  -C**2     -SC     C**2      SC     |
C        |  -SC       -S**2   SC        S**2   |
C
C   C-->COS (THETA) ;   S-->SIN (THETA
C
C   THE INPUTS NEEDED ARE:
C      THE STIFFNESS OF THE ELEMENTS AND THEIR INCLINATION IN THE SAME
C      ORDER
C
C ********************************************************************
      DO 5 I=1,NE
      READ (5,*) CK,THETA
      WRITE (6,3100)CK,THETA
 3100 FORMAT(5X,2(F8.2,5X),5X,'STF')
      THETA=3.141592*THETA/180.0
      STM(I,1,1)=CK*(COS(THETA))**2
```

```
      STM(I,1,2)=CK*(COS(THETA))*(SIN(THETA))
      STM(I,1,3)=-STM(I,1,1)
      STM(I,1,4)=-STM(I,1,2)
      STM(I,2,1)=STM(I,1,2)
      STM(I,2,2)=CK*(SIN(THETA))**2
      STM(I,2,3)=-STM(I,2,1)
      STM(I,2,4)=-STM(I,2,2)
      STM(I,3,1)=-STM(I,1,1)
      STM(I,3,2)=-STM(I,1,2)
      STM(I,3,3)=-STM(I,1,3)
      STM(I,3,4)=-STM(I,1,4)
      STM(I,4,1)=-STM(I,2,1)
      STM(I,4,2)=-STM(I,2,2)
      STM(I,4,3)=-STM(I,2,3)
      STM(I,4,4)=-STM(I,2,4)
    5 CONTINUE
      RETURN
      END
C
C
C
C
      SUBROUTINE GLOBAL(STM,NE,TABLE3,N2J,GSM)
      DIMENSION GSM(N2J,N2J),TABLE3(4,NE),STM(NE,4,4)
      INTEGER TABLE3



C ******************************************************************
C
C  THE GLOBAL STIFFNESS MATRIX IS A 2*NJ X 2*NJ MATRIX. THIS GIVES THE
C  TOTAL STIFFNESS DUE TO EVERY ELEMENT AT EACH JOINT
C       N2J= 2*NJ
C
C ******************************************************************
      DO 20 I=1,N2J
      DO 20 J=1,N2J
      GSM(I,J)=0
   20 CONTINUE
      DO 10 I=1,NE
      DO 5 J=1,4
      DO 5 K=1,4
      GSM(TABLE3(J,I),TABLE3(K,I))=STM(I,J,K)+GSM(TABLE3(J,I),TABLE3(K,I
     +))
    5 CONTINUE
   10 CONTINUE
      RETURN
      END
```

```
      SUBROUTINE COEMTX(GSM,N2J,NCL,A,NFRC)
      DIMENSION GSM(N2J,N2J),A(N2J,NCL)
C
C
C
C
C ******************************************************************
C
C
C ******************************************************************
      DO 5 I=1,N2J
         DO 5 J=1,N2J
            A(I,J)=GSM(I,J)
    5 CONTINUE
      DO 10 I=1,N2J
      A(I,NCL)=0
   10 CONTINUE
      DO 15 I=1,NFRC
      READ (5,*)NFC,FRC
      A(NFC,NCL)=FRC
   15 CONTINUE
      RETURN
      END
C
C
C
C
      SUBROUTINE REDUCE(A,N2J,NCL,NCONST,N)
      DIMENSION A(N2J,NCL),N(NCONST)
      SUBROUTINE REDUCE(A,N2J,NCL,NCONST,N)
      DIMENSION A(N2J,NCL),N(NCONST)
C
C
C
      DO 5 I=1,NCONST
      READ(5,*)N(I)
    5 CONTINUE
      DO 10 I=1,NCONST
         DO 15 J=1,N2J
         A(J,N(I))=0
   15    CONTINUE
         A(N(I),N(I))=1
   10 CONTINUE
      RETURN
      END
C
C
```

```
      SUBROUTINE FLIM(AB,N,NP,NDIM)
      DIMENSION AB(N,NP)
C ********************************************************************
C
C   THIS SUBROUTINE SOLVES A SET OF LINEAR EQUATIONS
C   THE GAUSS ELIMINATION METHOD IS USED WITH PARTIAL PIVOTING.
C   MULTIPLE RIGHT-HAND SIDES ARE PERMITTED. THESE SHOULD BE SUPPLIED
C   AS COLUMNS THAT AUGMENT THE COEFFICIENT MATRIX.
C   THE PARAMETERS ARE:
C            AB    COEFFICIENT MATRIX AUGMENTED WITH R.H.S. VECTOR
C            N     NUMBER OF EQUATIONS
C            NP    NUMBER OF COLUMNS IN THE AUGMENTED MATRIX
C            NDIM  FIRST DIMENSION OF MATRIX AB IN THE CALLING PROGRAM
C   THE SOLUTION VECTORS(S) ARE RETURNED IN THE AUGMENTATION COLUMNS
C   OF AB
C ********************************************************************
C   BEGIN THE REDUCTION
      NM1=N-1
        DO 35 I=1,NM1
C     FIND THE ROW NUMBER OF THE PIVOT ROW. WE WILL THEN INTERCHANGE
C     ROWS TO PUT THE PIVOT ELEMENT IN THE DIAGONAL.
        IPVT=I
        IP1=I+1
        DO 10 J=IP1,N
            IF (ABS(AB(IPVT,I)) .LT. ABS(AB(J,I))) IPVT=J
   10   CONTINUE
C   CHECK TO BE SURE THE PIVOT ELEMENT IS NOT TOO SMALL. IF SO PRINT A
C   MESSAGE AND RETURN
        IF (ABS(AB(IPVT,I)) .LT. 1.E-5) GO TO 99
C   NOW INTERCHANGE, EXCEPT IF THE PIVOT ELEMENT IS ALREADY ON THE
C   DIAGONAL
        IF (IPVT .EQ. I) GO TO 25
        DO 20 JCOL=I,NP
          SAVE=AB(I,JCOL)
          AB(I,JCOL)=AB(IPVT,JCOL)
          AB(IPVT,JCOL)=SAVE
   20   CONTINUE
C   NOW REDUCE ALL ELEMENTS BELOW THE DIAGONAL IN THE I-TH ROW. CHECK
C   TO SEE IF A ZERO ALREADY PRESENT. IF SO SKIP REDUCTION FOR
C   THAT ROW
   25   DO 32 JROW=IP1,N
            IF(AB(JROW,I) .EQ. 0.) GO TO 32
            RATIO=AB(JROW,I)/AB(I,I)
            DO 30 KCOL=IP1,NP
              AB(JROW,KCOL)=AB(JROW,KCOL)-RATIO*AB(I,KCOL)
   30   CONTINUE
   32   CONTINUE
```

```
   35  CONTINUE
C  WE STILL NEED TO CHECK AB(N,N) FOR SIZE
       IF (ABS(AB(N,N)) .LT. 1.E-5) GO TO 99
C  NOW WE BACK SUBSTITUTE
       NP1=N+1
       DO 50 KCOL=NP1,NP
          AB(N,KCOL)=AB(N,KCOL)/AB(N,N)
          DO 45 J=2,N
             NVBL=NP1-J
             L=NVBL + 1
             VALUE=AB(NVBL,KCOL)
             DO 40 K=L,N
               VALUE = VALUE-AB(NVBL,K)*AB(K,KCOL)
   40        CONTINUE
             AB(NVBL,KCOL)=VALUE/AB(NVBL,NVBL)
   45     CONTINUE
   50 CONTINUE
       RETURN
C   MESSAGE FOR NEAR SINGULAR MATRIX
   99 WRITE (6,100)
  100 FORMAT('0',' SOLUTION NOT FEASIBLE. A NEAR ZERO PIVOT IS
      ENCOUNTERED')
       RETURN
       END
C
C
C
C

       SUBROUTINE RESULT(A,N2J,NCL,N,NCONST)
       DIMENSION A(N2J,NCL),N(NCONST)

C *********************************************************************
C
C   THIS ROUTINE IS TO PRINT THE RESULTS
C
C *********************************************************************
       WRITE (6,1600)
 1600 FORMAT('1',44X,'DISPLACEMENT',14X,'REACTION FORCE')
       WRITE (6,1610)
 1610 FORMAT(45X,12('-'),14X,12('-'),)
       DO 5 I=1,N2J
          DO 10 J=1,NCONST
          IF (I .EQ. N(J)) GOTO 15
   10     CONTINUE
       WRITE(6,1500)I,A(I,NCL)
 1500 FORMAT('0',5X,'IN COORDINATE DIRECTION NO',2X,I3,8X,E13.6//)
       GOTO 20
```

```
   15 CONTINUE
      X=-A(I,NCL)
      WRITE(6,3000)I,X
 3001 FORMAT('0',5X,'IN COORDINATE DIRECTION NO',2X,I3,8X,E13.6//)
   20 CONTINUE
    5 CONTINUE
      RETURN
      END
      7,5,3,1
      1,2
      1,3
      1,4
      3,4
      2,5
      4,5
      2,4
      10.,0.
      10.,90.          Input data
      10.,45.
      10.,0.
      10.,45.
      10.,0.
      10.,90.
      9,1.
      4
      2
      1
```

Index